The Almanac of EDUCATION CHOICES

Jerry Mintz

EDITOR IN CHIEF

Raymond Solomon
Sidney Solomon

ASSOCIATE EDITORS

Alan Muskat   DATABASE MANAGER

A SOLOMON PRESS BOOK

MACMILLAN PUBLISHING USA
SIMON & SCHUSTER MACMILLAN
New York

PRENTICE HALL INTERNATIONAL
London   Mexico City   New Delhi   Singapore   Sydney   Toronto

DEDICATIONS

To OUIDA MINTZ
Whose help has been life-long
— Jerry Mintz

To CLARA FREEDMAN SOLOMON
Beloved devoted wife
— Sidney Solomon

To JUDY SOLOMON
Thy fountain be blessed
— Raymond Solomon

Macmillan Publishing USA
Simon & Schuster Macmillan
866 Third Avenue
New York, NY 10022

Library of Congress Catalog Card Number: 95-78509

ISBN: 0-02-860280-3

Printed in the United States of America

Printing Number
1 2 3 4 5 6 7 8 9 10

A Solomon Press Book

The paper meets the requirements of ANSI/NISO Z39.48-1992 (Permanence of Paper).

BOOK DESIGN BY SIDNEY SOLOMON AND RAYMOND SOLOMON

Contents

LISTING OF
ALTERNATIVE SCHOOLS AND PROGRAMS

Acknowledgments

Our aims in producing the Almanac are to promote communication among people in the world of educational alternatives, to work toward a more cohesive movement and ultimately make alternative education available to all learners. The Alternative Education Resource Organization was created to work toward these goals. It inspired and supported the development of the Almanac. AERO is the education arm of the 60-year-old School of Living, a nonprofit corporation. It publishes *AERO-GRAMME,* a quarterly networking newsletter.

This project has had consistent support from the Alternative Education Conference. All of the states which have alternative education organizations and participated in the Conference committed themselves to help. Through additional state education contacts and *AERO-GRAMME* readers, we established representatives in 42 states. They have worked hard to funnel information to us. We also received help from every state education department in the United States, and most provincial education departments in Canada. Our heartfelt thanks for this cooperation.

The following other alternative education groups provided us with invaluable support and resources:

> National Coalition of Alternative Community Schools
> Association of Waldorf Schools of North America
> Network of Progressive Educators
> National Coalition of Education Activists
> Montessori Foundation
> *Changing Schools* (a magazine)
> Holt Associates
> Coalition of Essential Schools
> School of Living
> *Public School Montessorian* (a magazine)
> Home Education Press
> Global Alliance for Transforming Education
> Magnet Schools of America
> Resource Center for Redesigning Education
> *Natural Life Magazine*
> International Association for the Study of Cooperation in Education
> Folk Education Association of North America
> Canadian Alliance of Homeschoolers
> North American Montessori Teachers Association
> National Association of Charter Schools

Much of the sorting and mailing of questionnaires and newsletters was done by energetic interns at the AERO office, including Mike Lepore, Tom Morley, Mike Denisenko, David Hammerman, Jenifer Goldman, Lisa Harris, Asiba, Sunny, and Wakan Tupahache. Their enthusiasm and help with a tedious job was indeed welcome.

Lauren Most helped coordinate the issue of *AERO-GRAMME* which first announced the project, and also began entering the data from the returned questionnaires.

Alan Muskat, a Princeton graduate interested in alternative education, communities and computers became a key asset as database manager. Through him we met efie womon, who also entered and edited data.

Traci Lachenmeyer first contacted us from California, and began editing, entering data, and swapping disks, eventually moving back to the New York area.

Carol Morley, a homeschool parent, edited virtually all of the Montessori questionnaires, and went on to do any other work we needed.

Another homeschool parent, Betty Lepore, also did editing.

David Sower of Floyd, VA, heard about the project through the intentional communities network, and also became an editor.

Debby Finn, in New York City, became our most recent editor.

Ouida Mintz coordinated most phone messages (which came in at all times of the day and night), and her advice and support were essential.

We are fortunate to include helpful articles written by some of the best-known leaders in alternative education. These include Ron Miller, founder of *Holistic Education Review* and Director of the Resource Center for Redesigning Education; Dave Lehman, Principal of the Alternative Community School (Ithaca, NY) and President of the New York State Alternative Education Association; Professor Mary Ann Raywid of Hofstra University and the Center for the Study of Educational Alternatives; Mary Ellen Sweeney; Pat Montgomery; Kathy Duffy; Andrew Smallman; Louanne Bierlein; and student Vadim Sheppel. Please see biographical notes about each of these contributors at the end of each article.

Kip Shaw, of Pageworks in Delhi, NY, handled the typesetting tasks with high professional skill and unfailing patience. Krishnendu Mandal cheerfully gave advice and assistance in solving computer-related problems.

We are grateful to Phil Friedman, Publisher of Macmillan Reference, for his publishing wisdom, advice, and cooperation during the many months of development of the *Almanac*. A hearty thank you, Phil.

We are deeply appreciative of the overall guidance as well as close attention to detail offered by Andrew V. Ambraziejus, managing editor of Macmillan Reference.

Finally, our thanks to the thousands who provided information to us through questionnaires, telephone calls, faxes, letters, lists and enthusiastic support.

The Whys and Hows of Alternative Education

Introduction
An Idea Whose Time Has Come

This is the first comprehensive directory of alternative education choices in the United States and Canada in paperback format. It is our hope that our collection of educational alternatives under one cover will communicate to the public the broad scope and availability of this movement, as well as foster communication and networking within it.

We have compiled and written the book as a call to action. Although it may be used by some for study and research, we expect that it will predominately serve to help those seeking to create a good educational environment for themselves, their children, or in which to teach. The book may be used as a guide to create a new school, a new program within an existing school or a home-based learning program.

What educational alternatives generally have in common is an approach that is more individualized, with more respect for the student, parent and teacher, and is more *experiential* and *interest based*. Once you decide that you are looking for alternatives to the traditional school system, you must find out which approach is most suitable for you.

You may want to explore one of the fifty boarding or residential alternatives in the book—a list of them can be found on page 311. Most of them are small, democratic, flexible. Many are not very expensive and some offer scholarships. But perhaps the best approach would be to visit several of the alternatives that are near where you live. Since we list the schools by State, and in ZIP CODE order within each State, you can look for the ones nearest your ZIP CODE and note the type of school when it is indicated. Virtually all welcome visitors. And seeing these schools first-hand is the best way to find out about them. Call ahead for an appointment. *Remember, we do not judge the quality or make any specific evaluations of the schools. That is entirely up to you.*

A wide variety of educational alternatives exists at the elementary, secondary and college levels. These generally fall into four major categories: public choice, public at-risk, independent (or private) and home-based.

The public school options in this book number in the thousands; these include entirely separate schools in their own settings as well as classes, programs and even semiautonomous "schools within schools." Public choice options are open to all students in their communities (though some have waiting lists). Among these are the magnet schools, which attract students to particular themes, such as science and performing arts. Public at-risk schools are geared toward students who are having difficulty with school and have special needs (including potential dropouts, pregnant teens, returning students, etc.).

Generally speaking, public school teachers must have state certification. Independent schools have more flexibility in staff selection and educational approach. Montessori schools, in one form or another, are the most plentiful; we list more than 2500. Most of these are private, but an increasing number are public. In addition, we list over 100 Waldorf schools, based on the teachings of Rudolf Steiner, 60 Quaker (or Friends) schools and over 500 other independent schools. The majority of independent schools offer at least partial scholarships.

Families who choose "none of the above" for educational, philosophical or religious reasons, or because there appears to be no nearby educational alternative, can decide to have home-based education. If you are interested in this option, you can find help by connecting with one of the more 700 home-based groups listed in the book. Some call themselves *unschoolers,* for they follow an approach based on interest, rather than a set curriculum. Others enroll in "umbrella" schools which provide a curriculum. (See homeschool resource section.) Those which are religious-based usually indicate so in their name, but most of those listed here are for homeschoolers of all backgrounds and philosophies.

There are also some interesting "gray" areas. For example, home-based educators have combined to create resource centers where they meet as often as four days a week, but their members are all home-based. In some states, public school districts have set up programs for homeschoolers whereby they are considered enrolled and have access to school resources and facilities. In Canada, some private schools receive public school funding. This is also being done in Milwaukee for low income students.

Above and beyond all this, it is possible, with help, to start an alternative school yourself! This is being done all over the world (see section on foreign schools) as groups of parents, teachers and students come together to form new independent schools, or new programs in existing schools. Another exciting area is opening up with the "Charter" schools; combining private initiatives and state funding, a charter school can be set up with specific purposes and supported without many of the usual state regulations. More than 11 states have passed enabling legislation. (See section on Charter schools for more information.) Help for starting or changing schools can be found in the resource section. The Alternative Education Resource Organization, which aided in the production of this book, is one such resource.

If you choose to create a new alternative, one of your first tasks will be to decide how decisions are to be made for the organization. This is crucial. As you browse through the listings, you will see that school governance can involve the local educational authority, a board, an administrator, teachers, parents and even the students themselves. Many combine these, for example, by having a policy-making board, with day to day decisions being made by a democratic school meeting. (See section on Starting a New Educational Alternative.)

It is being increasingly recognized that students learn better when they have real responsibility for their own education. In fact, some see this as a basic right. This philosophy is implemented in a wide variety of ways. Quaker schools work toward consensus at a school meeting in which all participants come to a "sense of the meeting." At Montessori schools students continually choose which materials they want to work with. In some independent community schools, the educational process and all basic decisions are made at a democratic school meeting, with each person having a say. There are schools in which the students participate in hiring their own teachers. An increasing number of schools base their curricula on the interests expressed by the learners, and some have noncompulsory class attendance.

Our advocacy of alternative styles in education does not negate the devotion and skills of the many thousands of excellent teachers and administrators in the mainstreams of schooling. This cataloging of educational alternatives does not imply that all that goes on in the mainstream educational systems is bad. There are many good programs and untold numbers of effective individual teachers and administrators in the traditional schools, as well as millions of parents, teachers and children who are happy with that choice. Also, everything does not always go perfectly in alternative schools, and results vary widely. Our point is to alert the general public to the fact that *these educational alternatives are choices available for their consideration.* Furthermore, many mainstream schools have incorporated methods which might be considered "alternative" so that the line between alternative and mainstream is becoming blurred. Perhaps that is good, for as Ted Sizer of the Coalition of Essential Schools has said, "I want to put an end to alternative education. What you offer should be available to all students."

We have compiled the *Almanac* because we feel it is of primary importance to help students learn how to learn, to stay open to that process and retain confidence in themselves as learners throughout their lives. Perhaps at one time it was possible to teach students just what was needed to be known for their lives, but with today's explosion of information, the best thing we can do is help students maintain openness, curiosity and flexibility as they face the challenges of the 21st century.

How to Use the Almanac

Although we have over 6,000 entries, that does not mean that we have found every single alternative school, program, or homeschool group; we hope to hear from those we missed, and those who create new alternatives, so we may list them in future editions. If you find an error in the listings or wish to include a new school or program in the next printing, write to Jerry Mintz, 417 Roslyn Rd., Roslyn Hts., NY 11577.

The schools, groups, and programs in this *Almanac,* although sometimes very different from each other, fall into categories which are generally considered to be educational alternatives. Our key purpose in listing them is to let the reader know they exist. Beyond that, we have given additional information, some of which came from the thousands of questionnaires which were returned to us. Some of it came from lists and other data sent to us by state education departments, Montessori, Waldorf, Quaker, community schools, and other alternative education organizations. Within tight space limitations, we have provided what we can.

We do not evaluate any of the schools or programs. These listings should not be considered definitive, just indicative. All the information has originated with the schools and programs themselves.

In the interest of space we have sometimes given just one listing for schools with multiple sites. On the other hand, you might find a listing for a school or program that has closed. We decided that it was better to err on that side than to delete all entries for which we have not had a confirmation, in order to give the reader more possible choices.

"CHOICE," "AT RISK," AND "GIFTED"

The terms *choice, at-risk,* and *gifted* are widely used to distinguish different types of schools or programs and the students served in each case.

First, most public alternatives are listed as either choice or at-risk. This does not necessarily mean that the latter are mandatory (i.e., court-ordered). While at-risk alternatives are geared toward a specific population, enrollment is often by choice and frequently open to not-at-risk students as well.

Second, what puts someone "at risk," and at risk of what? The student at risk is either in danger of falling behind or is already having trouble with school. This could be due to poverty, pregnancy, substance abuse, disability, etc. Often only the effects are known: poor performance, "discipline," attendance, etc. For students whose needs are not being met by regular school, at-risk alternatives are often the only thing that comes between failing and dropping out. Of course, there are many young people who decide to educate themselves, or otherwise lead lives outside of school, and are quite successful.

Although we believe that all people are gifted and talented, albeit in different and often unrecognized ways, there are public and private "magnet" schools that specialize in meeting the needs of the "gifted" or "talented" individual who may excel in academics, the arts or public speaking, etc.

DEFINITIONS

Competency-based: Students receive credit when they demonstrate proficiency in a given area.

Charter school: In certain states (including MN, CA, MA, and CO) private initiative and state funding can combine to set up schools with specific purposes and supported without many of the usual state regulations.

Childcare provided: Either during school (for the children of teen and adult parents) or before/after school (for primary age students).

Contract: student and teacher make an agreement/commitment to each other

GED: General Education Diploma. Also called high school equivalency, offered to students who pass a competency test.

Glasser: Advocates non-coercive education through behavior cards, level system.

Home-based: Programs controlled by parents for teaching their own children.

Homeschooling support groups: Offer advice, support, get-togethers, legal and other information, and often go on field trips.

Independent: Private, not part of a municipal or state system. However, independent schools sometimes contract with public systems to provide services.

International: Multicultural, multiethnic; also used by Montessori schools to refer to first generation U.S. citizens, i.e., those who parents are immigrants—recent ones, in fact.

Open-entrance, open-exit: No rigid enrollment calendar.

Orff Shulwork: An approach to music used primarily in Montessori schools.

Public at-risk: Programs geared for students with special needs who have experienced school problems.

Public choice: Programs potentially open to all students in a given area, although there are sometimes lotteries or waiting lists.

Student-centered: An approach based on the interest of the student rather than an arbitrary curriculum.

ABBREVIATIONS AND ACRONYMS

General

N, S, E, W, NE, NW, SE, SW north, south, east, west, etc.
E, J, M, S, Mag, H Elementary, Junior, Middle, Senior, Magnet, High
S/P School/Program
adt adult
AE alternative education
ALC Area Learning Center
alt Alternative
CC Community College
Cont Continuing
Ed Education
Inc Incorporated
Ind Independent

ft, pt, ht full-, part-, half-time
P/F pass/fail (grading)
prog program
req'd required
SE special education
St Saint
tech technology
V, voc vocational
x phone number extension (e.g., 444-5678 x129)

Postal

Ave, Blvd, Ct, Dr, Ln, Rd, St, Tr, PO, SR, RR avenue, boulevard, court, drive, lane, road, street, trail, post office, state route, rural route

Titles

Adm Administrator,–tive,–tion
Adms Admissions
Assn Association
Asst Assistant
Chair Chairman,–woman,–person
Comm Community
Coord Coordinator
CSW Certified Social Worker
Dept Department
Dev Development
Dir Director/Directress
Enrl Enrollment
Fac Faculty
Head Head of School, Headmaster, Headmistress
LD learning disability
Mgr Manager
PPS Pupil Personnel Services
Prin Principal
Reg Registrar
Sr Sister
Supt Superintendant
Tch Teacher

Special Features

AIM alternative instructional methods
ASL American Sign Language
A/V audio-visual
CAI computer assisted instruction
cur curriculum
ESL English for speakers of other languages
HSED HS Equivalency Diploma
IB International Baccalaureate
IEP, ILP individualized education/learning plan
gov governance
home ec home economics
JTPA Federal Job Training and Partnership Act
lang language
PASS Portable Assisted Study Sequence
PE physical education
voc vocational

State Departments and Private Organizations

__ prefix or suffix (e.g., N for "National . . .")
AEE Assn for Experiential Education
__AEYC __ Assn for the Ed of Young Children
__ANS __ Assn of Nonpublic Schools
__AANS, __ Assn of Academic Nonpublic Schools
AC Administrators Council
ACSI Assn of Christian Schools, International
AECI Assn for Early Childhood International
__AIS__ __ Assn of Independent Schools of . . .
AMI Assn Montessori Internationale
AMITOT AMI Teachers of Texas
__ASC __ Assn of Schools and Colleges
ASN Alternative Schools Network (Chicago)

AWSNA Assn of Waldorf Schools of N. America
BE Board of Education
BOCES Board of Cooperative Educational Services
CAP Community Action Program
CES Coalition of Essential Schools
CIS Council of Independent Schools
CME Contemporary Montessori Education
CMF Christian Montessori Fellowship
DE Department of Education
DFS Division of Family Services
DHR Department of Human Resources
DSS Department of Social Services
DHS Department of Health Services
DL&E Department of Labor and Education (SD)
__EA __ Education Agency
FCOE Friends Council on Education
FIS Federation of Independent Schools
FOM Friends of Montessori
FS Family Services
FTP Federation of Teaching Parents
HD Health Department
HEA Home Educators Association
HSGI HS Graduation Incentive (MN)
ISA__ Independent Schools Assn of . . .
ISD Independent School District
KC Kindergarten Council
MA Montessori Assn (also Massachusetts)
MAC Montessori Administrators Council
MAEO Michigan Alternative Education Organization
ME__ Montessori Educators of . . . (I: International)
MF Montessori Foundation
MIA Montessori Institute of America
__MS __ Montessori Society
MS__ Montessori Schools of . . . (A: America)
MSA Middle States Assn of Colleges and Schools
NAEYC National Assn for the Ed of Young Children
NAECP National Academy of Early Childhood Programs
NAEEC National Academy for Ed of Early Childhood
NAMTA North American Montessori Teachers Assn
NCME National Center for Montessori Education
__NE __ of New England
NIPSA National Independent Private Schools Assn
NWASC NW Assn of Schools and Colleges
OE Office of Education
PAMS Pan American MS
PIC Private Industry Council
PNMA Pacific Northwest MA
__PS __ Public Schools
RSF Religious Society of Friends
SACS Southern Association of Colleges and Schools
SB School Board
SNMC St Nicholas' Montessori Centre/College
SNMTA St Nicholas' Montessori Teachers Association
__SS __ Social Services
USD United/Unified Schools District
WASC Western Assn of Schools and Colleges

Starting a New Educational Alternative

New educational alternatives are constantly cropping up. The fact that we have cataloged so many thousands of educational alternatives here should tell you that many people have been dissatisfied with conventional educational systems. They have gone on to implement their dreams, creating a spectrum of choices for parents and children. You can do it too. Here's how.

There are three major aspects that have to be addressed in the creation of a new alternative: philosophy, legal requirements and support.

PHILOSOPHY

The first question is: Why do you need to start this new school or program? The answer to that question leads directly to the realm of philosophy. The alternatives in this book are generally based on the interest of the learner and center on respect for the student, parent and teacher in contrast with most mainstream philosophies. Many approaches are taken by alternative schools. Some of the forms of new alternatives being created today include parent cooperatives, homeschool resource centers, charter schools, public at-risk alternatives, public choice and magnet schools, Montessori and Waldorf Schools.

The governance of a new alternative, how it will make decisions, depends on many factors. If it is public, such as a charter school, the basic governance is defined by that state's charter law. If it is private, that governance could be determined by philosophy, such as Waldorf or Montessori, or how it was first organized. For example, if a group of parents started the school, it could be set up as a parents' cooperative. Decisions could be made by the whole group, democratically or through consensus. They could be made by representatives, or by an elected board. If the school is to operate as a democracy, potential students could be involved in the decision-making process from the beginning.

A decision must be made whether the alternative will be for-profit or not-for-profit. There are some restrictions on non-profit schools. A for-profit organization cannot receive tax-deductible contributions.

Also, some of the most successful alternatives have initially had as a leader or coordinator someone who embodies the values of the group, and who is a strong democratic empowerer. That person has the respect of the group, and the confidence and ability to empower the people around him or her to be involved with decision making and responsibility.

LEGAL REQUIREMENTS

Since education in the United States is primarily in the domain of the individual states, a first step in starting an alternative would be to examine the education laws in your state. For example, in New York and some other states, there is a Department of Non-Public Schools (within the State Department of Education) which is supportive of independent schools and homeschooling and will send you basic information about the legal requirements.

It is advisable not to go officially to any local or state authorities until you are armed with the facts. It might be prudent to talk first to people at a comparable new school or program in your state to find what their experience has been in dealing with state regulations. (If you ask someone in authority a question to which they do not have the answer or are misinformed, they could tell you that you cannot do something which is actually permissible.)

An early step should be contacting the relevant groups that are described in the resource section of this *Almanac*. Through them you will get helpful advice about the laws in your state, and they may lead you to additional resources. For example, you might contact Holt Associates or the National Homeschool Association for general information on how to homeschool, or the Alternative Education Resource Organization for basic information about starting a new independent or public alternative. Refer also to the table of basic legal requirements which you will find in this book.

In some cases the best way to deal with the authorities is to tell them what to do. If you have done your homework, they can simply follow your instructions. For example, in New York parents are only required to inform the local authorities of their intent to homeschool. In one case, since the family knew they were the first to homeschool in their district, they added to their letter to the school the instructions on which forms were to be sent and where they could get them. The school authorities followed their instructions with no problem.

In a state in which the law about private schools was vague, a group was starting an alternative school. Since they expected local school authorities would be defensive about the endeavor, they obtained a written opinion from the state's attorney general that they were legally schooling their students. When local authorities arrived to inform them that the students were truant, they were presented with the attorney general's letter. This suggests that if at all possible someone knowledgable about the law should be included in your initial organizing group.

GETTING STARTED

How do you get started? It seems that it is better to "strike while the iron is hot." One of the first Native American schools was organized after just one meeting. A parent asked, "Don't we need Federal funds to do this?" but he was told that their community had the resources and power to do it themselves. One week later the school was opened. That school and the many others it has spawned are in operation to this day, 25 years later.

There is no definitive manual for starting a new educational alternative. Each situation is unique and calls for a particular approach to meet those needs. In some situations there are guidelines which can be followed. For example, in Toronto, the Board of Education has procedures by which a new public alternative can be established by interested students, parents or teachers. Once these requirements are satisfied, the Board can provide space and teachers' salaries. Over 25 public alternatives have been established since the Seed School (the original one) was started in the early 70s. Sudbury Valley School has put out a "school starting kit," and dozens of independent alternatives have decided to follow the SVS model of completely democratic schools. Several states have passed Charter School legislation and have guidelines for their establishment. There are now over 150 charter schools, with enabling legislation passed in 11 states, and the movement is explosively expanding. Montessori and Waldorf schools are also being established with the help of several national groups.

Sometimes resources and approaches can be combined. One fast growing phenomenon is the homeschool resource center. As the homeschool movement grows, groups of homeschoolers have gone beyond informal support groups by creating centers which operate several days a week. You can be resourceful. One group has been meeting in a different home every day for 15 years. Another group arranged to use the space and equipment of a tutorial center which was not being used during the school day. These resource centers sometimes are able to avoid cumbersome private school laws because all students are being homeschooled and the parents take primary responsibility for their child's education. Some public school systems (mostly in California) have established programs for home-schoolers, thus enabling homeschooling to be a legitimate form of public education, and enabling their systems to receive state per-pupil funds to assist with curriculum design and provide facilities.

SUPPORT

Funding plays a significant role in determining what kind of alternative you can start. There are trade-offs involved in some of these decisions. For example, charter schools have public funding, but it is often hard to get the charter school approved. Even though regulations concerning those schools are generally waived or relaxed, there are inherent restrictions in operating a public school as opposed to an independent school. The most obvious is the separation of church and state, which is required of a public school. There is also no guarantee that the waivers of the present will always be in force. Nevertheless, if a school can get public funding, that is one way to stay financially afloat and offer the program to children of all income backgrounds. Some independent schools, such as Southside Family School in Minnesota, have established contracts with the public school system to pay for some of their children to be educated while still maintaining their independent status. In Milwaukee, a public fund has been established which pays for low income children to go to local private schools. In Indianapolis, the Golden Rule Bank finances a private "voucher" program which supports half of the cost of hundreds of low income students attending private schools.

If your group chooses to create an independent school, an effort should be made to find significant funding other than tuition. Many schools have found creative approaches to this problem. For example, the Free School in Albany, New York (more than 25 years old) bought up old row houses at auction for as low as $500. The parents, teachers and students renovated the buildings, and the income generated from them helps support the school. Highland Free School, in West Virginia, had somewhat depleted gas and oil wells donated to them, which they operate, and the income supports the school. Clonlara School, in Michigan, has built its interest in supporting home education into the Clonlara Home Based Education Program, which generates income to support their independent day school. They now supply curricular and other help to thousands of homeschoolers in every state.

If your school is to rely to some extent on tuition, you need to find out how many people in your area are interested in the approach which your group is espousing. Your philosophy can limit those numbers. On the other hand, if you are not clear about your philosophy, a poor hybrid could be created, or the group could become split. Tuition in most alternative schools is usually on a sliding scale in order to encourage a diversity of student population. The Manhattan Country School in New York City goes beyond that. In their school, which by design is 50% white and 50% minority, higher income students actually pay a higher percentage tuition, similar to a progressive tax. The fact that these schools do give extensive tuition reduction to low income students is often used in fundraising in their communities. Local merchants and individuals support these schools because they are seen as providing a service to their communities.

Some of the more effective fundraising sources for these schools include bingo, raffles, different types of art auctions, direct mailings, and walkathons. For example, when the Petrolia School in California lost public funding and was faced with the possibility of having to again bus their students two hours each way to the nearest public school, they organized a "trashathon." Sponsors pledged funds when the parents, students, and teachers cleaned the roadside trash from their school to the public school—also dramatizing the distance. This event has been repeated yearly since that time, raising $7000 in 1995.

Some schools have created intentional communities to support their school, and some intentional communities have started alternative schools for their children and others nearby. (Intentional communities refer to self-organized groups with a common interest, usually living on a jointly owned piece of land and cooperatively managed.) In those cases, operating costs are often negligible. People in the community offer their experience and help as if they were a large homeschooling family. Sometimes such communities hire teachers or resource people, but not always.

Communities and homeschooling families have the advantage of being able to have their educational programs operating 24 hours a day, so their approach can be more thorough and far-reaching. There are a small number of alternative schools which take boarding students (see boarding school section). Those schools have the same advantage of a 24-hour environment and are supported to some extent by income generated from boarding students. One such school, in Petrolia, California, began to take boarding students because they were so far from the nearest public school and needed more students to combine with the small number of local students.

A growing number of teachers are looking for schools or programs which allow them to really help children grow. In many cases they are willing to take the lower salaries of independent schools or homeschool groups. Of course, parent-teachers and volunteers are a part of the mix. When a new public alternative or charter is being created, it is often the case that the salaries are determined by the local teachers' union contract. Those programs can, however, also make use of parents and other volunteers.

A GROWING PHENOMENON

In analyzing the data, we have discovered existing alternative schools whose founding dates go all the way back to 1786. We also discovered another startling figure. When we plotted the founding dates, it turned out that there has been a gradual increase in the number of alternatives founded each year, starting with a low ebb in the early 50s. After reaching an initial peak in the late 60s and early 70s, there was a slight dip. But starting in the late 70s there has been a dramatic *increase* in foundings of educational alternatives, with over 60% of existing educational alternatives founded since the early 80s. Without much fanfare, this movement has been growing much faster than many people have believed. This is the key message for you: You only have to decide to do it and have the confidence that you can bring it to fruition.

Just keep in mind, all of the 6000 educational alternatives listed in this book were originally founded by interested educators, parents or students, some as recently as the past few months. Others are in process now. It is not necessary to establish an institution. If your new alternative helps only one child, it creates a living legacy.

— *Jerry Mintz*

Home Based Education
A Multi-faceted Phenomenon

FIRST STEPS

Homeschooling, for me, had an inauspicious beginning. The children of Kelsey Service (Nicol and Colin) were students in Clonlara School, the independent alternative school that my husband and I started in 1967. In 1971 just before the Service family moved from Michigan to northern California Kelsey announced, "There are no alternative schools in the part of California where we will live, so I've decided to educate the kids at home. I'll need you to help me with materials and such." So was I introduced to a concept that, at first blush, sounded new and unusual.

Several years later I was asked by some parents whose children had never attended any school at all whether Clonlara School could help them educate their children at home. Each year the numbers of inquiries grew. By 1979, the Clonlara School Home Based Education Program was officially started. It extended to home educators the services of a fully functioning day school.

I soon discovered that I was not alone in the uncharted landscape of homeschooling. For some time, John Holt had been encouraging people to teach children rather than opt for the more expensive and time consuming chore of starting their own schools.[1] Raymond Moore had been researching home schooling for many years before it became a household term.[2] Ed Nagel of the Santa Fe Community School was just then completing his successful fight for its existence.[3] He extended the services of the Community School as an umbrella school for home educators. Little did I know, in those early days, that my role would turn out to be riding shotgun for parents' choice.

QUAKES AND TREMORS

In 1979, an official from the Michigan State Department of Education contacted me to investigate Clonlara School's enrollment of homeschoolers, threatening to "close the school down" if the practice continued. This sent me to the University of Michigan Law Library to research the school code and compulsory attendance law. I discovered that home schooling was actually mentioned in approving tones by two Attorneys General. When I passed this information along, the reception from the Department of Education was blatantly hostile. As time went by they encouraged local school district officials to mistreat homeschoolers with impunity; they did all in their power to impede.

Education is a sacred cow. School officials assumed a proprietary stance as though the education of children was their exclusive domain and that a parent, lacking credentials and being ignorant of what schooling is all about, ought not to be trespassing. That a mere parent had the power to fulfill compulsory attendance laws by teaching at home was incomprehensible to many school folks; they resisted it mightily. Beyond and above the question of power lay the fact that money was lost to a public school for every student who stayed at home. A virtual war was waged upon homeschooling parents by institutional (government) school personnel. Ironic indeed, considering that public schools are, in point of fact, the "new kid on the block," historically speaking. Before compulsory education was devised, homes were the main, and only, schools.

Being the director, I was frequently called upon to intercede on behalf of parents with their local school officials. Yes, they did have the right. Yes, the student would get an education. No, the students would not be isolated from their friends and all social contacts. No, this was not a front for child abuse. Much of my time was spent traveling all over the country from one hot spot to another to testify in court or to address a local school committee. One district in Michigan refused to transfer students' school records when requested by Clonlara School, believing that this would somehow punish the parents and the school that helped them. Districts in various parts of the country took parents to court for "failure to send" their children to school. Criminal proceedings were leveled at parents and students for their crime of educating. *Parents were even sent to jail.*

In 1986, Clonlara filed suit against the State of Michigan Education Department (*Clonlara et al. v. Michigan Board of Education*). This, and two other cases (*People v. Bennett* and *People v. DeJonge*) went all the way to the Michigan Supreme Court. The court handed down decisions in May 1993 which are very favorable toward home educators. The power of the Department of Education was significantly diminished and the path for home educators became virtually unobstructed. Other states and other cases have produced similar results. Departments of Education in several states recognized the need to confer with all parties—teachers, administrators, and homeschool parents—to establish fair and equitable regulations. This rational approach defused potential battles surrounding parents' rights to teach their own children. State legislatures have taken up the task of writing and passing laws in still other states.

Meanwhile, back in the homes, parents and students sought out others who were choosing to home-educate and formed support groups for sharing, arranging excursions and social events and classes for children and families. Parents make plans and execute conferences on a local, state and national level. They coordinate curriculum fairs replete with vendors selling manipulative materials, paper, art supplies, textbooks and more. They arrange demonstrations, workshops, seminars, panel discussions, classes for adults and for children. All this without having to go through a larger school system for assistance or permission.

Parents edit newsletters, news sheets, and magazine as vehicles of communication amongst themselves and the general public. They form national organizations. The National Coalition of Alternative Community Schools (NCACS) expanded to include homeschoolers years ago. The National Homeschool Association (NHA) is a major grassroots organization. (See listing in this directory.) The first and consistently staunchest allies of home educators were and are librarians.

TURNAROUND

Fortunately, most home educators were not caught up in the tempest which resulted from the earlier animosities. Those who were engaged have rendered the path safe and simpler for all who followed with each successful court decision, with each successful lobbying effort, with each success in changing hostile attitudes.

The confrontation is over, except for a few occasional diehard school officials who rear up in proprietary roles. By now, most public school officials realize that home-based education is here to stay. They changed their tactics to include wooing parents and students back into the schools. Free textbooks are offered, enrollment in particular classes is possible, helping teachers are available, participation in field trips is encouraged, and more.

In several states dual enrollment is written into the regulations. Students who are educated at home can enroll for one or more classes in the public schools, space permitting. In the state of Washington public schools receive state funds for helping homeschoolers; the funds vary with the manner of help provided. A large number of parents who otherwise would never have considered homeschooling have been encouraged to enroll their children in public school for a few days a week and to do homeschooling on the other days.

Recently, in some states public school officials have taken to sending certain students home with the admonition that they do home-based education (expulsion with a smile, so to speak). Needless to say, these students are not wanted in the schools; they are becoming known as "pushouts." School officials hope this will help dropout rates go down and test scores stabilize, not to mention the possible reduction of behavior problems.

TO SCHOOL OR NOT TO SCHOOL

Some homeschooling parents choose to import the trappings of conventional schools into their homes. The kitchen or recreation room is transformed into a mini-classroom with chalkboards, desks and textbooks. These families are referred to as those who *school at home.* Others set the notion of school aside. They use everyday life as their curriculum. The interests, the needs and the capabilities of their children dictate their approach, and they frequently desire a relaxed approach to child rearing and education. These families are referred to as those who *unschool.*

Large numbers of Christian families adopt the school-at-home approach, but many opt for unschooling, inspired by the writings of Susan Schaeffer MacCaulay. In her book, *For The Children's Sake,* she draws heavily upon the teachings of Charlotte Mason, devout Biblical Christian and founder in the late 1800s of the House of Education, a teacher training college in Ambleside, England.

> The first proposition of Charlotte Mason's educational philosophy may seem merely a statement of the obvious. But I want to emphasize that . . . [I]t is a central truth . . . and if we ignore it, great sorrow and malpractice may result.
>
> Try a simple experiment. Take a small child on your knee. Respect him. Do not see him as something to prune, form, or mold. This is an individual who thinks, acts, and feels. He is a separate human being whose strength lies in who he is, not in who he will become.[4]

This "separate human being" is engaged in the process of growing and developing. His natural activity is exploring, she is active and interested, they are learning as much as possible about their surroundings, without being "instructed." Motion is the order of their day.

From the outside, it may appear that unschoolers lack a structure. For them, though, it is not a question of having or not having structure in their homeschool. The question is: *who does the structuring?* The board of education, the curriculum planning committee, the textbook publishers or the administration can call the shots in schools. In a homeschool the parents and students can structure their own time and choose activities that make sense to them. What is the family's learning style? What are the learners' goals, both present and future? The structure, then, is intrinsic; not extrinsic. The practices in conventional schools may be out of place in homes where faith in the personhood of the child is valued above the need to control, to train, to mold.

Alternative schools, like those in the National Coalition of Alternative Community Schools,[5] have for several decades now shown that the child who is unhurried learns better and retains more than children who are pressured, clocked and compared throughout their developmental years.

The most frequented sessions at the annual conference of the Clonlara School Home Based Education Program focus upon getting school out of the heads of the students and of the parent. This approach to child rearing appears to fly in the face of norms that most people take for granted. Children are looked upon as objects. They are somewhat automatically relegated to nursery schools or child care at about the age of three years, even when parents are not working outside of the home. Institutionalization of children has become as commonplace as institutionalizing the elderly in our society.

Can children learn without being taught? Do unschooled children grow into healthy adults? There are numerous living, walking, talking, thriving examples that they do.

In December 1994 a nineteen-year-old student graduated from the University of Michigan with a perfect 4.0 grade point average. He had gone from being home-educated to college at the age of fifteen. He is severely dyslexic; he reads, with great effort, at about a fifth grade level. How is it that he is able to achieve so remarkably, overcoming an obstacle of such magnitude? His mother, a single parent, read to him from his college textbooks for three hours each day. She plans to continue this practice throughout the next three years while he attends Yale law school.

Another student went to public school from an alternative school where she had never seen a textbook—age five through age twelve. She returned home at the close of her second day, her arms loaded with textbooks. "Look, Mom," she said with a smile, "they gave me all of these books, and when I finish these, they'll give me more!" She had been allowed to live and learn without coercion while her brain matured at each level of development, mastering the various tasks appropriate to each phase. At age twelve, when her brain was ready for abstract thought, when it was prepared to tackle reading and counting, she embraced it, naturally.

A different student asked his parents to remove him from public school when he was in the fifth grade. The reason? School was taking all of the time he would rather be spending in his favorite area—history. As a homeschool student he had time to be a docent at his town's historical museum and to study/learn in an uninterrupted fashion. When he was fourteen years old he was asked to advise Kevin Kostner's filmmaking team about historical facts needed to portray characters and actions in a film. He and his sister became very involved in films and because of this, the family moved to the west coast to be closer to the life work of the children.

Barry Lopez, National Book Award Winner, recently described his own early education to a homeschool parent at a book signing. She asked him what books he had read as a youth. He replied: "I didn't read very much. School didn't agree with me and I paid as little attention to it as possible. I played in the outdoors most of the time, observing animals and trying to catch them for pets. I climbed trees. I had perfect attendance in The Big School."

The time-honored philosophies and practices in the House of Education, in Ambleside, England, in A. S. Neill's Summerhill School (also in England), in Maria Montessori's *Casa de Bambini* (Italy), and in Rudolph Steiner's Waldorf Schools (Germany) inspired many founders of alternative schools during the 60s and 70s. So, likewise, do they inspire and guide parents who prefer home-based education. The focal point of their approach is the child, the child as a person; not as a thing. Education as *living*, not as schooling.

NO BOUNDS

Nor is the growth of homeschooling limited by national boundaries. Clonlara, for example, has served families in each American state and in twenty foreign countries. In Japan, where putting pressure on children is a societal norm, homeschooling is becoming almost as commonplace as in the United States. Tokyo Shure, an alternative school, started Home Shure, its program for homeschoolers (1993). In September 1994 the school sponsored a "Symposium on Home School" in Tokyo. About three hundred people purchased advance tickets; however, 899 people showed up for the day-long event.

Now, with the industrial age giving way to the information age, the world is the classroom in ways that would not have been possible before. The first-ever high school via the Internet, Clonlara School Compuhigh, was launched in late September 1994. Students and their mentors (teachers) communicate via e-mail and bulletin boards. Six classes are offered in this pilot phase: Algebra, American Government, Collaborative Writing, Computer Networking, Small Business, and World Geography. One teen who has become so immersed in the technology reported, "My Mom doesn't know what came over me: I never worked so hard in my life."[6] Another states, "Before Compuhigh, I wasn't able to focus on science and history. I would try to read different books on these subjects but they all seemed boring. Now . . . I have my mentor's guidance and encouragement . . . I'm actually studying these subjects, not just passing time towards my credits."[7]

From those early days of struggle, the homeschool movement has grown to include a very diverse population with a wide array of approaches. There is, obviously, room aplenty for individualizing, streamlining and experimenting. The terrain is vast; it can accommodate those who operate from a Biblical perspective, those of various faiths, those with no religious affiliations, those who imitate the controls of school, those who unschool, those who combine several of the above.

Homeschooling is not a new idea—it is as old as mankind! It is a living phenomenon, small enough to permit changes to occur with relative ease and large enough to embrace a wide variety of approaches and methods tailored to the individual. Above all, it allows creativity; parents and students are limited only by their imaginations.

NOTES

[1] John Holt, *Teach Your Own* (New York; Delacorte Press/Seymour Lawrence, 1981).

[2] "Better Late Than Early," was published by Readers Digest in 1975, followed by "Home Grown Kids" in 1984, followed by many more publications.

[3] Ed Nagel, *Cheez! Uncle Same* (Santa Fe: SFCS Publications, 1978) chronicles the Santa Fe Community School's successful struggle to survive and its case, *Santa Fe Community School et al., v. New Mexico State Board of Education et al.*

[4] Susan Schaeffer MacCaulay, *For The Children's Sake* (Westchester, Illinois: Crossway Books, 1984), p. 12.

[5] The NCACS is listed in this directory.

[6] Quote by Liberty Lloyd taken from *the Learning Edge,* newsletter of Clonlara School Home Based Education Program, Vol. 12, No. 2, December 1994/January 1995, p. 16.

[7] Quote by Dave Newberger, *The Learning Edge,* Vol. 12, No. 2, p. 16.

— *Pat Montgomery*

Pat Montgomery has logged over 45,000 hours in the classrooms of parochial, public, alternative and homeschools over the span of her educational career. She is the founder and director of Clonlara School and of Clonlara School Home Based Education Program in Ann Arbor, Michigan.

An Overview of State Laws
State Regulations on Homeschooling

Home educating is legal in every state in the United States. Over the years, in virtually every state there has been a flurry of activity concerning the regulations that govern homeschooling. Parents frequently researched the status of local regulations before moving from one state to another. In some cases, parents made a move based solely upon this variable. It was not always easy, since some state department of education personnel were found to explain the regulations inaccurately.

The best way to learn the regulations is to contact veteran homeschoolers in any given area. Local public librarians usually have the names and addresses of local homeschool support groups. Contact them to discover how practitioners are interpreting the regulations.

There is still work being done in some states on fine-tuning the regulations, so be prepared. The chart below may need to be updated in some cases.

— Pat Montgomery

State	Parent Qualification	Require Approval by School Officials	Require Testing	Require Notification
AL	None, if home is allied with a local church; otherwise parents may use a state certified teacher (tutor)			Y
AK		Y	Grades 4, 6, 8	Y
AZ			First year; every 3 years thereafter	Y
AR			Annually	Y
CA				Y
CO			Grades 3, 5, 7, 9, 11	Y
CT			Annual portfolio review	Y
DE				Y
FL			Annual test or evaluation by a teacher	Y
GA	High school diploma or equivalent		Every 3 years after grade 3	Y
HI			Grades 3, 6, 8, 10	Y
ID				
IL				V
IN				
IA			Annual test or portfolio	Y
KS				Y
KY				Y
LA		Y	Annually	Y
ME		Y	Annual test or review by teacher or support group	Y

Y (Yes); V (Voluntary); O/P (Optional)

16

State	Parent Qualification	Require Approval by School Officials	Require Testing	Require Notification
MD				Y
MA		Y	Annual test or progress reports during year	Y
MI*				V
MN			Annually	Y
MS				Y
MO				O/P
MT				Y
NE				Y
NV	Parent consults with certified teacher (25 hours during first year only) or enrolls in a correspondence school		Annual in grades 1–9, or report cards from approved correspondence school	Y
NH			Annual or written evaluation by a teacher	Y
NJ				
NM	High school diploma or equivalent			Y
NY			Grades 3, 5, 8	Y
NC	High school diploma or equivalent		Starting with 4th grade, annual test every other year	Y
ND†			Annually	Y
OH	High school diploma or equivalent or supervised by person with bachelor's degree.		Annual test or written review by teacher	Y
OK				Y
OR			Annually	Y
PA	High school diploma or equivalent		Grades 3, 5, 8	Y
RI		Y		Y
SC	High school diploma or equivalent	Y	Annually‡	Y
SD			Annually	Y
TN	High school diploma or equivalent; for teaching high school, a college degree		Grades 2, 5, 7, 9	Y
TX				Y
UT		Y		Y
VT			Annual assessment§	Y
VA			Annual test or progress assessment	Y
WA			Annually	Y
WV				Y
WI				Y
WY				Y
DC				Y

*Parents who have religious reasons (i.e., strongly held inner convictions) against using a state certified teacher need not do so; parents without these convictions must use a state certified teacher.

†Parent must hold a certificate, or have a high school education and be supervised by a certified teacher, or pass a national teacher exam.

‡Parents who enroll in the South Carolina Association of Independent Home Schools are exempt from the testing requirement.

§Parents have several choices: assessment by a certified teacher or by an approved Vermont school teacher, review by a teacher advisor from a commercial curriculum publisher along with a portfolio, or an annual standardized test.

Religion-Based Homeschooling

Imagine that Jane and John sit at their school desks. A chalkboard flanked by colorful bulletin boards adorns the wall to their right, but the other walls are given over to other furniture and decor belonging to the rest of the family: the schoolroom in this home has been carved out of a portion of the family room.

Mom begins school promptly at 8 a.m. with prayer and the Pledge of Allegiance. She provides individual instruction as needed, but, for the most part, Jane and John work in their Christian workbooks, completing multiple pages in each subject. A half hour to an hour each is dedicated to math, history, English, science, and Bible lessons. The children then take turns reading aloud to Mom and completing reading workbook exercises. Science and social studies each likewise receive their due, but the highlight of the day is music or art (taught on alternating days). Jane and John create Bible verse mobiles today, a project that gives them an enjoyable break from their workbooks.

People react in various ways to this picture of homeschooling. Some think it ideal, while others are dismayed at the rigidity. This is the stereotypical picture of the Christian homeschooling family in the minds of many, reinforced by pictures and stories in national magazines. Like most stereotypes, however, it does not accurately describe the majority of Christian homeschools. Christian homeschooling families may share a common theology but do not find the same common ground when it comes to educational philosophy. They range from those who are child-oriented (some readily accepting the label "unschoolers") to those who are regimented and traditional. Comments that homeschoolers are being railroaded into the same educational approach are unmerited because the notion that all independent, strong-minded parents would cooperate with a single notion of homeschooling is not proven by the facts.

Witness the exhibit hall at a typical Christian homeschool conference. A Beka, one of the very conservative publishers, has a table next to KONOS. KONOS has a unit study approach that tells parents to help their children dress up like Daniel Boone and go out in the woods to learn about trailblazing. KONOS scorns history and science textbooks in favor of "real" books. Math drills (pages and pages of timed fill-in-the-blanks) are sold next door to plastic math manipulatives that are used to teach everything from counting through calculus. At such convention exhibits, diversity is the rule rather than the exception, just as it is within homeschooling families.

While educational approaches used by Christian homeschoolers span the spectrum, there remains a dividing line between them and the non-Christian homeschoolers. That dividing line is original sin. Orthodox Christians must acknowledge the presence of original sin or else they negate the need for Jesus Christ to be their Savior. If they acknowledge that children are born with a sin nature, this philosophical position imposes upon parents a duty to help their children overcome their sin nature. This means that parents must train and influence their children in all areas of life. Those parents who believe a Rousseauian philosophy of innate goodness believe that by removing the inhibiting influences children will naturally blossom into good people through the freedom of self-discovery and self-determination.

The orthodox Christian view of the child is played out in homeschooling through parental control, albeit to varying degrees. Because the sin nature (resulting from original sin) is seen as a predisposition to act in sinful ways, Christian parents see teaching and training children to overcome that sin nature as an essential part of their role. In keeping with that mandate, some parents feel that training the mind and the will to be submissive and obedient is the highest priority, while others allow much greater leeway in adjusting schooling to fit the individuality of each child. The first type of parent is more likely to choose a rigid program that requires a disciplined approach, while the latter is likely to create a study unit to cater to a child's interest in raising rabbits. While the bunny rabbit-based study might be nontraditional and creative, it is still monitored and directed by the parent to some extent. This is different from a true "unschooling" approach where the child determines what he wants to learn, when he wants to learn, and even *if* he wants to learn. Christian parents do not relinquish responsibility for child training by delegating all such choices to their children.

We need to acknowledge at this point that there are non-Christian homeschooling parents who control their children's education. In fact, there is even greater diversity in homeschooling approaches outside the Christian realm. While many non-Christian homeschoolers can readily accept both unschooling and parent-directed schooling, orthodox Christians cannot because the unschooling approach denies a basic element of their faith. This philosophical divide is the reason that separates Christian homeschooling from other groups. Similarly, Mormons and Muslims have created their own groups for theological reasons important to them.

Obviously, there are people positioned at every place along a spectrum between parent-directed schooling and unschooling, as well as those who fall outside the spectrum (because they have no convictions about the nature of children). I have frequently used the label "orthodox Christianity" because we should differentiate between Christian homeschoolers who are operating from a *theological* base and those who are nominally Christian, operating from a Christian *cultural* base. Some parents operate from an authoritarian position because they believe that children need to be controlled simply to maintain order and accomplish goals, even though they lack Biblical convictions. Because many such parents come from culturally Christian families, they are labeled Christian *home educators* despite the lack of theological motivation. At the same time, a smaller population of nominal Christians has embraced a looser child-centered approach because, even though they call themselves Christians, they reject the orthodox doctrines of sin and redemption.

While it is difficult to define a typical Christian homeschooling family, some distinctions from other homeschoolers show up when we examine products marketed to the various homeschooling submarkets. The best place to see this is at an exhibit hall in conjunction with a homeschooling event. What you are unlikely to find at a Christian event exhibit are resources with a New Age slant approved public school reading, science and history texts. At most nonsectarian events, we won't find many of the major Christian publishers but an abundance of games, hands-on learning materials, craft items, woodworking sets, etc.

Because of the philosophical differences, it makes a great deal of sense to have conventions catering to specific theological viewpoints to eliminate confusion for those homeschoolers who are firm in their theology, yet not informed about homeschooling options.

This is also true when it comes to seminars and workshop presentations. Parents who have not thought through their philosophy of education and its foundation are at the mercy of persuasive speakers. Although the open-minded concern of those who sponsor events offering a full range of theological views is to be applauded, there is concern that many homeschoolers leave confused and overwhelmed.

Christian homeschooling organizations and events are the most visible because the majority of homeschoolers are Christians. Within the homeschooling movement, however, we are seeing a dramatic increase in the number of non-Christian families choosing the homeschool option for a host of societal and personal reasons. In an endeavor such as home education, which touches on the very fundamental issues of life, it makes sense for any home educator, whatever his or her philosophy, to have access to like-minded veterans who can answer questions and provide suggestions from a compatible philosophical perspective. Because of this, it makes sense to encourage diversity in the homeschool movement. The more groups and events there are to meet the specific needs of home educators from their own philosophical viewpoints, the more successful home educating families will be.

— Cathy Duffy

Cathy Duffy has been homeschooling her three sons since 1982 and is the author of *The Christian Home Educator's Curriculum Manuals* and *Government Nannies*.

Organic Curriculum

An increasing number of people in the movement for educational alternatives are embracing what can be called "organic curriculum." The phrase is almost an oxymoron and is meant to be somewhat ironic. Curriculum ordinarily describes a course of study which is imposed from the outside. Something organic grows from within itself. Organic curriculum, therefore, is a course of study which is based on the interests expressed by the learner.

How this process operates varies from school, to program, to homeschool family. Teachers at one school never offer classes, but wait for students to ask for them. At another teachers say, "You can't expect each child to rediscover all of human learning," and therefore they feel they must offer a variety of possibilities to the students, sometimes on a daily basis. At 70-year-old Summerhill (which pioneered the "free school" movement) class attendance is still noncompulsory and daily decisions are made democratically, but teachers do offer a regular curriculum from which the students can choose.

One commonality among these approaches is a belief that children innately want to learn and do not have to be "motivated." Indeed, this concept is backed up by modern brain research which shows that the brain is naturally aggressive and wants to learn, as indicated in Leslie Hart's book, *Human Brain and Human Learning*.[1] Of course, good teachers have always intuitively acted from this concept of building from the interest of the student.

Some call this approach unstructured, which shows a lack of understanding of freedom. Freedom, structure and self-discipline are intrinsically connected. One graphic illustration, by noted philosopher-physician Deepak Chopra,[2] describes an apparently chaotic and unstructured Pennsylvania Station at rush hour, with people madly dashing about in all directions. Yet, of course, that situation is very highly structured, with individuals knowing where they are starting and determining where they will end up. Another analogy is that someone may tell me that I am free to play Tchaikovsky's violin concerto, but I do not have the ultimate freedom to play it without a lot of hard work and self-discipline.

Educators today realize that they do not know what information will be needed by their students to survive and navigate in the 21st century. What they must do instead is help them learn how to find the resources to answer their own questions and to help them retain confidence in themselves as learners. There are various ways to do this. One way is by simply basing what students study on their own interests, underscoring that ultimately all knowledge is linked.

There is a process by which an individual or group can determine which things are of most interest to them at that time. Sometimes it is called organic curriculum, or just a question class. For a few minutes the participants brainstorm questions for which they would like answers. It is important that the coordinator of this process make it clear (by example if necessary) that all questions are welcomed and none are considered silly or stupid. After a list of a few dozen questions has been made, the questions are re-read. If done by an individual, the questions are rated by interest level on a scale of 1 to 10. If done in a group, a show of hands indicates the interest raised by the question.

One seemingly innocuous question, "Who invented buttons?" led to an interesting search of history. We discovered that women's clothes button on the left because when buttons first became the vogue 500 years ago, women used dressers who buttoned their clothes for them, most of whom were right-handed.

Other questions recently elicited from 9–12 year olds in a visit to the Free School in Albany, New York, included: Why do some men go bald? Why are little green pieces of paper worth so much? Why does time move faster the older you get? How can you have healthy hair if it is made of dead cells? Why do men have to be so macho? Why are we alive?

Needless to say, you do not have to know the answers to these questions to discuss and research them. They may lead to many places, even connect with each other, and the knowledge built from this kind of approach grows like a tree with roots, not disembodied facts floating in the air.

Living is learning, and an educator must help the student and parent remember that fact. Learning takes place all the time, and we must learn to value that. One important role which the educator may have is to help the student reflect upon and evaluate his or her experiences. For John Dewey, this was a very important aspect of learning, and it has been shown that through this process short-term learning can be reinforced and become integrated into long-term understanding. It is also important to remember that reflection not be forced on the student and thus damage the value of the experience.

Here are some concrete examples of organic learning:

Danny came into school one day and asked, "What do I need to do to get a pilot's license?" We called out around the school, "Whoever wants to be in Danny's pilot license class, get in the van." Six of us went to the airport and were told to go next door, where they did pilot training. After some description of the requirements to get a pilot's license, one of the pilots came into the room. "Why don't you show them what a cockpit on a plane looks like?" the manager asked the pilot. While we were examining the cockpit of the plane, the manager stuck his head out the door and said, "Why don't you take them for a spin?" Starting from Danny's question about how to get a pilot's license, we found ourselves flying over our school!

One 13-year-old had been homeschooling for a year, but he and his parents wanted help in getting away from the traditional curriculum. Using a series of processes, including the "question class," we found out he was interested in learning about business, veterinary medicine and organic farming, among other things. We introduced him to some importers-wholesalers in New York City, and he set up a little business, selling to people in his home town in Virginia. He set up internships with a veterinarian, and at an organic farm, which he eventually managed part-time. He also started taking classes in acupuncture. He learned how to build houses with his step-father.

The point is that we need to stop being self-limiting in our definition of the education process. Several alternative schools which have been around a long time have recently done studies on their graduates. From the results it seems clear that they have become adults who know how to meet their own needs, be leaders, help other people, and evolve and change as the times change. They know how to teach themselves.

— Jerry Mintz

City and Country School

I go to City and Country School. It is a private school in Manhattan. Before I came here I went to public school in Kharkov, in the Ukraine. I am ten years old and I have been going to City and Country for about a half a year.

One thing that really surprised me about my school was on the first day one of the boys stood up on a chair and the teacher didn't do anything to him. But in my old school in the Ukraine they probably would have called his parents into the school and he would have been in a lot of trouble.

The kids are free in my school. But still they can't do just anything they want. They don't have to wear shorts. They can wear anything they want. They don't have to wear a uniform. They don't have to sit straight. Nobody commands them—"Do this, do that." Of course they have lessons. We study, but in a free way. In my old school if we wanted to say something we couldn't just call out. If you called out it would count as a disciplinary problem. In our school, almost in every lesson we can answer the question or ask a question without raising our hand.

We are learning things in a very different way. For example, we are now learning fractions. They did give us a textbook, but they also gave us real blocks exactly the same size and shaped the same way as shown in the textbook. We could even take them home, and they helped us to understand fractions. In all my classes they make it more interesting by making it more real.

Each class has a job, from the 7-year-olds to the oldest (about 13 years old). Last year the nine-year-olds ran the school supply store. They even made video commercials to teach them how to do it. They give us jobs to help us learn how to take responsibility and be ready for the future.

After school, after 3 o'clock, you can stay until 5 o'clock. We can go to art, shop, science, computer, library or to the yard. When 5 o'clock comes I feel tired and I want to go home. But in the morning I like to get to school early. I love my school.

— *Vadim Shepel*

Public Alternative Schools and Programs

Following the initial development of nonpublic, or "independent" alternative schools (typically called "free schools" in the beginning), which were so strongly tied to and reflective of the "counterculture" of the 1960s, "public" alternative schools have grown enormously in number since their beginnings in the late 1960s and early 1970s. In his excellent article "A History of Public Alternatives" (which appeared in the March 1976 *New Schools Exchange Newsletter*, the first major voice of the free and alternative schools), Joe Nathan, quoting Mario Fantini, described this important turning point as follows: ". . . the real impact of private free schools has not been to achieve radical reform outside the system of public schools, but rather to stimulate a more progressive, albeit moderate reform within the public schools."

These often have been (and are still today) alternative high schools to which students could (and can) choose to apply, such as Philadelphia's Parkway Program and New York's City as School, which were designed to extend learning to the greater communities in which schools reside. Also in the early 1970s, the School of Education at the University of Massachusetts received a major U.S. government grant to develop a National Alternative Schools Program. During its five year history NASP produced a national directory, published a newsletter (*Applesauce*), issued a number of reports on such topics as the financing of public alternative schools, sponsored conferences, and helped start several public alternative high schools. At a similar time there were major funds from the National Institute for Education, given particularly to Minneapolis, Berkeley and Seattle-Tacoma school districts to help them develop public alternative high schools. But, small groups of parents (and sometimes students) were also effective in getting public open schools or alternative schools in their communities, such as the St. Paul Open School, Louisville's Brown Open School, Cambridge Alternative School, Berkeley Other Ways School, Los Angeles Area Alternative School and our own Ithaca (NY) Alternative Community School.

Then there have been the *magnet* schools, begun in the 1970s, more typically elementary schools, each with a specific curricular theme or focus, drawing students from all sectors of a given community, and often designed to address new legal requirements for school desegregation. Other elementary public alternative schools were inspired by schools in England, among them the infant schools, or the integrated or open classroom schools. Also, there have been a number of *schools within schools*—a few classrooms and a handful of teachers in one wing or section of a larger building, usually a high school or junior high, typically with only a partial curriculum for which greater flexibility and freedom from the conventional curriculum is provided. And, more recently, there has been the development of public alternative schools for students with "behavioral problems"—sometimes referred to as "soft jails" and not often welcomed as part of the same alternative education movement—and those for students "at-risk," or potential dropouts, for whom the alternative may involve one classroom and limited choice. All of these various types of public alternative schools or programs are found in this *Almanac*. Since 1970 teachers and administrators, and sometimes parents and students, of these various public alternatives have been meeting annually at conferences held throughout the country, early on under the aegis of the now defunct International Consortium for Options in Public Education (ICOPE) of the Department of Education at Indiana University. Currently such national gatherings are sponsored by the various statewide alternative education organizations (of which there presently are more than 20). In 1992 the 22nd annual conference was hosted by the Virginia Alternative Educators Association in Williamsburg, Virginia, and the 1993 conference in Colorado was hosted by the group Colorado Options in Education. In 1994 the conference was in Des Moines, Iowa, and in 1995 the 25th annual meeting was held in Bloomington, Indiana. The statewide alternative education organizations are loosely affiliated through the editorial board of the *Changing Schools* publication which is a current national voice for alternative schools.

The effects of public alternatives have been analyzed by various people and various studies throughout the most recent twenty- to thirty-year history of such schools. It is important to remember that these schools have their roots in the Progressive Education movement of the turn of the century. *The Eight Year Study* published in 1942 was and still is one of the most definitive studies which compared the college records of some 1500 students from nontraditional schools with those from traditional schools—finding the former group did as well as or better than the latter on all measures. In this 1976 article, Joe Nathan summarized the early effects of early public alternatives as follows:

1. They have made "life more bearable for thousands of young people, age 5 to 18, who are in them."
2. They have provided students with "the opportunity to learn from a variety of people, not just certified teachers."
3. Students have had "opportunities to spend more time out of the school building taking local or even cross-country field trips, and serving as interns at local community agencies or businesses."
4. "The feeling that someone other than their family really cares about them is a new experience for an astonishing number of students;" it has been the feeling of belonging that many have about their school.
5. Another "effect on many students has been to convince them that they can have more impact on both their own and the lives of others . . . alternative schools help them learn how participation in social action and service projects make them feel they can have a positive influence on their communities."
6. "Many public alternatives have helped increasing numbers of young people learn how to analyze community problems and deal with at least some of them."
7. Effectively serving the needs of staff, "Alternative school teachers find different ways of using resources and greater flexibility . . . can spend more time on individual student evaluations because they don't have to fool with figuring grades . . . [and] have the opportunity to get a few copies of various materials, rather than having to accept class sets of required texts."

Similar findings have continued to be reported as described in the "highlights" of an extensive study of 1200 public alternative secondary schools published in 1982 by Mary Anne Raywid of Hofstra University, "The Current Status of Schools of Choice in Public Secondary Education": high staff morale, better student-teacher relations, no greater cost, kids like alternatives, attendance goes up, and "the most outstanding features of alternative schools are human relationships and instructional activities—not equipment, nor facilities, nor curriculum . . . Alternative schools are pioneering new organizational structures, innovative forms of social control, and new varieties of learning activities." And more recently in his 1990 book, *Public Alternative Education,* Central Washington University Education Professor Tim Young concludes, after a thorough analysis of the research to date, that: (1) students have more positive attitudes toward school, (2) their school attendance improves, and (3) their achievement improves as the result of their attending public alternative schools.

Most importantly, throughout the past twenty-plus years, educators in these public alternative schools have all been doing things differently. As Mary Anne Raywid recently explained in her article in the fall 1990 issue of *Changing Schools,* the debate continues over the question of ". . . whether it was individual freedom or whether it was communitarianism and collective decision making instead, that is the real essence of alternative schooling— or whether action learning takes precedence over curricular relevance as the more critical defining element." Raywid pointed out further ongoing debates over the mission of public alternative education. ". . . did it intend to institutionalize diversity by providing a mechanism enabling and inviting schools to differ from one another—or was alternative education the vanguard that would point the way, showing what *all* schools ought to be like?"

Perhaps Jonathan Kozol has captured the full meaning for those of us carrying on the struggle as public alternative educators in his Introduction to the republication of his 1972 book originally entitled *Free Schools,* (then in 1982 retitled *Alternative Schools: A Guide for Educators and Parents*).

> The Free School [or Alternative School] was conceived, not as an instrument by which to flee from history, but rather as a visible metaphor for many values, visions, and ideals that seemed to some of us to be essential in the struggle to assure the psychological and intellectual survival of our children.

Those of us in public alternative education are continuing to keep the metaphor alive!

— *Dave Lehman*

Dave Lehman is the Principal of the Alternative Community School (Ithaca, NY) and President of the New York State Alternative Education Association.

Charter Schools
A Serious Challenge to the Status Quo

Imagine your dream school in which you and your colleagues have complete control over the budget and for which nearly all laws and rules have been eliminated: no more Carnegie Units, policy manuals, district collective bargaining agreements, and textbooks selected from on high. Imagine groups of individuals—teachers, parents, students, community leaders—sitting down together on a regular basis to design and implement this dream. No more excuses; no more passing the buck. Just lots of freedom, responsibility and hard work to ensure appropriate student learning is occurring. Is this an impossible scenario within our country's public school system? Difficult, yes, but not impossible, given the recent passage of charter school legislation in a growing number of states.

What are these entities called charter schools? Why have they come to be? And, what impact are they having on the lives of teachers, students and parents?

Generally, a charter school is a public educational entity operating under a charter, or contract, that has been negotiated among the *organizers* who design and run the schools (e.g., local school board, state board of education), and a sponsor who oversees the provisions of the charter. The school is "public" in that it cannot be selective in student admissions, cannot charge tuition, must be nonsectarian and is held accountable for student results. It is also a school of choice for teachers, students and parents; if the school fails to attract these individuals, or violates any terms of its charter, it goes out of business. In exchange for this enhanced accountability, these schools are freed from most state laws and local board policies (except for issues such as health, safety, civil rights, fiscal and pupil accountability), and are granted full authority over nearly all funding that follows their students. The inherent elements of choice, true site-based decision making, deregulation/decentralization and enhanced accountability—all within a public setting—have made charter schools a very attractive reform initiative for policymakers, educators and parents alike.

As of mid-June 1995, 17 states had enacted some type of charter school legislation, with the first state being Minnesota in 1991. Each state's law is different, but eight are considered "stronger" laws whereby charter schools can generally be organized by a variety of individuals or groups; can be sponsored by public entities other than the local school board (or there is a strong appeal process); are legally and financially autonomous within their districts; and are automatically exempt from most state and local laws/rules. These states include: Arizona, California, Colorado, New Hampshire, Massachusetts, Michigan, Minnesota and Texas. In most of the other states charter-type schools are essentially no more than enhanced site-based decision-making experiments in that they remain part of the school district, having to seek individual rather than blanket waivers.

Charter legislation remains under consideration in a number of states, and odds are high there will be several additional states on the list by the time this book is published. Given the popularity of charter schools as a reform effort, the issue is often not *if* a given state will enact such legislation but *how strong* the measure will be. Charter schools do, however, have their opponents. These often include groups such as school board associations and teacher unions who have a large stake in the status quo and are concerned about allowing too much emphasis on this new, unproven strategy.

What are these schools like and what impacts are beginning to surface? First, no two charter schools are alike; they come in every size, shape and flavor. Unlike the "one-size-fits-all" scenario typically found across school districts, many charter schools offer the best of what alternative education has to offer (e.g., smaller schools; experiential learning; teachers who want to work with students in nontraditional settings)—with the added features of true site control, limited rules/regulations to follow and a contract to show results. Some have a special emphasis (such as science or the arts); others serve a special population such as dropouts. Some are housed in nontraditional educational facilities such as community recreational halls or old church buildings. Others are housed in "regular" school buildings, having converted from an existing school rather than starting from scratch. A few examples of the over 200 charter schools approved and/or in operation include: *I'Tom Escuela of Centro de Amistad,* a trilingual/tricultural (Spanish/English/Yaqui) community-based K–12 school located in and run by the town of Guadalupe, AZ; *City Academy,* a school for dropouts aged 12–21 housed in a community park recreational center in St. Paul, MN; *Northlane Math and Science Academy,* a hands-on focused school housed in a home/garage in Freeland, MI serving students aged 6–12; *Boston Renaissance Charter School,* a K–5 inner-city school open 210 days per year, 12 hours per day, utilizing the Edison Project design; the *Community of Learners,* a middle school in Durango, CO, focused on student-centered and self-directed learning; and the *Choice 2000 On-line High School,* operating a complete educational program through "cyberspace" using file servers based in Perris, CA.

Given the newness of this reform activity, no formal studies or data exist on the impact of such schools. Instead, informal reports are revealing numerous positive stories and a few not-so-positive findings as well. General trends reveal that:

- *Numerous "at-risk" students are being served by charter schools.* Many schools have chosen to focus on pupils who had not been successful in the traditional public school setting.

- *Unique community and/or business charter school partnerships are being formed.* For example, the *Skills for Tomorrow Charter School,* a vocational/technical school in Minnesota, is being run with support from the Teamsters Union. Several charter schools are being operated or co-operated by universities (e.g., the *Pueblo School for the Arts and Science* in Colorado; the *Saginaw Chippewa Academy* in Michigan).

- *Unique learning environments are being created in response to student and parental desires.* Numerous charter schools utilizing multi-age/multi-grade, Montessori-type, or back-to-basics programs have been established in response to parents. As one example, the *Community Involved Charter School,* a college-preparatory school in Colorado, is serving some of the over 1,000 students who had previously been on a waiting list for a similar program in the area.

- *Unique opportunities for teachers have also surfaced.* In every charter school, teachers are involved in all key operational decisions. In at least one school (Minnesota's *New Country Charter School*), a group of certified teachers have formed a cooperative and are contracting out their teaching services to the school.

- *Larger percentages of existing funds are being focused on instructional activities.* Through the use of creative volunteers and other efforts, some charter schools are saving money on the business side of schooling. For example, the *Vaughn Next Century Learning Center* in Los Angeles realized a $1.2 million surplus (out of a $4.6 million budget) in addition to lowering class sizes and backfilling a district-wide teacher pay cut. These funds were used in part to purchase and raze two adjacent crack houses and to build additional classrooms.

- *Ripple effects across the broader system are becoming visible.* Conceptually, charter schools are intended to not only serve the students within their walls but to help initiate other changes. To some degree this is beginning to occur. For example, a Montessori-type program is now being offered by one Minnesota district after parents sought to establish such a program under the charter law. In response to Massachusetts' charter law, the Boston Public Schools and its teacher union initiated a process for creating their own charter-like schools. These types of activities could have occurred without charter school legislation, but the pressure to do so was not present.

- *Charter schools are not immune from problems.* A few events underscore the fact that charter school laws have glitches to be worked out. Mismanagement can occur. Michigan's initial charter school was found to have violated their state constitution in part because it usurped the state board's power to oversee public education. Some charter schools have had difficulty managing administrative operations and securing buildings and capital equipment. Indeed, the charter of one school, the Los Angeles–based Edutrain Charter School, was revoked due to financial mismanagement.

Overall, charter schools are not for the faint of heart. Involvement in their creation, governance, and day-to-day operation requires a large investment of time and energy and a high tolerance for ambiguity. They are also not a panacea for K–12 educational reform. They instead represent a serious challenge to many long held truths regarding instructional practices, governance, regulation and accountability. As Yvonne Chan, principal of *Vaughn Next Century Learning Center,* noted in a *Time* magazine article (October 31, 1994), "The charter takes the handcuffs off the principal, the teacher and the parents—the people who know the kids best. In return, we are held responsible for how kids do" (p 54). Perhaps Nick Reisinger, a 12-year-old student in Michigan's *Northlane Academy* charter school sums it up best: "Here we get to talk about things instead of just listening to some boring teachers. I don't feel like 'duh, what am I doing here?' anymore" (*Time,* p. 53).

— Louann A. Bierlein

Louann A. Bierlein is assistant professor/researcher in the Louisiana Education Policy Research Center at Louisiana State University, as well as an education reform policy consultant who has been following the national charter school movement for a number of years.

The Lessons of the Community Involved Charter School, Lakewood, Colorado

ONE GROUP'S CHARTER SCHOOL EFFORTS

Since January of 1991, I have worked with a small group of conscientious parents and educators to propose a new alternative school in a public school district that has one of the most famous alternative programs in the country, the 25-year-old Jefferson County Open School—with a waiting list of over 1,000. Prior to the charter school concept coming to Colorado, we had presented our ideas to a school district that was strapped for funds and not interested in adding to their fiscal burden. The passage of the Charter Law on May 11, 1993, provided us with the leverage necessary to be taken seriously. Subsequently, on March 9, 1994, we were the seventh charter school to be approved in Colorado. Fourteen charter schools of various philosophical and curricular emphasis are now open (March 1995).

On September 6, 1994, we opened our doors to 459 students, grades K–12. We continue to learn lessons through the evolution of our school. Our plans on paper have not always turned out as anticipated. Often there are surprise deviations from the original plans. We have the following tips for groups in the planning and then implementation process of a charter school:

TIME   Spend adequate time talking about a shared vision. We have found that quick decisions result in negative repercussions.

INCLUSION   Involve key players (parents, teachers, students, community members) when developing the vision and reaching consensus. Roles need to be clearly defined and the committees that make recommendations to a steering committee or coordinating committee need to know that up front. The efforts need to be coordinated by a central committee or person or combination thereof.

NETWORKING   Join with other parents and teachers in your district or area who are planning schools of choice or charter schools, regardless of their philosophical bent. We have found much support from other parents and educators who are promoting choice—and some of those people support educational philosophies radically different from ours. Our common denominator is not curricular emphasis but school choice. We have learned from each other by trading information, and we have had added support to one another when the waters became murky.

CENTRAL OFFICE RELATIONS   We have been fortunate in our dealings with district personnel. We have purposefully established and maintained conciliatory relations with our district personnel. They have gone the extra mile for us. When the going was rough recently, they were there to support us.

SIZE   One lesson we have learned concerns optimal school size. We are a K–12 program and we reached for 500 students. We have discovered that 420 students is the optimal size for our program. It allows us to offer the diversity we seek. (Deborah Meier, from Central Park East, advocates staff small enough to sit around a table.) With 23 teachers and 4 support staff we are unable to sit around even the largest conference table. Stages of group development are complicated and prolonged with large numbers of students and staff.

GOVERNANCE   Experiment with various administrative models. Our administrative steering committee makes final decisions from recommendations made by all other committees. Our program has to be coordinated, especially in light of our large school size. Final decisions are laborious and time consuming and the procedures need to be streamlined. Some members of other committees resent the fact that they aren't able to make final decisions.

ACCOUNTABILITY   In our new charter school we were naive to presuppose that all students and employees would give their 100% effort. Teacher accountability systems should be well thought out in the proposal stage. We did not anticipate the employee accountability problems we have encountered and we are shoring up this issue for future situations.

The charter school law calls for true site-based management. Persons engaged in this endeavor are equipped, for the most part, with old-world skills. We are asking persons with traditional skills to participate in a new world. Be prepared for the forming, storming, norming and performing stages of group development with as many democratic procedures as possible. We have found that we also must have faith in the evolution of the program and process because numerous details and situations arise for which we had not pre-planned. Despite the challenges, this opportunity is truly the personal and professional chance of a lifetime.

— *Mary Ellen Sweeney*

The Research Record

Alternative schools have been studied more for their organizational arrangements and processes than for their outcomes. There are several important and related reasons for this. First is the interest in making business and industrial organizations work well—as reflected in the corporate excellence literature of the last dozen years. Second is the discovery in the early 1970s that the way a school is organized and structured may have as much to do with its success as do the quality of its program and instruction. Third is that alternative schools offer the clearest extant example of organizational departure from the standard model of schools. Amid all the present talk of restructuring, it has been said, alternatives provide our most definitive example of what restructured schools might look like.

As the study of schools as organizations has developed over the past decade, one attribute after another has been identified as crucial: organizational climate, culture, downscaling and personalization, worker commitment and satisfaction, visionary leadership, shared decision-making. And as research came to focus on one of these components after another, some inquirers have looked at alternative schools to see whether and in what form these attributes were observable there. The findings have been positive and informative.

One of the most recent emphases to emerge in organizational research on schools (a product of the last seven or eight years) has to do with the nature and extent of "professional community" within a school. It appears that the more developed the professional community, the greater the likelihood of success in dealing with students and helping them achieve. Research on professional community asks about the kind of relationships that exist among staff, the extent to which teachers work together and discuss their work and the extent to which they share a common sense of the school's mission and goals.

Two recent national studies have found alternative schools outstanding in this regard. One, a study of sixteen high schools conducted by Stanford's Center for Research on the Context of Secondary School Teaching, found a Michigan alternative school to stand head and shoulders above the other fifteen on most of the indicators related to professional community. Indeed, they found Horizons High School to exceed national means by as much as two or three standard deviations on a number of the measures used. The study's final report indicated that teachers at Horizon have a greater influence on policy than at any other site; that teacher collaboration time is more extensive than at any other site; that they have high marks for their principal's leadership; and their job satisfaction is among the highest encountered in the study.[1]

A second study, conducted by the University of Wisconsin's Center on the Organization and Restructuring of Schools, took a longitudinal look at restructured schools. It found the alternative school in its study to be the most mature and effective example of professional community. Moreover, the alternative appeared to be the study's most successful example of a restructured school.[2]

Still another study which appears to offer substantial support for the organizational features of alternative schools is an extensive inquiry carried out in New York. It compared the impacts of two types of magnet schools on students: one, where the magnet students were not separated from others, save in their specialized courses, and were otherwise part of a standard comprehensive high school; and the other type where the students were grouped together in a school which operated separately, with its own students and teachers.[3] The second type was found far more effective than the first with respect to both dropout prevention and student accomplishment. The study's authors attribute the success to the fact that the students in the second type of magnet program had the opportunity to take more courses in the magnet area. So theirs is a curricular rather than an organizational explanation but, from what they have described, an organizational explanation of the advantage is at least equally plausible. The second type of program was able to change the daily experience of students, whereas the first one was not. In the first type of magnet, the failure to separate students from students outside the program meant that not everybody was there by choice—and thus not everybody shared the interests that attracted the choosers. The result was that school climate and culture, and student sense of affiliation, changed very little.

The study points to the importance of several factors that figure prominently in most alternative schools. The first is that alternative schools tend to elicit strong affiliation from those connected with them. They are, as some have called them, "membership" schools or "communities" which students feel they have joined. Youngsters typically exhibit strong ties to the school, its teachers, and to one another.[4]

A second factor suggested by the New York study (although not acknowledged there) is that curriculum may not occupy the sort of importance for students that it holds for adults in a school. One prominent researcher, John Goodlad, has said that even for the adults working there, as well as for the students, the most important thing about a school is not academics, but the way in which one's daily life unfolds and is lived there.[5] Alternative schools acknowledge this in the spirit they bring to "doing" school, the climate that is carefully sustained in most, the activities they provide, and the way people—all people, students as well as staff—are treated within them.

The third thing the magnet school study suggests is the importance of choice—not only one's own choice, but the fact that *everyone* is there by choice. It makes for quite a different kind of setting than that in which some or all are assigned.

Both magnets and alternative schools have a record of trying to interest and genuinely engage youngsters in learning. At the secondary level, magnets tend to do so by featuring content in which students have a particular interest. Alternatives tend more often, though not exclusively, to engage students in the school environment and in the activities through which content is presented. One type of alternative that has been popular since the early days of public school alternatives, for instance, is the city-as-school concept in which students learn directly from observation (as in courtrooms) and participation (as in internships). Other activities that have been widely adopted have included independent study opportunities, mentorships and service learning arrangements.[6]

Alternative schools are also known for the dramatic turnarounds they have brought to the lives of individual youngsters whose previous school performance has ranged from poor to disastrous. It is not always the case by any means, but alternative school teachers can tell stories of kids who had hated schools and teachers, and who blossomed in the alternative. Such stories don't ordinarily impress researchers who tend to look instead for hard, well-substantiated evidence, involving comparison groups and, preferably, large numbers. This sort of evidence is harder to come by (and perhaps less important to alternative school audiences who are inclined to emphasize individuality and particularity anyway, over the typicality and generalizations researchers seek) but gradually the hard evidence is piling up.

One analysis[7] summed up the situation this way: "Virtually all studies that compare magnet and nonmagnet schools show that students in magnet schools have higher achievement, better attendance and dropout rates and, overall, better school performance." Increasingly, studies are ruling out the explanation that the magnet students were smarter, or more accomplished to start, or more highly motivated. A study done in Montgomery County, MD, in 1988 compared two sets of youngsters matched at the outset for their educational achievement and apparent potential, at the time when one group entered a magnet school and the other continued in the regular program. The investigators found that the magnet students accomplished more—and that the longer they remained in the magnet school, the greater the contrast became with the performance of their regular school counterparts.[8]

More recently, their findings were confirmed on a large scale by a study of 816 magnet school students in four cities. Long-term magnet students (for seven years or more) were matched with shorter term magnet students (under three years) as to sex, race, and entering achievement levels. The study found that the long-termers did better on all the indicators checked: grades, test scores, attendance, behavior, participation in extracurricular activities and school awards. Moreover, it was ascertained that this was the case with weaker as well as stronger students and independent of the theme of the magnet school.[9]

By virtue of their well-known holistic orientation, alternative schools are interested, however, in much more than academic achievement. They are concerned with the kind of experience school represents for students and how the students feel about their school. Here, too, the research is very positive. One large study that sought to determine how well schools respond to the needs of their students found alternative high schools to far surpass conventional ones, in the eyes of both teachers and students. Indeed, even the *lowest* scoring alternative schools were judged to be far better at meeting student needs than were the *highest* scoring conventional ones![10] And constituent satisfaction rates associated with alternative schools have long been known to outshine those of comparable traditional schools in the same locale for parents as well as students and teachers.[11]

Follow-up studies show that these positive sentiments prove to be long-lasting. Graduates don't later turn sour, and they don't conclude afterward that their school had not prepared them for what was to come.[12] For instance, a study of one famous alternative school—the Village School, in Great Neck, NY—polled all of its graduates, some from as long as ten and fifteen years earlier. It compared their views and sentiments regarding their high school with those of the graduates of one of the district's other high schools. After having graduated, the alternative school alumni were consistently more positive about their alma mater than were the graduates of the conventional high school.[13]

Another kind of follow-up study also testifies to the superiority of alternative schools. It has long been observed that a larger percentage of students from alternative schools than from other comparable local schools tend to go on to college—suggesting that they are more positively disposed toward education, and/or more convinced of their own capacity to handle higher education, than are other local youngsters. A study of the graduates of one of the nation's best-known high schools, which happens to be an alternative school—Central Park East Secondary School in New York City—showed that more than 90% of their students graduate in either four or five years (while on average only 55% of the city's students do so). Of these, 95% go on to college and, it appears, very few of those who start fail to finish. CPESS has a dropout rate of only 5%.[14] To make clear the significance of such figures, it must be added that the school is in Spanish Harlem, an area where 96% of the students come from minority families and almost 80% of them qualify for free or reduced cost lunches. CPESS is a member, in fact a charter member, of the Coalition of Essential Schools, a much respected national network seeking to restructure schools. Ted Sizer, the Coalition's founder, reports that some of its most successful schools are alternatives.

Thus it appears that the research record amassed by alternative schools may eventually come to equal that of progressive education, one of their ideological forebears. The famous Eight-Year Study, which examined the effects of 30 innovative Progressive high schools of the 1930s, concluded that the graduates of such schools had decided advantages over the graduates of conventional high schools.[15] They were more likely to succeed in college than were their counterparts and, in fact, the more innovative their high schools and the farther they departed from the conventional, the greater the advantage of their students. The carefully designed Eight-Year Study was widely acknowledged to have made the case for the innovative schools of its day. Now, taken collectively the documented studies like those cited here, the superiority of alternative schools can be acknowledged.

NOTES

[1] See Center for Research on the Context of Secondary School Teaching. "Report of Survey Findings to Horizon High School, Wyoming, Michigan." Stanford University and Michigan State University, March 1991; and M. W. McLaughlin and J. E. Talbert, "Contexts That Matter for Teaching and Learning." Stanford: Center for Research on the Context of Secondary School Teaching, March, 1993.

[2] M.A. Raywid, "Professional Community and Its Yield at Metro Academy," in *Professionalism and Community: Perspectives on Reforming Urban Schools*, edited by K.S. Louis and S.D. Kruse. Thousand Oaks, CA: Corwin, pp. 45–95.

[3] R. L. Crain, A. Heebner, and Y. P. Si, *The Effectiveness of New York City's Career Magnet Schools. An Evaluation of Ninth Grade Performance Using an Experimental Design*. Berkeley: Center for Research in Vocational Education, 1992.

[4] See G. A. Smith, ed., *Public Schools That Work: Creating Community*. New York: Routledge, 1993; and G. G. Wehlage, R. A. Rutter, G. A. Smith, N. Lesko, and R. R. Fernandez, *Reducing the Risk: Schools as Communities of Support*. Philadelphia: Falmer, 1989.

[5] J. I. Goodlad, *A Place Called School: Prospects for the Future*. New York, McGraw Hill, 1984

[6] See M. A. Raywid, *The Current Status of Schools of Choice in Public Secondary Education*. Hempstead, NY: Project on Alternatives in Education, Hofstra University, 1982; and M.A. Raywid, "Synthesis of Research on Schools of Choice," *Educational Leadership*, April 1984, pp. 70–78.

[7] M. Musumeci and R. Szczypkowski, *New York State Magnet School Evaluation Study. Final Report*. Larchmont, NY: Magi Educational Services, 1991, p. 55.

[8] J. Larson and B. Allen, *A Microscope on Magnet Schools: 1983 to 1986*, Vol. 2: *Pupil and Parent Outcomes*. Rockville, MD: Montgomery County Public Schools, 1988.

[9] Musumeci and Szczypkowski, *New York State Magnet School Evaluation Study.*

[10] T. Gregory and G. Smith, "School Climate Findings," *Changing Schools* 11(2) (Spring, 1983): 8–10.

[11] See M.A. Raywid, "The Mounting Case for Schools of Choice," in *Public Schools by Choice*, edited by J. Nathan. Distributed by Free Spirit Press of Minneapolis. 1989, pp. 13–40.

[12] See, e.g., J. Nathan, *Attitudes Toward High School Education Held by Graduates of a Traditional and an Alternative Public School in St. Paul, Minnesota*. Doctoral dissertation. University of Minnesota, 1981.

[13] Clancy, P., "A Study of the Graduates of a Suburban Alternative High School." Hofstra University, 1988.

[14] Paul Schwarz, "Dear Students, Parents and Staff," *Newsletter* #31, Central Park East Secondary School, May 17, 1993.

[15] Aikin, W.M., *The Story of the Eight-Year Study*. New York: Harper & Bros., 1942.

— *Mary Anne Raywid*

The Use of Computers in Educational Alternatives

When a group of parents and I created the Puget Sound Community School, no one in our group considered himself/herself a technology expert. But we were united in our belief that a basic understanding of computers, especially computer networking, would be an invaluable skill for 21st century adults. We felt that the Internet offers a type of interaction that is typically missing in traditional educational settings, allowing students the freedom to explore alternative learning methods while giving them access to a vast arsenal of information in a matter of seconds. Content can be delivered in the form of text, graphics, sound and/or full-motion video whenever and wherever it is requested, thus catering to the unique learning styles of individual students. So, recognizing that our job as parents and educators was to encourage motivated, skillful, lifelong learners, providing students access to the Internet was a priority.

This is not to say that we designed a school in which students interact with each other only through their home computers; on-line education is but one of the experiences we offer. The foundation of our school is community-based education, which means involving young people in the activities of the community instead of sequestering them from these activities. To facilitate this, we designed our school without a school building. Thus students can regularly interact with each other and members of the community in a variety of public locations. They attend classes in places like libraries, parks and places of business; they are involved in weekly field trips and apprenticeships; and they can participate in community service projects. Believing that learning is best fostered by self-motivation, we do not require our students to participate in any activity in which they lack interest, and we endeavor to provide as many activities as possible that they request. Further, if interested, they can participate in all facets of our administration, from organizing projects to serving as board members.

From the outset then, the basic tenet of our philosophy has been to help students discover and pursue what was important to *them*. We wanted to create a school that encouraged self-motivated exploration, feeling that the best way for individuals to discover their own unique paths was to be fully responsible for their choices and actions. With computer networking, we felt it was best to provide each student a personal Internet access, some basic how-to instructions and let them go at it on their own.

The most popular activity the students have discovered is connecting their computers to a common computer, typically one some distance from their homes in and around Seattle. When they do that, they can interact and talk with others who have also connected to the same computer, just "talking" or playing fantasy-based games. One of our students is even participating in an on-line apprenticeship with a computer engineer who lives in Ohio. They pick a time each week to connect to her system where the student is learning how to do programming.

Imagine students from any part of the world regularly participating in a live, interactive class and you will begin to get a sense of what is possible. Geography, for instance, takes on a greater meaning when you are actually interacting with your classmates from France, Japan and Australia. A greater respect for cultural diversity is nurtured as students learn to communicate with people from a variety of backgrounds.

At a school social gathering a parent shared a story about his son who had a difficult time keeping up with others on the computer network because he wasn't able to type fast enough. He asked his father for pointers on how to increase his typing speed and accuracy and is now motivated to use a typing tutor program. This is from a 13-year-old student who throughout his schooling had refused to write.

Although our Internet service provider is in Seattle, we can connect to our account from any on-line computer in the world and have the same services as we get at home. We can also tap into other computers that provide a variety of services for both students and teachers. One particular service in Illinois allows users to post questions to scientists on a variety of topics. This is an example of how the Internet provides students the opportunity to access experts in any field, closing the gap that often exists between the academic and professional worlds.

Another valuable use of the Internet is through e-mail. Teachers can send private notes to students, at any time, that they then can read in the comfort and privacy of their own homes. These notes include such things as homework reminders, scheduling changes, surveys, and requests for information. We have also connected interested students to keypals (the Internet term for a penpal) all over the world. Early on we made contact with a school in Italy looking for middle school-aged students with whom they could correspond and practice written English.

Another e-mail service we have used this year is called MEMORIES. Started by a veteran of World War II in the United Kingdom, the idea of the MEMORIES project is to allow students from all over the world to interview World War II survivors via e-mail.

One of the more exciting of our Internet projects is our school's involvement in the World Wide Web. The Web is expanding Internet resources to include pictures, video clips and sounds. This allows students with Web access to connect to places like the Louvre and to "see" the Mona Lisa. While I don't want to imply that this replaces actual hands-on experiences, it provides opportunities for students to explore world resources.

We have our own site on the Web, called a Home Page, which allows us to provide information about our school to millions of Internet users worldwide. All of our school newsletters are archived on our Home Page, as is information about our services and programs. We also post messages to enrolled families and have programmed our page so visitors can easily send us an e-mail message. We have linked the Home Pages of other organizations to our page, thus allowing, for example, a student who is studying whales to access the Center for Whale Research.

We teach our students the programming language that allows them to create their own pages that become part of the Web. They can include such things as photographs, audio messages, and samples of their artwork on their individual pages. They can also conduct surveys and receive e-mail from others who connect to their pages. Students with their own Home Pages are no longer writing for just their teachers. They are involved instead in a project that allows them to write for a real audience of people of all ages in the global community.

We are not the only organization providing students with on-line educational opportunities. In Michigan, the Clonlara School, an organization that for many years has assisted homeschooled students from all over the world, has developed Compuhigh. The idea behind Compuhigh was conceived by Stan Kanner as a means of utilizing the advantages of homeschooling in connection with the classes he taught at the Alternative Learning Center, a program of the Fairmont, West Virginia Public Schools. Compuhigh offers students a variety of individualized on-line courses based on the concepts of freedom of choice and active participation by students.

To participate, students first enroll at Clonlara. The next step is to connect to the Delphi computer network which is providing Compuhigh its Internet access. Once enrolled, the students' initial point of entry to Compuhigh is the School Lobby. The School Lobby contains an on-line bulletin board for students and mentors to read and post Compuhigh messages. There are various classrooms that correspond to each course being offered. Each classroom contains a bulletin board for course messages, a forum for ongoing class discussions and a database for uploading and downloading relevant files. Students learn from each other and from the mentors who facilitate the courses. A key component of Compuhigh is the interactive experience; students are participating from all over the world.

In its first year Compuhigh has attracted 25 students, one from as far away as Moscow. To this point, all of the students are homeschoolers, although Kanner is open to extending Compuhigh's services to include students in alternative schools. He said that although the students are connecting from far-away locations, it feels like a "real" school. Like other on-line projects, part of the beauty of Compuhigh is that it allows students to process information and participate in a discussion in a manner that meets their own unique learning styles.

Another cutting edge program is being offered in Chula Vista, California. In 1988 the Sweetwater Union High School District started an innovative computer-based program for at-risk students. Developed by Tom Williams, the district's Director for Alternative Education, the program is now providing nearly 3000 students with a computer-interactive individualized learning program that has helped to dramatically lower student drop-out rates. The district has developed eight student learning centers located on high school campuses. Each center is connected to NovaNET (based in Tucson) which allows instructors to select the most appropriate on-line curriculum resources for individual students from thousands of subject areas. When successfully completed, these individualized courses provide up to 40 percent of a student's grade in the subjects being covered.

To capitalize on the success demonstrated by at-risk students, Sweetwater's Wide-Area Learning Coordinator, Dennis Renfro, created a program in 1993 for the district's high achievers. Participants in this program not only use the resources of NovaNet to complete their basic core curriculum but have gone on to access world-wide databases as well as to create their own on-line forums for poetry, short stories, current events and other subjects. Students involved in the program receive honors-level credit while participating at district learning centers, off-site classrooms and at home.

We have now entered a post-industrial age in which strength comes to those who can act independently and know how to access and use information. In so doing, the role of students has changed. No longer empty vessels on the conveyor belt of education waiting to be filled, students are active participants in the creation of knowledge and meaning. In terms of computer literacy, those learning to use this technology will have the skills necessary for success in the 21st century.

— *Andrew Smallman*

Andrew Smallman, the recipient of thirteen years of traditional schooling, founded and directs the Puget Sound Community School, affording students the trust, respect and responsibility he feels were missing from his education. His e-mail address is pscs@speakeasy.org, and the school home page address is http://www.speakeasy.org/~pscs/.

Alternative Education
A Brief History—and Today's Major Trends

Why are there "alternative" schools? Our system of public schooling was first organized in the 1830s to provide a common, culturally unifying educational experience for all children. Yet, from the very beginning, certain groups of educators, parents and students themselves have declined to participate in this system. Their reasons are various and the forms of schooling—and nonschooling—that they have chosen instead are equally diverse. The history of alternative education is a colorful story of social reformers and individualists, religious believers and romantics. Despite their differences, however, they share an especially strong interest in young people's social, moral, emotional and intellectual development, and, more deliberately than most public school programs, they practice educational approaches that aim primarily to nourish these qualities.

Historians of public education have described how, during the period between 1837 (when Horace Mann became the first powerful leader of a state education agency) and the early twentieth century (when new scientific theories were applied to psychology, learning and organizational management), a particularly narrow model of schooling became solidly established as the "one best system" of public education. According to this model, the purpose of schooling was to overcome cultural diversity and personal uniqueness in order to mold a loyal citizenry and an effective workforce for the growing industrial system. Education aimed primarily to discipline the developing energies of young people for the sake of political and social uniformity as well as the success of the emerging corporate economy. In the early twentieth century, these goals were concisely expressed by the term "social efficiency," which was often used by educational leaders.

Many people are attracted to alternative schools and home education because they feel that this agenda of "social efficiency" does not allow for such values as individuality, creativity, democratic community life and spiritual development. Indeed, Horace Mann's efforts to centralize public schooling were opposed from the start by religious leaders and other critics who argued that education is a community, family and personal endeavor, not a political program to be mandated by the state. For example, many of the Transcendentalist thinkers of the mid-nineteenth century—Emerson, Thoreau, Alcott, Brownson, Ripley—argued against the rigidity of public schooling; and several of them started their own alternative schools. The Temple School in Boston, run by Bronson Alcott between 1834 and 1838 (with his daughter Louisa May as one of the students) is an outstanding historical model of alternative education. Alcott rejected the teaching methods of his time (rote memorization and recitation) and encouraged Socratic dialogue, with a deeply moral and spiritual emphasis.

The roots of many twentieth century alternative school movements go back to three European philosopher/educators: Jean-Jacques Rousseau, Johann Heinrich Pestalozzi and Friedrich Froebel. In his 1762 book *Emile,* Rousseau argued that education should follow the child's natural growth rather than the demands of society, which, he claimed, tend to thwart all that is organic, natural and spiritual. This emphasis on the innate development of human nature became the primary philosophical basis for many alternative movements in education. It has influenced progressive educators as well as generations of libertarian thinkers. In the early 1800s, the Swiss humanitarian Pestalozzi opened schools for orphans, adopting Rousseau's principles. His work inspired educators in Europe and America (including Alcott). One of his disciples, Joseph Neef, emigrated to the U.S. and founded child-centered schools in three states between 1809 and 1827. Froebel was another teacher at Pestalozzi's school, and later became famous as the founder of the kindergarten concept. It is not well known that Froebel envisioned all levels of schooling as being nourishing "gardens" for children's spontaneous development.

This philosophical tradition strongly influenced Francis Parker, who, with John Dewey, originated the progressive education movement late in the nineteenth century. A public school superintendent, head of a teacher education program, and popular speaker and author, Parker believed that education should serve the needs of children and conform to their styles of thinking and learning. Although Parker himself (and many subsequent progressive educators) tried to reform the "one best system" from within, during the first two decades of this century his influence spread to many alternative schools such as those associated with progressive educators like Margaret Naumberg, Helen Parkhurst and Caroline Pratt, among others.

At the same time, two European educational pioneers designed alternative methods with roots going back to Rousseau, Pestalozzi and Froebel. Maria Montessori was an Italian pediatrician/psychiatrist who studied child development with a meticulous scientific eye as well as a deep religious faith in the divine essence of the human being. She opened her first "children's home" in 1907. Rudolf Steiner was an Austrian philosopher/mystic who developed a spiritual science called Anthroposophy that he applied to the fields of medicine, agriculture, architecture and the arts, as well as education. He founded the first Waldorf school in 1919. Both of these methods have evolved into important international movements for educational change.

It was during the 1960s that alternative education grew into a widespread social movement. During this decade, of course, countercultural themes that had always been marginal and virtually invisible—racial justice, pacifism, feminism and opposition to corporate capitalism—exploded into public view. Mass demonstrations, alternative lifestyles and publications, and the urban riots and assassinations of that period led to a deep examination of modern society and institutions. Educators and other writers—including Paul Goodman, John Holt, Jonathan Kozol, Herbert Kohl, George Dennison, James Herndon and Ivan Illich—launched passionate attacks against the "one best system" and its agenda of social efficiency. The period between 1967 and 1972, especially, was a time of crisis for public education, when student demonstrations, teacher strikes, and a deep questioning of traditional assumptions shook the system to its core. In these few years alone, over 500 "free schools"—nonpublic schools based on countercultural if not revolutionary ideas— were founded. Open classrooms and magnet schools (public schools of choice) were introduced. And the spirit of Rousseau, Pestalozzi and Froebel began to seep into academic and professional circles, leading, by the end of the 1970s, to approaches that came to be called "humanistic" and "holistic" education.

The counterculture did not prevail; over the past twenty years, "traditional" values have been strongly reasserted in politics and in education. The 1983 report by President Reagan's Commission on Excellence in Education, *A Nation at Risk*, was a powerful statement of the traditional goals of American public schooling—social efficiency and economic growth—and it led to a tidal wave of political grandstanding, legislative mandates and frantic "restructuring" mainly intended to produce better disciplined citizens and workers for a competitive global economy. George Bush's "America 2000" agenda became Bill Clinton's "Goals 2000" program (now enacted into law) which continued this top-down movement to harness the young generation's energies to the needs of the corporate economy. Those who worked for progressive, child-centered or humanistic education within the system during the heyday of the counterculture have found little support for their vision in recent years. Many have turned to altenative settings.

Within the public system there are now many alternative programs for students "at risk" of dropping out because they are so completely alienated by the impersonal routines of much conventional schooling. And there are still significant pockets of progressive educators and related groups—such as those promoting whole language and cooperative learning—who remain determined to infuse public education with more democratic, humanistic purposes. But despite these oases of student-centered learning, the educational climate during the past decade has been affected by ever tighter state and federal control over learning, leading to still further testing, politically mandated "outcomes" and national standards. There is some hope in the relatively new concept of "charter schools," which allows parents and innovative educators to receive public funding with less bureaucratic intervention, although it remains to be seen how much freedom such schools will be allowed if national standards begin to be enforced.

As government school systems become increasingly yoked to the purposes of the corporate economy, it is likely that thousands more families and educators will turn to the more democratic and person-centered values represented by most alternative schools and home education. For the past century and a half, alternative schools have been isolated countercultural enclaves with little influence on mainstream educational thinking and policy. But in the "postindustrial" or "postmodern" era that appears to be emerging now, the industrial-age model of "social efficiency" is possibly starting to become obsolete.

Perhaps, as Ivan Illich envisioned in his 1970 book *Deschooling Society* and James Moffett describes in his recent book *The Universal Schoolhouse,* the idea of a public school system may have outlived its usefulness. According to these and other authors, in a democratic, information-rich society, learning should take place everywhere in the community. Young people should have access to mentors who nourish their diverse personal interests and styles of learning. We have a long way to go before this sort of system is in place, but if our society does in fact move in this direction, it may well be the alternative educators who show the way.

MAJOR APPROACHES IN ALTERNATIVE EDUCATION

MONTESSORI SCHOOLS   Maria Montessori (1870–1952), the first woman physician in Italy, was working with retarded and emotionally disturbed children around the turn of the century when she discovered that they, as well as normal children, learn best through their senses by working with concrete materials. Building on the earlier work of Eduard Seguin, who had taught deaf-mute children, Montessori devised a set of manipulative learning materials that invite children to explore colors, shapes, textures, sounds, language and even geometric relationships. For example, she designed a series of beautifully colored glass beads to develop numerous mathematical skills. Children responded to these materials enthusiastically, and in her "prepared environment" Montessori and her follow-ers have consistently found children developing intense concentration, self-confidence and a strong interest in learning to read, write and understand their world.

In the Montessori classroom, children are grouped in 3-year age spans and are intro-duced to materials and activities according to their developmental stages and "sensitive periods" of special interest in the environment. They are then free to practice indepen-dently or in small groups for much of the day—a Montessori classroom resembles a busy workshop with activity taking place in every direction. At the same time, Montessori edu-cators emphasize care, courtesy and orderliness within the environment. The Montessori approach is well developed at the elementary level and is becoming increasingly popular in public magnet schools.

WALDORF SCHOOLS   Waldorf education was conceived by the Austrian philosopher Rudolf Steiner (1861–1925) as a means of cultural and spiritual renewal after the devastation of the First World War. Steiner believed that modern Western society had placed too much emphasis on external, materialistic values, at the expense of the imaginative, creative innermost spirit of the human being. The Waldorf curriculum draws upon the mytholo-gies, legends and arts of the great civilizations through history to awaken the creative and emotional life within each child. Since Steiner emphasized the close relationship between children and the adults who are their mentors and models, a group of students stays together with the teacher every year from first through eighth grades; and these teachers are trained to be unusually perceptive of children's temperaments and learning styles.

Teaching methods are carefully designed to match the phases of psychological/spiritual development that Steiner identified. For example, since young children learn primarily through sensation, teachers pay close attention to the use of color, form and music in the environment; and natural materials such as wood, wool and cotton are always used rather than anything plastic or artificial. Early elementary children take in the world primarily through images and feelings, so for these ages Waldorf teachers recite vivid stories and present the curriculum poetically rather than through dry textbook facts. Young children learn through movement, imitation and play, so the teacher leads the class through numerous games, dances and exercises (such as counting or reciting poems while clapping or marching) and introduces them to a unique form of expressive movement, eurhythmy, that Steiner invented. At all stages, imagination and artistic expression are cultivated to the fullest extent possible.

QUAKER SCHOOLS   Quaker schools—elementary, secondary, and college programs—have for many years been counted among the outstanding progressive schools in the United States. In part this is because the Quaker faith has tended to attract many liberal, progressive followers with a deep interest in social justice, peace and democratic social change. In their schools they emphasize student-centered learning based on personal expe-rience and inquiry, a caring and democratic school culture, multicultural and interracial harmony, as well as intellectual ability. But the essence of Quaker education, and the reason that progressive people find Quakerism spiritually nourishing, lies deeper. The founder of the sect in seventeenth century England, George Fox, taught that each individual contains a seed of the divine—what he called "that of God in every one." Each person has access to an "Inner Light" which may, if one learns to "center down" and quiet egotistic desires, reveal important facets of Truth. Given this perspective, education, like worship, becomes a process of personal seeking supported by a caring, nurturing community. The pursuit of truth is not to be prescribed by authority but is, to use Fox's own word, "experimental."

SOME INTERESTING DEVELOPMENTS IN PUBLIC EDUCATION

COOPERATIVE LEARNING.   This is a teaching strategy based on extensive research in social psychology and educational practice which shows that young people enjoy working together and can learn very effectively in groups. The leading authors and consultants within the Cooperative Learning (CL) movement, such as Roger and David Johnson, Yael and Shlomo Sharan, Robert Slavin and Spencer Kagan, have influenced thousands of teachers and devised numerous special techniques for organizing collaborative groups of learners and building classroom communities. For example, they provide effective ways for teams to work together to research a particular topic, or for group members to learn from each other's areas of interest. An advanced model called Group Investigation gives students a great deal of responsibility for pursuing their own learning goals and supporting their peers in doing the same.

CL has the potential to be far more than a set of techniques, however; and many of its practitioners and advocates (for example, Mara Sapon-Shevin, Nancy Schniedewind and Alfie Kohn) are raising serious questions about the destructively competitive nature of schooling and society at large. For more information, including an extensive resource guide, contact the International Association for the Study of Cooperation in Education, Box 1582, Santa Cruz, CA 95061-1582.

WHOLE LANGUAGE.   The Whole Language movement has grown rapidly over the past few years among English teachers who have grown dissatisfied with the monotonous methods of basal readers (condensed, lifeless textbooks with carefully controlled vocabularies), "drill-and-skill" workbooks and other mechanical, uncreative ways of teaching literacy. The Whole Language approach is based on research by Ken Goodman and others in the field of psycholinguistics, which suggests that children best learn to read and write the same way they learned to walk and talk—by plunging in and doing it! Whole Language teachers provide a language-rich environment (real books, storytelling, discussions, journal and letter writing) and emphasize that reading and writing are meaningful activities—ways of communicating our experience to each other—not simply verbal skills or abstract intellectual abilities. By making classrooms meaningful, relevant and exciting to students, Whole Language teachers have begun to examine many of the assumptions underlying conventional schooling, even outside the boundaries of teaching language. Many Whole Language teachers have joined networks and organizations to push for reforms in school management and curriculum design. For more information contact Richard C. Owen Publishers, P.O. Box 585, Katonah, NY 10536.

DEVELOPMENTAL EDUCATION.   A growing number of public school educators are beginning to take seriously what Rousseau pointed out in *Emile* and what educational pioneers like Montessori and Steiner knew so well—children's physical, emotional and intellectual growth unfolds in distinct stages, and there are particular ways of engaging young people that are most appropriate for each stage of development. (Young children do not thrive on math workbooks. Few children learn well while sitting in rows of hard seats. Children should not have their imagination, sociability or curiosity deadened by an abstract, artificially segmented curriculum.) Developmental education takes several forms, such as the "responsive classroom" model developed by the Northeast Foundation for Children (71 Montague City Rd., Greenfield, MA 01301) and now being successfully applied in dozens of schools; the "multiage continuous progress classroom" promoted by the Society for Developmental Education (Ten Sharon Road, Box 577, Peterborough, NH 03458); and the "integrated day" program (popular in the early 1970s as the "open class-room" model and still taught in a few progressive teacher education programs).

A new but very promising developmental theory is the Natural Learning Rhythms (NLR) approach being implemented by the Center for Educational Guidance (P.O. Box 445, North San Juan, CA 95960). Based on years of family counseling experience and wide-ranging research in psychology and education, NLR describes the stages of cognitive, emotional and spiritual growth in great detail and explains how adults can respond to the needs of children most appropriately at each stage. NLR uses terms such as "BodyBeing" and "EmotionalBeing" to describe children's evolving experience and suggests specific activities (such as rites of passage) for helping children through the often difficult transitions from one stage to the next.

MULTIPLE INTELLIGENCES AND LEARNING STYLES.   In 1983, psychologist Howard Gardner of Harvard University introduced his theory of multiple intelligences in his book *Frames of Mind.* In a short time, this theory has inspired numerous educational innovations and experiments around the country. Gardner argued that there are at least seven modes of knowing the world, but that conventional schooling only addresses one or two of them. A truly effective education should engage spatial, musical, interpersonal and other forms of intelligence and thus enable students who are stronger in these areas to thrive. Learning would include a variety of experiences and activities, not just verbal questioning and reading of texts. Other educational researchers have examined learning "styles" and concluded that there are wide differences between people in the ways they process information. They have called upon educators to design diverse and flexible learning environments so that students with a whole range of learning styles can feel comfortable and experience success. For more information about multiple intelligences and learning styles, contact New Horizons for Learning, P.O. Box 15329, Seattle, WA 98115.

FOR FURTHER READING

Luvmour, Sambhava and Josette. *Natural Learning Rhythms: How and When Children Learn.* Berkeley: Celestial Arts, 1993.

Miller, Ron, *What Are Schools For? Holistic Education in American Culture,* Brandon, VT: Holistic Education Press, 1992.

Moffett, James. *The Universal Schoolhouse: Spiritual Awakening Through Education.* San Francisco: Jossey Bass, 1994.

Smith, Gregory. *Education and the Environment: Learning to Live with Limits.* Albany: SUNY Press, 1992.

Wood, George. *Schools that Work: America's Most Innovative Public Education Programs.* New York: Dutton, 1992.

These books are available from *Great Ideas in Education,* P.O. Box 298 Brandon, VT 05733.

— Ron Miller

Ron Miller is the founder of *Holistic Education Review* and is the Director of the Resource Center for Redesigning Education.

Listing of Alternative Schools and Programs

Alabama

Fellowship of Christian Home Educators
PO Box 563, Alabaster, AL 35007
205-664-2232

EPIC Elementary
1000 Tenth Ave S, Birmingham, AL 35205
Louise Caskey, 205-581-5155
Type: magnet
K-5th grade
Philosophy.

Ramsay Alternative School
1800 Thirteenth Ave S, Birmingham, AL 35205
Robert Atkins Jr, 205-933-2420
Type: magnet
9-12th grade
Gifted and talented.

Creative Montessori, Inc (1968)
1650 28th Ct S, Birmingham, AL 35209
Barbara R. Spitzer, Dir, 205-879-3278
Non-profit; tuition: $225-355/mo
17 teachers, 200 students, ages 3-12
Affiliations: AMS, AMI, SNMC
Governance by board
French; PE; soccer field; gym; childcare; urban location.

St Theresa Montessori School
1800 Collier Dr, Midfield, AL 35228-2706

East Lake UMC Academy
1603 Great Pine Rd, Birmingham, AL 35235
Type: home-based

Joseph S. Bruno Montessori Academy (1982)
5509 Timber Hill Rd, Birmingham, AL 35242
Theresa B. Sprain, 205-995-8709
Non-profit; tuition: $195-285
11 teachers, 7 assistants, 206 students
Affiliation: AMS
Governance by administrator
Extensive facilities and materials in (esp. physical and earth) science and biology; completely equipped classrooms in new buildings on 12 acres; rural location; transportation; interns accepted.

CHEF: Christian Home Education Fellowship of Alabama
3423 19th St, Tuscaloosa, AL 35401
Arné Williams or Wayne & Connie Atchinson, Pres
Database of AL contacts, schools and support groups.

University Place School
221 18th St, Tuscaloosa, AL 35401
Linda Albritton
Type: Montessori

Montessori School of Tuscaloosa
919 23rd Ave E, Tuscaloosa, AL 35404-3013

Tuscaloosa Academy
420 26th St N, Tuscaloosa, AL 35406-2722
Type: Montessori

Country Day Montessori School
4500 Crabbe Rd, Northport, AL 35476-2025

Fellowship Christian Support Group
PO Box 583, Double Springs, AL 35553
Rosemary Wright, 205-489-2636
Type: home-based

Crossroads Center
809 Church St NE, Decatur, AL 35601
Michael Ferguson, 205-552-3054
Type: public choice

Athens Support Group
16373 H'ville/Brownsville Ferry Rd, Athens, AL 35611
Randy & Dawn Wilson
Type: home-based
Way Home Christian School, area coordinator.

Children's House Montessori
PO Box 2237, Florence, AL 35630

Florence/Sheffield Area Support Group
1701 Lake Pickwick Dr, Sheffield, AL 35660
Joel Rainer, 205-381-6245
Type: home-based

The Country Day School (1987)
1930 Slaughter Road, Madison, AL 35758

Debby Clark, Admissions Dir, 205-772-8086
Type: Montessori; tuition: $250/400/mo.
15 teachers, 155 students, ages 3-12
Affiliations: NIPSA, NAYEC, Daycare Directors Assoc
Governance by administrator
Hands-on approach; Mortenson Math; Spanish; whole language; computers; fine arts (art, music, classics); portfolio assessment; childcare; suburban location.

Anderson Montessori Academy
7887 Highway 72 W, Madison, AL 35758-9559

Montessori Learning Center (1990)
2334 Pansy, Huntsville, AL 35801
Brenda Tackett, Owner/Dir, 205-534-6296
Tuition: $190/330/mo
4 teachers, 1 assistant, 50 students, ages 3-6
Affiliation: AMS
Governance by administrator
Childcare; urban location; interns accepted.

Mrs Rhonda's Montessori School
3102 Leeman Ferry Rd SW, Huntsville, AL 35801-5330
Rhonda Pennel

Children's House of Montessori
2605 Leeman Ferry Rd SW, Huntsville, AL 35801-5611

Montessori School of Huntsville (1965)
1220 Blevins Gap, Huntsville, AL 35802
Marcia Ramsey, Adm, 205-881-3790
Non-profit; tuition: $1,620/2,475/yr
5 teachers, 3 assistants; student ages 3-9
Affiliation: AMS
Governance by administrator, board
Childcare; suburban location; interns accepted.

Montessori Academy in Bailey Cove
1695 Shady Cove Cir SE, Huntsville, AL 35802-2753
Murty Vardhani

Lee High School
606 Forrest Circle, Huntsville, AL 35811
Tom Owens, 205-536-8136
Type: magnet
9-12th grade
Creative and performing arts and pre-engineering.

Homeschooling Network
PO Box 742, Tallahassee, AL 36078
205-283-5018

Islamic Home School Association of North America
(1988)
RR 1 Box 240, Tuskegee, AL 36083-9127
Anisa Alzoubi, 919-832-1960
Bi-monthly newsletter; networking.

Tuskegee Institute Montessori School
School Of Education, Tuskegee Institute, AL 36088-1693

Montessori Academy
1025 S Hull St, Montgomery, AL 36104-5141

Carver Creative & Performing Arts Center
2001 W Fairview Ave, Montgomery, AL 36108
Cheryl Carter, 205-269-3813
Type: magnet
10-12th grade
Creative & Performing Arts.

Covenant Academy
1147 Freemont St, Montgomery, AL 36111
Lauren Coats, 205-284-1574
Type: home-based
Umbrella.

Greengate Montessori School
3265 McGehee Rd, Montgomery, AL 36111-2301

Christian Educators at Home in Anniston (CHEAHA)
2044 Alexandria-Jacksonville Rd, Jacksonville, AL 36265
Dennis & Nancy Smith, 205-848-9944, 831-5355

Marietta Johnson School of Organic Education
8 Marietta Dr, Box 1555, Fairhope, AL 36532
Mary Bradshaw, 205-925-9347
Type: independent

Baldwin County Home Educators
PO Box 1645, Robertsdale, AL 36567
Gail Hinton

Child Day Care Association of Mobile
457 Conti St, Mobile, AL 36602-2407
Type: Montessori

Dunbar Magnet of the Performing Arts
500 St Anthony St, Mobile, AL 36603
Freddie Sigler, 205-690-8255
4-8th grade
Creative & Performing Arts.

Old Shell Rd Elementary
1705 Old Shell Rd, Mobile, AL 36604
Bobby Glenn Smith, 205-473-6571
Type: magnet
K-3rd grade
Creative and performing arts.

Montessori Academy (1973)
18 Pierpont Dr W, Mobile, AL 36606
Anne C. Brandon, Dir, 205-478-7219
Non-profit; tuition: $220-360/mo
3 teachers, 6 assistants, 84 students, ages 18 mo-6 yrs
Urban location.

Homeschool Advocates
5962 Chalet Dr N, Mobile, AL 36608
205-344-3239

Montessori Spring Hill Children's House
4307 Old Shell Rd, Mobile, AL 36608

Weinacker's Montessori School (1969)
227 Hillcrest Rd, Mobile, AL 36608
John P. B. Weinacker, 344-8755, FAX: 342-0712
Tuition: $150-285/mo
4 teachers, 4 assistants, 68 students, ages infant-9
Governance by administrator
Preschool Spanish; childcare; urban location; interns accepted.

The Sunshine House
Hwy 90 W, Mobile, AL 36609
Type: Montessori

Montessori Children's House
462 Yevonne Curve E, Mobile, AL 36609-2309

Southwest Alabama Home Educators
6721 Timbers Dr W, Mobile, AL 36695
Fred/Kathy Dryer, 205-639-9452

Auburn/Opelika Christian Home Educators
PO Box 2171, Auburn, AL 36830

Children's Montessori School
231 E Drake Ave, Auburn, AL 36830-3917

St Joseph School
General Delivery, Holy Trinity, AL 36859-9999
Type: Montessori

Chattahoochee Valley Homeschoolers Support Group
Phenix City, AL 36867
Bruce/Donna Potenza, 205-298-1229

Alaska

Denali Elementary School
148 E 9th Ave, Anchorage, AK 99501-3699
Susan Moore
Type: Montessori

Steller Secondary School (1974)
2508 Blueberry, Anchorage, AK 99503
Donald Shackelford, 907-279-2541
Type: public choice
250 students, 9–12th grade
Governance by democratic school meeting
Seminar approach; community involvement; work
    experience.

SEARCH
2650 E Northern Lights Blvd, Anchorage, AK 99508-0000
Barbara Garrison, 907-278-9631
7–10th grade

Anchorage Montessori School
1200 E 27th Ave, Anchorage, AK 99508-3303
Betsey Howard

School Within a School
East HS, 4025 E 24th Ave, Anchorage, AK 99510
Type: public choice

Alaska Private and Home Educators
Box 141764, Anchorage, AK 99514
907-753-3018

Hillside Montessori
7340 Hillside Way, Anchorage, AK 99516
Lorrie Lundquist-Yeagle

Nikolaevsk School
PO Box 39010, Ninilshik, AK 99556
Kenneth Moore, Prin, 907-235-8972
K–12th grade

Homeschoolers of Cordova
PO Box 782, Cordova, AK 99574-0782
907-424-3943

Mat-Su Alternative High School
600 E Railroad Ave, Suite 6, Wasilla, AK 99654
Peter Burchell, 907-373-7775
9–12th grade

Kenai Alternative School
152 Park Ave, Soldotna, AK 99669
Rick Matiya, 907-262-6315
K–12th grade

Fairbanks Montessori School
2014 30th Ave, Fairbanks, AK 99701
Kristie Yunker

**Directory of Global Education Resources in North
    America**
(See Resource Section)

Juneau Montessori Center
750 Saint Ann's Ave, Douglas, AK 99801
Deanna Claus

Centralized Correspondence School
3141 Channel Dr #100, Juneau, AK 99801-7897
Marylou Purvis, Prin, 907-465-2835, FAX: 465-2935
K–12th grade

Revilla High School (1972)
3131 Baranof Ave, Ketchikan, AK 99901
Shelley Stallings, Educator, 907-225-6681
Type: public at-risk
4 teachers, 45-52 students, ages 14-21, 9–12th grade
Governance by teachers and principal
Teacher qualifications: AK Certification
Field study of forestry, archeology, karst, fisheries, wildlife
    biology; camping on remote island; multi-aged classes;
    non-compulsory class attendance; rural location; trans-
    portation; interns accepted.

Arizona

Khalsa School (1971)
346 E Coronado Rd, Phoenix, AZ 85004
Satwant Singh Khalsa, 602-252-3759
Type: Montessori, non-profit; tuition: $225/345/mo
6 teachers, 10 assistants, 100 students, ages infant-9
Affiliations: AZ Child Care Assn, FOM; accreditation: AZ DHS
Governance by teachers and administrators
Holistic education; Spanish; yoga; gymnastics; swimming;
    computers; creative dance; drama; art; childcare; urban
    location; interns accepted.

Reed Montessori School (1971)
1124 N 3rd St, Phoenix, AZ 85004
Rita Ramirez, Dir, 602-252-1953
Non-profit; tuition: $160-285/mo
1 teacher, 2 assistants, 30 students, mainly international, ages
    3-6
Affiliation: AMI
Governance by board
Childcare; interns accepted.

Sunrise Montessori Academy
844 North 9th Ave, Phoenix, AZ 85007-2316
Aleena Meyer

Arcadia Montessori Schools
5115 E Virginia Ave, Phoenix, AZ 85008-1628

Montessori Childrens Home
516 W Bethany Home Rd, Phoenix, AZ 85013-1554

North Central Montessori School
6730 N 7th St, Phoenix, AZ 85014-1003

Villa Montessori
4535 N 28th St, Phoenix, AZ 85016-4998
Marilyn Burbach

Phoenix Special Programs (1969)
3132 W Clarendon Ave, Phoenix, AZ 85017
Robert A. Dye, Supt; Eleanor Marine, Registrar, 602-263-2601,
    FAX: 602-265-7179
Type: independent, non-profit; tuition: $80 per half credit

40 teachers, 3000 students, ages 11+, 7-12th grade
Affiliation: NCASC
Governance by principal and board
Teacher qualifications: AZ Certification
Correspondence courses; full curriculum available.

Montessori Day Schools (1981)
9215 N 14th St, Phoenix, AZ 85020
Margaret M. Huffman, 602-943-7672, FAX: 902-395-0271
Tuition: $260/375/mo
16 teachers, 9 assistants, 224 students, ages infant-18
Accreditation: AMS
Governance by administrator
4 large campuses in Phoenix area; sports; music; dance;
    childcare; suburban location; interns accepted.

Montessori Center School
8625 N 19th Ave, Phoenix, AZ 85021

Phoenix Learning Alternatives Network (PLAN) (1989)
8835 N 47th Pl, Phoenix, AZ 85028
Nancy Sherr, 602-483-3381, FAX: -6299
Type: home-based, non-profit; cost: $24/yr,$10/mo activity
    fee
Student ages infant-16
Weekly activities on yearly theme; hands-on approach; non-
    sectarian, eclectic; newsletter; suburban location.

Maryvale High School
3415 N 59th Ave, Phoenix, AZ 85033
Rene Diaz, 602-271-2503
Type: magnet
9-10th grade
Leadership education; community service.

South Phoenix Montessori
1300 S 10th St, Phoenix, AZ 85034-4516

South Mountain High School
5401 S 7th St, Phoenix, AZ 85040
Art Lebowitz, 602-271-2884
Type: magnet
9-12th grade
Visual and performing arts; law; aerospace.

Sigueme
PO Box 54171, Phoenix, AZ 85078
Type: Montessori

Good Earth Montessori (1978)
734 N Robson, Mesa, AZ 85201
Nelleke Van Savooyen, Dir, 602-833-2622
Tuition: $205/370
2 teachers, 3 assistants, 35 students, ages 3-6
Governance by administrator
Located in small old house; suburban location; interns
    accepted.

Bethany Home Educators (1980)
2720 S Flint Circle, Mesa, AZ 85202
Lyn Codier, Secretary, 602-820-5050
Cost: $15/yr membership fee
290 teachers, 1,000 students, ages 5-17, K-12th grade
Governance by board
Teacher qualifications: Affidavit; Iowa Test scores
Iowa Tests for ages 8+; resources; workshops; field trips; edu-
    cational fairs; speech meets; spelling bees; urban location

Tempe Montessori School (1978)
410 S El Dorado Rd, Mesa, AZ 85202
Irma Letson, Adm, 602-966-7606
Tuition: $3,762/yr
10 teachers, 100 students, ages 2.5-12
Affiliation: AMI
Governance by teachers and principal
Teacher qualifications: AMI credential
Farm animal pets; German; French; optional religious ed; no
    letter grades; non-compulsory class attendance; multi-

aged classes; extensive field trips; suburban location;
interns accepted.

Mesa Montessori
2830 South Carriage Lane, Mesa, AZ 85202-7801
Lillian D Busch

Arizona Families for Home Education
639 E Kino Dr, Mesa, AZ 85203
602-964-7435

Montessori International School
1930 E Glencove St, Mesa, AZ 85203

Arizona LDS Home Centered Learners
3360 E Florian, Mesa, AZ 85204
Jessica Russell, 602-924-9369
Home school support group of approximately 150 families.
    Religious orientation is Latter-Day Saint. They publish a
    monthly newsletter called The Liahona.

Montessori Children's Centre
2834 E Southern Ave, Mesa, AZ 85204-5517
Tammy and Diane

Casa De Montessori
745 S Extension Rd, Mesa, AZ 85210-2212

Adobe Montessori School
1700 W Warner Rd, Chandler, AZ 85224-2676

Rainbow Montessori School (1980)
6520 E Cactus Rd, Scottsdale, AZ 85254
Doris or Robin Rasmussen, 602-998-0024
Tuition: $240-370/mo
5 teachers, 20 assistants, 151 students, ages infant-9
Affiliations: NAMTA, AMS
Governance by administrator
Computers; Spanish; Yamaha music; ethnic luncheons; inter-
    national mix; childcare; urban location; interns accepted.

Families For Home Education
PO Box 4661, Scottsdale, AZ 85261
602-941-3938

Joyful Child
(See Resource Section)

Fountain Hills Montessori School
15055 N Fountain Hills Blvd, Fountain Hills, AZ 85268-2330
Carrie Jackson

Alpha Omega Institute (1991)
404 W 21st St, Tempe, AZ 85282
Trish Tackleson, VP of Finance, 602-731-9411, FAX: 602-438-
    2702
Type: independent
175 students, ages 5-14, pre K-8th grade
Governance by board
Curriculum; service; supplies

Awakening Seed School
1130 W 23rd St, Tempe, AZ 85282
Bill Glover, 602-829-1479
Type: independent
Student ages 3-10
Student publishing; global responsibility; creative problem
    solving.

Sunrise Montessori School (1979)
14233 N 47th Ave, Glendale, AZ 85306
Mary Ellen Marion, Dir, 602-843-6053
Tuition: $155-310/mo
2 teachers, 5 assistants, 88 students, ages toddler-12
Affiliation: NAMTA
Governance by administrator
Complete traditional program; Spanish; childcare; suburban
    location.

SPICE (1992)
104-14 W Mulberry Dr, Avondale, AZ
Susan Taniguchi, 602-877-3642
Type: home-based
Suburban location.

Pinal County Public Schools (1993)
PO Box 769, Florence, AZ 85323
Dr Peggy Roush, 602-868-6565, FAX: 602-868-4671
Type: public choice
400 students

Mountainside Montessori
29022 N 62nd St, Cave Creek, AZ 85331
Lucy Kastelic

World University (1967)
Box 2470, Desert Sanctuary Campus, Benson, AZ 85602
Dr. Howard John Zitko, President, 602-286-2985, FAX: 602-286-2985
Non-profit
Governance by board
Schools in USA, Italy, Nigeria, Japan, and India; tutorial; experiential; soul-oriented; each school is independent; parent institution, World U Roundtable, founded in 1947, has annual conference; interns accepted.

Wood Canyon School (1992)
PO Box 781; 54 Wood Canyon, Bisbee, AZ 85603
David Skinner, Dir, 602-432-3995
Type: independent, non-profit; tuition: shared expenses
2 teachers, 6 students, ages 6-18
Affiliations: NCACS, NALSAS, RGEA
Governance by faculty, student reps; parent cooperative
96 acres; seasonal streams; outdoor survival; fine arts; no letter grades; non-compulsory class attendance; multi-aged classes.

Cochise County Families for Home Education
PO Box 533, St David, AZ 85630
602-720-4134

Casas Adobess Montessori
665 W Roller Coaster Rd, Tucson, AZ 85704-3817

Carden School of Tucson (1980)
5260 N Royal Palm Dr, Tucson, AZ 85705
Nette F. Jeppson, Dir, 602-293-6661
Type: independent, non-profit; tuition: $1,750/yr
12 teachers, 95 students, ages 4-14, K-8th grade
Governance by principal
Teacher qualifications: Carden Ed Foundation training
Christian; language; arts; patriotism; urban location.

Montessori Schoolhouse
1127 N 6th Ave, Tucson, AZ 85705

Tucson High School
400 N Second Ave, Tucson, AZ 85705
John Hoge, 602-822-2480
Type: magnet
9-12th grade
Science, math, cumputers, and performing arts.

Reaching Their Highest Potential
430 S Essex Ln Dept N8a, Tucson, AZ 85711
Type: Montessori

New Morning Montessori
1135 N Craycroft Rd, Tucson, AZ 85712

Holladay Elementary
1110 E 33rd St, Tucson, AZ 85713
Nora Grig, 602-798-2737
Type: magnet
4-6th grade
Visual and performing arts.

Senior High Accomodations (1971)
115 N Fremont, Tucson, AZ 85716
Fred McConnell, 602-798-8663
Type: public at-risk
2 teachers; student ages 15-22, 9-12th grade
Governance by faculty and student representatives, democratic school meeting
Contracts; experiential; community use; multi-aged classes; extensive field trips; non-compulsory class attendance; urban location

Kino Learning Center
6625 N First Ave, Tucson, AZ 85718
602-297-7278
Type: independent

Highland Free School (1970)
510 S Highland St, Tucson, AZ 85719
Nicholas Sofka, Director, 602-623-0104
Type: independent, non-profit; tuition: $340/mo, scholarships
3 teachers, 30 students, ages 4.5-12, ungraded
Governance by parent advisory committee open to all
Teacher qualifications: certified teachers
Holistic approach; computer center; creative audio and video activities; music; Spanish; innovative adventure playgrounds; goats, ducks, geese; no letter grades; multi-aged classes; extensive field trips; urban location; interns accepted.

Project MORE (1973)
440 S Park Ave, Tucson, AZ 85719
Robert J Mackey, Dir, 602-798-2806
Type: public choice/at-risk
8 teachers, 200 students, partly at-risk, ages 14-22, 9-12th grade
Affiliation: NCASC
Governance by teachers, principal, board.
Teacher qualifications: AZ Certification
Multi-aged classes; field trips required; academic probation; urban location; limited transportaion; interns accepted.

Zephyr Press
(See Resource Section)

Tucson Home Education Network (THEN)
7521 E Lurlene Dr, Tucson, AZ 85730

Arches (1987)
PO Box 11482, Tucson, AZ 85746
Sarah Evans, 602-883-7436
Type: home-based, non-profit; cost: $20/yr
Emphasizes spiritual knowledge.

Hands-On Science
(See Resource Section)

Hermosa Montessori School (1978)
12051 E Fort Lowell/ 8800 E 22nd St, Tucson, AZ 85749/ 85710
Sheila Stolov, Dir, 602-749-5518, 296-9537
Tuition: $220-345/mo
8 teachers, 6 assistants, 160 students, ages 3-12
Governance by an administrator and democratic school meeting
Teacher qualifications: certification
Two 10-acre campuses; authentic Montessori program; nature studies; art; music; movement; Spanish; childcare; urban & rural locations; interns accepted.

Sunrise
PO Box 190, Whiteriver, AZ 85941
Dave Jones, 602-338-4844
Type: public choice
20 students, HS
Community service; vocational; school-developed business; childcare.

Flagstaff Junior Academy
2401 W Hwy 66 #10, Flagstaff, AZ 86001
Type: Montessori

Twin Peaks Montessori School
2717 N Center St, Flagstaff, AZ 86001

Home School Advantage
(See Resource Section)

Prescott College
220 Grove Ave, Prescott, AZ 86301
Derk Janssen, 602-778-2090

Primavera School
1410 Copper Basin Rd, Prescott, AZ 86301
Carol Darrow, 602-445-5382

The Garden Street Learning Center
134 Garden St, Prescott, AZ 86301
Marilyn King
Type: Montessori

Parents Association of Christian Home Schools
HC 63 Box 5530, Mayer, AZ 86333-9712

Wind, Sand and Stars Sedona Montessori
90 Deer Trail Dr, Sedona, AZ 86336-5120
Claudine Mohoney

Circle of Angels (1988)
PO Box 3452, West Sedona, AZ 86340
Leia & Douglas Stinnett, Dirs, 602-282-0580
Type: home-based

Students mainly spiritually focused
Spiritual education; ready-to-use manual of lesson plans;
    teacher-training; no letter grades.

Veade Valley School (1948)
3511 Veade Valley School Rd, Sedona, AZ 86351
Roy E. Grimm, Head, 602-284-2272, FAX: 284-0432
Type: independent, boarding, non-profit; tuition: $17,325/yr,
    scholarships
24 teachers, 125 students, ages 13–18, 9–12th grade
Affiliations: NAIS, AEE
Governance by board
Teacher qualifications: prefer BA/MA
Emphasis on anthropology, intercultural understanding, envi-
    ronmental stewardship; classical college prep; experiential
    pedagogy; multi-aged classes; extensive field trips; rural
    location; interns accepted.

Montessori Schoolhouse
1325 Ramar Rd, Bullhead City, AZ 86442
Lynn Zubrick

Window Rock
PO Box 559, Ft Defiance, AZ 86504
Tom Hatch, Director, 602-729-5705 x479
Type: public at-risk
4 teachers, 53 students, mainly at-risk, ages 14–20, HS
Governance by board
Teacher qualifications: state certification
Focus on Navajo culture; computer lab; self-paced; multi-
    aged classes; extensive field trips; rural location; trans-
    portation; interns accepted.

Arkansas

Lakeside Montessori School
609 W 15th St, Pine Bluff, AR 71601
Mark Willett

Montessori School of Pine Bluff
611 W 23rd Ave, Pine Bluff, AR 71601

El Dorado Watson Educational Center
1401 E Center St, El Dorado, AR 71730
Sue Castleberry, 501-864-5091
Students mainly at-risk
Experiential; community service required

South Conway County Program
2220 Prince St, Conway, AR 72032
Raymond Simon, Supt, 501-329-8849
Ten-day alternative to suspension; addresses affective and
    cognitive skills; interpersonal relations; parent involvement;
    community resources

Arkansas Christian Home Education Association
PO Box 4410, North Little Rock, AR 72116-2110
501-753-9164

Crystal Hill Elementary Magnet
5001 Doyle Venable Dr, N Little Rock, AR 72118
Wanda Ruffins, 501-753-4323
Student ages 4+,-6th grade
Written, oral, visual communications.

Montessori School of North Little Rock, Inc
Kierre & Perin Rd, N Little Rock, AR 72118

Hilltop Montessori School
3 Kierre Dr, North Little Rock, AR 72118-2303

Children's House Montessori School (1973)
4023 Lee Ave, Little Rock, AR 72205
Nancy Hall, Dir, 501-664-5993
Tuition: $125–205/mo
5 teachers, 4 assistants, 77 students, ages infant-9
Affiliation: AMS; accreditation: AMI
Governance by administrator
Homey; spacious grounds; multi-cultural; music; dance;
    childcare; urban location; interns accepted.

Dunbar Junior High School
1100 Wright Ave, Little Rock, AR 72206
Nancy Volsen, 501-324-2440
Type: magnet
7–9th grade
Gifted and talented; international.

Mann Arts & Math Junior High School
1000 E Roosevelt, Little Rock, AR 72206
Marian Lacey, 501-228-2450
Type: magnet
7–9th grade

Montessori Cooperative School
2101 Main St, Little Rock, AR 72206-1573

Tanglewood Montessori School
7217 Ohio St, Little Rock, AR 72207-5023

Infant Toddler Montessori School (1978)
7205 Illinois St, Little Rock, AR 72207-6033
Jyothi R. McMinn, Dir/Owner, 501-666-7249, FAX: 664-8847
Tuition: $9–18/day
3 teachers, 3 assistants, 54 students, ages infant-6
Affiliations: AMI, AMS, NCME, AAWS; accreditation: NAEYC

Governance by administrator
International and peace studies; visiting international faculty; interns accepted.

Little Rock Montessori School
3704 Woodland Hts, Little Rock, AR 72212
John Harris, Bd Pres, 501-225-2428
Non-profit; tuition: $195/240/mo
4 teachers, 7 assistants, 78 students, ages infant-6
Affiliation: AMI
Governance by parent cooperative
Childcare.

Joseph Pfeifer Kiwanis Camp (1929)
5512 Ferndale Cutoff, Little Rock, AR 72216
Sanford Tollette, 501-821-3714
Students mainly at-risk, ages 9-13, 4-6th grade
Summer program; year-round alternative classroom

Children's House Montessori
PO Box 5105, Little Rock, AR 72225

Forrest City
334 Graham St, Forrest City, AR 72335
Emerson Hall, Supt, 501-633-1485
Students mainly at-risk
Low ratio; GED classes; specialized individual instruction addresses special needs; childcare

Madison Montessori School
PO Box 170, Madison, AR 72359-0170
Vhaness W Chambers

Lee County Program
55 N Carolina St, Marianna, AR 72360
James Davis, Supt, 501-295-7100
7-12th grade
Behavior modification; social adjustment; supervision; intense instruction in core subjects

Crowley's Ridge Christian Parent Education Association
4303 Brenda, Jonesboro, AR 72401
501-972-0243
Type: home-based

Jonesboro Program
1307 S Flint St, Jonesboro, AR 72401
Bill Beasley, Supt, 501-933-5800
ES
Intensive, positive, individualized academic, social services.

The Children's House
300 E Nettleton Ave, Jonesboro, AR 72401-4123
Type: Montessori

Batesville Montessori School, Inc
PO Box 2595, Batesville, AR 72503-2595

Montessori Children's Schoolhouse (1979)
415 N 2nd, Harrison, AR 72601
Karen Shrum, Adm, 501-741-1141
Non-profit; tuition: $160-200/mo
6 teachers, 6 assistants, 128 students, ages infant-12
Affiliation: NAMTA
Governance by board
French activities; custom designed facilities; childcare; rural location; interns accepted.

Clear Spring School (1974)
Box 142, Eureka Springs, AR 72632
Molly Seeligson, Dir, 501-253-7888, FAX: 253-7590
Type: independent, non-profit
6 teachers, 4 assistants, 56 students, ages 3-12, pre K-6th grade
Governance by board
Teacher qualifications: college degree
One on one learning; computer use beginning in first grade; German; handbells; in a 12-acre wooded area, close to downtown; no letter grades; multi-aged classes; extensive field trips; rural location; interns accepted.

Fayetteville High School Within a School
1001 Stone, Fayetteville, AR 72701
Mr Wistry
Type: public

S-W-S (1993)
1001 Stone St, Fayetteville, AR 72701
Wisty Rorabacher or Gilda Pierce, 501-444-3050
Type: public choice
2 teachers, 50 students, ages 15-19, 10-12th grade
Governance by democratic school meeting
Design own course work; freedom to identify, pursue personal interests; multi-aged classes; non-compulsory class attendance; extensive field trips

Uptown School (1972)
108 N West Ave, Fayetteville, AR 72701
501-444-3042
Students mainly at-risk
Governance by administrators
Teacher qualifications: AR Certification
Separate campus; graduation credits; multi-aged classes; interns accepted.

Montessori Children's House
57 E Township St, Fayetteville, AR 72703-2814

Headwater School (1976)
Rt 1, Pettigrew, AR 72752
Kate Kuff, Pres, Board of Dirs, 501-861-5613
Type: independent, home-based, non-profit; cost: $6/day, scholarships
5 teachers, 40 students, ages 2-17
Governance by democratic school meeting, parent cooperative
Located in Ozark Mountains; outdoor education; co-op games; multi-disciplinary projects; with 1, 2, or 3-day attendance, combines home education with group experience; global and environmental awareness; no letter grades; non-compulsory class attendance; multi-aged classes; extensive field trips; interns accepted.

Springdale Learning Center & "Nite" School (1989)
1103 Emma Ave, Springdale, AR 72764
John Dollarhide, 501-750-8832, FAX: 750-8811
Type: public at-risk
8 teachers, 175 students, mainly at-risk, ages 15-50, 9-12th grade
Governance by principal
Teacher qualifications: BA, state certification
Urban location.

Comprehensive Health Education Program
PO Box 645, Paris, AR 72855
Ann Sneed, Dir, 501-963-6531
Student ages 7-18
Social skills development

Ft Smith Montessori School (1968)
3908 Jenny Lind, Ft Smith, AR 72903
Jacqie Mollenhauer, Dir, 501-646-7225
Non-profit; tuition: $1,350/2,250
6 teachers, 93 students, ages 3-12
Affiliations: AMS, NAMS
Governance by administrator and board of trustees
Childcare; urban location.

St Scholastica Montessori
PO Box 3489, Fort Smith, AR 72913-3489

4-A School
PO Box 9050, Texarkana, AR 75505-9050
Robert McDonald, Dir, 501-772-4792
Students mainly at-risk
Social skills; counseling; resource speakers; field tours

California

Drew Junior High School
8511 Compton Ave, Los Angeles, CA 90001
213-583-6961
Type: magnet
7-9th grade
Gifted and high ability.

Russell Elementary School
1263 E Firestone Blvd, Los Angeles, CA 90001
213-582-5034
Type: magnet
1-6th grade
Gifted and high ability.

Simon Rodia High School (1965)
2315 E 103rd St, Los Angeles, CA 90002
Michael Wardlow, Prin, 213-567-3804, FAX: 213-567-4346
Type: public at-risk
3 teachers, 110 students, mainly at-risk, ages 15-18, 9-12th
   grade
Governance by principal
Teacher qualifications: CA secondary credential, LA USD
   teacher pool
Multi-aged classes; urban location.

Thomas Riley High School (1971)
1524 E 103rd St, Los Angeles, CA 90002
Mary Ann Shiner, Prin, 213-563-6692, FAX: 566-6379
Type: public at-risk
15 teachers; student ages 13-18, 7-12th grade
Governance by teachers and principal
Teacher qualifications: secondary certification
3 locations; academics; child birth and parenting skills; multi-
   aged classes; urban location; transportation.

Burroughs Junior High School
600 S McCadden Pl, Los Angeles, CA 90005
213-938-9146
Type: magnet
7-9th grade
Gifted and high ability.

32nd St USC School
822 W 32nd St, Los Angeles, CA 90007
213-748-8007
Type: magnet
1-9th grade
Performing and visual arts.

Adams Junior High School
151W 30th St, Los Angeles, CA 90007
213-744-1502
Type: magnet
7-9th grade
Gifted and high ability.

Audobon Junior High School
4120 11th Ave, Los Angeles, CA 90008
213-299-2882
Type: magnet
7-9th grade
Gifted and high ability.

Hillcrest Elementary
4041 Hillcrest Dr, Los Angeles, CA 90008
213-296-6867
Type: magnet
1-6th grade
Enriched studies; music.

David Roberti Child Development Center
1156 East Vernon Ave, Los Angeles, CA 90011-3719
Type: Montessori

The Accelerated School Charter
450 North Grand Ave, Los Angeles, CA 90012
Joe Rao, 213-625-6040
Type: charter
Students mainly at-risk, K-6th grade
Affiliation: CA BE
Inner city; capital improvements funded largely by teacher-
   obtained grants.

EDUTRAIN (1994)
1100 S Grand Ave, Los Angeles, CA 90015
Keith Turnage, 213-687-9771
Type: charter
850-1500 students, 7-12th grade
Affiliation: CA BE
Academic/voc; counseling and social services; family
   outreach.

Baldwin Hills Elementary
5421 Rodeo Rd, Los Angeles, CA 90016
213-937-7223
Type: magnet
1-6th grade
Gifted and high ability.

and Work Center (AEWC) (1987)
1320 W Third St, Los Angeles, CA 90017
Wendy Reddish, Program Director, 213-625-6649
Type: public at-risk; scholarships
62 teachers, 2300 students, ages 14-19, HS
Affiliation: LAUSD/Adult Division
Governance by school-based shared decision making
Teacher qualifications: ability to work with high-risk youth
23 locations; lab approach; voc training; competency-based;
   independent study; multi-aged classes; urban location.

Mid City Alternative School
3100 W Adams Blvd, Los Angeles, CA 90018
213-731-9346
Type: magnet
K-12th grade

Euclid Elementary
806 Euclid Ave, Los Angeles, CA 90023
213-263-6792
Type: magnet
1-6th grade
Gifted and high ability.

Stevenson Junior High School
725 S Indiana St, Los Angeles, CA 90023
213-262-4101
Type: magnet
7-9th grade
Gifted and high ability.

Westwood Elementary School
2050 Selby Ave, Los Angeles, CA 90025
Michelle Bennett, 310-474-7788
Type: charter
Affiliation: CA BE
Conversion to family model; thematic, experiential.

Southern California Montessori School
1430 S Centinela Ave, Los Angeles, CA 90025-2501

Hollywood High School
1521 N Highland Ave, Hollywood, CA 90028
213-461-7139
Type: magnet
9-12th grade
Performing arts.

El Sereno Junior High School
2839 N Eastern Ave, Los Angeles, CA 90032
213-223-2441
Type: magnet
7-9th grade
Gifted and high ability.

Los Angeles County High School for the Arts
5151 State University Dr, Los Angeles, CA 90032
Bo Vitolo, Prin; Alistair Hunter, Asst Prin, 213-343-2787, FAX: -2549
Type: public choice
485 students, ages 15-18, 10-12th grade
Affiliation: ALCOE/CSULA
Governance by shared decision making committees, principal, faculty and student representatives, board
On CSULA campus; CSULA courses; performance; exhibits; extensive field trips; interns accepted.

Multnomah St Elementary
2101 N Indiana Ave, Los Angeles, CA 90032
213-224-8098
Type: magnet
1-6th grade
Highly gifted.

Hamilton High School
2955 Robertson Blvd, Los Angeles, CA 90034
310-836-1262
Type: magnet
10-12th grade
Humanities.

Palms Junior High School
10860 Woodbine St, Los Angeles, CA 90034
310-837-5001
Type: magnet
6-8th grade
Gifted and high ability.

Play Mountain Place (1948)
6063 Hargis St, Los Angeles, CA 90034
Gaile Price, Director, 213-870-4381
Type: independent, non-profit; tuition: call, scholarships
10 teachers, 84 students, ages 2-13
Governance by teachers and principal, board; student input is encouraged, expected; final decision by board.
Teacher qualifications: experience in humanistic educational techniques
A "country school in the city"; non-authoritarian consensus-based problem-solving, decision-making, communication skills; student body reflects the community, culturally and economically; no letter grades, non-compulsory class attendance; multi-aged classes; urban location; interns accepted.

Acacia Montessori School
10520 Regent St, Los Angeles, CA 90034-6304
Also at 2820 Ponce Ave, Belmont.

Community Elementary
5954 Airdrome St, Los Angeles, CA 90035
213-935-7288
Type: magnet
K-6th grade
Humanities; social sciences.

Open School
6085 Airdrome St, Los Angeles, CA 90035
213-937-6249
Type: magnet
1-6th grade
Individualized.

The Open Charter School
6085 Airdrome St, Los Angeles, CA 90035
Lillian Gephart, 213-937-6249

Type: charter
K-6th grade
Affiliation: CA BE
Magnet school conversion; cluster approach; team teaching; emphasis on technology.

Bancroft Junior High School
929 N Las Palmas Ave, Los Angeles, CA 90038
213-464-3174
Type: magnet
7-9th grade
Television; theater; fine arts.

Eagle Rock Elementary
2057 Fair Park Ave, Los Angeles, CA 90041
213-258-5342
Type: magnet
3-6th grade
Gifted and high ability.

Eagle Rock High School
1750 Yosemite Dr, Los Angeles, CA 90041
213-254-7767
Type: magnet
7-9th grade
Highly gifted.

Eagle Rock Montessori School
1439 W Colorado Blvd, Los Angeles, CA 90041-2320

Arroyo Seco Alternative School (1972)
4805 Sycamore Tr, Los Angeles, CA 90042
J. Sherrard, Asst Prin, 213-254-5141, FAX: 344-0235
Type: public choice
22 teachers, 500 students, ages 5-14, K-8th grade
Teacher qualifications: state credential
Open structure; dedicated to academic excellence and multi-cultural education; students must be able to work independently; community-based learning; parents, students, teachers participate in decision-making; multi-aged classes; extensive field trips; urban location; transportation; interns accepted.

Crenshaw High School
5010 11th Ave, Los Angeles, CA 90043
213-296-5370
Type: magnet
10-12th grade
Gifted and high ability.

Loyola Village Elementary/LMU
8821 Villanova Ave, Los Angeles, CA 90045
310-670-0480
Type: magnet
1-6th grade
Performing and visual arts.

Fairfax High School
7850 Merose Ave, Los Angeles, CA 90046
213-651-5200
Type: magnet
10-12th grade
Visual arts.

Wonderland Ave Elementary
8510 Wonderland Ave, Los Angeles, CA 90046
213-654-4914
Type: magnet
1-6th grade
Gifted and high ability.

74th St Elementary
2112 W 75th St, Los Angeles, CA 90047
213-753-2338
Type: magnet
1-6th grade
Gifted and high ability.

Pluralistic School
851 Wellsley, Los Angeles, CA 90049
Joel Pelcyger, Director

Westland School (1949)
16200 Mulholland Dr, Los Angeles, CA 90049
Janie Lou Hirsch, Dir, 310-472-5544, FAX: 310-472-5807
Type: independent, non-profit; tuition: $7,400/yr,
    scholarships
16 teachers, 130 students, ages 5–12, K–6th grade
Governance by board
Integrated; social studies-based; experiential; block building;
    no letter grades; extensive field trip; interns accepted.

Montessori of West Los Angeles
PO Box 49325, Los Angeles, CA 90049-0325

Turningpoint School
1300 North Sepulveda Blvd, Los Angeles, CA 90049-1656
Deborah Richman
Type: Montessori

Home Education League of Parents (HELP) (1989)
3208 Cahuenga Blvd W, Suite 131, Los Angeles, CA 90068
Terri Endsley, Exec Dir, 800-582-9061
Supports affiliated, autonomous chapters; newsletter;
    unschooling philosophy.

Horizons High School (1991)
6740 E Suva St, Bell Gardens, CA 90201
Paul F. McKernan, Tch in charge, 213-726-1225 x 6191, FAX:
    213-887-7837
Type: public choice
2 teachers, 24 students, ages 15–18, HS
Affiliation: Montebello USD
Governance by teachers and principal
Teacher qualifications: credential
Site-based decision-making; outcome-based activities; pro-
    jects; work experience; post graduation assistance; subur-
    ban location.

Moreno High School (1971)
241 Moreno Dr, Beverly Hills, CA 90212
Joseph S. Wianecki, Dir, 310-201-0661 x456, FAX: 556-4319
Type: public at-risk
2 teachers, 40 students, ages 15–18, 9–12th grade
Governance by board
Counseling; no letter grades; multi-aged classes; urban
    location.

Compton Lynwood Child Development Center
530 W Alondra Blvd, Compton, CA 90221
Type: Montessori

Culver City Independent Study
11450 Port Rd, Culver City, CA 90230

Montessori School of Downey
11822 Downey Ave, Downey, CA 90240

Montessori Children's Academy
9062 Firestone Blvd, Downey, CA 90241-5318
Janet Morton

Ameston Elementary
1048 W 149th St, Gardena, CA 90247
310-327-3716
Type: magnet
1–6th grade
Television; theater; fine arts.

Moneta High School (1972)
1230 W 177th St, Gardena, CA 90248
Adele Bloom, Prin, 310-329-4139, FAX: 310-352-4027
Non-profit
3–4 teachers, 85–97 students, mainly at-risk, ages 16–20
Affiliation: Los Angeles USD
Governance by teachers, principal
Teacher qualifications: CA certification

Contract-based; self-paced; computers; diploma program;
    some SE services; multi-aged classes; interns accepted.

Santa Monica Montessori Institute
27473 Pacific Coast Hwy, Malibu, CA 90265
Type: Montessori teacher education

Independent Study Program (1982)
1301 Artesia Blvd, Manhattan Beach, CA 90266
Judi James, Coord, 372-1730
Type: public at-risk
13 teachers, 440 students, ages 14+, 9–12th grade
Governance by teachers, principal
Interns accepted.

Manhattan Academy (1975)
1740 Mahattan Beach Blvd, Manhattan Beach, CA 90266
Gail Burch, 310-374-1804
Type: Montessori; tuition: $425-745/mo
6 teachers, 5 assistants, 102 students, ages infant–12
Accreditation: AMI
Governance by administrator
Self-concept, creativity; childcare; suburban location; interns
    accepted.

Marquez Charter School
16821 Marquez Ave, Pacific Palisades, CA 90272
Jacqueline Ota, 610-454-4019
Type: charter
K–5th grade
Affiliation: CA BE
Conversion; thematic, cooperative.

Palisades Charter High School
15777 Bowdoin St, Pacific Palisades, CA 90272
Merle Price, 310-454-0611
Type: charter
Affiliation: CA BE
Conversion.

Palisades Elementary Charter
800 Vie De La Paz, Pacific Palisades, CA 90272
Terri Lynn Arnold, 310-454-3700
Type: charter
K–5th grade
Affiliation: CA BE

Temescal Canyon High School (1976)
777 Temescal Cyn Rd, Pacific Palisades, CA 90272
Kay Lachter, Prin, 310-454-0315, FAX: 310-459-8560
Type: public at-risk
3 teachers, 81 students, ages 15–18, 9–12th grade
Governance by leadership council, principal, teachers, classi-
    fied member, parent member
Teacher qualifications: CA credential
Work experience; poet conducts literary sessions, has pub-
    lished students' work; counseling group for girls in abusive
    relationships; extensive field trips; multi-aged classes

Redondo Shores High School (1993)
1000 Del Amo Blvd, Redondo Beach, CA 90277
Judi James, Coord, 213-798-8690
Type: public at-risk
5 teachers, 134 students, ages 16–19, 10–12th grade
Governance by teachers, principal

Enthusiasm for Learning Foundation
(See Resource Section)

Redondo Beach Alternative Program (1993)
1401 Inglewood Ave, Redondo Beach, CA 90278
Sandy Clifton, 310-379-5449, FAX: 310-798-8659
Non-profit
Suburban location.

State St Elementary School
3211 Santa Ana St, South Gate, CA 90280-2305
Type: Montessori

Morning Glory School
2522 Lincoln Blvd, Marina Del Rey, CA 90291
Zarina Paroo
Type: Montessori

Westside Alternative School
104 Anchorage St, Marina del Rey, CA 90292
310-821-2019
Type: magnet
K–12th grade

Independent Study
401 S Inglewood Ave, Inglewood, CA 90301

The University of Children (1986)
1518 Centinela Ave, Inglewood, CA 90302
Lore Geissler, Adm, 310-677-4406
Type: Montessori; tuition: $275–520/mo
4 teachers, 7 assistants, 107 students, ages infant–9
Affiliations: NCME, AMS, AMI,, NAEYC
Governance by administrator
Childcare; urban location.

Canyon Charter School
421 Entrada Dr, Santa Monica, CA 90402
Joyce Landsverk, 310-454-7510
Type: charter
ES
Affiliation: CA BE

Montessori Institute of Los Angeles
2918 Santa Monica Blvd #D, Santa Monica, CA 90404
Type: Montessori teacher education

Thoreau Montessori School
1508 17th St, Santa Monica, CA 90404-3402

Santa Monica Montessori School
1619 20th St, Santa Monica, CA 90404-3817

Santa Monica Alternative School House (SMASH) (1973)
2802 4th St, Santa Monica, CA 90405
Jim Cantor, Teaching Prin, 310-396-2640, FAX: 452-4353
Type: public choice
6 teachers, 180 students, ages 5–14, K–8th grade
Affiliation: SMM USD
Governance by teachers, principal, parents, students
Teacher qualifications: CA credential
Community of learners; no letter grades; extensive field trips;
    multi-aged classe; interns accepted.

Santa Monica Waldorf School (1988)
1512 Pearl St, Santa Monica, CA 90405
Beth Resch, 310-450-0349
Non-profit; tuition: $6,400-7,200/yr, scholarships
5 teachers, 4 assistants, 47 students, ages 3–10, pre K–4th
    grade
Affiliation: AWSNA
Governance by board of trustees
Teacher qualifications: Waldorf teacher training
Emphasizes imagination, creativity in all areas; each subject
    pursued intensively for several weeks; no letter grades;
    suburban location; interns accepted.

Montessori Institute of Los Angeles, Inc (1968)
PO Box 265, Santa Monica, CA 90406
Estela C. Palmieri, Dir of Training, 310-395-5676
Type: higher education, non-profit; tuition: $4,800/course
20 students, mainly international
Accreditations: AMI, MACTE
Governance by board
AMI 3-6 Primary Diploma summer course; approved by CA
    Supervisor of Public Instruction; urban location.

GreenMeadows Montessori
4627 Greenmeadows Ave, Torrance, CA 90505-5505

Peninsula Montessori School
3646 Newton St, Torrance, CA 90505-6635
Claudia Krikorian

Whittier Friends School (1974)
6726 S Washington Ave, Whittier, CA 90601
Sharon G. Rollins, 310-945-1654
Type: Quaker, non-profit; tuition: $3,400/yr, scholarships
1 teacher, 30 students, ages 6–13, 7th grade
Affiliation: Friends Council on Education
Governance by administrator, board
Teacher qualifications: credential
Latest technology; whole-classroom learning; conflict man-
    agement-based approach; extensive field trips; multi-aged
    classes; urban location.

Primente Montessori School
10947 South Valley Home Ave, Whittier, CA 90603-3041
Millie Primanti

East Whittier City School District
14535 E Whittier Blvd, Whittier, CA 90605
Dr Ron Oliver
Type: Montessori

Franklin Community School
5777 S Lockleed Ave, Whittier, CA 90606
Marsha A Brown, Prin, 310-692-1497, FAX: 908-0332
Type: public at-risk
2 teachers, 1 assistant, max 34 students, mainly at-risk, ages
    11–14, 6-9th grade
Governance by teachers, principal, student reps.
Multi-aged classes; counselor; max 17/class; JTPA; parenting
    classes; suburban location; transportation.; interns
    accepted.

HCL (1980)
PO Box 4643, Whittier, CA 90607
Susan Jordan, Dir, 310-696-4696
Type: home-based; cost: $196/family
600 students, ages 5–18, K–12th grade
Affiliations: NCACS, NHA, NALSAS
Governance by principal
Administrative unit

Children's House
8271 Gay St, Cyprus, CA 90630
Ann Perrah, 714-995-2054
Type: independent

Contract Independent Study
123 S Montebello Blvd, Montebello, CA 90640

Fremont Elementary (1991)
200 W Madison Ave, Montibello, CA 90640
213-721-2435
Type: public choice
23 teachers, 700 students, mainly at-risk, ages 5–10, K–4th
    grade
Governance by teachers, principal.
No letter grades; multi-aged classes; suburban location;
    transportation.

PASS Program (1990)
12820 Pioneer Blvd, Norwalk, CA 90650
Jerry McCamly, Team Leader, 310-868-0431 x5209, FAX: 802-
    1596
Type: public at-risk; scholarships
11 teachers, 550 students, ages 13–20, HS
Governance by teachers and principal
Teacher qualifications: state certification
CAI; independent study; suburban location.

Christian Home Educators
Box 2009, Norwalk, CA 90651-2009
800-564-2432, 310-864-2432

Home And Independent Study
9333 Los Lomas Ave, Pico Rivera, CA 90660

Ruben Salazar Continuation (1968)
9515 Haney St, Pico Rivera, CA 90660

Anne Eichman, Alt Ed Dir, 310-801-5128
Type: public at-risk
7 teachers, 170 students, ages 16-18, 10-12th grade
Governance by teachers and principal
Teacher qualifications: BA
Self-paced; job development; multi-aged classes; suburban location; interns accepted.

ABC Secondary Independent Study
16534 S Carmenita Rd, Cerritos, CA 90701
Type: public choice

Montessori Center
12914 Wolverton Ln, Cerritos, CA 90701
Hasmita Parekh

Tracy High School
12222 Cuesta, Cerritos, CA 90701
George Hershey, Prin, 310-926-7136
Type: public at-risk
20 teachers, 350 students, ages 16-19, 10-12th grade
Governance by teachers and principal
Thematic instruction; student, family services; career ed; suburban location.

Montessori School of Bell Flower
5840 Premiere Ave, Lakewood, CA 90712
Deborah Zampa

American Montessori Consulting
(See Resource Section)

Dodson Junior High School
28014 Montereina, San Pedro, CA 90732
310-833-4877
Type: magnet
7-9th grade
Gifted and high ability.

Harbor Math & Science Elementary
1214 Park Western Pl, San Pedro, CA 90732
310-831-3253
Type: magnet
1-6th grade
Gifted and High Ability.

South Shores/CSUDH
2060 W 35th St, San Pedro, CA 90732
310-832-6596
Type: magnet
1-6th grade
Performing and visual arts.

Brighter Days Montessori
1903 W Summerland St, San Pedro, CA 90732-2526

Ambler Ave Elementary
319 E Sherman Dr, Carson, CA 90746
310-532-4090
Type: magnet
1-6th grade
Gifted and high ability.

Stevenson Elementary
515 Lime Ave, Long Beach, CA 90802
Julie Mendell, 310-437-0407
Type: magnet
K-5th grade
Performing arts.

Bay Shore School
PO Box 13038, Long Beach, CA 90803
310-434-3940
Type: home-based
Independent study.

Hamilton Middle School
1060 E 70th St, Long Beach, CA 90805

Ross Shickler, 310-602-0302
Type: magnet
6-8th grade
Visual arts and technology.

Lindberg Middle School
1022 E Market St, Long Beach, CA 90805
Dennis Lyman, 310-424-2845
Type: magnet
6-8th grade
Visual and performing arts.

Hughes Middle School
3846 California Ave, Long Beach, CA 90807
Gary Graves, 310-595-0831
Type: magnet
6-8th grade
Talent achievement program.

Butler Elementary
1890 Orange Ave, Long Beach, CA 90808
Charlotte Smith, 310-591-7477
Type: magnet
3-8th grade
Creative and performing arts.

Montessori School-Eureka
5306 E Arbor Rd, Long Beach, CA 90808
Leonard F. Pijpaert, 310-421-5505
Tuition: $300-330/mo
4 teachers, 10 assistants, 135 students, ages 3-12
Affiliation: AMI; accreditations: CA DSS,
Governance by administrator
Support activities in piano, computers, sports, gymnastics, dance and karate; childcare; suburban location; interns accepted.

Audio Memory Publishing
(See Resource Section)

Long Beach Educational Partnership High School (1988)
125 E 8th St, Long Beach, CA 90813
Frederick Kimbrel, Asst Prin, 310-495-1397
Type: public choice
9 teachers, 500 students, mainly at-risk, ages 15-18, 9-12th grade
Governance by board
Teacher qualifications: state credential
Cooperative effort between Long Beach USD and Ultimate Resources Inc. to recover youths who have dropped out of the regular comprehensive HS; modified independent study; urban location.

Constellation Community Charter Middle School
701 Locust Ave, Long Beach, CA 90813-4316
Rachel Schwenn, 310-436-9931
Type: charter
6-8th grade
Affiliation: CA BE

Fremont Elementary
4000 E 4th St, Long Beach, CA 90814
Jacquelyn Dodge, 310-439-6873
Type: magnet
K-5th grade
Conservatory of music.

Bixby Elementary
5251 E Stearns St, Long Beach, CA 90815
Naomi Blackmore, 310-498-3794
Type: magnet
K-5th grade
Structure of the intellect.

Montessori at Long Beach
2301 Ximeno Ave, Long Beach, CA 90815-1839
Barbara McClean

Montessori Children's House
5550 E Atherton St, Long Beach, CA 90815-4008

Pasadena Waldorf School (1979)
209 E Mariposa St, Altadena, CA 91001
Nancy Thurlbeck, Enrl Dir, 810-494-9564
Non-profit; tuition: $4,378-5,379/yr, scholarships
22 teachers, 162 students, ages 4.9-12, K-8th grade
Affiliation: AWSNA
Governance by faculty and board
Teacher qualifications: Waldorf training
Classical curriculum; suburban location.

Walden School
1999 Mar Vista Ave, Altadena, CA 91001-3127
Type: Montessori

Rancho High Independent Study
150 S 3rd Ave, Arcadia, CA 91006

Wonder Years Montessori School
141 W Las Tumas Dr, Arcadia, CA 91007
Sandhya Ray

Park Alternative Center (1984)
c/o Monrovia USD, 325 E Huntington Dr, Monrovia, CA 91016
Dr Ellen A. Lavin, 818-357-0320
Type: home-based public choice
3 teachers, 80 students, mainly at-risk, ages 5-18, K-12th grade
Governance by teachers and principal
Teacher qualifications: state certification
Independent study for HS; homeschooling; suburban location.

Montrose Christian Montessori
2710 Piedmont Ave, Montrose, CA 91020
Linda Di Giovanni

Arcadia Montessori School
PO Box 767, Arcadia, CA 91066-0767

Pacific Oaks Children's School (1945)
714 W California Blvd, Pasadena, CA 91105
Margaret Heritage, Dir
Type: Quaker, non-profit; tuition: $1,080-8,100/yr
45 teachers, 225 students, ages infant-9, pre K-3rd grade
Affiliation: Pacific Oaks College
Governance by principal, faculty and student representatives, and board
Teacher qualifications: MA for faculty, BA for head teachers in ECE or CD
Anti-bias; emphasis on environment, self-esteem, choice making; parental involvement; arts; special needs; humanistic; Pacific Oaks College students work with children; two campuses, located in Cultural Heritage neighborhoods; no letter grades; multi-aged classes; childcare; suburban; interns accepted.

Sequoyah School (1958)
535 S Pasadena Ave, Pasadena, CA 91105
Hannah Maclaren, 818-795-4351, FAX: 818-795-8773
Type: independent, non-profit; tuition: $5,400, scholarships
17 teachers, 166 students, ages 5-14, K-8th grade
Governance by democratic school meeting
Teacher qualifications: BA/BS, certification; open ed, montessori, alt ed experience preferred
23,000 volume library; integrated curriculum; arts, science, camping/field studies; computers in all classrooms; science lab facility; no letter grades; multi-aged classes; extensive field trips; childcare; urban location; interns accepted.

Victory Montessori Schools
444 S Sierra Madre Blvd, Pasadena, CA 91107

Network of Progressive Educators
(See Resource Section)

Glendale Montessori Elementary
1212 N Pacific Ave, Glendale, CA 91202
Nina O'Brian and Marta Tyler

St Anne Montessori School
1479 E Broadway, Glendale, CA 91205

Options for Youth
2529 Foothill Blvd, Suite 1, La Crescenta, CA 91214
John Hall, 213-957-4280
Type: 3 yr charter
7-12th grade
Store-front serving drop outs since 1987.

Oak View High School (1982)
5701 E Conifer St, Oak Park, CA 91301
Larry Misel, Alt Ed Dir, 818-707-7919
Type: public at-risk
4 teachers, 50 students, mainly at-risk, ages 14-19, 9-12th grade
Governance by teachers and principal
Teacher qualifications: state credential
A California Model School; college and non-college paths; suburban location; interns accepted.

Montessori School of Agoura
28124 Driver Ave, Agoura, CA 91301-2643

Welby Way Elementary
23456 Welby Way, West Hills, CA 91307
818-992-8229
Type: magnet
1-6th grade
Gifted and high ability.

Beginning Montessori Children's House
7475 Fallbrook Ave, West Hills, CA 91307-1502

Santa Susana School
22280 Devonshire St, Chatsworth, CA 91311
Dr Marilyn Lucky
Type: Montessori

Montessori Children's House of Newbury Park (1986)
1360 S Wendy Dr, Newbury Park, CA 91320-5532
Pam Nelson, Dir, 805-499-7495
Non-profit; tuition: $275-315/mo
4 teachers, 3 assistants, 44 students, ages 3-9
Quiet, natural setting; across from Santa Monica Rec. Area; interns accepted.

Balboa Blvd Elementary
17020 Labrador St, Northridge, CA 91325
818-349-4801
Type: magnet
1-6th grade
Gifted and high ability.

Highland Hall School
17100 Superior St, Northridge, CA 91325
Christine Meyer
Type: Waldorf

Casa Montessori
17633 Lassen St, Northridge, CA 91325-1400
Sakura Long

Vena Ave Elementary
9377 Vena Ave, Arleta, CA 91331
818-896-9551
Type: magnet
1-6th grade
Gifted and high ability.

Pacoima Junior High School
9919 Laurel Canyon Blvd, Pacoima, CA 91331
818-899-5291
Type: magnet
7-9th grade
Television; theater; fine arts.

Canterbury Ave Elementary
13670 Montague St, Pacolma, CA 91331
818-892-1104
Type: magnet
1-6th grade
Gifted and high ability.

Cleveland High School
8140 Vanalden Ave, Reseda, CA 91335
818-349-8410
Type: magnet
9-12th grade
Humanities.

Vaughn Next Century Learning Center
13330 Vaughn St, San Fernando, CA 91340
Yvonne Chan, 818-896-7461
Type: charter
1024 students, pre K-6th grade
Affiliation: CA BE
Conversion; multi-track year-round calendar w/ early childhood education and child care.

Fenton Avenue School
11828 Gain St, Lake View Terrace, CA 91342
Joseph Lucente Jr, 818-896-7482
Type: charter
1180 students, pre K-6th grade
Affiliation: CA BE
Conversion; multi-track, year-round; 3 hr/wk parental involvement required.

Park Montessori
13130 Herrick Ave, Sylmar, CA 91342
Grace Park

Sepulveda Junior High School
15330 Plummer St, Sepulveda, CA 91343
818-891-5859
Type: magnet
7-9th grade
Gifted and high ability.

Porter Junior High School
15960 Kingsbury St, Granada Hills, CA 91344
818-891-1807
Type: magnet
7-9th grade
Gifted and high ability.

San Jose St Elementary
14928 Clymer St, Mission Hills, CA 91345
818-361-4325
Type: magnet
1-6th grade
Highly gifted.

Rivendell Montessori School
10651 Vinedale St, Sun Valley, CA 91352-2825

Learning Post High Independent Study
23007 W Dalbey Dr, Valencia, CA 91355

Portola Junior High School
18720 Linnet St, Los Angeles, CA 91356
818-708-2865
Type: magnet
7-9th grade
Highly gifted.

Montessori World
2685 Calle Abedul, Thousand Oaks, CA 91360
David Browne

Little Oaks Montessori
101 N Skyline Dr, Thousand Oaks, CA 91361

International Association of Progressive Montessorians
2509 E Thousand Oaks Blvd #340, Thousand Oaks, CA 91362
Lori and Lowell Byrne

JFK School Within a School
27845 Beacon St, Castaic, CA 91384
Jane Lopez
Type: public choice

Valley Alternative Magnet (1973)
6701 Balboa Ave, Van Nuys, CA 91406
Terry Morton, Prin, 818-342-6133
Type: public choice
20 teachers, 540 students, ages 5-18, K-12th grade
Affiliation: LA USD
Governance by principal, teachers, parents, students
Community service; career internships; concurrent enrollment in community colleges; speakers bureau; extensive field trip; interns accepted.

Fairfield School
16945 Sherman Way, Van Nuys, CA 91406-3614
Howard Spike
Type: Montessori

Kester Ave Elementary
5353 Kester Ave, Van Nuys, CA 91411
818-787-3026
Type: magnet
1-6th grade
Gifted and high ability.

Van Nuys High School
6535 Cedros Ave, Van Nuys, CA 91411
818-781-2371
Type: magnet
10-12th grade
Performing arts.

Tripod Montessori School
2901 Keystone St, Burbank, CA 91504

Earhart High School
5355 Colfax Ave, N Hollywood, CA 91601
Susan Allen, Prin, 818-769-4877, FAX: 818-980-1794
Type: public at-risk
4 teachers, 120 students, mainly at-risk, ages 15-19, 10-12th grade
Governance by teachers, principal, and clerical rep
Teacher qualifications: CA Credential
Structured and individualized classes; special ed; student volunteer program; multi-aged classes.

North Hollywood High School
5231 Colfax Ave, N Hollywood, CA 91601
818-769-8510
Type: magnet
10-12th grade
Highly gifted.

GoodEarth Montessori School (1991)
2593 Chino Hills Pkwy, Chino Hills, CA 91709
Sofi Kasubhai, Adm, 909-393-0998
Tuition: $285-330/mo
6 teachers, 11 assistants, 156 students, ages 2.5-6
Affiliation: NCME
Governance by administrator
Teacher qualifications: Montessori training
Individualized education; childcare; suburban location; interns accepted.

Buena Vista High School (1965)
13509 Ramona Ave, Chino, CA 91710
Jon L. Sweat, Prin, 909-628-9903
Type: public choice
11 teachers, 270 students, partly at-risk, ages 14-19, 9-12th grade
Governance by board

Student advisory groups meet weekly with staff to set curriculum and goals; model teen parenting program; multi-aged classes; childcar; interns accepted.

Montessori Academy of Claremont
PO Box 1150, Claremont, CA 91711
Sandra Schmidt

Montessori Children's Center
4066 Las Casas Ave, Claremont, CA 91711-2323

Riverside Area Home Learners
c/o Gibson, 13171 Spur Branch Cir, Corona, CA 91719
909-245-0902

Children's Montessori Center
2791 Green River Rd # 112, Corona, CA 91720
Misreen A Firdjy

Montessori School of Pai Plaza (1991)
1400 W 6th St, #112, Corona, CA 91720
Mina Patel, Dir, 909-734-0555
Tuition: $250/350/mo
2 teachers, 4 assistants, 50 students, mainly international, ages 3-6
Governance by administrator
Safe environment; plentiful materials; computer; music; gymnastics; dance; childcare; urban location; interns accepted.

Ramona Community School
3548 Doe Springs, Carona, CA 91720-3603
Cheri Spies Havens
Type: Montessori

ET2 Educlional Clinic (1986)
15540 E Fairgrove Ave, La Puente, CA 91744
Michael Keith, Coord, 818-855-3132
Type: public at-risk
23 teachers, 400 students, ages 13-18, 8-12th grade
Governance by teachers, principal
Teacher qualifications: CA credential
Assessment-based; individualized; goal setting; job placement, readiness; HS completion; urban location.

Valley Alternative High School (1993)
14162 E Lomitac Ave, La Puente, CA 91744
Rob Arias, Prin, 818-855-3855, FAX: 818-855-3719
Type: public/independent choice/at-risk
13 teachers, 450 students, ages 13-19, 7-12th grade
Governance by teachers and principal
Open school concept; technology-driven curriculum; suburban location; transportation; interns accepted.

Montessori Child Development Center (1974)
15207 Los Robles Ave, Hacienda Heights, CA 91745
Carolyn S. Mueller, Exec Adm, 968-8207
8 teachers, 4 assistants, 184 students, ages infant-12
Affiliation: AMI
Governance by administrator
Air conditioning; year-round swimming lessons; field trips; French; Spanish; music; keyboard; arts; suburban location; interns accepted.

Genesis Program (1989)
904 N Willow Ave, La Puente, CA 91746
Rita Leroux, Director, 818-918-3266, FAX: 918-3491
Type: public at-risk
2 teachers, 33 students, ages 14-19, 7-12th grade
Affiliations: Cal Poly, Pomona, Azusa Pacific College, Girl Scouts, United Way, JTPA
Governance by teachers and principal
Teacher qualifications: state certification
Multi-aged classes; urban location; transportation; interns accepted.

Rowland Heights Montessori Institute
18760 E Solima Rd, Rowland Height, CA 91748
Dora Nedic

Meher Montessori School (1972)
2009 S Garfield Ave, Monterey Park, CA 91754
Gail Shaeffer, Dir, 213-724-0683
Tuition: $430/mo
5 teachers, 12 assistants, 130 students, ages 3-12
Affiliation: NAMTA; accreditation: AMI
Governance by administrator
Teacher qualifications: 20 years experience
Multi-cultural; childcare; suburban location; interns accepted.

Mujeres Y Hombres Nobles (1992)
1260 S Monterey Pass Rd, Monterey Park, CA 91754
Annie Cabrera, Asst Prin, 213-262-2263, FAX: 213-262-4043
Type: public at-risk
10 teachers, 150 students, ages 10-18, 7-12th grade
Affiliation: LA Co Office of Ed
Governance by consortium model, including community-based organizations, parents, faculty and students.
Teacher qualifications: multiple subject state credential
Community services homebase; counseling; health and welfare services, referrals; urban location.

Village Montessori Academy (1985)
23431 Golden Springs Dr, Diamond Bar, CA 91765
Sofi Kasubhai, Adm, 909-860-4001
Tuition: $285/330/mo
5 teachers, 6 assistants, 100 students, mainly international, ages infant-6
Affiliations: AMS, NAEYC, SCAEYC, NCME
Governance by administrator
Interns accepted.

Pacific Ackworth Friends School
6210 Temple City Blvd, Temple City, CA 91780
Nancy Blomeyer, Dir, 818-287-6880
Type: Quaker

Del Paso High School
476 S Lemon Ave, Walnut, CA 91789
Dr Richard Stevens, Prin, 909-594-0776
Type: public choice/at-risk
11 teachers, 200 students, ages 15-18, 9-12th grade
Affiliations: WASC, CCEA
Governance by board
Teacher qualifications: credentials
Continuation; CA model school; no letter grades; multi-aged classes; suburban location; transportation; interns accepted.

Independent Study
1717 W Merced, W Covina, CA 91790

Century High School (1932)
20 Marengo Ave, Alhambra, CA 91801
Jacqueline Coulette, Prin, 818-308-2250, FAX: -2597
Type: public at-risk
8 teachers, 250 students, ages 16-18, 9-12th grade
Affiliation: WASC
Governance by teachers, principal
Teacher qualifications: CA credential
Up to 30 advisees per teacher/advisor; model drug/alcohol program; petting zoo

Oneonta Montessori School
2221 W Poplar Blvd, Alhambra, CA 91801

Friendly Foreign Language Learning
(See Resource Section)

Clear View Elementary Charter School
455 Windrose Way, Chula Vista, CA 91910
Ginger Hovenie, 619-498-3000
Type: charter
K-6th grade
Affiliation: CA BE

Discovery School
1100 Camino Biscay, Chula Vista, CA 91910
Fred Elliot, 619-656-0797
Type: charter
K-6th grade
Affiliation: CA BE

Hilltop Learning Center (1991)
555 Claire Ave, Chula Vista, CA 91910
Anita Minor, 619-425-4593
Type: public at-risk
4 teachers, 180 students, ages 14-19, 9-12th grade
Governance by teachers, principal
Flexible; client-centered; business-like environment; computer-based; independent study; JTPA outreach; service learning; counseling; multi-aged classes; interns accepted.

Castle Park Learning Center (1988)
1395 Hilltop Drive, Chula Vista, CA 91911
Jim Finnerty, 619-691-6205
Type: public at-risk
5 teachers, 240 students, ages 14-19, 9-12th grade
Governance by teachers, principal
Flexible; client-centered; business-like environment; computer-based; independent study; JTPA outreach; service learning; counseling; multi-aged classes; interns accepted.

Chula Vista/Del Ray Learning Center (1992/1986)
1034 4th Ave, Chula Vista, CA 91911
Patrick Judd, Coord, 619-691-5801
Type: public at-risk
5 teachers, 100 students, ages 14-19, 9-12th grade
Governance by teachers, principal
Flexible; client-centered; business-like environment; computer-based; independent study; JTPA outreach; service learning; counseling; multi-aged classes; tech-prep course; interns accepted.

Job Training Partnership Act (1991)
467 1/2 Moss St, Chula Vista, CA 91911
Dedra Wilson, Mgr, 619-691-5824
Type: public at-risk
1 teacher, 104 students, ages 14-18, 9-12th grade
Teacher qualifications: certification
3 locations; partnerships, apprenticeships, internships; support services; school to work transition; paid work experience, training; pre-employment skills; work maturity; multi-aged classes; childcare

Mueller Elementary School
715 "I" St, Chula Vista, CA 91911
Bill Collins, 619-422-6192
Type: charter
K-6th grade
Affiliation: CA BE

Centro de Ensenanza Montessori
PO Box 7818, Chula Vista, CA 91912
Norma Callado

Bonita Vista Learning Center (1993)
751 Otay Lakes Rd, Bonita, CA 91913
David Ashley, Coord, 619-691-6111
Type: public at-risk
2 teachers, 80 students, ages 14-19, 9-12th grade
Governance by teachers, principal
Flexible; client-centered; business-like environment; computer-based; independent study; JTPA outreach; service learning; counseling; multi-aged classes; interns accepted.

Mar Vista Learning Center (1987)
505 Elm Ave, Imperial Beach, CA 91932
Nancy Cummins-Slovic, 619-691-5849
Type: public at-risk
5 teachers, 240 students, ages 14-19, 9-12th grade
Governance by teachers, principal
Flexible; client-centered; business-like environment; com-

puter-based; independent study; JTPA outreach; service learning; counseling; multi-aged classes; interns accepted.

Taproot Montessori School
5173 Guava Ave, La Mesa, CA 91941-3614
Ann Katzenmeyer

Lemon Grove Elementary
1750 Madera St, Lemon Grove, CA 91945

Sweetwater Learning Center (1986)
2900 Highland Ave, National City, CA 91950
Andy Sanchez, 619-691-5430
Type: public at-risk
8 teachers, 320 students, ages 14-19, 9-12th grade
Governance by teachers, principal
Flexible; client-centered; business-like environment; computer-based; independent study; JTPA outreach; service learning; counseling; multi-aged classes; interns accepted.

Waldorf School of San Diego (1981)
3327 Kenora Dr, Spring Valley, CA 91977
Charlotte Dukich, Adm, 619-589-6404
Non-profit; tuition: $4,000/yr, scholarships
14 teachers, 75 students, ages 3.5-11, pre K-5th grade
Affiliation: AWSNA
Governance by faculty and board
Teacher qualifications: college degree, Waldorf training
Unhurried, stress-free; age-appropriate; no letter grades; suburban location; interns accepted.

Carlsbad Montessori School
740 Pine Ave, Carlsbad, CA 92008-2427
Pam Crisman

Casa Montessori de Carlsbad
3470 Madison St, Carlsbad, CA 92008-5032
Pamela Crisman

Cajon Valley Junior High School
395 Ballantyne St, El Cajon, CA 92020
Linda Fisher, 619-588-3092
Type: magnet
7-8th grade
Fine arts (FAME).

Chaparral High School (1959)
1600 N Cuyamaca St, El Cajon, CA 92020
Dr Barbara A. Stanley, Prin, 619-448-1401, FAX: 596-2815
Type: public at-risk
22 teachers, 450 students, mainly at-risk, ages 14-17, 9-12th grade
Governance by teachers and principal
Teacher qualifications: same as comprehensive high schools in district
Non-competitive; self-directed; self-paced; success-oriented, positive environment; transportation for SE students; multi-aged classes; suburban location; interns accepted.

Cooperative Home Education Program Center
750 E Main St Bldg 2, El Cajon, CA 92020

Flying Hills Elementary
1251 Finch St, El Cajon, CA 92020
Richard Pangborn, 619-588-3132
Type: magnet
3-6th grade
Fine arts (FAME).

Sunset High School (1966)
684 Requeza, Encinitas, CA 92024
Terry Hendlin, 619-753-3860, FAX: 619-753-8469
Type: public at-risk
8 teachers, 182 students, ages 13-19, 9-12th grade
Governance by principal and board
Teacher qualifications: CA Credential
Support groups; multi-aged classes; suburban location; interns accepted.

Encinitas Migrant Infant-Toddler
915 Capri Rd, Encinitas, CA 92024-1214
Type: Montessori

Montessori Children's House
616 N Highway 101, Leucadia, CA 92024-2042

North Coast Montessori Center, Inc (1983)
2122 Encinitas Blvd, Encinitas, CA 92024-4304
Linda Campbell, Owner-Administrator, 619-753-9400
Tuition: $2,750/4,200/yr
4 teachers, 2 assistants, 50-60 students, ages 3-6
Governance by administrator
Teacher qualifications: AMS credential
Childcare; suburban location; interns accepted.

Montessori Children's Nest
1170 Arcadia Rd, Encinitas, CA 92024-4602

Masters Academy Montessori
275 Santa Fe Dr, Encinitas, CA 92024-5130

Montessori School of La Jolla
7427 Fay Ave, La Jolla, CA 92037-5041
Carol Sherlock

Learning Forum/Supercamp
1725 South Hill St, Oceanside, CA 92054
Bobbi Deporter
Type: independent

Plato High Independent Study
2111 Mission Ave (Annex), Oceanside, CA 92054

Ocean Shores High School (1972)
3131 Oceanside Blvd, Oceanside, CA 92056
Dr R. J. Williamson, Coord, 619-439-3142, FAX: -5588
Type: public at-risk
12 teachers, 270 students, ages 15-18
Governance by board
Interns accepted.

Old Mission Montessori School
4070 Mission Ave, Oceanside, CA 92057-6402
Debbie Cisneros and Maggie Sullivan

Abraxas High School (1972)
12450 Glen Oak, Poway, CA 92064
Andy Patapow, Prin, 619-748-5900, FAX: 679-1739
Type: public at-risk; scholarships
18 teachers, 250 students, ages 16-19, 9-12th grade
Affiliation: PUSD
Governance by principal, board
Teacher qualifications: multi-subject credential
Self-paced; support groups; frequent reviews; multi-aged
  classes; contracts; urban location; transportation; interns
  accepted.

Montessori Child Development Center (1978)
14911 Espola Rd, Poway, CA 92064
Marijane Sattler, 619-748-1727, FAX: 619-748-8995
Non-profit; tuition: $359/427/mo
4 teachers, 4 assistants, 60 students, ages 3-6
Affiliations: AMS, NAEYC
Governance by board of trustees
In converted old farm house; outdoor education includes
  farm animals and gardens; childcare; rural location; interns
  accepted.

Country Montessori School
12642 Monte Vista Rd, Poway, CA 92064-2522
Elizabeth Bahn

Montessori Children's House
703 9th St, Ramona, CA 92065
Allison Welch

Montessori at Fairbanks Country Day
PO Box 8953, Rancho Santa Fe, CA 92067

Foothills High School (1983)
158 Cassou Rd, San Marcos, CA 92069
Bob Henricks, Prin, 619-591-4134
Type: public choice/at-risk
3 teachers, 180 students, mainly at-risk, ages 14-18, 9-12th
  grade
Governance by principal, board
Teacher qualifications: CA credential
Independent study; teen parenting/pregnancy; childcare;
  rural location.

Santee Elementary
Box 719007, Santee, CA 92072

Santa Fe Montessori School
1010 Solana Dr; PO Box 745, Solana Beach, CA 92075
Nancy Sager and Connie Zylstra

Chinaberry Book Service
(See Resource Section)

Casa Montessori Schools (1982)
1930 Sunset Dr, Vista, CA 92083
Avril Warthen, 619-758-2434
Tuition: $2,500-4,150/yr
6 teachers, 4 assistants, 100 students, ages 3-12
Governance by administrator
Two locations, one with sports field; music; Spanish; German;
  computer; suburban location; interns accepted.

Cooperative Learning Center (1993)
454 Papaya St, Vista, CA 92083
Alonna Farrar, Educational Adm, 619-726-3020
Type: home-based
16 teachers, 24 students, ages 6-15
Governance by parent cooperative
Teacher qualifications: Parents who want one-on-one learn-
  ing experience with their children
Interest-centered; skills/knowledge exchange; field trip;
  interns accepted.

Memorial Christian School
1830 Anna Ln, Vista, CA 92083
Annette Brown
Type: Montessori

Guajome Park Academy
1234 Arcadia Ave, Vista, CA 92084
Rene Townsend, 619-726-2170
Type: charter
6-12th grade
Affiliation: CA BE

Vista Academy of the Performing Arts
600 N Santa Fe, Vista, CA 92084
Rodney Goldenberg, 619-941-0880
Type: magnet
K-5th grade
Performing Arts.

Ivy High School (1974)
PO Box 368, Fallbrook, CA 92088
Marc Steffler, Prin, 619-723-6395, FAX: 619-723-6392
Type: public at-risk
5 teachers, 130 students, ages 14-19, 10-12th grade
Governance by principal, teachers, board
Full service continuation HS; flexible schedule, programs;
  individualized; close teacher/student/parent relationship;
  rural location; transportation; interns accepted.

Kids' Edition of Continental Newstime (1992)
341 W Broadway, Suite 265, San Diego, CA 92101
Gary P. Salamone, Editor-in-Chief, 619-492-8696, 202-452-
  7453
Daily fax-only educational aid; brief courses; distributed to
  ages 6-12; children's daily newspaper.

St Vincent de Paul Life Skills
1501 Imperial Ave, San Diego, CA 92101
Nadean Burinton, Literary Specialist, 619-233-8500 x1500-1,
    FAX: 235-9707
Type: independent, non-profit
5 teachers; students mainly at-risk
Governance by life skills staff, village adm
Teacher qualifications: ABE credential; ESL, employment
    certificate
Multi-sensory, multi-dimensional interactive teaching;
    content-based goals; social services; referrals; multi-aged
    classes; no letter grades; non-compulsory class atten-
    dance; interns accepted.

The Charter School of San Diego
1807 Robinson Ave, Suite 205, San Diego, CA 92103
Mary Bixby, 619-686-6666
Type: 1 yr charter
6–12th grade
Affiliation: CA BE
Charter renewable to 4 yrs; developed by UCSD & SD Business
    Roundtable.

Walden Academy Charter School
4100 Normal St, San Diego, CA 92103-2682
Bertha O. Pendleton, 619-293-8418
Type: charter
K–6th grade
Affiliation: CA BE

Montessori School of San Diego
1323 W Spruce St, San Diego, CA 92103-5328

Futures High School (1990)
1450 Frazee Rd #301, San Diego, CA 92108
Sarita Bland, Dir, 619-297-5311, FAX: 619-297-5313
Type: independent; tuition: $3,700/yr
8 teachers, 30 students, ages 12–19, 7–12th grade
Governance by teachers and principal
Teacher qualifications: credential preferred
Independent study; suburban location; interns accepted.

Institute for Mutual Instruction
(See Resource Section)

Muir Alternative School
3390 Armstrong, San Diego, CA 92111
Samuel Wong, 619-268-1954
Type: magnet
K–12th grade
Humanistic studies.

Baker School
4041 T Steet, San Diego, CA 92113
Maria Garcia, 619-264-3139
Type: magnet
K–6th grade
Music conservatory.

Bethune School
6835 Benjamin Holt Rd, San Diego, CA 92114
Michael Giafaglione, 619-267-2271
Type: magnet
K–6th grade
Structure of the intellect.

O'Farrell Community School
6130 Skyline Dr, San Diego, CA 92114
Robert Stein, 619-293-8418
Type: charter
6–8th grade
Affiliation: CA BE

Darnell E-Campus
6020 Hughes St, San Diego, CA 92115
Loyal Carlon, 619-582-1822
Type: charter

K–4th grade
Affiliation: CA BE
Conversion; extensive parental involvement.

National Center for Montessori Education
Elementary Course, 4454 Pocahontas, San Diego, CA 92117
Type: Montessori teacher education

Montessori School of San Diego at Coronado
901 C Ave, Coronado, CA 92118-2607

Mission Bay Montessori Academy (1968)
2640 Soderblom Ave, San Diego, CA 92122
Mary Gaber, Dir, 619-457-5895
24 teachers, 10 assistants, 380 students, ages 3–12
Affiliations: NAMTA, AMI, AMS
Governance by administrator
On 18 secluded acres; computers; Spanish; extracurriculars;
    active parent involvement; suburban location; interns
    accepted.

Montessori School of Mira Mesa
11167 Westonhill Dr, San Diego, CA 92126
Sandra Manning

Priority Montessori Materials
(See Resource Section)

Albert Einstien School
PO Box 434136, San Ysidro, CA 92143
Christina A De Leon
Type: Montessori

Centro de Education Montessori
PO Box 434915, San Ysidro, CA 92143
Claudia Mondaca

Pinocho
PO Box 430172, San Ysidro, CA 92143-0172
Adriana Martinez
Type: Montessori

Montgomery Learning Center (1986)
3250 Palm Ave, San Diego, CA 92154
Lee Beca, 619-691-5489
Type: public at-risk
6 teachers, 260 students, ages 14–19, 9–12th grade
Governance by teachers, principal
Flexible; client-centered; business-like environment; com-
    puter-based; independent study; JTPA outreach; service
    learning; counseling; multi-aged classes; interns accepted.

Southwest Learning Center (1990)
1685 Hollister St, San Diego, CA 92154
Mike Pineda, 619-691-6230
Type: public at-risk
4 teachers, 180 students, ages 14–19, 9–12th grade
Governance by teachers, principal
Flexible; client-centered; business-like environment; com-
    puter-based; independent study; JTPA outreach; service
    learning; counseling; multi-aged classes; interns accepted.

The Waldorf Charter School
PO Box 6061, San Diego, CA 92166
Cliff and Bambi Schmidt, 619-223-6196
Type: charter
K–8th grade
Affiliation: CA BE

The Cheerful Cherub
(See Resource Section)

Twin Palms High School (1970)
190 N Fifth St, Blythe, CA 92225
Dave Distel, Prin, 619-922-4884, FAX: 619-922-1177
Type: public at-risk
4 teachers, 88 students, ages 16–18, 10–12th grade
Governance by teachers and principal

Teacher qualifications: Experience, teaching area flexibility
Continuation HS; variable credits; no letter grades; rural location; interns accepted.

Midway High School (1979)
601 W Main St, Calipatria, CA 92233
Homer Stiff, Prin, 619-348-2430, FAX: 619-344-8926
Type: public at-risk
1 teacher, 20 students, mainly at-risk, ages 16–20, 9–12th grade
Accreditation: WASC
Governance by principal and board
Teacher qualifications: high school multiple subject credential or higher
Contracts; tutorial; diploma; multi-aged classes; urban location; transportation.

Mt San Jacinto High School
30-800 Landau Blvd, Cathedral City, CA 92234
V. Richard Savarese, Prin, 619-324-7199
Type: public at-risk
18 teachers, 450 students, 9–12th grade
Governance by principal
Teacher qualifications: CA credential
CA model school; multi-aged classes; extensive field trips

Washington Charter School
45-768 Portola Ave, Palm Desert, CA 92260
Carol Harlock, 619-862-4350
Type: charter
K–5th grade
Affiliation: CA BE

Montessori School of the Valley
43250 Warner Trail, Palm Desert, CA 92260-8245
Elaine Maloney

Independent Study (1977)
1555 Alejo, Palm Springs, CA 92262
Donald T. Aikens, Adm, 619-323-8047
Type: public choice
5 teachers, 150 students, mainly at-risk, ages 5–19, K–12th grade
Governance by principal and board
Teacher qualifications: Elementary and secondary experience
Parent involvement required; suburban location.

Yucca Mesa Charter School
3380 Avalm Ave, Yucca Valley, CA 92284
Eva Kinsman, 619-228-1777
Type: charter
K–6th grade
Affiliation: CA BE
Governance by school-based management council.
Elementary school conversion; parental programs.

Central High School (1969)
405 N 2nd Ave, Barstow, CA 92311
Richard L. Brown, Prin, 619-256-0611, FAX: 619-256-1436
Type: public at-risk; scholarships
7 teachers, 150 students, ages 16–18, 9–12th grade
Governance by informal student body

Independent Study Program
1000 Armory, Barstow, CA 92311

Independent Study Program (1984)
551 S Ave "H", Barstow, CA 92312
Martelle Huff, Coord, 619-256-6517
Type: public choice
6 teachers, 170 students, partly at-risk, ages 5–53, K–12th grade
Governance by principal, district coordinator.
Teacher qualifications: CA Certification, non-emergency
Individualized; urban location.

Bear Valley Charter School
PO Box 1607, Big Bear Lake, CA 92315

Jim Comlossy, 909-866-5721
Type: charter
6–8th grade
Affiliation: CA BE
Emphasis on social responsibility; parental involvement required.

Cato School of Reason
4075 Nielson Rd, Phelan, CA 92329
Dan L. Steele, 619-868-5309
Type: charter
K–12th grade
Affiliation: CA BE

CC-PALS (CA Coalition of People for Alternative Learning Situations) (1982)
PO Box 291786, Phelan, CA 92329
Debbie Bartle, State Dir, 619-868-2860
Regional and bi-annual state meetings; newsletter.

International Montessori Institute
38395 Trifone Rd, Sage, CA 92343-9693
Type: Montessori teacher education

Cole Elementary
1331 Cole Ave, San Bernardino, CA 92346
Rosalyn Doug, 714-862-5611
Type: magnet
K–6th grade
Music intensives; reading clinic.

Mountain High School (1979)
PO Box 430, Lake Arrowhead, CA 92352
Flo Mullendore, Prin, 909-337-0842
Type: public at-risk
4 teachers, 100 students, mainly at-risk, ages 16–20, 9–12th grade
Governance by board
Teacher qualifications: CA Credential
Extended family atmosphere; 94% average daily attendance; multi-media art programs; incentive grants; no letter grades; interns accepted.

Excelsior Academy
9258 Malpaso Rd, Phelan, CA 92371
Dr Kurt Harper, 619-868-5400
Type: charter
K–12th grade
Affiliation: CA BE
Emphasis on technology; off-site learning; six-week bus trip.

Burke Montessori School (1985)
524 Via Vista Dr, Redlands, CA 92373
Dee Burke, Adm, 909-793-7065
Tuition: $248/mo
1 teacher, 12 students, ages 3–6
Governance by administrator

Montessori in Redlands (1976)
1890 Orange Ave, Redlands, CA 92373
Margie J. Armantrout, Dir, 909-793-6989
Non-profit; tuition: $340-520/mo
11 teachers, 13 assistants, 242 students, ages infant–12
Accreditation: AMI
Governance by board of trustees
In grapefruit grove adjacent to park, historic district; one hour to mountains, desert or ocean; childcare; rural location; interns accepted.

Johnson Center at University of Redlands (1969)
PO Box 3080 1200 E Colton Ave, Redlands, CA 92373-0999
Yasuyuki Awada, Dir, 909-335-4071, FAX: 909-793-2029
Boarding, non-profit; tuition: $15,760/yr, scholarships
140 students
Accreditation: WASC
Governance by community consensus
Teacher qualifications: PhD, ABD

Students negotiate learning contracts with faculty; no letter grades; student designed curriculum and majors; suburban location.

Mojave High School (1987)
16633 Lemon St, Hesperia, CA 92392
Arlene Gluck, 619-948-3999
Type: public at-risk
12 teachers, 240 students, ages 16-22, 9-12th grade
Governance by principal
Teacher qualifications: certification
Incentives for attendance, achievement; self-esteem programs; rap groups; speaker program; designated model school by CA DE in 1993; no letter grades; multi-aged classes; extensive field trip; interns accepted.

High Desert Center (1988)
15733 First St, Victorville, CA 92392
Susan Wells-Massengale, Dir, 619-955-3440, FAX: 245-3512
Type: public choice
13 teachers, 300 students, mainly at-risk, ages 13-20, 7-12th grade
Governance by principal, teachers, board and student reps
Continuation; SB65 drop-out clinic; GED prep; open entry/exit; no letter grades; multi-aged classes; suburban location; interns accepted.

California Elementary
2699 California St, San Bernardino, CA 92405
Manuel Salinas, 714-887-2501
Type: magnet
K-5th grade
Creative and performing arts; vanguard.

Marshall Elementary
3288 G St, San Bernardino, CA 92405
Alvina Pawlik, 714-882-3376
Type: magnet
K-6th grade
Multi-cultural.

Burbank Elementary
198 W Mill St, San Bernardino, CA 92408
Susan Vargas, 714-884-9404
Type: magnet
K-6th grade
Junior journalists.

9th Street Elementary
555 E Olive St, San Bernardino, CA 92410
Paul Shirk, 714-381-0889
Type: magnet
K-6th grade
Music intensives.

Alessandro Elementary
670 Ramona Ave, San Bernardino, CA 92411
Tom Crist, 714-885-3281
Type: magnet
K-5th grade
Single track year-round; vanguard-gifted and talented.

Rio Vista Elementary
1451 California, San Bernardino, CA 92411
Carolyn Livingson, 714-884-3281
Type: magnet
K-5th grade
Vanguard; artists in residence.

The Weaver Curriculum (1986)
2752 Scarborough, Riverside, CA 92503
909-688-3126, FAX: 909-351-9625
For Christian and homeschools.

Arachi Montessori Children's House
4174 Mobley Ave, Riverside, CA 92505-1732
Pat Arachi

Riverside Unified Independent Study
6735 Magnolia Ave, Riverside, CA 92506
Type: public choice

Helen Hunt Jackson Alternative School/
Alessandro High School (1970)
26866 San Jacinto St, Hemet, CA 92544
Jim Smith, Prin, 909-765-5193, -5182, FAX: 765-5195
Type: public choice; scholarships
11 teachers, 200/400 students, mainly at-risk, ages 12-19, 7-12th grade
Accreditation: WASC
Governance by principal, board
Teacher qualifications: credential
HHJ: independent study; small classes; computer lab; bilingual program; non-compulsory class attendance; AHS: model continuation school; work experience; applied business; SE inclusion; no letter grades; multi-aged classes; interns accepted.

March Mountain High School (1968)
24551 Dralaca Ave, Moreno Valley, CA 92553
Jon Gaffney, Prin, 909-485-5700, FAX: 909-485-5652
Type: public choice/at-risk
26 teachers, 900 students, ages 14-19, 9-12th grade
Governance by school council, principal
Teacher qualifications: CA credential
Continuation; independent study; GED prep; multi-aged classes; variable credits; suburban location.

Moreno Valley Community Learning Center
13911 Parris Blvd, Moreno Valley, CA 92553
Vernon Coleman, 909-485-5600
Type: charter
1-12th grade
Affiliation: CA BE

Creekside (1992)
24105 Washington Ave, Murrieta, CA 92562
Dr Albert Ross, Prin, 909-696-1409, FAX: 909-696-1455
Type: public at-risk
4 teachers, 120 students, ages 15-19, 9-12th grade
Governance by principal, faculty, student representatives
Teacher qualifications: fully credentialed
Tailored to each student; alternative content, delivery and time frame; pregnant/parenting teens component; suburban location; transportation; interns accepted.

Choice 2000 On-Line School
215 N "A" St, Perris, CA 92570
Judy Smith, 909-943-6369
Type: charter
9-12th grade
Affiliation: CA BE

Temecula Learning Center
31350 Rancho Vista Rd, Temecula, CA 92592
Pat Novotney, 909-676-2661
Type: charter
K-12th grade
Affiliation: CA BE

University Montessori
17 Calabria Lane, Foothill Ranch, CA 92610
Wendy Metrakos

Valley View High School (1990)
689 Wildcat Way, Brea, CA 92621
Katie Plass, Coord, 714-990-7559, FAX: 714-529-2137
Type: public choice
2 teachers, 50 students, mainly teen parents, ages 15-19
Teacher qualifications: CA credential
Independent study; accelerated learning; parenting; employment

Montessori Universe of the Child
400 West Fir St, Brea, CA 92621-6422

Shekinah Curriculum Cellar
(See Resource Section)

Center, Monte Vista High School
390 Monte Vista Ave, Cost Mesa, CA 92627
Carole Castaldo, Prin, 714-760-3450, FAX: 760-3426
Type: public choice
10 teachers, 350 students, ages 14-19, 9-12th grade
Governance by board
Non-compulsory class attendance; suburban location; interns accepted.

Center, Back Bay High School
300 Monte Vista Ave, Costa Mesa, CA 92627
Carole Castaldo, Prin, 714-760-3450, FAX: 760-3426
Type: public at-risk
4 teachers, 100 students, mainly at-risk, ages 14-19, 9-12th grade
Governance by board
Suburban location; interns accepted.

The Sycamore Tree
(See Resource Section)

Montessori on the Lake (1987)
23311 Muirlands, Lake Forest, CA 92630
Sue Matsu, 714-855-5630
Tuition: $330-470/mo
25 teachers, 40 assistants, 432 students, mainly international, ages toddler-15
Affiliation: NCME
Governance by teachers and administrators
Suburban location; interns accepted.

Casa dei Bambini Montessori School
25435 Trabuco Rd # C5, El Toro, CA 92630-2738

Aliso Montessori
24291 Muirlands Blvd # 1/#2, El Toro, CA 92630-3000

North Orange County Community College District/Adult Education (1965)
1000 North Lemon St, Fullerton, CA 92632
Nilo Lipiz, ESL Co-Ord, 714-871-4030, FAX: 738-7853
Type: public choice
55 teachers, 34,000 students, mainly multi-ethnic, ages 18+
Governance by administration
Teacher qualifications: bachelor's degree
Adult ed: ESL, ABE, HS/GED, DSPS, Seniors, Medical, vocational, etc; tuition-based programs: computer, foreign language, others; no letter grades; urban location; interns accepted.

Arborland Montessori Children's Academy (1988)
1700 W Valencia Dr, Fullerton, CA 92633
Sueling Chen, Prin, 714-871-2311, FAX: 714-773-1532
Tuition: $310-385/mo
5 teachers, 5 assistants, 122 students, ages 3-12
Accreditation: AMI
Governance by administrator
Small class size; hands-on activities; computer; Spanish; piano; music; choir; gymnastics; swimming; dance; martial arts; optional hot lunches; childcare; urban location; interns accepted.

Alternative and Continuing Education Program
780 Beechwood 1, Fullerton, CA 92635
Jean Klinghoffer, 714-870-3775
Type: public choice
730 students, ages 14+

Rainbow PreSchool
12914 Hazel Ave, Garden Grove, CA 92641
Sunja Oak
Type: Montessori

Montessori School
6921 Belgrave Ave, Garden Grove, CA 92645
Noreen Begole

Montessori Greenhouse School
5856 Belgrave Ave, Garden Grove, CA 92645-1729
Charles and Joy Turner

Huntington Beach Alternative
16666 Tunstall Ln, Huntington Beach, CA 92647
Type: independent

Montessori Child Development Center
16692 Landau Lane, Huntington Beach, CA 92651
Ellen Goodman

Community Learning Center
21601 Tree Top La, Laguna Beach, CA 92651
Kathie Reynolds or Libley Coleman, 714-497-7793
Type: independent

Montessori School of Laguna Beach
340 St Ann Dr, Laguna Beach, CA 92651
Ishwar Chainani

Home Study Alternative School
PO Box 10356, Newport Beach, CA 92658
Gaylen McGee, Dir
Cost: $100-150/sem
K-8th grade
Designed by certified teachers; comprehensive; lesson instructions; assistance always available; students placed according to ability; multidisciplinary

Waldorf School of Orange County
2627 Vista Del Oro, Newport Beach, CA 92660-3548
Mechtild Howard

Montessori of Orange
2261 N Orange Olive Rd, Orange, CA 92665-2746
Kathleen Glassman

Marygrove Montessori
419 S Glassell St, Orange, CA 92666-1905

Santiago Middle School (1995)
515 N Rancho Santiago Rd, Orange, CA 92669
Mary Ann Owsley, 714-997-6366
Type: charter
7-8th grade
Affiliation: CA BE

Primanti Montessori Schools
5003 E Chapman Ave, Orange, CA 92669-4211
Lisa Koch

El Camino Real High School (1976)
1351 E Orangethorpe, Placentia, CA 92670
Glen Collard, Prin, 714-996-1971
Type: public at-risk
15 teachers, 280 students, ages 16-18, 9-12th grade
Affiliation: WASC
Governance by principal
Teacher qualifications: CA credential
Office practices; community service required; flexible scheduling; suburban location; interns accepted.

La Entrada High School (1989)
1351 E Orangethorpe Ave, Placentia, CA 92670
Glen Callard, Prin, 996-1971
Type: public at-risk
2 teachers, 80 students, ages 16-18, 10-12th grade
Governance by principal
Teacher qualifications: CA Certification
Independent study strategies; suburban location.

Montessori Children's World
431 E Palm Dr, Placentia, CA 92670-3296

Academia Montessori
3415 S El Camino Real, San Clemente, CA 92672

Kagan's Cooperative Learning
(See Resource Section)

Montessori School of Tustin
PO Box 15791, Tustin, CA 92681

Rancho Santa Margarita Montessori
30075 Comercio, Rancho Santa Margarita, CA 92688
Anne Munz

Silverado High School (1973)
25632 Diseno Dr, Mission Viejo, CA 92691
Dr Barry Lietz, 714-586-8800
Type: public at-risk
14 teachers, 250 students, ages 14–19, 9–12th grade
Affiliation: Saddleback Valley USD
Governance by principal, teachers, board
State computer academy; multi-aged classe; interns
  accepted.

Appletree Montessori
25542 Jeronimo Rd, Mission Viejo, CA 92691-2724

Pathfinder High School of Independent Study
26440 La Alameda #350, Mission Viejo, CA 92691-6319
Terry & Margaret Ann Mccarty
Type: independent

Horizon Education (1983)
848 N Parton, Santa Ana, CA 92701
Ellen Wilson, 714-547-2423, FAX: 714-547-2344
Type: public at-risk
75 teachers, 2000 students, ages 12–19, 7–12th grade
Governance by Adm of Alt Ed, Prin
Teacher qualifications: CA credential
Community-based; career education; counseling; teen par-
  enting; mobile outreach classroom; state-of-the-art tech-
  nology; multi-aged classe; interns accepted.

Foothill Montessori School
18692 E 17th St, Santa Ana, CA 92705-2700

Valley Vista High School (1968)
9600 Dolphin St, Fountain Valley, CA 92708
Richard Maynard, Prin, 714-964-7760, FAX: 964-3045
Type: public at-risk
15 teachers, 265 students, ages 14–18, 10–12th grade
Governance by teachers, principal and board
ESL; SE; school-centered curricula; safe environment; urban
  location.

Fountain Valley Christian Montessori
18110 Magnolia St, Fountain Valley, CA 92708-5605

Backyard Scientist
(See Resource Section)

IUSD, Montessori Early Childhood Education (1986)
31 West Yale Loop, Irvine, CA 92714
Feland L. Meadows, PhD, Co-ord, 714-551-1647/643-8174,
  FAX: 714-786-7521/831-7786
Non-profit; tuition: $0-420/mo
13 teachers, 14 assistants, 255 students, mainly international,
  ages 3–9
Accreditations: PAMS, Nat'l U, OBEMLA, CA DE, Irvine USD
Governance by teachers and administrators
Serve Chinese, Japanese, Hispanic, Vietnamese, Korean,
  Persian and English-speaking students in their home lan-
  guage and English; childcare; suburban location; interns
  accepted.

San Joaquin High School (1990)
311 W Yale Loop, Irvine, CA 92714
Ann Beirne, 714-857-2682
Type: public choice
10 students

Village Montessori School
4552 Sandburg Way, Irvine, CA 92715-2735

University Montessori School
101 Russell Pl, Irvine, CA 92715-4052

Santiago Hills Elementary School
29 Christamon, Irvine, CA 92720
Type: Montessori

Montessori Child Develoment Center
1692 Landau Lane, Hunting Beach, CA 92749

Polaris High-Independent Study
501 Crescent Way, Anaheim, CA 92803

Beavercreek Montessori School
632 S Andover Dr, Anaheim, CA 92807-4608

Montessori Children's House (1988)
559 Aliso St, Ventura, CA 93001
Bonnie M. Gordon, 805-653-5759
Tuition: $225/255/mo
1 teacher, 1 assistant, 14 students, mainly international, ages
  3–6
Affiliations: NCME, Orff Shulwork
Governance by administrator
Spanish; art; childcare; suburban location; interns accepted.

Community Alliance Program (1990)
5109 Loma Vista Rd, Ventura, CA 93003
Lawrence Keegan, 805-654-2602, FAX: 805-658-0853
Type: public choice
15 students

Ventura Montessori School
PO Box 3719, Ventura, CA 93006-3719

Bedford Open School (1976)
1199 Bedford Dr, Camarillo, CA 93010
Julie Cavaliere, Prin, 805 484-5116
Type: public choice
11 teachers, 223 students, ages 5–12, K–6th grade
Governance by principal, teachers, parents, students
Teacher qualifications: CA credential
Enrichment courses; learning lab; hands-on experiences;
  artist-in-residence for music, art, dance; perceptual motor
  lab; Education Through Music; no letter grades.

Fillmore Community High School (1980)
Box 697, Fillmore, CA 93016
Phil Catalano, 805-524-2271, FAX: 805-524-4625
Type: public at-risk
150 students, ages 12+, 7–12th grade
Affiliation: WASC
Governance by board
Independent study; adult diploma; GED; ESL; no letter grades;
  multi-aged classes; rural location.

Landmark
(See Resource Section)

Laurel Springs School (1990)
PO Box 1440, Ojai, CA 93023
JoAnn LeClere, Registrar, 805-646-2473, FAX: 805-646-0186
Type: home-based
21 teachers, 250 students, ages 5–18, K–12th grade
Governance by principal
Teacher qualifications: BA or BS
Parent as primary teacher; students assigned to correspon-
  dence teacher

Oak Grove School
220 W Lomita Ave, Ojai, CA 93023
Mary Louise Sorem, HS Dir, 805-646-8236, FAX: -6509
Type: independent, boarding, non-profit
Pre K–12th grade
Affiliations: Krishnamurti Schools, NAIS; accreditations: CAIS,
  WASC
ES: no letter grades, nature study, arts; HS: college prep,
  interscholarstic sports, camping, travel; rural location.

Ojai Valley Children's House (1973)
806 W Baldwin Rd, Ojai, CA 93023
Rosemary Stone, Reg/Office Mgr, 805-649-2525, FAX: 646-
1543
Type: Montessori; tuition: $2,000-4,070/yr
6 teachers, 6 assistants, 115 students, ages toddler-12
Accreditation: Montessori World Ed Inst
Ten acres of oak- and garden-studded grounds; concerts and
field trips an integral part of varied curriculum; childcare;
rural location.

Independent Studies
309 S K St, Oxnard, CA 93030

Rose Ave Elementary
220 S Driskill Ave, Oxnard, CA 93030
Dennis Johnson, 805-487-3918
Type: magnet
K-6th grade
Gifted and talented.

Oratory School
112 E De La Guerra St #44, Santa Barbara, CA 93101-2205
Marian Galvin
Type: independent

Santa Barbara Montessori
1500 State St, Santa Barbara, CA 93101-2514

Montessori Public School Systems
518 Casitas Rd, Canta Barbara, CA 93103
Nancy Williams

Jodi House Montessori School
916 Garcia Rd, Santa Barbara, CA 93103-2124
Jane Granite

Peabody Charter School
3018 Calle Noguera, Santa Barbara, CA 93105
Pat Morales, 805-549-7042
Type: charter
K-6th grade
Affiliation: CA BE
Parents commit 3 hrs/wk to school service.

Waldorf School of Santa Barbara
2300-B Garden St, Santa Barbara, CA 93105
Gita Labrentz

Montessori Center School (1965)
3970 La Colina Rd, Santa Barbara, CA 93110
Carla Mathieu, Dir, 805-682-5648
Non-profit; tuition: $4,800-5,900/yr
18 teachers, 18 assistants, 295 students, ages infant-12
Governance by teachers and administrators, board
8 acres; library; auditorium; music and art studios; childcare;
suburban location; interns accepted.

Open Alternative School
4025 Foothill Rd, Santa Barbara, CA 93110-1209
Carol Preston, 805-962-3826
Type: public choice

Santa Barbara Charter School
6100 Stow Canyon Rd, Goleta, CA 93117
Wendy Kanter, 805-687-0809
Type: charter
K-8th grade
Affiliation: CA BE
Co-op.

Sunrise/Adelante High School (1982)
209 N Park Ave, Avenal, CA 93204
Richard L. Swanson, PhD, 209-386-4162, FAX: -5303
Type: public at-risk
4 teachers, 65 students, ages 13-18, 7-12th grade
Affiliation: Reef Sunset USD
Governance by teachers, principal

Teacher qualifications: CA credential
Multi-aged classe; interns accepted.

BEST Educational Systems
PO Box 1128, Ojai, CA 93204
Rene Martinez
Type: Montessori

Ygnacio Valencia High School (1979)
1925 Randolph, Delano, CA 93215
Dr Efrain Rodriguez, Prin, 805-725-4000, FAX: 721-9390
Type: public choice
9 teachers, 230 students, mainly at-risk, ages 14-18, 9-12th
grade
Governance by principal
Teacher qualifications: CA Credential, BA or BS
Work at home under contract; multi-aged classes; rural
location.

Exeter Independent Study/
233 E Maple, Exeter, CA 93221

Pioneer Primary, Middle
8810 14th Ave, Hanford, CA 93239
Hugh Lee, 209-584-8831
Type: charter
700 ES students, K-8th grade
Affiliation: CA BE
Conversion of two elementaries; competency-based.

Summit Continuation High School (1983)
3284 Erskine Creek Rd; PO Box 3797, Lake Isabella, CA 93240
Vickie Johnston, Site Supervisor, 619-379-3997, FAX: -6234
Type: public at-risk
2 teachers, 45 students, ages 16-19, 10-12th grade
Governance by teachers and principal
Teacher qualifications: credential
Independent study; rural location; transportation; interns
accepted.

Oak View High School (1989)
6449 De Woody, Caton, CA 93242
Thomas Kent, Prin, 209-923-4000
Type: public at-risk
1 teacher, 16 students, ages 14-19, 9-12th grade
Governance by principal, board
Teacher qualifications: CA credential
Individualized; multiple intelligences programs; multi-aged
classes

McFarland Independent School (1980)
5899 Fifth St, McFarland, CA 93250
Kathleen J. Heisey, Adm, 805-792-6312, FAX: -2447
Type: independent at-risk, non-profit
6 teachers, 140 students, mainly at-risk, ages 13+, 9-12th
grade
Affiliation: McFarland USD
Governance by teachers, principal, board
Teacher qualifications: secondary credential, voluntary
assignment
Electives; multi-aged classes; rural location.

San Joaquin High School (1980)
599 Fifth St, McFarland, CA 93250
Kathleen J. Heisey, Prin, 805-792-3178, FAX: -2447
Type: public at-risk
6 teachers, 75 students, ages 13-20, 9-12th grade
Governance by teachers, principal, board
Teacher qualifications: secondary teaching credential
Self-paced; small groups; vocational; multi-aged classes; rural
location.

Tulare Tech Prep (1993)
426 N Blackstone, Tulare, CA 93274
Dr William Pendleton, 209-688-1815, FAX: 685-8286
Type: public at-risk
4 teachers, 51 students, mainly at-risk, ages 14-18, 9-12th
grade

Governance by board
Teacher qualifications: CA teaching credential in subject area
1-room classroom; 4-teacher team teaching, tech-based with CORD applied academic curr; job shadowing/work exp; college and specialty classes at regular HS available; multi-aged classes; rural location; interns accepted.

Greenhouse Montessori School- Chinowth
4143 S Dans St, Visalia, CA 93277-7901

Charter Oak School
PO Box 1725, Visalia, CA 93279
Neva C. Wright, 209-798-1954
Type: charter
1-8th grade
Affiliation: CA BE

Visilia Independent Study
315 E Acequia St, Visilia, CA 93291

Vista East High School (1979)
815 Eureka St, Bakersfield, CA 93305
Fuchsia Ward, Asst Prin, 805-323-9006, FAX: 805-631-0559
Type: public at-risk
16 teachers, 300 students, ages 14-18, 9-12th grade
Governance by principal
Teacher qualifications: credential
Personalized; counseling; model drug intervention program; community service; multi-aged classes; interns accepted.

Thorner Elementary
5501 Thorner, Bakersfield, CA 93306
Shirley Walston, 805-631-5490
Type: magnet
K-6th grade
Creative and performing arts.

Bessie Owens Junior High School
815 Potomac Ave, Bakersfield, CA 93307
Dennis Patrick, 805-631-5420
Type: magnet
K-6th grade
Gifted and talented education.

Mt Vernon Elementary
2161 Potomac Ave, Bakersfield, CA 93307
Lillian Tafoya, 805-631-5380
Type: magnet
K-6th grade
Creative and performing arts.

Friends School
7300 Ming Ave, Bakersfield, CA 93309
Katie Jennings, 805-833-6860
Type: Quaker

PBVUSD
3100 Actis St, Bakersfield, CA 93309
Lydia Zimmerman
Type: Montessori

Montessori Children's Center
3234 Belle Terrace, Bakersfield, CA 93309-4102
Anjali Sinha

Montessori Children's School (1983)
4200 S Higuera St, San Luis Obispo, CA 93401
Mary Kern, Adm, 805-544-6691
Tuition: $2,750/3,250/yr
3 teachers, 2 assistants, 56 students, ages 3-9
Affiliations: NAMTA, MWEI
Governance by administrator
Drama; art; music; puppetry; excursions to local performances; woodworking; Spanish; French; yoga; Native American study; summer programs; childcare; suburban location; interns accepted.

The New Dawn
1768 14th St, Los Osos, CA 93402

Ranae Turner
Type: Montessori

Pacific Beach High School (1967)
11950 Los Osos Valley Rd, San Luis Obispo, CA 93405
R D Christensen, Prin, 805-541-1216
Type: public choice
4 teachers, 80-100 students, ages 16-18, 10-12th grade
Governance by principal
Teacher qualifications: CA certification
Rural location; interns accepted.

Lucia Mar Independent Study Center (1983)
227 E Bridge St, Arroyo Grande, CA 93420
Karen Mork, Tch, 805-473-4238
Type: public choice/at-risk
2 teachers, 60 students, partly at-risk, ages 13-18, 9-12th grade
Governance by principal.
Teacher qualifications: multi-subject certification
Multi-aged classes; non-compulsory class attendance; no letter grades; rural location.

Arroyo Grande School
275 N Halcyon Rd, Arroyo Grande, CA 93420-2524
Type: Montessori

Central Coast Homeschoolers (1990)
7600 Marchant Ave, Atascadero, CA 93422
Barbara Alward, 462-0726
Non-profit
2 teachers, 2 students, ages 7-10
Affiliation: Homeschool Assn of CA
Governance by teachers; Prin
Student-centered; no preset curriculum; rural location.

Children's House Montessori School
3025 Monterey Rd, Atascadero, CA 93422-1849

Clarence Ruth Elementary School
501 N W St, Lompoc, CA 93436-5099
Type: Montessori

Maple High School (1967)
Carob St, Vandenberg AFB, CA 93437
Hector Samaniego, Prin, 805-734-5666
Non-profit
7 teachers, 100 students, mainly pregnant minors
Affiliation: Lompoc USD
Governance by teachers, principal
Teacher qualifications: CA credential
Competency-based; no letter grades; multi-aged classes; childcar; interns accepted.

Children's Montessori School of Lompoc, Inc (1981)
PO Box 3510, Lompoc, CA 93438
Jim Murphy, Dir, 805-733-2290
Non-profit; tuition: $1,925/3,410/yr
2 teachers, 1 assistant, 35 students, ages 3-12
Affiliation: AMI
Governance by board of trustees
After-school art, dance, piano, voice, computer; choir; marine biology; childcare; suburban location.

Community Education Center (1983)
251 E Clark Ave, Santa Maria, CA 93455
Fred Miller, Prin, 805-937-6358, FAX: 805-934-4743
Type: public choice
35 teachers, 1500 students, mainly at-risk, ages 13+, 9-12th grade
Affiliation: CSU
Governance by shared decision making
Teacher qualifications: California certification
Delta program; teen parenting; concurrent adult education; wilderness trip; alternative ed work center; GAIN; work study; RECAP; BICEP; SAW; unscheduled school day; non-compulsory class attendanc; interns accepted.

West Mall Alternative School
6495 Lewis Ave, Atascadero, CA 93465
Dan Ross, Prin, 805-462-0309, FAX: 805-466-2941
Type: public/independent home-based at-risk
7 teachers, 125 students, mainly at-risk, ages 5–19, K–12th
  grade
Governance by principal
Independent study; teachers assist parents in home-lesson
  planning, teaching; rural location.

Eagle Canyon High School (1993)
964 Old County Rd, Templeton, CA 93465
Douglas Nix, Prin, 805-434-1528
Type: public at-risk
4 teachers, 25 students, ages 14–18
Governance by teachers and principal
Teacher qualifications: CA credential
Rural location.

Palisade Glacier High School (1972)
PO Box 938, Big Pine, CA 93513
John K. Helmbold, Prin, 619-938-2001
Type: public at-risk
3 teachers, 45 students, ages 16–19, 9–12th grade
Affiliation: Bishop Joint Union HS District
Governance by principal
Teacher qualifications: CA certification, experience
Independent study; teen parenting; counseling; child devel-
  opment classes; career guidance; multi-aged classes

Desert Montessori Academy
44503 North Fern Ave, Lancaster, CA 93534-3408
Sharon Davis

Independent Study
45024 3rd St, Lancaster, CA 93535

Heritage Montessori School
934 N Heritage Dr, Ridgecrest, CA 93555-5517
Helen DeVere

Rare Earth High School (1986)
PO Drawer CC, Rosamond, CA 93560
Dr Lawrence Jones, Prin, 805-256-5095, FAX: 256-1247
Type: public at-risk
7 teachers; students mainly at-risk, ages 8–18, 3–12th grade
Governance by principal
Teacher qualifications: CA certification
Continuing education with behavior modification; no letter
  grades; interns accepted.

Enterprise Alternative Independent Study
1550 Herndon, Clovis, CA 93612

Sierra Vista High School (1984)
1327 E El Monte, Dinuba, CA 93618
Maryann Boylan, Prin, 209-591-5732, FAX: 209-591-3334
Type: public at-risk
3 teachers, 120 students, ages 13–18, 9–12th grade
Governance by board
Teacher qualifications: CA certification
National drug-free school; model continuation HS; multi-
  aged classe; interns accepted.

Kingsburg Jt High
1415 Marion St, Kingsburg, CA 93631

San Luis High School
125 7th St, Los Banos, CA 93635
M. E. Barr, Prin, 209-826-8410, FAX: 826-2252
Type: public at-risk
6 teachers, 172 students, ages 16–18
Governance by principal, board
Teacher qualifications: CA credential
Multi-aged classe; interns accepted.

Duane E. Furman High School
1903 Modoc, Madera, CA 93637

Kim Logan, 209-675-4482
Type: public choice

Chawanakee Home School/Independent Study (1988)
PO Box 707, North Fork, CA 93643
Doug Waltner, Mgr, 209-877-2215, FAX: 209-877-2377
Type: public choice
2 teachers, 30 students, K–8th grade
Affiliation: CCIS
Governance by board
Teacher qualifications: CA credential
Homeschoolers participate in band, sports, science classes;
  monthly art activities; parent meetings; no letter grades;
  non-compulsory class attendance; extensive field trips

Mountain Home School
50200 Rd 427, Oakhurst, CA 93644
Bob Guizar, 209-683-2024
Type: charter
K–8th grade
Affiliation: CA BE

El Portal High Independent Study
Box 210, San Joaquin, CA 93660

Cutler-Drosi Alternative Programs (1989)
41855 Rd 128, Drosi, CA 93674
Carolyn Kehrli, 209-528-4703, FAX: 209-528-3132
Type: public at-risk
12 teachers, 195 students, ages 14–18, 9–12th grade
Governance by teachers, principal
Extensive field trips; multi-aged classe; interns accepted.

Roosevelt High School
4240 E Twarf, Fresno, CA 93702
Jane Hammaker, 209-441-3777
Type: magnet
9–12th grade
Visual and performing arts.

George M. DeWolf High School (1959)
2021 N Clark St, Fresno, CA 93703
Gerry Catanzarite, EdD, Prin, 209-441-3233, FAX: 209-323-
  7400
Type: public at-risk
16 teachers, 325 students, ages 15–19, HS
Affiliation: Fresno USD
Governance by principal
Teacher qualifications: California credential
Adventure-based education program; ropes course; in coop-
  eration with Fresno City College; urban location.

Bullard Talent Elementary
4950 N Harrison, Fresno, CA 93704
Clytee Ramsey, 209-441-6831
Type: magnet
K–8th grade
Performing arts.

Whole Language Umbrella
(See Resource Section)

West Park Academy Charter School
2695 S Valentine Ave, Fresno, CA 93706
Bernard Hanlon, 209-233-6501
Type: charter
Pre K–8th grade
Affiliation: CA BE
Conversion; interdisciplinary.

Fresno Valley High School
1540 M St, Fresno, CA 93721
Kelly Martin, 209-237-7215
Type: independent; tuition: $2,500/yr, scholarships
12 students, mainly at-risk, ages 15–20, 9–12th grade
For those who "fall between the cracks" in PS; emphasis on
  community, critical thinking, accountability.

Manchester GATE Elementary
2307 E Dakota, Fresno, CA 93726
Nancy Hensel, 209-441-6741
Type: magnet
K–6th grade
Gifted and talented.

Pioneer Christian Academy (1991)
5533 E Swift Ave, Fresno, CA 93727
Marshall Fritz, President, 209-292-1776, FAX: 209-292-7582
Type: independent; tuition: sliding scale
Student ages 5–19, K–12th grade
Affiliation: Quality Schools Consortium
Governance by democratic school meeting
Multi-denominational; Christ chosen virtues, student chosen
   academics; an extension of home, assisting parents in
   raising their children; no letter grades; non-compulsory
   class attendance; multi-aged classes; extensive field trips;
   suburban location; interns accepted.

Children's Place Montessori School
5094 E Tulare Ave, Fresno, CA 93727-3929

Creative Teaching Materials
(See Resource Section)

Ala Carte, International School
1030 Kentfield Dr, Salinas, Ca. 93901-1064
Type: independent

Pacific Montessori Association
PO Box 2051, Salinas, CA 93902-2051

Marina Education Center (1993)
390 Caronel Ave, Marina, CA 93908
Ron Breding, Prin, 384-3305
Type: public choice/at-risk
20 teachers, 250 students, mainly at-risk, ages 6–25, 5–12th
   grade
Governance by principal, faculty and student reps
Teacher qualifications: CA credential
Multi-aged classes; continuing ed; suburban location; interns
   accepted.

Montessori Learning Center, Inc
30 Hitchcock Rd, Salinas, CA 93908-9341

Waldorf School of Monterey
PO Box 221057, Carmel, CA 93922
Victoria Lohman

Center at King City Joint Union High School
505 N Third Street, King City, CA 93930
Ed Bullard, Prin, 408-385-4661, FAX: 408-385-0695
Type: public choice/at-risk
15 teachers, 600 students, mainly at-risk, ages 15–60, 9–12th
   grade
Governance by principal, faculty and student representatives,
   board
Teacher qualifications: secondary credential & voluntary
   placement
Independent study; CAI; competency-based; multi-aged
   classes; rural location; transportation.

Kinderhaus Montessori School
501 El Dorado St, Monterey, CA 93940-4608

Cypress High School (1965)
PO Box 1031, Monterey, CA 93942-1031
Vicki Phillips, Prin, 408-899-7026, FAX: 408-899-0628
Type: public at-risk
9 teachers, 150 students, ages 14–18, 9–12th grade
Governance by teachers and principal
Self-esteem; goal setting; decision making; responsibility;
   named CA model school in 1992; multi-aged classes; subur-
   ban location; transportation.

Critical Thinking Press
(See Resource Section)

P. G. Center for Independent Study (1984)
555 Sinex Ave, Pacific Grove, CA 93950
Bruce H. Henderson, Dir/Supervisor, 408-646-6512, FAX: -6500
Type: home-based public choice
1 teacher, 25 students, ages 6–20, K–12th grade
Affiliation: Pacific Grove USD
Governance by teachers, principal, and board
Teacher qualifications: certified
Access to Monterey Bay Aquarium, ocean environments, lan-
   guage institutes, Naval Library, historical museums,
   galleries.

Gonzales Union HSD (1979)
690 Main St, Soledad, CA 93960
Linda Coyne, Prin, 408-678-3066, FAX: 408-678-0162
Type: public choice, at-risk; scholarships
15 teachers, 1,000 students, ages 13+
Teacher qualifications: Credential
Pinnacles Continuation HS; independent study; adult ed;
   Regional Occupation Programs; CAI; rural location; trans-
   portation; interns accepted.

College of Notre Dame Early Learning Center
1500 Ralston Ave, Belmont, CA 94002-1908
Adyllia Linka
Type: Montessori

Peninsula Montessori
1151 Vancouver Ave # A, Burlingame, CA 94010-5674
JoAnne Bailey

Burlingame Montessori School
2109 Broadway, Burlingame, CA 94010-5675
Lynette Muhic

Kinderlings
978 Highland Cir, Los Altos, CA 94022
Carolyn Courture
Type: Montessori

Montessori School of Los Altos
201 Covington Rd, Los Altos, CA 94022

The Learning Community at Los Altos HS (1971)
201 Almond Ave, Los Altos, CA 94022
Gary Bacon, Coord, 415-960-8869
Type: public choice
1 teacher, 25 students, ages 14–18, 9–12th grade
Governance by board
Balanced, whole-person approach; student-centered; personal and group experience; students participate in curriculum development; strong service component;
   multi-aged classes; interns accepted.

Waldorf School of the Peninsula (1984)
401 Rosita Ave, Los Altos, CA 94022
Brenda Aronow, Business Mgr, 415-948-8433
Non-profit; tuition: $4,200-16,000/yr, scholarships
8 teachers, 101 students, ages 4.9–13, K–7th grade
Affiliation: AWSNA
Teacher qualifications: Waldorf certification preferred
Suburban location.

Peninsula School (1925)
Peninsula Way, Menlo Park, CA 94025
Carol Young-Holt, Director, 415-325-1584
Type: independent; tuition: $3,530-5,470, scholarships
19 teachers, 21 assistants, 254 students, ages 3–14, K–8th
   grade
Governance by staff/parent cooperative with board of
   directors
Teacher qualifications: foundation in child development, CA
   credential or equivalent
Emphasis on the arts, with afternoon choices of weaving,

clay, fine arts, wood shop, jewelry-making; play is highly valued; ETV video, "Why do These Kids Love School?" based on school; no letter grades; multi-aged classes; extensive field trips; suburban location; interns accepted.

Saint Joseph's Montessori School
150 Valparaiso Ave, Menlo Park, CA 94025
Janet Wildey

Green Oaks Montessori
490 Willow Rd, Menlo Park, CA 94025-2716
Kathy Hassan

Menlo Montessori
3300 Alpine Rd, Menlo Park, CA 94028-7525

Millbrae Montessori School
797 Santa Margarita Ave, Millbrae, CA 94030-1164

Montessori Gardens
1120 Rose Ave, Mountain View, CA 94040-4058

Nienhuis Montessori USA
(See Resource Section)

Western Montessori School
323 Moorpark Way, Mountain View, CA 94041-1621

Garfield Charter School
815 Allerton St, Redwood City, CA 94063
Ronald Crates, 415-365-1550
Type: charter
K-6th grade
Affiliation: CA BE

Edison Montessori School
750 Dartmouth Ave, San Carlos, CA 94070

Math Products Plus
(See Resource Section)

San Carlos Charter Learning Center
1250 San Carlos Ave #102, San Carlos, CA 94070
Sue Steelman-Bragato, 415-598-8192
Type: charter
Student ages 9-12
Affiliation: CA BE
Community-integrated.

Early Learning Institute Second Generation
850 Gateway Blvd, South San Francisco, CA 94080-7021
Dr Charles Bernstein
Type: Montessori

Sunnyvale School District Montessori Program
830 W McKinley, Sunnyvale, CA 94086
Betsy Reeves

Rainbow Montessori
790 E Duane Ave Bldg # 5, Sunnyvale, CA 94086-3359

Montessori School
622 Old San Francisco Rd, Sunnyvale, CA 94086-7960

Santa Clara Valley Homeschoolers
795 Sheraton Dr, Sunnyvale, CA 94087

Lakewood School
750 Lakechime Dr, Sunnyvale, CA 94089
Donna Myers
Type: Montessori

John Swett Elementary
727 Golden Gate Ave, San Francisco, CA 94102
Kay Nomura, 415-241-6320
Type: magnet
K-5th grade
Visual and performing arts.

Tenderloin Community Children's Center
302 Eddy St, San Francisco, CA 94102-2607
Type: Montessori

Sand Paths Academy
525 Bryant St, San Francisco, CA 94107-1222
Type: Montessori

Binet Montessori
1715 Octavia St, San Francisco, CA 94109
Daniel Binet, 415-567-4000
Tuition: $400-550/mo
5 teachers, 5 assistants, 125 students, ages 3-9
Accreditation: AMS
Governance by administrator
50 weeks/year; childcare; urban location; interns accepted.

Royal Day School
1 Daniel Burnham Ct, San Francisco, CA 94109-5455
Type: Montessori

Montessori House of Children
1187 Franklin St, San Francisco, CA 94109-6813

Global Voice Education Project for C Band Satellite
(See Resource Section)

New College of California (1971)
766 Valencia St, San Francisco, CA 94110
Katrina Fullman, Adms Coord, 415-626-0884
260 students, adult ages
School of Humanities; Public Interest Law School; Graduate School of Psychology; Weekend College; seminars; undergraduate thesis; journal work; credit for life experience.

Center For Independent Study
1000 Cuyuga Ave, San Francisco, CA 94112

Rivendell School
4512 Irving St, San Francisco, CA 94112
Li Moon
Type: independent

S. F. Community Elementary
125 Excelsior St, San Francisco, CA 94112
Paul Reinhertz, 415-469-4739
Type: magnet
K-8th grade

Live Oak School
117 Diamond St, San Francisco, CA 94114
Kirk Fisher

San Francisco Waldorf School
2938 Washington St, San Francisco, CA 94115
Monique Grund

Royal Montessori School
1550 Eddy St, San Francisco, CA 94115-4165

California Institute of Integral Studies
765 Ashbury St, San Francisco, CA 94117
Type: higher education
Has on-campus and on-line programs.

Synergy School (1973)
975 Grove, San Francisco, CA 94117
Elena Dillon, Adms Dir, 415-567-6177
Type: independent, non-profit; tuition: $4,700/yr, scholarships
8 teachers, 94 students, ages 5-12, K-6th grade
Governance by teacher cooperative
Teacher qualifications: elementary credential, experience
Empowers students to become self-confident, creative learners; no letter grades; multi-aged classes; extensive field trips; urban location; interns accepted.

Multicultural Education c/o Caddo Gap Press
(See Resource Section)

Montessori Children's House
25 Lake St, San Francisco, CA 94118-1422

Children's School of San Francisco
420 9th Ave, San Francisco, CA 94118-2913
Type: Montessori

Big City Montessori School
240 Industrial St, San Francisco, CA 94124-1917
Meighan Tideman

Maria Montessori School (1972)
678 Portola Dr, San Francisco, CA 94127
Ursula Thrush, Head, 415-731-8188, FAX: 415-566-4311
Non-profit; tuition: $350/470/mo
6 teachers, 2 assistants, 74 students, mainly international,
    ages 3–15
Affiliations: MACTE, NAMTA
Governance by administrator
Traditional Montessori with emphasis on peace ed; childcare;
    suburban location; interns accepted.

International Studies Academy
693 Vermont St, San Francisco, CA 94131
Tom Ruiz, 415-695-5866
Type: charter
Educationally disadvantaged, senior high
Affiliation: CA BE
Inner city conversion; 23% LEP; on-site program for hearing
    impaired.

San Francisco Charter Early Childhood School
73 Arbor St, San Francisco, CA 94131
Sydney Gurewitz Clemens, 415-586-7338
Type: charter
Pre K–3rd grade
Affiliation: CA BE
Whole language, literature-based.

School of the Arts Alternative High School
700 Font Blvd, San Francisco, CA 94132
Yvonne McClung, 415-469-4027
Type: magnet
9–12th grade
Performing Arts.

Montessori Children's Center
755 Font Blvd, San Francisco, CA 94132-1795

Saybrook Institute Graduate School (1971)
450 Pacific, 3rd Fl, San Francisco, CA 94133
J. Bruce Francis, PhD, Pres, 415-433-9200, FAX: 415-433-9271
Type: higher education, non-profit; tuition: $9,500/yr,
    scholarships
80 teachers, 300 students, ages 35–63
Governance by board
Psychology; human science; distance learning format taught
    by internationally known scholars.

San Francisco Montessori School
300 Gaven St, San Francisco, CA 94134-1113

Ohlone
950 Amarillo, Palo Alto, CA 94303
415-856-1726

Creative Montessori Learning Center
1425 Bay Rd, Palo Alto, CA 94303-1109

Chrystie's Creche
3711 Ross Rd, Palo Alto, CA 94303-4551
Chrystie Tzugaris
Type: Montessori

Horrall Elementary School
949 Ocean View Ave, San Mateo, CA 94401-3462
Type: Montessori

Little Montessori School
27 10th Ave, San Mateo, CA 94401-4304

Neighborhood Montessori School
1333 Rosewood, Belmont, CA 94402

Bright Beginnings Montessori School
30 Hobart Ave, San Mateo, CA 94402
Joanne Adan

Meadow Heights Elementary School
PO Box K, San Mateo, CA 94402-0058
Type: Montessori

San Mateo Montessori
15 14th Ave, San Mateo, CA 94402-2407
Eleanor Spare

Hillsborough Montessori Children's House
315 Tulane Dr, San Mateo, CA 94402-3237
Eleanor Spare

Parkside Elementary School
1685 Eisenhower St, San Mateo, CA 94403-1098
Type: Montessori

Discovery Montessori School
1601 Oakwood Dr, San Mateo, CA 94403-3918
Bonnie Mathisen

Child Unique Montessori School
2226 Encinal Ave, Alameda, CA 94501
Cindy Acker

Island High School (1967)
2437 Eagle Ave, Alameda, CA 94501
Ed Tucker, Prin, 510-748-4024, FAX: 510-769-7417
Type: public at-risk
10 teachers, 170 students, ages 15–19, 9–12th grade
Governance by principal
Teacher qualifications: credential
Teen parenting; ROP food service program; mainstreamed

Bayside Montessori Association
1523 Willow St, Alameda, CA 94501-2716

Rising Star Montessori School
770 Santa Clara Ave, Alameda, CA 94501-3102
Ann Gavey

Montessori School of Alameda
1247 Park Ave, Alameda, CA 94501-5235
Dr Pamela Lanaro

Prospects High
625 W 4th St, Antioch, CA 94509
Type: public choice

La Paloma High School (1974)
6651 Lone Tree Way, Brentwood, CA 94513
Jerry Hardt, Prin, 510-634-2888, FAX: 510-634-1687
Type: public at-risk
8 teachers, 130 students, ages 15–18, 9–12th grade
Governance by board
1993 CA DE Continuation Model HS Excellence Awar; interns
    accepted.

Alhambra Montessori
2771 Treat Blvd, Concord, CA 94518

Crossroads High School
1266 San Carlos Ave, Concord, CA 94518
Betty Potts, Adm, 510-933-1123
Type: public at-risk
2 teachers, 40 students, mainly at-risk, ages 14–19, 9–12th
    grade
Governance by principal, faculty and student representatives
Teacher qualifications: secondary credential
Parenting, pre/post-natal health, childbirth, survival skills,
    career orientation; multi-aged classes; suburban location.

Nueva Vista High School (1991)
1101 Alberta Way, Concord, CA 94518
Julie Hernandez, Adm, 510-689-1487
Type: public choice/at-risk
2 teachers, 40 students, mainly at-risk, ages 13–19, 9–12th grade
Governance by principal, faculty and student representatives, democratic school meeting
Community service, vocational, aviation programs; individualized and group learning; multi-aged classes; extensive field trips; suburban location.

Concordia School
2353 5th Ave, Concord, CA 94518-1112
Alice Marshall
Type: Montessori

Horizons School
2730 Salvio St, Concord, CA 94519
Doug Cook, Adm, 510-687-0374
Type: independent, non-profit
9 teachers, 235 students, mainly at-risk, ages 12–18, 7–12th grade
Governance by principal
Teacher qualifications: CA certification

Adelante High School (1992)
2450 Grant St, Concord, CA 94520
Marti Howell, Adm, 510-798-1168
Type: public at-risk
5 teachers, 85 students, mainly at-risk, ages 14–17, 9–12th grade
Governance by teachers and principal
Teacher qualifications: expertise in subject areas
Necessary Small High School; "On Location" program combines classwork with off-campus projects; "On Campus" is more traditional; multi-aged classes; suburban location; interns accepted.

Myrtle Farm Montessori School
4980 Myrtle Dr, Concord, CA 94521-1436
Krista Ericson

Prospect High School (1991)
3100 Oak Park Blvd, Pleasant Hill, CA 94523
Noreen Doyle, Adm, 510-945-7902
Type: public at-risk
2 teachers, 40 students, ages 14–18, 9–12th grade
Governance by teachers and principal
Teacher qualifications: must teach multiple subjects
Counselor-trained faculty; self-esteem; productive hour concept; coop learning; computers; no letter grades; multi-aged classes; suburban location; interns accepted.

Willow High School (1970)
PO Box 816; 1650 Crockett Blvd, Crockett, CA 94525
Darlene Rourke, Lead Tch, 510-787-1286
Type: public at-risk
1 teacher, 20 students, ages 16–18, 9–12th grade
Governance by teachers, principal
Teacher qualifications: CA certification
Flexible learning format; teen parenting; working students; no letter grades; multi-aged classes

Fountainhead Montessori (1973)
115 Estates Dr, Danville, CA 94526
Sarah Zimmerman, Pres/Adm, 510-820-1343
Non-profit; tuition: $3,050-6,050/yr
20 teachers, 27 assistants, 447 students, ages infant–9
Affiliations: AMS, NAEYC
Governance by administrator
Childcare; suburban location; interns accepted.

Das Montessori Kinderhaus
101 Sonora Ave, Danville, CA 94526-3833

Bright Star Montessori
7140 Gladys Ave, El Cerrito, CA 94530
Swarna Matz, Dir, 233-5330
Non-profit; tuition: $3,600-5,100/yr
9 teachers, 10 assistants, 139 students, mainly international, ages infant–15
Accreditation: AMS
Governance by administrator
Childcare; suburban location; interns accepted.

Sem Yeto High School (1967)
421 Madison St, Fairfield, CA 94533
Edward E. Welsh, Prin, 707-421-4271
Type: public choice/at-risk
12 teachers, 290 students, ages 16–19, 9–12th grade
Affiliation: WASC
Governance by board
Teacher qualifications: CA secondary credential
Close supervision; multi-aged classes; suburban location; interns accepted.

Vista Alternative School (1985)
4455 Seneca Park Ave, Fremont, CA 94536
Mary Douglass, 510-657-7028, FAX: 510-657-5535
Type: public choice
11 teachers, 260 students, ages 5–21, K–12th grade
Affiliations: Fremont USD, CCIS
Governance by teachers and principal
Teacher qualifications: CA credential
Homeschooling component with certificated guidance of parents as teachers; independent study; JHSers meet in small groups; SHSers work individually; suburban location.

Vista Alternative (1985)
4455 Seneca Park, Fremont, CA 94538
Mary Douglass, 510-687-9155, FAX: 510-657-5535
Type: public choice/at-risk
9 teachers, 250 students, ages 5–21, K–12th grade
Governance by teachers and principal
Teacher qualifications: CA credential
Independent study; tutorial; suburban location; interns accepted.

Montessori School of Fremont (1975)
1901 Washington Blvd, Fremont, CA 94539
Tess Buenaventura, Dir, 510-490-0919, FAX: 510-489-3913
Tuition: $250-395/mo
4 teachers, 5 assistants, 89 students, mainly international, ages toddler–6
Affiliations: AMI, NAMTA, MAC-USA
Governance by teachers and administrators
Rich cultural resources; computer ed; extensive ESL, parent ed; childcare; suburban location; interns accepted.

Hayward Unified
24411 Amador St, Hayward, CA 94540-5000
Type: public choice

Montessori School of Hayward
1101 Walpert St, Hayward, CA 94541
Dr Pamela Lanaro

Montessori Children's School
1620 East Ave, Hayward, CA 94541-5315

Montessori School of Castro Valley
19234 Lake Chabot Rd, Castro Valley, CA 94546-2902
Dr Pamela Lanaro

Montessori Children's House
915 Colina Ct, Lafayette, CA 94549

Diablo Valley Montessori
3390 Deer Hill Rd, Lafayette, CA 94549-3258
Barbara Grillo

Montessori Children's House of Lafayette
955A Moraga Rd, Lafayette, CA 94549-4524
Naome Dragstedt

Marshall
4602 Almond Cir, Livermore, CA 94550
Type: Montessori

Vineyard High Independent Study
685 Las Positas Blvd, Livermore, CA 94550
Type: home-based public choice

Valley Montessori School
460 North Livermore Ave, Livermore, CA 94550-2929
Mary Ellen Cordiss

Montessori School & Educational Foundation
5966 Greenridge Rd, Castro Valley, CA 94552-1818

Martinez Independent Study (1980)
600 F St, Martinez, CA 94553
Kathy Prout, Asst Dir, 510-228-5156, FAX: 510-228-6989
Type: public choice
4 teachers, 115 students, ages 5+, K–12th grade
Affiliation: CA Consortium
Governance by principal
Homeschooling support; multi-aged classes; extensive field
     trips

Montessori Children's Center
33170 Lake Meade Dr, Fremont, CA 94555
Naseem Meer

Montessori House of Children
22 Wakefield Dr, Moraga, CA 94556-1216
Vera Depass

Sunrise Montessori of Napa Valley (1978)
PO Box4077, Napa, CA 94558
Janice Tres, Co-owner/Adm, 707-253-1105
Tuition: $225-335/mo
8 teachers, 7 assistants, 110 students, ages infant–9
Two campuses; childcare; suburban and rural location.

Temescal High School
2447 Old Sonoma Rd, Napa, CA 94558
Darlene Lance, Prin, 707-253-3791
Type: public at-risk
5 teachers, 100 students, partly at-risk, ages 16–18, 10–12th
     grade
Governance by teachers, principal
Teacher qualifications: credential
Integrated, project approach; varied schedule; art; adopted
     by Sunrise Rotary Club; no letter grades; multi-aged classe;
     interns accepted.

Crossroads High Independent Study
Box 385, Newark, CA 94560
Type: home-based public choice

Newark Independent Study
5715 Musick Ave, Newark, CA 94560

Contra Costa Alternative High School
10 Irwin Way, Orinda, CA 94563
Joel Weber, 510-254-0199
Type: independent; tuition: $400-600/mo, scholarships
40 students, 9–12th grade
Focuses on social awareness, self-exploration; multi-cultural;
     large variety of electives; suburban location.

Montessori Children's House of Pinole
2281 Johanna Ct, Pinole, CA 94564-1816

Grasp Independent Study
809 Black Diamond St, Pittsburg, CA 94565
Type: public choice

Amadora Valley Adult School
4659 Bernal Ave, Pleasanton, CA 94566
Jean Kaput, Asst Dir, 510-426-4280, FAX: 510-846-5317
Type: public choice
Governance by principal, board

Teacher qualifications: CA credential
Interns accepted.

YMCA Child Development Center
200 Lake Ave, Rodeo, CA 94572
Sandra Farmer
Type: Montessori

Montessori Children's House of Rodeo
355 Parker Ave, Rodeo, CA 94572-1124
Johanna Lowe

St Helena Montessori School (1971)
1328 Spring St, St Helena, CA 94574
Ms Heil, Adm, 707-963-7642
Non-profit; tuition: $2,200-3,550/yr
3 teachers, 3 assistants, 58 students, ages 3–12
Affiliations: AMI, NAMTA
Governance by administrator, board
Catholic; Catechesis of the Good Shepherd; French; com-
     puter; art; Orff-Shulwerk music; gymnastics; suburban
     location.

Montessori Family Center
960 Dowdell Ln, St Helena, CA 94574-1452
Patricia Goldstein

Lincoln High
2600 Teagarden St, San Leandro, CA 94577
Janet McCarthy, Prin, 510-667-3594
Type: public at-risk
6 teachers, 90 students, ages 16–18, 9–12th grade
Governance by teachers, principal
Teacher qualifications: CA credential
Volunteer service; regional occupational programs connec-
     tion; personal, group counseling; variable credit

Montessori School at Washington Ave
14795 Washington Ave, San Leandro, CA 94578
Dr Pamela Lanaro

Montessori School of San Leandro
16292 Foothill Blvd, San Leandro, CA 94578-2105
Dr Pamela Lanaro

Independent Study
820 Bockman Rd, San Lorenzo, CA 94580

Venture School (1978)
3280 E Crow Canyon Rd, San Ramon, CA 94583
Norman Abraham, Prin, 510-275-0402, FAX: 510-275-0171
Type: public choice, home-based
19 teachers, 504 students, mainly at-risk, ages 5–53, K–12th
     grade
Governance by principal, board
Teacher qualifications: California credential
Independent study; individualized goals; extensive field trip;
     interns accepted.

Hacienda Child Development
4671 Chabot Dr, Pleasanton, CA 94588
Type: Montessori

Parkmead Alternative Learning School
1920 Magnolia, Parkmead, CA 94595
510-939-2900
Type: public choice
6 teachers, 175 students, K–5th grade
5 hrs/mo parent participation required.

Jingletown Charter Middle School
2601 E 9th St, Oakland, CA 94601
Clemintina Duron, 510-532-6751
Type: charter
6–8th grade
Affiliation: CA BE
ESL.

Oakland Montessori School
3636 Dimond Ave, Oakland, CA 94602-2213

Casa Montessori School
5062 Dublin Ave, Oakland, CA 94602-2605

Cole Elementary
1011 Union St, Oakland, CA 94607
Jaqueline Phillips, 510-444-7733
Type: magnet
4-6th grade
Performing arts.

East Bay Waldorf School
1275 61st St, Emeryville, CA 94608
Sherry McCarthy

Pacific Rim International School (1989)
5521 Doyle St, Emeryville, CA 94608
Christina Cheung, Dir, 510-849-1889
Type: Montessori; tuition: $385-505/mo
5 teachers, 1 assistant, 48 students, mainly international,
    ages 2-8
Affiliations: NAEYC, IRA, NAMTA, NCME, AMS
Governance by administrator
English-Mandarin bilingual and multi-cultural program; child-
    care; urban location; interns accepted.

Jardin Montessori School
3239 Elm St, Oakland, CA 94609

Park Day School (1976)
368 42nd St, Oakland, CA 94609
Tom Little, Dir, 510-653-0317, FAX: -0637
Type: independent, non-profit; tuition: $5,600/yr,
    scholarships
12 teachers, 200 students, ages 5-12, K-6th grade
Governance by consensus of staff and board
Teacher qualifications: experience in alternative school
    settings
Cloistered garden setting; activities-based curriculum;
    emphasis on multi-cultural, diversity elements in diverse
    population; central teacher involvement in long-range
    planning; no letter grades; extensive field trips; urban loca-
    tion; interns accepted.

Grand Lake Montessori
723 Santa Ray Ave, Oakland, CA 94610-1722

Casa Dei Bambini Montessori School
281 Santa Clara Ave, Oakland, CA 94610-2623
Helen Sears

Oakland High School
1023 MacArthur Blvd, Oakland, CA 94611
Joanne Grimm, 510-451-1208
Type: magnet
10-12th grade
Visual arts.

Piedmont Independent Learning High School (1981)
760 Magnolia Ave, Piedmont, CA 94611
Tra Holloway Boxer, Prin, 510-420-3702, FAX: 654-7374
Non-profit
5 teachers, 32 students, mainly at-risk, ages 15-19, 9-12th
    grade
Governance by principal
Flexible; mastery-based; open entry/exit; individual assess-
    ments, contracts; multi-aged classe; interns accepted.

Applegarden Montessori School
5667 Thornhill Dr, Oakland, CA 94611-2156
Naome Dragstedt

Arts School
5263 Broadway Ter, Oakland, CA 94618
Type: public choice

My Own Montessori (1986)
5723 Oak Grove Ave, Oakland, CA 94618
Gena K. Lawrence, Adm, 510-652-5979
Non-profit; tuition: $400-620/mo
2 teachers, 2 assistants, 28 students, ages 3-6
Accreditation: AMS
Governance by board
Childcare; urban location; interns accepted.

Rockridge Montessori School
6118 Harwood Ave, Oakland, CA 94618-1340

Mountain Boulevard Preschool (1983)
4432 Mountain Blvd, Oakland, CA 94619
Dennis or Eleni Wanken, 510-482-2850, FAX: 510-482-0326
Type: Montessori; tuition: $695/mo
3 teachers, 4 assistants, 45 students, ages 3-6
Affiliations:, NAEYC; accreditation: AMS
Childcare; transportation; interns accepted.

Skyline High School
12250 Skyline Blvd, Oakland, CA 94619
Thomas Lorch, 510-531-9161
Type: magnet
10-12th grade
Performing arts.

Cedar Creek Montessori Day Care (1979)
1600 Sacramento St, Berkeley, CA 94702
Kerry Woodward, Dir, 510-525-1377
Tuition: $590/mo
2 teachers, 2 assistants, 38 students, ages 3-6
Accreditation: AMS
Governance by administrator
Art; nature studies; interns accepted.

Encampment for Citzenship (1946)
2530 San Pablo Ave, Suite B-10, Berkeley, CA 94702
Doug Harkness, 415-548-8908
Type: independent, non-profit; tuition: $2,400/yr,
    scholarships
50 students, ages 16–19
Six-week summer camp; focus on current social, political
    issues; workshops; community service; arts and politics.

Montessori Family School (1981)
1850 Scenic Ave, Berkeley, CA 94703
Jane Wechsler, Dir, 510-848-2322
Non-profit; tuition: $3,700-6,250/yr, scholarships
12 teachers, 8 assistants, 123 students, ages 2-12
Affiliation: AMS; accreditations: NAEYC,
Governance by teachers and administrators
Borders UCBerkeley; cultural diversity; summer program;
    parent involvement required; childcare; urban location;
    interns accepted.

Family Forum
1035 Pablo Ave #5, Albany, CA 94706
Grace Orenstein
Type: Montessori

Montessori Children's School
661 San Luis Rd, Berkeley, CA 94707

Montessori School of Kensington
52 Arlington, Kensington, CA 94707
510-527-1278
Tuition: $405/555/mo
4 teachers, 5 assistants, 52 students, ages infant-9
Affiliations: AMS,
Governance by administrator
Adjacent to University of California gardens, local library,
    recreation center, park, and tennis courts; childcare; subur-
    ban location; interns accepted.

Northern Alameda/Western Contra Costa Homeschool Support Group (1988)
1090 Miller Ave, Berkeley, CA 94708
Ann Kositsky-Haiman, 510-527-5091
Non-profit
Regular meetings.

Concepts to Go
Dept M, PO Box 10043, Berkley, CA 94709
Ruth Ingram
Type: Montessori

Berkeley Montessori School
2030 Francisco St, Berkeley, CA 94709-2198
Curt Chamberlain

West County Montessori
716 Appian Way, El Sabrante, CA 94803

Keystone Montessori
801 Park Central St, Richmond, CA 94803-1225
Linda Shehabi

El Sobrante School
1060 Manor Rd, El Sobrante, CA 94803-1398
Type: Montessori

Kappa High School (1992)
4300 Cutting Blvd, Richmond, CA 94804
Dr Richard B. Blaettler, Prin, 510-234-0281
Type: public at-risk
4 teachers, 100 students, ages 15–18, 9–12th grade
Governance by principal
Tutoring; portfolios; computer labs; TAP; role model speakers; job shadowing/mentoring; breakfast program; multi-aged classe; interns accepted.

Montessori Kinderhaus
5638 Bayview Ave, Richmond, CA 94804-4827

Vista High Independent Study
2625 Barnard Rd, Richmond, CA 94806
Type: public choice

Middle College High School (1993)
2600 Mission Bell Dr, San Pablo, CA 94806
Myra Silverman, Prin, 510-235-7800 x411
Type: public choice
80 students

Seaview School
2000 Southwood Dr, San Pablo, CA 94806-1039
Type: Montessori

Columbia Pacific University
1415 3rd St, San Rafael, CA 94901
Cynthia Sirkin, 800-227-0119
Non-residential programs for BA, MA, PhD; credit for life experience; no letter grades.

Montessori School of Central Marin
317 Auburn St, San Rafael, CA 94901-5209
Dr Pamela Lanaro

Marin Waldorf School
755 Idylberry Dr, San Rafael, CA 94903
Karen Rivers

Montessori Special Education Institute
PO Box 6633, San Rafael, CA 94903

Montessori de Terra Linda
620 Del Ganado Rd, San Rafael, CA 94903-2306
Jim Cummesky

Creekside Montessori School
PO Box 570, Bolinas, CA 94924-0570

Marin Montessori School (1963)
5200 Paradise Dr, Corte Madera, CA 94925-2107
Jane Calbreath, Off Coord, 415-924-5388, FAX: 415-924-5305
Non-profit; tuition: $3,480-4,990/yr
8 teachers, 7 assistants, 179 students, mainly international, ages infant–12
Affiliations: NAMTA, ISBMA; accreditation: AMI
Governance by board of directors
Natural bayfront environment; childcare; suburban location.

Cascade Canyon School
2626 Drake Rd, Fairfax, CA 94930-0879
Anne Evans, Director, 415-459-3464, FAX: 415-459-1189
Type: independent, non-profit; tuition: $4,500-5,500, scholarships
3 teachers, 36 students, ages 5–14, K–8th grade
Affiliation: NCACS
Governance by parent cooperative, board
International education with several foreign languages, multi-cultural community service, sister school program via E mail and visits overseas; no letter grades; non-compulsory class attendance; multi-aged classes; extensive field trips; suburban location; interns accepted.

Rainbow Bridge Montessori School
21 William St, Cotati, CA 94931-4235
Juli Inman

Tamiscal High School (1990)
599 William Ave, Larkspur, CA 94939
Debrah Stewart, 415-927-3465
Type: public choice
100 students, partly at-risk, ages 14–19, 9–12th grade
Governance by teachers, principal
College prep; independent study

Ross Academy Montessori (1966)
7 Thomas Dr, Mill Valley, CA 94941
Claire Haeger, 415-383-5777
Tuition: $230-420/mo
5 teachers, 2 assistants, 75 students, ages infant–6
Affiliation: NAMS; accreditation: AMS
Governance by administrator
Gymnastics, dance, music optional; childcare; suburban location; interns accepted.

Penngrove Montessori
11201 Main St, Penngrove, CA 94941

Marin Horizon School
305 Montford Ave, Mill Valley, CA 94941-3388
Type: Montessori

Montessori School of Novato (1985)
1915 Novato Blvd, Novato, CA 94947
Susan Young, Adm, 415-892-2228
Tuition: $290/380
2 teachers, 44 students, ages infant–6
Affiliation: AMI
Governance by administrator
Childcare.

Nova Independent Studies (1990)
720 Diablo, Novato, CA 94947
Tom Ovens, Lead Tch; Jim Campagna, Prin, 415-897-7653
Type: public choice
5 teachers, 135 students, ages 5–18, K–12th grade
Affiliation: Novato Unified Schools
Governance by teachers, principal
Teacher qualifications: district requirements
Weekly individual student/teacher meetings; contract learning; community service; no letter grades; interns accepted.

Carpe Diem High School (1992)
201 Fair St, Petaluma, CA 94952
Susan Rodkin, Prin, 707-778-4796
Type: public at-risk

3 teachers, 30 students, ages 14-18, 9-12th grade
Governance by teachers and principal
Mini-field trips: 3-4 students, one teacher for career exploration, community involvement; multi-aged classes; suburban location.

Montessori Schools of Petaluma (1975)
825 Middlefield Dr, Petaluma, CA 94952
Tom Sipes, Dir, 707-763-9222
Non-profit; tuition: $260-474/mo
7 teachers, 7 assistants, 135 students, ages infant-12
Governance by teachers and administrators
Childcare; suburban location; interns accepted.

Marin School
PO Box 504, Petaluma, CA 94953-0504
Type: Montessori

Sonoma Mountain High School (1992)
333 Casa Grande Rd, Petaluma, CA 94954
Marilyn Stratford, Prin, 707-778-4738
Type: public at-risk
3 teachers, 30 students, ages 14-17, 9-12th grade
Governance by teachers, principal
Integrated block curriculum; mini field trips; high level of technology; personal student-staff connections; multi-aged classes

Early Work
(See Resource Section)

San Anselmo Montessori School
100 Shaw Dr, San Anselmo, CA 94960-1904

Slide Ranch
2025 Shoreline Hwy, Muir Beach, CA 94965
Suzanne Connolly, Dir, 414-381-6155
Type: independent, non-profit; tuition: variable, scholarships
50 students, K-12th grade
Principles of ecology; farm, wild lands, ocean environments; 1-day and overnight; experiential.

Sparrow Creek Montessori School (1973)
304 Caledonia St, Sausalito, CA 94965
Judith Bang-Kolb, 415-332-9595
Non-profit; tuition: $390/mo, scholarships
3-4 teachers, 22 students, ages 3-6
Governance by board of trustees
Art; year-round garden; childcare; suburban location; interns accepted.

Children's Cultural Center of Marin (1971)
620 Drake Ave, Sausalito, CA 94965-1107
Elice Webster, 415-332-1044, FAX: 332-1058
Type: Montessori; tuition: $595/mo
5 teachers, 8 assistants; student ages infant-9
Affiliation: NAMTA; accreditation: AMS
Daily French; extensive computer ed; Japanese; global studies; suburban location; transportation; interns accepted.

Liedloff Continuum Network
(See Resource Section)

Santa Cruz Montessori School (1964)
6230 Soquel Dr, Aptos, CA 95003
James M. Moore, Head, 408-476-1646, FAX: 408-476-2703
Non-profit; tuition: $3,200-4,650/yr
10 teachers, 15 assistants, 258 students, ages infant-15
Affiliations: NAMTA, AMI, MAC; accreditation: AMI/USA
Governance by teachers. administrators, board
2-acres with access to Monterey Bay; creative conflict resolution; Great Books literature; Central Coast Writer's Workshop; childcare; suburban location; interns accepted.

Fawnhaven Montessori Pre-School
6401 Freedom Blvd, Aptos, CA 95003-9607
Barbara Hendricks

South Street Centre (1987)
PO Box 227, Boulder Creek, CA 95006
Betsy Herbert; Estelle Fein, Co-Dirs, 408-338-2540
Type: home-based; cost: Variable
7 teachers, 60 students, ages 5-16, K-12th grade
Affiliation: San Lorenzo Valley SD
Governance by teachers and Prin
Teacher qualifications: Interest in learning process
Workshops; conferences; link for developing community-based education; contracted by local SD for some service; suburban location; interns accepted.

AMI Montessori House of Children
124 W Latimer Ave, Campbell, CA 95008-1105

San Jose Montessori School
564 Hawthorne Ave, Campbell, CA 95008-2117

Central Bay High School (1991)
13994 Castroville Blvd, Castroville, CA 95012
Rich Castello, Prin, 408-633-4790
Type: public at-risk
2 teachers, 24 students, mainly teen parents, ages 14-18
Affiliation: NMCUSD
Governance by teachers, principal, board
Childcare

Villa Montessori, Inc (1964)
20900 Stevens Creek Blvd, Cupertino, CA 95014
Renee Davis, Dir/Adm, 408-257-3374
Non-profit; tuition: $2,350/yr
2 teachers, 2 assistants, 60 students, mainly international, ages 3-6
Affiliation: AMS
Governance by board of trustees
Mandarin, Spanish, Croatian, Russian, German, French, and Dutch speaking staff; suburban location.

One World Montessori School, Inc (1979)
20220 Suisun Dr, Cupertino, CA 95014-4428
Pascale Marion, Office Mgr, 408-255-3770
Tuition: $325-670/mo
11 teachers, 12 assistants, 203 students, mainly international, ages infant-12
Affiliations: AMI, AMS
Governance by board
Emphasis on cultural subjects; multi-cultural student body and teaching staff; childcare; suburban location; interns accepted.

Monarch Montessori Christian
11700 Upland Way, Cupertino, CA 95014-5106

Quality Education Resources
(See Resource Section)

Charter School Number 25
6134 Hwy 9, Felton, CA 95018
Eric Schoffstall, 408-336-5167
Type: charter
K-12th grade
Affiliation: CA BE
Integrating existing homeschool and White Oak HS; individualized.

Natural Alternative
328 Redwood Dr, Felton, CA 95018
Susan Morin, 408-335-0765
Type: home-based
Student ages 2-6
Positive enrichment through play; home/outdoor environment; emphasis on natural rhythms and personality development.

South Valley Homeschoolers Association
7273 Carr Pl, Gilroy, CA 95020
Sheri Russell

Casa Di Mir Montessori Ele School
200 Prospect Ave, Los Gatos, CA 95030
Wanda Whitehead

Casa Maria Montessori School
PO Box 1906, Los Gatos, CA 95031-1906

Milpitas Independent Study
1500 Escuela Parkway, Milpitas, CA 95035

Home Educator's Almanac
(See Resource Section)

Wilson High School (1992)
1840 Benton Ave, Santa Clara, CA 95050
Dr Daniene Marciano, Vice Prin, 408-984-6442, FAX: -8250
40 students

Rainbow Montessori
1725 De La Cruz Blvd # 6, Santa Clara, CA 95050-3011

Pioneer Montessori
400 N Winchester Blvd, Santa Clara, CA 95050-6317

Santa Clara Valley School (1995)
890 Pomeroy Ave, Santa Clara, CA 95051
Stuart Williams-Ley, Staff Member, 408-296-2072
E-mail Freekids@aol.com, WWW SCVS@webpage.com
Type: independent; tuition: $4,700 (1st), 3,700 (2nd), 2,700
   (3rd), 2,800 pt/yr
Student ages 5-19, ungraded
Sudbury Valley School model.

Home School Association of California (1987)
PO Box 2067, Santa Clara, CA 95055-2067
Mary Griffith, Editor, CA Homeschooler, 707-765-5375
Non-profit
Newsletter.

Bayside Children's College
609 Pacific Ave, Santa Cruz, CA 95060
Karen Ancic, Director, 408-454-0370
Type: independent

Cities in Schools Learning Center
133 Mission St, Santa Cruz, CA 95060
Dr Terry Jones, 408-429-3800
Type: charter
9-12th grade
Affiliation: CA BE

Global Youth Academy (1972)
819 1/2 Pacific Ave, Santa Cruz, CA 95060
Steve Myers, 408-423-4451, FAX: 408-423-3081
Type: independent, non-profit; tuition: $5,700/yr,
   scholarships
6 teachers, 37 students, ages 12-18, 6-12th grade
Affiliation: CAN
Governance by principal, democratic school meeting, board
Teacher qualifications: varies by subject
Year-round; emphasis on world-citizenship, creativity, personal growth; extensive international travel; 3 Golden Bell
   awards won; optional letter grades; multi-aged classe;
   interns accepted.

Pacific Village School
518 Meder St, Santa Cruz, CA 95060
Paul Manners, 408-429-9209, FAX: 426-9607
Type: independent; tuition: $3,465 (1st)/yr
4 teachers, 7-30 students, ages 5-19, ungraded
Sudbury Valley School model; kitchen, large deck; 3 acres
   shared with Catalpa Farm community includes 3 art
   studios, workshop, and organic garden.

Santa Cruz Waldorf School (1976)
2190 Empire Grade, Santa Cruz, CA 95060
Stephen Spitalny, Chair, 408-425-0519
Non-profit; tuition: $4,500-4,800/yr, scholarships

180 students, ages 4.75-14, K-8th grade
Affiliation: ASWNA
Governance by faculty
Teacher qualifications: Waldorf training
Multi-cultural emphasis; community service; suburban/rural
   location; transportation; interns accepted.

The ARK School (1979)
313 Swift St, Santa Cruz, CA 95060
Leonard Cowan, Counselor; Joan Thompson, Secretary, 408-
   429-3434
Type: public choice/at-risk
10 teachers, 210 students, mainly at-risk, ages 14-19, 9-12th
   grade
Governance by teachers and principal
Teacher qualifications: CA Certification
Community involvement; no letter grades; multi-aged
   classes; extensive field trips; suburban location; interns
   accepted.

**International Association for the Study of Cooperation
in Education**
(See Resource Section)

Alternative Family Education Home Studies (1991)
300 La Fonda, Santa Cruz, CA 95062
Dr Terry Jones, 408-429-3052, FAX: 408-429-3303
5 teachers, 125 students, K-12th grade
Governance by teachers, principal, parent cooperative
Teacher qualifications: state certification
Non-compulsory class attendance; extensive field trips;
   urban location.

Children's Art Foundation, Stone Soup Magazine
(See Resource Section)

The Vineyard School
2317 Vine Hill Rd, Santa Cruz, CA 95065
JoAnn King, Director, 408-438-7320
Type: independent

Agape Montessori Childdren's Home
19732 Solana Dr, Saratoga, CA 95070

Notre Dame Montessori (1966)
15100 Norton Rd, Saratoga, CA 95070
Kathy Genereux, Adm, 408-867-1663
Non-profit; tuition: $215/mo
7 teachers, 64 students, ages 3-6
Accreditation: AMS
Governance by administrator
Rural location; interns accepted.

Linscott Charter School
220 Elm St, Watsonville, CA 95076
Vera Algoet, 408-728-6301
Type: charter
125 students, K-5th grade
Affiliation: CA BE
Principal replaced by fiscal officer and instructional leader.
Conversion; may expand to pre K-12.

Horace Mann Elementary
55 N Seventh St, San Jose, CA 95112
Milly Powell, 408-988-6237
Type: magnet
K-5th grade
Student-centered.

Pioneer Plus High School (1992)
1290 Blossom Hill Rd, San Jose, CA 95118
Bob Heinrich, Counselor, 408-264-4428
Type: public at-risk
2 teachers, 40 students, ages 14-19, 9-12th grade
Affiliation: San Jose USD
Governance by teachers and principal
Variable credit; individual studies classes available.

American Montessori School
19950 McKean Rd, San Jose, CA 95120

Castillero Middle School
6384 Leyland Park Dr, San Jose, CA 95120
E. Orta-Camilleri, 408-998-6385
Type: magnet
6-8th grade
Visual and performing arts.

Broadway High School (1982)
1088 Broadway Ave, San Jose, CA 95125
Kerm Hartley, Prin, 408-998-6215, FAX: 408-288-8039
Type: public at-risk
15 teachers, 300 students, ages 13–19, HS
Governance by principal
Teacher qualifications: CA credential
Teen parenting; GED prep; work experience; drug/alcohol day
    treatment; ESL; urban location; transportation.

Willow Glen Plus (1992)
2001 Cottle Ave, San Jose, CA 95125
Fred Morales, Counselor, 408-264-4422
Type: public at-risk
2 teachers, 40 students, ages 15.5–18, 10–12th grade
Governance by principal
Teacher qualifications: CA secondary credential
Focus on changing failure behaviors; close parent contact;
    multi-aged classes; field trips; counseling; suburban loca-
    tion; transportation; interns accepted.

Educational Options (1962)
1671 Park Negles, San José, CA 95126
Susan Truitt-Valdez, 408-998-6127, FAX: 408-998-8814
Type: public at-risk
43 teachers, 4000 students, ages 5–19, K–12th grade
Affiliation: San José USD
Governance by principal
Teacher qualifications: certification
Business, college partnerships; independent study; no letter
    grades

Herbert Hoover Middle School
1635 Park Ave, San Jose, CA 95126
Patti Gregory, 408-998-6274
Type: magnet
6-8th grade
Visual and performing arts.

Lincoln High School
555 Dana Ave, San Jose, CA 95126
Oreen Gernreich, 408-998-6300
Type: magnet
9-12th grade
Visual and performing arts.

San Jose Unified School District
1605 Park Ave, San Jose, CA 95126
Norris Hill, Magnets Mgr
Type: Montessori

Trace Elementary
651 Dana Ave, San Jose, CA 95126
Rosanne Adona, 408-998-6257
Type: magnet
3-5th grade
Visual and performing arts.

Cory Elementary
2280 Kenwood Ave, San Jose, CA 95128
Mei Kamenik, 408-998-6219
Type: magnet
K-2nd grade
Visual and performing arts.

Peninsula Homeschoolers
4795 Lage Dr, San Jose, CA 95130
408-379-6835

Pegasus High School (1991)
1776 Educational Park Dr, San Jose, CA 95133
Tim McDonough, Prin, 408-729-3967, FAX: 926-6785
Type: public at-risk
6 teachers, 120 students, mainly at-risk, ages 16–20, 10–12th
    grade
Governance by teachers and principal
Self-contained facility; 1:20 ratio; 3.5-hour day; in-class and
    independent study; earn credits toward graduation or
    transfer back to comprehensive HS; urban location; interns
    accepted.

HeadsUp! Child Development Centers
2841 Junction Ave, Suite 100, San Jose, CA 95134
Type: Montessori

Capitol High School Program (1990)
760 Hillsdale Ave, San Jose, CA 95136
Kathie Hodges, Coord, 408-723-6550, FAX: 266-6531
Type: public at-risk
3 teachers, 72 students, mainly at-risk, ages 16–19, 11–12th
    grade
Independent study; voc training; extensive field trips; urban
    location.

Casa Di Mir Montessori Elementary School
PO Box 4804, San Jose, CA 95150-4804
Nancy Curran

West Valley Montessori School
PO Box 611686, San Jose, CA 95161

Kohl Open Elementary
6325 N Alturas, Stockton, CA 95205
Bud West, 209-953-3020
Type: magnet
K-6th grade
Open School.

Stockton School Magnet Assistance
1144 E Channel St, Stockton, CA 95205
Joanne Miller, Dir
Type: Montessori

Hamilton Middle School
2245 E 11th St, Stockton, CA 95206
Edna Romos, 209-953-4701
Type: magnet
7-8th grade
Creative and performing arts; pre-IB.

Hazelton Elementary
535 W Jefferson St, Stockton, CA 95206
Petrina Romo, 209-953-4212
Type: magnet
4-6th grade
Gifted and talented.

James Monroe Elementary
2236 E 11th St, Stockton, CA 95206
Barbara Chan, 209-953-4271
Type: magnet
4-6th grade
Creative and performing arts.

Taft Elementary
419 Downing, Stockton, CA 95206
Margarita Ortega, 209-953-2011
Type: magnet
Student ages 3+,-6th grade
Montessori.

Creative Beginnings Montessori (1986)
6002 Plymouth Rd, Stockton, CA 95207
Sarah Wentworth, Owner/Dir, 209-474-8711
Tuition: $205/mo
1 teacher, 1 assistant, 21 students, mainly international, ages
    3-6

Affiliations: AMS, NAYEC
Governance by administrator
Diverse, both ethnically and financially; urban location; interns accepted.

Independent Study Center
2010 W Swain Road, Stockton, CA 95207

Alternative Cluster (1992)
22 S Van Buren, Stockton, CA 95209
Andres Torres, Acting Prin, 209-953-4306
Type: public at-risk
25 teachers, 625 students, ages 14-18, 9-12th grade
Governance by teachers and principal
Multi-aged classes; urban location.

New World Montessori (1980)
2367 Waudman Ave, Stockton, CA 95209
Shirley Garey, Owner, 209-952-8854
Tuition: $115-400/mo
3 teachers, 25 students, ages infant-6
Affiliations: NCME, NAMTA; accreditation: NCME
Governance by administrator
Childcare; suburban location; interns accepted.

Adelita Migrant Child Development Center
14320 E Harney Lane, Lodi, CA 95230
Type: Montessori

Sue Brock Migrant Infant Center
333 W Mathews Rd, French Camp, CA 95231
Margarita Cervantes
Type: Montessori

Artesi II Child Development Center
777 W Mathews Rd, French Camp, CA 95231-9764
Type: Montessori

Independent Study
815 W Lockeford St, Lodi, CA 95240

Independent Study K-8 Program (1983)
420 S Pleasant Ave, Lodi, CA 95240
Pamela Loechler, Tch, 209-331-7245
Non-profit
3 teachers, 76-90 students, ages 5-14
Governance by board
Teacher qualifications: credential
Monthly teacher visits; field trips; newsletter; art class; weekly computer lab; non-compulsory class attendance; extensive field trips

Calaveras Unified Alterative Education- Sierra Hills
Box 178, San Andreas, CA 95249
Type: public choice

Escalon Independent Study Center
1520 E Yosemite Ave, Escalon, CA 95320

The Eagle's Nest
(See Resource Section)

Irwin High School (1990)
20384 Geer Ave, Hilmar, CA 95324
John C. Johnson, Teaching Prin, 209-667-0276
Type: public at-risk
3 teachers, 50 students, ages 15-19, 9-12th grade
Governance by board
4-hour day; remedial; individualized; childcare; rural location; transportation.

Sierra Waldorf School
19234 Rawhide Rd, Jamestown, CA 95327
Karen Brock

Lindberg Educational Center (1987)
311 E North St, Manteca, CA 95336
Debbie Houck, 209-825-3100, FAX: same
Type: public choice
500 students

Alexander Street Montessori (1982)
21 E Alexander St, Merced, CA 95340
Jan Child, Head, 209-383-1232
Non-profit; tuition: $1,980/4,180/yr
1 teacher, 2 assistants, 30 students, ages 3-6
Governance by board
Large yard with flower and vegetable gardens; arbor; swimming pool; nature activities; pets; seasonal celebrations; childcare.

Independent Study
Box 2187, Merced, CA 95344

Homeschoolers For Peace
Box 74, Midpines, CA 95345
Pam & Craig Gingold, 209-742-6802

Yosemite Area Homeschoolers/ Homeschoolers for Peace
PO Box 74, Midpines, CA 95345

Duncan-Russell High School (1969)
164 W Grantiline Rd, Tracy, CA 95376
Cynthia Johannes, Prin, 209-831-5220
Type: public at-risk
7 teachers, 135 students, ages 16-18, 9-12th grade
Governance by principal, board
Teacher qualifications: certification
Teachers are counselors; weekly academic, attendance reports; parent contacts; no letter grade; interns accepted.

Excel High School (1992)
315 E 11th St, Tracy, CA 95376
Barbara Shreve, lead teacher, 209-831-5135, FAX: 209-836-3347
Type: public at-risk
2 teachers, 40 students, ages 14-18, 9-12th grade
Affiliation: Tracy High School
Governance by teachers and principal
Abbreviated school day; self-paced; hands-on learning; urban location.

Montessori Services
(See Resource Section)

Summerfield Waldorf School (1974)
155 Willowside Rd, Santa Rosa, CA 95401
Leslie Sheldon, Office Mgr, 707-575-7194
Non-profit; tuition: $3,800-5,230/yr, scholarships
31 teachers, 365 students, ages 5-18, K-12th grade
Affiliation: AWSNA
Governance by teachers
Teacher qualifications: 2-yr Waldorf training
32 acres; working organic farm; wildlife preserve; farming, gardening integrated into curriculum; extensive field trips; rural location; interns accepted.

Sonoma County Charter School (1994)
1825 Willowside Rd, Sonoma, CA 95401
Jim Hamilton, 707-544-1651
Type: charter
K-6th grade
Affiliation: CA BE
Non-graded; local business involvement; at need/low achieving student focus.

College Oak Montessori School
1925 W College Ave, Santa Rosa, CA 95401-4440

Consensus Classroom, Inc (1991)
7899 St Helena Rd, Santa Rosa, CA 95404
Linda Sartor, Facilitator/Consultant, 707-538-5123
Non-profit
Publicizes, instructs in consensus decision making model.

Montessori Elementary School
1569 Brush Creek Rd, Santa Rosa, CA 95404-2099
Peggy Colgan

Montessori Visions
1625 Franklin Ave, Santa Rosa, CA 95404-2506

Bennett Valley Charter School
2250 Mesquite Dr, Santa Rosa, CA 95405
Lyle Graf, 707-542-2201
Type: charter
K-6th grade
Affiliation: CA BE
Home study with parent as teacher and progess monitored
   monthly by resource teacher.

Paxundr Corp
1270 Franquette, Santa Rosa, CA 95405
Gayle Cavender
Type: Montessori

Rancheria High School (1978)
Box 457, Boonville, CA 95415
Val Muchowski, 707-895-3543, FAX: 707-895-2665
Type: public at-risk
2 teachers, 16 students, ages 14-34, 9-12th grade
Governance by principal
Teacher qualifications: certification
Individualized; multi-aged classes; rural location.

Waldorf School of Mendocino County (1972)
6280 3rd St, Box 349, Calpella, CA 95418
Star Gilley, Office Mgr, 707-485-8719
Non-profit
135 students, K-8th grade
Governance by teachers and Board of Directors
Hebrew; woodworking; gardening; band; chorus; eurythmy;
   no letter grades; extensive field trips; rural location.

R. H. Lewis Independent Study
Box 6630, Clearlake, CA 95422
Type: public choice

Richard H. Lewis School (1982)
PO Box 6630; S Center Dr, Clearlake, CA 95422
Mary Ann Penson, Dir, 707-994-2045
Type: public choice
5 teachers, 80 students, mainly at-risk, ages 5-18, K-12th
   grade
Governance by director
Teacher qualifications: CA Credentials
Students attend weekly, work at home; rural location.

The Eel River School
PO Box 218, Covelo, CA 95428
Kate Lane, 707-983-6708
Type: charter
20-30 students, K-12th grade
Affiliation: CA BE

Osprey Learning Center Independent Study
Box 129, Garberville, CA 95440
Type: public choice

**Mountain View High School/ Center for Independent
   Study**
1024 Prince St, Healdsburg, CA 95448
Elizabeth Burmudez, 707-431-3449
Type: public choice

Laytonville High School (1992)
PO Box 868, Laytonville, CA 95454
Mark Iacuaniello
Type: public choice
18 students

Acorn School
PO Box 387, Point Arena, CA 95468
Ellen Lockwood, 707-882-2274
Type: public choice

Nonesuch School
4004 Bones Rd, Sebastopol, CA 95472
Type: independent

Montessori Children's House
500 N Main St, Sebastopol, CA 95472-3407

Pleasant Hill Montessori School
789 Pleasant Hill Rd, Sebastopol, CA 95472-4027

Family English Literacy Program (1991)
3273 Airway Dr, Santa Rosa, CA 95473
4 teachers, 2 assistants, 85-120 students, mainly at-risk
Governance by director
Teacher qualifications: experience in adult ESL or in working
   with children, multi-cultural sensitivity
Adult ESL at 2 sites: Woodland for Mexicans, W. Sacramento
   for Russians; intergenerational activities; Social Service
   referrals; interns accepted.

Hearthsong
(See Resource Section)

Mandala Montessori School
960 Lark Ave, Sonoma, CA 95476

NCME
4043 Pepperwood Ct, Sonoma, CA 95476
Karen Lecy
Type: Montessori

Sonoma Valley Charter School
721 W Napa St, Sonoma, CA 95476
Marilyn Kelly, 707-935-6023
Type: charter
K-8th grade
Affiliation: CA BE

Sonoma Valley Waldorf School (1987)
PO Box 2063, Sonoma, CA 95476
Tiare Newport Wicklund, 707-996-0996
Non-profit; tuition: $4,080-5,220/yr, scholarships
3 teachers, 45 students, ages 3-8, pre K-2nd grade
Governance by teachers, board, and administrator
Teacher qualifications: Waldorf Institute training
Multi-aged classes; urban location.

Vintage Country Day School (1985)
PO Box 1514, Sonoma, CA 95476
Penny B. Aguer, Prin, 996-6560
Type: Montessori, non-profit; tuition: $230-355/mo
3 teachers, 3 assistants, 48 students, ages 3-12
Affiliation: AMS
Governance by administrator, board
Suburban location; interns accepted.

Montessori School of Sonoma
PO Box 760, Sonoma, CA 95476-0760

Young School
180 East Napa St, Sonoma, CA 95476-6710
Anthony Bell
Type: Montessori

Mariposa School (1969)
Box 387, Ukiah, CA 95482
Hannah Wild, 707-462-1016
Type: independent; tuition: $2,000-3,400, sliding scale
45 students, ages K-5
Hands-on approach, teaches students to experience nature
   in their everyday lives; conflict resolution part of curricu-
   lum; active parent involvement; rural location.

New School of Ukiah
433 N State St, Box 296, Ukiah, CA 95482
King Collins, 707-468-5537
6-12th grade

Ukiah Unified
1056 N Bush St, Ukiah, CA 95482
Type: public choice

Whale Gulch Elementary Independent Study
76811 Usal Rd, Whitethorn, CA 95489

Independent Study
249 N Main, Willits, CA 95490
Type: public choice

New Horizons/ Community as Classroom
371 E Commercial St, Willits, CA 95490
Thayer Craig, 707-459-6521
Type: public choice
Also houses City-as-School program.

Mistwood Montessori (1980)
1801 10th St, Eureka, CA 95501
Patti Frink, Owner, 444-8100
Tuition: $175/285/mo
3 teachers, 3 assistants, 75 students, ages 3–6
Governance by administrator
Music; Spanish immersion; childcare; suburban location.

Equinox School
470 Union St, Arcata, CA 95521
707-822-4845

Gateway Community School (1982)
1464 Spear Ave, Arcata, CA 95521
Duke Cairns, Teacher, 707-822-4721
Type: independent; tuition: $2,000/yr
4 teachers, 29 students, ages 5–11, K–5th grade
Governance by parent cooperative, democratic school
    meeting, board
Focuses on self-esteem, empowerment with responsibility,
    cooperation, community involvement, and environmental
    awareness; no letter grades; multi-aged classes; extensive
    field trips; interns accepted.

Mad River Montessori (1980)
PO Box 4334, Arcata, CA 95521
Robin Renshaw, 707-822-4027
Non-profit; tuition: $150/250/mo
1 teacher, 2 assistants, 36 students, ages 3–6
Governance by board
Rural location; interns accepted.

Michael Olaf Company
(See Resource Section)

Northern Humboldt Adult School (1971)
2755 McKinleyville Ave, McKinleyville, CA 95521
Kenny Richards, Prin; Jackie Hammer, Coord, 707-839-1613
Type: public choice
5 teachers, 600 students
Affiliation: N Humboldt Union HS District
Governance by principal
Teacher qualifications: CA credential, CBEST
3 locations; GED prep; enrichment classes; independent
    study; multi-aged classes

Petrolia High School (1983)
Box 197, Petrolia, CA 95558
Seth Zuckerman, Director, 707-629-3509
Type: independent, boarding, non-profit
10 teachers, 24 students, ages 14–18, 9–12th grade
Governance by teachers and principal, democratic school
    meeting, board
Year starts with 2 week backpacking; 6 week intercultural trip
    with home stay, often in Mexico; involvement in local envi-
    ronmental restoration efforts; individually designed project
    month; extensive field trips; rural location.

Humboldt Homeschoolers
688 S Whaven Dr, Trinidad, CA 95570
Paige Smith, 707-677-3290
Inclusive; loosely organized; newsletter; rural location.

Quest Independent Learning Center (1986)
332 Finley St, Auburn, CA 95603
Robert Klein, Counselor, 916-885-2401, FAX: 916-885-9371
Type: public choice
10 teachers, 206 students, ages 14–19, 9–12th grade
Affiliation: WASC
Governance by teachers; principal
Teacher qualifications: CA credential
Community-based; Trees for Mother Earth project on Navajo
    Reservatio; interns accepted.

Village Faire for Educators
10594 Combie Rd #106515, Auburn, CA 95603
Lorna Wood
Type: Montessori

Deterding Elementary School
6000 Stanley, Carmichael, CA 95608
Penny Scribner, 916-575-2338
Type: charter
K–6th grade
Affiliation: CA BE

Village Montessori Schools
5033 Fair Oaks Blvd, Carmichael, CA 95608-6039
Karen Arnold

Valley Oak Montessori Children's House
7545 Tad Lane, Citrus Heights, CA 95610

Countryside Montessori
7416 Northlea Way, Citrus Heights, CA 95610-6525

Isabel S. Naranjo Migrant Child Development Center
180 Sequoia Ave, Courtland, CA 95615
Type: Montessori

Davis Montessori School (1989)
2907 Portage Bay W, Davis, CA 95616
Karen Fejta, Owner, 916-753-2030, FAX: 916-756-1210
Tuition: $3,250/3,500/yr
5 teachers, 2 assistants, 80 students, ages 3–12
Affiliation: AMS
Governance by administrator
Spanish and computer enrichment for ages 4+; music
    weekly; parent participation welcome; childcare; suburban
    location; interns accepted.

Davis Waldorf School (1986)
3100 Sycamore Ln, Davis, CA 95616
Kathy Zablan, Adm, 916-753-1651
Non-profit; tuition: $4,675/yr, scholarships
10 teachers, 95 students, ages 4.75–13, K–7th grade
Affiliation: AWSNA
Teacher qualifications: completion of R. Steiner's teacher
    training courses
Rigorous academics; language arts; history; Spanish; German;
    handwork; woodwork; music; gardening in biodynamic
    farm; rural location.

Independent Study Program (1990)
526 B St, Davis, CA 95616
Katie Goetzinger, Prin, 916-757-5333
Type: public choice
6 teachers, 120 students, mainly at-risk, ages 5–18, K–12th
    grade
Governance by teachers, principal, board
Teacher qualifications: CA certification
Includes homeschooling program.

LaRue Park Children's House
50 Atrium Way, Davis, CA 95616
Karen Fejta
Type: Montessori

Montessori Country Day
1811 Renoir Ave, Davis, CA 95616-0508

PLENTY (1974)
PO Box 2306, Davis, CA 95617
Charles Haren, Program Dir, 916-753-0731, FAX: 916-762-0731
Type: higher education, non-profit
Student ages 20+
Affiliation: York University
Governance by board of directors and staff
Teacher qualifications: Successful community development
    facilitators
Community education, development; overriding concern for
    indigenous people, environment; students participate in
    disaster relief, alternative energy, micro-economic devel-
    opment, reforestation, health care, agriculture; no letter
    grades; interns accepted.

Redbud Montessori
PO Box 1562, Davis, CA 95617-1562

Elk Grove Montessori School
8842 Williamson Dr, Elk Grove, CA 95624
Norman Lorenz

Little London Montessori
9132 Elk Grove Blvd, Elk Grove, CA 95624

Transitions at Elk Grove High School (1992)
9800 Elk Grove-Florin Rd, Elk Grove, CA 95624
Patty Jungkeit, Tch-In-Charge, 916-686-7741
Type: public at-risk
4 teachers, 60 students, ages 14–16, 9–10th grade
Governance by teachers, principal, board
Teacher qualifications: CA credential
Weekly teacher conference; bi-weekly parent contact; coun-
    seling support groups; community service project; interns
    accepted.

Esparto Child Development Center
705 Omega St, Esparto, CA 95627
Type: Montessori

Esparto Homeschoolers
PO Box 305, Esparto, CA 95627
916-787-3613

Madison High (1980)
Box 69, Esparto, CA 95627
Barbara Evans, Prin, 916-787-3907
Type: public choice
3 teachers, 35–40 students, ages 15–19, 9–12th grade
Governance by teachers, principal

Rudolf Steiner College
9200 Fair Oaks Blvd, Fair Oaks, CA 95628
Gayle Davis
Type: Waldorf

Sacramento Valley School
9341 Fair Oaks Blvd; PO Box 1123, Fair Oaks, CA 95628
Kaye Lynn Peterson, Admissions Clerk, 916-962-3681
Type: independent, non-profit; tuition: $2,700/yr
3 teachers, 14 students, ages 5–19, K–12th grade
Governance by democratic school meeting
Teacher qualifications: first volunteer, then be elected by
    school meeting
Sudbury Valley School model; self-directed, free interaction
    in safe community environment; exchanges; apprentice-
    ships; non-compulsory class attendance; multi-aged
    classes; extensive field trips; no letter grades; suburban
    location.

Sacramento Waldorf School (1959)
3750 Bannister Rd, Fair Oaks, CA 95628
Margaret Preston, Adm, 916-961-3900, FAX: -3970
Non-profit
370 students, ages 5–19, K–12th grade
Affiliation: AWSNA
No letter grades in lower school; extensive field trips; subur-
    ban location.

Association of Waldorf Schools
(See Resource Section)

Village Montessori Schools
4305 Bannister Rd, Fair Oaks, CA 95628-6918

Folsom Middle School
500 Blue Ravine Rd, Folsom, CA 95630
Robert Mange, 916-983-4466
Type: charter
Junior high
Affiliation: CA BE
Year-round, multi-track based on State Frameworks; commu-
    nity service.

Folsom Montessori School
502 Riley St, Folsom, CA 95630-3029
Lise Witthaus

Steward Ship
(See Resource Section)

Mountain Home Alternative
Box 395, Oakhurst, CA 95644

Carlin C. Coppin Elementary School
150 E 12th St, Lincoln, CA 95648
Scott Leaman, 916-645-6390
Type: charter
580 students, K–6th grade
Affiliation: CA BE
K–6 conversion with management by the existing system;
    School Site Council with parental involvement.

Creekside Oaks Charter Elementary School
2030 First St, Lincoln, CA 95648
Jeannine Wheeler, 916-645-6380
Type: charter
K–6th grade
Conversion.

Horizon Instructional Systems
870 J St, Lincoln, CA 95648
Randy Gashler, 916-645-6399
Type: charter
K–adult
Affiliation: CA BE
Governance by board of 4 parents, 2 teachers, one adult ed
    faculty member, and one community member.
Home study by parent/school contract.

Lincoln High North (1991)
1081 7th St, Lincoln, CA 95648
Dale Pence, Prin, 916-645-6360
Type: public at-risk
2 teachers, 25 students, ages 16–18, 10–12th grade
Governance by board
Teacher qualifications: CA credential
School within school; rural location.

Lincoln High School
1081 7th St, Lincoln, CA 95648
Dale Pence, 916-645-6360
Type: charter
700 students
Conversion.

Phoenix High School (1978)
870 J St, Lincoln, CA 95648
Bob Noyes, Prin, 916-645-6395, FAX: 916-645-6356
Type: public at-risk; scholarships
3 teachers, 60 students, ages 16–18, 10–12th grade
Governance by principal
Teacher qualifications: credential
Competency-based; variable credit; extensive field trips;
    multi-aged classe; interns accepted.

Sunrise Montessori School
8449 Sunrise Blvd, Roseville, CA 95661-5349

Cedar Springs Waldorf School (1989)
6029 Gold Meadows Rd, Placerville, CA 95667
Lauren Cushman, Administrator, 916-642-9903
Non-profit; tuition: $3,100-3,600/yr, scholarships
19 teachers, 80 students, ages 4-11, K-4th grade
Affiliation: AWSNA
Governance by faculty and board consensus
Teacher qualifications: BA/BS+ 2 yrs Waldorf training
Working toward becoming a working farm school; hands-on, minds-on approach; Spanish; Japanese; multi-aged classes; rural location; interns accepted.

Charter Community School and Extended Day Program
6767 Green Valley Rd, Placerville, CA 95667
Marta Reyes, 916-621-2543
Type: charter
K-12th grade
Affiliation: CA BE
Conversion; individualized.

Louisiana Schnell Elementary School
2871 Schnell School Rd, Placerville, CA 95667
Cathryn Morgan, 916-622-6244
Type: charter
500 students, 32% AFDC, K-5th grade
Affiliation: CA BE

Montessori of Placerville (1974)
100 Placerville Dr/PO Box 87, Placerville, CA 95667
Nancy A. Weddle, Owner/Dir, 916-626-5330
Tuition: $170-225/mo
3 teachers, 1 assistant, 40 students, ages 3-6
Affiliations: CH ADD, NAEYC
Governance by administrator
Peace education; movement area; rural location; interns accepted.

Rite of Passage School
6767 Green Valley Rd, Placerville, CA 95667
Wally Newberry, 916-622-7130
Type: charter
6-12th grade
Affiliation: CA BE

Bluestocking Press
(See Resource Section)

American Montessori Academy
1050 Douglas Blvd, Roseville, CA 95678-2714

Sheridan Elementary School
PO Box 268, Sheridan, CA 95681
Beth Anderson, 916-633-2599
Type: charter
100 students, K-5th grade
Affiliation: CA BE
K-5 conversion; serving as a placeholder for an amended charter.

Cameron Park Montessori School (1974)
4645 Buckeye Rd, Shingle Springs, CA 95682
Deanna Gardner, Owner/Dir, 916-677-1776
Tuition: $175/250/mo
5 teachers, 6 assistants, 102 students, ages 3-9
Affiliations: NCME, NBA
Governance by administrator
Teacher qualifications: Montessori training
Montessori materials; childcare; rural location; interns accepted.

ACE at Markham (1991)
101 Markham Ave, Vacaville, CA 95688
Ricki Gaudie, 707-453-6230
Type: public choice
4 teachers, 120 students, ages 5-12, K-6th grade

Governance by parent cooperative
Parent participation required; lifelong research skills; co-op learning; no letter grades; multi-aged classes; suburban location; interns accepted.

Country High School
343 Brown St, Vacaville, CA 95688
Muzetta M. Thrower, Prin, 707-453-6215
Type: public at-risk
9 teachers, 185 students, mainly at-risk, ages 15-19, 9-12th grade
Governance by democratic school meeting
Teacher qualifications: state credential
Teen mothers program with nursery; catering through Foods/Economics classes; computer lab; multi-media art classes; multi-aged classes; urban location; interns accepted.

Montessori Children's School
201 Beard St, Vacaville, CA 95688
Debbie Challburg

West Sacramento School for Independent Study
1712 Evergreen St, W Sacramento, CA 95691

Wheatland High School
1010 Wheatland Rd, Wheatland, CA 95692
Michael Edwards, 916-633-3100
Type: charter
Affiliation: CA BE

SPICE Homeschool Support Group
PO Box 282, Wilton, CA 95693
Bonnie Sellstrom or Loni Rossbach, 916-687-7053
Gatherings; no formal rules or elected leaders.

Winters Child Development Center
100 Myrtle Ave, Winters, CA 95694
Type: Montessori

Independent Learning Center (1988)
1016 1st St, Woodland, CA 95695
Sandi Redenbach, Coord, 916-666-0264, FAX: 916-756-5537
Type: public at-risk; scholarships
2 teachers, 50 students, ages 14-18, 9-12th grade
Affiliation: Woodland Joint Unified
Governance by coordinator/teacher
Self-esteem building; responsibility training; community service; career counseling; student contracts; law-related education; independent stud; interns accepted.

Yolo Parent Child Center
1285 Lemen Ave, Woodland, CA 95695-3311
Type: Montessori

Woodland Montessori Children's House
1738 Cottonwood St, Woodland, CA 95695-5137
Pamela Barrow-Lynn

Contract Independent Study
Box 14429, S Lake Tahoe, CA 95702
Type: public choice

Live Oak Waldorf School
410 Crother Rd; PO Box 57, Applegate, CA 95703
Ellyn Hilliard, Coord, 916-878-8720
Non-profit; tuition: $3,800/yr, scholarships
12 teachers, 190 students, ages 4-13, K-8th grade
Affiliation: AWSNA
Governance by board, faculty and student representatives
Teacher qualifications: prefer Waldorf training
1st Waldorf in US with pledge contribution funding; no one denied due to financial limitations; rural location; interns accepted.

Auburn Discovery Montessori School
PO Box 5019, Auburn, CA 95713
Mariann Lokvig, Owner, 916-823-9577

Tuition: $238/364/mo
7 teachers, 4 assistants; student ages 3-12
Affiliation: NCME
Governance by administrator
Childcare; interns accepted.

Little London Montessori School
9124 Bruceville Rd, Elk Grove, CA 95757
Savi Godamunne

Educational Futures Project
(See Resource Section)

Mankato Wilson Campus School Remembered: Video
(See Resource Section)

Visual and Performing Arts Centre (1984)
2315 34th St, Sacramento, CA 95817
Connie Mockenhaupt, Coord, 916-454-6238, FAX: -6270
Type: public choice
14 teachers, 500 students, ages 14-18, 9-12th grade
Governance by principal, coordinator assists
Teacher qualifications: Specialized training, experience
Extensive field trip; interns accepted.

C. K. McClatchy High School
3066 Freeport Blvd, Sacramento, CA 95818
William Dionisio, 916-553-4400
Type: magnet
9-12th grade
Humanities.

Discovery Montessori School (1973)
5613 G St, Sacramento, CA 95819
Shirley Skadar-Smith, MEd, Exec Dir, 916-739-1462
Non-profit; tuition: $230-420/mo
2 teachers, 4 assistants, 32 students, mainly international,
    ages 3-6
Affiliations: AMS, NCME, NAEYC; accreditation:
Governance by administrator and board of trustees
Spanish and culture part of curriculum; childcare; urban loca-
    tion; interns accepted.

Camellia Waldorf School (1989)
5701 Freeport Blvd, Sacramento, CA 95822
Meredith Johnson, Business Mgr, 916-427-5022
Non-profit; tuition: $3,200-4,700/yr, scholarships
5 teachers, 42 students, ages 4-9, K-3rd grade
Affiliation: AWSNA
Governance by faculty and board
Urban location; interns accepted.

Edward Kemble Elementary
7495 29th St, Sacramento, CA 95822
Rovida Mott, 916-399-5025
Type: magnet
K-6th grade
GATE: gifted and talented education.

South Land Park Montessori School, Inc (1973)
6400 Freeport Blvd, Sacramento, CA 95822-5904
Steve Hempel, Office Mgr, 916-391-5380, FAX: 916-391-2678
Tuition: $2,400-3,950/yr
9 teachers, 9 assistants, 160 students, ages 3-15
Affiliation: AMS
Governance by administrator
Childcare; suburban location; interns accepted.

Bowling Green Elementary School
4211 Turnbridge Dr, Sacramento, CA 95823
Dennis Mah, 916-399-5426
Type: charter
814 students, pre K-6th grade
Affiliation: CA BE
'93- conversion.

Las Flores High School (1987)
5900 Bamford Dr, Sacramento, CA 95823

Barbara Hyatt, 916-422-5604
Type: public choice
10 students

Rio Cazadero High School
7825 Grandstaff Dr, Sacramento, CA 95823
Ron Rule, Prin, 916-422-3058
Type: public at-risk
10 teachers, 252 students, ages 14-19, 9-12th grade
Governance by teachers and principal
Teacher qualifications: CA certification
Classes (3 hrs/day) change quarterly; collegiate schedule;
    suburban location; interns accepted.

William Daylor
6131 Orange Ave, Sacramento, CA 95823
James Ross, Prin, 916-427-5428
Type: public at-risk
Governance by teachers, principal
Interns accepted.

Jonas Salk Alternative Middle School
2950 Hurley Way, Sacramento, CA 95825

Florin Elementary
7300 Kara Dr, Sacramento, CA 95828
M'Lissa Ann Gardner, 916-383-0530
Type: at-risk charter
Pre K-2nd grade
Affiliation: CA BE

Insights (1992)
7956 Cottonwood Ln, Sacramento, CA 95828
Priscilla Marsh, 916-689-8600
Type: public at-risk
5 teachers, 60 students, ages 14-16, 9-10th grade
Governance by teachers and principal
No F's given if no credit earned; urban location.

Montessori Country Day at Riverlake (1991)
7575 Rush River Dr, Sacramento, CA 95831
Pam Barrow-Lynn, Owner/Adm, 916-427-1900
Tuition: $31/day-335/mo
4 teachers, 20 assistants, 110 students, mainly International,
    ages Infant-6
Accreditation: AMS
Governance by administrator
Modern classrooms and materials; childcare; interns
    accepted.

John Still Creative Center
2250 John Still Dr, Sacramento, CA 95832
Rachel Wallin, 916-399-5375
Type: magnet
K-8th grade

Natomas Charter School (1994)
3700 Del Paso Rd, Sacramento, CA 95834
Charlie Leo, 916-535-7630
Type: charter
814 students, 7-9th grade
Affiliation: CA BE
Work-study.

Countryside Montessori School
5590 Madison Ave, Sacramento, CA 95841-3114

Mariposa Waldorf School (1980)
12833 Colfax Hwy; PO Box 1210, Cedar Ridge, CA 95924
Patricia Montijo, Adm, 916-272-8411
Non-profit; tuition: $2,895-3,095/yr, scholarships
14 teachers, 105 students, ages 4-11, K-5th grade
Affiliation: AWSNA
Governance by faculty and board
2-5 week alternating subject blocks; school festivals; rural
    location.

Whiz Kidz (1992)
277 East Ave, Chico, CA 95926
Norman Rose, PhD, 916-898-8446
Type: home-based; cost: $55/mo
2 teachers, 55 students, ages 4-14
CAI; games; art; music; publishing

Montessori Children's Center
3105 Esplanade, Chico, CA 95926-0202
Paula Kenyon

Chico Montessori Children's House
814 Glenn St, Chico, CA 95928-4001

Colusa Unified
817 Colus Ave, Colusa, CA 95932
Type: public choice

Grass Valley Charter School (1990)
10840 Gilmore Way, Grass Valley, CA 95945
Susan Byerrum, Coord, 916-273-8723
Type: public choice
5 teachers, 110 students, ages 5-13, K-8th grade
Governance by teachers, principal
Teacher qualifications: CA credential
Homeschool support; textbooks; supplies; enrichment
    classes; field trips; parent education workshops; no letter
    grades; non-compulsory class attendance; multi-aged
    classes; extensive field trips.

Sierra Mountain High (1980)
140 Park Ave, Grass Valley, CA 95945-7202
Earle Conway, Prin, 916-272-2635
Type: public choice, at-risk
12 teachers, 220 students, mainly at-risk, ages 14-18, 9-12th
    grade
Governance by prinipal, staff, with input by students.
Teacher qualifications: CA credential
Alternative calendar; has 9th and 10th grade in daytime, inde-
    pendent study school for adolescents and adults in
    evening; emphasis on four A's: acceptance, appreciation,
    affection, and attention; multi-aged classes, extensive field
    trips; rural location; interns accepted.

Ready Springs Union Elementary
10862 Spenceville Rd, Penn Valley, CA 95946

Ready Springs Union Elementary School
10872 Spenceville Rd, Penn Valley, CA 95946
Greg Peterson, Dir, 916-432-1141
Type: charter
K-8th grade
Affiliation: CA BE
Home study and tutorial; integrated curriculum; parental ed.

Indian Valley High School (1980)
Box 743, Greenville, CA 95947
Loana Gakle, Prin, 916-284-6099
Type: public at-risk
1 teacher, 15 students, ages 15-19, 10-12th grade
Rural location.

Sierra Mountain High School (1988)
12338 McCourtney Rd, Grass Valley, CA 95949
Russ Jones, 916-273-4431
Type: public choice
100 students

Live Oak Center (1988)
2207 Pennington Rd, Live Oak, CA 95953
Joy Allingham, Prin, 707-695-1835
Non-profit
4 teachers, 136 students, ages 5+, K-12th grade
Governance by board
Opportunity education; Valley Oak Continuation HS; indepen-
    dent study; adult education; Even Start Family Literacy;
    gifted-talented education

Ananda School
14616 Tyler Foote Rd, Nevada City, CA 95959
Bruce Malinor or Susan Dermand, 916-292-3775
Type: independent; tuition: $195/mo.
60 students, ages 14+
Affiliations: Foundation for Life, Sharing Nature Assn
Education for Life Workshops; teaching math; children's
    literature.

Global Friends School Program
13075 Woolman Lane, Nevada City, CA 95959
Eric Joy, 916-477-1277
Type: Quaker, non-profit; tuition: flexible
Student ages 14-19, 9-12th grade
Affiliation: Friends Council on Education
Governance by friends meeting
Academics within context of real life issues, experiences;
    learning with heart and hands as well as head; travel,
    service within diverse cultural settings; multi-aged classes;
    extensive field trips; rural location; interns accepted.

John Woolman School (1963)
13075 Woolman Ln, Nevada City, CA 95959
916-273-3183, FAX: 916-273-9028
Type: Quaker, boarding; tuition: $14,900/yr, scholarships
35 students, ages 14-17, 9-12th grade
Affiliation: NAIS
Governance by teachers, principal, board
Teacher qualifications: credentials, experience
Emphasizes truthfulness, simplicity, non-violence, respect,
    listening to the Spirit Within; nurtures inquiry, creativity,
    physical work, service; multi-aged classes; rural location.

Nevada City Charter School
215 Washington St, Nevada City, CA 95959
John A. Halverson, 916-265-1820
Type: charter
K-8th grade
Affiliation: CA BE

Nevada City Elementary
700 Hoover Lane, Nevada City, CA 95959

Nevada City Home Study Charter School
215 Washington St, Nevada City, CA 95959
Dennis C. Dobbs, 916-256-6444
Type: charter
K-8th grade
Affiliation: CA BE

Magic Meadow School
PO Box 29, N San Juan, CA 95960
Type: home-based

Pathfinder (1984)
PO Box 445, N San Juan, CA 95960
Keith Alpaugh, Dir, 916-292-3623, FAX: 916-292-3558
Type: independent, non-profit; tuition: $280/mo,
    scholarships
2 teachers, 12 students, ages 8-12
Governance by board
Teacher qualifications: working knowledge of Natural
    Rhythms developmental theory
Student-directed; family involvement; wholistic; environmen-
    tal; no letter grades; multi-aged classes; non-compulsory
    class attendance; extensive field trips; rural location;
    interns accepted.

Twin Ridges Alternative Charter School
PO Box 529, N. San Juan, CA 95960
Paul Alderere, 916-292-4221
Type: charter
K-8th grade
Affiliation: CA BE
Homeschool plan by student, parent, and resource teacher.

Twin Ridges Elementary
Box 529, N San Juan, CA 95960
Chris Dach, 916-265-9051
Type: home-based public choice

Lewis Carroll Montessori
9391 Rices Texas Hill Rd, Oregon House, CA 95962
Janet Carter

Prospect Alternative Center for Education (1968)
2060 2nd St, Oroville, CA 95965
Dorence Young, Tch, 916-538-2330
Type: public at-risk
10 teachers, 240 students, mainly at-risk, ages 14–18, 9–12th
  grade
Governance by teachers, principal, board
Teacher qualifications: credential
Continuation; independent study; teen parenting; opportunity school; work-study; no letter grades; multi-aged
  classes; childcar; interns accepted.

Home Tech (1995)
5655 Recreation Dr, Paradise, CA 95969
Laura Dearden, 916-872-6400
Type: charter
K–6th grade
Affiliation: CA BE

Great Explorations (1993)
2085 E Main St, Quincy, CA 95971
Gloria Potvin, 916-283-1553
Type: independent; tuition: $100/mo, scholarships
1 teacher, 12–25 students, ages 5+, K+
Governance by parent cooperative
Teacher qualifications: MA, language literacy, 12 years
  experience
Based on GATE principals: holistic, experiential; educational
  enrichment program; no letter grades; multi-aged classes;
  rural location; interns accepted.

Albert Powell Continuation High School
1875 Clark Ave, Yuba City, CA 95991
Mike Hogan, Counselor, 916-741-5210
Type: public at-risk
10 teachers, 240 students, mainly at-risk, ages 16–19,
  10–12th grade
Governance by teachers and principal
Individualized; multi-aged classes.

Churn Creek High School (1993)
3411 Churn Creek Rd, Redding, CA 96002
Allen Eggleston, Prin, 223-5177
Type: public at-risk
3 teachers, 70 students, ages 16–19, 10–12th grade
Governance by principal
Teacher qualifications: CA credential
Operates afternoons and evenings.

Shady Oaks Montessori School
1410 Victor Ave, Redding, CA 96003-4819

Mountain View High School (1984)
37579 Mountain View Rd, Burney, CA 96013
Max A. Best, Prin/Dir, 335-3852
Type: public at-risk
4 teachers, 75 students, ages 6–18, K–12th grade
Governance by principal, board
Multi-aged classes

Mt Lakes High School (1992)
PO Box 818, Shasta Lake, CA 96019
Dr Mario Johnson, Prin, 916-275-7000, FAX: -7006
Type: public at-risk
9 teachers, 150 students, ages 16–18+, 10–12th grade
Governance by principal, board
Teacher qualifications: Multiple or single subject CA credential
Pregnant minor/teen parenting program; rural location;
  transportation.

Sandhill Crane School (1989)
PO Box 160, Fall River, CA 96028
916-336-6582
Type: independent, boarding; tuition: $5,000/yr
2 teachers, 3 students, ages 9–15
Affiliations: Kempo International, Ch'uan Tao Assn
Governance by benevolent director
Teacher qualifications: outstanding athlete, min 7 yrs training
  in Chinese martial arts
Does not advocate material gain, ego enhancement; vehicle
  is mind-body training of Chinese martial arts; no letter
  grades; multi-aged classes; extensive field trips; rural location; interns accepted.

Jefferson High School (1992)
720 Rockfellow Dr, Mt Shasta, CA 96067
Richard C Holmes, Prin, 916-926-0425
Type: public at-risk
3 teachers, 50 students, mainly at-risk, ages 15–18, 9–12th
  grade
Governance by principal.
Individualized; self-paced; interns accepted.

Kids Art
(See Resource Section)

Even Start
1135 Lincoln St, Red Bluff, CA 96080
Phil Hopkins, Dir, 916-527-5811
Non-profit
9 teachers, 140 students
Affiliation: Head Start
Governance by teachers and director
Teacher qualifications: C Best Test
GED prep; ESL; no letter grades; childcare; rural location;
  transportation.

Salisbury Continuation High School (1970)
1415 Burkeley St, Red Bluff, CA 96080
Dick Garcia, Prin, 916-529-8766, FAX: 916-529-8840
Type: public at-risk
4 teachers, 80 students, ages 16–18, 10–12th grade
Governance by teachers, principal, board
No letter grades; rural location; transportation; interns
  accepted.

Alta Montessori
PO Box 2527, Kings Beach, CA 96143-2527

Tahoe Montessori House
848 Glorene Ave, South Lake Tahoe, CA 96158
Susan Ward

Santan High School (1971)
1006 Otterbein St, Rowland Heights, CA 96748
Luciario de Sylva, Prin, 818-965-5971
Type: independent choice/at-risk
14 teachers, 300 students, ages 15–18, 9–12th grade
Affiliation: WASC
Governance by principal.
Teacher qualifications: CA credential, dedication to students
  and profession
Competency-based; continuous progress; individualized; CAI;
  counseling/guidance; advanced courses; drop-out recovery; pregnant teens; transportation; suburban location;
  interns accepted.

Vacaville Independent Charter School
751 School St, Vacaville, CA 98688
Judith Cook, 707-453-6140
Type: charter
K–12th grade
Affiliation: CA BE

Colorado

Arvada New Child Montessori School
6454 Simms St, Arvada, CO 80004-2650

Catholic Home Educators
556 Oakland Ct, Aurora, CO 80010
Laura Franceschi, 303-367-9317

Carousel Academy for Children
1440 Elmira St, Aurora, CO 80010-3217
Type: Montessori

East Academy
1275 Frazier St, Aurora, CO 80011
Linda Fenstermacher, 303-340-0630

Homeschoolers of Central Aurora
3049 Wheeling St, Aurora, CO 80011
Michele Fox, 303-360-6653

Independent Network of Creative Homeschoolers
c/o Woodhouse, 724 Victor St, Aurora, CO 80011
303-340-3185, 751-6421

The Discovery School (1995)
18393 E LaSalle Place, Aurora, CO 80013
Bob Hamilton-Pennell, 303-680-2035
Type: charter
144 students, 1-6th grade
Affiliation: Aurora Public Schools
Expanding to K-8th.

Over the Rainbow Child Care
16750 E Iliff Ave, Aurora, CO 80013-1135
Type: Montessori

"I" Team Estate (1968)
4360 S Pitkin, Aurora, CO 80015
John McCluskey, Teacher/Coordinator, 303-690-2594
Type: public at-risk
4 teachers, 65 students, ages 16–21, 11–12th grade
Affiliation: Cherry Creek Schools
Governance by teachers and principal
Teacher qualifications: SE/VE certification
Co-op ed; classes culminate in outings; community climate
    essential; no letter grades; multi-aged classes; extensive
    field trips; suburban location; interns accepted.

Jefferson Academy
9955 Yarrow St, Broomfield, CO 80020
Michael Munice, 303-438-0111
Type: charter
190 students, K-6th grade
Affiliation: Jefferson County R-1
Core Knowledge curriculum.

A Child's Adventure Land Montessori House
7205 W 120th Ave, Broomfield, CO 80020-2358

Christian Single Home Educators' Network
5560 E 60th Ave #256, Commerce City, CO 80022
Marci Groblebe, 303-288-9581

Lester Arnold High School (1972)
6500 72nd Ave, Commerce City, CO 80022
Larry Nichols, 303-289-2983, FAX: 303-289-7167
Type: public choice
18 teachers, 410 students, mainly at-risk, ages 16–21, 9–12th
    grade
Governance by principal
Teacher qualifications: CO certification
Individualized; outcome-based; comprehensive integrated
    approach; no letter grades; interns accepted.

Louisville Montessori School
461 Tyler Ave, Louisville, CO 80027-2700
Judith Cole

Alternative Center for Education
3455 W 72nd Ave, Westminster, CO 80030
Carole Bieshaar, Asst Prin, 303-428-2575, FAX: -2142 (CEP)
Type: public at-risk
11 teachers; students mainly at-risk, ages 14–21, 9–12th
    grade
Governance by board and principal
Teacher qualifications: state certification
Enrichment days, flexible scheduling, 18-day grading
    periods/attendance contracts; outcome-based; experi-
    ence-based; small classes; multi-aged classes; extensive
    field trips; suburban location; transportation; interns
    accepted.

Colorado Home Educator's Association
3371 W 94th Ave, Westminster, CO 80030
Clark Echols

Foothills Academy
4725 Miller St, Wheatridge, CO 80033
Mary Faddick, 303-431-0920
Type: independent; tuition: $4,350, scholarships
131 students, ages K-8
Academic and social achievements are celebrated; basic skills,
    art, music, foreign language, outdoor ed program;
    monthly "mini-society" marketplace; visiting artists; exten-
    sive field trips.

Academy Charter School
809 N Park St, Castle Rock, CO 80104
Kathy Consigli, 303-660-4881
350 students, K-7th grade
Governance by elected parents.
Core knowledge curriculum.

Christian Homes Educating for Excellent Results
Castle Rock, CO 80104
303-688-2286

Colorado's Finest Alternative High School (1980)
2323 W Baker Ave, Englewood, CO 80110
Tom Synnott, Prin, 303-934-5786
Type: public choice
774 students

Montessori at Denver Tech Center (1990)
5460 DTC Pkwy, Englewood, CO 80111
Patrice K. Plainbeck, 290-8843
Tuition: $380–470/mo
3 teachers, 4 assistants, 56 students, ages 3–12
Accreditations: AMS, CO DSS
2 acres; library; computer lab; cooking; Orff music; childcare;
    suburban location; transportation; interns accepted.

Options-Littleton Public Schools (1992)
6558 S Acoma St, Littleton, CO 80120
303-387-3580, FAX: 303-347-3590
Type: public at-risk
Governance by teachers and principal
Small classes; community; wilderness experiences; extensive
    field trips; suburban location; interns accepted.

Hillcroft Academy, Ltd
7018 S Prince St, Littleton, CO 80120-3536
Type: Montessori

Montessori Children's House Of Littleton
71 E Panama Dr, Littleton, CO 80121-2333
Marjorie Ewing

Montessori Children's Academy
2819 W Belleview, Littleton, CO 80123
Linda Hurja and Kathy Porter

Sci-Tech Academy
6500 W Coal Mine Rd, Suite 101, Littleton, CO 80123
John and Barbara Ziegler, 303-972-7433
Type: charter
100 students, 6–11th grade
Affiliation: Jefferson County R-1
College prep; expanding to K–12 with 500 students.

Columbine Montessori Preschool
6653 W Chatfield Ave, Littleton, CO 80123-5834

Montessori School at Lone Tree (1985)
9396 Ermindale Dr, Littleton, CO 80124
Jean Pilon, Adm, 303-799-8540
Tuition: $274–528/mo
5 teachers, 11 assistants, 120 students, ages 3–6
Affiliation: AMS
Governance by administrator
Summer program with full science and nature study; extensive field trips; suburban location; interns accepted.

Montessori School of Douglas County
9396 Erminedale Dr, Littleton, CO 80124-8939
Jean Pilon

Core Knowledge Charter School
10423 Parker Rd, Parker, CO 80134
Laurel Iakovakis, 303-840-7070
Type: charter
165 students
Affiliation: Douglas County SD
Core Knowledge curriculum including second language; resources shared with Academy Center.

Front Range Eclectic Educators
5732 Stetson Ct, Parker, CO 80134
Pat Mason, 303-841-9494
Type: home-based

Parker Montessori Educational Institute
10750 E Victorian Dr, Parker, CO 80134
Jami Boarman, Prin, 303-841-4325, FAX: 303-841-5878
Non-profit; tuition: $2,100-5,700/yr
15 teachers, 12 assistants, 144 students, ages infant–12
Affiliations: AMS, ASCD, AMI, NAMTA, NAEYC
Governance by board
Childcare; suburban location; interns accepted.

Renaissance School (1995)
15922 Parkside Dr, Parker, CO 80134
Shirley Jenkins, 303-841-4585
Type: charter
228 students, ES
Individualized; multi-aged, multi-lingual classes.

Colorado Home Schooling Network
7490 W Apache, Sedalia, CO 80135
303-688-4136

Colorado Home Educators Association
1616 17th St Suite 372, Denver, CO 80202
303-441-9938

Montessori at Greenwood
5670 Greenwood Plaza Blvd, Englewood, CO 80202

Colorado Options
201 E Colfax Ave, Denver, CO 80203
Type: Montessori

SAFE School (1994)
1925 Blake St, Denver, CO 80203
Mike Clem, 303-295-3164
Type: charter

5 teachers, 90 students, ages 11–21, 6–12th grade
Governance by faculty & student reps, board
Teacher qualifications: CO cert
Formerly HS Redirection; no letter grades; non-compulsary class attendance; multi-aged classes; extensive field trips; transportation.

Center for International Studies (1985)
West High School, 951 Elati St, Denver, CO 80204
Dr Daniel P Lutz, Prog Mgr, 303-620-5364, FAX: 303-620-5412
Type: public choice
11 teachers, 200 students, ages 14–18, 9–12th grade
Governance by teachers and principal
Teacher qualifications: international experience, international studies academic background
Project and experiential learning; focus on international affairs, cross cultural communication skills; interdisciplinary projects; languages; volunteer service; high academic standards; urban location; interns accepted.

Emily Griffith Opportunity School (1985)
1250 Welton St, Denver, CO 80204
Mary Ann Parthum, Prin, 303-572-8218
1576 students, mainly at-risk, ages 17–21
Open-entry/exit; individualized; competency-based; self-paced; vocational skills.

Mitchell Elementary
1350 E 33rd Ave, Denver, CO 80204
Dr Martha Urioste, 303-296-8412
Type: magnet
Student ages 3+,–6th grade
Montessori.

Second Chance Program (1986)
1250 Welton St, Denver, CO 80204
George F. Adian, PhD, Asst Prin, 303-575-4738, FAX: 303-575-4840
Type: public choice
16 teachers, 307 students, ages 17–21, HS
Affiliation: Denver Public Schools
Governance by teachers, principal, board
Teacher qualifications: state certification
Open-entry/exit; outcome-based; GED; vocational; multi-aged classes; urban location.

Barrett Elementary
2900 Richard Allen Ct, Denver, CO 80205
Daphne Hunter, 303-388-5841
Type: magnet
1–2nd grade
Highly gifted.

British Primary School
410 23rd St, Denver, CO 80205
Paul Biwer, Prin, 303-295-7869

Clayton Charter School
3605 Martin Luther King Blvd, Denver, CO 80205
Meera Mani, 303-331-0650
Type: at-risk charter
88 students, 6–8th grade
Affiliation: Denver Public Schools
Expanding to 6–12; High/Scope curriculum incorporates family social services.

Denver School of the Arts (1991)
3240 Humboldt, Denver, CO 80205
303-764-6817, FAX: 303-294-9049
Type: public choice
7 teachers, 410 students, ages 11–18, 6–12th grade
Affiliation: Network Performing Arts
Governance by teachers, principal, democratic school meeting
Teacher qualifications: degree in subject area, professional experience
Two art forms per year: writing, dance, vocal music, instru-

mental music, theater, technical theater/design, visual arts; process emphasized over performance; special ed; multi-aged classes; extensive field trips; urban location; transportation; interns accepted.

Harrington Elementary
3230 E 38th Ave, Denver, CO 80205
Sally Edwards, 303-333-4293
Type: magnet
K-5th grade
Highly gifted.

Mitchell Montessori Elementary (1986)
1350 E 33rd Ave, Denver, CO 80205
Dr Martha Urioste, 303-296-8912, FAX: 303-292-5349
Type: Public choice Montessori
25 teachers, 560 students, ages 3-15
Affiliations: AMS, AMI
Governance by committee
Teacher qualifications: Montessori training
Strong parent participation; supportive community partnership; no letter grades; multi-aged classes; urban location; transportation; interns accepted.

Garfield Montessori School
1557 Garfield St, Denver, CO 80206-1912

Christian Home Educators of Colorado
1015 S Gaylord #226, Denver, CO 80209
303-777-1022

Montessori School of Washington Park
320 S Sherman St, Denver, CO 80209
Sharon Wolf

Denver Waldorf School
735 E Florida, Denver, CO 80210
Ina Jaehnig

St Anne's Episcopal School
2701 South York St, Denver, CO 80210-6032
John Comfort
Type: Montessori

Fred N. Thomas Career Education Center (1976)
2650 Eliot St, Denver, CO 80211
Bill Smith, Prin, 303-964-3000, FAX: 303-964-3004
Type: public choice
66 teachers, 800-1,000 students, ages 14-18, 9-12th grade
Affiliation: Denver PS
Governance by collaborative decision making committee
Teacher qualifications: certified, vocationally licensed
30 career prep programs; career interest surveys, assessments; interns accepted.

The Montessori Connection
2413 W 32nd Ave, Denver, CO 80211-3321

Jefferson County Open School
7655 W 10th Ave, Lakewood, CO 80215
Prin, 303-233-4878
Type: public choice
620 students, pre K-12th grade
Governance by democratic school meeting
Self-directed learning; team teaching; active parental involvement; evaluations and continuous progress; "Walkabout Program," a series of passages, completed for graduation; multi-aged classes; no letter grades; extensive field trips; urban & suburban location.

McLain High School Alternative Cooperative Education (1970)
2001 Hoyt St, Lakewood, CO 80215
Patricia Mishler, Head, 303-238-8171, FAX: 303-233-6875
Type: public at-risk; scholarships
9 teachers, 190 students, ages 16-20, 9-12th grade
Affiliation: Jefferson County Schools
Yearly river raft trip; no letter grades; multi-aged classe; interns accepted.

Pinyon Court School
(See Resource Section)

Garden Place Academy
4425 Lincoln St, Denver, CO 80216
Stan Reynolds, Prin, 303-295-7785
International Baccalaureate.

Wyman Elementary
1690 Williams St, Denver, CO 80218
Wanda Lenox, 303-320-1632
Type: magnet
1-5th grade
Highly gifted.

Gust Elementary
3440 W Yale Ave, Denver, CO 80219
Joy Wilson, 303-935-4613
Type: magnet
1-5th grade
Highly gifted.

Southwest Montessori Preschool
3805 W Walsh Pl, Denver, CO 80219-3241

Eclipse Program at Denver Children's Home
1501 Albion St, Denver, CO 80220
David Dunn or Linda Lindsay, 303-399-4890
Type: independent, boarding, non-profit
15 teachers, 60 students, mainly at-risk, ages 11-18, 7-12th grade
Governance by teachers and principal
Integrated; thematic; internships; community service, placement; experiential; multi-aged classes; extensive field trips; urban location; interns accepted.

Eclipse/Independent Redirection
1501 Albion, Denver, CO 80220
Linda Lindsay, Dir, 303-399-4890, FAX: 303-399-9846
Type: public at-risk, boarding
24 teachers, 135 students
Governance by teachers, principal, students. parents
Emotional support; community-based and therapeutic day programs; multi-cultural; extensive field trips; multi-aged classes; interns accepted.

Gove Montessori Middle School (1993)
4050 E 14th Ave, Denver, CO 80220
Pauline McBeth, Prin, 303-355-1676
Type: public choice
2 teachers, 35 students, ages 11-13, 7th grade
Governance by collaborative decision making committee
Teacher qualifications: Montessori training
No letter grades; multi-aged classes; extensive field trips; urban location; transportation; interns accepted.

Montessori Children's House of Denver (1991)
1467 Birch St, Denver, CO 80220
Gina Abegg, Dir, 303-322-8324
Tuition: $250/385/mo
2 teachers, 10 assistants, 47 students, ages 3-6
Affiliation: AMS
Governance by teachers and administrators
Organic gardening; inner-city nature study; multi-cultural; cultural studies; ecology and peace education; childcare; urban location; interns accepted.

Thurgood Marshall Charter Middle School (1995)
1640 Kearney St, Denver, CO 80220
Cordia Booth, 303-399-9131
Type: charter
220 students, 6-8th grade
Focus on academic rigor, bilingual competence and student self-discipline.

Cottage "I" Team (1968)
6444 E Floyd Ave, Denver, CO 80222
Orvin Breningstall, Team Leader, 303-757-6213

Type: public at-risk
4 teachers, 5 students, ages 16–21, 11–12th grade
Affiliation: Cherry Creek HS
Governance by team of teachers with student input
Teacher qualifications: MA in behavior disorders
Experiential; student need/interest-based; outdoor ed; com-
munity involvement; extensive field trips; no letter grade;
interns accepted.

Ellis Elementary
1651 S Dahlia, Denver, CO 80222
Tony Knight, 303-756-8363
Type: magnet
1–2nd grade
Highly gifted.

Montessori School of Denver
1460 S Holly St, Denver, CO 80222-3510
Sonnie McFarland or Karen Middleton

Denver Youth Academy
1240 W Bayaud, Denver, CO 80223
Anthony Perea, 303-698-2300
Type: at-risk charter
120 students, 6–8th grade
Affiliation: Denver Public Schools
Individualized.

Post Oak School
83 W Archer Pl, Denver, CO 80223-1617
Type: Montessori

**George Washington Computer Magnet High School and
International Baccalaureate Program**
655 S Monaco Pkwy, Denver, CO 80224
Ted Brucker; Suzanne Geimer, 303-394-8705; 399-2214

Changing Schools Newsletter
c/o Colorado Options in Education
(See Resource Section)

Montessori Child Discovery Center
1975 S Garrison St, Lakewood, CO 80227-2204

Montessori Academy of Bear Creek
9300 W Dartmouth Place, Lakewood, CO 80227-4407
Ann Bell

Alternative #1 High School (1980)
1200 E 78th Ave, Denver, CO 80229
Toni Finley, Secretary, 303-287-9400, FAX:-1864
Type: public at-risk
9 teachers, 150 students, ages 16–21, 9–12th grade
Governance by principal
Teacher qualifications: certification
Graduation by demonstration; multi-aged classes; urban loca-
tion; transportation.

North Suburban Homeschoolers
9156 N Clermont, Thornton, CO 80229
Teri Daniel, 303-287-9878

Academy of Charter Schools
4400 E 107th Place, Thornton, CO 80233
John Kircher, 303-252-0692
Type: charter
300 students, K–12th grade
Affiliation: Adams 12 Five Star District
Multiple campuses; Core Knowledge curriculum for K–6.

Expeditionary School
3750 S Magnolia Way, Denver, CO 80237
Barbara Volpe, 303-861-8661

McGlone Elementary Montessori ECE
4500 Crown Blvd, Denver, CO 80239
Dr J Maalis Hagen

Community Involved Charter School
7700 W Woodward Dr, Lakewood, CO 80277
Dr Mary Ellen Sweeney, 303-985-7092

Type: charter
500 students, K–12th grade
Affiliation: Jefferson County R-1
College-prep.

Mapleton Montessori school (1979)
700 Highland Ave, Boulder, CO 80302
Dede Coogan Beardsley, Adm, 303-449-4499
Non-profit; tuition: $1,840-4,000/yr
3 teachers, 4 assistants, 60 students, ages 3–6
Governance by administrator
Childcare; interns accepted.

Naropa Institute (1974)
2130 Arapahoe Ave, Boulder, CO 80302
Marta Shaman, Adms Counselor, 303-444-0202, FAX: -0410
Type: higher education, non-profit; tuition: $8,000/yr
803 students
Governance by board
Accredited; Buddhist contemplative tradition; arts; writing;
literature; contemplative and transpersonal psychology;
environmental studies; religion; gerontology and long-
term mgmt; education; dance; suburban location.

Naropa Institute-Early Education BA (1990)
2130 Arapahoe Ave, Boulder, CO 80302
Marta Shaman, Adms Counselor, 303-444-0202
Type: higher education, non-profit; tuition: $265/cr,
scholarships
6 teachers, 15 students
Governance by board
Joins Buddhist and holistic approaches in movement, medi-
tation, arts, child development, parenting, contemplative
teaching; Waldorf, Montessori, Shambhala; internship at
Alaya Preschool; urban location.

September School
1902 Walnut St, Boulder, CO 80302
Brus Westby, Prin, 303-443-9933
Type: independent, non-profit; tuition: $4,275/yr,
scholarships
19 teachers, 96 students, partly at-risk, ages 14–19, 9–12th
grade
Governance by teachers and principal, board
Teacher qualifications: 75% of teachers certified
Integrates academics with performing and visual arts; wilderness training; group and individual counseling; strong
family-oriented evaluation conferences; multi-aged
classes; extensive field trips; interns accepted.

The New High School (1993)
889 17th St, Boulder, CO 80302
Rona Wilensky, Prin, 303-447-5401, FAX: 303-938-1742
Type: public choice
400 students, ages 14–19
Teacher qualifications: CO certification
Graduation by exhibition; multiple entry points; community
service required; teaching for understanding; integrated
learning; suburban location; interns accepted.

University Hill Elementary
956 16th St, Boulder, CO 80302
Jo Ann Trujillo Hays & Jeannie Jacobson, Leadership Team,
303-442-6735, FAX: 939-9439
Type: public choice
22 teachers, 380 students, mainly multi-ethnic, ages 5–10,
K–5th grade
Governance by teachers and parents with student
involvement
Teacher qualifications: experience-based philosophy; bilingual
Experience-based philosophy (Dewey); integrated curriculum
built on students's interests and strengths; anti-bias;
Family Resource School; bilingual program (half of school);
training and internships for Univ of CO students; no letter
grades; multi-aged classes; extensive field trips; urban
location; interns accepted.

Boulder Valley Alternative Middle School
6096 Baseline Rd, Boulder, CO 80303
303-499-6800

Countryside Montessori
5524 Baseline Rd, Boulder, CO 80303
Nancy Ahlstrand, Dir, 303-494-3100
Non-profit; tuition: $500/mo
4 teachers, 4 assistants, 36 students, partly at-risk, ages 2.5-6
Accreditation: AMS
Governance by administrator
Emphasis on cultural studies; suburban location; interns accepted.

Friends' School (1987)
5465 Pennsylvania, Boulder, CO 80303
Marjorie Larner, Program Dir, 303-666-8886
Type: Quaker, non-profit; tuition: $2,200-5,500/yr, scholarships
12 teachers, 97 students, ages 2-11, pre K-5th grade
Governance by teachers and principal
Whole-person; interest-based; conflict resolution; student-directed, teacher-guided; environmental focus; no letter grades; extensive field trips; interns accepted.

Montessori Education Center of the Rockies (1978)
3440 Longwood Ave, Boulder, CO 80303
Virginia H. Hennes, Dir, 303-494-3002
Type: higher education, non-profit; tuition: $3,000/yr
10 teachers, 20-30 students
Affiliation: AMS
Governance by board of trustees
One-year teacher education program, preschool and toddler level: 8 wks of academics in the summer followed by 9 mos of student teaching; no letter grades; suburban location.

Mountain Shadows Montessori (1976)
4154 N 63rd, Boulder, CO 80303
Marlene Skovsted, Adm, 303-530-5353
Non-profit; tuition: $2,832-4,512/yr
6 teachers, 7 assistants, 135 students, ages 3-12
Affiliations: NAMTA, MTAC; accreditation: AMI
Governance by teachers and administrators
Childcare; rural location; interns accepted.

Paddock Alternative School (1991)
805 Gillaspie Dr, Boulder, CO 80303
Ann Kane, Lead Tch, 303-447-5580
Type: public choice
10 teachers, 128 students, ages 5-12, K-5th grade
Governance by council of teachers and parents
Teacher qualifications: CO certification
Small classes; Spanish; no letter grades; extensive field trips; multi-aged classes; interns accepted.

Association for Experiential Education
(See Resource Section)

Boulder Montessori School
3300 Redstone Rd, Boulder, CO 80303-7139
Karen Olson

In Other Words
(See Resource Section)

Shining Mountain Waldorf School (1982)
987 Locust Ave, Boulder, CO 80304
Nancy Jane, Enrl Coord, 303-444-7697, FAX: 444-7701
Boarding, non-profit; tuition: $3,500-5,850/yr, scholarships
25 teachers, 326 students, ages 4-18, K-12th grade
Affiliation: AWSNA
Governance by teachers, principal, and board
Teacher qualifications: Waldorf training, certification
8 acres; extensive field trips; summer school; rural location; interns accepted.

Washington Bilingual Alternative Elementary
1215 Cedar Ave, Boulder, CO 80304
Tony Vigil, 303-449-6618

Jarrow Montessori School
3900 Orange Ct, Boulder, CO 80304-0753
Marguerite Humphrey

Bitsy Montessori Day Care Center
1937 Upland Ave, Boulder, CO 80304-0934
Christine Adams

Kids Discover Magazine
(See Resource Section)

Montessori School of Lakewood (1978)
5925 W 1st Ave, Lakewood, CO 80401
Janice Norton Kruse, 303-232-7030
Tuition: $1,850-3,200/yr
4 teachers, 7 assistants, 115 students, ages infant-12
Governance by administrator
Childcare; suburban location; interns accepted.

Children's World Learning Center
573 Park Point Dr, Golden, CO 80401-5737
Type: Montessori

Montessori School of Golden Head
714 Cheyenne St, Golden, CO 80401-5834

Summit County Home Schoolers
Dillon, CO 80435
303-468-9412

Mountain Area Home Educators
Evergreen, CO 80439
303-838-6377

Montessori Children's House of Evergreen
PO Box 2468, Evergreen, CO 80439-2468
Betsy Hohe

Summit Alternative School (1986)
Frisco, CO 80443
Demi Garner, 303-668-3522
Type: public choice
2 teachers, 35 students, partly at-risk, ages 14-20, 9-12th grade
Governance by principal and democratic school meeting
Within traditional HS; student-directed; extensive field trips; rural location; transportation; interns accepted.

Idaho Springs Home Educators
Idaho Springs, CO 80452
303-567-4800

Pinewood School
(See Resource Section)

Olde Columbine High School (1982)
1200 S Sunset, Longmont, CO 80501
William R. Blick, Prin, 303-772-3333, FAX: 651-7446
Type: public at-risk
5 teachers, 85 students, ages 14-20, 9-12th grade
Governance by students
Teacher qualifications: CO Certification
Urban location; transportation; interns accepted.

Pleasant Hill Academy (1988)
1130 Francis St #7045, Longmont, CO 80501
Linda Kreibick, Reg, 303-772-8828
Type: home-based, non-profit; cost: $35/family
Student ages 5-90, K-12th grade
Governance by board
Family designed and taught; use of community resources; diversity in evaluation; statewide branches.

St Vrain Valley Alternative Middle School
820 Main St, Longmont, CO 80501
Ken Poppe, 303-682-9377

Gateway Montessori School
1500 9th Ave, Longmont, CO 80501-4228

Eagle Rock School (1993)
Box 1770, Estes Park, CO 80517
Robert Burkhardt, Head, 303-588-0600, FAX: 586-4805
Type: independent, boarding, non-profit; tuition: free
20 teachers, 96 students, partly at-risk, ages 15–18, HS
Affiliation: Honda
Governance by teachers, principal, democratic school
    meeting, board
650 acres; 1 mile from Rocky Mountain National Park; inte-
    grated; stresses service learning, outdoor ed, environmen-
    tal stewardship, cross-cultural understanding; no letter
    grades; multi-aged classes; extensive field trips; interns
    accepted.

Wyoming Homeschoolers
615 S Loomis, Ft. Collins, CO 80521

Children's House Montessori School
113 N Shields St, Fort Collins, CO 80521-2418

Centennial High School (1976)
330 E Laurel St, Fort Collins, CO 80524
Dr Bill Lamperes, Prin, 303-493-4129
Type: public at-risk
14 teachers, 180 students, mainly at-risk, ages 14–21,
    10–12th grade
Governance by principal, faculty, students, parents
Teacher qualifications: CO License/Certification
Students must maintain commitment to pledge card; multi-
    aged classes; urban location; interns accepted.

Harris Bilingual Alternative Elementary
501 E Elizabeth, Ft. Collins, CO 80524
303-482-7902
K–5th grade

Homeschoolers Under God
1749 Hastings Dr, Fort Collins, CO 80526

Northern Colorado Home School Association
4633 Skyline Dr, Fort Collins, CO 80526
303-493-2243; 669-6234

Ferguson High School (1972)
804 E Eisenhower, Loveland, CO 80537
Howard C. Wenger, Prin, 303-667-5881, FAX: 669-0772
Type: continuation, non-profit
7 teachers, 105 students, ages 25–50, 9–12th grade
Governance by democratic school meeting
Teacher qualifications: CO certification
Special 1-wk classes; daily leadership; college schedule; after-
    noon, night classes; multi-aged classes; suburban location;
    interns accepted.

Agape Family Schools
5108 Edgewood Ct, Loveland, CO 80538
303-669-2581
Type: home-based

Mary Blain Elementary Key School (1991)
860 E 29th St, Loveland, CO 80538
Randy Zila, Prin, 303-669-2973, FAX: 303-669-1785
Type: public choice
35 teachers, 485 students, ages 5–11, K–5th grade
Governance by shared decision making
Class rotation with single aged class and teacher; multi-aged
    classe; interns accepted.

We Are Teaching Our Children At Home
Brighton, CO 80601
303-659-9282

Brighton Montessori School
203 South 3rd Ave, Brighton, CO 80601-2011
Joyce Acre

Charter School for the Gifted and Talented
12323 Claude Court, Eastlake, CO 80614
Nancy Hall, 303-450-3936
Type: charter
125 students, 1–5th grade
Affiliation: Adams 12 Five Star District
Expanding to pre K–12 with 500 students; focus on science-
    math-technology.

EastLake Montessori School
12585 Third St, Eastlake, CO 80614

Weld Opportunity School (1987)
1112 9th Ave, Greeley, CO 80631
Bonnie Peterson, Dir, 303-351-7472
Type: public at-risk
5 teachers, 65 students, ages 15–19, 9–12th grade
Governance by teachers, principal
Teacher qualifications: CO certification
Work experience; pregnancy prevention; teen parenting;
    peer support; counseling; career exploration; life skills;
    multi-aged classe; interns accepted.

Montessori Early Learning Center
529 22nd St, Greeley, CO 80631-7134

University of Northern Colorado Laboratory School
Greeley, CO 80639
303-351-2321

Morgan County Homeschoolers Network
Brush, CO 80723
303-867-4461

Sterling Alternative High School (1982)
201 S 11th Ave, Sterling, CO 80751
Darrell Smith, Prin, 303-522-5079, FAX: 303-522-5084
Type: public at-risk
3 teachers, 32 students, ages 15–19, 9–12th grade
Governance by teachers, principal
Shared decision making; monthly review of academic, per-
    sonal development; parent involvement; multi-aged classe;
    interns accepted.

Community Learning Center (1990)
425 W Alabama, Fountain, CO 80817
Robert Vise, Dir, 719-382-7429, FAX: 719-382-7338
Type: public at-risk
2 teachers, 35 students, ages 16–12, 9–12th grade
Governance by principal; board
Vocational; counseling; portfolios; work/study; multi-aged
    classes; suburban location; transportation; interns
    accepted.

Teller County Home Education Association
Woodland Park, CO 80863
719-687-8676

Program (1981)
Box 99, Woodland Park, CO 80866
Rose Martin, 719-687-8450, FAX: 719-687-3880
Type: public at-risk
1 teacher, 25–40 students, ages 16–19, 10–12th grade
Governance by student gov't, democratic school meeting
Support groups; work-study; no letter grades; multi-aged
    classes

Palmer Night School (1981)
301 N Nevada Ave, Colorado Springs, CO 80903
Jack Terry, Dir, 303-520-2850
Type: public choice/at-risk
6 teachers, 120-300 students, ages 16–20, 9–12th grade
Governance by principal and board
Teacher qualifications: CO Certification
For pregnant teens/mothers and students who work days;
    multi-aged classes; urban location; interns accepted.

Educational Opportunity Program (1970)
730 N Walnut, Colorado Springs, CO 80905
RH Pete Freeman, Prin, 719-630-0240, FAX: 719-630-0243
Type: public choice
14 teachers, 250 students, mainly at-risk, ages 16-20, HS
Affiliation: School District #11
Governance by principal
Teacher qualifications: CO certification
Personalized, small group instruction; personal, academic
    goal setting; flexible schedule; urban location; interns
    accepted.

Harrison Second Chance (1988)
2755 Janitell Rd, Colorado Springs, CO 80906
Jim Reid, Coord/Prin, 719-576-8226, FAX: 576-6980
Type: public choice/at-risk
1 ft, 10 pt teachers, 80 students, mainly at-risk, ages 14-21,
    9-12th grade
Governance by teachers and principal
Teacher qualifications: current employment in district,
    interview
Volunteer tutors from local colleges; required work and/or
    community service; no SE; suburban location.

The Golden Mountain Schools (1975)
306 W Brookside, Colorado Springs, CO 80906
Rai Christiansen, Dir, 729-632-0872
Type: Montessori; tuition: $2,100-4,000/yr
6 teachers, 6 assistants, 100 students, ages 3-9
Affiliations: MTAC, AMS
Governance by administrator
Teacher qualifications: 30 yrs experience
French 4 times/wk an integral part of curriculum; peace,
    music ed in preschool; childcare; urban location; interns
    accepted.

Born to the Golden Mountain Montessori Child Center
306 W Brookside St, Colorado Springs, CO 80906-2156
Rae Christiansen

Belleau Montessori School
3131 Pennsylvania, Colorado Springs, CO 80907

A Montessori School
6480 Coolwell Dr, Colorado Springs, CO 80908-3324

Colorado Springs Homeschoolers
2906 Marilyn Rd, Colorado Springs, CO 80909
719-598-8444

Widefield Alternative High School (1987)
615 Widefield Dr, Colorado Springs, CO 80911
Dave Turner, Dean, 719-392-3481, FAX: 719-390-4372
Type: public at-risk
4 teachers, 60 students, ages 16-21, 10-12th grade
Governance by board
Teacher qualifications: state certification
Credit per class; work/study; 20-day sessions; community
    environment; suburban location.

Woodland Hills Montessori School (1984)
3215 Woodland Hills Dr, Colorado Springs, CO 80918
Dr Jackie Howell, 719-594-0611
Tuition: $190/330/mo
13 teachers, 75 students, ages 3-9
Governance by board
Teacher qualifications: CO Certification
Childcare.

Woodman Montessori School
6985 Blackhawk Pl, Colorado Springs, CO 80919-1124

Colorado Springs Homeschool Support Group
PO Box 26117, Colorado Springs, CO 80936-6117
719-598-2636

The Connect School
107 E 7th, Pueblo, CO 81002

Judy Mikulas, 719-542-0224
Type: charter
6-8th grade
Affiliation: Pueblo County SD70
School without walls using multiple community resources.

Keating Education Center (1982)
215 E Orman Ave, Pueblo, CO 81003
Jim Wessely, 719-549-7371
346 students
Second chance; evening classes; work study for teen
    mothers, out of school students.

Pueblo Home School Association
2616 Lambert, Pueblo, CO 81003
MaryLou Greene, 719-545-5649

Pueblo School for the Arts and Sciences
1745 Acero, Pueblo, CO 81004
Dr Sam Pantleo, 719-549-2737
Type: charter
300 students, K-9th grade
Affiliation: Pueblo 60 SD
Based on Paideia model; operated by U. Southern CO.

Pueblo Montessori Center
110 Calla Ave, Pueblo, CO 81005-1205
Leslie Kelham and Becky Chaussen

Sonshine Support Group
Lamar, CO 81052
719-336-7990
Type: home-based

Ignacio Second Chance (1986)
PO Box 460, Ignacio, CO 81137
Paulette Giambattista, Dir, 303-563-9417, FAX: -4524
Type: public at-risk
3 teachers, 60 students, ages 15-21, 9-12th grade
Governance by teachers and principal
Individual guided study; multi-aged classes; rural location.

New Horizons (Second Chance) High School (1986)
PO Box 72, La Jara, CO 81140
Jean Kelley, 719-274-4220
50 students, mainly returning to school, HS
Individual study; cont ed; health, career ed required.

Monte Vista Community School (1973)
345 E Prospect Ave, Monte Vista, CO 81144
719-852-2212, FAX: 719-852-6184
Type: public choice/at-risk
1 teacher, 20 students, mainly at-risk, ages 15-53
Accreditation: Colorado State
Governance by director
Teacher qualifications: CO certification
Competency-based; GED prep; self-directed; field trips; rural
    location; transportation; interns accepted.

Chaffee County High School (1989)
PO Box 2027, Buena Vista, CO 81211
Dick Couch, Dir, 719-395-4064
Type: public at-risk
3 teachers, 40 students, ages 16-23, 10-12th grade
Governance by principal, faculty and student reps
Teacher qualifications: CO Certification
Point, attendance contract; 80 hrs service learning required;
    no letter grades; rural location.

Collegiate Peaks Home Educators
Buena Vista, CO 81211
719-395-2069

Exploratory School-Lincoln Elementary
420 Myrtle, Canon City, CO 81212
Molly Merry, 719-275-7445

The Exploratory School (1992)
420 Myrtle Ave, Canon City, CO 81212
Molly Merry, Tch, 719-269-3785
Type: public choice
2 teachers, 60 students, 5-6th grade
Governance by teachers, principal
Project-based learning; traditional and alternative experiences; student-directed; experiential

Gunnison Valley Homeschoolers
Gunnison, CO 81230
303-641-0870

Christian Parents Who Are Teaching at Home
Durango, CO 81301
303-884-4122

Community of Learners
201 E 12th St, Durango, CO 81301
Sandy Davis, 303-259-0328
Type: charter
60 students, 6-8th grade
Affiliation: Durango 9-R SD
Expanding to 6-12; student-centered, self-directed.

Home Education for Excellence in Durango (HEED)
917 CR 216, Durango, CO 81301
Maureen Clerici, 303-247-2725

La Plata Montessori School
2899 Holly Ave, Durango, CO 81301-4416

The EXCEL School
PO Box 1350, Durango, CO 81302
James Ewing, 303-259-0203
Type: charter
120 students, 6-9th grade
Affiliations: Durango 9-R SD, Fort Lewis College
Expanding to 6-12; area professional development center.

Battle Rock Charter School
12247 C.R.G., Cortez, CO 81321
Stephen Hanson, 303-565-3237
Type: charter
ES

Southwest Open High School (1985)
PO Box 1420, Cortez, CO 81321
Richard Fulton, Prin, 303-565-1150, FAX: 303-565-1203
Type: public choice/at-risk
6 teachers, 80 students, mainly at-risk, ages 15-21, 9-12th grade
Governance by principal, faculty, student reps, board, democratic school meeting
Teacher qualifications: CO Certification
Experiential; community-based; mentorships; outdoor ed; teen parenting; no letter grades; non-compulsory class attendance; multi-aged classes; rural location; interns accepted.

San Juan Home Educators
Montrose, CO 81401
303-249-6765

Delta County Support Group
Paonia, CO 81428
303-527-4323
Type: home-based

Lamborn Valley School
1559 4110 Dr, Paonia, CO 81428
Addie Cranson, 303-527-3165
Type: independent, home-based; cost: variable
16 students, ages 3-18
Part of intentional community with some outside boarding students; learning related to student experience and interest; organic farm and orchard; work projects; travel-study trips; $120/yr for homeschoolers.

The Children's Cooperative Homeschool (1992)
PO Box 335, Ridgway, CO 81432
Jeanne Stewart, Dir/Tch, 303-626-5279
Non-profit; cost: $200/mo, scholarships
1 teacher, 9 students, ages 5-6, ES
Affiliation: NCACS
Governance by parent co-op and teacher
Teacher qualifications: CO Certification; MA in Teaching Elem Ed
Field trips; rural location

R-5 High School (1970)
310 N 7th St, Grand Junction, CO 81501
303-242-4350, FAX: 303-242-4465
Type: public at-risk
12 teachers, 235 students, ages 16-21, 10-12th grade
Affiliation: Mesa SD #51
Governance by teachers and principal
Teacher qualifications: degree, vocational certification
Multi-aged classes; extensive field trips; interns accepted.

The Children's Cottage
441 Kennedy Ave, Grand Junction, CO 81501
Type: Montessori

Home Education League of Parents
PO Box 4865, Grand Junction, CO 81502
Peggy Nishikowa
Non-profit
Affiliation: West River Academy enrollment
Governance by co-ordinators directed through national level
14 families; inclusive; suburban location.

National Association of Private Nontraditional Schools and Colleges
(See Resource Section)

Montessori School of Grand Junction
2405 Apricot Ct, Grand Junction, CO 81506-8450
Beth Long

Aspen Children Center
315 C Ave, Aspen, CO 81611
Type: Montessori

Aspen Sprouts
315 A A B C, Aspen, CO 81611
Type: Montessori

Aspen Waldorf School (1991)
PO Box 1563, Aspen, CO 81612
Patty Fox, 303-925-7938
Non-profit; tuition: $3,500/yr, scholarships
3 teachers, 27 students, ages 3-12, pre K-4th grade
Affiliation: AWSNA
Governance by faculty and student representatives and board
Teacher qualifications: BA, Waldorf training
Extensive field trips; suburban location; transportation; interns accepted.

Eagle County Charter Academy
PO Box 21-330, Avon, CO 81620
Patti Anderson, 303-949-0656
Type: charter
4 teachers, 64 students, 5-7th grade
Affiliation: Eagle County SD
Trimester block scheduling.

Mountain Sage School
PO Box 1241, Carbondale, CO 81623
Pricilla Dickinson, 303-963-9647
Type: independent; tuition: $2,680/yr, scholarships
12 students, ages K-2
Affiliation: NCACS
Will add a grade each year; individualized; Friday field trips, overnights, ski trips.

Mt Sopris Montessori School
PO Box 366, Carbondale, CO 81623-0366
Mark Ross

Aspen Community School (1970)
1199 Lenado Rd; PO Box 336, Woody Creek, CO 81656
George Stranahan, Head, 303-923-4080, FAX: 303-923-6207
Type: independent, non-profit; tuition: up to $6,900/yr,
    scholarships

14 teachers, 106 students, ages 2.5–14, pre K–8th grade
Affiliation: NCACS
Governance by board and parent cooperative
Log schoolhouse on mesa overlooking Rocky Mtns; rooted in
    community; fluid curriculum; respect for differences;
    apprenticeships with artist and woodworker in residence;
    multi-aged classes; extensive field trips; no letter grades;
    rural location; transportation; interns accepted.

Connecticut

**The Educational Association of Christian
    Homeschoolers (TEACH)**
(See Resource Section)

Alternative Education School (1986)
240 Stafford Ave, Bristol, CT 06010
Edward Mongeon, Dept Chair, 203-584-7709
Type: public choice
5 teachers, 48 students, mainly at-risk, 7–10th grade
At Bristol Community Center; individualized; experiential; life
    skills, awareness; field trips.

Wilderness School (1974)
PO Box 298, E Hartland, CT 06027
Tom Dyer, Dir; Dorothy Soden, Business Mgr, 203-491-3528,
    566-4761
Type: public
Student ages 13.5–16
Base camp/courses in natural settings; 20-day wilderness
    course.

The Alternative School (1981)
Housatonic Valley Regional HS, Falls Village, CT 06031
William DeVoti, Tch/Coord, 203-824-5123
Type: public choice
2 teachers, 14 students, mainly at-risk, 9–12th grade
Experiential; outdoor adventure; community shadowing;
    magazine.

ABLE (Alternative Behavioral Learning Environment)
    (1982)
134 W Middle Tpk, Manchester, CT 06040
Marilyn Fabian, Judith Spicker, Tchs, 203-647-3521
Type: public choice
2 teachers, 15 students, mainly at-risk, 10–12th grade
In-house; short-term intervention.

Vertices at Manchester High School (1976)
134 E Middle Tpk, Manchester, CT 06040
Sue Hardy, John Stedman, Tchs, 203-647-3509
Type: public choice
2 teachers, 30–35 students, mainly at-risk, 10–12th grade
In-house; mainstream re-entry program.

Hans Christian Anderson Montessori
212 Bolton Center Rd; PO Box 9218, Bolton, CT 06043-7637
Kathy Hoyt

Alternative Vocational Education (AVE)
New Britain High School
110 Mill St, New Britain, CT 06051
Paul N. Eshoo, Coord, 203-225-6351
Type: public choice
10 teachers, 30–38 students, mainly at-risk, 11–12th grade
In-house; machine tech; drafting and blueprint;
    telecommunications.

Montessori Children's House, c/o Ethel Walker School
Bushy Hill Rd, Simsbury, CT 06070

Freeman's Montessori Schoool
895 Main St, South Glastonbury, CT 06073-2218
Alberta Freeman

Enfield Montessori
1370 Enfield St, Enfield, CT 06082
Sr Mary Anastasia, Prin, 203-745-5847
Non-profit; tuition: $1,400-1,600
5 teachers, 5 assistants, 122 students, ages 3–12
Affiliation: NAMTA; accreditation: CT
Governance by board
Suburban location; interns accepted.

Montesorri Children's House
PO Box 194, West Simsbury, CT 06092-0194
Type: Montessori

Alternate Learning Center at Sage Park Middle School
    (1980)
25 Sage Park Rd, Windsor, CT 06095
Anita W. Baten, Tch, 203-688-6415
Type: public choice
1 teacher, 1 assistant, 30–35 students, mainly at-risk, 7–8th
    grade
Study and organizational skills; peer counseling.

Alternative Center for Education (ACE)
Windsor High School (1981)
50 Sage Park Rd, Windsor, CT 06095
Thomas G. Martin, Jr, Vice Prin, 203-688-8334
Type: public choice
2 teachers, 15 students, mainly at-risk, 9–10th grade
In-house; individualized; tutorial; human relations; career
    planning.

Windsor Montessori (1983)
114 Palisado Ave, Windsor, CT 06095-2531
Darlene Dulchinos, Dir, 203-285-1426
Non-profit; tuition: $290/320/634/mo
4 teachers, 1 assistant, 38 students, ages infant–6
Affiliation: AMS; accreditation: NAECP
Large building; gym; 2 playgrounds; childcare; suburban loca-
    tion; interns accepted.

Small Group Instruction
Windsor Locks HS, Windsor Locks, CT 06096
Edgar J. Gorman, Spec Serv Dir, 203-627-1480
Type: public choice
Students mainly at-risk, HS
In-house; early graduation for potential drop-outs; voc; mod-
    ified work experience.

TMR Program at Regional School #7 (1976)
Central Ave Ext, Winsted, CT 06098
Pat Keener, SE Dept Chair, 203-379-8525

Type: public choice
1 teacher, 2 assistants, 7 students, mainly at-risk, ages 13-21
In middle school; individualized; voc; perf arts; life skills.

Hartford Board of Education
249 High St, Hartford, CT 06103
Alice A Davis
Type: Montessori

Watkinson School (1881)
180 Bloomfield Ave, Hartford, CT 06105
Kay Montgomery, Adms Dir, 203-236-5618, FAX: 233-8295
Type: independent, non-profit; tuition: $13,550/yr,
scholarships
36 teachers, 175 students, ages 10-19, 6-12+
Affiliation: CES
Governance by board
Teacher qualifications: BS minimum, compatible philosophy
Special support for gifted, LD; early college courses at U of
Hartford; pre-professional arts program; independent
study; suburban location; interns accepted.

Synergy Alternative High School Program (1973)
110 Long Hill Dr, E Hartford, CT 06108
Dr Betti Colli, Coord, 203-282-3160
Type: public choice
6 teachers, 1 assistant, 80 students, mainly at-risk, 9-12th
grade
Informal; cooperative work experience; survival-type
encampments; reality-therapy peer support; daily contract; weekly all-school meeting; student/staff discipline
committee.

Alternate Day Program (1977)
51 Willow St, Wethersfield, CT 06109
Francis H. Stuart, PPS/SE Dir, 203-563-8181 x214
Type: public choice
3 teachers, 1 assistant, 20 students, mainly at-risk, 9-12th
grade
Daily peer counseling; psychiatric consultation; checklist level
system.

ASK Program at Hall High School (1975)
975 N Main St, W Hartford, CT 06117
James Solomon, Coord, 203-232-4561
Type: public choice
2 teachers, 50 students, mainly at-risk, 10-12th grade
In-house; team taught English and social studies classes only;
informal academic and personal counseling.

Montessori School of Greater Hartford (1964)
64 St. James St, West Hartford, CT 06119
Carol Kuszik, 203-236-4565, FAX: 203-233-1070
Non-profit; tuition: $3,090/6,890
6 teachers, 9 assistants, 110 students, mainly international,
ages 3-9
Governance by board of trustees
Childcare; suburban location.

Alternative Learning Center (1977)
21 Valley St, Willimantic, CT 06226
Roz Rosen, Dir, 203-423-0233
Type: public choice
5 teachers, 2 assistants, 55 students, mainly at-risk, 7-12th
grade
Small, flexible and intimate environment; student-operated
bakery business.

Alternative Learning Program for Students (1983)
610 Wauregan Rd, Danielson, CT 06239
Mike Vose or Bill Scalise, Co-Chairs, 203-774-7836
Type: public choice
2 teachers, 1 assistant, 25 students, mainly at-risk, 9-12th
grade
Drop-out intervention; emphasis on independent study, self-
direction; computers.

Natchaug Democratic School (1993)
164 Main St, Hampton, CT 06247
Jed Katch, 203-455-0505
Type: independent, non-profit; tuition: $3,500, 2,500 second,
1,500 3rd
2 teachers, 10 students, ages 5-19, 1-12th grade
Governance by democratic school meeting
Teacher qualifications: expertise in one or more areas; certification not necessary
Students choose what they want to learn, when, how, and
with whom; larger community used through visitations
and apprenticeships with businesses, universities; no letter
grades; non-compulsory class attendance; multi-aged
classes; rural location.

Mount Hope Montessori School (1961)
PO Box 267, Mansfield Center, CT 06250
Florence Caillard, Dir, 203-423-1070
Non-profit; tuition: $4,000/yr
3 teachers, 5 assistants, 72 students, mainly international,
ages 3-6
Governance by board
Rural location.

Oak Grove Montessori School (1981)
132 Pleasant Valley Rd, Mansfield Center, CT 06250
Karen Drazen, Dir, 203-456-1031
Non-profit; tuition: $3,996-4,140/yr
5 teachers, 2 assistants, 72 students, ages 3-12
Affiliations: AMS, MSCT
Governance by board
Whole language program; passive solar, earth berm building;
childcare; interns accepted.

Study Circles Resource Center
(See Resource Section)

Montessori Discovery School
218 Dudley St, Norwich, CT 06360
Patrice Champeigne

Norwich High School (1984)
Mahan Dr, Norwich, CT 06360
Nancy Elizabeth Young, Dir, 203-823-4213
Type: public choice
4 teachers, 50 students, mainly at-risk, 9-12th grade
Individualized; school gov and leadership opportunities; voc.

Montville Alternative High School (1977)
300 Norwich/New London Tpk, Uncasville, CT 06382
Richard Bilda, Prin, 203-848-7816
Type: public choice
3 teachers, 1 assistant, 35 students, mainly at-risk, 9-12th
grade
Silk screening and chair caning subsidize field trips.

Waterford High School Satellite Program (1981)
15 Rope Ferry Rd, Waterford, CT 06385
Kate Novato, Burke Reagan, Co-Tchs, 203-442-9401 x46
Type: public choice
2 teachers, 1 assistant, 20 students, mainly at-risk, 9-12th
grade
In-house; individualized; highly structured; small groups; voc;
work experience; counseling; behavior modification.

Horizons: Branford High School (1990)
185 E Main St, Branford, CT 06405
Robert C Gaiser, Adm, 203-488-7291
Type: public choice/at-risk
8 teachers, 65 students, mainly at-risk, ages 14-20, 9-12th
grade
Affiliation: CT Assn of Alt Schs & Progs
Governance by teachers, administrator, students.
Teacher qualifications: CT Certification
Interns accepted.

Wightwood School
56 Stony Creek Rd, Branford, CT 06405
Bill Kaplan, Head, 203-481-0363
Type: independent, non-profit; tuition: $5,595-7,195/yr,
scholarships
100 students, pre K–8th grade
Integrated; topic-centered; experiential; family-oriented; art;
Spanish; overnight, week-long trips; problem solving; environmental science.

Shoreline School of Montessori
675 East Main St, Branford, CT 06405-2934
Robin Barron

Boulder Knoll Montessori School
660 Boulder Rd, Cheshire, CT 06410-3216

Clinton Elementary Schools Integrated Day (1981)
c/o Joel School, Glenwood Circle, Clinton, CT 06413
Daniel Hesford, Coord; Kopi Saltman, Jim Snow, Prins, 203-
669-5768
Type: public choice
14 teachers, 325 students, K–5th grade
In-house; multi-grade groups; students stay with teacher for
more than 1 yr; no letter grades.

Connecticut Home Educators Association (1983)
PO Box 250, Cobalt, CT 06414
Linda Schroth, Pres, 203-267-4240

Programmed Alternative Learning (PAL)
Fairfield Public Schools (1978)
760 Stillson Rd, Fairfield, CT 06430
Mary Michael, Housemaster, 203-255-8308
Type: public choice
5 teachers, 1 assistant, 25 students, mainly at-risk, 6–12th
grade
For very emotionally disturbed students; extensive student,
parent counseling; work experience.

Hunt Ridge Montessori
4670 Congress St, Fairfield, CT 06430-1721

Montessori Center for Early Learning
148 Beach Rd, Fairfield, CT 06430-6002
Belen Orejas Fernandez

Fairfield Montessori School
100 Mona Ter, Fairfield, CT 06430-6422

The Learning Cooperative at Fairfield High School (1978)
755 Melville Ave, Fairfield, CT 06432
Kenneth Tavares, Adm, 203-255-8350, FAX: 366-1371
Type: public at-risk
3 teachers, 30 students, mainly at-risk, ages 14–19, 9–12th
grade
Governance by board
In-house; individualized; small classes; family-like environment; work experience; community service reqd; multi-
aged classes; suburban location.

Montessori School of Madison
213 Green Hill Rd, Madison, CT 06443-2103
Sharon Timek

Integrated Day at Memorial Middle School (1977)
Hubbard St, Middlefield, CT 06455
Maureen Hamilton, Judith O'Hare, Tchs, 203-349-3489
Type: public choice
5 teachers, 100 students, 5–6th grade
In-house; individualized; experiential; individual project
research; vertical age grouping; cooperative group work;
narrative evaluations or letter grades.

Center for Creative Youth
Wesleyan University, Middletown, CT 06459
Joan Hickey, Dir, 203-347-9411 x2684
Type: public choice
25 teachers, 22 assistants, 200 students

Residential summer program; music; creative writing;
theater; dance; visual arts; technical theater.

Newtown Montessori School
40 Dodgingtown Rd, Newtown, CT 06470
Myriam Woods, Head
Non-profit; tuition: $3,050/5,000/yr
3 teachers, 3 assistants, 90 students, ages 3–9
Affiliations: AMS, NAEYC; accreditation: CAIS
Governance by board
Childcare; suburban location; transportation; interns
accepted.

Program at North Branford High School (1977)
49 Caputo Rd, N Branford, CT 06471
John DeCaprio, Prin, 203-484-0421
Type: public
3 teachers, 15 students, 9–12th grade
In-house; work experience; individualized.

Oxford Alternative Program at Great Oak Middle School
(1982)
222 Governor's Hill Rd, Oxford, CT 06483
Donna Fusco, Tch, 203-888-5418
Type: public choice
1 teacher, 7 students, mainly at-risk, 7–8th grade
In-house; experiential; individual or small group setting.

Seymour High School (1978)
2 Botsford Rd, Seymour, CT 06483
Edward Rostowsky, Asst Prin, 203-888-2561
Type: public choice
1 teacher, 10–15 students, mainly at-risk, 9–12th grade
In-house; small groups; work-study.

Program (1988)
N Summit St, Southington, CT 06489
Michael Donahue, Lead Tch, 203-628-3223
Type: public choice
7 teachers, 25–40 students, mainly at-risk, 9–12th grade
For current or potential drop-outs; small classes; computer,
food service, marketing and retail studies.

ROPE at Southington High School (1971)
720 Pleasant St, Southington, CT 06489
Joel Davis, Dir of Secondary Ed, 203-628-0331
Type: public choice
2 teachers, 35 students, mainly at-risk, 10–12th grade
For drop-outs and youths working full-time.

Parents Place and Kids Connection
420 Center St, Wallingford, CT 06492
Nancy Freyberg, Dir, 203-265-1253
Type: independent
Spiritually centered; parents, students, teachers develop integrated programs based on collaboration, inclusion, democratic decision-making, peaceful conflict resolution, care
for others and the earth.

SAFE/SA Program (1979)
490 Chapel St, Stratford, CT 06497
Wayne Theriault, 203-385-4298
Type: public choice
3 teachers, 40 students, mainly at-risk, 9–12th grade
Work/study; independent study; volunteer work.

Career High School (1983)
21 Wooster Pl, New Haven, CT 06511
Charles J Williams, 203-787-8400
Type: public choice
36 teachers, 385 students, 9–12th grade
Affiliation: NEASC
Emphasis on business/computers and allied health; intern-
ships; partnership with Yale-New Haven Hospital.

Cooperative High School (1980)
800 Dixwell Ave, New Haven, CT 06511
Edward Linehan, Coord, 203-777-5923, -5924

Type: public choice
17 teachers, 240 students, 9–12th grade
Visual arts; vocal music; creative writing; theatre; dance; ind study; career planning; thematic approach; team teaching.

Educational Center for the Arts/ACES (1972)
55 Audubon St, New Haven, CT 06511
Robert D. Parker, Dir, 203-777-5451
Type: public choice
20 teachers, 165 students, 9–12th grade
Dance; music; visual arts; theatre; poetry/prose; letter grades or narrative evaluations.

High School in the Community (HSC) (1970)
45 Nash St, New Haven, CT 06511
Patricia Morgillo, Facilitator, 203-787-8635,-8636
Type: public choice
13 teachers, 230 students, 9–12th grade
Team teaching; inter-disciplinary courses; experiential; intensive guidance; peer support group; advocacy policy; student/parent/staff policy council.

Betsy Ross Arts Elementary
185 Barnes Ave, New Haven, CT 06513
Brenda Hollard, 203-787-8974
Type: magnet
5–8th grade

Cold Spring School
263 Chapel St, New Haven, CT 06513
Irene Fiss, Director, 203-787-1584
Type: independent; tuition: $6,700-8,500/yr, scholarships
110 students, ages 5-12, K–6th grade
Multi-cultural, diverse student body; active participation in community affairs; optional long-day program; Spanish language and culture program.

Jepson Non-Graded School
375 Quinnipiac Ave, New Haven, CT 06513
Johanna Wilson, 203-787-6077
Type: magnet
Ungraded
Cooperative learning technology.

Children's House Of Montessori
351 Mckinley Ave, New Haven, CT 06515-2026
C Patricia Totalo

al Program-Day Session (1977)
One Circle St, W Haven, CT 06516
Bert Siclari, Dir, 203-932-5701 x36
Type: public choice
3 teachers, 1 assistant, 70 students, mainly at-risk, 10–12th grade
In-house.

Polly T. McCabe Center (1966)
390 Columbus Ave, New Haven, CT 06519
Elizabeth S. Celotto, Coord, 203-787-8758,-6423
Type: public choice
14 teachers, 150-200 students, mainly at-risk, 6–12th grade
For pregnant/parenting students and drop-outs; pre- and post-natal exercises; social/emotional, medical, and career counseling.

Sound School (1981)
60 S Water St, New Haven, CT 06519
George E. Foote, Coord, 203-787-6937
Type: public choice
11 teachers, 200 students, 9–12th grade
Oceanography; marine biology; ecology; field research; merchant marine history; boat building/maintenance; navigation; boat shop; 66-foot ketch.

West Hills Elementary & Middle School
311 Valley St, New Haven, CT 06519
Janice Romo, 203-787-8613
Type: magnet

K-8th grade
Individualized.

Free-To-Be-Me! Montessori Early Development Center
PO Box 216, Bridgeport, CT 06601-0216

Park City Alternative (1973)
135 Park Ave, Bridgeport, CT 06602
Cliff Scheinkman, Coord, 203-576-8245
Type: public choice
5 teachers, 60 students, mainly at-risk, 10–12th grade
At U. Bridgeport; internships; liaison with CT National Bank.

Bridgeport Montessori Center
210 Congress St, Bridgeport, CT 06604-4007

Paddy Bear Montessori Infant Toddler School
790 Central Ave, Bridgeport, CT 06607-1705

Bridgeport Montessori School
165 Logan St, Bridgeport, CT 06607-1931

Harding Prep (1973)
389 Kossuth St, Bridgeport, CT 06608
Clifford Scheinkman, Coord; Richard Sakowitz, Head Tch, 203-576-7178
Type: public choice
5 teachers, 50 students, mainly at-risk, 9–10th grade
Drop-out intervention; in Benjamin Franklin Center.

Hall Neighborhood House
52 Green St, Bridgeport, CT 06608-2425
Patricia Howell
Type: Montessori

Trumbull Alternate School (TAS) (1972)
6254 Main St, Trumbull, CT 06611
Anthony Minotti, SE Dir, 203-268-1595
Type: public choice
2 teachers, 15-20 students, mainly at-risk, 9–12th grade
Progress monitored through daily point system checksheet; career ed; work experience.

Alternate Education Program at Ledyard High School
24 Gallup Hill Rd, Ledyard, CT 06634
Anne A. Park, Dir, 203-464-9600
Type: public choice
13 teachers, 85 students, mainly at-risk, ages 16+, 9–12th grade
In-house; evening diploma program.

Alternate School
201 Birch St, Waterbury, CT 06704-3808
Therese P. Guay, Prin, 203-574-8029
Type: public choice
12 teachers; students mainly at-risk, 7–12th grade
Vocational.

Alternative Learning Program at Long River Middle School (1986)
Columbia Ave, Prospect, CT 06712
Holly Norton, Tch or Gary Gombar, Prin, 203-758-4421
Type: public choice
1 teacher, 1 assistant, 10 students, mainly at-risk, 6–8th grade
In-house; individualized; highly structured; small groups; community service.

Wolcott High School Alternative Program (1985)
457 Bound Line Rd, Wolcott, CT 06716
Joseph DiLeo, SHAPE Coord, 203-879-1434
Type: public choice
1 teacher, 25 students, mainly at-risk, 9–12th grade
In-house; for potential drop-outs; point system rates behavior; credited counsel class.

Beatrice Ayer Patton School
Skyline Ridge Rd, Bridgewater, CT 06752
Mother Catarina Boyer
Type: Montessori

at Mary I. Johnson School
Whittemore Rd, Middlebury, CT 06762
Joan M. Quilter, PhD, Student Serv Dir, 203-758-1729
Type: public choice
4 teachers, 1 assistant, 20 students, mainly at-risk, 9–12th
   grade
Small group structured environment.

Washington Montessori School
16 Church St, New Preston, CT 06777-1599
Patricia Werner

Montessori School Of Northwestern Conneticut
5 Knife Shop Rd, Northfield, CT 06778-2603

Southeast School Center for Alternative Learning (1979)
196 Oak Ave, Torrington, CT 06790
Gary Lambour, Prin, 203-489-2298
Type: public choice
5 teachers, 4 assistants, 35–40 students, mainly at-risk,
   7–12th grade
Intensive, highly motivational; counseling and guidance; voc;
   career exploration; adventure/experiential ed.

Watertown Alternative School (1977)
324 French St, Watertown, CT 06795
Colleen Spieler, Dept Head, 203-274-5411 x344
Type: public choice
4 teachers, 3 assistants, 42 students, mainly at-risk, 9–12th
   grade
In-house; individualized; mainstream re-entry or graduation.

Carden Education Foundation
(See Resource Section)

Alternative Center for Education (1977)
Locust Ave, Danbury, CT 06810
Joseph Pepin, Dir, 203-797-4762
Type: public choice
8 teachers, 90+ students, mainly at-risk, 9–12th grade
Individualized; emphasis on community service.

Anderson Montessori
PO Box 122, Danbury, CT 06813-0122

Alternate Learning Program at Darien High School (1975)
High School Lane, Darien, CT 06820
William Devlin, Team Leader, 203-655-3981 x13
Type: public choice
3 teachers, 25 students, mainly at-risk, 10–12th grade
In-house; small classes; contracts; class meetings; student
   ethics council; community service required.

Town & Country Montessori School
Florida Rd Box 127, Georgetown, CT 06829

Community Learning Program at Greenwich High School (1977)
10 Hillside Rd, Greenwich, CT 06830
Jane Carlin, Senior Tch, 203-625-8010, FAX: 203-863-8888
Type: public choice/at-risk
2 teachers, 25 students, mainly at-risk, ages 15–21, 10–12th
   grade
Governance by teachers, principal; democratic school
   meeting
Outdoor adventure; responsibility for self, others; college
   prep; internships; community service; ethnic, economic
   diversity; multi-aged classes; suburban location.

Montessori School
52 Brookside Dr, Greenwich, CT 06830

The Whitby School
969 Lake Ave, Greenwich, CT 06831-3095
Betsy Benham
Type: Montessori

Mead School (1969)
Box 1517, Greenwich, CT 06836
Norman Barron, 203-637-3800, FAX: 203-637-5917
Type: independent, non-profit; tuition: $8,000, scholarships
50 teachers, 230 students, ages 6–15
Affiliations: CAIS, NAIS
Governance by principal, board
Recognizes various types of intelligence equally; high
   parental involvement; supports physical, emotional and
   cognitive; exchanges with inner city schools; no letter
   grades; non-compulsory class attendance; multi-aged
   classes; extensive field trips; suburban location;
   transportation.

Briggs Center for Vocational Arts (BCVA)
350 Main St, Norwalk, CT 06851
John H. Henshall, Dir, 203-847-7137
Type: public choice
20 teachers, 200 students, mainly at-risk
Individualized; self-paced; voc; counseling; teen parent
   program.

Montessori School of Redding
25 Cross Hwy, Redding, CT 06875
Ingrid Moe

Montessori Academy of Abingdon
5 Taporneck Ct, Ridgefield, CT 06877
Rhonda Kindig

Priyamont Montessori School
21 King Lane, Ridgefield, CT 06877-4404

Ridgefield Montessori School
40 Florida Rd # 185, Ridgefield, CT 06877-6111

Educational Reform Group
(See Resource Section)

Helen Gander Friends Nursery School
317 New Canaan Rd, Wilton, CT 06897
Marjorie Walton, 203-762-5669
Type: Quaker

The Montessori School (1963)
34 Whipple Rd, Wilton, CT 06897
203-834-0440, FAX: 203-761-9386
Non-profit; tuition: $3,736-6,800
11 teachers, 6 assistants, 217 students, ages infant–12
Accreditation: AMI; CT AIS
Governance by board
Childcare; suburban location.

Tri-Town Alternative at Middlebrook Middle School (1985)
131 School Rd, Wilton, CT 06897
Robert Feldkircher, Dir, 203-762-8388
Type: public choice
10 teachers, 25 students, mainly at-risk, ages 16+
Evenings for students working full-time.

Wilton Montessori
345 Belden Hill Rd, Wilton, CT 06897

LF Community Learning Program
37 Cascade Rd, Stamford, CT 06903
Jane Carlin, 203-329-0869
Type: public choice

Youth Employment & Education Program (1978)
137 Henry St, PO Box 929, Stamford, CT 06904
Kras Hristoff-Carlucci, Dir, 203-323-2171, 359-3524
Type: public
HS
In-house; career planning; job placement; voc; counseling;
   tutoring; teen parent program; P/F grading; contracts.

Executive High School Internship Program
Stamford Public Schools (1975)
55 Strawberry Hill Ave, Stamford, CT 06905
Frances L. Howes, Coord, 203-977-4265,-4531
Type: public choice
25-30 students, 11-12th grade
In-house; semester-long internships in public and private organizations; management theory; peer support; P/F contracts; career counselors.

The Vicarage School of Montessori
40 London Dr, Hamden, CT 26517
Donna Fronte, Dir, 288-2116
Tuition: $96-160/mo
2 teachers, 8 assistants, 80 students, ages infant-9
Affiliations: IMS, NAEYC
Governance by administrator
Science; geography; musical instruments; community activities; childcare; suburban location; transportation; interns accepted.

Delaware

Paul M. Hodgson Vocational-Technical High School
2575 Summit Bridge Rd, Newark, DE 19702
Steven Godowsky, Prin, 302-834-0993, FAX: 834-0598
Type: public choice
986 students, ages 13-21, 9-12th grade
Affiliation: CES
Governance by board/district
Teacher qualifications: state qualifications/certification
Senior Project: An Exhibition of Achievement; core interdisciplinary teams; school management team; employability rating with grades; academic/vocational integration; Common Planning time-schoolwide teams; suburban location; transportation; interns accepted.

CACC Montessori School
PO Box 892, Hockessin, DE 19707
Dorothy Conte, Dir, 302-239-2917, FAX: -0432
Non-profit; tuition: variable
5 teachers, 11 assistants, 125 students, mainly international, ages infant-6
Affiliation: AMS; accreditation: NAEYC
Governance by administrator and board of trustees
Suburban location; interns accepted.

Hockessin Friends Preschool
PO Box 192, Hockessin, DE 19707
Nancy Blockilinger, 302-239-2223
Type: Quaker

Hockessin Montessori School
7200 Lancaster Pike; PO Box 580, Hockessin, DE 19707-0565
Gina Reeves

The Children's House
175 Sawin Lane, Hockessin, DE 19707-9713
Fred and Elinore Barney
Type: Montessori

Christina School District
83 E Main St, Newark, DE 19711
Iris Metts, Supt of Schools
Type: Montessori

Newark Center For Creative Learning (1971)
401 Phillips Ave, Newark, DE 19711
Ann L. Brown, Director, 302-368-7772
Type: independent, non-profit; tuition: $3,951 (siblings 80%), scholarships
11 teachers, 92 students, ages 5-14, K-8th grade
Governance by parent cooperative
Teacher qualifications: none required; parents like ed or grad degree
Oldest students spend week at outdoor skills center, apprentice one afternoon a week at local businesses; many outside visitors; no letter grades; multi-aged classes; extensive field trips; suburban location; interns accepted.

Delaware Home Education Association
11 Bristol Knoll Rd, Newark, DE 19711-2122
302-368-3427

Independence School
1300 Paper Mill Rd, Newark, DE 19711-3408
Type: independent

Tri-State Homeschoolers Association
PO Box 7193, Newark, DE 19714-7193

Elementary Workshop (1971)
502 Pine St, Wilmington, DE 19801
Lillian A. Shah, Dir, 302-656-1498, FAX: 302-656-1485
Type: Montessori, non-profit; tuition: $4,100/yr, scholarships
10 teachers, 105 students, ages 3-12
Affiliation: AMS
Governance by principal, teachers, board
Model school; active parent co-op; scholarship program insures multi-racial/cultural student population; no letter grades; multi-aged classes; urban location; interns accepted.

Red Clay Consolidated School District
1400 Washington St, Wilmington, DE 19801
Patricia Reinbold
Type: Montessori

People's Settlement Preschool
408 E 8th St, Wilmington, DE 19801-3699
Type: independent

Willmington Friends School
101 School Rd, Wilmington, DE 19803
Carol Ramsey, 302-576-2900
Type: Quaker

Pilot School, Inc (1957)
100 Garden of Eden Rd, Wilmington, DE 19803-1599
Doris LeStourgeon, Dir, 302-478-1740, FAX: 302-478-1746
Type: independent, non-profit; tuition: $11,524/yr, scholarships
37 teachers, 159 students, mainly at-risk, ages 5-14, ungraded
Affiliations: NAIS, DAIS, NAPSEC, CEC
Governance by principal and board
Teacher qualifications: degree
Individualized; psychologist; language therapist; music therapist; educational diagnostician; eclectic approach; no letter grades; suburban location; interns accepted.

Educational Enrichment Center, Inc
730 Halstead Rd, Wilmington, DE 19803-2228
Type: independent

Montessori Learning Centre
2313 Concord Park, Wilmington, DE 19803-2911
Gilda De Berardinis

Oakwood Clonlara School
228 Waverly Rd, Wilmington, DE 19803-3135
Type: independent

Design-A-Study
(See Resource Section)

The Children's House, Inc (1974)
2400 W 17th St, Wilmington, DE 19806
Elinore and Frederick Barney, Owners, 302-429-9244
Type: Montessori; tuition: $3,130-3,990/yr
3 teachers, 3 assistants, 41 students, ages Infant-9
Affiliations: AMS, NKAD, DAEYC
Governance by administrator, parent cooperative
Safe setting; childcare; urban location; interns accepted.

Children's House
5 Yale Rd/Cooper Farm, Wilmington, DE 19808-2205
Ardeth Savage
Type: Montessori

EUREKA! Learning Community, Inc
6 Ridgewood Circle, Wilmington, DE 19809-2813
Type: independent

Wilmington Montessori School
1400 Harvey Rd, Wilmington, DE 19810-4200
Marie Dugan

Early Childhood Laboratory School
1200 N Du Pont Hwy, Dover, DE 19901-2277
Type: independent

The Little School, Inc
308 N Queen St, Dover, DE 19901-3026
Type: independent

Dover Montessori Country Day School
1 Dover Air Park, Dover, DE 19901-9236

Rose Valley School
160 Rose Valley Rd, Dover, DE 19901-9713
Type: independent

Joshua's Choice School
RD 1, Box 418, Ellendale, DE 19941-9617
Type: independent

King's Kids Academy
RD #5, Gox 130, Georgetown, DE 19947-9426
Type: independent

Community Learning Institute, Inc
RD #1, Box 307-P, Hartly, DE 19953-9511
Type: independent

The Child Craft Company
1307 Laurel Hwy, Seaford, DE 19973
Type: independent

The Idea Patch
451 Clayton Blvd, Smyna, DE 19977-1207
Type: independent

Florida

Gibbs High School
850 34 St S, St Petersburg, FL 22711
Barbara Shorter, 813-893-5452
Type: magnet
9-12th grade
Performing arts.

Amelia Island Montessori (1974)
Amelia Island Plantation, Amelia Island, FL 32034
Dr Jim Morgan, Adm, 904-261-6610
Non-profit; tuition: $1,275-3,320/yr
6 teachers, 6 assistants, 124 students, ages infant-9
Affiliation: AMS; accreditation: FLKC
Governance by board of trustees
Heavily wooded area; language, music, arts and crafts, and
    etiquette optional; childcare; suburban location.

Citizen's High School
188 College Dr, Box 1929, Orange Park, FL 32067-1929
904-276-1700
Type: public choice

Montessori School of Ormond Beach
50 Coolidge Ave, Ormond Beach, FL 32074
Susie White

Discovery School
413 Ponte Vedra Blvd, Pontevedrabeach, FL 32082
Suzy Dalt
Type: Montessori

Stonesoup School (1979)
Star Rt 1, Box 127, Crescent City, FL 32112
Deborah Rogers, 904-698-2516
Type: independent, boarding, non-profit; tuition: $700/mo,
    scholarships
3 teachers, 10 students, ages 8-18,-12th grade

Affiliation: NCACS
Governance by democratic school meeting
Free school approach to learning and living; freedom tem-
    pered with responsibility and independence, cooperation;
    encourages self-reliance, character development; self
    paced tutorials; on 50 acres with lake; no letter grades;
    non-compulsory class attendance; multi-aged classes;
    extensive field trips; rural location; interns accepted.

Florida Parent Education Association
Rt 4, PO Box 60-H, Interlachen, FL 32148
904-684-4940
Type: home-based

Seaside Montessori School
264 Division St, Ormond Beach, FL 32174-6208

Halifax Montessori School
51 Coolidge Ave, Ormond Beach, FL 32174-6247

Pierson Montessori Center (1990)
592 S Volusia Ave, Pierson, FL 32180
David Cipolloni, 904-749-4420, FAX: 904-749-1002
Non-profit; tuition: $60-70/wk
3 teachers, 20 assistants, 80 students, mainly international,
    ages infant-6
Affiliations: AMS, Comite de Hispano
Governance by administrator
Primarily serving Mexican farmworker community; bilingual
    curriculum; rural location; interns accepted.

Fishweir Elementary
3977 Herschel St, Jacksonville, FL 32205
Josephine Fiveash, 904-389-2230
Type: magnet
K-5th grade
Creative arts.

Normandy Elementary
6803 Arques Rd, Jacksonville, FL 32205
Anoola Lott, 904-781-0511
Type: magnet
Student ages 4+,-5th grade
Community outreach.

J. Allen Axsen Elementary
1221 E 16th St, Jacksonville, FL 32206
Janice Hunter, 904-353-7225
Type: magnet
K-5th grade
Montessori.

Duval County Public Schools
1701 Prudential Dr, Jacksonville, FL 32207
Betty White
Type: Montessori

Pine Forest Elementary
3929 Grandt Rd, Jacksonville, FL 32207
Margaret McCaughey, 904-398-7181
Type: magnet
K-5th grade
Performing arts.

Martin Luther King Elementary
8801 Lake Placid Dr, Jacksonville, FL 32208
Constance Hall, 904-768-8239
Type: magnet
K-5th grade
Gifted and talented; college prep.

James Weldon Johnson Middle School
1840 W 9th St, Jacksonville, FL 32209
Mary Brown, 904-630-6640
Type: magnet
6-8th grade
Gifted and talented.

Stanton College Prep High School
1149 W 13th St, Jacksonville, FL 32209
Jerry Gugel, 904-630-6760
Type: magnet
9-12th grade
Gifted and talented.

A Child's Place (1988)
3718 Salisbury Rd/3105 Southside Blvd, Jacksonville, FL 32216
Catherine Selhoust, 904-733-5797
Type: Montessori; tuition: $370-470
94 students, ages infant-6
Affiliations: NAMTA, N FL MTA; accreditation: NAEYC
Governance by administrator
Teacher qualifications: AMS, AMI, SNMC
Serves children of professional working parents; involved with local corporate community; Reed Grants for specific program expansion; childcare; urban location; interns accepted.

Hogan Spring Glen Elementary
6736 Beach Blvd, Jacksonville, FL 32216
Susan Schandelmaker, 904-725-1044
Type: magnet
K-5th grade
Community outreach.

San Mateo Elementary
600 Baisden Rd, Jacksonville, FL 32218
Marilyn Myrick, 904-757-4766
Type: magnet
K-5th grade
Gifted and talented.

Oakwood Country Day
PO Box 23950, Jacksonville, FL 32241-3950
Type: Montessori

Discovery Montessori School (1990)
485 6th Ave N, Jacksonville Beach, FL 32250
Karin Clark, Adm, 904-247-4577
Non-profit; tuition: $930/3200
3 teachers, 3 assistants, 53 students, ages infant-toddler & 6-9
Affiliation: AMS
Governance by board of directors
Neighborhood setting; outstanding materials; Atlantic Ocean beach nearby; childcare; suburban location.

Montessori Tides (1986)
533 2nd Ave N, Jacksonville Beach, Fl 32250
Kathy Graham, Dir, 904-241-1139
Tuition: $1,820/yr
2 teachers, 4 assistants, 54 students, ages 3-6
Affiliation: AMS; accreditation: FKC
Governance by administrator
Quiet beach location; suburban location; interns accepted.

Crown Point Elementary
3800 Crown Point Rd, Jacksonville, FL 32257
Sherry Adams, 904-262-0960
Type: magnet
K-5th grade
Creative and expressive arts.

Schluck School
3221 Apalachee Pkwy, Tallahassee, FL 32301
Carolyn Schluck
Type: independent

Hurricane Island Outward Bound (1964)
Tallahassee, FL 32303
J. M. Howard, Staff Specialist, 904-224-2752, FAX: 904-922-6721
Type: independent, non-profit
10 teachers, 1,000 students, mainly at-risk, ages 13-18, 6-12th grade
Governance by board, administrators, staff specialists, director
Teacher qualifications: FL DE requirements, 1st aid, experience in alternative setting
One of four programs nationally; wilderness, urban, service expeditions; credit for peer counseling, outdoor ed, life mgmt skills, environmental science, reading, history; 28-80-day courses; multi-aged classes; rural location.

Magnolia School
2705 W Thorpe St, Tallahassee, FL 32303
Susan Smith, 904-385-3834
Type: independent; scholarships
35-40 students, ages 5-11

School for Applied Individualized Learning (SAIL) (1975)
725 N Macomb St, Tallahassee, FL 32303
Rosanne Wood, 904-488-2468, FAX: 904-922-8483
Type: public choice; scholarships
17 teachers, 218 students, ages 14-19, 9-12th grade
Affiliation: FAASE
Governance by democratic school meeting
Teacher qualifications: FL certification
Environmental science magnet program; Spanish/Latin American history; computer applications; video productions; student court; college dual enrollment; multi-aged classes; extensive field trip; interns accepted.

Montessori School Of Tallahassee
1212 Stone Rd, Tallahassee, FL 32303-3626

Children's House Montessori School
5072 Easy St, Tallahassee, FL 32303-7912

Florida Association for Schools at Home
1000 Devil's Dip, Tallahassee, FL 32308
904-878-2793

Full Flower Education Center (1987)
1816 Mahan Dr, Box 2493, Tallahassee, FL 32308
Irwin Friedman, Director, 904-878-8476
Type: independent, non-profit
4 teachers, 27 students, ages 5-13, K-8th grade
Governance by teachers and principal
Teacher qualifications: love to teach and love children
Intent is to establish a safe environment in which students
    discover what they truly love to do with their lives; no
    letter grades; multi-aged classes; extensive field trips; sub-
    urban location; interns accepted.

Huckleberry School
RR 3, Box 705A, Tallahassee, FL 32308
Laura Wharton
Type: independent

Montessori Cooperative Early School
2521 Mahan Dr, Tallahassee, FL 32308-5405

Grassroots Free School (1972)
2458 Grassroots Way, Tallahassee, FL 32311-9012
Patrick Seery, Coord, 904-656-3629
Type: independent, non-profit; tuition: sliding scale,
    scholarships
6 teachers, 40 students, ages 5-18
Affiliations: NCACS, AERO
Governance by democratic school meeting & parent
    cooperative
Based on Summerhill model; 20 min from Capitol; theater
    productions; whole language; integrated, interest-based
    curricula; independent study; cooperative learning; no
    letter grades; non-compulsory class attendance; multi-
    aged classes; extensive field trips; rural location; interns
    accepted.

A. D. Harris (1977)
819 E 11th St, Panama, FL 32401
Anita Goodman, Prin, 904-872-4590
Type: public at-risk
24 teachers, 300 students, ages 12-21, 6-12th grade
Governance by teachers, principal, board
Teacher qualifications: certification
Performance based; work experience; small classes; school-
    within-a-school; extensive field trips; transportation;
    interns accepted.

Dozier School
Hwy 276, Marianna, FL 32446-8955
Billy Baxter, 904-482-9181
Type: public at-risk

Creative Learning Center
3151 Hyde Park, Pensacola, FL 32503
Mary Lee Porter
Type: Montessori

Petree Pre-K Center
916 E Fairfield Dr, Pensacola, FL 32503-2817
Type: Montessori

O. J. Semmes Elementary School
1250 E Texar Dr, Pensacola, FL 32503-4073
Type: Montessori

Spencer Bibbs Elementary School
2005 N 6th Ave, Pensacola, FL 32503-4521
Gena Keszthelyi
Type: Montessori

Learning Skills Center (1985)
5000 W Mobile Hwy, Pensacola, FL 32506
Hetty Krucke, 904-457-1627
Type: independent, home-based, non-profit; cost: $275/mo,
    scholarships
5 teachers, 35 students, mainly at-risk, ages 10-18, 4-12th
    grade

Governance by board
Individualized; grades by request; accredited HS; teachers and
    students work on having a relationship that counts in their
    lives; extensive field trips; suburban location.

Montessori Early School (1977)
20 Jamison St/1010 N 12th Ave, Pensacola, FL 32507
Mary Gaudet, Adm, 904-456-8735
Tuition: $1,930-2,880/yr
7 teachers, 8 assistants, 155 students, ages infant-12
Affiliation: AMS
Governance by co-owners and teachers
Accomodates students with special needs; childcare; subur-
    ban location; interns accepted.

Florida Parent Education Associaton
9245 Woodrun Rd, Pensacola, FL 32514
Dr. Larry Walker
Type: home-based

A BEKA Correspondence School
(See Resource Section)

West Florida Home Education Support League
PO Box 11720, Pensacola, FL 32524
904-477-0333

Montessori Children's House
RR 3 Box 476, Crestview, FL 32536

Montessori Learning Center of Ft Walton
204 Hospital Dr NE, Ft Walton Beach, FL 32548-5067

Montessori Children's Schoolhouse
8 Pfeiffer St, Gulf Breeze, FL 32561-4410
Karen Blake

Waldorf School of Gainesville (1979)
921 SW Depot Ave, Gainesville, FL 32601
Kathleen Katz, Adm, 904-375-6291
Non-profit; tuition: $2,300-3,200/yr, scholarships
10 teachers, 60 students, ages 3-10, 1-4th grade
Governance by faculty and board
German, Spanish; ESL; after school care; festivals; urban
    location.

Alachua County Home Schoolers
1929 NW 42nd Pl, Gainesville, FL 32605
Kim Hooie, 904-372-8260

Flowers Montessori School
3111 NW 31st Ave, Gainesville, FL 32605-2125

Millhopper Montessori (1977)
8505 NW 39th Ave, Gainesville, FL 32606
Christine Miller, 904-375-6773
Tuition: $290-350/mo
4 teachers, 4 assistants, 940 students, ages infant-9
Accreditations: FL CIS, FL KC
Governance by administrator
State of the art facility; childcare; suburban location; interns
    accepted.

Community Home School
6715 NW 63rd Ave, Ocala, FL 32606
Bob & Nora Whitcomb

Alachua Home School Group
512 Forest St, Alachua, FL 32615
904-462-3930

Hogtown Homeschoolers
180 SW 21-A Rd, Archer, FL 32618
904-622-9735

Jordan Glen School (1974)
12425 SW 154th St, Archer, FL 32618
Jeff Davis, Director, 904-495-2728
Type: independent; tuition: $2,700/yr, scholarships

8 teachers, 84 students, ages 5-14, K-8th grade
Governance by board made up of parents, teachers, principal
Teacher qualifications: education degree, masters in some
   areas
Values individual differences; believes that the joy of living
   and love of learning need never be separated; encourages
   process of exploration and discovery, meaningful academic
   study; multi-aged classes; suburban location; interns
   accepted.

Family Learning Center
(See Resource Section)

Homeschooling Today
(See Resource Section)

Florida Parent Education Association
2901 SW 41st St, Ocala, FL 32674
Gary Regoli, Director
Type: home-based

Altamonte Montessori School
482 Osceola St, Altamonte Springs, FL 32701-7845
Muriel Owens

Grace Home Schoolers
115 Wolf Trail, Casselberry, FL 32707
407-695-3270

School Within A School
Apopka HS, 555 W Martin St, Apopka, FL 32712
Type: public

Children's House
509 E Pennsylvania Ave, Deland, FL 32724-3616
Type: Montessori

Twinkle Stars Montessori School
238 S Amelia Ave, Deland, FL 32724-5914
Virginia Harris-Myrie

Deltona Group
350 Blythville Ave, Deltona, FL 32725
407-860-2318
Type: home-based

Family Centered Learning of Central Florida
1091 Ridge Rd, Longwood, FL 32725
407-332-8502
Type: home-based

North Lake Education Center (1990)
42630 State Rd 19, Altoona, FL 32726
Dorothy McCoo, Prin, 904-669-7979
Type: public at-risk
10 teachers, 130 students, ages 10-14, 6-8th grade
Governance by teachers and principal
Teacher qualifications: FL certification
Students may progress to the next teacher and unit every 21
   days; multi-aged classes; rural location; transportation;
   interns accepted.

Maitland Preparatory
1221 Trinity Woods Ln, Maitland, FL 32751-3159
Type: Montessori

Wymore Career Education Center
100 E Kennedy Blvd, Eatonville, FL 32751-5348
407-644-7518
Type: public choice

Family Learning Exchange
2020 Turpentine Rd, Mims, FL 32754
Type: home-based

Chuluota First Home Schoolers
2060 Miracle Ln, Chuluota, FL 32766
305-366-3270

Crooms School of Choice
2200 W 13th St, Sanford, FL 32771-1636
407-322-6022
Type: public choice

Lake Fern Montessori Academy (1981)
257 Aquinaldo Ave, Titusville, FL 32780
Roxanne L. Richards, 407-268-3365
Tuition: $115/220/230/mo
1 teacher, 4 assistants, 71 students, ages 3–9
Affiliations: NAMTA, AMS
Governance by administrator
Teacher qualifications: FL certification
2.5 acres of natural habitat; nature studies; vegetable garden;
   fruit trees and plants; childcare; urban location; interns
   accepted.

HETE: Home Educators Teaching for Eternity
7853 Clarcona Ocoee Rd, Orlando, FL 32792
407-578-6251

Parkland Home Educators
517 Roughbeard Rd, Winter Park, FL 32792
Beth Girard, Co-Dir, 407-657-7560
50+ families registered; field trips; math/science fair; spelling
   bee; family game night; variety show; worlds fair; monthly
   parent meetings.

YES Program at Astronaut High School
800 War Eagle Blvd, Titusville, FL 32796-2398
Sherry M Johnson, Dir, 407-264-3000
Type: public at-risk
3 teachers, 45 students, ages 16+, 10-12th grade
Competency-based; CAI.

Beeman Park Montessori School
2300 Ridge Ave, Orlando, FL 32803-1636

Montessori Children's House of St James
505 E Ridgewood St, Orlando, FL 32803-5620

Florida at Home
(See Resource Section)

Montessori Casa dei Bambini
2500 S Bumby Ave, Orlando, FL 32806-5013

Discovery Days Montessori
5304 Alpha Dr # 10, Orlando, FL 32810-4422

Family Training Fellowship
6828 W Livingston, Orlando, FL 32835
407-332-8502
Type: home-based

Buena Vista Academy (1990)
11601 Ruby Lake Rd, Orlando, FL 32836
Jean Cross, Adm, 407-238-0014
Non-profit; tuition: $3,100/yr
61 students, mainly international, ages 6-15
Governance by administrator, parent cooperative, board
Fosters creative thinking and learning; suburban location.

Montessori World School (1981)
11693 Ruby Lake Dr, Orlando, FL 32836
W. Nora Yee, Adm, 407-239-6027
Tuition: $1,800/3,375/yr
6 teachers, 3 assistants, 106 students, ages 3–6
Affiliations: AMS, NAMTA
Governance by administrator
Quiet wooded setting; field trips to area attractions; child-
   care; suburban location; interns accepted.

Florida Parent Educators Association (1984)
406 Dartmouth Ave, Melbourne, FL 32901
Monte F. Hancock, MS, Chair, 407-723-1714
4,000 member families.

Children's House of Montessori (1986)
1340 Wickham Rd S, W Melbourne, FL 32904
Sue King, 404-724-2740, FAX: 407-725-7463
Tuition: $170/220/mo
1 teacher, 1 assistant; students mainly international, ages 3-6
Governance by administrator
Interns accepted.

Country Day Montessori School
365 East Dr, Indian Harbor Beach, FL 32937
Cynthia Thomas

Especially for Children
1230 Banana River Dr, Indian Harbor Beach, FL 32937-4162
Cynthia Thomas
Type: Montessori

Suntree Montessori School
2990 Business Center Blvd, Melbourne, FL 32940
Cynthia Thomas

Rockledge Montessori School
3000 S Fistie, Rockledge, FL 32940
Cynthia Thomas

Montessori School of Frederick
210 Carib Dr, Merritt Island, FL 32952-3647

Island Montessori School
655 Oleander St, Merritt Island, FL 32952-3747

Vero Beach Support Group
1016 21st Ct, Vero Beach, FL 32960
407-562-4380
Type: home-based

J. W. Johnson School
735 W 23rd St, Hialeah, FL 33010-2141
J. Molina
Type: Montessori

Montessori Children's House of Miami Lakes
6381 Miami Lakeway NE, Miami Lakes, FL 33014
Charlene Thibodeau

Joella C. Good Elementary
6350 NW 188 Tr, Miami, FL 33015
Rosemarie Jaworski, 305-625-2008
Type: magnet
Student ages 4+,-K
Montessori.

Apple Tree Montessori
7755 NW 178th St, Miami, FL 33015-3859
Susan Levine

Sunrise Montessori Holistic School
2360 W 68th St # 10, Hialeah, FL 33016-5501
Armando Elias

Rainbow Montessori School
3351 N SR 7, Hollywood, FL 33021-2708
Gila Burke

Hollywood Hills Private School
5516 Hollywood Blvd, Hollywood, FL 33021-6458
Type: Montessori

Hilltop Montessori Elementary
2921 SW 56th Ave, Hollywood, FL 33023-5301

Avocado Elementary
16969 SW 294 St, Homestead, FL 33030
Carol S. Bernstein, 305-247-4942
Type: magnet
K-2nd grade
Gifted program.

Kingswood Montessori Academy (1968)
20130 SW 304th St, Homestead, FL 33030
Elizabeth Calabrese, 305-248-2308, FAX: same
Tuition: $2,300/3,300/3,700/yr
4 teachers, 6 assistants, 106 students, ages infant-12
Affiliation: Dade ANS; accreditation: AISFL
Governance by administrator
5 wooded acres in the Redlands; childcare; rural location;
   interns accepted.

Naranja Elementary School
13990 SW 264 St, Naranja, FL 33032
Johanna Teague, 305-258-3401
Type: magnet
4-5th grade
Gifted program.

Ocean Reef Schoolhouse
Plaza Bldg Box B-108, 31 Ocean Reef Dr, Key Largo, FL 33037
Type: Montessori

Montessori Childrens House
99341 Overseas Hyw, Key Largo, FL 33037-4246
Carol Hilton

Montessori Children's School of Key West, Inc
1214 Varela St, Key West, FL 33040-3314
Elizabeth Shewan

Nathan Young School
14120 NW 24th Ave, Opa Locka, FL 33054
E. Pace
Type: Montessori

Opa-Locka Elementary
600 Ahmad St, Opa-Locka, FL 33054
Dr S. Frank McKoy, 305-688-4605
Type: magnet
2-5th grade
Gifted program.

Rainbow Park Elementary
15355 NW 19 Ave, Opa-Locka, FL 33054
Henry Haddon, 305-688-4631
Type: magnet
4-6th grade
Expressive arts.

Golden Glades School
16520 NW 28th Ave, Opa Locka, FL 33054-6493
A. Jackson
Type: Montessori

Parkway Middle School
2349 NW 175 St, Miami, FL 33055
Robert Edwards, 305-624-9613
Type: magnet
7-8th grade
Humanities.

North Carol City Elementary
19010 NW 37 Ave, Opa-Locka, FL 33056
Barbara Hawkins, 305-624-2615
Type: magnet
K-6th grade
Gifted program.

Off Campus Alternative Programs
1400 NE 6th St #8, Pompano Beach, FL 33060-6536
Charles Hilgenfeldt, 305-786-7818
Type: public at-risk

North Broward School
3701 NE 22nd Ave, Lighthouse Point, FL 33064-3934
Type: Montessori

Coral Springs Montessori Preschool (1991)
11380 W Sample Rd, Coral Springs, FL 33065
John Freda, Dir, 305-344-0027

3 teachers, 3 assistants, 68 students, mainly international, ages 3-6
Affiliation: AMS
Interns accepted.

The Learning Experience of Coral Springs
3811 Coral Springs Dr, Coral Springs, FL 33065-2399
Type: Montessori

Dade County Division Of Magnet Schools/Programs
1444 Biscayne Blvd #303, Miami, FL 33132
Miriam Stoudt
Type: Montessori

New World School of Arts
300 NE 2 Ave, Miami, FL 33132
Dr Mandy Offerle, 305-237-3135
Type: magnet
10-12th grade

Southern Montessori Institute
3060 Orange St, Coconut Grove, FL 33133
Type: Montessori teacher education

Charles R. Drew Elementary
1775 NW 60 St, Miami, FL 33133
Frederick Morley, 305-624-1495
Type: magnet
4-6th grade
Expressive arts.

Crestview Elementary
2201 NW 187 St, Opa-Locka, FL 33133
Jill Witlin, 305-624-1395
Type: magnet
1-5th grade
Writing.

Carrollton School of the Sacred Heart
3747 Main Hwy, Miami, FL 33133-5907
Type: Montessori

Sheandoah School
1023 SW 21st Ave, Miami, FL 33135-5049
M. Elias
Type: Montessori

Phyllis Wheatley School
1801 NW 1st Pl, Miami, FL 33136-1795
D. Pascal
Type: Montessori

Design & Architecture High School
4001 NE 2 Ave, Miami, FL 33137
Jacq. Hinchey-Sipes, 305-573-7135
Type: magnet
7-12th grade
Design & Architecture.

Montessori School of Miami Beach
7141 Indian Creek Dr, Miami Beach, FL 33141-3030

Allapattah Middle School
1331 NW 46 St, Miami, FL 33142
Maria Jerkins, 305-634-9787
Type: magnet
6-8th grade
Media arts.

Charles Drew Middle School
1801 NW 60 St, Miami, FL 33142
Gail Senita, 305-633-6057
Type: magnet
7-8th grade
Visual and performing arts.

Olinda Elementary
5536 NW 2l Ave, Miami, FL 33142
Lenora Smith, 305-633-0308

Type: magnet
1-6th grade
Gifted program.

Orchard Villa School
5720 NW 13th Ave, Miami, FL 33142-2699
C. McCalla
Type: Montessori

Alexander School, Inc
6050 SW 57th Ave, Miami, FL 33143
James R. McGhee, Adm, 305-665-6274, FAX: 305-665-7726
Type: Montessori; tuition: $3,850-7,310/yr
17 teachers, 30 assistants, 477 students, mainly international, ages infant-12
Accreditations: FCIS, FKC, AISF, AMS
Governance by administrator
State of the art computer lab; childcare; suburban location; transportation; interns accepted.

Ludlam Elementary
6639 SW 74 St, S Miami, FL 33143
Donald Schwartz, 305-667-5551
Type: magnet
K-6th grade
Gifted program.

South Miami Elementary
6800 SW 60 St, S Miami, FL 33143
Rexford Darrow, 305-667-8847
Type: magnet
4-6th grade
Expressive arts.

South Miami Middle School
6750 SW 60 St, S Miami, FL 33143
Ms Ivery or Ms Valdez, 305-661-3481
Type: magnet
7-9th grade
Center for the arts.

The Children's House
7701 SW 76th Ave, Miami, FL 33143-4125
Susan Menendez
Type: Montessori

Sunset Montessori School
7430 Sunset Dr, Miami, FL 33143-4130
Janet Haigney

Lillie C Evans (1990)
1891 NW 75th St, Miami, FL 33147
Geraldine W. Tisdol, 305-691-4973
Type: Public choice Montessori
2 teachers, 2 assistants, 56 students, mainly at-risk, ages 3-9
Governance by teachers, administrators, democratic school meeting
Urban location; interns accepted.

St Christopher's Montessori School
95 Harbor Dr, Key Biscayne, FL 33149-1499
Catherine Hubbell

Miami Northwestern High School
7007 NW 12 Ave, Miami, FL 33150
Dr James Monroe, 305-836-0991
Type: magnet
9-12th grade
Visual and performing arts.

Martin Luther King School
7124 NW 12th Ave, Miami, FL 33150-3693
B. Nixon
Type: Montessori

Holmes School
1175 NW 67th St, Miami, FL 33150-4198
J. Goa
Type: Montessori

Everglades Elementary
8375 SW 16 St, Miami, FL 33155
Dr Stanley Dansky, 305-264-4154
Type: magnet
K-5th grade
Gifted program.

Lego Resource Center
3245 SW 60th Ave, Miami, FL 33155
Robert Alan, Dir
Tuition: $322/mo
Apprenticeships in powerboat maintenance, landscaping,
    dentistry, and vegetarian cooking; multi-aged classes; no
    letter grades; interns accepted.

South Miami High School
6856 SW 53 St, Miami, FL 33155
Judith Weiner, 305-666-5871
Type: magnet
9-12th grade
Media arts.

Wagner Montessori School (1989)
6330 SW 40th St, Miami, FL 33155
Andrew K. Wagner, Adm, 305-661-6434, FAX: 305-663-9274
Tuition: $2,965/2,965/4,995/yr
3 teachers, 4 assistants, 71 students, ages infant-9
Affiliations: AMS, NAEYC
Governance by administrator
CAI; childcare; suburban location; interns accepted.

Killian Montessori School
8640 SW 112th St, Miami, FL 33156-4325
Janice Kimrey

Perrine Elementary
8851 SW 168 St, Perrine, FL 33157
Rosemary Fuller, 305-235-2442
Type: magnet
K-4th grade
Creative arts.

R. R. Moton Elementary
l8050 Homestead Ave, Perrine, FL 33157
Yvonne Hinson, 305-235-3612
Type: magnet
5-6th grade
Expressive arts.

Winhold Montessori School
17700 Old Cutler Rd, Miami, FL 33157-6326
Eleanor Winhold

Star Bright Child Development
1253 NE 112th St, Miami, FL 33161
Type: Montessori

Barry University
11300 NE 2nd Ave, Miami Shores, FL 33161
Dr Ijya C. Tulloss, Dir, 305-899-3714, FAX: 899-3630
Affiliation: AMS; accreditation: MACTE
Governance by board of trustees
Master's awarded with teaching certificate; computer lab;
    bookstore.

Von Wedel Montessori School (1968)
11820 NE 13th Ave, N Miami, FL 33161
R. A. or Tamara Von Wedel, 305-893-9876
Tuition: $2,350-3,700/yr
4 teachers, 1 assistant; student ages 3-9
Accreditation: AMS
Governance by administrator
Traditional Montessori program; 2 acres of greenery; swim-
    ming pool; 2 large preschool classrooms; childcare; no
    letter grades; suburban location; interns accepted.

Montessori Children's House
9718 Bird Rd, Miami, FL 33165-4032

Scotts Lake Montessori Magnet (1988)
1160 NW 175th St, Miami, FL 33169
Dr Linda Levene, Head Tch; Christell Rocach, Prin, 305-624-
    1493, FAX: 305-625-2567
18 teachers, 3 assistants, 265 students, mainly international,
    ages 4-11
Governance by administrator
Teacher qualifications: FL certification
Childcare; transportation; interns accepted.

Pine Villa Elementary
21799 SW 117 Ct, Goulds, FL 33170
Melvin Dennis, 305-258-5366
Type: magnet
Student ages 4+,-4th grade
Montessori.

Mays Middle School
11700 Hainlin Mill Dr, Miami, FL 33170
Robert Stinson, 305-233-2300
Type: magnet
6-8th grade
Visual and performing arts; humanities.

F. C. Martin Elementary
14250 Boggs Dr, Richmond Hghts, FL 33176
Ossie Hollis, 305-238-3688
Type: magnet
5-6th grade
Gifted program.

Two Ragamuffins in Perpetual Search-mode (TRIPS)
(See Resource Section)

Caribbean Elementary
11990 SW 200 St, Miami, FL 33177
Carmen Suarez, 305-233-7131
Type: magnet
K-4th grade
Gifted program.

Montessori School Of Kendall
11860 SW 80th St, Miami, FL 33183-4821

Florida Associationof Alternative School Educators
(See Resource Section)

Bethune Elementary
2400 Meade St, Hollywood, FL 33220
Linda Arnold, 305-926-0860
Type: magnet
K-5th grade
Visual and performing arts.

Norland Middle School
1235 NW l92 Tr, Miami, FL 33269
John F. Gilbert, 305-653-1210
Type: magnet
7-9th grade
Center for the arts.

Parkway Middle School
3600 NW 5th Ct, Ft Lauderdale, FL 33311
Willie Dudley, 305-797-4550
Type: magnet
6-8th grade
Visual and performing arts; computers; high technology.

Summit Private School (1981)
1725 Davie Blvd, Ft Lauderdale, FL 33312
Judy Dempsey, 305-523-9489
Type: Montessori; tuition: $295-395/mo
9 teachers, 4 assistants, 123 students, ages infant-12
Affiliation: AMS
Governance by administrator
Swimming; gymnastics; dance; drama; karate; computer;
    childcare; urban location; interns accepted.

Blake School
7001 W Sunrise Blvd, Plantation, FL 33313-4427
Type: Montessori

Nova Blanche Forman Elementary School (1965)
3521 SW Davie Rd, Fort Lauderdale, FL 33314
Margaret Underhill, Prin, 305-370-1788, FAX: -1655
Type: public choice
57 teachers, 960 students, ages 5-11, K-5th grade
Governance by school Improvement Team (including parents)
Teacher qualifications: BA, certification in elem ed
A Research and Development Center that has piloted many
    county projects, e.g., the original ESL, Saludos and GOTCHA
    programs, Behavior Change Program, Study-Travel, and
    primary multi-age classes; urban location; transportation;
    interns accepted.

Montessori Children's House
6590 SW 39th St, Fort Lauderdale, FL 33314-2416

Jacaranda School
8250 Peters Rd, Plantation, FL 33324-3298
Type: Montessori

Three Village Montessori
1400 Indian Ter, Fort Lauderdale, FL 33326-2771
Cheri Kaplan

North Andrews Gardens
345 NE 56 St, Ft Lauderdale, FL 33334
Sidney Ditkowsky, 305-928-0370
Type: magnet
K-5th grade
Visual and performing arts.

Walker Elementary
1001 NW 4th St, Ft Lauderdale, FL 33334
Lucy Thomas, 305-765-6878
Type: magnet
K-5th grade
Visual and performing arts.

Children's Garden Montessori
201 E Commercial Blvd, Fort Lauderdale, FL 33334-1625

Little Flower Montessori
533 E Oakland Park Blvd, Fort Lauderdale, FL 33334-2151
Mary Cronin Byrd

Children's House of the Palm Beaches
211 Trinity Place, West Palm Beach, FL 33401
Dr Helena Valldejuli-ButlerLois Carter
Type: Montessori

Little School of Rosarian Academy
807 North Flagler Dr, West Palm Beach, FL 33401-3705
Marie Schultz
Type: Montessori

Wee Wisdom Montessori School
1957 S Flagler Dr, West Palm Beach, FL 33401-7715

Village Montessori
21 W 21st St, Riviera Beach, FL 33404-5501

South Olive Elementary School
7101 S Olive Ave, West Palm Beach, FL 33405-4769
Type: Montessori

Hillwood Private School-Montessori
1366 Victory Dr, West Palm Beach, FL 33406

Palm Beach County Public Schools (1993)
3314 Forest Hill Blvd, A-210, West Palm Beach, FL 33406-5813
Patricia M. Hollings, Coord, 407-434-8347
Type: public choice
160 students

School of the Arts, Middle & High
3701 N Shore Dr, W Palm Beach, FL 33407
Edward Duhy, 407-881-4698
Type: magnet
7-11th grade
Dance/Music/Theatre/Visual & Performing Arts/Communica-
tions.

Sabal Palm School
4400 N Australian Ave, West Palm Beach, FL 33407-3699
Joanne R. Cochran, Prin, 407-881-4797
Type: public at-risk
9 teachers, 250 students, ages 10-16, 4-10th grade
Affiliation: Palm Beach City Commissioners
Governance by teachers and principal
Teacher qualifications: In-field academic, vocational
    certification
Level system; rewards and incentives for appropriate behav-
    ior; tutoring; multi-aged classes; urban location; interns
    accepted.

Childrens Montessori House
4015 Spruce Ave, West Palm Beach, FL 33407-4215

Montessori Unlimited
10277 Allamanda Blvd, Palm Beach Gardens, FL 33410
Elisabeth Goossens

Holland Northlake Day School
8788 N Military Trail, Palm Beach Gardens, FL 33410-6240
Diann Holland
Type: Montessori

Montessori Children's Center (1989)
353 Hiatt Dr, Palm Beach Gardens, FL 33418-7106
Mary C. Sandrini, Administrator, 407-626-9222, FAX: 407-626-
    0418
Tuition: $375/425/450
2 teachers, 10 assistants, 65 students, ages infant-6
Affiliation: IMS
Governance by administrator
Custom designed facilities equipped with Nienhuis Montes-
    sori teaching materials; childcare; suburban location;
    interns accepted.

Montessori Academy
12532 Cobblestone Way, Boca Raton, FL 33428-2419

Claremont Montessori School (1985)
2450 NW 5th Ave, Boca Raton, FL 33431
Nancy Hallenberg, Dir, 407-394-7674
Non-profit; tuition: $4,800/yr
2 teachers, 1 assistant, 22 students, ages 6-12
Affiliation: AMS
Governance by board
Montessori apparatus; camping skills taught from age 6-HS;
    new 8,000 sq-ft facility; suburban location.

Summit Private School of Boca Raton (1985)
3881 NW 3rd Ave, Boca Raton, FL 33431
Jeanne Hudlett, Adm, 407-338-5020, FAX: 407-338-5021
Type: Montessori; tuition: $330-435/mo
10 teachers, 6 assistants, 172 students, ages infant-9
Affiliations: AMS, NCME
Governance by administrator
Children's garden; fish and turtle ponds; American History
    studied in authentic tipi; childcare; urban location; interns
    accepted.

Children's House of Boca Raton (1988)
100 Pine Circle, Boca Raton, FL 33432
Dr Kathleen L. Bowser, Dir, 407-391-0074
Type: Montessori; tuition: $3,100/4,500/yr
6 teachers, 2 assistants, 50 students, ages 3-6
Affiliations: NAMTA, NAEYC, SACUS; accreditation: AMS
Governance by administrator
Multi-aged classes; no letter grades; urban location; interns
    accepted.

Addison Academy
19860 Jog Rd, Boca Raton, FL 33434-4454
Type: Montessori

Deerfield Park Elementary
627 SW 3nd Ave, Deerfield Beach, FL 33441
Carolyn Eggelletion, 305-481-5777
Type: magnet
K-5th grade
Visual and performing arts.

S. D. Spady Elementary
330 NW 8th Ave, Palm Beach, FL 33444
Mavis Allred, 407-243-1558
Type: magnet
K-5th grade
Montessori.

Unity Wee Wisdom Montessori School
624 N H St, Lake Worth, FL 33460-2946

Northern Private Schools
1822 High Ridge Rd, Lake Worth, FL 33461-6172
Type: Montessori

Guardian Angels Montessori School
1325 Cardinal Ln, Lantana, FL 33462-4205

Oliver's Academy
PO Box 4041, Tequesta, FL 33469
Laura Ingman, Secretary, 407-340-0759
Type: independent; tuition: variable
19 students, pre K-12th grade
Bible-based; family-oriented; cooperative; emphasizes self-
    teaching.

School of Choice
541 Rardin Ave, Pahokee, FL 33476-2399
407-924-6470
Type: public choice

Gulf Stream School
3600 Gulf Stream Rd, Gulf Stream, FL 33483-7499
Nancy Froio
Type: Montessori

Montessori Unlimited/West Glades Montessori
20400 Cain Blvd, Boca Raton, FL 33498-6746
Elisabeth Goossens

Holy Name Academy
12117 Wichers Rd, Dade City, FL 33525
Sr Roberta Bailey
Type: Montessori

Countryside Montessori Academy
16720 Tobacco Rd, Lutz, FL 33549

Priory Early Childhood Center
Drawer H, St Leo, FL 33574-4002
Type: Montessori

Sarasota Public Schools Montessori Program
Booker MS, 2250 Myrtle St, Sarasota, FL 33580
Diane Riva

The Learning Tree Montessori School
305 S Melville Ave, Tampa, FL 33606

Beach Park Private School
4200 W North A St, Tampa, FL 33609-2269
Ann and Dick Winkler
Type: Montessori

Montessori Country Day School (1983)
5705 Interbay, Tampa, FL 33611
Polly Nelson, Dir, 813-831-4378
Tuition: $1,800/2,300/3,400/yr
3 teachers, 3 assistants, 55 students, ages infant-6

Accreditation: AMI
Governance by administrator
Large yard includes gardens, swings, tree houses, chicken
    coops, rabbit hutches, large deck; convenient to Hyde
    Park, Davis Islands, Palma Ceia and South Tampa; urban
    location; interns accepted.

The Montessori House Day School (1970)
7010 Hanley Rd, Tampa, FL 33614
Kay H. Murrell, Head Dir, 813-884-7220, FAX: 813-961-8639
Tuition: $2,350/3,500/yr
1 teacher, 1 assistant, 30 students, ages 3-6
Affiliations: NAMTA, HAANS; accreditations: AMS, FL CIS, FL KC
Governance by administrator
MTTI satellite site; trees; grass; basketball court; fitness mate-
    rials; childcare; suburban location; interns accepted.

Under the Rainbow Montessori Learning Center
79l6 N Himes Ave, Tampa, FL 33614

Montessori Academy of Temple Terrace
5804 Gibson Ave, Temple Terrace, FL 33617-1252
Sonia Johnson

Montessori Early Learning Institute
3823 W Hudson Ln, Tampa, FL 33624
Sonia Johnson

The Montessori House Day School (1980)
5117 Ehrlich Rd, Tampa, FL 33624
Kay H. Murrell, Head Dir, 813-961-9295, FAX: 813-961-8639
Tuition: $2,430-3,870/yr
9 teachers, 5 assistants, 142 students, ages 3-12
Affiliations: NAMTA, HAANS; accreditations: AMS, FL CIS, FL KC
Governance by administrator
Full complement of Montessori materials; faculty develop-
    ment; 3 acres; outdoor equipment; gardens; basketball
    court; aerobics court; childcare; suburban location; interns
    accepted.

Montessori In The City
3218 W Bay To Bay Blvd, Tampa, FL 33629-7106
Ann and Dick Winkler

Montessori Children's House of Tampa Palms
15347 Amberly Dr, Tampa, FL 33647-2144
Yvonne Kuhn

Montessori By The Sea
1603 Gulf Way, Saint Petersburg Beach, FL 33706-4237
Sue Haynie

Sunflower School
5313 27th Ave S, Gulfport, FL 33707
Molly Barnes, 813-321-7657
Type: independent; tuition: $2,850/yr, scholarships
50 students, ages 4-12
Environmental, community emphasis; art; music; drama;
    Spanish; computers; homeschooler advice, materials,
    books; no letter grades.

Tri-County Coordinated Child Care
PO Box 1269, Highland City, FL 33846-1269
Type: Montessori

Lifetime Books and Gifts
(See Resource Section)

Edison Learning Center
3243 Clifford St, Ft Myers, FL 33901-3514
Type: independent

Gulf Coast Homeschool
2454 Burton Ave, Ft Myers, FL 33907
813-936-5182

Montessori School of Ft Myers (1969)
2151 Crystal Dr, Ft Myers, FL 33907
Charlie or Linda Touton, Adms, 813-936-4515

Tuition: $2,150/3,400/yr
3 teachers, 3 assistants, 60 students, ages 3-12
Affiliation: AMS; accreditations: FLKC, NIPSA
Governance by administrator
Multi-cultural staff, students; childcare; urban location;
   interns accepted.

Wright Montessori Academy
37 Barkley Cir, Fort Myers, FL 33907-7531

Lee County Schools
3800 Michigan Ave, Fort Myers, FL 33916
Beth Godwin, Dropout Prev Coord, 813-334-6221, FAX: 332-
   4839
Type: public choice/at-risk
120 teachers, 1400 students, mainly at-risk, ages 10-23,
   4-12th grade
Teacher qualifications: FL Certification
Teen parenting; accelerated credit; no letter grades; extensive field trips; urban, suburban and rural locations; transportation; interns accepted.

Bonita Montessori School
27040 Imperial St, Bonita Springs, FL 33923
Kathy Leitch, Dir, 813-992-5138, FAX: 813-481-5413
Tuition: $2,250-2,565/yr
2 teachers, 2 assistants, 30 students, ages 3-6
Affiliations: AMS, NAEYC
Governance by administrator
Private wooded location; active parent involvement; inclu-
   sive; peace curriculum; childcare; suburban location;
   interns accepted.

Florida Parent Education Association
609 Greenwood, Lehigh Acres, FL 33936
Steve Shelfer, Dir
Type: home-based

Central Sun Montessori Inc
1291 Hilltop Dr, Naples, FL 33940-3323

Cedar Montessori School (1983)
10904 Winterview Dr, Naples, FL 33942
Roy Marshall, Administrator, 813-597-7190
Non-profit; tuition: $2,530-3,700/yr
5 teachers, 7 assistants, 136 students, ages infant-12
Non-discriminatory; childcare.

New Challenge School (1990)
16529 Joppa Ave, Port Charlotte, FL 33948
Gregg Sinner, Prin, 813-625-0080, FAX: 813-625-3409
Type: public at-risk
10 teachers, 180 students, ages 14-20, HS
Governance by prin; faculty, student reps; democratic school
   meeting; board; parent coop; county office
Teacher qualifications: Florida certification-any field/level
Raywid Type I ed alt for teen parents, others; multi-aged
   classes; suburban location; transportation; interns
   accepted.

Montessori School of Charlotte County, Inc (1979)
4344 Pinnacle St, Punta Gorda, FL 33980
Maja B. Wolfe, Head, 813-629-7710
Tuition: $285/mo
2 teachers, 1 assistant, 25 students, ages 3-9
Governance by administrator
Extra Spanish lessons; gymnastics; pre-ballet; childcare; sub-
   urban location; interns accepted.

Panama Support Group at Ft Amador
PSC Box 1578, APO Miami, FL 34001
Type: home-based

Center for Education (1976)
6024 26th St W, Bradenton, FL 34207
Janice Mattina, 813-753-4987
Type: Montessori; tuition: $2,200-3,245/yr
7 teachers, 4 assistants, 136 students, ages 3-12

Governance by administrator
Words in Color reading program; childcare; suburban location; interns accepted.

Gulf Coast Marine Institute
301 7th St E, Bradenton, FL 34208-1139
Janice Norrie, 813-741-3102
Type: public at-risk

Countryside Montessori School (1984)
5237 Ashton Rd, Sarasota, FL 34233
Kitty Williams, Dir, 904-922-4949
Tuition: $4,400/yr
9 teachers, 150 students, ages 3-12
Affiliation: AMS
Governance by board of trustees
Teacher qualifications: Montessori Certification
Located on organic farm; environmental principles; foreign
   language; music; art; creative movement; no letter grades;
   extensive field trips; non-compulsory class attendance;
   multi-aged classes; suburban location; interns accepted.

New Directions
4409 Sawyer Rd, Sarasota, FL 34233-1808
813-361-6580
Type: public choice

New College
5700 N Tamiami Tr, Sarasota, FL 34243-2197
Jim Feeney, 813-359-4200

Ideal High School
1130 Indian Hill Blvd, Venice, FL 34293
813-486-2131
Type: public at-risk

Cornerstone School (1982)
2313 SE Lake Weir St, Ocala, FL 34471
Carol Montag, Dir, 904-351-8840
Type: independent, non-profit; tuition: $1,750/yr,
   scholarships
12 teachers, 118 students, ages 3-10, pre K-5th grade
Affiliations: FCIS, NPE
Governance by principal, parent cooperative, board
Whole language; literature-based reading; curriculum suspended for 5-day, thematic mini-courses with mixed
   groups; no letter grades; extensive field trips; rural location; interns accepted.

Phoenix Center of Marion County
2091 NE 35th St, Ocala, FL 34479-2900
904-732-6542
Type: public choice

Wider Horizons School (1986)
4060 Castle Ave, Spring Hill, FL 34609
Dr Domenick or Julie Maglio, 904-686-1934
Type: Montessori; tuition: $7.50-17/day
5 teachers, 150 students, ages infant-15
Accreditation: NIPSA
Governance by administrator
Research curriculum approach; childcare; suburban location;
   transportation.

The Home School Shopper
(See Resource Section)

Belleair Montessori School
905 Ponce De Leon Blvd, Clearwater, FL 34616-1019

Florida Parent Education Association
14739 Mocking Bird Ln E, Clearwater, FL 34620
Type: home-based

Ainsworth Montessori Academy
5990 142nd Ave N, Clearwater, FL 34620-2806

Lake Fern Academy (1975)
22126 Shoreside Dr, Land O Lakes, FL 34639-4626
Nettie Rossi, Owner, 813-264-5362
Type: Montessori; tuition: $2,730-4,410/yr
7 teachers, 4 assistants, 122 students, ages infant-12
Affiliation: AMS
Governance by administrator
Year-round; quarterly breaks; "camps" during breaks enhance
   special areas of study; childcare; suburban location; interns
   accepted.

ESP Publishers, Inc
(See Resource Section)

Montessori Learning Circle
9618 Denton Ave, Hudson, FL 34667-4339
Mary Bowman

Palm Harbor Montessori School
2313 Nebraska Ave, Palm Harbor, FL 34683-3944
Christine Norbom

World of Knowledge: A Montessori School
1935 Abacus Rd, Holiday, FL 34690-5540
Rene Womelsdorf

Open Door Private School of Pinellas Co, Inc
710 Scotland St, Dunedin, FL 34698
Lucy N. Basso Smith, 813-733-8202
Type: home-based; cost: $100/yr
50 students, K-12th grade
Administrative/record keeping office for homeschoolers; info
   on resources, scholarships, field trips, testing.

Dunedin Montessori Academy
637 Michigan Blvd, Dunedin, FL 34698-2618
Lydia Banome

Lee Education Center (1988)
207 N Lee St, Leesburg, FL 34748
Dr Joyce Driver, 904-787-0043
Type: public at-risk
10 teachers, 150 students, ages 12-19, 6-12th grade
Governance by teachers and principal
Teacher qualifications: FL certification
Competency-based; multi-aged classes; suburban location;
   interns accepted.

Leesburg Montessori School
415 Lee St, Leesburg, FL 34748-5082

Montessori NEST
608 S 9th St # D, Leesburg, FL 34748-6378
Merry Hadden

Sun Grove Montessori School (1978)
5610 Oleander Ave, Ft Pierce, FL 34982
Barbara Scott, Adm, 407-464-5436
Non-profit; tuition: $200-335/mo
4 teachers, 4 assistants, 75 students, mainly international,
   ages 3-9
Affiliations: NAMTA, MTA, NCME
Governance by administrator, board of trustees
Complete Montessori; gardening project with UF Coop Ext;
   Edu-Kinestetics; effective parenting classes; ungraded;
   childcare; suburban location; interns accepted.

Treasure Coast Homeschoolers
5902 Sea Grape Dr, Ft Pierce, FL 34982
LaWanda Sutherland, 407-465-8521

Martin Downs Montessori
3001 SW Mill Creek Way, Palm City, FL 34990-3155

Georgia

Avendale High School
1192 Clarendon Rd, Avendale Estate, GA 30002
Amers Kitchens, 404-289-6766
Type: magnet
8-12th grade
Center for performing arts.

Friends School of Atlanta (1991)
112 Adair St, Decatur, GA 30030
Waman W. French, Head, 404-373-8746
Type: Quaker, non-profit; tuition: $5,000/yr
15 teachers, 92 students, ages 4.5-11, K-6th grade
Affiliation: Friends Council on Education
Governance by board
Developmental approach; manipulatives, experiences build
   concepts for learning; philosophy of peace, justice, simplicity, diversity, community; no letter grades; multi-aged
   classes.

Lullwater School (1973)
705 S Candler St, Decatur, GA 30030
Dr Joan K Teach, 404-378-6643, FAX: 404-377-0879
Type: independent, non-profit; tuition: $5,900, scholarships
9 teachers, 60 students, mainly at-risk, ages 4.5-14, K-9th
   grade
Affiliations: AIGE, CEC
Governance by board
Teacher qualifications: BS, certification; specialization, MS
   preferred
Confluent education, interrelated curriculum; continuous

progress; multi-racial, holistic; supportive of ADD and LD
students; multi-aged classes; extensive field trips; urban
location.

TAPS Program
320 N McDonough St, Decatur, GA 30030
George Hickman, 404-370-4438
Type: public choice
For students who fall just below gifted classification; 1 day/
   week; identical to state's program; transportation.

DeKalb County Magnet Programs
3770 N Decatur Rd, Decatur, GA 30032
Charles Hutcheson, Exec Dir, 404-297-2307
Type: public choice
4th grade
Atherton Writing Academy (4th grade; computer literacy);
   Clifton Computer Education (4-7th grade; one worksta-
   tion/student); Avondale ES Academy for Performing Arts
   (K-7th grade); Avondale HS Center for Performing Arts (5
   year); Kittridge MagS for High Achievers (emphasis on cre-
   ativity, critical thinking, independence, communication);
   Browns Mill MagP for High Achievers (emphasis on global
   ed, foreign language, and computer technology); Hooper
   Alexander Spanish MagP; Towers HS Foreign Language
   MagP (3 hrs/day earns 2 yrs credit in 1); Canby Lane
   Academy of Mathematics, Science, and Technology (4-7th
   grade, lab settings); Snapfinger Academy of Mathematics,
   Science, and Technology (4-7th grade, lab settings).

Story Book School, Inc
3471 Glenwood Rd, Decatur, GA 30032-4407
Type: Montessori

Northwoods Montessori World of Children
1879 Columbia Dr, Decatur, GA 30032-5908

Atlanta Network
c/o Paymer, 1158 McConnell Dr, Decatur, GA 30033
Type: home-based

Arbor Montessori School
2998 Lavista Rd, Decatur, GA 30033-1308

Occupational Education Center–South
3303 Panthersville Rd, Decatur, GA 30034
Larry Ladner, 404-241-9400
Type: public choice
500 students

A Child's Campus
2780 Flat Shoals Rd, Decatur, GA 30034-1034
Type: Montessori

Atherton Elementary
1674 Atherton Dr, Atlanta, GA 30035
Paul Warner, 404-284-6662
Type: magnet
K-7th grade
Arts; writing academy.

Progressive School System
2637 Panola Rd, Lithonia, GA 30058
Type: Montessori

Montessori Education Center #2
81 Bankhead Hwy SW, Mableton, GA 30059-2509

The Hands-On Math
353 Lemon St, Marietta, GA 30060
JoAnn Crimm, 404-424-3674
Type: public choice
ES

Casa DiBambini Montessori
4010 Lower Roswell Rd, Marietta, GA 30068-4058

Country Brook Montessori School (1987)
2175 Norcross Tucker Rd, Norcross, GA 30071
Leroy Moffitt, 404-446-2397, FAX: 404-448-2805
Tuition: $250-375/mo
6 teachers, 6 assistants, 98 students, mainly international,
    ages 2-12
Affiliations: AMS, NAMTA, MACTE; accreditation: NCME
Governance by administrator
Spanish; computers; multi-cultural enrollment; located in
    high-tech area in fast growing county; teacher training
    facility for NCME; childcare; urban location; interns
    accepted.

The Hammond School
11273 Elkins Rd, Roswell, GA 30076-1202
Type: Montessori

High Meadows
PO Box 859, Roswell, GA 30077
Sheryl Smith, 404-993-2940
Type: independent; tuition: $4,140/yr
275 students, pre K-12th grade

National Center for Montessori Education
(See Resource Section)

Covered Bridge Montessori School (1981)
3941 Covered Bridge Rd, Smyrna, GA 30082
Barbara Moffitt, 404-434-3181, FAX: 404-434-1128
Tuition: $230-375/mo
7 teachers, 14 assistants, 136 students, ages infant-9
Affiliation: MACTE-MEG; accreditation: NCME

Governance by administrator
On 3 acres in wooded subdivision; pool; childcare; suburban
    location; interns accepted.

NCME Atlanta / National Reporter
3951 Covered Bridge Rd, Smyrna, GA 30082
Barbara Moffitt, Dir
Type: Montessori

Stone Mountain Montessori
4700 E Ponce De Leon Ave, Stone Mountain, GA 30083-1230

Rockbridge Montessori School
4733 Rockbridge Rd, Stone Mountain, GA 30083-4248

Aurora Montessori Academy
4451 Hugh Howell Hwy, Tucker, GA 30084

Montessori School at Brookstone
1680 Brookstone Walk, Acworth, GA 30101-4572
Tudy Cook

Star Student Program
123 Brown St, Carrollton, GA 30117
Patricia Stokes, 404-834-1868
Students mainly at-risk, 5-6th grade
Weekly tutorial; emphasis on rewarding success.

Douglas County Programs
9030 Hwy 5, PO Box 1077, Douglasville, GA 30133
Randy Brittain, 404-920-4000
Gifted; vocational; co-op; JTPA; evening HS; joint HS/college
    enrollment; adult ed.

Montessori School of Douglas County Inc
8014 Duralee Ln, Douglasville, GA 30134-2539

International Academy
4160 Vansant Rd, Douglasville, GA 30135
Aghdas Kashi
Type: Montessori

Duluth Montessori School
2997 N Peachtree St, Duluth, GA 30136-2745

Cobb County Homeschoolers
813 Wyntuck Dr, Kennesaw, GA 30144

Montessori Children's House of Cobb Academy
2871 Cherokee St, Kennesaw, GA 30144-2823

Montessori Children's House of Kennesaw
3238 Cherokee St, Kennesaw, GA 30144-2901

Rome Montessori, Inc
PO Box 807, Rome, GA 30161

Montessori School of Rome (1982)
1499 Dodd Blvd, Rome, GA 30161-6643
Swarna Kumar, 706-232-7744
Tuition: $210/275/mo
4 teachers, 7 assistants, 72 students, ages infant-6
Governance by administrator
Childcare.

Sunshine Montessori School
1110 N 5th Ave, Rome, GA 30165-2604

Blackstock Montessori (1980)
87 Blackstock Rd, Villa Rica, GA 30180
R. O'Neil Duffy, Adm, 404-459-6797
Non-profit; tuition: $2,250-3,260/yr
6 teachers, 4 assistants, 98 students, ages infant-12
Affiliation: AMS
Governance by administrator
Custom designed building; 10 wooded acres; pilot sutdy for
    AMS/SAC; childcare; rural location; transportation; interns
    accepted.

Herbst Homeschool (1983)
6473 Hickory Flat Hwy, Woodstock, GA 30188
Jill Herbst, 404-516-4826
Non-profit
1-2 teachers, 3 students, ages 5-15, K-9th grade
Non-regimented; suburban location.

Park View Montessori (1989)
6689 Bells Ferry Rd, Woodstock, GA 30188
Kathy Faircloth, Owner/Dir, 404-926-0044
Tuition: $53.50-99.50/wk
5 teachers, 132 students, ages infant-6
Affiliation: MEGA
Governance by administrator
Childcare; suburban location; interns accepted.

REACH
617 Colony Ct, Woodstock, GA 30188
Vicki Scott
Type: home-based

Medlock Bridge Montessori School
10100 Medlock Bridge Pky, Alpharetta, GA 30201
Robin Hanson

Montessori Internationale
10250 Haynes Bridge Rd, Alpharetta, GA 30202
Cindy Savage

Preston Ridge Montessori (1988)
3800 N Point Pkwy, Alpharetta, GA 30202
Dolores R. Gang, 404-751-9510
Tuition: $3,195-5,265/yr
7 teachers, 7 assistants, 109 students, ages 3-12
Affiliations: AMI, NAMTA; accreditation: MIA
Governance by administrator and board of trustees
Childcare; transportation; interns accepted.

Nesbit Ferry Montessori
9330 Nesbit Ferry Rd, Alpharetta, GA 30202-5345

Georgia Home Education Association
245 Buckeye Ln, Fayetteville, GA 30214
404-461-3657

Lee Crest Academy, Inc
402 Bates Ave, Fayetteville, GA 30214-1906
Type: Montessori

Montessori Woods
1305 Cone Circle, Grayson, GA 30221
John Long

First Presbyterian Montessori Kindergarten
120 Broad St, La Grange, GA 30240-2704

Gwinnett Vocational Center at Oakland
990 McElvaney Lane, Lawrenceville, GA 30244
Roger Sarter, 404-963-7936
Type: public choice
HS

Educating Speakers of Other Languages
52 Gwinnett Dr, Lawrenceville, GA 30245
Liz Rieken, 404-513-6641
Type: public choice

Gwinnett Vocational Center at Parkview
1000 Cole Dr, Lilburn, GA 30247
Roy Rucks, 404-921-4592
Type: public choice
HS

Teaching Our Peers (TOP)
166 Holly Smith Dr, McDonough, GA 30253
Andrea L Green, 404-957-3945
Type: public at-risk

Georgians for Freedom in Education (1983)
209 Cobb St, Palmetto, GA 30268
Billie Jean Bryant, Coord, 404-463-3719 or 463-1073
Non-profit
Non-sectarian; newsletter; monitors legislation; promotes
    grassroots lobbying; seminars; workshops.

Peachtree City Montessori
232 Stevens Entry, Peachtree City, GA 30269-3320
Leslie Bryan

Montessori Education Center of Gwinnett
PO Box 692, Snellville, GA 30278
Trudy Friar

The Children's House
2350 Wisteria Dr, Snellville, GA 30278-2658
Type: Montessori

Montessori Children's Hall
2123 Easy St, Snellville, GA 30278-2839

Montessori Institute of Atlanta
2355 Virginia Pl NE, Atlanta, GA 30305
Type: Montessori teacher education

North Atlanta High School
2875 Northside Dr NE, Atlanta, GA 30305
Judith Rogers, 404-842-3108
Type: magnet
9-12th grade
International studies; arts.

Downtown Learning Center
1080 Euclid Ave, Atlanta, GA 30307
Robert Morrison, 404-330-4161
Type: public choice
HS
Traditional curriculum; contracts.

Fernbank Science Center
(See Resource Section)

Horizons School
1900 Dekalb Ave, Atlanta, GA 30307
Dr Lorraine Wilson, Co-Adm, 404-378-2219, FAX: 404-373-
    3650
Type: independent, boarding, non-profit; tuition: $3,800-
    8,000/yr, scholarships: work, need
14 teachers, 145 students, ages 4-18, pre K-12th grade
Affiliation: NCACS
Governance by democratic school meeting; some decisions
    by administration
Campus designed and built by students and staff; alt eval
    methods in some classes; college prep; whole-person
    approach; multi-aged classes; extensive field trips; urban
    location; interns accepted.

The Children's Garden (1987)
2089 Ponce de Leon Ave, Atlanta, GA 30307
Susan Jones, Grade II Tch, 404-371-9470
Type: Waldorf, non-profit; tuition: $2,000-4,000/yr,
    scholarships
8 teachers, 44 students, ages 3-9, nursery, K, II
Affiliation: AWSNA
Governance by faculty and board
Teacher qualifications: Waldorf training and/or experience
Only school in Atlanta with play kindergarten, nursery school,
    and arts daily; urban location; interns accepted.

Southwest Montessori
2407 Cascade Rd SW, Atlanta, GA 30311-3225

B. T. Washington High School
45 Whitehouse Dr SW, Atlanta, GA 30314
Robert Lowe, 404-752-0728
Type: magnet
9-12th grade
Health professions; multi-cultural; humanities.

Southside Comprehensive High School
801 Glenwood Ave SE, Atlanta, GA 30317
Joseph Carpenter, 404-624-2064
Type: magnet
9–12th grade
Information process and decision making.

Atlanta Northeast Montessori School Inc
2193 Johnson Ferry Rd NE, Atlanta, GA 30319-2503

Ben Franklin Academy
Clifton Rd, Atlanta, GA 30322

Creative Learning Montessori
1108 Heatherstone Dr, NE, Atlanta, GA 30324-4642

First Montessori School of Atlanta
5750 Long Island Dr NW, Atlanta, GA 30327-4844

East Cobb Montessori, Inc
5730 Pinebrook Rd NE, Atlanta, GA 30328-5224

Benjamin Franklin Academy (1987)
1585 Clifton Rd, NE, Atlanta, GA 30329
Wood Stonehurst, Head, 404-633-7404, FAX: 321-0610
Type: independent, non-profit; tuition: $11,800/yr,
   scholarships
60 students, mainly at-risk
Affiliations: GAIS, AAIS, SAIS, CES
Governance by board
Teacher qualifications: GA certificate
For those who are "out of step with conventional schools";
   consensus decision-making; urban location.

Montessori Child Dev Centers
PO Box 15281, Atlanta, GA 30333

Occupational Education Center-North
1995 Womack Rd, Dunwoody, GA 30338
Frank Hall, 404-394-0321
Type: public choice
450 students

Montessori Children's House of NE Atlanta
2635 Fairlane Dr, Doraville, GA 30340-3225

Northwoods Montessori School (1971)
3340 Chestnut Dr, Atlanta, GA 30340-3239
Elizabeth Samples, Executive Director, 404-457-7261
Non-profit; tuition: $2,985/4,170/yr
9 teachers, 9 assistants, 157 students, ages 3–12
Affiliations: NAMTA, MAC; accreditation: AMI
Governance by administrator
Traditional Montessori program; childcare; urban location.

Four Seasons School
2459 Dresden Dr NE, Chamblee, GA 30341-5218
Type: Montessori

**Atlanta Montessori International Teacher Training
   Center**
820 Loridans Dr, Atlanta, GA 30342
Type: Montessori teacher education

North Side Atlanta Homeschoolers
c/o Jane Kelley, 4141 Wieuca Rd NE, Atlanta, GA 30342

Montessori Center of Buckhead, Ltd
3725 Powers Ferry Rd NW, Atlanta, GA 30342-4422

Tri-Cities High School
2575 Harris St, Atlanta, GA 30344
Hershel Robinson, 404-669-8200
Type: magnet
9–12th grade
Visual and performing arts.

Georgia Home Educators
PO Box 88775, Dunwoody, GA 30356
404-451-4130

Foxfire Teacher Outreach
(See Resource Section)

Free to Learn at Home
4439 Lake Forest Dr, Oakwood, GA 30566
404-536-8077

Hall County Home Educators
PO Box 1283, Oakwood, GA 30566

Athens Montessori School
3145 Barnett Shoals, Athens, GA 30605-4327
Warren McPherson

Individualized Language Arts (ILA) Project
501 Central Ave, Dalton, GA 30720
Barbara S. Rous, 706-226-6369
K–12th grade
"Writing-across-the-curriculum."

Christians Concerned for Education / Still Waters
330 Concord Ln, LaFayette, GA 30728
706-397-2941
Type: state home-based

Innovative Program Center
(See Resource Section)

Briarwood Montessori School
3155 Thomson Hywy, Warrenton, GA 30828-6354

A. R. Johnson Health Science and Engineering HS,
John S. Davidson Fine Arts School (5–12th grade)
3146 Lake Forest Dr, Augusta, GA 30909
Bert Thomas, 404-737-7150
Type: public choice, HS

Walden Hall Christian Montessori
3615 Wheeler Rd, Augusta, GA 30909-1825

The CSRA Home Education Association
PO Box 204756, Augusta, GA 30917
300+ members; also covers parts of SC; monthly legal
   updates.

GAIA Permaculture Community (1978)
Rt 1 Box 74, Mauk, GA 31058
Alton Deville, Founder, 912-649-7700
Type: higher education, non-profit
2 teachers, 7 students, mainly at-risk, ages 22–40
Governance by community leader and students
Tending garden, poultry, goats; designing solar homes; build-
   ing straw bale cottages; aquifer conservation; erosion pre-
   vention; group decision making; cooperation with
   surrounding community.

Bloomindage Elementary
Main St, Bloomingdale, GA 31302
Amelia Poppell, 912-748-4403
Type: magnet
K–5th grade
Learning styles; performing and fine arts.

Liberty Educational Alternatives Division (LEAD)
5 Shipman Ave, Hinesville, GA 31313
Chris Chalker, 912-876-3795

Bartow Elementary
1804 Stratford St, Savannah, GA 31401
Dora Myles, 912-651-7331
Type: magnet
K–5th grade
Gifted and talented.

Optional Program with Training (OPT)
208 Bull St, Savannah, GA 31401
Edward G. Miller, 912-651-7000
Students mainly at-risk
Tutorial; CAI; self-paced; competency-based; GED/diploma
   prep.

Savannah-Chatham Cty Magnet Schools
208 Bull St, Savannah, GA 31401
Lillie Ellis, 912-651-7233
Type: public choice
The Biological Sciences Academy at Downtown W ES; The
    Business, Legal, Financial and Performing Arts Academy at
    SHS; The Gifted and Talented Academy at Bartow ES; The
    Computer Science and Video Technology Academy at E
    Broad St ES; The Charles Ellis Montessori Academy (K–5, no
    letter grades); The Academy of Performing and Fine Arts at
    Gadsden ES (partnership with the Savannah College of Art
    and Design and Savannah Symphony Orchestra); The Sci-
    ences and Mathematics Academy at Haven ES (astronomy,
    rocketry, space and environmental science, long-term
    research projects, Math-a-thon, Young Astronauts Club
    (works with Coastal Rocketry Association to design and
    launch model rockets), and a permanent greenhouse and
    weather station; extensive field trips); The Computer
    Science Academy at Hodge ES; The Honors, International
    Studies, and Foreign Language Academy at Spencer ES
    (Japan, Germany, Spain, and France); The Computer
    Science Academy at Hubert MS (modems, satellite dish);
    The Biological and Medical Professions Academy at Beach
    HS; Gould ES (Olympic theme; nature trail); Hesse ES (com-
    puters, video); Howard ES (individualized; CAI); Pooler ES
    (extensive CAI); Windsor Forest ES (curriculum integrates
    music, poems, rhymes, games, songs, and dances; perfor-
    mances); Jenkins HS (nationally recognized robotics, with
    lasers and lithograph; emphasis on physical sciences; tech-
    nicians and engineers from Gulfstream Aerospace Corp);
    transportation.

Shuman Middle School
415 Goebel Ave, Savannah, GA 31404
Roland James, 912-651-7085
Type: magnet
6–8th grade
Performing arts; communications.

Parent & Child Montessori Learning Center
1407 E 41st St, Savannah, GA 31404-3525
Paula Washburn

Charles Ellis Elementary
220 E 49th St, Savannah, GA 31405
Anne Monaghan, 912-651-7250

Type: magnet
K–5th grade
Montessori academy.

Savannah Montessori School
6610 Abercorn St, Savannah, GA 31405-5827

Green Heart School
2611 Salcedo Ave, Savannah, GA 31406
Type: Montessori

Montessori Academy
8415 Cresthill Ave, Savannah, GA 31406-6113

Seminole Montessori School
2499 Seminole Trail, Waycross, GA 31501

Children's Montessori School
810 Newcastle St, Brunswick, GA 31520

Montessori Guidance Center
136 Dunbarton Dr, St Simons Island, GA 31522-1015
Susan Williamson

Lowndes County Alternative Program
1112 N St Augustine Rd, Valdosta, GA 31601
Dennis Tipton, 912-245-2250
Type: public choice
HS
After school credit classes.

Americus/Sumter County Alternative School
802 Ashby St, Americus, GA 31709
Connie Caruthers, Dir, 912-924-3605,-6045
Student age 4, pre K
Individualized.

**Vocational Office Training (VOT) and Diversified
    Cooperative Training (DCT)**
439 Firetower Rd, Leesburg, GA 31763
Marie Wright and Larry Murkerson, 912-759-6264
Type: public choice
HS

Colquitt County Alternative School
5th St SW, Moultrie, GA 31768
Richard Warren, Dir, 912-890-6206
Diploma-earning; evenings.

Hawaii

Hawaii Military Families in Home Education
113 Nijmegen Rd, Fort Ord, HI 93941-1524
Gail Thomas
Other contact: Mary Lyons; 183 20th Ave, Honolulu, HI; 808-
    422-7949.

Pali-uli Waldorf School (1988)
PO Box 1338, Kealakekua, HI 96704
Shelley Hoose, Adm, 808-322-3316
Tuition: $3,600-4,000/yr, scholarships
5 teachers, 65 students, ages 3-12, pre K-6th grade
Affiliation: AWSNA
Governance by board and faculty through administrator
Teacher qualifications: college degree, Waldorf training
Traditional Waldorf curriculum; Hawaiian studies; multi-aged
    classes; rural location; interns accepted.

Hale O Ulu
91-1841 D Ft Weaver Rd, Ewa, HI 96706
Ann Kawahara

Christian Homeschoolers of Hawaii
91-824 Oama St, Ewa Beach, HI 96706
Arleen Alejado, 808-689-6398

CORAL Ohana O Maui (1993)
4150 Hana Hwy, Haiku, HI 96708
Elizabeth Werthiem, 808-573-0978
Type: independent, non-profit; tuition: $225-450/mo
5 teachers, 48 students, ages 4-15, ungraded
Governance by democratic school meeting
Teacher qualifications: staff chosen by students and staff
On rural Maui; student motivated activities; outdoor explo-
    rations to waterfalls, beaches; drumming, dance, song;
    school is new and evolving; no letter grades; non-
    compulsory class attendance; multi-aged classes; rural
    location.

Ohana Community Center
880 Hana Hwy, Haiku, HI 96708
Type: home-based

Tropical Homeschooler Newsletter
(See Resource Section)

St Joseph's Montessori Preschool (1991)
999 Ululani St, Hilo, HI 96720
Nancy Graber, Dir, 808-961-0424
Non-profit; tuition: $300/350/mo
2 teachers, 4 assistants, 45 students, ages 3–6
Affiliations: NCEA, AMS
Governance by administrator
Large classrooms; in heart of Hilo; childcare; interns
accepted.

Christ Lutheran Montessori (1964)
595 Kapiolani St, Hilo, HI 96720-3997
Christa Murufas, Dir, 808-935-6468
Tuition: $250/330/345/mo
3 teachers, 2 assistants, 52 students, mainly international,
ages 3–9
Governance by administrator and board of trustees
Childcare; suburban location; interns accepted.

Hale O Kamali'i Montessori School
326 Desha Ave, Hilo, HI 96720-4817
Marie Roberts

Hale 'O Ho' oponopono (1972)
PO Box 376, Honaunau, HI 96726
Pat Bento, Site Mgr, 808-328-9166, FAX: 808-328-8917
Type: public at-risk
6 teachers, 30 students, ages 14–19, 9–12th grade
Teacher qualifications: BA, experience with at-risk
Vocational; counseling; HS curriculum; multi-aged classes;
rural location; transportation; interns accepted.

Carey School
260 N Kainalu Dr, Kailua, HI 96734-2396
Type: Montessori

Kamuela & Kona Montessori Schools (1980)
PO Box 1604, Kamuela, HI 96743
Virginia Hammon, Head, 808-885-4141, FAX: 808-885-4994
Non-profit; tuition: $3,040-5,600/yr
14 teachers, 9 assistants, 166 students, ages infant–12
Affiliations: AMS, NAEYC, GATE
Governance by board, teachers, administrators
Peace ed by nurturing self-esteem, self-discipline, indepen-
dence, self-motivation, responsibility; childcare; interns
accepted.

Kohala Montessori
PO Box 1793, Kumuela, HI 96743
Cheri Spies Havens

Haiku Hale O'Keiki Montessori School
46-283 Kahuhipa St, Honolulu, HI 96744
Patricia Gooch

Kapaa Elementary School
4886 Kawaihau Rd, Kapaa, HI 96746
Joan Sahw, Staff Facilitator
Type: Montessori

St Catherine's School
5021 Kawaihau Rd, Kapaa, HI 96746-2097
Carol West
Type: Montessori

Ka Papa Honua O Keawanui (1979)
HC-01 Box 471, Kaunakakai, HI 96748
Rose L. Moreno, Site Mgr, 808-558-8945, FAX: -8979
Type: public at-risk
3 teachers, 25 students, ages 14–18, 7–12th grade
Teacher qualifications: BA, experience with at-risk
Vocational; counseling; HS curriculum; multi-aged classes;
rural location; transportation.

Malamalama School
HCR2 13031, Keaau, HI 96749
Office Mgr
Type: Waldorf

Montessori Hale O Keiki (1991)
PO Box 2348, Kihei, HI 96753
Elaine O'Colmain, Dir, 808-874-7441, FAX: same
Non-profit; tuition: $3,720/3,900/yr
3 teachers, 3 assistants, 48 students, mainly international,
ages 3–6
Affiliations: AMS, NAEYC, HAEYC, Kinei Comm Assn, Chaminade
U; accreditation: HIDHS
Governance by board
Gymnastics; Kindermusik; Hawaiian studies; computers; child-
care; suburban location; interns accepted.

Kanai Waldorf School (1986)
PO Box 818; 4480 Hookui Rd, Kilauea, HI 96754
Ann Simpson, Adm Dir, 808-828-1144, FAX: 825-1110
Non-profit; tuition: $4,000/yr
10 teachers, 94 students, ages 3–12, pre K–6th grade
Governance by board
Form drawing; modeling; German; Music; Hawaiian Studies;
handwork; multi-aged classes; rural location.

Ka'imi Naaua'O Montessori School
PO Box 1419, Kapaau, HI 96755-1419

Montessori School of Maui (1978)
PO Box 1435, Makawao, HI 96768
Jing Wong, 808-871-2682, FAX: same
Non-profit; tuition: $3,630-4,100/yr
5 teachers, 4 assistants, 121 students, mainly international,
ages 3–12
Governance by administrator, board of trustees
Hawaiian and Japanese cultural resource teachers; childcare;
rural location; interns accepted.

Hawaii Island Home Educators
PO Box 851, Mountain View, HI 96771
Connie Siler, 808-968-8076; 968-8434

Kids Lib News
(See Resource Section)

Kalani Honua
RR 2, Box 4500, Pahoa, HI 96778
Cynthia Albers
Type: independent

Open Sky Home Education (1985)
PO Box 915, Alaili Rd, Pahoa, HI 96778
Micheal Sunandra, 808-965-9474, 936-2561
Non-profit
2–3 teachers, 3–10 students, ages 3–11
Governance by parent cooperative and democratic school
meeting
Teacher qualifications: sensitive, playful, aware, honest
Rooted in natural bonding, trust, and cooperation; geodesic
toys; camping; Kids Lib Newsletter; handcrafts; extensive
field trips; non-compulsory class attendance; rural loca-
tion; interns accepted.

Marti Jones
PO Box 1490, Pahoe, HI 96778
Marti Jones
Type: Montessori

Montessori Country School
PO Box 1203, Pahoa, HI 96778-1203
Marie Rieck

Montessori of Maui
Baldwin Ave, Paia, HI 96779
Jing Wong

Mililani Montessori Center
Wahiawa Site 11679, California Ave, Wahiawa, HI 96786

Friends Learning at Home
PO Box 3476, Mililani, HI 96789
Linda Inouye, 808-625-0445

St John's Mililani Montessori Center
95-370 Kuahelani Ave, Mililani, HI 96789-1103
Linda Durocher

Haleakala Waldorf School
RR 2 Box 790, Kula, HI 96790
Rosemary K. Moore, Adm Dir, 808-878-2511, FAX: -3341
Non-profit; tuition: $4,850/yr
16 teachers, 175 students, ages 4-13, pre K-8th grade
Affiliation: WANA
Governance by board and teachers
Teacher qualifications: experience, Waldorf training, BA
Ecology; community service; exchanges with sister schools
  worldwide; extensive field trips; suburban location; trans-
  portation; interns accepted.

Maui Alternative Learning Center (1977)
c/o Baldwin HS, 1650 Kaahumanu Ave, Wailuka, HI 96790
Sydney Jamison, Teacher
Type: public at-risk
1 teacher, 18 students, ages 14-19, HS
Affiliation: HI DE
Governance by teachers and principal
Teacher qualifications: state certification
7 networked computers; Josten's Life Skills program; state
  funded work-study; multi-aged classes; extensive field
  trips; suburban location; transportation.

Hawaii Homeschool Association
66960 Kuewa Dr, Waialua, HI 96791

**HAPPY (Homeschool Adventures: Program for Parents
  and Youngsters)** (1989)
777 Kolani St, Wailuku, HI 96793
Gail Nagasako, Founder, 808-242-8225, FAX: 808-242-7020
Weekly field trips.

Cities in Schools
94-366 Pupupani St #209, Waipahu, HI 96797
Fay Uyeda

Kawaiahao Child Care Center
872 Mission Lane, Honolulu, HI 96813-5051
Wendy Lagreta
Type: Montessori

Chaminade U Montessori Teacher Education Program
3140 Waialae Ave, Honolulu, HI 96816
Louise Bogart

Distance Learning
3645 Waialae Ave, Honolulu, HI 96816
Vicki Kajioka

L Robert Allen Montessori Center (1982)
1365 Kaminaka Dr, Honolulu, HI 96816
Sylvia Carey, 808-735-4875, FAX: 808-735-4870
Non-profit; tuition: $3,300/3,800/yr
3 teachers, 4 assistants, 36 students, ages 3-6
Affiliation: AMS; accreditations: MACTE, WASC, HIDE

Governance by board of trustees
Multi-ethnic; view of Diamond Head; Japanese; Orff and
  Suzuki instruction; childcare; urban location; interns
  accepted.

Elementary School Guidance Program (1987)
1887 Makuakane St, Honolulu, HI 96817
Wally Lau, Dir, 808-842-8627, FAX: -0080
Non-profit
2 teachers, 400 students, ages 5-12, K-6th grade
Teacher qualifications: BA, experience
Promotion of school success; prevention; guidance; heterogeneous grouping; minimal labeling of at-risk; rural
  location.

Malama o ke Ola (Caring for Life) (1978)
1850 Makuakane St, Bldg C, Honolulu, HI 96817
Rick Campbell, Program Mgr, 808-842-8632, FAX: -8515
Type: public at-risk
7 teachers, 300 students, ages 12-16, 7-11th grade
Governance by principal
Teacher qualifications: BA
Hawaiian culture; self-awareness; communication, school sur-
  vival skills; experiential; suburban location.

St Philomena's Child Center
3300 Ala Laulani St, Honolulu, HI 96818-2837
Type: Montessori

Montessori Center of Pearl Harbor
45 Makalapa Dr, Honolulu, HI 96818-3110

Calvary by the Sea School
5339 Kalanianaole Hwy, Honolulu, HI 96821
Jane Stegmaier
Type: Montessori

Star of the Sea Early Learning Center
4449 Malia St, Honolulu, HI 96821-1138
Lisa Foster
Type: Montessori

Kilohana United Methodist Pre-school
5829 Mahimahi St, Honolulu, HI 96821-2120
Type: Montessori

Montessori Community School
1515 Liholiho St, Honolulu, HI 96822
Patsy Tom

Montessori Elementary
3225 Pakanu St, Honolulu, HI 96822

Maryknoll Elementary School-Montessori Center
1722 Dole St, Honolulu, HI 96822-4997

Honolulu Waldorf School (1961)
350 Ulua St, Honolulu, HI 96825
Michael Preston, Faculty Chair, 808-377-5471
Tuition: $4,000-5,500/yr, scholarships
25 teachers, 226 students, ages 3-14, pre K-8th grade
Affiliation: AWSNA
Governance by college of teachers and board
Languages; non-academic kindergarten; comprehensive,
  non-elective curriculum; suburban location; interns
  accepted.

Idaho

Sandpoint Montessori School
1004 Ruth Ave, Sandpoint, ID
Heidi Gonzales

Alternative Junior High School (1978)
252 Pershing St, Pocatello, ID 83201
Paul Matthews, 208-233-1161
Type: public at-risk
4 teachers, 30 students, mainly at-risk, ages 12-15, 7-9th
grade
Governance by teachers, principal and board
Teacher qualifications: BS, ID Certification, ability
Highly structured; students required to complete 4 levels of
responsibility; min 10 weeks; rural location; transportation;
interns accepted.

Teen Parent Center (1989)
240 E Maple, Pocatello, ID 83201
Sheryl Brockett, Prin, 208-232-2994
Type: public at-risk
5 teachers, 60 students, mainly at-risk, ages 12-21, 7-12th
grade
Governance by teachers, principal, and board
Teacher qualifications: certified in subject area
Support services integrated with Health and Welfare, Job
Service and Health Department; childcare; multi-aged
classes; urban location; transportation.

Bonneville School
320 N 8th Ave, Pocatello, ID 83201-5713
Type: Montessori

Second Chance High School
1328 S Meridian, Blackfoot, ID 83221
Guy Gladden, Dir, 208-785-8825, FAX: -8893
Type: public at-risk
7 teachers, 130 students, mainly at-risk, ages 14-21, 9-12th
grade
Governance by teachers, principal, board
Teacher qualifications: ID Certification
Strong voc; 1:18 ratio; extensive community support; multi-
aged classes; childcare; suburban location; transportation;
interns accepted.

Montessori Place
775 Lincoln Dr, Idaho Falls, ID 83401-4920

Continuation High School (1974)
1767 Blue Sky Dr, Idaho Falls, ID 83402
Aaron L Maybon, Prin, 208-525-7795, FAX: same
Type: public choice
20 teachers, 300 students, ages 16-24, 9-12th grade
Governance by principal, board.
Teacher qualifications: ID Certification
Teen parenting; childcare; counseling; college rep; multi-
aged classes; 90% attendance rule; urban location.

Alternative High School
135 N Bridge, St Anthony, ID 83445
Richard Law, Dir, 208-624-3416

Bridgeview Alternative High School
PO Box 790, Salmon, ID 83467
Jay Skeen, Head Tch, 208-756-6277

Lewiston High School
1114 9th St, Lewiston, ID 83501
Jim Wilund, Prin, 208-746-2331
Type: public

Alternative High School
714 Jefferson, Box 430, Grangeville, ID 83530
Janice Ingrahm, Clerk, 208-983-0940

Caldwell Alternative High School (1981)
1117 Arthur St, Caldwell, ID 83605
Michele Travis, Adm Asst, 208-455-3325, FAX: 455-3341
Type: public at-risk
7 teachers, 120 students, mainly at-risk, ages 14-21, 9-12th
grade
Governance by principal.
Teacher qualifications: ID Certification
Multi-aged classes; open entry; individualized; self-paced;
mastery learning; no homework; art; homeless student
assistance; rural location; transportation; interns accepted.

Black Canyon Alternative (1990)
315 S Johns, Emmett, ID 83617
Amy Linville, Head Tch, 208-365-5552, FAX: -5085
Type: public choice
5 teachers, 65 students, mainly at-risk, ages 16-21, 9-12th
grade
Governance by teachers and principal
Interns accepted.

Heartland Center (1991)
PO Box 967, 411 South Hwy 55, McCall, ID 83638
Ralph Colton, PhD, Dir, 208-634-3686
Type: public at-risk
1 teacher, 12-18 students, ages 14-21, HS
Affiliation: SW ID PIC
Governance by board with student assistance
Teacher qualifications: certification
100% attendance policy; urban location.

Meridian Academy (1989)
2311 E Lanark, Boise, ID 83642
Marilyn Renolds, Superviser, 208-887-4759
Type: public choice, at-risk
12 teachers, 150 students, mainly at-risk, HS
Governance by principal, faculty and student reps
Rural location; interns accepted.

Cloverdale Montessori
4765 Goldenrod, Meridian, ID 83642
Ron Dingwall

Boise Montessori Center
2999 Moore St, Boise, ID 83702-2140

Scientific Wizardry Educational Products
(See Resource Section)

Elementary Montessori School
1004 Shoshone St, Boise, ID 83705-2340
Christel Nordhausen

Boise Evening High School (1975)
6001 Caggia, Boise, ID 83709
Bob Nisbett, Prin, 208-322-3723
Type: public choice
12 teachers, 300+ students, mainly at-risk, ages 16+, 9-12th
grade
Governance by principal and board
Teacher qualifications: certification
Multi-aged classes; urban location.

Idaho Home Educators (1980)
Box 4022, Boise, ID 83711
208-482-7336
Non-profit
Governance by parents
Resource store for help in choosing curriculum; no letter
grades; extensive field trips; suburban location.

Echo Springs Transition Studies Center (1993)
105 N 1st Ave, Suite 229, Sandpoint, ID 83805
Doug Kim-Brown, 208-265-0208, FAX: 263-6908

Type: higher education; tuition: $1,600+/mo
Student ages 18–24
Empower, assist students in identifying their interests and
assessing their strengths and weaknesses.

Home Educators of Idaho
3618 Pine Hill Dr, Coeur d'Alene, ID 83814
208-667-2778

Project CDA (Creating Dropout Alternatives) (1978)
725 Hazel Ave, Coeur d'Alene, ID 83814
Roger Hansen, 208-667-7460
Type: public at-risk
16 teachers, 234 students, ages 14–20, 8–12th grade
Governance by principal, faculty and student representatives
Teacher qualifications: ID certification
Emphasizes student responsibility; student/staff/parent part-
nerships; self-governing school community; rural location;
interns accepted.

Mortenson Company
PO Box 98, Hayden Lake, ID 83835
Jerry Mortensen
Type: Montessori

Homeschooling on the Polouse (1993)
802 White Ave, Moscow, ID 83843
Peg Harver-Marose, 208-882-1593
See WA listing of same name.

New Vision Alternative High School (1990)
Box 40, Post Falls, ID 83854
Colleen Kelsey, Head Tch, 208-773-3941, FAX: -3218
6 teachers, 65 students, ages 14–21, 9–12th grade
Governance by head teacher, faculty and student representa-
tives, and democratic school meeting
Teacher qualifications: experience with at-risk
outcome-based; family atmosphere; rural location

Snow Valley Academy
HCR 5 Box 76F, Priest River, ID 83856
Marnie Mason, 208-448-1869
Type: independent

Sandpoint Waldorf School
PO Box 95, Sand Point, ID 83864
Andrea Lyman

Lake Pend Oreille High School (1989)
1005 N Boyer, Sandpoint, ID 83864
Leonard Parenteau, Prin, 208-263-6121, FAX: 265-5734
Type: public at-risk
7 teachers, 70 students, mainly at-risk, ages 15–19, 9–12th
grade
Governance by teachers and principal
Teacher qualifications: certification, experience with at-risk
youth
Vocational, technology programs competency-based; group,
individual counseling; community involvement; multi-aged
classes; rural location; transportation; interns accepted.

Illinois

Montessori Learning Center
15 E Palatine Rd, Arlington Heights, IL 60004

Northwest Suburban Montessori School (1964)
800 N Fernandez, Arlington Heights, IL 60004
Rosemary Kreuser, 708-259-6044
Non-profit; tuition: $190-465/mo
5 teachers, 16 assistants, 182 students, ages infant–6
Governance by administrator, board
3-year modern art program; weekly arts/crafts and gymnastics for a fee; suburban location; interns accepted.

Christian Liberty Academy Satellite Schools
(See Resource Section)

Arlington Heights Little Peoples Montessori School
1234 N Arlington Heights Rd, Arlington Heights, IL 60004-
4741

Creative Care Children's Center
415 N Hough St, Barrington, IL 60010-3028
Type: Montessori

Crystal Lake Montessori
8617 Ridgefield Rd, Crystal Lake, IL 60014

Deerfield Montessori School (1966)
760 North Ave, Deerfield, IL 60015
Lisa Kambich, Assoc Dir, 708-945-7580, FAX: 708-948-5136
Non-profit
, mainly international, ages infant–6
Affiliations: AMS, ILMS
Governance by administrator and board of trustees
4 sites: Deerfield (2), Riverwoods, Glenview; ponds; woods;
nature trails; small animals; gardens; music; dance; foreign
language; summer program; childcare; suburban location;
interns accepted.

Westminster School
824 Waukegan Rd, Deerfield, IL 60015-3206
Type: Montessori

Children's Learning World Montessori School
PO Box 1231, Des Plaines, IL 60017-1231
Rosemary Fish

Glencoe Montessori School
395 Jefferson Ave, Glencoe, IL 60022-1877
Dr James Tulloss

Country Meadows Montessori (1981)
100 S Cemetery Rd, Gurnee, IL 60031-4439
Catherine Ozark, Owner, 708-244-9352
Non-profit; tuition: $230-400/mo
6 teachers, 14 assistants; student ages 3–12
Affiliation: AMS
Governance by board of trustees
On 3.8 acres in restored barn; childcare; rural location; interns
accepted.

Montessori Center of Highland Park
1731 Deerfield Rd, Highland Park, IL 60035-3704

Highland Park Montessori School
1301 Clavey Rd, Highland Park, IL 60035-4539
Carol Lee

Forest Bluff School
121 E Sheridan Pl, Lake Bluff, IL 60044-2632
Type: Montessori

Montessori School of Lake Forest (1965)
13700 W Laurel, Lake Forest, IL 60045
Lissa Hektor, Adm, 708-918-1000, FAX: 907-918-1304
Non-profit; tuition: $184/wk-5,564/yr

16 teachers, 10 assistants, 190 students, ages infant-12
Affiliation: AMI; accreditations: AMS, ILBE
Governance by administrator, board
Orff music; Spanish; after-school German, French, drama, art, gymnastics; childcare; suburban location; interns accepted.

Steppingstone Montessori School
101 S Beck Rd, Lindenhurst, IL 60046-9655

Montessori School of Long Grove
Box 1115 RFD, Long Grove, IL 60047
Kris Mills

Montessori World of Discovery
1660 Checker Rd, Long Grove, IL 60047

Children's Corner Developmental Center (1992)
888 E Belvidere Rd #107, Grayslake, IL 60048
June Glogovsky and Lorna Collar, Owners, 708-548-2880
Type: Montessori; tuition: $185-370
140 students, ages 3-6
Affiliation: AMS
Governed by owner partnership
Gymnastics; foreign language; suburban location.

Libertyville Montessori
PO Box 654, Libertyville, IL 60048-0654
Marjorie Cramer

Progressive Path School
510 Broadway, McHenry, IL 60050
Liz Berg, 312-497-3647
Type: independent
16 students, pre K-ES

Alexander Graham Bell Montessori School
2020 E Camp McDonald Rd, Mount Prospect, IL 60056-1727
Barbara Harris

Park View Montessori School
805 N Burning Bush Ln, Mount Prospect, IL 60056-1913

Career Publishing Inc
(See Resource Section)

Montessori Country Day School
200 W Maple Ave, Mundelein, IL 60060-1739

Children's House of the North Shore
1220 S Lake St, Mundelein, IL 60060-3706
Irene Voros
Type: Montessori

New Beginnings Montessori School
1401 S Lake St, Mundelein, IL 60060-4208
Carol Cossitt

Countryside Montessori School
1985 Pfingsten Rd, Northbrook, IL 60062-5853
Annette B Kulle

Barrington Montessori School
140 Patricia Ln, Palatine, IL 60067
Norma J Cicci

Dawn Gate- A Montessori School
728 S Wilke Rd, Palatine, IL 60067-7629

Montessori Edu-Care Centers
1004 N Cumberland Ave, Park Ridge, IL 60068-2047

Montessori Adventure to Learning Center
304 S Palatine Rd, Prospect Hts, IL 60070

Anatomical Chart Company
(See Resource Section)

Shimer College (1853)
PO Box A 500, Waukegan, IL 60079
David B. Buchanon, Adms Dir, 708-623-8400, FAX: 249-7171

Boarding, non-profit; tuition: $12,000/yr, scholarships
20 teachers, 120 students, ages 15+
Governance by democratic school meeting
Small classes; no lectures or textbooks; early entrance option; weekend adult program; many homeschoolers accepted; suburban location.

Carman Elementary
520 Helmholz, Waukegan, IL 60085
Isabelle Buckner, 708-336-3100
Type: magnet
K-5th grade
Concerned citizen leadership; service.

Glenwood Elementary
2500 Northmoor, Waukegan, IL 60085
Robert Moran, 708-336-3100
Type: magnet
K-5th grade
Individually challenging.

North Elementary
410 Franklin, Waukegan, IL 60085
Sylvia Zon, 708-336-3100
Type: magnet
K-5th grade
Learning resource academy.

Robert E. Abbott Elementary
1319 Washington, Waukegan, IL 60085
Rita Melius, 708-336-3100
Type: magnet
6-8th grade
Project Discovery; gifted.

Thomas Jefferson Elementary
600 S Lewis, Waukegan, IL 60085
Allan Mismash, 708-336-3100
Type: magnet
6-8th grade
Gifted program.

Washington Elementary
110 S Orchard, Waukegan, IL 60085
Barbara Prendergast, 708-336-3100
Type: magnet
K-5th grade
Citizenship; community involvement.

Waukegan Montessori School
PO Box 133, Waukegan, IL 60085

Whittier Elementary
801 N Lewis Ave, Waukegan, IL 60085
Laurie Rickerd, 708-336-3100
Type: magnet
K-5th grade
Early childhood center; activity-based learning.

Clark Elementary
601 Blanchard, Waukegan, IL 60087
Bernice Gehris, 708-336-3100
Type: magnet
K-5th grade
Global understanding through continental studies.

Oakdale Elementary
2230 McAree Rd, Waukegan, IL 60087
David Mackie, 708-336-3100
Type: magnet
K-5th grade
Global education.

Buffalo Grove Montessori School
950 Ellen Dr, Buffalo Grove, IL 60089-3707
Deborah LaPorte

Ronald Knox Montessori (1963)
2031 Elmwood Ave, Wilmette, IL 60091
Usha Bala, Ed Adm, 708-256-2922
Non-profit; tuition: $1,020-2,120/yr
8 teachers, 10 assistants, 199 students, ages infant-6
Affiliations: AMS, ILMS, AMT, NAMTA, NAEYC
Suburban location; interns accepted.

Rose Hall Montessori School
1140 Wilmette Ave, Wilmette, IL 60091-2604

St Francis Xauvier's Little Children's House
808 Linden Ave, Wilmette, IL 60091-2711
Type: Montessori

Forest Bluff Montessori School
1063 Cherry St, Winnetka, IL 60093
Haley C Nate

Montessori Childrens House
525 Sunset Ridge Rd, Northfield, IL 60093-1025

**Transitional Care program at Northwest Coonen High
    School** (1982)
101 S Jefferson St, Woodstock, IL 60098
Joyce A Gallery, Coord, 815-338-7360, FAX: 337-5510
Type: independent at-risk, non-profit; tuition: $125/sem
4 teachers, 20-30 students, ages 14-18, 9-12th grade
Governance by teachers, principal, student reps.
Teacher qualifications: flexibility, high tolerance level, team
    worker
Clinically based; daily group life skills class; therapeutic recre-
    ation; counseling; multi-aged classes; levels/privileges;
    rural location; interns accepted.

Community Montessori School
640 McHenry Ave, Woodstock, IL 60098-2923

Crystal Lake Montessori School
8700 Crystal Springs Rd, Woodstock, IL 60098-8058
Pamela Zirko

Illinois Christian Home Educators
PO Box 261, Zion, IL 60099

Discovery Montessori Center
PO Box 6, Bloomingdale, IL 60108-0006

Montessori School of DeKalb
321 Oak St, DeKalb, IL 60115-3369
Beverly Ann Smith

Children's House Montessori School
417 W Main St, West Dundee, IL 60118
Elizabeth Maliska

Forest Park Montessori School
16 Lathrop Ave, Forest Park, IL 60130-1009
Karla Ozima

La Leche League International
(See Resource Section)

Geneva Board of Education School District #304
400 McKinley Ave, Geneva, IL 60134
Adm Office, Dist 304
Type: Montessori

Mansio Mens
102 Howard St, Geneva, IL 60134-2318
Carolee Watts
Type: Montessori

Hansel & Gretel Haus
1 N 450 Park Blvd, Glen Ellyn, IL 60137
Annie Carlson
Type: Montessori

New Morning Children's House
400 N Walnut St, Itasca, IL 60143-1735
Joyce Czerwinskyyj
Type: Montessori

Creative Montessori Learning Center
550 S Edgewood St, Lombard, IL 60148-2822
Soumini Pillai

Alpha Montessori School
1625 S Mannheim Rd, Westchester, IL 60154-4318
Leanoore Dean

St Charles Board of Education School District 303
1304 Rongheimer Rd, St Charles, IL 60174
Child Study Office
Type: Montessori

Montessori Children's Academy (1981)
706 E Park Blvd, Villa Park, IL 60181
Chibi Lu Teng, Owner, 708-832-4423
Tuition: $15-35/day
3 teachers, 4 assistants, 45 students, ages infant-6
Affiliation: AMS; accreditation: ILBE
Governance by teachers and administrators
Childcare; interns accepted.

Seton Academy
350 N Westmore Ave, Villa Park, IL 60181
Type: Montessori

Wheaton Montessori Children's House
1970 Gary Ave, Wheaton, IL 60187-3029
Ms Vicks

Montessori Learning Center
1015 W Golf Rd, Hoffman Estates, IL 60194-1339
Rochelle Gutstadt

Montessori School of North Hoffman (1988)
1200 Freeman Rd, Hoffman Estates, IL 60195
Mrs Motlagh, PhD, Dir, 708-705-1234
Non-profit; tuition: $170-650/mo
7 teachers, 5 assistants, 129 students, ages infant-12
Affiliation: AMS
Governance by administrator
Specifically designed environment features lofts and fixtures
    at child's level; foreign language, art, music, Suzuki violin;
    childcare; suburban location; interns accepted.

Acarath Montessori School
22 Kristin Dr, Schaumburg, IL 60195-3302

Chiaravalle Montessori (1965)
425 Dempster St, Evanston, IL 60201
Linda Dolnick, Adms Dir, 708-864-2190, FAX: -2206
Non-profit; tuition: $1,260-10,370/yr
30 teachers, 30 assistants, 381 students, ages infant-15
Affiliations: NAMTA, NAEYC, IL BE; accreditations: AMS, ISACS
Governance by administrator, board
In national historic landmark building; large gym; auditorium;
    art studio; music room; near Lake Michigan, public trans-
    portation, city playground; childcare; suburban location;
    interns accepted.

Child Care Center of Evanston
1840 Asbury Ave, Evanston, IL 60201'
Blair Grumman
Type: Montessori

American Science and Surplus
(See Resource Section)

HOUSE
806 Oakton, Evansville, IL 60202
Ann Wasserman, 708-328-6323
Type: state home-based
Urban location

Intercultura Foreign Language Immersion Montessori
1145 Westgate St, Oak Park, IL 60301-1029
Dr Michael Rosanova

Children's Garden (1980)
165 N Lombard Ave, Oak Park, IL 60302
Roshan Mawani, Dir, 708-383-6570
Type: Montessori; tuition: $2,650-4,620/yr
2 teachers, 5 assistants, 40 students, ages 3-6
Affiliations: NAEYC, CAEYC, AMS
Governance by administrator
Spanish; Math Their Way; childcare; suburban location;
   interns accepted.

West Suburban Montessori School
1039 S East Ave, Oak Park, IL 60304

Alcuin Montessori School (1961)
7970 Washington Blvd, River Forest, IL 60305
Marianne Dunlap, Ed Dir, 708-366-1882
Type: Montessori, non-profit; tuition: $1,540-4,015/yr
13 teachers, 12 assistants, 273 students, ages infant-15
Affiliations: NAMTA, MAC/USA, AMI/EAA, AMI/USA; accreditation:
   IL DE
Governance by board
Classic Montessori school; childcare; suburban location;
   interns accepted.

Woodlite Design
PO Box 385, Elmwood, IL 60421-0385
Type: Montessori

Flossmoor Montessori (1966)
740 Western Ave, Flossmoor, IL 60422
Lawrence Lewis, Adm, 708-798-4600
Non-profit
Affiliation: ILMS; accreditation: AMI
Governance by administrator, board
Suburban location; interns accepted.

St Joseph's Earth Child School
925 Braemar Rd, Flossmoor, IL 60422-2205
Type: Montessori

Casa Montessori
3344 Knollwood Ln, Homewood, IL 60430-2710

Joliet Montessori School
1600 Root St; 3113 Heritage Dr, Joliet, IL 60435

Montessori West School
1711 Burry Circle, Joliet, IL 60435-2079

Suburban Lithuanian Montessori (1983)
14911 127th St, Lemont, IL 60439
Dana Dirvonis, 708-257-8891
Non-profit; tuition: $1,200/yr
1 teacher, 2 assistants, 30 students, ages 3-6
Affiliations: Lithuanian MS of America, Inc
Governance by board of trustees
Language and culture; interns accepted.

New Beginnings Christian Montessori Preschool
151 E Briarcliff Rd, Bolingbrook, IL 60440-3070
Patricia Stephens

St Dennis Montessori School
229 E 12th St, Lockport, IL 60441-3502

Education Service Network (1978)
1320 Union St, Morris, IL 60450
Jeffrey A, May, Dir, 815-941-3231, FAX: 815-942-5384
Type: public choice
10 teachers, 400 students, mainly at-risk, ages 14-21, 9-12th
   grade
Governance by director of vocational education
Teacher qualifications: state certification
Evenings; small classes; emphasis on student's culture; sub-
   urban location.

Oaklawn Montessori School
8901 S 52nd Ave, Oak Lawn, IL 60453-1307
Norma De La Cruz Froio

Garden Gates Montessori School
91st & 82nd Ave, Hickory Hills, IL 60457

Hands-On History
(See Resource Section)

Hickory House Montessori
8222 W 95th St, Hickory Hills, IL 60457-1942

Montessori Schools, Inc
7926 W 103rd Ave, Palos Hills, IL 60464

S W Suburban Montessori School
12219 86th Ave, Palos Park, IL 60464

Southwest Suburban Montessori (1970)
8800 W 119th St, Palos Park, IL 60464
Kathy Williams, Ed Adm, 708-448-5332
Non-profit; tuition: $632/1,714/2,370/yr
6 teachers, 9 assistants, 157 students, ages toddler-6
Affiliations: AMS, IMS; accreditation: NAEYC
Governance by administrator and board of trustees
Spanish instruction weekly; gym; handicap accessible; com-
   puters; testing available; parent rap sessions and work-
   shops; rural location; interns accepted.

Illinois Montessori Children's House
303 Illinois St, Park Forest, IL 60466
Ms Piunti

Laren Montessori School
425 E 164th St, South Holland, IL 60473-2216
Susan Considine

Palos-Worth Montessori School
7100 W 112th Ave, Worth, IL 60482

Creative Art Work
27 S Calumet, Aurora, IL 60506
Regina Barnett
Type: Montessori

Fox Valley Montessori School (1968)
850 N Commonwealth, Aurora, IL 60506
Robert Bates, Exec Dir, 708-896-7557
Non-profit; tuition: $35/day
18 teachers, 147 students, ages 2-12
Affiliation: AMS
Governance by board of trustees
Teacher qualifications: Montessori certification
Guided by respect for each individual; focus on real life skills;
   no letter grades; non-compulsory class attendance; multi-
   aged classes; suburban location; interns accepted.

Illinois Mathematics and Science Academy (1986)
1500 W Sullivan Rd, Aurora, IL 60506-1039
708-801-6000
Type: magnet, boarding
Student ages 13-18, 10-12th grade
State-funded; mentorships; near Fermi Accelerator Lab.

Batavia Board of Education School Dist 101
12 W Wilson, Batavia, IL 60510
Adm Office
Type: Montessori

Carmel Montessori Academy & Children's House
595 S River Rd, Batavia, IL 60510
Arthur Basler

Montessori Academy (1971)
595 S River St, Batavia, IL 60510
Mary Yahnke, Dir, 708-879-2586
Non-profit; tuition: $250-513/mo
3 teachers, 6 assistants; student ages 3-12

Affiliation: AMS; accreditation: IMS
Governance by administrator
6 acres; 3 buildings; gym/auditorium; childcare; suburban
location; interns accepted.

Seton Little People's School
5728 Virginia Ave, Clarendon Hills, IL 60514-1607
Sue Buntrock
Type: Montessori

Precious Child Montessori School
3910 Highland Ave, Downers Grove, IL 60515

Montessori of Woodridge
6953 Woodridge Dr, Woodridge, IL 60517-2009
Patricia Whyte

Montessori School of Hinsdale
302 S Grant, Hinsdale, IL 60521
Desmond Perry

MECA-SETON Montessori Teacher Education Program
302 S Grant St, Hinsdale, IL 60521-4053
Celma Pinho Perry or Desmond Perry

Montessori Children's House
8532 Wedgewood Dr, Burr Ridge, IL 60521-6353

Creative World Montessori
Edgewood & Goodman, La Grange, IL 60525
Gundrun Olson

Edgewood Children's Academy
1515 W Ogden Ave, La Grange Park, IL 60525-1721
Type: Montessori

Du Page Montessori School
23 W 600 Warrenville Rd, Lisle, IL 60532
Robert Breen

Woodridge Montessori
4510 River Dr, Lisle, IL 60532

Rosehill Children's Academy
1910 Maple Ave, Lisle, IL 60532-2164
Type: Montessori

Oakview Montessori Children's House
5325 Oakview Dr, Lisle, IL 60532-2357
Alice Sosnowski

Montessori School of Lisle
23 W 550 Hobson Rd, Naperville, IL 60540
Barbara Gleespen

Carmel Montessori Academy
3 S 238 Rt 59, Warrenville, IL 60555
Carmen LaFranzo

Montessori Children's House
238 Rt 59, Warrenville, IL 60555

Montessori School of Western Springs
4601 Franklin Ave, Western Springs, IL 60558-1572
Elizabeth Steves

Downers Grove Montessori School
909 Oakwood Dr, Westmont, IL 60559-1073

New Morning Montessori Children's House
234 S Adams St, Westmont, IL 60559-1904

Montessori Moppet Centre
25 W 530 75th St, Naperville, IL 60565
Judith Hojnackie

Wilcox & Follett
(See Resource Section)

Notre Dame De Chicago Academy
1338 W Flournoy St, Chicago, IL 60607-3328
Type: Montessori

Montessori of Holy Family
1019 S May St, Chicago, IL 60607-4232

First Immanuel Lutheran Montessori
1124 S Ashland Ave, Chicago, IL 60607-4604
Concetta McCartney

Institute for Latino Progress
2570 S Blue Island, Chicago, IL 60608
Gabriela Perez, 312-890-0055, FAX: 312-890-1537
700 students, ages 18+, HS
Affiliation: ASN
Adult ed; diploma/GED prep; college prep, bilingual, and voc
classes; leadership development.

Garfield Alternative High School
220 W 45th Place, Chicago, IL 60609
Oye Khale, 312-924-0543, FAX: 312-924-0546
160 students
Affiliation: ASN
Vocational training; language arts; college prep.

Franklin Magnet Elementary & Middle School
225 W Evergreen Ave, Chicago, IL 60610
Alice M. Maresh, 312-534-8510
K-8th grade
Performing and creative arts.

Holy Trinity Montessori
1900 W Taylor St, Chicago, IL 60612-3732
Patricia Litberg

Disney Magnet Elementary
4140 N Marine Dr, Chicago, IL 60613
Raphael Guajardo, 312-534-5840
Student ages 4+,-8th grade
Open classroom.

Jane Addams Resource Corporation
1800 W Cuyler, Chicago, IL 60613
Mary LaPorte, 312-871-1151
Student ages 16-21
Affiliation: ASN
Learning program for out-of-school youth; GED and college
prep; career awareness; employment; metal-worker
training.

Lake View Academy
716 W Addison, Chicago, IL 60613
Deborah Bayly, 312-281-3065
Tuition: $750-4,500/yr
20 students
Affiliation: ASN
Whole-person emphasis.

Latino Youth Alternative High School
2200 S Marshall Blvd, Chicago, IL 60613
312-281-3065
Affiliation: ASN
Emphasis on community and cultural awareness.

Search School
640 W Irving Pk, 3rd Flr East, Chicago, IL 60613
Audrey Giske
Type: Montessori

The Southern School (1969)
1447 W Montrose, Chicago, IL 60613
Margaret Tucker, Exec Dir or Betty Luckey, Dir, 312-477-2895,
FAX: 477-2996
Type: independent at-risk/SE, non-profit
8 teachers, 50 students, mainly with behavior problems, ages
12-21
Governance by principal, board.
Teacher qualifications: Certified Type 10 in SE
Therapeutic day school, combining social services and acade-
mics; urban location; interns accepted.

Chicago Waldorf School (1974)
1651 W Diversey, Chicago, IL 60614
Connie Starzynski, Adms Dir, 312-327-0079, FAX: -4544
Non-profit; tuition: $4,800/yr, scholarships
26 teachers, 300 students, ages 3.5-14, pre K-8th grade
Affiliation: AWSNA
Governance by college of teachers
Teacher qualifications: Waldorf training
Full Waldorf curriculum; strong parent-community support;
    urban location.

The Ancona School
4770 S Dorchester, Chicago, IL 60615
Bonnie L. Wishne, 312-924-2356, FAX: 312-924-8905
Type: Montessori; tuition: $2,800-5,500/yr
Affiliation: ASN
Governance by parent cooperative
Spanish; arts; computers; multi-cultural emphasis; urban
    location.

Urban Life Center
5004 S Blackstone, Chicago, IL 60615
Scott E. Chesebro, 312-523-2333
Affiliation: ASN
Field placements.

Children's House at Harper Square
4800 S Lake Park Ave, Chicago, IL 60615-2044
Joan Alofs
Type: Montessori

South Harper Montessori
8358 S Stony Island Ave, Chicago, IL 60617-1759

Bobby Hebert Montessori School
33 E 83rd St, Chicago, IL 60619

South Harper Montessori School
9029 S Harper Ave, Chicago, IL 60619-7901

Accounters Community Center
1155 W 81st St, Chicago, IL 60620
Dr. Reggie McClinton, PhD, 312-602-2050
Type: public at-risk
Student ages 2-14, pre K-9th grade
Affiliation: ASN
Comprehensive, community-based youth services; crisis
    intervention; temporary living arrangements; foster care;
    drug and alcohol services; emergency food pantry; urban
    location.

Montessori School
9421 S Longwood Dr, Chicago, IL 60620-5643

Benjamin E. Mays Academy (1963)
6800 S Wentworth Ave, Chicago, IL 60621
Judith A. Starks, Dir, 312-602-5466, FAX: 312-602-5243
Type: public at-risk; tuition: variable
10 teachers, 325 students, ages 16+, HS
Affiliation: City Colleges of Chicago
Teacher qualifications: Bachelor's degree minimum
Multi-aged classes; urban location.

DeDiego Community Acadamy
1313 N Claremont Ave, Chicago, IL 60622
Lawrence McDougald, 312-534-4451
Type: magnet
K-8th grade
Fine and performing arts.

Near North Montessori School
1434 W Division, Chicago, IL 60622
Jacqueline Bergen, 312-384-1434
Tuition: $4,535/yr
400 students, ages 3-13, pre K-8th grade
Affiliation: ASN

Bethel School
4215 West End, Chicago, IL 60624
Hazel Nelson, 312-533-3636, FAX: 302-533-3635
Type: public choice; tuition: $1,250/yr
200 students, ages 3-13, K-8th grade
Affiliation: ASN

Flower Vocational-Essential School (1911)
3545 W Fulton Blvd, Chicago, IL 60624
Bettie D. Stewart, Essential Coord, 312-534-6756, FAX: 312-
    534-6938
Type: public choice
57 teachers, 720 students, partly at-risk, ages 14-20, HS
Affiliations: U of I, DePaul
Governance by local school council, teachers, principal
Teacher qualifications: IL Certification
College prep; hands-on training in one of 7 on-site, student-
    run businesses; entrepreneurial training; urban location;
    interns accepted.

Lawndale Community School
3400 W Grenshaw, Chicago, IL 60624
Linda Berg, 312-826-6330
51 students
Affiliation: ASN

Delano Child-Parent Center
3905 W Wilcox St, Chicago, IL 60624-2833
Type: Montessori

Good News Educational Workshop
7645 N Paulina, Chicago, IL 60626
Linda Ballas, 312-764-2228, FAX: 312-262-2293
scholarships
60 students, ages 3-13
Affiliation: ASN
Racially and economically diverse population; computers;
    arts; Spanish; field trips and camping; hands-on; emphasis
    on problem solving and non-violent conflict resolution.

North Shore Academy for Children
6711 N Sheridan Rd, Chicago, IL 60626-4532
Type: Montessori

Christian Montessori School
10 W 110th St, Chicago, IL 60628

Lindblom Technical High School (1919)
6130 S Wolcott Ave, Chicago, IL 60628
Betty J. Miller, CES Coord, 312-535-9300, FAX: -9314
Type: public choice
40 teachers, 680 students, ages 13-17, 9-12th grade
Governance by local school council
Teacher qualifications: bachelor's degree
Portfolio assessment; freshman portfolio exhibitions; team
    teaching; interdisciplinary instruction; socratic seminars;
    cooperative learning; student as worker, teacher as coach;
    urban location; interns accepted.

Tiny Tots Montessori School
901 E 104th St, Chicago, IL 60628
Mildred Bradley

Florence Foster Montessori Academy
11023 S Halstead St, Chicago, IL 60628-3908

Lithuanian Montessori Children's Center (1963)
2743 W 69th St, Chicago, IL 60629
Liuda Germanas, 312-476-4999
Non-profit; tuition: $1,200/yr
1 teacher, 1 assistant, 18 students, ages 3-6
Affiliations: Lithuanian MS of America, Inc
Language and culture; urban location; interns accepted.

Varnas Montessori Center
3038 W 59th St, Chicago, IL 60629-2542

Curie Metropolitan High School
4959 S Archer Ave, Chicago, IL 60632
Robert B. Schneider, 312-535-2100
Type: magnet
9-12th grade
Performing and creative arts.

Chicago Urban Day School
1248 W 69th St, Chicago, IL 60636-3599
Georgia Jordan
Type: Montessori

American School
(See Resource Section)

Parkway Community House
500 E 67th St, Chicago, IL 60637
Laura Holmes, 312-493-1306, FAX: 312-493-9392
Affiliation: ASN
Governance by principal
Adult basic ed; GED prep; literacy.

The Blue Gargoyle Youth Service Center
5655 S University Ave, Chicago, IL 60637
Barbara Cramer, 312-955-4108
Affiliation: ASN
Vocational services; computer assistance; counseling; adult
    literacy; GED; U of C volunteers.

Serendipity Children's House
2625 N Laramie Ave, Chicago, IL 60639-1625
Type: Montessori

Alternative Schools Network
(See Resource Section)

Prologue Learning Center
1105 W Lawrence, Chicago, IL 60640
Nancy Jackson, 312-728-7221, FAX: 312-728-3865
60 students, ages 16+
Affiliation: ASN
Emphasis on basic skills, realistic life planning; GED prep;
    career assessment; job placement.

Uptown Community Learning Center
4409 N Broadway, Chicago, IL 60640
312-769-2085
Affiliation: ASN

St Bartholomew Montessori Preschool
4941 W Patterson Ave, Chicago, IL 60641-3512

Montessori Elementary School (1979)
10149 Utica Ave, Evergreen Park, IL 60642
Norine Colby, Head, 708-499-3238
Non-profit; tuition: $2,000-3,600/yr
3 teachers, 3 assistants, 52 students, ages 3-12
Affiliations: NAMTA, MF, MAC/USA; accreditations: AMS, ASN
Governance by teachers and administrators
German; French; interns accepted.

Montessori Elementary and Preschool (1979)
14911 W 127th, Lemont, IL 60642
Norine Colby, Head, 708-257-1110
Non-profit; tuition: $4,000/4,600 (ages 6-12); varies for
    younger children
3 teachers, 3 assistants, 59 students, ages 3-12
Affiliations: AMS, NAMTA, MAC, ASN
Governance by teachers and administrators
German and French for 6-12 year-old students; interns
    accepted.

Beverly Montessori School (1967)
9916 S Walden Pkwy, Chicago, IL 60643
Virginia Maciulis, Dir, 312-239-7635
Non-profit; tuition: $1,360/yr
6 teachers, 9 assistants, 152 students, ages 3-6
Affiliation: AMS

Governance by administrator
Urban location; interns accepted.

Clissold Elementary School
2350 W 110th Pl, Chicago, IL 60643
Nicki Ruiz
Type: Montessori

Vanderpoel Magnet Elementary & Middle School
9510 S Prospect Ave, Chicago, IL 60643
E. Robert Olson, 312-535-2690
K-8th grade
Humanities.

Council Oak Montessori School
11030 S Longwood Dr, Chicago, IL 60643-4042
Marsha Enright

Academy of Scholastic Achievement
4651 W Madison St, Chicago, IL 60644
Gladys Simpson, 312-921-1315, FAX: 312-921-1121
Affiliation: ASN
Open entry; college prep; child/parent center; voc;
    counseling.

Aspira Alternative High School
2555 N Kimball, Chicago, IL 60644
Robb Michael, 312-772-0950, FAX: 312-486-9280
60 students, ages 16-20, HS
Affiliation: ASN
Drop-out retrieval; transition to "regular" HS; basic academic
    and social skills stressed; job placement; counseling.

Learning Network
5911 W Midway Park, Chicago, IL 60644
Luther Syas, 312-378-7076, FAX: 312-378-8190
1-8th grade
Affiliation: ASN
Basic skills; single and teen parent family counseling; adult
    ed; computer literacy; word processing.

Edgebrook-Wildwood Montessori Preschool
6736 N Loleta Ave, Chicago, IL 60646-1424

Casa Infantil Day Care Center
2222 N Kedzie, Chicago, IL 60647
Type: Montessori

Centro Latino Universidad Popular
2750 W North Ave, Chicago, IL 60647
Olivia Flores Godinez, 312-772-0836
Affiliation: ASN

Dr Pedro Albizu Campos High School (1972)
1671 N Claremont, Chicago, IL 60647
Marvin Garcia, Dir, 312-342-8022, FAX: 342-6609
Type: independent, non-profit; tuition: $500/yr, scholarships
8 teachers, 60 students, mainly Puerto Rican/Latino, ages
    14-18, 9-12th grade
Affiliation: ASN
Governance by faculty/student/parent board
Intensive; community-oriented; emphasis on Puerto Rican
    history and culture; extensive field trips; urban location;
    interns accepted; also has Consuelo Lee Corretjer Day Care
    Center.

Ruiz Belvis Cultural Center
1632 N Milwaukee Ave, Chicago, IL 60647
Rafael Arzuaga, 312-235-3988
Affiliation: ASN
Emphasis on Puerto Rican culture, history and community
    affairs; GED; ESL; Spanish literacy; plastic/graphic arts; salsa
    dance; musical instrument classes; counseling; after-school
    tutoring.

South Shore Montessori School
2555 E 73rd St, Chicago, IL 60649

Sullivan House High School (1970)
7305 S Clyde, Chicago, IL 60649
Meryl Domina, Prin, 312-324-5014
Type: public at-risk
10 teachers, 60 students, mainly at-risk, ages 14–23, HS
Affiliation: Alternative Schools Network
Governance by director with extensive input from faculty and students
Teacher qualifications: BA/BS, IL Certification or experience in AE
"Last chance" school; supportive services; career planning; literacy ed; no letter grades; extensive field trips; urban location; interns accepted.

The Neighborhood Institute's Career Education and Employment Center
2255 E 75th St, Chicago, IL 60649
Barbara Searles, 312-933-2040
Affiliation: ASN
GED prep; voc counseling; job placement.

Westside Holistic Family Center
4909 W Division, Chicago, IL 60651
Conna Blasingame, 312-921-8777, FAX: 312-921-1045
Affiliation: ASN
Adult ed; employment; GED tutoring; computer assistance; counseling.

Ted Lenart Regional Gifted Center
8445 S Kolin Ave, Chicago, IL 60652
William Harnedy, 312-535-2322
Type: magnet
1–8th grade
Regional Gifted Center.

Keller Gifted Elementary Magnet Center
3020 W 108th St, Chicago, IL 60655
Ruth Muth, 312-535-2636
1–6th grade
Regional Gifted Center.

Brickton Montessori (1986)
8622 W Catalpa, Chicago, IL 60656
Deborah A. Kelley, Prin, 312-714-0646
Non-profit; tuition: $3,340-5,490
10 teachers, 20 assistants, 172 students, ages infant–12
Affiliations: ISBE, IACNPS, IMS; accreditations: AMS, IL BE
Governance by board
Year-round; childcare; urban location; interns accepted.

World of Discovery Montessori School
12253 S McDaniel St, Alsip, IL 60658-2545
Mariam Fuillen

Kassers Childrens House
2449 W Peterson Ave, Chicago, IL 60659-4112
Kathleen Kasser
Type: Montessori

Alternatives, Inc
1126 W Granville, Chicago, IL 60660
Judy Gall, 312-973-0578
Affiliation: ASN
Individual, family, and group counseling; employment program; crisis intervention and advocacy; substance abuse prevention workshops.

Rogers Park Montessori School (1966)
1244 W Thorndale Ave, Chicago, IL 60660
Marsha Hahn, Adm, 312-271-1700
Non-profit; tuition: $2,400-5,720/yr
11 teachers, 7 assistants, 127 students, ages infant–9
Affiliation: AMS
Governance by board
Music; developmental gymnastics; childcare; urban location; interns accepted.

Kankakee Valley Montessori School
196 S Harrison Ave, Kankakee, IL 60901-4043
Tami Kacmar

Lincoln Cultural Center Montessori
240 Warren Ave, Kankakee, IL 60901-4319

Steuben Primary Center
520 S Wildwood Ave, Kankakee, IL 60901-5365
Type: Montessori

St Peter Montessori
320 Elmwood Ave, South Beloit, IL 61080-1929

Elmhurst- Lombard Montessori
550 S Edgewood, Rockford, IL 61102

Lathrop Elementary (1957)
2603 Clover Ave, Rockford, IL 61102
Jill Coffman, Prin, 815-966-3285
Type: Public choice Montessori
5 teachers, 1 pt assistant, 478 students, ages 3–12
Governance by administrator
Houses both traditional and Montessori classes; suburban location; transportation.

Montessori Learning Path (1983)
410 8th St, Rockford, IL 61104
Mary Schoembs, Adm, 815-964-1700
Non-profit; tuition: $160/404/mo
5 teachers, 2 assistants, 68 students, ages 3–6
Affiliations: Rockford Regional Daycare Dirs Assn, AMS
Governance by board of trustees
Parent cooperation; urban location; interns accepted.

Rockford Public Schools
201 S Madison St, Rockford, IL 61104
William Bowen
Type: Montessori

Montessori Children's House of Rockford
4700 Augustine Dr, Rockford, IL 61107

Montessori Learning Center of Rockford, Inc. (1984)
1390 N. Mulford Rd, Rockford, IL 61107
Emma Lou Mulnix, Adm, 815-226-0111
Non-profit; tuition: $1,625-2,700/yr
5 teachers, 7 assistants, 102 students, ages 3–15
Affiliation: AMS
Governance by board
Childcare; urban location; interns accepted.

Open Court Publishing
(See Resource Section)

Villa Montessori School (1979)
3010 26th Ave, Moline, IL 61265
Renee M. Detloff, Head, 309-764-7047, FAX: same
Non-profit; tuition: $3/hr-2,200/yr
12 teachers, 18 assistants, 180 students, ages infant–9
Affiliations: AMS, QCAEYC, NAEYC; accreditation: ISACS
Governance by administrator
Spanish and Japanese studies for all; childcare; suburban location; interns accepted.

Rainbow Re-Source Center
(See Resource Section)

Farm Country General Store
(See Resource Section)

Montessori School of Peoria
200 S Church St, Washington, IL 61571-2717

Montessori School of Bloomington-Normal
5 Kensignton Circle, Bloomington, IL 61704-7602

Pontiac Montessori School
102 E Michigan Ave #E, Pontiac, IL 61764-1158
Dorothy Rodgers

The Montessori School of Champaign-Urbana (1963)
1403 Regency Dr E, Savoy, IL 61874
Rita Young, Adm, 217-356-1818
Tuition: $210-414/mo
5 teachers, 5 assistants; student ages 3-6
Affiliations: AMS, IL BE
Governance by board
New facility; Spanish; ASL; music lessons available; interns
accepted.

Enriched GED Program (1989)
5800 Godfrey Rd, Godfrey, IL 62035
Holly Novara, Coord
Type: independent
7 teachers, 72 students, ages 16-18
Affiliation: Lewis & Clark CC
Governance by board
Teacher qualifications: MA
College credit.

Montessori Children's House of Alton
5800 Godfrey Rd, Godfrey, IL 62035-2426
Laurie Milnor or Parents Assn

Edwardsville Montessori School
4401 Hwy 162, Granite City, IL 62040
Mary Beth McGivern

Children's House- St Clair
400 Joseph Dr, Belleville, IL 62221-1632
Type: Montessori

Belleville Alternative Night School (1976)
2600 W Main, Belleville, IL 62223
618-233-5094, FAX: 618-233-7586
Type: public at-risk
33 teachers, 195 students, mainly at-risk, ages 15-21, 9-12th
grade
Governance by teachers, principal, parent advisory board
Voc, community, parenting ed; work transition; counseling;
multi-aged classes; suburban location.

Beck Optional Education Program (1985)
6137 Beck Rd, Red Bud, IL 62278
James W. Heil, Dir, 618-473-2222, FAX: 618-473-2292
Type: public at-risk
7 teachers, 60 students, ages 15.5-21, 9-12th grade
Affiliations: North Central, ISBE
Governance by teachers, principal, board
Teacher qualifications: IL Certification
Vocational; small classes; on-on-one instruction; community
service; multi-aged classes; rural location; transportation;
interns accepted.

Fearon Teacher Aids
(See Resource Section)

Futures Unlimited (1977)
250 E William St, Decatur, IL 62523
Randall Taylor, Director, 217-429-1054
Type: public at-risk
8 teachers, 120 students, mainly at-risk, ages 13-19, 7-12th
grade
Affiliation: Macon Co Ed Service Region
Governance by teachers and principal
Teacher qualifications: state certification
Parenting; family living; sociology; traditional academics; MS
completion; multi-aged classes; urban location.

Montessori Ganderfeather's Children's House (1990)
6758 Minder Rd, Rochester, IL 62563
Jill Persinos, Adm, 217-498-8609
Tuition: $110-350/mo
2 teachers, 1 assistant, 45 students, ages infant-12
Affiliation: AMS
Governance by administrator
Located on a rural farm; barnyard animals; Earth education;
childcare; interns accepted.

Children's Village
860 S Main St, Jacksonville, IL 62650-3012
Type: Montessori

Montessori Children's of Springfield
4147 Sandhill Rd, Springfield, IL 62702-1114

John Hay Montessori Children's House
200 N 11th St, Springfield, IL 62703-1004

Montessori Schoolhouse (1987)
717 Rickard Rd, Springfield, IL 62704
Gail Parker, Owner/Adm, 217-787-5505
4 teachers, 3 assistants, 56 students, ages infant-15
Affiliation: AMS
Governance by administrator
Spanish; swimming pool; multi-cultural staff; childcare; urban
location; interns accepted.

St Nicholas Montessori Preschool
326 S Douglas Ave, Springfield, IL 62704-1725

Springfield Public Schools Program (1976)
2530 E Ash St, Springfield, IL 62707
Dr. Linda W. Seltzer, Supervisor, 217-525-3275
Type: public at-risk
25 teachers, 700 students, mainly at-risk, ages 11-21, 5-12th
grade
Governance by teachers and principal
Teacher qualifications: state SE certification
Individualized, integrated; whole-person approach with community agencies' support; urban location; transportation;
interns accepted.

Matrix Institute
PO Box 4487, Springfield, IL 62708-4487
Type: Montessori

Carbondale New School
RR 5 Pleasant Hill Rd, Carbondale, IL 62901
Linda M. Rohling, Dir
Type: independent; tuition: $2,250/yr, scholarships
54 students, pre K-8th grade
Parental involvement.

Cairo Montessori Pre-School
PO Box 521, Cairo, IL 62914-0521

Emerson Elementary School
3101 Elm St, Cairo, IL 62914-1399
Dr Elaine Bonifield
Type: Montessori

Montessori School of Southern Illinois
507 N 9th St, Murphysboro, IL 62966-1841

Indiana

Anderson Community Program
30 W 11th St, Anderson, IN 46016
Sheila Decaroli, 317-641-2157
Type: public at-risk

Countryside Learning Center
PO Box 3030, Anderson, IN 46018-3030
Type: Montessori

Montessori Academy
620 Kinzer Ave, Carmel, IN 46032-2311

Noblesville Montessori House
954 Mulberry St, Noblesville, IN 46060

Country Children's House
2225 Dakota Dr, Noblesville, IN 46060-9075
Type: Montessori

I Can! Montessori School
14506 Crystal Creek Dr, Noblesville, IN 46060-9506
Mr or Ms Rhodes

Montessori Children's House
222 S 4th Ave, Beech Grove, IN 46107-1915

Hancock-S. Madison Joint Services (1993)
820 N Broadway, Greenfield, IN 46140
Fritz Kolmerton, 317-462-9527
Type: public choice
150 students

Child's World Montessori Pre-School
199 W Pearl St, Greenwood, IN 46142-3534
Joyce Probst

Greenwood Montessori School
824 N Madison Ave, Greenwood, IN 46142-4127

Indiana Association of Home Educators
1000 N Madison Ave Suite S2, Greenwood, IN 46142-4158
317-865-3013

Foreign Language Magnet (1984)
1500 E Michigan St, Indianapolis, IN 46201
David Banks, Dir, 317-226-3964, FAX: 317-226-3932
Type: public choice
160 teachers, 2100 students, ages 14-18, HS
Affiliation: North Central
Governance by principal
Teacher qualifications: Degree, IN certification
Six instruction levels; companion history courses; immersion; language maintenance; college credit courses; travel and study abroad; foreign teaching; multi-aged classes; extensive field trips; interns accepted.

Key Renaissance Middle School
1401 E 10th St, Indianapolis, IN 46201
Patricia Bolanos, 317-226-4297
Type: magnet
6-8th grade
Theme-based.

Francis Parker Montessori School (1979)
2353 Columbia Ave, Indianapolis, IN 46205
Jean Harrell, Prin, 317-226-4256, FAX: 226-3370
Type: public choice
30 teachers, 470 students, ages 3-12, pre K-5th grade
Affiliation: I PS
Governance by principal
Teacher qualifications: state certification, IPS Montessori training
Outdoor learning lab; close student-teacher partnership; strong parent organization; self-paced; no letter grades; multi-aged classes; 9 week grading periods; urban location; interns accepted.

Rousseau McClellan IPS #91
5111 N Evanston Ave, Indianapolis, IN 46205
Melissa Keller, principal, 317-226-4291
Type: Public choice Montessori
24 teachers, 364 students, ages 5-11, K-5th grade
Governance by principal, board
Teacher qualifications: state certification; system-based Montessori training.
Multi-aged classes; extensive field trips; no letter grades; urban location; transportation; interns accepted.

Montessori Activity Center
3819 N Delaware St, Indianapolis, IN 46205-2647

A Children's Habitat (1972)
4550 N Ilinois St, Indianapolis, IN 46208
Judy Weingartner, teacher, 317-283-7525
Type: Montessori, non-profit
3 teachers, 1 assistant, 45 students, ages 3-6
Governance by parent cooperative
Childcare; suburban location; interns accepted.

Montessori Centres, Inc (1964)
563 W Westfield Blvd, Indianapolis, IN 46208
Evelyn Froehlich, Pres, 317-257-2224
2 teachers, 3 assistants, 45 students, mainly international, ages 3-9
Affiliation: CIMTA
Governance by board
Spanish speakers; near Children's Museum and Butler U; Kolbe resources for gifted.

Shortridge Middle School
3401 N Meridian St, Indianapolis, IN 46208
Al Finnell, 317-226-4010
Type: magnet
6-8th grade
Arts; mulitcultural; humanities.

Children's House
2401 W 39th St, Indianapolis, IN 46208-3271
Type: Montessori

Horizon Middle School
2310 E 30th St, Indianapolis, IN 46218
Sharon Wilkins, 317-226-4350
Type: public
65 students, mainly at-risk, 7-8th grade
Community involvement.

Broad Ripple High School
1115 Broad Ripple Ave, Indianapolis, IN 46220
Larry McCoud, 317-226-3784
Type: magnet
9-12th grade
Humanities; performing and visual arts.

Little Friends Child Care (1985)
3030 E Kessler Blvd, Indianapolis, IN 46220
Karen Kosoglov, Dir, 317-251-5690
Type: independent, non-profit; tuition: $89-111/wk
11 teachers, 73 students, ages 1-6
Governance by board
Teacher qualifications: teaching degree or child care experience
State licensed; parent advisory group; extensive field trips; suburban location; interns accepted.

Decatur Vocational Enrichment Center (1984)
5251 Kentucky Ave, Indianapolis, IN 46221
Elizabeth A. Gut, 317-856-7511

Type: public at-risk
4 teachers, 50 students, ages 14–19, 9–12th grade
Affiliation: Decatur Central HS
Governance by teachers and principal
No letter grades; suburban location.

Stephen Foster #67 Elementary
553 N Somerset Ave, Indianapolis, IN 46222
John Airola, 317-226-4267
Type: magnet
K–5th grade
Montessori.

Wayne Township Alternative Junior High (1986)
2001 Bridgeport Rd, Indianapolis, IN 46231
Jerry Stephens, Dept Chair, 317-243-5507
Type: public at-risk
3 teachers, 45 students, ages 12–16
Governance by teachers and principal
Teacher qualifications: IN license
Alternative to expulsion; multi-aged classes; transportation.

Discovery at Indian Creek (1986)
10833 E 56th St, Indianapolis, IN 46236
Dr Karen Gould, Prin, 317-823-4497, FAX: 823-0973
Type: public choice
29 teachers, 541 students, ages 6–11, 1–5th grade
Governance by teachers, principal, parents, board
Teacher qualifications: Bachelor's
Science themes; integrated curriculum; use of technology;
   parental involvement; university collaboration as professional development school; nature center; active learning;
   alternative assessments; extensive field trips; interns
   accepted.

Learning Unlimited (1976)
1801 E 86th St, Indianapolis, IN 46240
Jay Hill, EdD, Dir, 317-259-5301, FAX: 317-259-5369
Type: public choice
14 teachers, 325 students, ages 15–18, 9–12th grade
Governance by principal, faculty and student reps, board
Humanities-based school-within-a-school; semester long
   community projects; contracts with community resource
   persons and teachers; projects integrated into academic
   classes; suburban location; interns accepted.

Wayne Enrichment Center (1976)
5248 W Raymond, Indianapolis, IN 46241
Ellen Jose, Chair, 317-248-8685, FAX: 243-5537
Type: public at-risk
6 teachers, 150 students, ages 14–19, 9–12th grade
Affiliation: Indianapolis Dept of Empoyment & Training
Governance by teachers and principal
Teacher qualifications: state certification
Integrates employment/life skills; work-study; community
   service; no letter grades; suburban location; interns
   accepted.

Montessori Learning Center
11056 Westfield Blvd, Indianapolis, IN 46280

Lake County Christian Home School Association
11202 Parrish, Cedar Lake, IN 46303
219-365-5267

Chesterton Montessori School
270 E Burdick Rd, Chesterton, IN 46304-9303
Terry Cavollo

Montessori Children's Schoolhouse
5935 Hohman Ave, Hammond, IN 46320-2425
Kathleen Hill, principal-Administrator, 219-932-5666
8 teachers, 15 assistants, 231 students, ages infant–9
Affiliation: ILMS; accreditation: AMS
Governance by board
Urban location; interns accepted.

Montessori Children
1814 Bluebird Ln, Munster, IN 46321-3427

Montessori School Woodmar Church of God
1421 173rd St, Hammond, IN 46324-2860

Calumet Region Montessori
2109 57th St, Hobart, IN 46342-5629

Montessori School of Michigan City
5388 N Bleck Rd, Michigan City, IN 46360
Pamela K Smith

Montessori School of Porter Country
505 Marquette St, Valparaiso, IN 46383-2598

Porter County Career Center
1005 N Franklin St, Valparaiso, IN 46391
Kathy Spears, Prin, 219-531-3170, FAX: 219-531-3173
Non-profit; tuition: variable
5 teachers, 100–150 students, ages 16–19, 9–12th grade
Governance by superintendent and principal
Credit for work; max 10 students/class; independent study;
   no letter grades; non-compulsory class attendance; multi-
   aged classes; urban location.

Montessori School of Elkhart
416 E Crawford St, Elkhart, IN 46514-2764

Montessori School House
58433 City Rd 105, Elkhart, IN 46517-9452

Discovery House Preschool
419 S 5th St, Goshen, IN 46526-3925
Type: Montessori

Youth Educational Service Program (YES) (1986)
c/o Starke Circuit Ct, Knox, IN 46534
John Baldwin, 219-772-9151
3 teachers, 12 students
For expelled students under court jurisdiction; group
   counseling.

The Montessori Academy (1969)
15767 Day Rd, Mishawaka, IN 46565
Donna Durish, Head, 219-256-5313, FAX: 219-256-5499
Non-profit; tuition: $620–4,265/yr
13 teachers, 14 assistants, 314 students, ages infant–15
Affiliation: NAMTA; accreditations: AMS, MACTE
Governance by board of trustees
Extracurriculars; computer lab; PE; childcare; suburban loca-
   tion; interns accepted.

**Wawasee Community Substance Abuse Outreach
   Program**
#1 Warrior Path, Syracuse, IN 46567
Karen Parr, 219-457-3147
1 teacher, 4–5 students, 6–12th grade
Alternative to expulsion; counseling; job or volunteer work
   required.

Whitko Community AIM School
2043 N Detroit St, Warsaw, IN 46580
Dave McGuire, 219-267-8875
Type: public at-risk

Montessori Child Development Center
601 E Smith St, Warsaw, IN 46580-4540

The Montessori Center (1982)
1236 Lincoln Way E, South Bend, IN 46601
Marianne Surges, Adm, 812-289-1222
Non-profit; tuition: $1,450–2,500/yr
2 teachers, 3 assistants, 50 students, ages 3–6
Affiliation: AMS
Governance by administrator
Flexible program; childcare; urban location; interns accepted.

Montessori School of South Bend, Inc
1302 E Indiana Ave, South Bend, IN 46613-3230

Little Flower Montessori School
624 N Notre Dame Ave, South Bend, IN 46617

Montessori School
3002 S Michigan, South Bend, IN 46618

Countryside Montessori
53287 Ironwood Rd, South Bend, IN 46635-1385

Steuben County MSD Alternative School
400 S Martha, Angola, IN 46703
Lisa Ulery, 219-665-1360
Mainly returning students, ages 15-22, 9-12th grade
Half-day of work assisting social worker, teacher, etc.

Wells County Alternative School (1992)
120-22 LaMar St, Bluffton, IN 46714
Ron Harnish, Dir/Tch, 824-0474
Type: public at-risk
4 teachers, 32 students, ages 16-21, 9-12th grade
Governance by teachers and principal
Teacher qualifications: IN license
Teachers are tutors; self-paced; rural location.

Adams County Center for Educational Success
654 N 12th St, Decatur, IN 46733
Barbara Baker, Dir, 219-724-4434
Type: public choice
3 teachers; students mainly involved in special life challenges
Afternoons of work, community service, or childcare.

Wells County al Center
PO Box 386, Ossian, IN 46777
Dr Michael Sailsbery, 219-622-4125
Type: public at-risk

Ralph Bunche Elementary
1111 Green St, Fort Wayne, IN 46803
Connie Murphy, 219-425-7323
Type: magnet
Student ages 4+,-5th grade
Montessori.

Montessori Academy of Fort Wayne
2726 Lynn Ave, Fort Wayne, IN 46805-3842

Weisser Park-Whitney Young ES Fine Arts Magnet (1978)
902 Colerick St, Ft Wayne, IN 46806
Daniel A. Bickel, Prin, 219-425-7483
Non-profit
47 teachers, 750 students, ages 4-12, pre K-5th grade
Affiliation: Ft Wayne Comm. Schools
Governance by teachers, principal
Teacher qualifications: IN certification
Enriched basics program; extensive use of technology; integrated multi-cultural emphasis; extensive field trips; multi-aged classe; interns accepted.

Children's Cottage
2820 Reed St, Ft Wayne, IN 46806-1204
Type: Montessori

Martin Luther King Montessori School
326 E Wayne, Ft Wayne, IN 46807
Cathy Cullen

Franke Park Biological Science Magnet (1988)
828 Mildred Ave, Ft Wayne, IN 46808
Jean Linville, Prin, 219-425-7336
Type: public choice
24 teachers, 514 students, ages 5-11, K-5th grade
Governance by principal
Large outdoor education area; hands-on-science lab; greenhouse; gardens; ampitheater; wetland; adjacent to park/zoo; extensive field trip; interns accepted.

Three Rivers Montessori (1967)
724 W 4th St, Ft Wayne, IN 46808-2609
Starr Watts, Joan Hayden, Co-Dir, 219-426-6143
Non-profit; tuition: $187/200/315/mo
5 teachers, 7 assistants, 92 students, ages infant-6
Affiliation: AMS
Governance by board of trustees
Computer education; foreign languages; Oalcroze Eurythmics; gymnastics; childcare; urban location.

Fort Wayne Area Home Schools
13428 Old Auburn Rd, Fort Wayne, IN 46816
Ron & Sharon Hoot

Montessori Children's House of Kokomo, Inc
PO Box 4052, Kokomo, IN 46904-4052

Allen School Alternative Program
1240 S Adams St, Marion, IN 46952
Susan Bove, 317-662-2546
Type: public
Students mainly disruptive, K-4th grade
Intervention model; behavior modification in-service; structured time-out room.

River Falls Christian Association of Home Educators
PO Box 482, Charlestown, IN 47111
812-256-6446

McDowell Education Center (1972)
2700 McKinley Ave, Columbus, IN 47201
Paul G. Riddle, Dir, 812-376-4451, FAX: 376-4512
Type: public at-risk
45 teachers, 450-500 students, ages 16-20, 9-12th grade
Governance by teachers, principal, democratic school meeting
Teacher qualifications: IN certification
Vocational; multi-aged classes; extensive field trips; outcome-based; rural location.

Jackson County Christian Home Educators
528 E 16th St, Seymour, IN 47274
812-523-1532

Montessori House for Children
313 N Chinquapin Way, Muncie, IN 47304-3642

Friends Preschool
418 W Adams St, Muncie, IN 47305
Shelly Stewart, Head Tch, 317-288-5133
Type: Quaker

ACE Program (1986)
1300 Spartan Dr, Connersville, IN 47331
Kathy McCarty, Coord, 317-825-4110, FAX: 827-0836
Type: public at-risk
5 teachers, 72 students, ages 15-19, 8-12th grade
Governance by teachers and principal
Teacher qualifications: IN certification
Individual curriculum plans; self-directed; credit for work completed; suburban location; transportation.

North Campus Alternative School (1975)
80 Glenwood St, New Castle, IN 47362
Karen P. Marcum, Dir, 317-521-7237, FAX: 317-521-7268
Type: public at-risk
11 teachers, 170 students, mainly IDEA handicapped, ages 12-21, 7-12th grade
Governance by teachers; principal
Teacher qualifications: IN SE License
Competency-based; psychologist; counselor; no letter grades; multi-aged classes; level system; rural location; transportation; interns accepted.

Children's School (1971)
607 W Main St, Richmond, IN 47374
Laurence Boggess, Head Tch, 317-966-5767
Type: Quaker, non-profit; tuition: $1,800/yr, scholarships

5 teachers, 50 students, ages 4–11, K–5th grade
Affiliation: Friends Council on Education
Teacher qualifications: BA or higher
No letter grades; multi-aged classes; suburban location;
    interns accepted.

Meramec Montessori Children's Center
PO Box 64, Yorktown, IN 47396-0064

Bloomington Montessori (1968)
1835 S Highland Ave, Bloomington, IN 47401
Jeanne G. Jerden, Exec Asst, 812-336-2800
Non-profit; tuition: $165-370/mo
4 teachers, 11 assistants, 147 students, ages 3–12
Affiliation: AMS
Governance by board
Suburban location; interns accepted.

Harmony School (1974)
Box 1787, Bloomington, IN 47402
Steve Boncheck, Director, 812-334-8349, FAX: 812-334-8349
Type: independent, non-profit; tuition: sliding scale, 80% on
    scholarships
17 teachers, 200 students, ages 3–21, pre K–12th grade
Affiliations: Coalition of Essential Schools, NCACS
Governance by democratic school meeting
Teacher qualifications: all have BA-PhD, 60% certified, no spe-
    cific qualifications
Based on the principal that the role of education in a democ-
    racy is to sensitize young people to the delicate balance
    between individual growth and community responsibility;
    no letter grades; multi-aged classes; extensive field trips;
    suburban location; interns accepted.

School of Education, Alternative Teacher Education
Indiana University, Bloomington, IN 47405
Tom Gregory, 812-876-9362
Type: higher education

LEARN
7633 Shilo Rd, Unionville, IN 47468
Type: home-based

Padanaram Village School (1972)
RR 1, Box 478, Williams In, IN 47470
Steven Fuson, Schoolmaster, 812-262-7252
Type: independent, boarding, non-profit; no tuition
9 teachers, 60 students, ages 5–18, K–12th grade
Governance by teachers and principal, parent cooperative
Community shares goods communally; 3 R's and strong cur-
    ricula are blended with arts, hands-on learning, community
    life; no letter grades; multi-aged classes; extensive field
    trips.

Vincennes Community
300 N 6th St, Vincennes, IN 47591
Dr Joan Beckman, Asst Supt, 812-882-3668
MS, HS
Alternative to suspension/expulsion.

Southern Indiana Support Group
PO Box 388, Princeton, IN 47670
812-385-4176
Type: home-based

Richmond Community Out of School Option
300 Hab Etchison Blvd, Richmond, IN 47674
Dr Karen Montgomery, 317-973-3300

6–8th grade
Short-term, intensive intervention as alternative to expulsion.

McCutchanville Montessori
8100 Petersburg Rd, Evansville, IN 47711-1777

Stanley Hall Enrichment Center (1988)
800 S Evans, Evansville, IN 47713
Patricia C. Cato, Prin, 812-465-8281
Type: public at-risk
5 teachers, 110 students, ages 15–21, 10–12th grade
Governance by teachers; principal
Teacher qualifications: Licensed and/or endorsed
Student-centered; self-paced; multi-aged classes; life skills;
    career awareness; community service; urban location;
    interns accepted.

Montessori Academy
4611 Adams Ave, Evansville, IN 47714
Roxanne Crouch

Terre Haute Montessori School
4310 S 11th St, Terre Haute, IN 47802-4318
Frances Murphy

Vigo County Juvenile Center Educational Services
961 Lafayette Ave, Terre Haute, IN 47804
Beverly Spear, 812-462-4224
Students mainly detained
Tutoring; counseling.

Wabash Valley Homeschool Association (1984)
2515 E Quinn Ave, Terre Haute, IN 47805
Barbara Palmer, 466-9467
Governance by parent cooperative

Montessori School
St Mary of Woods College, St Mary Of The Woods, IN 47876-
    1001

Rising Star Montessori School
413 Teal Rd, Lafayette, IN 47905-2311

Montessori School of Greater Lafayette
PO Box 2311, W Lafayette, IN 47906
Anita McKinney

Montessori School of Crawfordsville
1850 Ladoga Rd, Crawfordsville, IN 47933-3743

Indian Trials Career Center (1987)
807 N 6th St, Monticello, IN 47960
Carl Van Meter, Director, 219-583-9639
Type: public at-risk
2 teachers, 30 students, ages 11–21, 6–12th grade
Affiliation: Twin Lakes School Corp
Governance by teachers, principal, board
Teacher qualifications: state certification
Individualized; CAI; outcome-based; multi-aged classes; no
    letter grades; non-compulsory class attendance; rural loca-
    tion; transportation; interns accepted.

Upbeat Alternative School
RR 1, Oxford, IN 47977
Dale Jones, 317-884-1600
Students mainly teen parents, pregnant, other special needs,
    7–12th grade
Individualized entry/exit criteria.

Iowa

SHEEP
9400 NE 46th Ave, Altoona, IA 50009
Angela Sweiter
Type: home-based

Laurel Tree Montessori Preschool
3727 Calhoun Ave, Ames, IA 50010-4104

Bondurant-Farrar Summer School (1984)
300 Garfield, Bondurant, IA 50035
Warren Kyer, 515-967-7819
1 teacher, 15 students, JH
Half-day; self-paced; remediation; rural location.

DMACC Academic Achievement Center (1972)
1125 Hancock Dr, Boone, IA 50036
Jinny Silberhorn, Dir, 515-432-7203 x 1020
Type: public at-risk
7 teachers; students partly at-risk, ages 17+, HS
Teacher qualifications: BA
Urban location.

Network of Iowa Christian Home Educators
Box 158, Dexter, IA 50070
800-723-0438, 515-830-1614

Indianola Learning Center (1992)
1301 E 2nd Ave, Indianola, IA 50125
Michael A. Baethke, 515-961-9580
Type: public choice
5 teachers, 60–65 students, HS
Vocational; teen parenting; student-based discipline; community involvement; competency-based; self-paced; urban location.

Caring Connection (1988)
1602 S 2nd Ave, Marshalltown, IA 50158
Anne Peglow, 515-752-4535
Type: public choice
13 teachers, 600 students, all
Independent and home study; contracting; mentoring; childcare; ESL; self-evaluation; pass/fail, no-grade options; special ed; vocational; teen parenting; urban location.

SAFE–Student Alternative Formula Education (1989)
216 Sherman, Murray, IA 50174
James F. Rhoads, 515-447-2517
Type: public choice
4 teachers, 50 students, mainly Native American, JH, HS
Competency-based; self-paced; independent study; GED; remediation; contracting; special ed; vocational; rural location.

Basics & Beyond Alternative School (1991)
600 N 2nd Ave W, Newton, IA 50208
James Fenton, 515-791-0700 x1700
Type: public choice
8 teachers, 80 students, HS
Competency-based; self-paced; independent study; teen parenting; community studies, contracting; childcare; career/vocational; no letter grades; urban location.

Jasper County Support Group
1510 S 8th Ave, Newton, IA 50208
Pastor Jim Black
Type: home-based

Reading Recovery, Reading/Writing Lab, Math Lab
1800 Grand Ave, Des Moines, IA 50211
Sharon Castelda, Chap 1 Supervisor, 515-242-7731, FAX: 515-242-7550
Type: public at-risk
78 teachers, 3000 students, ages 6–12, 1–6th grade

Teacher qualifications: reading endorsements
Urban location.

CAP (Clarke Alternative Program) (1985)
800 N Jackson, Osceola, IA 50213
Joe Shelton, 515-342-6505
Type: public choice
1 teacher, 30–35 students, HS
Flexible schedule; site-based; individualized study; 2 diploma types; arranged, regular school, and correspondence courses; work/study; childcare.

PASS Perry High School (1989)
18th & Lucinda, Perry, IA 50220
Kirk Waggie, 515-465-4656
1 teacher, 63 students, mainly at-risk, HS
Teen parenting; independent study; computer-based; personalized; peer tutoring; pass/fail option; career/vocational; urban location.

Perry Learning Center (1993)
1200 18th St, Perry, IA 50220
Eugene Brady, Prin, 515-465-2997, FAX: 515-465-2426
Type: public at-risk
1 teacher, 20 students, mainly at-risk, ages 16–20, 10–12th grade
Governance by principal
Multi-aged classes; rural location.

Story County Support Group
Roland, IA 50236
Claudia Nielsen, 515-388-4677
Type: home-based
Meets 1st Tuesday of month.

Roland-Story Elementary
900 Hillcrest Dr, Story City, IA 50248
Jane A. Todey, 515-733-4386
1 teacher, 10 students, mainly Asian, ES-HS
Student volunteers/assistants; mentoring; peer tutoring; ESL; personalized program.

Sayre Elementary and Middle School
1700 Vine St, West Des Moines, IA 50265
Barbara Sayre
Type: Montessori

Montessori Children's House
1025 28th St, West Des Moines, IA 50265-2124

Iowa Coalition for Home Educators
PO Box 6055, Des Moines, IA 50309
515-262-8547

Montessori Learning Center
4533 University Ave #E, Des Moines, IA 50311-3359

Des Moines Alternative High School-North (1993)
1801 16th St, Des Moines, IA 50314
Vince Lewis, Prin, 515-244-0448, FAX: 244-0448
Type: public choice
200 students, mainly at-risk, ages 15–20, 9–12th grade
Governance by principal, teachers
Work experience credit; support groups; multi-aged classes; childcare; interns accepted.

Des Moines South Alternative High School (1969)
1000 SW Porter, Des Moines, IA 50315
Vince Scavo, 515-285-3323
Type: public choice
44 teachers, 350 students, pre-K, HS
Separate building; computers; independent study; contracting; teen parenting; mentoring; childcare; self-evaluation; vocational; urban location.

Phillips Traditional School
1701 Lay St, Des Moines, IA 50317
Linda Hansen, Prin, 515-265-3406
Type: public choice
23 teachers; student ages 5-12, K-5th grade
Governance by principal
Teacher qualifications: excellent service
No letter grades; interns accepted.

Bureau of Federal School Improvement, Dept of Education
(See Resource Section)

Montessori Children's Center
8509 Alice Ave, Des Moines, IA 50325-7111

Cerro Cordo County Support Group
626 10th NE, Mason City, IA 50401
Dennis or Nancy Erickson
Type: home-based

Mason City Alternative School (1975)
19 N Illinois, Mason City, IA 50401
David A. Ciccetti, 515-421-4427
Type: public choice
7 teachers, 80-100 students, HS
Competency-based; independent study; computers;
    teaming; contracting; peer tutoring; Share-Time Program;
    childcare; special ed; vocational; teen parenting; urban
    location.

St Ansgar ABE/GED (1976)
206 E 8th St, St Ansgar, IA 50472
Larry Pheggenkuhle, 515-736-4329
1 teacher, 3-5 students, JH, HS
Evening GED prep; no letter grades.

Gordon Willard Center
104 S 17th St, Fort Dodge, IA 50501
Jerry Einwalter, Coord/Tch, 515-576-7305, FAX:-1988
Type: public choice
5 teachers, 65 students, mainly at-risk, ages 15-21, 9-12th
    grade
Affiliation: IA AE Assn
Governance by advisory board of students, parents,
    community
Teacher qualifications: IA Certification
Individual education plans; self-paced; on-site work/study;
    social skills; 80% attendance required; rural location; trans-
    portation; interns accepted.

Student Support Services-Iowa Lakes Community College (1972?)
3200 College Dr, Emmetsburg, IA 50536
Melba Byrkeland, 712-852-3554, FAX: 712-852-2152
Type: public at-risk; tuition: $76/wk
3 teachers; student ages 17+, 12+
Governance by board
Teacher qualifications: certification
Psycho-social approach; supervised housing; rural location;
    interns accepted.

Storm Lake Senior High School (1989)
621 Tornado Dr, Storm Lake, IA 50588
Steve Berry, 712-732-8065
2 teachers, 49 students, JH, HS
Independent study; computer-based work; teaming; peer
    tutoring; ESL; self-evaluation; SE; urban location.

Webster City Alternative School (1973)
1000 Des Moines St, Webster City, IA 50595
Mary Crystal, 515-832-2648
2 teachers, 2-26 students, JH, HS
After-school M-Th; credits toward graduation at Webster City
    HS; teen parenting; independent study; computers; self-
    paced; urban location.

Casa Montessori School, Inc (1982)
9204 University Ave, Cedar Falls, IA 50613
Patricia Poage, Dir, 319-277-8121
Non-profit; tuition: $230-295/mo
2 teachers, 2 assistants, 36 students, ages 3-9
Governance by administrator

Malcolm Price Laboratory School (1986)
19th & Campus St, Cedar Falls, IA 50613-3593
Linda Fernandez, 319-273-2202
Type: independent
95 teachers, 600 students, all
Affiliation: Univ of N Iowa
Competency-based; special ed; performing arts; self-paced;
    cooperative learning; computers; learning packets;
    teaming; non-graded through grade 8; teen parenting;
    urban location.

Expo II (1973)
PO Box 848, Waverly, IA 50677
Jean Klunder, 319-352-2630
1 teacher, 20 students, HS
Academic instruction; independent study; self-paced.

Independent Learning Center (1968)
844 W 4th St, Waterloo, IA 50702
Charmaine Carney, 319-234-5745
6 teachers, 315 students, HS
Affiliation: Hawkeye CC
School year and summer drop-in center, 13 hrs/day, M-F;
    independent study; computer-based work; self-paced;
    home study; GED; urban location.

EXPO High School (1975)
927 Franklin St, Waterloo, IA 50703
W. Ray Richardson, Dir, 319-291-4842
Type: public at-risk
16 teachers, 245 students, ages 14-21
Affiliation: NCA
Governance by teachers, principal, board
No letter grades; extensive field trips; multi-aged classe;
    interns accepted.

Creston Alternative School (1981)
107 N Maple, Creston, IA 50801
Angela Scallon, 515-782-4375
Type: public choice
1 teacher, 15 students, HS
Storefront; personalized program; contracting; urban
    location.

LeMars Community/WIT-ILC (1990)
410 5th Ave SW, LeMars, IA 51031
Jim Patera, 712-546-4153
Type: public choice
2 teachers, 50 students, HS
Affiliation: W Iowa Tech
In printing business building; half-day; competency-based;
    self-paced; contracting; peer tutoring; urban location.

Whiting Community School (1988)
Whiting, IA 51063
Gary Funkhouser, 712-458-2468
2 teachers, 10 students, ages 3-4, pre-K
Afternoon program; student volunteers; special ed; urban
    location.

Central Campus Individual Learning Center (1971)
1121 Jackson St, Sioux City, IA 51105
Dr Paul VanderWiel, 712-279-6073
12 teachers, 450-550 students, HS
Affiliation: W Iowa Tech
Competency-based; self-paced; independent study; teen
    parenting; special ed; vocational; GED; ESL; urban location.

Carroll Alternative School (1992)
2809 N Grant Rd, Carroll, IA 51401

Gary D. Currie, 712-792-8010
Type: public choice; tuition: if outside district
3 teachers, 17 students, HS
Pre-employment training; independent study; computers; learning packets; 1/3 credit every 30 school days; no letter grades; suburban location.

Ida County Support Group
Ida Grove, IA 51445
Sue Goodenow, 712-364-2209
Type: home-based
Meets 3rd Monday of month.

Independent Learning Center (1979)
Lewis Central H S, Hwy 275, Council Bluffs, IA 51503
Curt Peterson, 712-366-8240
Type: public choice
1 teacher, 24 students, HS
Competency-based; self-paced; independent study; urban location.

Iowa Western Community College Adult Learning Center (1972)
620 N 8th St, Council Bluffs, IA 51503
Margot Fetrow, Coord, 712-325-3266, FAX: 325-3424
Type: public choice
13 pt teachers, 900 students, mainly at-risk, ages 16+
Governance by teachers and principal
Teacher qualifications: college grad
GED prep; ESL; ABE; self-paced; skills improvement in reading, writing, math at all levels; no letter grades; non-compulsory class attendance; multi-aged classes; suburban location.

Kanesville High School (1974)
807 Ave G, Council Bluffs, IA 51503
Romola Fritz, 712-328-6510
Type: public choice
14 teachers, 275 students, HS
Computers; SE; teen parenting; childcare; no letter grades; vocational; urban location.

Harlan Flexible Education Center (1991)
2712 12th St, Harlan, IA 51537
Amy Stallman, Adm; Kent Klinkefus, Prin, 712-755-3568, FAX: 712-755-7413
Type: public at-risk
1 teacher, 1 assistant, 18 students, ages 16–21, 9–12th grade
Affiliation: IA Western CC
Governance by teachers and principal
Teacher qualifications: secondary education certification
Require 80% mastery; independent study; self paced; work- and volunteer-for-credit programs; rural location.

Central Alternative High School (1973)
39 Bluff St, Dubuque, IA 52001
David Olson, 319-588-8395
Type: public choice
17 teachers, 275 students, JH, HS
Separate building; service learning; expeditionary learning; teaming; contracting; teen parenting; weekly visits by mental health and social work specialists; special ed; urban location.

Dubuque Montessori School, Inc Slattery Center
Flora Park, Dubuque, IA 52001

MAC: Maquoketa Alternative Classroom
PAR: Prevention & Retention Program (1973)
600 Washington, Maquoketa, IA 52060
Debbra J. Carson, Dir, 319-652-2451 x39
Type: public choice; tuition: if outside district
3 teachers, 40 students, mainly at-risk, HS
OBE, structured, individualized; mentorships; On-The-Job training; business partnerships help student transition from school-to-work; self-evaluation; rural location.

Allamakee Community District
1105 3rd Ave NW, Waukon, IA 52172
Dr Joe Schmitz
Type: Montessori

CEC Alternative Schools (1978)
509 S Dubuque, Iowa City, IA 52240
Diana Paulina, 319-339-6809, FAX: 319-339-5702
Type: public at-risk
8 teachers, 100 students, ages 13–21, 7–12th grade
Governance by democratic school meeting
Teacher qualifications: state certification
Work-study; video/art studios; art museums; leaders in district tech; shared decision making; no letter grades; multi-aged classes; extensive field trips; transportation; interns accepted.

Johnson County Support Group
Iowa City, IA 52240
Diana Brahn; Leslie Johnson, 319-645-2918, 338-4522
Type: home-based
Meets 1st Monday of month, 8-9 pm.

Willowind School
226 S. Johnson, Iowa City, IA 52240-5146
Ruth Manna
Type: independent

Little Shadow Montessori School
416 Fairchild St, Iowa City, IA 52245-2822

Montessori School of Iowa City
502 Reno St, Iowa City, IA 52245-3039
Patricia Hanick

Cedar Valley Montessori School
3rd Ave & 23rd St, Marion, IA 52302

Marion Learning Center (1978)
600 10th Ave, Marion, IA 52302
Jerry Hora or Jacquie Oster, 319-377-2216
2 teachers, 220 students, ages 14+, HS
Self-paced; GED; HS diploma; serves Linn-Mar, Marion, Central City, North Linn, Springville, Alburnett, Center Point districts.

Lincoln Alternative School (1990)
102 E North, Stanwood, IA 52337
Lou Grimm, 319-945-3341
Type: public choice
1 teacher, 9 students, JH, HS
Academic curriculum; self-paced; independent study; rural location.

STC Partnership Center (1990)
205 W 3rd St, Tama, IA 52339
Donna Downs Hempy, Proj Mgr, 515-484-3085, FAX: 515-484-3924
Type: public at-risk
4 teachers, 45 students, ages 12+, 6–12th grade
Affiliation: S Tama Co Schools
Governance by board
Teacher qualifications: certification
Tutoring; GED; ESL; learning lab; employment, recreational, and supportive human services; rural location; interns accepted.

Kirkwood Learning Center (1974)
111 Westview Dr, Washington, IA 52353
Sandy Weller, 653-4655, FAX: 653-6243
Type: public choice/at-risk
1 teacher, 175-200 students, partly at-risk, ages 15-74
No letter grades; multi-aged classes; rural location.

West Campus (1981)
Hwy 22E, PO Box 150, Wellman, IA 52356
Valli Domsic, 319-646-2093
Type: public choice

1 teacher, 20 students, HS
Competency-based; independent and home study; vocational; teen parenting; GED; no letter grades; urban location.

Metro High School (1974)
1212 7th St SE, Cedar Rapids, IA 52401
Dr Mary Wilcynski, Prin, 319-398-2193
Type: public at-risk
36 teachers, 620 students, mainly at-risk, ages 14–21, 9–12th grade
Affiliation: NCA
Governance by teachers and principal
Teacher qualifications: BA in education
Academics, electives, Vocademics (e.g., food service, on-site day care, laundry, recycling center, bike repair shop); credit awarded via a narrative evaluation by attendance, work performance and behavior; twice cited by US DOE as Blue Ribbon School; no letter grades; multi-aged classes; extensive field trips; urban location; interns accepted.

Johnson School (1976)
355 18th St SE, Cedar Rapids, IA 52403
Laurinda Fitzgerald, 319-398-2174
Type: public choice
4 teachers, 100 students, 1–5th grade
Focus on fine arts; urban location.

Kirkwood Lincoln Learning Center (1985)
9th St & 18th Ave SW, Cedar Rapids, IA 52404
Jan McBurney, 319-366-0142
Type: public choice
5 teachers, 20–40 students, HS
Affiliations: Prairie HS, Kirkwood Adult HS
Separate building; flexible hours; ESL; correspondence courses; independent and home study; GED; computers; community studies; career/vocational; urban location.

Monroe County Support Group
Albia, IA 52531
Erlene Gangsted; Bonnie Hall, 515-923-7912, 932-5680
Type: home-based
Meets 3rd Friday of month.

Davis County Alternative School (1990)
102 High St, Bloomfield, IA 52537-1738
Dee Altheide, 515-664-2200 x156
Type: public choice
2 teachers, 20 students, mainly Native American, HS
Affiliation: Davis Cty HS
Flexible hours; summer courses; academic assistance; no letter grades; independent study; rural location.

University Alternative High (1985)
1200 Market, Burlington, IA 52601
Raymond Eilenstine, 319-753-2701
8 teachers, 135–150 students, HS
Independent study; career/voc; self-paced; in separate building; childcare.

Creative Learning Center (1974)
1733 Ave I, Fort Madison, IA 52627
Beverly Link, 319-372-8093

Type: public choice
4 teachers, 85 students, HS
In two-story frame house; self-paced; independent study; community studies; teen parenting; urban location.

Montessori Country School
835 Ave A, Fort Madison, IA 52627-2859

Learning Center (1978)
2285 Middle Rd, Keokuk, IA 52632
Barb Harrison, Dir, 319-524-2542
Type: public at-risk
2 teachers, 50 students, mainly at-risk, ages 14–21, 9–12th grade
Affiliation: Keokuk Community School
Governance by teachers and principal
Teacher qualifications: Iowa subject are certification
Independent study, correspondence courses, career/vocational classes, and personalized educational programs; urban location.

Lincoln Alternative High School
732 11th Ave S, Clinton, IA 52732
Richard Grugin, Prin, 319-242-4073, FAX: 243-2415
Type: public at-risk
10 teachers, 120 students, mainly at-risk, ages 14–21, 9–12th grade
Governance by teachers and principal
Teacher qualifications: state secondary certification
Teacher considered a "family leader"; emphasis on self-growth and positive social values; support groups on young parenting, substance abuse, sexual abuse, and children of alcoholics; multi-aged classes; urban location; transportation; interns accepted.

CEP (Continuing Education Program) (1988)
152 Colorado St, Muscatine, IA 52761
R. L. Casini, 319-263-6141
Type: public choice
1 teacher, 150 students, HS
Affiliations: Muscatine CC, Muscatine HS
Self-paced; independent study; diploma.

Kirkwood Education Center
N Cedar St, Tipton, IA 52772
HS
Affiliation: Kirkwood CC
GED, Kirkwood Adult Ed diploma, or Tipton Comm School diploma; flexible hours.

Montessori House of Children
1918 W 16th St, Davenport, IA 52804
Margaret A Callett

2001 Alternative Program (1990)
1002 W Kimberly Rd, Davenport, IA 52806
Roger Fuerstenberg, 319-386-5840, 391-9161
Type: public choice
11 teachers, 275 students, HS
11 am–9 pm; traditional class structure with cooperative learning; remediation; computer-based work; urban location.

Kansas

Montessori Children's House of Lawrence
1900 University Dr, Lawrence, KS 66044-4554

Sunshine Acres Preschool
2141 Maple Ln, Lawrence, KS 66046-3299
Type: Montessori

Raintree Montessori School
4545 Clinton Pky, Lawrence, KS 66047-1913

Project STAY (Second Time Around for Youth)
1620 Rose, Leavenworth, KS 66048
Cynthia Bixby, Dir, 913-684-1580
3 teachers, 88 students
Individualized learning contracts; work/study; community
service; group studies.

Phase V Program (1972)
1800 W Dennis, Olathe, KS 66061
Jim Houghton, Dir, 913-780-7250
250-300 students, mainly at-risk
Night classes; min. attendance, productive work required.

Children's House
1024 W Fairwood Ln, Olathe, KS 66061-2414
Type: Montessori

BaSE (Basic Skills Education)
15100 W 127th, Olathe, KS 66062
Paige May, 913-780-7270
1 teacher, 56 students
Teacher qualifications: certification
9 week study skills curriculum; daily monitor required;
monthly parent meetings; independent study.

Final Focus at Olathe South High School
1640 E 151st St, Olathe, KS 66062
Zeny Schmidt, 913-780-7160
11 students, 11th grade
Affiliation: Olathe AVTS
Career education; vocational training; guest speakers; field
trips; simulations; weekly grade, attendance reviews.

Student HELP Clinic
315 N Lindenwood, Olathe, KS 66062
Walter Carter, 913-780-7002
Students mainly at-risk, ES-HS
Study, social skills; self-concept class; evaluation services;
tutoring; parenting class.

Lawrence Area Unaffiliated Group of Homeschoolers
(LAUGH) (1992)
RR 1, Box 496, Perry, KS 66073
Barbara J. Michener, 913-597-5579
Non-sectarian.

Kansans for
19985 Renner Rd, Spring Hill, KS 66083
913-686-2310
Type: state home-based

Associated Youth Services, Inc
3111 Strong, PO Box 6145, Kansas City, KS 66106
Pamela Wiens, Dir of Ed & Emp Training, 913-831-2820
Type: independent, non-profit
5 teachers, 2 assistants, 80 students, mainly at-risk, ages
13-21, 6-12th grade
Affiliations: KSBE, KS City, JTPA
Summer, night courses; individualized; pre-employment
skills; job placement assistance; on-staff social worker.

Career Opportunity Center
800 S 55th St, 2nd Flr, Kansas City, KS 66106
Carolyn Conklin, Dir, 913-596-1534

4 teachers, 300 students, ages 16+, HS
Open entry/exit; individualized instruction; contracts; self-
paced; no letter grades.

Center for International Studies
6649 Lamar, Shawnee Mission, KS 66202
David W. Wolfe, Dir, 913-384-6800
5 teachers, 2 assistants, 114 students, HS
Language, culture, geopolitical studies in Arabic, Chinese,
Japanese, Russian; study at multinational corporations, art
galleries, museums; summer program; cabaret concerts,
festivals; evening courses; International Marketplace.

Enthusiasm for Learning Foundation
(See Resource Section)

Shawnee Mission Program
5900 Lamar, Shawnee Mission, KS 66202
Dr Charles Jackard; Ron Bates, 913-789-3520
50 teachers, 600 students, mainly at-risk, 7-12th grade
Group counseling; personalized instruction; max 15 students/
class; day and night classes; teen mothers required 1
hr/day nursery care; RN on staff; childcare.

Christian Home Educators Confederation of Kansas
PO Box 3564, Shawnee Mission, KS 66203

Discovery Montessori
5603 Neiman, Shawnee Mission, KS 66203

Johnson City Preschool
6810 W 80th St, Overland Park, KS 66204
Type: Montessori

Overland Park Montessori
8029 Overland Park Dr, Shawnee Mission, KS 66204-3779

The Phoenix Montessori School (1992)
2013 W 104th St, Leawood, KS 66206
Alice Blackford, Dir, 381-1250
Non-profit; tuition: $255-305/mo
1 teacher, 1 assistant, 20 students, ages 3-6
Affiliation: AMI
Governance by board
Full range of Montessori materials; custom designed build-
ing; large outdoor play area; interns accepted.

Belmont Schools
PO Box 6212, Leawood, KS 66206-0212
Hal Swanson
Type: Montessori

Highlawn Montessori
3531 Somerset, Prairie Village, KS 66208
Carolyn Godfrey, Adm, 913-649-6160
Non-profit; tuition: $2,295/yr
4 teachers, 5 assistants, 93 students, ages 3-6
Governance by administrator, board
Teacher qualifications: AMI Certification
Traditional Montessori setting; extended day for ages 4.5-6;
childcare; multi-aged classes; suburban location; interns
accepted.

La Petite Academy
14 Corp Woods, 8717 W 110th St #300, Overland Park, KS
66210
Marketing Dept
Type: Montessori

Pre-Vocational Careers Class at Valley Heights Jr-Sr HS
(1983)
Rt 1, Blue Rapids, KS 66411
Ann Walter, 913-363-2508
1 teacher, 4 students, mainly LD, JH, HS

Learning strategies and remediation class; 9-mo job, life skills class; job placement and training; post graduation support services.

School of Success
1st & Kickapoo, Hiawatha, KS 66434
Rosemary Schooler, c/o Hiawatha HS, 600 Redskin Dr, 913-742-2119,-3312
Type: public choice
1 teacher, max 10 students, adult ages
Individualized; work/study; goal is employment or higher ed; counseling; time clocks record attendance; contracts; HS diploma.

K S Haugh Center (1981)
1833 Elmdale Ave, Junction City, KS 66441
Bernice Bullard, 913-762-3698
Type: public at-risk

Manhattan Parent Educators
1002 Houston, Manhattan, KS 66502
913-539-3641
Type: home-based

Here to Encourage the Learning Process (HELP)
Wamego High School
801 Lincoln, Wamego, KS 66547
Carol Wyatt, Dir, 913-456-2214
45 students
Resource room; study, career skills; trained peer tutors receive credit.

Topeka Program
1900 Hope, Topeka, KS 66604
James Dodge, 913-271-6813
20 teachers, 130 students, mainly at-risk
Individualized; small class size; open entry; support programs; child development courses; comprehensive intervention program; childcare.

Topeka West High School Program
2001 Fairlawn, Topeka, KS 66604
Dr Robert McFrazier, Prin, 913-272-1643
Students mainly at-risk
Individualized.

Discovery School
1701 SW Collins Ave, Topeka, KS 66604-3218
Jan Schiesser
Type: Montessori

Highland Park High School Program
2424 California, Topeka, KS 66605
Dr Susan Rogers, 913-266-7616
1 teacher, max 36 students, mainly at-risk
Individualized; small groups.

STARS at Topeka High School (1990)
800 W 10th St, Topeka, KS 66612
Bill Bagshaw, 913-232-0483 x29
60 students
Social work; video production; newspaper; mentorships; consultations; social worker; volunteer tutors; interns accepted.

Topeka High School Program
800 W 10th, Topeka, KS 66612
William Bagshaw, 913-232-0483
2 teachers, 27 students, mainly at-risk
Develops personal, academic skills.

Windows Reading Program at Topeka High School
800 W 10th, Topeka, KS 66612
Mary McGinty, 913-232-0483
Students mainly at-risk
Program as independent study or enrichment; personalized reading list; required oral, written reports.

Campus Center
620 Constitution St, Emporia, KS 66801-2847
Dr Wesley C. Jones
4 teachers, 18 students, ages 10–18
Mental Health Ctr of E Central KS, Flint Hills Special Co-op staff; family nights; individual case managers; summer program; runs 11 months/year with abbreviated school schedule in summer.

Renwick Secondary Extended Learning Program
PO Box 68, Andale, KS 67001
Carmen May, Gifted Ed Coord, 316-445-2521
1 teacher, 21 students, HS
Independent projects; career shadowing; mentorships; advanced literature; Odyssey of the Mind; Stock Market Game; Citizen Bee; scholars' bowls; drama productions; film festival; college counseling; ACT/SAT prep.

Academic Enrichment
715 E Madison, Derby, KS 67037
Nancy L. Bolz, Coord, 316-788-8580
5 teachers, 60 students
7 week minimum; tutorial assistance; grades monitored weekly; self esteem, goal setting, decision making, and responsibility are stressed; individual attention is paramount.

BCCC Community Resource Center Alternative School
613 N Main, El Dorado, KS 67042
Sue Choens, Coor/Instructor, 316-321-4030
Tuition: variable
4 teachers; HS
Affiliations: Butler Cty CC, Local District
3 locations; partly self-directed; multi-aged classes; smoking area.

First Step Industries
900 W 12th, Newton, KS 67114
Dr Bill Harrington, 316-284-6280
2 teachers, 46 students, mainly differently-abled, HS
Shop work; construction; daily evaluation determines school credit and paycheck amount, through system of profit-sharing.

Newton Alternative Learning Center
218 E 7th St, Newton, KS 67114
Marlin Frey, Prin, 316-284-6231
2 teachers, 70–75 students, mainly at-risk, ages 16+
Flexible scheduling; individualized.

Webster Community School
900 E 12th St, Winfield, KS 67156
Kathy Rogers, 316-221-5170
3 teachers, 66 students, 3–5th grade
Focus on community; research projects, activities; field trips; family involvement; hands-on learning; group interactions, cooperation.

Teaching Parents Association (1980)
PO Box 3968, Wichita, KS 67201
Jim Farthings, Pres, 316-945-0810, FAX: 316-685-1617
Type: home-based, non-profit
Governance by parent cooperative and board
Mostly conservative Christian; open to all; newsletter; meetings; regular activities.

Downtown Law, Public and Social Service Magnet High School
455 N Main, 9th Flr, Wichita, KS 67202
Clare Korst, Prin, 316-833-4265
7 teachers, 100 students, 11–12th grade
Located in City Hall; internships; case studies; community service; mentorships; stresses good citizenship.

Emerson Elementary
2330 W 25th, Wichita, KS 67203
Marilyn Tilton, 316-833-3565
Type: magnet
K–5th grade
Open learning.

Rounds Montessori School
Box 8245, Wichita, KS 67206

Wichita Collegiate School
9115 E 13th St N, Wichita, KS 67206-1298
Type: Montessori

Celebration Montessori Center, Inc (1983)
2711 E Douglas, Wichita, KS 67211
Margaret W. Sandlin, Adm, 316-683-3149
Tuition: $155/mo
1 teacher, 3 assistants, 75 students, ages 3–6
Governance by administrator
Montessori math approach: bead cabinet and decimal
   system; urban location; interns accepted.

Mayberry Middle Magnet School
207 S Sheridan, Wichita, KS 67213
Linda S. Wilson, 316-833-3500
600 students
Emphasis on Global Education; technology; foreign language
   required.

Metro-Meridian Alternative High School
301 S Meridian, Wichita, KS 67213
Mary J. Whiteside, Prin, 316-833-3535
200 students, mainly at-risk
Individualized; self-paced; no failing grades given.

Northeast Magnet High School
1847 N Chautauqua, Wichita, KS 67214
Jim McNiece, 316-833-2300
415 students, 9–12th grade
Focus on science technology and visual arts; computers;
   interdisciplinary team-taught approach; humanities core;
   foreign language required.

Wells Alternative Middle School
3601 S Pattie, Wichita, KS 67216
Karen Cahow, 316-833-2995
100 students, mainly special needs

Lewis Elementary
3030 S Osage, Wichita, KS 67217
Eileen Copple, 316-833-3860
Type: magnet
K–5th grade
Open learning.

Brooks Middle Magnet
3802 E 27th St N, Wichita, KS 67220
Brenda E. Moore, Prin, 316-833-2345
825 students
Global Education; Science Technology; foreign language;
   parent, community involvement; tutoring; parent-teacher-
   student conferences; goal setting.

Buckner Elementary
3530 E 27th St N, Wichita, KS 67220
Nancy Roth, 316-833-2365
Type: magnet
1–5th grade
Performing arts.

Wichita Friends School, Inc (1991)
PO Box 9584, Wichita, KS 67277
Shelli Kodel, Head, 316-729-0303
Type: Quaker, non-profit; tuition: $2,300, scholarships
4 teachers, 44 students, ages 5–11, K–5th grade
Governance by board
Teacher qualifications: certification
Interdenominational; hands-on; class size limited to 20;
   multi-aged classes; suburban location; interns accepted.

Hesston/Canton Home Educators Association
Rt 1 Box 136, Canton, KS 67428
Connie Bunn, 316-367-8205

EXCEL (Extra-Curricular Educational Learning)
5056 E K-4 Hwy, Gypsum, KS 67448
Jackie Frevert, Coord, 913-536-4286
Type: public choice
6 teachers, 65 students, 5–12th grade
After-school tutorial program; 1:4–7 ratio; focus on academic
   skills, self-confidence, motivation.

**Kanopolis Middle School Individual Improvement
   Program**
PO Box 37, Kanopolis, KS 67454
Paula Bigham, 913-472-4477
1 teacher; 5–8th grade
Tutorial program; weekly study skills class required for grades
   5–7.

Montessori Children's House
PO Box 1791, Hutchinson, KS 67501

Central Kansas Home Educators
Route 1, PO Box 130, Lyons, KS 67554
Mike and Elaine Williamson

Community Based Education at Lyons High School
601 American Rd, Lyons, KS 67554
Larry Walker, Coord, 316-257-5114
10–12 students, mainly special needs
Work-study program.

Kathryn O'Loughlin McCarthy Elementary School
1401 Hall, Hays, KS 67601
Tanya Channell, Prin, 913-623-2510
Type: public choice
20 teachers, 288 students, K–5th grade
Affiliation: Fort Hays State Univ
Emphasis on technology, computers, research; multimedia
   CAI; hands-on, non-textbook math; same teacher for 2
   years; parent involvement; no letter grades; childcare.

Project SOS (Second Opportunity for Students) (1977)
1900 1st Ave, PO Box 460, Dodge City, KS 67801
Betty Allen, 316-227-1617
2 teachers, 75 students, HS
Affiliation: DC HS
Self-paced; credit-earning; extensive CAI; work experience;
   support group meetings; childcare.

Ti In
PO Box 99, Ingalls, KS 67853
John O'Brien, 316-335-5136
1 teacher, 28 students
Foreign language; marine science; psychology; astronomy;
   sociology; anatomy; physiology.

Kentucky

Creative Education Center (1985)
110 N 5th St; PO Box 154, Bardstown, KY 40004
Janet MacLean, Dir, 502-348-6022
Type: independent, non-profit; tuition: $2,000/yr,
   scholarships
6 teachers, 46 students, ages 6-18, 1-12th grade
Governance by teachers, principal, parent cooperative, board
School without failure; self-paced; individualized; multi-ability,
   multi-aged classes; extensive field trips; rural location;
   interns accepted.

Children's House Montessori
6710 Wolf Pen Branch Rd, Harrods Creek, KY 40027

Lagrange Montessori
5th St, Oldham County, KY 40031

Nazareth Montessori Children's Center
PO Box 44, Nazareth, KY 40048-0044
Pat Hill, SCN

Fairdale High School
1001 Fairdale Rd, Louisville, KY 40118
Marilyn M. Hohmann, 502-473-8248
Type: magnet
9-12th grade
Magnet career academy.

Saint Martin Montessori
639 S Shelby St, Louisville, KY 40202-1657

Central High School
1130 W Chestnut St, Louisville, KY 40203
Harold E. Fenderson, 502-473-8226
Type: magnet
9-12th grade
Magnet career academy.

Coleridge Taylor Elementary School
1115 W Chestnut St, Louisville, KY 40203-2090
Type: Montessori

Louisville Montessori Center
2316 Bonnycastle Ave, Louisville, KY 40205
Kaki Robinson

Hayfield Montessori School
2000 Tyler Ln, Louisville, KY 40205-2922

Mercy Montessori School
2181 Tyler Ln, Louisville, KY 40205-2953

Ursuline Montessori
3105 Lexington Rd, Louisville, KY 40206-3061

Waggener High School
330 S Hubbards lane, Louisville, KY 40207
Kathy Hopper, 502-473-8340
Type: magnet
9-12th grade
Magnet career academy.

DuPont Manual High School
120 W Lee St, Louisville, KY 40208
Beverly Keepers, 502-473-8241
Type: magnet
9-12th grade
Magnet career academy.

Noe Middle School
121 W Lee St, Louisville, KY 40208
Ron Crutcher, 502-473-8307
Type: magnet
6-8th grade
Visual and performing arts.

Youth Performing Arts High School
1517 S Second St, Louisville, KY 40208
Beverly Keepers, 502-473-8355
Type: magnet
9-12th grade

Saint Columba Montessori
2208 Dixie Hwy, Louisville, KY 40210-2244

St Charles Montessori
2708 W Chestnut St, Louisville, KY 40211

John F. Kennedy Elementary School
3807 Young Ave, Louisville, KY 40211-2340
Jacqueline Austin
Type: Montessori

JCPS/Gheens Professional Development Academy
4425 Preston Hwy, Louisville, KY 40213
Ann Bruce
Type: Montessori

Kentucky Home Schoolers
3310 Illinois Ave, Louisville, KY 40213
502-636-3804

Doss High School
7601 St Andrews Church Rd, Louisville, KY 40214
Gordon E. Milby, 502-473-8239
Type: magnet
9-12th grade
Magnet career academy.

Kenwood Montessori School
4601 S 6th St, Louisville, KY 40214-1405

Iroquois Middle & High School
4615 Taylor Blvd, Louisville, KY 40215
James Decker, 502-473-8269
Type: magnet
6-12th grade
Initiative program.

Southern High School
8620 Preston Hwy, Louisville, KY 40219
Steven D. Stallings, 502-473-8330
Type: magnet
9-12th grade
Magnet career academy.

Seneca/Binet High School
3510 Goldsmith Lane, Louisville, KY 40220
Charles Hill (Binet), 502-473-8209
Type: magnet
9-12th grade
Magnet career academy.

Moore High School
6415 Outer Loop, Louisville, KY 40228
Warren Shelton, 502-473-8304
Type: magnet
9-12th grade
Magnet career academy.

Westport Middle School
8100 Westport Rd, Louisville, KY 40242
Jim Stone, 502-473-8346
Type: magnet
6-8th grade
Humanities; fine art.

Pleasure Ridge Park High
5901 Greenwood Rd, Louisville, KY 40258
Charles Miller, 502-473-8311

Type: magnet
9–12th grade
Magnet career academy.

Fern Creek High School
9115 Fern Creek Rd, Louisville, KY 40291
John Sizemore, 502-473-8251
Type: magnet
9–12th grade
Magnet career academy.

Jeffersontown High School
9600 Old Six Mile Lane, Louisville, KY 40299
Harold Russell, 502-473-8275
Type: magnet
9–12th grade
Magnet career academy.

Visitation Montessori School of Cardome
PO Box 594, Georgetown, KY 40324

Children's Montessori School
PO Box 545, Georgetown, KY 40324-0545

Montessori's House of Children
109 Berry Ave, Versailles, KY 40383-1454
Tony and Rene Guagliardo

Kentucky Home Education Association
PO Box 81, Winchester, KY 40392-0081

Danville Montessori School
PO Box 651, Danville, KY 40423-0651

Fayette County Public School
701 E Main St, Lexington, KY 40502
Carol Hiler
Type: Montessori

Southern Hills Montessori
2356 Harrodsburg Rd, Lexington, KY 40503-1795

Community Montessori School
166 Crestwood Dr, Lexington, KY 40503-2690
Janet Ashby

Wellington Academy
628 Wellington Way, Lexington, KY 40503-2734
Type: Montessori

The Lexington School
1050 Lane Allen Rd, Lexington, KY 40504-2099
Type: Montessori

Bluegrass Elementary & Middle School
475 Price Rd, Lexington, KY 40508
Ed Brand, 606-251-9497
Type: magnet
4–8th grade
Performing arts.

St Peter Claver Montessori
485 W 4th St, Lexington, KY 40508-1366

Providence Montessori School
1209 Texaco St, Lexington, KY 40508-2026

Children's House Kindergarten
135 Walton Ave, Lexington, KY 40508-2315
Type: Montessori

Montessori School of Frankfort (1978)
104 Cove Spring Rd, Frankfort, KY 40601
Cindy McKee, 502-875-3331

Non-profit; tuition: $145/205/mo
2 teachers, 1 assistant, 37 students, ages 3–9
Governance by administrator
4.5 park-like acres; swimming and gymnastics at YMCA; child-care; rural location; interns accepted.

St Camillus Montessori (1992)
709 E Center St, Corbin, KY 40701
Sr Mary Bezold, Dir, 606-528-9501
Non-profit; tuition: $950-1,450
1 teacher, 2 assistants, 30 students, mainly international, ages 3–6
Affiliations: NAMTA, NCEA
School within a school of 320 pre K-HS students; Spanish; accelerated program; AP classes; rural location; interns accepted.

Covington Children's House
1044 Scott St, Covington, KY 41011-3159
Type: Montessori

Northern Kentucky Montessori Center, Inc (1967)
232 Beechwood Rd, Ft Mitchell, KY 41017
Kitty K. Salter, Ed Dir, 606-331-3725, FAX: 606-282-4705
Non-profit; tuition: $1,900/yr
11 teachers, 30 students, ages 3–6
Affiliation: AMS; accreditation: KYDE
Governance by administrator, board
4 acres; individualized approach emphasizes self-development, self-confidence; suburban location; interns accepted.

Villa Early Learning Center
2402 Amsterdam, Villa Hills, KY 41017
Sr Mary Peter
Type: Montessori

Martha Arnett's Montessori Center
PO Box 18317, Erlanger, KY 41018-0317

St Anne Montessori School
River Rd Rt 8, Melbourne, KY 41059

Speedwell Montessori School
1907 Ky Ave, Paducah, KY 42001

Murray Montessori School
212 N 15th St, Murray, KY 42071-1844

Brighten Green Montessori School
436 Plum Springs Rd, Bowling Green, KY 42101-9165

Montessori Children's House
2800 Bill Dedmon Rd, Bowling Green, KY 42101-9421

Community Montessori School
PO Box 422, Glasgow, KY 42142-0422
Kathy Khatib

Triplett School
801 Old Hartford Rd, Owensboro, KY 42301
Rick Tripplett
Type: Montessori

The Montessori Method
405 N Main St, Somerset, KY 42501-1408

LORD/Elizabethtown Montessori School
(See Resource Section)

Christian Home Educators of Kentucky
691 Howardstown Rd, Hodgenville, KY 42748
502-358-9270

Louisiana

Montessori of the Riverlands
3601 River Rd, Destrehan, LA
Cynthia Pastor, Head, 504-785-8733
Tuition: $200–300/mo
2 teachers, 2 assistants, 45 students, ages 3–6
Accreditation: Board of Elementary and Secondary Education
Governance by administrator
Childcare; rural location; interns accepted.

Montessori School of Metarie
5220 Irving, Metarie, LA 70003

Montessori Learning Center
6220 Hodgson St, Metairie, LA 70003-4261

Alpha Montessori
301 Canal St, Metairie, LA 70005-3632

Family Resource Head Start Center
4219 N Rampart, New Orleans, LA 70017
Jeannine Thomas
Type: Montessori

Career Opportunity Preparation Education (COPE)
67 E Chalmette Circle, Chalmette, LA 70043
Marilyn Kimball, 504-271-2533
Remedial; vocational technology courses; career counseling; exit to regular HS or GED prep.

GED Preparation Alternative Program
67 E Chalmette Circle, Chalmette, LA 70043
Marilyn Kimball, 504-271-2533
Students must earn a CAT grade equivalent score of 8.5+ in reading, language, and mathematics; class max 25 students.

Montessori West
3520 Claire Ave, Gretna, LA 70053

Stepping Stones Montessori
552 Terry Pkwy, Gretna, LA 70056-4047

Realizing Educational Achievement for Life (REAL)
501 Manhatten Blvd, Harvey, LA 70058
Dianna Dyer, 504-367-3120
ES-HS
Remedial program; GED; Career Center.

Eight and 1/2 & Performance-Based Diploma Programs
PO Box 46, Luling, LA 70070
Dr James Taylor, Carolyn Woods, 504-785-6289
12 teachers, 140 students, 9–12th grade
Affiliation: Destrehan HS and Hahnville HS
8 1/2: computers; counseling; mainstreamed for health, PE, elective; exit to regular HS; PBD: basic academic and vocational skills; comparative eval; CAI; counseling.

Eight and 1/2 Program
PO Box 338, Lutcher, LA 70071
Caldonia S. Ceasar, 504-869-5375
7-8th grade
Mainstreamed for health, PE, one elective; daily counseling; reading instruction.

Plaquemines Parish Alternative School
PO Box 70, Port Sulphur, LA 70083
Louise Danielson, Phoenix HS, 504-564-2743
Students mainly at-risk, MS
Developing self-esteem, job skills; classes at Vo-Tech.

Urban League Street Academy
1806 Canal St, New Orleans, LA 70112
Murphy Sanchez, Program Mgr, 504-523-3560
Student ages 16+, HS

Program open to all, but directed towards young male dropouts who are public housing residents; GED; values ed; counseling.

New Orleans Free School (1971)
3601 Camp St, New Orleans, LA 70115
Dr. Robert Ferris, principal, 504-896-4065, FAX: 504-896-4065
Type: public choice
12 teachers, 325 students, mainly low-income, ages 5–15, K-8th grade
Affiliation: Teach for America
Governance by teachers and principal
Teacher qualifications: certification, or alternative LA certification
Meaningfulness, connections, engagement, inquiry, creativity, increased experience; no letter grades; multi-aged classes; extensive field trips; urban location; interns accepted.

New Child Montessori School
3915 Perrier St, New Orleans, LA 70115-3730

Our Lady of the Elms
1938 General Pershing St, New Orleans, LA 70115-5434
Type: Montessori

Audubon Montessori School
428 Broadway, New Orleans, LA 70118
Jill Otis

St Francis of Assisi
611 State St, New Orleans, LA 70118
Sr M Joanne Ladwig
Type: Montessori

University Montessori School
7508 Burthic Rt, New Orleans, LA 70118

Happy Times Nursery
1602 S Carrollton Ave, New Orleans, LA 70118-2826
Type: Montessori

Children's House Montessori School
3800 Eagle St, New Orleans, LA 70118-3404

Lake Vista Montessori School
6645 Spanish Fort Blvd, New Orleans, LA 70122

St Joseph Alpha
1200 Mirabeau Ave, New Orleans, LA 70122-1945
Type: Montessori

Hoadley School
475 Oak Ave, New Orleans, LA 70123
Type: Montessori

Educational Success Through Alternative to Suspension (ESTAS) Program
5931 Milne Blvd, New Orleans, LA 70124
Mary Thompson, 504-483-6492
7-8th grade
Individualized; max 1:15 ratio.

New Orleans Montessori School
6432 Bellaire Dr, New Orleans, LA 70124-1442

New Orleans Science and Mathematics High School
980 Navarre Ave, New Orleans, LA 70124-2710
Dr Barbara MacPhee, Prin, 504-483-4145
HS
Activity-based; integrated math, science; half-day program.

Children's Place
6317 Argonne Blvd, New Orleans, LA 70124-3901
Type: Montessori

Uptown Montessori School
6213 1/2 S Tonti St, New Orleans, LA 70125-4226

Lake Forest Montessori
8258 Lake Forest Blvd, New Orleans, LA 70126-3318

Lafourche Parish Alternative School
PO Box 879, Thibodaux, LA 70302
Lorene S. Watkins, 504-446-5631
Students mainly at-risk, HS
At Central and North Vocational Training Centers; GED.

Ascension Parish Alternative Program
PO Box 189, Donaldsonville, LA 70346
Roy W. Stern, Brd Member, 504-473-7981
Students mainly at-risk, ages 16+, HS
4 academic courses; special ed resource course.

Eighth Grade Transitional Program
PO Box 189, Donaldsonville, LA 70346
Shelby Robert, Asst Supt, 504-621-2300
Teacher qualifications: LA certification
Reading; math; life-coping skills; PE; electives; exit to regular
   HS or GED program.

Curriculum Alternative Track
PO Box 5097, Houma, LA 70361
Bill Simons, 504-876-7400
Student ages 16-21
HS diploma or GED.

Genesis
PO Box 5097, Houma, LA 70361
Bill Simons, 504-876-7400
Students mainly at-risk, 9-12th grade
For students having difficulty in school, or drop-outs; regular
   curriculum for 5 hours; supervised study/tutorial for 30
   min/day.

Alternative Diploma Program
PO Drawer B, Napoleonville, LA 70390
James D. Blanchard, Supervisor, 504-369-7251
Student ages 16+
GED; elective courses; PE.

Tangipahoa Parish Magnet High School
111 J W Davis Dr, Hammond, LA 70401
Karl R. Ingram, Prin, 504-542-5634
Student ages 16+
Evening classes.

University Montessori of Hammond
702 N Magnolia St, Hammond, LA 70401-2526

Oak St Montessori
312 N Oak St, Hammond, LA 70401-3217

PM Senior High School
PO Box 310, Bogalusa, LA 70429
Chip Conerly, 504-735-1392
Students mainly adults and at-risk
HS diploma; refreshers in English, math, arts, humanities, for
   those pursuing postsecondary education.

Montessori Children's House
10 Karen Dr, Covington, LA 70433

Covington Montessori School
116 N Monroe St, Covington, LA 70433-2656
Colleen Ryan

Three Rivers Academy
14253 Highway 190, Covington, LA 70433-7307
Art Williams, 504-892-3126
For those with learning or emotional problems to function as
   students and citizens; day and resident options; group,
   individual therapy.

Career Opportunity Preparation Education
PO Box 940, Covington, LA 70434
Dr Maria Guilott, 504-892-2276
Students mainly at-risk
Vocational training; Carnegie units; GED and trade/industry
   certificate option.

**Alternative to Suspension, Expulsion, Absenteeism, and
   Drop-Out (SEAD)**
PO Box 540, Greensburg, LA 70441
Mary B. Smith, 504-222-4349
Students mainly at-risk, 6-12th grade
Increased self-esteem; close coordination with regular
   teacher; exit to regular school; guidance.

New Covenant Weekday School
4375 Hwy 22, Mandeville, LA 70448
Diane Ferguson, Dir, 504-626-5988
Type: Montessori, non-profit; tuition: $230/mo
2 teachers, 2 assistants, 38 students, ages 3-6
Affiliation: AMS
Governance by church session

Magnolia Montessori
170 N 7th St, Ponchatoula, LA 70454-3305
Terry Ann McMahon

Montessori Chateau
40804 Chinchas Creek Rd, Slidell, LA 70461
Neil J. Songy, Adm, 504-643-8507
Tuition: $160-220/mo
5 teachers, 5 assistants, 92 students, ages infant-6
Affiliations: AMS, LMS
Governance by administrator

Lafayette Parish Middle School Transitional Program
PO Drawer 2158, Lafayette, LA 70502-2158
Tammy Frey, 318-232-0681
Student ages 15+, 5-8th grade
Remedial reading, mathematics, language arts; GED.

The Children's Community School
211 J.B. Rd, Lafayette, LA 70506
Cheryl Fell
Type: independent

Melody Montessori Tiny Tot School
620 Saint Louis St, Lafayette, LA 70506-4416

Vermilion Parish GED Preparation Alternative Program
2200 S Jefferson St, Abbeville, LA 70510
Susan V. Richard, 318-898-5722
5 hrs GED prep; elective courses; exit to adult ed.

JTPA Alternative Program
220 S Jefferson St, Abbeville, LA 70511
Dr Jane Abshire, 318-898-5770
Counseling; educational support; GED; career ed; class max:
   15; health; PE; vocational; Carnegie credit.

Children's House Acadiana
3725 Pinhook Rd, Broussard, LA 70518-5551
Type: Montessori

Alternative Program for GED Preparation
PO Box 170, Centerville, LA 70522
Amar Lancon, 318-836-9661
Student ages 15+
Computer-assisted; counseling; GED; vocational; exit to
   regular HS or adult ed.

Jefferson Davis Alternative Program
PO Box 640, Jennings, LA 70546
Johnnie Adams, 318-824-1834
20 students, 7-8th grade
At Lake Arthur HS and Fenton HS; reading; mathematics.

Alternative Curriculum to Success
1204 LeMaire St, New Iberia, LA 70560
Judith Guidry, Dale Henderson, 318-364-7641
4 academic classes; 2-hour vocational block; GED.

Project Completion
PO Box 859, St Martinville, LA 70582
Elizabeth Judice, 318-394-6261
Student ages 16+, HS
At Breaux Bridge, St Martinville, Cecilia; basic work skills; personal, career counseling; health, PE, electives at HS.

Alternative Center for Education (ACE)
1101 Te Mamou Rd, Ville Platte, LA 70586
Fannie Soileau, 318-363-6651
Students mainly at-risk, ages 14+
Academic instruction; vocational and pre-employment skills training; counseling; GED.

GED Program for At-Risk Students
PO Box 438, Washington, LA 70589
Andrew C. Leon, 318-826-7360
Students mainly at risk, JH, HS
Vocational training.

Calcasieu PM High School
PO Box 800, Lake Charles, LA 70602
Garland Hamic, Jr, Asst Supt, 318-491-1670
Students mainly at-risk
HS diploma; M-Th 5-9 pm.

GED Alternative Program
PO Box W, Cameron, LA 70631
Adam Conner, 318-775-7393
Students mainly at-risk
Regular (Carnegie units) and GED classes.

Academic/Disciplinary Alternative Placement (ADAP)
PO Box 1090, DeRidder, LA 70634
J. R. Hickman, Asst Prin, 318-463-3266
Students mainly at-risk
At DeRidder HS; for expelled, suspended students; tutorials; make up work, tests; Carnegie units; exit to regular HS.

Little Learners Montessori (1978)
73 Center Circle, Sulphur, LA 70663
318-625-9357
Tuition: $60-235/mo
3 teachers, 1 assistant, 42 students, ages infant-6
Affiliations: AMI, AMS, NAMTA
Governance by administrator
Childcare; suburban location.

Louisiana Citizens for Home Education
3404 Van Buren, Baker, LA 70714
504-775-5472

Alternative Program for At-Risk Public School Students
PO Box 1130, Livingston, LA 70754
Raiford Leader
Students mainly at-risk, ages 14+, 6-12th grade
GED; individual, group counseling; job development and peer facilitation training.

West Feliciana High Pre-GED and GED Alternative/Drop-Out Prevention Program
PO Box 580, St Francisville, LA 70775
Rodney A. Lemoine, 504-635-4561
Students mainly at-risk, ages 15+, JH, HS
After 1-year readiness curriculum, JH students go to regular HS or GED prep.

St Francisville Montessori
PO Box 118, Saint Francisville, LA 70775-0118

Scotlandville Magnet High School
9870 Scotlandville Ave, Baton Rouge, LA 70801
Freddie Williams, 504-775-3715
Academic prep; engineering program.

Office of Youth Development
504 Mayflower, Bldg 6, Baton Rouge, LA 70802
Gail Rambin, 504-342-2655
Students mainly at-risk
GED prep at correctional facilities in Monroe, Baton Rouge, Bridge City.

Polk Elementary School
408 E Polk St, Baton Rouge, LA 70802-7272
Type: Montessori

Howell Park Elementary School
6125 Winbourne Ave, Baton Rouge, LA 70805-6200
Type: Montessori

Baton Rouge Magnet High School
2825 Government St, Baton Rouge, LA 70806
Lois Anne Sumrall, Prin, 504-383-0520
Type: public choice
College prep; visual and performing arts.

LaPrintaniere Montessori School
5064 Perkins Rd, Baton Rouge, LA 70808-3441

Montessori Children's House
5640 Highland Rd, Baton Rouge, LA 70808-6554

Montessori School of Baton Rouge (1965)
8227 Wimbledon Ave, Baton Rouge, LA 70810
Leanne Smith, Adm, 504-766-9942
Non-profit; tuition: $1,610-2,905/yr
4 teachers, 2 assistants, 59 students, ages 3-6
Accreditations: LADE, LAMA
Governance by board
French; Orff music; culture studies involve parents and community; childcare; urban location; interns accepted.

Howell Park Elementary Montessori Parent Organization
4615 Dickens Dr, Baton Rouge, LA 70812
c/o Susan B Albin

Montessori NEST School
124 McGehee Dr, Baton Rouge, LA 70815
Shirley Maughan

Michele's Nursery
12380 Old Hammond Hwy, Baton Rouge, LA 70816-1020
Type: Montessori

Tanglewood Elementary School
9352 Rustling Oaks Dr, Baton Rouge, LA 70818-4799
Type: Montessori

Baton Rouge Marine Institute
PO Box 2950, Baton Rouge, LA 70821
Mary Ellen Jordan, 504-922-5400
6 teachers, 42 students, mainly adjudicated, ages 14-18
Goals: reduced or eliminated criminal involvement, rehabilitation, increased academic levels and skills; exit to regular school, vocational training, job, military.

Juvenile Continuing Education Program
1050 S Foster Dr, Baton Rouge, LA 70821
Audrey Hampton, 504-922-5518
Students mainly at-risk, 6-10th grade
Individualized by entrance exams; exit to regular HS or adult ed.

PM School
PO Box 2950, Baton Rouge, LA 70821
Mary Ellen Jordan, 504-922-5406
Students mainly at-risk, ages 17+
At Glen Oaks HS and Capitol HS; evening classes; diploma.

Christian Home Educators Fellowship of Louisiana
PO Box 74292, Baton Rouge, LA 70874
504-642-2059

Kinder Haus Montessori (1984)
5201 W Napoleon Ave, Metairie, LA 71001
Pat Lacoste, Ed Dir, 504-454-2424
Tuition: $80-95/wk
6 teachers, 9 assistants, 71 students, ages infant-6
Governance by administrator, democratic school meeting
Childcare; suburban location; interns accepted.

Herndon Magnet Elementary
11845 Gamm Rd, Belceher, LA 71004
Dean Washam, 318-221-7676
K-5th grade
Fine and performing arts.

Bossier Achievement Center
PO Box 2000, Bossier City, LA 71006-2000
Dominic Salinas, Supervisor, 318-965-2281
Students mainly at-risk
Self-paced; teacher-directed; computers; independent study;
    academic; vocational; 12-month program.

Montessori Farm School
5111 US Hwy 80 E, Haughton, LA 71037-7921

Webster Parish Alternative School
209 Clerk, Minden, LA 71055
West Moses, 318-377-7052
Students mainly at-risk, JH, HS
Individual counseling; diploma or exit to adult ed.

Caddo Parish Magnet High School
1601 Viking Dr, Shreveport, LA 71101
Ascension Smith, 318-221-2501
9-12th grade
Fine and performing arts.

Hamilton Terrace Learning Center/Caddo PM School
1105 Louisiana Ave, Shreveport, LA 71101
John Baldwin, 318-222-4518
Affiliation: Caddo Career Ctr
HS courses; counseling; community service; cultural enrich-
    ment; pre-vocational training; GED; Adult Basic Ed.

Central Elementary
1627 Weinstock St, Shreveport, LA 71103-3063
Type: Montessori

Montessori School for Shreveport (1964)
2605 C E Galloway Blvd, Shreveport, LA 71104
Therese Misra, Adm, 318-861-6777
Non-profit; tuition: $1,850-2,800/yr
9 teachers, 171 students, ages toddler-12
Affiliation: AMS
Governance by board
Childcare; interns accepted.

Klenter Montessori School
3452 Broadmoor Blvd, Shreveport, LA 71105-2026

Caddo Parish Middle School
7635 Cornelious Dr, Shreveport, LA 71106
Lel McCullough, 318-868-6588
Type: magnet
6-8th grade
Fine and performing arts.

South Highlands Magnet Elementary
831 Erie St, Shreveport, LA 71106
Pamela Byrd, 318-865-5119
K-5th grade
Fine and performing arts.

Christian Center School
207 Idema St, Shreveport, LA 71106-6557
Type: Montessori

J B Harville Alternative School
6660 Quilen Rd, Shreveport, LA 71108

Margaret A. Brown, 318-621-9724
Students mainly at-risk
7 sites for MS and HS: 5 w/voc, diploma or re-entry; 2 for
    adjudicated students.

New Life Montessori
4445 Meriwether Rd, Shreveport, LA 71109-8409

Montessori Children's House
1959 Airline Dr, Bossier City, LA 71112-2407

Children's House of Monroe
2102 Valencia Ave, Monroe, LA 71201-2547
Type: Montessori

Children's House
1201 Stubbs Ave, Monroe, LA 71201-5621
Type: Montessori

A Performance-Based Diploma Program
PO Box 4180, Monroe, LA 71211
Maria Maggio, 318-325-0601
Students mainly at-risk
Drop-out prevention/retrieval; alternative to college prep;
    GED.

Opportunity Learning Center
PO Box 4180, Monroe, LA 71211
Maria Maggio, 318-325-0601
Students mainly at-risk, 6-9th grade
Carnegie units; exit to regular HS or GED program.

Morehouse Parish Alternative Program
PO Box 872, Bastrop, LA 71220
Jimmy Sistrunk, Supervisor, 318-281-5784
Students mainly at-risk
Academic, pre-vocational instruction for 13 year old potential
    drop-outs;14-15 year-olds prep for 9th grade; GED prep,
    career training for 16+.

Good Shepherd Early Childhood Dev Center
Box 442, 1404 1st St, Lake Providence, LA 71254-0442
Type: Montessori

West Carroll Parish al Program
PO Drawer 1318, Oak Grove, LA 71263
John Mercer, Supt, 318-428-2378
Student ages 16+, HS
GED; health; PE; vocational; electives; exit to regular HS, adult
    ed, postsecondary ed, or job; placement assistance.

Wildflower Montessori School
700 W Woodward Ave, Ruston, LA 71270
Rene Hunt

Woodland Hills Hospital School
6200 Cypress St, W Monroe, LA 71294
Patricia Johnson, Ed Coord, 318-396-5900
7-12th grade
Classes limited to 10; individualized; flexible schedule; coun-
    seling; medical treatment.

High School GED Program
PO Box 1230, Alexandria, LA 71301
Tommy Smith, 318-487-0888
HS
Expanded vocational, elective and academic experiences;
    individualized; GED prep.

PM High School
PO Box 1230, Alexandria, LA 71301
Tommy Smith, 318-487-0888
Student ages 17+, HS
HS diploma; evenings; refresher courses.

Montessori Learning Center
1304 Beech St, Alexandria, LA 71301-6001

Montessori Educational Center (1978)
1717 Jackson St, Alexandria, LA 71301-6433
Rosemary Robertson-Smith, 318-445-0138
Non-profit; tuition: $1,170/1,980/yr
6 teachers, 108 students, ages 3-12
Affiliations: AMS, IMS, NCME; accreditations: LADE, LAMA
Governance by teachers, administrators, board
Childcare; urban location; transportation; interns accepted.

Ewell Aiken Optional School
3443 Prescott Rd, Alexandria, LA 71303
Richard Bushnell, Prin, 318-442-1846
Student ages 14+, 5-12th grade
Individualized; CAI; self-paced.

Alternative Secondary Curriculum Program
PO Box 308, Jonesville, LA 71343
Norma White, Supervisor, 318-339-9505
Reading; GED; health; PE; 3-hour vocational block.

Alternative Vocational Curriculum (AVC) Program
PO Box 308, Jonesville, LA 71343
Norma White, Mary Gene Trunzler, 318-339-9505,-9579
Students mainly at-risk
Carnegie credits; vocational courses; exit to regular HS, GED
    program, another AVC program, employment.

Alternative Learning Experiences Reshape Thinking
    (ALERT)
201 Tunica Dr W, Marksville, LA 71351
John H. Wyatt, 318-253-5982
Students mainly at-risk, ages 16+
Affiliation: Avoyelles Vo-Tech School
Educational, support services for expelled students; voca-
    tional, diploma, and GED programs; exit to homebase
    school.

Grant Parish High School GED Program
PO Box 208, Colfax, LA 71417
Kenneth E. Deen, 318-627-3274

Student ages 16+
GED; academic or vocational courses for Carnegie credit; exit
    to regular HS or adult ed.

Beauregard/Vernon Home School Association
714 Tilley Rd, Leesville, LA 71446
Burwell, 318-535-9102
Inclusive.

Vernon Parish Alternative School
502 Berry Ave, Leesville, LA 71446
J. W. Pope, 318-239-3401
Students mainly at-risk, HS
Computer-assisted; small group instruction; personal, acade-
    mic, vocational counseling.

Alternative High School Program
200 Hwy 3110, S By-Pass, Natchitoches, LA 71457
Julia Hildebrand, 318-352-2358
HS
GED; vocational training.

Louisiana School for Mathematics, Science and the Arts
715 College Ave, Natchitoches, LA 71457
Dr Art Williams, 318-357-3176
Instruction via telecommunications to local schools through-
    out LA.

Natchitoches Parish Alternative School
1016 Keyser Ave, Natchitoches, LA 71457
Trudy Howell, Brd Member, 318-352-2358
Student ages 16+
Voc; individualized.

Winn Parish High School Alternative Program
PO Box 430, Winnfield, LA 71483
Jerry Bamburgh, 318-628-6936
Student ages 16+, HS
Carnegie units; GED.

Maine

Experiential Education Alternative (1990)
Noble High School, Berwick, ME 03904
Jon Appleby or Thomas Ledue, Tchs, 207-698-1320
Type: public choice
3 teachers, 30 students, mainly at-risk, ages 13-18, 8-12th
    grade
Governance by teachers and principal
Rural location.

BEAT (1986)
23 Maplewood ave, Biddeford, ME 04005
Harry Strother, Head Tch
Type: public at-risk
1 teacher, 2 assistants, 15 students, ages 12-15, 6-8th grade
Governance by teachers, principal.
Teacher qualifications: ME Certification
3 classes; films; PE; suburban location.

Program
Brunswick Junior High School
Barrows St, Brunswick, ME 04011
Linda Blakeman, 207-729-1669
Type: public at-risk

Union Street (1985)
35 Union St, Brunswick, ME 04011
Beth Schultz, Lead Teacher, 207-729-0001

Type: public at-risk
2 teachers, 1 assistant, 28 students, ages 14-19, 9-12th
    grade
Affiliations: AEA of ME, NCACS
Governance by teachers and principal
Teacher qualifications: MA in Ed or working toward one
Individualized; trust/community building field trips; Outward
    Bound component; interdisciplinary; alternative assess-
    ments; respect, accountability, tolerance emphasized; sub-
    urban location; interns accepted.

Cooperative Alternative School (1989)
340 Foreside Rd, Falmouth, ME 04011
Steve Gargiulo, Dir, 207-729-6609
Type: public choice
2 teachers, 18 students, partly at-risk, ages 14-18, 7-12th
    grade
Governance by supervisory council
Teacher qualifications: teaching and alternative experience
Work-study; film-making; Outward Bound; Project Adven-
    ture; occupational, career study; earned "personal days";
    multi-aged classes; extensive field trips; suburban location;
    transportation; interns accepted.

Alternative Learning Center (1980)
Main St, Cumberland Center, ME 04021
Doreen Thompson, Coord, 207-829-4836

Type: public at-risk
1 teacher, 1 assistant, 45 students, mainly at-risk, ages 12–20, 7–12th grade
Governance by principal, board, superintendent
Teacher qualifications: ME Certification
In house near JHS and HS; partial day program; work-study community service; independent study; support groups; experiential activities; peer tutoring; CAI; creative visualization for learning; creativity, relaxation, transformation of anger; multi-aged classes; suburban location; interns accepted.

Pequawket Valley Alternative Program (1991)
152 Main St, Fryeburg, ME 04037
Dave Sturdevant or Dede Frost, Dirs, 207-935-3344
Type: public at-risk
4 teachers, 15 students, ages 15–21, HS
Affiliation: Fryeburg Academy
Governance by faculty and student reps
Experiential; east coast ecology and community service projects; competency-based; no letter grades; non-compulsory class attendance; interns accepted.

Royal Academy
PO Box 1056 51 West Gray Rd, Gray, ME 04039.
Shirley Minster, 207-657-2800, Fax 657-2404
Type: home-based; cost: $240–400
Student ages K–12
Program and custom designed curriculum for families in the United States or overseas; flexible; focuses on students' previous knowledge, parental and student goals.

The School Around Us (1970)
RR 1, Box 1912 Log Cabin Rd, Kennebunkport, ME 04046
Claudia Berman, 207-967-3143
Type: independent, non-profit; tuition: $2,200, scholarships
4 teachers, 34 students, ages 4–12, pre K–6th grade
Affiliation: NCACS; accreditation: state of ME
Governance by parent cooperative
Teacher qualifications: excitement, commitment to self-growth
School meeting uses consensus model; developmental approach; interdisciplinary curriculum; 4-acre wooded location; emphasis on outdoors, community involvement, the arts, real work; concern for the environment and world community; no letter grades; non-compulsory class attendance; multi-aged classes; extensive field trips; rural location; interns accepted.

Windham Real School (1984)
55 High St, Windham, ME 04062
Arthur DiRocco, PhD, Dir, 207-892-4462
Type: public at-risk; tuition: $17,500/yr
5 teachers, 42 students, ages 13–20, 7–12th grade
Affiliation: Boy Scouts
Governance by board
Teacher qualifications: state certification
Adventure-based counseling; experiential education; rural location; transportation; interns accepted.

Sanford Alternative School (1986)
2R Main St, Sanford, ME 04073
Michael Fallon, 207-940-5135
Type: public at-risk
2 teachers, 20 students, ages 13–17, 8–10th grade
Governance by teachers and principal
Teacher qualifications: ME certification
Experiential; community-based; rural location.

at Scarborough HS
PO Box 370, Scarborough, ME 04074
Bill Haskell, 702-883-4315
Type: public at-risk

Southern Maine Home Education Support Network
(1985)
76 Beech Ridge Rd, Scarborough, ME 04074

207-883-9621
Non-profit
Family activities, events; nonsectarian, diverse group; about 100 member families.

Sebago Lake Homeschoolers Support Group
RR 2 Box 54, Sebago Lake, ME 04075
207-642-4368

The Merriconeag School (1984)
PO Box 336; S Freeport Rd, South Freeport, ME 04078
Tricia Tonks, Business Mgr, 207-865-3900
Type: Waldorf, non-profit; tuition: $2,400-6,500/yr, scholarships
17 teachers, 98 students, ages 3.5–11, K–4th grade
Affiliation: AWSNA
Governance by faculty
Teacher qualifications: Waldorf training
Suburban location; interns accepted.

Bonny Eagle (1988)
700 Saco Rd, Standish, ME 04084
Sam Jordan/Diane Beringer, Teachers, 207-929-3831
Type: public at-risk
2 teachers, 25 students, ages 14–17, 8–10th grade
Affiliation: ME Alt Ed Assoc
Governance by teachers and principal
Teacher qualifications: ME certification
Four mandatory components: individualized academics, community service, experiential (Outward Bound type), counseling (individual/group); suburban location; interns accepted.

New Country School (1972)
RR1, Box 6, West Baldwin, ME 04091
Jennifer Frick, Director, 207-625-4962
Type: independent, non-profit; scholarships
4 teachers, 29 students, ages 3–12, pre K–6th grade
Governance by parent cooperative
Teacher qualifications: Experience
Fifty acres of wood and bogland used for nature and land study; Japanese intern teaches language and culture; ski program; students help at local food pantry; five mini-group projects per semester; no letter grades; non-compulsory class attendance; multi-aged classes; extensive field trips; interns accepted.

West School Prep Program (1968)
57 Douglas St, Portland, ME 04102
William C Shuttleworth, Dir, 207-874-8225, FAX: 207-874-8154
Type: public at-risk
10 teachers, 50 students, ages 9–19, 4–12th grade
Governance by teachers and principal
Teacher qualifications: ME certification
Work opportunities; individualized; experiential; extensive field trips; urban location; interns accepted.

Association of Maine
25 Granite St, Apt 12, Portland, ME 04104
Tina Clark
Type: state home-based

Maine Homeschool Association (1987)
PO Box 9715-199, Portland, ME 04104
207-353-3588
Nonsectarian; membership-supported.

Pine Grove Child Development Center (1986)
32 Foreside Rd, Falmouth, ME 04105
B. J. Fifield, 207-781-3441
Type: Montessori; tuition: $351-499/mo
3 teachers, 3 assistants, 91 students, ages 3-6
Affiliations: NAEYC, AMS
Governance by administrator
Childcare; suburban location; interns accepted.

South Portland Alternatives (1989)
637 Highland Ave, South Portland, ME 04106
Tom Hyland, Dir, 207-767-7729, FAX: 207-767-7713
Type: public choice
1 teacher, 1 assistant, 30 students, mainly at-risk, ages 14–20, 9–12th grade
Governance by democratic school meeting (program); faculty/students/adm (high school)
Maine Studies of Native Cultures includes building a kayak; interdisciplinary courses; work with satellite imagery technology; multi-aged classes; urban location; transportation; interns accepted.

Casco Bay Montessori School
440 Ocean St, South Portland, ME 04106-6612

Fairview School
Minot Ave, Auburn, ME 04210
Donn Marcus
Type: Montessori

Franklin Alternative High School (1978)
Pine St, Auburn, ME 04210
David T. Eretzian, Prin, 207-782-3242
Type: public at-risk
6 teachers, 90 students, mainly at-risk, ages 15–20, 9–12th grade
Governance by teachers, principal, democratic school meeting
Teacher qualifications: ME Certification
Rural location; transportation; interns accepted.

Homeschool Associates of New England
(See Resource Section)

Poland Community School
HCR Box 20, Poland, ME 04273
Donald McGlauflin, 702-998-4934
5–8th grade

Center for Alternative Learning (1991)
59 Congress St, Rumford, ME 04276
Zebunnisa Weidler, John Schoen, teachers, 207-364-5604
Type: public at-risk
2 teachers, 20 students, mainly at-risk, ages 14–18, 9–12th grade
Governance by teachers and principal
Teacher qualifications: secondary certificate, experience with at-risk youth
1.5 room school with traditional and innovative courses; students must meet attendance, credit and behavior guidelines; multi-aged classes; extensive field trips; special integrated classes; urban location; interns accepted.

River Valley Alternative School (1987)
RR 1, PO Box 1220, Turner, ME 04282
Ric French, Supervisor, 207-225-3478
Type: public choice
3 teachers, 55 students, mainly at-risk, ages 14–20, 9–12th grade
Governance by teachers and principal
Teacher qualifications: BS, certification
Rural location; transportation; interns accepted.

Cony High Alternative Program for Students (CHAPS)
(1986)
104 Cony St, Augusta, ME 04330
Nancy Ruark, 402-626-2460
Kennebec County
Type: public choice
4 teachers, 45 students, mainly at-risk, ages 14–19, HS
Entrance requirements: application, interview, enrolled in Cony HS.
Governance by principal
Teacher qualifications: ME certification
Employment for credit; point reward system; opportunities to explore areas of special interest; work portfolios; urban location.

Gardiner Regional Middle School (1989)
Cobbossee Ave, Gardiner, ME 04345
Alan R. Smith, 207-582-1326
Type: public choice
54 teachers, 630 students, ages 11–14, 6–8th grade
Governance by principal

Bangor Montessori School
30 Otis St, Bangor, ME 04401
Amy Peterson-Roper

Penobscot Job Corps (1979)
1375 Union St, Bangor, ME 04401
207-990-3000, FAX: 942-9829
Type: public at-risk, boarding; scholarships
23 teachers, 330 students, mainly at-risk, ages 16–24
Affiliations: Training & Dev Corp, Dept of Labor
Teacher qualifications: bachelor's degree
College prep; ESL; voc; remedial studies; community resources; culturally diverse staff with educational hands-on experience; tutorials; multi-aged classes; rural location; interns accepted.

Reach School, Inc (1987)
PO Box 1366, Bucksport, ME 04416
Richard W Crampton, Dir, 207-469-7147
Type: independent, non-profit
2 teachers, 21 students, mainly at-risk, ages 13–19, 7–12th grade
Governance by board
Teacher qualifications: ME certification
Students responsible for own education; point systems; accountability; family atmosphere; rural location; transportation; interns accepted.

Hampton Academy
Box 279, Hamden, ME 04444
Ellen Pariser, Alt Ed Teacher, 207-862-6249
Type: public at-risk
1 teacher, 1 assistant, 16 students, mainly at-risk, ages 14–21, 9–12th grade
Governance by teachers and principal
Personal growth; credit for work; fine arts, including photography; course credit through fulfilling competency-based objectives; small classes; based on Glasser's Reality Therapy; students take responsibility for attendance; multi-aged classes; extensive field trips; rural location; interns accepted.

Stillwater Montessori School
RFD 2, Box 1300, Old Town, ME 04468-2165
Joe and Joanne Alex

Rural Education Program, HOME Coop
PO Box 10, Orland, ME 04472
Karen Saum, 207-469-7961
Type: higher education
4-yr baccalaureate-equivalent certificate in community economic development; designed for and by students.

Chewonki Foundation
RR 2 Box 1200, Wiscasset, ME 04578
Don Hudson, 207-882-7323
Environmental education; summer camp; wilderness trips; residential program; traveling natural science lessons; academic study for 11th grade

College of the Atlantic
105 Eden St, Bar Harbor, ME 04609
Hancock, 207-288-5015
Goal is to increase awareness of environmental problems and teach skills of human ecology necessary to solve them.

The Bay School
PO Box 269, Blue Hill, ME 04614
Michaela Colquhoun
Type: Waldorf

Peninsula Area Homeschooling Association
PO Box 235, Deer Isle, ME 04627

Gentle Wind School
(See Resource Section)

Mount Desert Island Homeschoolers (1992)
C/O Box 189A Richmond Rd, West Tremont, ME 04690
Kathy Van Gorder, 207-244-3615
24 students, ages 1-7

Brook Farm Books
(See Resource Section)

Hurricane Island Outward Bound (1964)
PO Box 429, Rockland, ME 04841
Peals Wrobel, Dir, 207-594-1401, FAX: 594-9425
Type: independent, non-profit; tuition: variable, scholarships
120 teachers, 1,000 students
Affiliations: Outward Bound, Inc
Governance by board
Develops self-esteem, self-reliance, concern for others and
   for environment; sailing, kayaking, rock-climbing, ropes
   courses; 4 programs nationally; no letter grades; non-
   compulsory class attendance.

Children's House
63 Pearl St, Camden, ME 04843
Martha Monahan
Type: Montessori

The Community School (1973)
Box 555-79 Washington St, Camden, ME 04843
Emanual Pariser, Dora Lievow, Co-Directors, 207-763-3000
Type: independent, boarding, non-profit; tuition: $17,000/yr,
   scholarships
6 teachers, 8 students, mainly at-risk, ages 16-21, HS
Affiliations: NCACS, Nat Dropout Prev Net
Governance by democratic school meeting; faculty determines inalterable rules
"Real" work in community, maintenance, and meeting room
   and board costs; applied home ec; conflict resolution and
   anger mgmt; competency-based; new book: Changing
   Lives: Voices From a School that Works; no letter grades;
   multi-aged classes; extensive field trips; rural location;
   interns accepted.

Riley School (1972)
Box 91, Glen Cove, ME 04846
Glenna W. Plaisted, Director, 207-596-6405
Type: independent, non-profit; tuition: $3,700-5,200,
   scholarships
11 teachers, 63 students, ages 4-14, ungraded
Affiliations: NEAS&C, ISANNE
Governance by principal, board
Teacher qualifications: strong background in child develop-
   ment; experience
Integrated curriculum; interest-based; community service;
   independent study; narrative evaluations; team teachiing;
   environmental studies; no letter grades; multi-aged
   classes; extensive field trips; interns accepted.

Homeschoolers of Maine
HC 62, PO Box 24, Hope, ME 04847
207-763-4251

Northeast Montessori Institute
PO Box 68, Rockport, ME 04856
Helen DeVere
Type: Montessori teacher education

Georges Valley High School (1978)
PO Box 192, Thomaston, ME 04861-0192
Celeste Frisbee, 207-354-2502, FAX: -2369

Type: public choice
33 teachers, 300 students, ages 13-19, 9-12th grade
Governance by board
Client-oriented; work-study; community service; modified
   schedule; contracts; ind study; adult ed; Outward Bound;
   rural location; transportation; interns accepted.

Ashwood School (1986)
PO Box 129, West Rockport, ME 04865
Sarah McBrian, Pres, Board of Trustees, 207-236-8021
Type: Waldorf, non-profit; scholarships
7 teachers, 56 students, ages 4-10, K-4th grade
Governance by faculty and board of trustees
Teacher qualifications: Waldorf training
Rural location.

Kennebec Montessori School
PO Box 866, Waterville, ME 04901
Adele Carey

Waterville Alternative (1987)
21 Gilman St, Waterville, ME 04901
Bernard Peatman, Dir, 207-873-5595
Type: public at-risk
5 teachers, 40 students, mainly at-risk, ages 13-19, 6-12th
   grade
Governance by principal
Teacher qualifications: state certification
Students may avail themselves of all activities, courses and
   facilities of regular HS; self-esteem and goal-setting programs; multi-aged classes; rural location; transportation.

National Audubon Society Expedition Institute (1981)
PO Box 365, Belfast, ME 04915
Karen Woodsum, Office Mgr, 207-338-5859
Type: independent higher education, boarding; tuition:
   $9,300/yr, scholarships
4 teachers, 20 students, HS, college, graduate school
Affiliation: Leslie College
Governance by consensus
Explores 1 region of US & Canada each sem; environmental
   ed degrees; values-based, holistic approach; non-
   authoritarian; self-paced, directed and evaluated; camping,
   hiking, canoeing.

Toddy Pond School
217 High St, Belfast, ME 04915
Andrea Stark, 207-525-4495
Type: independent; tuition: $2,000/yr, scholarships
22 students, ages 5-12
Governance by parent cooperative
Thematic approach with independent study; rural location.

TRANET: Transnational Network for Alternative/
   Appropriate Technologies
(See Resource Section)

Crossroads Learning Center (1984)
63 Water St, Skowhegan, ME 04976
Penny McGovern, Dir, 207-474-7175
Type: public at-risk
7 teachers, 54 students, mainly at-risk, ages 14-20, 9-12th
   grade
Governance by principal, faculty and student representatives
Teacher qualifications: ME Certification
Competency-based and traditional classes; toward diploma
   or GED; focus on the needs of the whole student; multi-
   aged classes; rural location; transportation; interns
   accepted.

Maryland

Henry Ferguson
14600 Berry Rd, Accokeek, MD 20607
John Dade, 301-292-5000
Type: magnet
2–5th grade
Talented and gifted.

Alternative School
Radio Station Rd, La Plata, MD 20646
William G. McCall, 932-1855
Type: public choice

St Mary's Community School
441 Autumnwood Dr, Mechanicsville, MD 20659
Lynn Erwin
Type: Montessori

Parents for Home Education
13020 Blairmore St, Beltsville, MD 20705
301-572-5827

Glenarden Woods
Echols Ave, Lanham, MD 20706
Oretha Bridgwaters, 301-772-6611
Type: magnet
2–6th grade
Talented and gifted.

Thomas Johnson Middle School (1993)
5401 Barker Pl, Lanham, MD 20706
John Robinson, Prin; Susan Wilkerson, Specialist, 301-459-5800
Type: Public choice Montessori
1 teacher, 19 students, ages 12–15
Accreditation: MDBE
Governance by administrator
Urban location; transportation; interns accepted.

Christian Family Montessori School (1982)
3628 Rhode Island Ave, Mt Rainier, MD 20712
Vernice W. Townsend, Adm, 201-927-7122
Tuition: $1,540/2,210/yr
4 teachers, 4 assistants, 84 students, ages toddler–12
Governance by administrator, board
Full Montessori program; Catachist of the Good Shepherd; urban location; interns accepted.

Little Friends for Peace
4405 29th St, Mt Rainier, MD 20712
Mary Joan Park
Type: Montessori

Bowie Montessori Children's House (1967)
5004 Randonstone Ln, Bowie, MD 20715
Anne Byron-Riley, 301-262-3566
Non-profit
7 teachers; students mainly international, ages 3–15
Affiliation: AMI
Governance by board
Childcare; suburban location; interns accepted.

Heather Hills
12605 Heming Lane, Bowie, MD 20716
Patricia Brooks, 301-262-3013
Type: magnet
2–6th grade
Talented and gifted.

Tall Oaks Vocational High School (1988)
2112 Church Rd, Bowie, MD 20716
Burt Poulis, 301-249-2900
Type: public choice
200 students

Mitchelville Children's School
12112 Central Ave, Mitchelville, MD 20721
Ms Harvey
Type: Montessori

Julia Brown Montessori School (1967)
9450 Madison Ave, Laurel, MD 20723
Adm, 301-498-0604
4 teachers, 6 assistants, 115 students, mainly international, ages 3–12
Affiliation: AMS; accreditations: MDBE, DHR
Governance by administrator
Traditional Montessori school; extracurriculars; childcare; suburban location; interns accepted.

Friends Community School (1986)
4601 Calvert Rd, College Park, MD 20740
Jane Manring, Tch-Dir, 301-699-6086
Type: Quaker, non-profit
10 teachers, 120 students, ages 5–11, K–6th grade
Affiliation: Adelphi Friends Meeting
Governance by friends meeting
Teacher qualifications: values consistent with Friends, experience.
Conflict resolution; portfolio assessment; multi-disciplinary, long-term projects; flexible teaching assignments; service projects; Math Their Way; no letter grades; multi-aged classes; extensive field trips; suburban location; interns accepted.

Doswell E Brooks Elementary (1986)
1301 Brooks Rd, Capital Hts, MD 20743
Margaret Williams, Prin; Susan Wilkerson, Specialist, 301-735-0470
Type: Public choice Montessori; tuition: $1,400 (ages 3–4)
11 teachers, 4 assistants, 275 students, ages 3–12
Accreditation: MDBE
Governance by administrator
Urban location; transportation; interns accepted.

Capitol Heights
601 Suffolk Ave, Capitol Height, MD 20743
Thelma Butler, 301-420-3430
Type: magnet
2–6th grade
Talented and gifted.

Central
200 Cabin Branch Rd, Capitol Height, MD 20743
William Watkins, 301-336-8200
Type: magnet
9–12th grade
Humanities; international studies.

Walker Mill
800 Karen Blvd, Capitol Height, MD 20743
Joan Brown, 301-366-8855
Type: magnet
7–8th grade
Talented and gifted.

Beddow School
8600 Loughran Rd, Fort Washington, MD 20744
Trudy Beddow
Type: Montessori

Flintstone Elementary (1986)
800 Comanche Dr, Oxon Hill, MD 20745
Dr Delores Smith, Prin; Susan Wilkerson, Specialist, 301-567-3142
Type: Public choice Montessori; tuition: $1,400 (ages 3–4)
11 teachers, 4 assistants, 275 students, ages 3–12

Accreditation: MDBE
Governance by administrator
Urban location; transportation; interns accepted.

Valley View
5500 Danby Ave, Oxon Hill, MD 20745
Inez Sadler, 301-839-3444
Type: magnet
2-6th grade
Talented and gifted.

Andrew Jackson
3500 Regency Parkway, Forestville, MD 20747
William Simmons, 301-736-9700
Type: magnet
7-8th grade
French immersion; humanities; international studies.

Longfields
3300 Newkirk Ave, Forestville, MD 20747
Yvonne Crawford, 301-736-6671
Type: magnet
2-6th grade
Talented and gifted.

Suitland
5200 Silver Hill Rd, Suitland, MD 20747
Sterling Marshall, 301-568-7770
Type: magnet
9-12th grade
University HS; visual and performing arts.

Henson Valley Montessori School
7007 Allentown Rd, Temple Hills, MD 20748
Robin Knight, HVMS

Œkos
PO Box 10, Glenn Dale, MD 20769
Paul Epstein and Teresita Leimer
Type: Montessori

Glenn Dale Early Childhood Education Center
6700 Glenn Dale Rd, Glenn Dale, MD 20769-9407
Judy Hoyer
Type: Montessori

Blue Mountain Book Peddler
(See Resource Section)

Prince George's Board of Ed Montessori Magnet Office
14201 School Ln, Upper Marlboro, MD 20772
Susan Wilkerson

New City Montessori School (1968)
3120 Nicholson St, Hyattsville, MD 20782
Shirley Windsor, Adm, 301-559-8488
Non-profit; tuition: $2,625-3,800/yr
3 teachers, 2 assistants, 60 students, ages 3-9
Affiliation: AMI
Governance by board
Between U of MD, Catholic U; near two subway stations; childcare; suburban location; interns accepted.

Paint Branch Montessori School (1975)
3215 Powder Mill Rd, Adelphi, MD 20783
Patricia Barshay, 301-937-2244
Tuition: $2,648-4,142/yr
7 teachers, 5 assistants, 95 students, ages 3-12
Affiliations: NAMTA, Elementary Teachers of Classics
Governance by administrator
Wooded area; nature trails; PE; art; music; ASL; childcare; suburban location; interns accepted.

Willowbrook Children's House
8151 15th Ave, Hyattsville, MD 20783-3501
Gloria Harvey
Type: Montessori

Kenmoor
3211 82nd Ave, Landover, MD 20785
Peter Bray, 301-722-1040
Type: magnet
2-6th grade
Talented and gifted.

Matthew Henson Elementary/Montessori (1986)
7910 Scott Rd, Landover, MD 20785
Sherra Chappelle, Prin, or Susan Wilkerson, Co-ord, 301-772-1922
Type: public choice; tuition: $1,000
11 teachers, 3 assistants, 275 students, ages 3-12
Governance by administrator, board
Computer lab; nearby woods; access to DC museums; suburban location; transportation; interns accepted.

Oakcrest
929 Hill Rd, Landover, MD 20786
James Chase, 301-336-8020
Type: magnet
2-6th grade
Talented and gifted.

Thomas G. Pullen
700 Brightseat Rd, Landover, MD 20786
Kathy Kurtz, 301-808-1260
Type: magnet
K-8th grade
Creative and performing arts.

Bethesda Montessori School (1982)
7611 Clarendon Rd, Bethesda, MD 20814
Gertrude A. Burr, Dir, 301-986-1260
Tuition: $4,250/yr
3 teachers, 4 assistants; student ages 2.5-6
Affiliation: AMI; accreditation: MD DE
Governance by administrator
Childcare; suburban location.

Lone Oak Montessori School
10100 Old Georgetown Rd, Bethesda, MD 20814
Patricia Swann

World Future Society
(See Resource Section)

Oneness Family Peace School
6701 Wisconsin Ave, Chevy Chase, MD 20815
Andy Kutt
Type: Montessori

Holden Montessori Day School
5450 Massachusetts Ave, Bethesda, MD 20816
Mary Ann Atwell

New Age Montessori School
4728 Western Ave, Bethesda, MD 20816

Washington Waldorf School
4800 Sangamore Rd, Bethesda, MD 20816
Ann Finucane

Abingdon Montessori School
5144 Massachusetts Ave, Bethesda, MD 20816-2740

Farrell Montessori School
6601 Bradley Blvd, Bethesda, MD 20817
Maureen van Emmerik

Walden Montessori Academy (1987)
7730 Bradley Blvd, Bethesda, MD 20817
Linda Grodin, Dir, 301-469-8123
Tuition: $3,300-5,500/yr
2 teachers, 3 assistants, 62 students, ages infant-6
Affiliation: AMS
Governance by administrator
Childcare; suburban location; interns accepted.

Triune Teaching Program (1992)
5206 Wissioming Rd, Bethesda, MD 20846
Mardy Burgess, 301-229-9577, FAX: 301-229-9578
Type: public at-risk
2 teachers, 16 students, ages 13–16, 8th grade
Governance by principal
Multi-cultural; Triune Brain Model; cooperative learning; classroom management; higher order mentoring; urban location.

Franklin Montessori School
10500 Darnestown Rd, Rockville, MD 20850
Pamela Trumble

Regional Institute for Children and Adolescents
15000 Broschart Rd, Rockville, MD 20850
Joan Benz, 251-6900
Type: public choice

Green Acres School
11701 Canville, Rockville, MD 20852
Type: independent

Norbeck Montessori School
4500 Muncaster Mill Rd, Rockville, MD 20853
Elizabeth Bissett

Apple Montessori School
11815 Seven Locks Rd, Potomac, MD 20854
Lynn Oboler and Marian Pepper

Anchor Montessori School
11204 Tara Rd, Potomac, MD 20854-1348
Linda Grodin

Manor Montessori School
10500 Oaklyn Dr, Potomac, MD 20854-3936
Marie Fonseca and Kathy Damico

Sandy Spring Friends School
16923 Norwood Rd, Sandy Spring, MD 20860
Stephen Gessner, 301-774-7455
Type: independent

Mater Amoris Montessori School
18501 Mink Hollow Rd, PO Box 97, Ashton, MD 20861-0097
Charlottee Kovach

Gaithersburg Internationalle Montessori School
429 W Diamond Ave, Gaithersburg, MD 20877

Flower Hill Country Day
8507 Emory Grove Rd, Gaithersburg, MD 20877-3731
Type: Montessori

Gerber Children's Center
1199 Quince Orchard Blvd, Gaithersburg, MD 20878
Kathy Fletcher
Type: Montessori

Butler School
15120 Turkey Foot Rd, Gaithersburg, MD 20878-3960
Rila Spellman
Type: Montessori

Village Montessori Schools
20301 Fulks Farms Rd, Gaithersburg, MD 20879
Jeanne MacDougall

Good Shepherd Montessori School
8921 Warfield Rd, Gaithersburg, MD 20882

Evergreen Montessori School
10101 Connecticut Ave, Kensington, MD 20895-3803
Lynn Pellaton

Casa De Montessori
709 Hobbs, Silver Spring, MD 20904

Home Study International
12501 Old Columbia Pike, Silver Spring, MD 20904
Robert Burnette, Dir of Student Services, 800-782-4769, FAX: 301-680-6577
Non-profit; scholarships
62 teachers, 2,200 students, ages 4+, pre K–college
Affiliation: Columbia Union College
Governance by board
State approved; accredited by National Home Study Council.

Thornton Friends School (1973)
13925 New Hampshire Ave, Silver Spring, MD 20904
Douglas R. Price, Head, 301-384-0320
Type: Quaker, non-profit; tuition: $8,745/yr, scholarships
12 teachers, 74 students, ages 13–18, 6–12th grade
Affiliation: Friends Council on Education
Governance by faculty members, board
Socratic pedagogy; drama; co-ed interscholastic soccer, basketball, softball; extensive field trips; multi-aged classes; middle school (gr 6–8) opening in Fall '94 for 20–30 addt'l students; interns accepted.

The Barrie School (1932)
13500 Layhill Rd, Silver Spring, MD 20905
Judy Yormick, 301-894-6200, FAX: 301-871-6406
Type: Montessori; tuition: $5,045-7,430/yr
54 teachers, 474 students, ages toddler–18
Governance by board of trustees, administrator
45 wooded acres; strong humanities; hands-on; foreign travel; community service; childcare; suburban location; transportation; interns accepted.

The Institute for Advanced Montessori Studies
13500 Layhill Rd, Silver Spring, MD 20906
Judy Yormick
Type: Montessori teacher education

Aspen Hill Montessori School
3820 Aspen Hill Rd, Wheaton, MD 20906-2904
Lance Gilbert

International Montessori Society
912 Thayer Ave, Silver Spring, MD 20910
Lee Havis, 301-589-1127
Type: Montessori resource, higher education; tuition: $2,100
1 teacher, 30 students
Governance by board
Independent study, correspondence to prepare for Montessori teaching; primary and elementary levels; Trust Tutoring Program.

Spring Bilingual Montessori School
2010 Linden Ln, Silver Spring, MD 20910-1703
Anne Neri

Home Study Institute
(See Resource Section)

Ellicott City Children's House
3604 Chatham Rd, Ellicott City, MD 21042-3920
Geri Herber
Type: Montessori

Children's Manor Montessori School
10495 Fair Oaks, Columbia, MD 21044
Dr Pradeep Ghosh

Columbia Montessori School (1972)
10518 Marble Faun Ln, Columbia, MD 21044
Maria E Garcia, Dir, 410-995-0337
Tuition: $320-560/mo
4 teachers, 4 assistants, 60 students, mainly international, ages infant–6
Affiliation: AMS
Governance by administrator
Traditional; childcare; interns accepted.

Love of Learning Montessori (1983)
10840 Little Patuxent Parkway, Columbia, MD 21044
Anulda Torres, Dir, 301-596-4412, FAX: same
Tuition: $385-523/mo
6 teachers, 65 students, mainly international
Affiliations: DHR, MDDE
Governance by administrator
Multi-cultural staff; childcare; suburban location.

Bryant Woods Montessori
10449 Green Mountain Circle, Columbia, MD 21044-2457
Penny Friedberg

Julia Brown Montessori (1974)
9760 Owen Brown, Columbia, MD 21045
Adm, 410-730-5056
4 teachers, 7 assistants, 100 students, mainly international,
     ages 3-6
Affiliation: AMS; accreditations: MDBE, DHR
Governance by administrator
Traditional Montessori school; extracurriculars; childcare; sub-
     urban location; interns accepted.

Maryland Home Education Association
9085 Flamepool Way, Columbia, MD 21045
410-730-0073

Children's House Montessori
9660 Basket Ring Rd, Columbia, MD 21045-3421
Mildred Stovall

Pretty Boy Elementary School
19810 Middleton Rd, Freeland, MD 21053
Dr Sue Rathbone
Type: Montessori

The Glen Burnie Homeschool Support Group
6514 Dolphin Ct, Glen Burnie, MD 21061
301-850-4496

The Montessory Society of Central Maryland (1962)
10807 Tony Dr, Lutherville, MD 21093
Marcia A. Hettinger, Adm, 410-321-8555, FAX: 410-321-8566
Type: Montessori, non-profit; tuition: $3,780-6,825/yr
22 teachers, 22 assistants, 371 students, mainly International,
     ages Infant-12
Affiliation: NAMTA; accreditations: MSA, AMS
Governance by administrator
Childcare; suburban location; interns accepted.

Towson Children's House
1710 Dulanly Valley Rd, Lutherville, MD 21093
Marcia Hettinger
Type: Montessori

Arlington Echo Outdoor Education Center
975 Indian Landing Rd, Millersville, MD 21108
Russell Heyde, 222-3822
Type: public choice

Montessori Foundation
(See Resource Section)

North Country Home Educators (1992)
1688 Belhaven Ct, Pasadena, MD 21122-3722
Nancy Greer, Resource Librarian, 410-437-5109
Inclusive; parent meetings; social activities; monthly newslet-
     ter; free membership.

Montessori Society of Westminster
c/o St Benjamin's Church, Krider's Cemetary Rd, Westminster,
     MD 21157
Kathy Grout

Westminster Alternative Programs (1991)
125 Airport Dr, Suite 18, Westminster, MD 21157
Peg Kulow, 410-848-4441, FAX: 410-848-5058
Type: public choice
9 students

School For the Arts #415
706-712 Cathedral St, Baltimore, MD 21201
David Simon, 410-396-1185
Type: magnet
9-12th grade

Willow Country Day School
233 E Rodwood St, Baltimore, MD 21202
Type: Montessori

Odong Ridge Montessori School
2118 Pine Ave, Baltimore, MD 21207-2826
Fred Eustis

Waldorf School of Baltimore
4701 Yellowwood Ave, Baltimore, MD 21209
Jo Karp

Calvert School Home Instruction Department (1987)
105 Tuscany Rd, Baltimore, MD 21210
Susan Weiss, Prin, 410-243-6030, FAX: 410-366-0674
Non-profit; cost: $250-700/yr, scholarships
55 teachers, 10,000 students, ages 5-14, K-8th grade
Governance by board of trustees, head master, principal
Students worldwide; Day School as experimental lab for
     course development; professional guidance; integrated
     curriculum; French; music; art; classical lit.

Friends School
5114 N Charles St, Baltimore, MD 21210
W. Byron Forbush, Head, 410-435-2800
Type: Quaker

Francis M. Wood Alternative Secondary Center
100 N Calhoun St, Baltimore, MD 21223
John R. Nauright, Jr, 396-1290
Type: public choice

Harbor City Learning Center
1001 W Saratoga St, Baltimore, MD 21223
Gary Unfried, 396-1513
Type: public choice

Community Career Center in Catonsville
16 Bloomsbury Ave, Baltimore, MD 21228
Robert L. Cullison, 887-0934
Type: public choice

Community Career Center in Rosedale
Old Philadelphia Rd, Baltimore, MD 21228
Robert L. Cullison, 887-0934
Type: public choice

George F. Bragg Nature Study Center
6601 Baltimore National Pike, Baltimore, MD 21228
Benjamin Wallace, Naturalist, 747-8336
Type: public choice

Montessori School
1532 E Fort Ave, Baltimore, MD 21230

Inner Harbor Children's House
100 W Henrietta St, Baltimore, MD 21230-3610
Marcia Hettinger
Type: Montessori

Heritage Montessori School (1981)
9515 Belair Rd, Baltimore, MD 21236
Catherine Szeto, Owner/Dir, 410-529-0374
Tuition: $2,675-3,600/yr
3 teachers, 3 assistants, 67 students, ages infant-9
Affiliation: AMS
Governance by administrator
Childcare; suburban location; interns accepted.

Anne Arundel County Learning Center
600 Adams Park, Annapolis, MD 21401
James Lyons, 222-1639
Type: public choice

Chesapeake Montessori School
30 Old Mill Bottom Rd N, Annapolis, MD 21401
Anne Locke or Paula Shipley

Montessori International Children's House
1641 N Winchester Rd, Annapolis, MD 21401-5850
Jean Burgess, Dir

Easton Montessori School
2 Martin Ct #3, Easton, MD 21601
Susan Pugh, Head, 410-822-7827
Non-profit; tuition: $3,250/4,375
1 teacher, 1 assistant, 25 students, ages 3-6
Affiliation: AMI
Governance by administrator and board of trustees
Rural location; interns accepted.

Cambridge Montessori School
309 Glenburn Ave, Cambridge, MD 21613-1531
Beth Lynch

Friendship Montessori School, Inc
25528 Worton/Lynch Rd, Worton, MD 21678

Maryland Association of Christian Home Educators
Box 3964, Frederick, MD 21701
301-663-3999

Banner School
1730-A North Market Ave, Fredrick, MD 21701
Type: Montessori

Alpha Plus
(See Resource Section)

Eagle Voice Center
(See Resource Section)

Willow Country Day School
1134 Long Corner Rd, Mt Airy, MD 21771
Karen Plaskow
Type: Montessori

Massachusetts

Amherst Montessori School
27 Pomeroy Ln, Amherst, MA 01002
Bruce Marbin, Dir, 413-253-3101
Non-profit; tuition: $320-441/mo
3 teachers, 4 assistants, 52 students, ages 3-6
Affiliation: MSMA; accreditation: AMI
Governance by board
Student-centered; nature studies; childcare; rural location;
   interns accepted.

Hampshire College
Amherst, MA 01002
Admissions Office, 413-582-5471, FAX: -5631
Boarding, non-profit; tuition: $19,490/yr, scholarships
100 teachers, 1079 students, ages 16-45
Close collaboration between students and faculty; multidisciplinary learning; emphasis on independent research and
   creative work; member of Five Colleges Consortium; no
   letter grades; rural location.

The Common School
521 S Pleasant St Box 52, Amherst, MA 01004
Mark Segar, 413-256-8989
Type: independent

The Learning Cooperative (1993)
6 University Dr #240, Amherst, MA 01004-6000
Caroline Adams, 413-253-0444
Type: home-based

Hartsbrook School (1981)
94 Bay Rd, Hadley, MA 01035
Catherine Hopkins, Faculty Chair, 413-586-1908
Type: Waldorf; tuition: $3,625-4,650/yr, scholarships
22 teachers, 200 students, ages 4-14, pre K-8th grade
Affiliation: AWSNA
Governance by teachers, board
Teacher qualifications: BA, Waldorf teacher training and/or
   expertise in specific subject
Balances humanities, sciences, arts; foreign language, begin-
   ning grade 1; no letter grades; suburban location; interns
   accepted.

Western Massachusetts Hilltown Charter School
Edward St, Haydenville, MA 01039
Dr William Cutler, 413-268-3384

Type: charter
35-60 students, K-4th grade
Affiliation: MA Executive Office of Ed
Reggio Emilia philosophy; rural location.

Holyoke Street School
130 Race St, Holyoke, MA 01040
413-536-2160
Type: independent
Students mainly at-risk

Magnet Middle School for Arts
325 Pine St, Holyoke, MA 01040
Selicita Elghadi, 413-534-2132
6-8th grade
Visual & performing arts.

Morgan Elementary
596 S Bridge, Holyoke, MA 01040
413-534-2083
Type: magnet
K-2nd grade
Pre-k Piaget; Montessori ungraded.

Morgan Montessori Kindergarten Program
596 S Bridge St, Holyoke, MA 01040-5953

Children's House Montessori
929 Northampton Hwy, Holyoke, MA 01040-9660

Folk Education Association of America
(See Resource Section)

Montessori Children's House
118 Riverdale St, W Springfield, MA 01089-4603

Experiment With Travel
Box 4884, Springfield, MA 01101-4884
Type: independent

Springfield Public Schools
195 State St, Box 1410, Springfield, MA 01102-1410
Teresa Regina
Type: Montessori

Montessori Internationale
56 Hopkins Pl, Longmeadow, MA 01106-1943

Elias Brookings Elementary
367 Hancock St, Springfield, MA 01107
Mary Anne Herron, 413-787-7200
Type: magnet
K–8th grade
Whole-student approach.

Lincoln Elementary School
732 Chestnut St, Springfield, MA 01107
Enrique Figueredo, 413-787-7314
Type: magnet
K–5th grade

Frank H. Freedman Elementary
90 Cherokee Dr, Springfield, MA 01109
Beverly A. Brown, 413-787-7443
Type: magnet
K–5th grade
Whole-student approach.

Homer Street Elementary
43 Homer St, Springfield, MA 01109
Robert Brown Jr, 413-787-7526
Type: magnet
K–5th grade
Whole-student approach.

William N. DeBerry Elementary
670 Union St, Springfield, MA 01109
Barbara Jefferson, 413-787-7582
Type: magnet
K–5th grade
Education Today for Tomorrow.

Massasoit Montessori School
455 Island Pond Rd, Springfield, MA 01118

Montessori School of Springfield
1644 Allen St, Springfield, MA 01118-1818

Pioneer Valley Montessori School (1964)
1524 Parker St, Springfield, MA 01129
Laura Geryk, Head/Dir, 413-547-0342
Non-profit; tuition: $2,256-4,252/yr
4 teachers, 4 assistants, 98 students, ages 3–12
Affiliations: MSMA, NAEYC; accreditations: AISNE, AMS
Governance by administrator, board
Childcare; suburban location; transportation; interns accepted.

Hibbard Alternative
280 Newell St, Pittsfield, MA 01201
Laurie Bell
Type: home-based

Home Education Resource Center
505 East St, Pittsfield, MA 01201
Cindy Chandler, 413-499-5836
25 students, ages 2-16
Community guest lecturers; resource list; field trips; books and materials.

Berkshire Homeschoolers Group (1980)
217 Old State Rd, Berkshire, MA 01224
Judith A. Coons, 413-443-1770
Non-profit
Testing; proposal writing; field trips; rural location.

Rudolf Steiner School of Great Barrington
35 W Plain Rd, Great Barrington, MA 01230
Virginia Flynn
Type: Waldorf

Montessori Berkshire (1979)
32 Pixley Hill Rd, Housatonic, MA 01236
Bonny Campbell, Dir, 413-274-3407
Non-profit; tuition: $3,000/yr
1 teacher, 2 assistants, 27 students, ages 3-6

Affiliations: AMS, MSMA
Governance by board of trustees
Rural location; interns accepted.

Massachusetts Home Learning Association (1987)
PO Box 1976, Lenox, MA 01240-4976
Maggie Sadoway, 413-637-2169
Newsletter; legal fact sheet for MA ($1); homeschooling information packet ($5).

Ashley Falls Program
PO Box 339, Sheffield, MA 01257
Eileen Brennan, Tch, 413-229-8778, FAX: 413-229-2913
Type: public choice
1 teacher, 22 students, ages 8–10, 3-4th grade
Affiliation: Undermountain Elementary
Governance by teachers, principal
Student ombudsman is arbiter of classroom conflicts; 2 students cook lunch each day; groupings vary; daily parent assistance; no letter grades, multi-aged classes; extensive field trips; rural location; transportation; interns accepted.

SALE: Specialized Alternative Learning Environment
PO Box 339, Sheffield, MA 01257
413-229-8778, FAX: 413-229-2913
Type: public choice
1,100 students, ages 3–22, pre K-12th grade
Governance by faculty, student reps, parent co-op, teachers, principal
Comprehensive; therapeutic; integrated; multi-aged classes; rural location; transportation; interns accepted.

Buxton School (1928)
PO Box 646, Williamstown, MA 01267
C. William Bennett, 413-458-3919, FAX: -9427
Type: independent, boarding, non-profit; tuition: $19,500/yr, scholarships
16 teachers, 80 students, ages 14–18, 9-12th grade
Governance by teachers and principal
Teacher qualifications: Bachelor's
Work program; the arts; students maintain school; entire school travels to major city for research projects and to perform touring play; no letter grades; extensive field trips; multi-aged classes; rural location.

Institute for International Cooperation and Development (1986)
PO Box 103, Williamstown, MA 01267
Josefin Jonsson, Adm Dir, 413-458-9828, FAX: 413-458-3323
Type: public choice; tuition: $3,200-4,300/yr, scholarships
6 teachers, 60 students, ages 18+
Affiliation: Scandinavian folk HS's
Organizes 6-12 mo travel, study and solidarity courses; street-children school in Zimbabwe; treeplanting in Mozambique; rural construction projects in Nicaragua, Brazil; rural location.

NE Foundation For Children
(See Resource Section)

Full Circle School (1973)
Box 45410, 21 Parmenter Rd, Bernardston, MA 01337
Michael Muir-Harmony, Teacher/Director, 413-648-9842
Type: independent, non-profit; tuition: $5,000/yr, scholarships
5 teachers, 60 students, ages 2.9-12, ungraded
Governance by board
Teacher qualifications: similar philosophical beliefs
Libertarian school where liberty is viewed not as a byproduct, but as an essential ingredient of education; integrity of childhood is respected; no letter grades; non-compulsory class attendance; multi-aged classes; extensive field trips; rural location.

Assumption Montessori School
N Main St, Box 128, Petersham, MA 01366

Rowe Camp & Conference Center
King Highway Rd Box 273, Rowe, MA 01367
413-339-4954
Type: higher education

Apple Country Homeschooling Association
PO Box 246, Harvard, MA 01451
508-456-8515

Harvard Elementary School Kindergarten
27 Massachusetts Ave, Harvard, MA 01451
Type: Montessori

Montessori Children's House of Auburn
135 Bryn Mawr Ave, Auburn, MA 01501-1605

Touchstone Community School
54 Leland St, Grafton, MA 01519
Dick Zajchowski
Type: independent

Maria Montessori School
21 Grove St, Millbury, MA 01527-2623

Francis W. Parker Charter School
234 Massachusetts Ave, Harvard, MA 01541
John Stadler, 508-456-8988
Type: charter
100 students
Affiliation: MA Executive Office of Ed
CES philosophy and application of TQM principles.

The Montessori Center of Shrewsbury
55 Oak St, Shrewsbury, MA 01545-2733
Nancy Corkum

Montessori Children's House (1976)
370 Worcester St, Southbridge, MA 01550
508-764-4032
Non-profit; tuition: $1,360-3,000/yr
11 teachers, 11 assistants, 35 students, ages 3-6
Accreditation: AMS
Governance by parent cooperative
Suburban location.

Treetops Montessori School
Baker Pond Rd, Dudley, MA 01571
Nancy Corkum

Worcester Area Homeschooling Organization
246 May St #2, Worcester, MA 01602
617-755-9553

City View Elementary
80 Prospect St, Worcester, MA 01605
Donald Shea, 508-799-3670
Type: magnet
K-6th grade
Discovery of self and world.

Burncoat Senior High School
179 Burncoat St, Worcester, MA 01606
William Hynes, 508-799-3300
Type: magnet
9-12th grade
Performing arts.

Burncoat St Elementary
526 Burncoat St, Worcester, MA 01606
Joseph Monfredo, 508-799-3537
Type: magnet
K-6th grade
Fine and performing arts.

Worcester Arts Magnet Elementary
315 St Nicholas Ave, Worcester, MA 01606
Margaret Vinditti, 508-799-3575
4-6th grade
Performing arts.

Worcester Charter School at Assumption College
500 Salisbury Rd, Worcester, MA 01615-0005
Mary Anderson, 508-762-5615 x426
Type: charter
500 students, K-4th grade
Affiliation: MA Executive Office of Ed
Edison Project school using "House System"; extended day and year.

Metro West Homeschoolers
25 Carter Dr, Framingham, MA 01701
508-877-6536

Sudbury Valley School (1968)
2 Winch St, Framingham, MA 01701
Mimsy Sadofsky, 508-877-3030, FAX: 788-0674
Type: independent, non-profit; tuition: $3600/2,575
(2nd)/1550 (3rd child)
11 teachers, 140 students, ages 4-20
Affiliation: NEASC
Governance by democratic school meeting
Teacher qualifications: students select staff invited to return each year
Students initiate; staff and equipment answer their needs; all ages mix freely; each staff and student has one vote at weekly meeting; school-starting kit; no letter grades; non-compulsory class attendance; multi-aged classes; suburban location.

Oak Meadow Montessori School
723 Massachusetts Ave, Boxborough, MA 01719-1413

Pincushion Hill Montessori School (1961)
30 Green St, Ashland, MA 01721
Christine Kovago, Dir, 508-881-2123
Non-profit; tuition: $2,750-5,500/yr
3 teachers, 3 assistants, 70 students, ages 3-9
Affiliations: AMI, AMS, MA Assn
Governance by administrator
Childcare; suburban location.

Concord Montessori (1975)
61 Birch Dr, Concord, MA 01742-2626
508-369-1455
Non-profit; tuition: $960-2,400/yr
5 teachers, 5 assistants, 78 students, ages infant-6
Affiliation: NAMTA
Governance by administrator
Suburban location; interns accepted.

Miller Elementary School (1973)
Woodland St, Holliston, MA 01746
Marcia Pinkham or Dr Anne Toule, Prin, 429-0668
Type: Public choice Montessori
10 teachers, 268 students, ages 3-12
Governance by administration
French Immersion; parents choose Montessori or traditional; transportation; interns accepted.

St Anne Montessori
720 Boston Post Rd E, Marlboro, MA 01752-3799
Sr Marie Joseph

Eliot Montessori School
5 Auburn St, South Natick, MA 01760-6064
Maggie Bryant or Bonnie James

The Life Experience School (1972)
2 N Main St, Sherborn, MA 01770
Lewis M. Randa, Dir, 508-655-2143, FAX: 655-5031
Type: Quaker; tuition: $18,000/yr
5 teachers, 15 students, mainly at-risk, ages 8-22
Affiliation: UN U for Peace; Harvard Div School
Governance by faculty and student representatives, board
Teacher qualifications: BS in SE or related field
No letter grades; extensive field trips; interns accepted.

Apple Valley Montessori School
80 Woodside Rd, Sudbury, MA 01776-3430
Audrey Newton

Barat Montessori School
5 Damon St, Cochituate, MA 01778-4807

Julie Billiart's Children's House
8 Summer St, Woburn, MA 01801
Type: Montessori

Woburn Montessori School
7 Kosciusko St, Woburn, MA 01801-3863

Merrimack Montessori School
55 Saltonstall Rd, Haverhill, MA 01830-4189

Georgetown School Department
1 Library St, Georgetown, MA 01833
Larry S. Borin, Supt, 508-352-5777, FAX: 508-352-5778
Type: public/independent choice
90 teachers, 1100 students, ages 5–19, K–12th grade
Governance by board
Comprehensive computer lab; 65 stations linked with Novell
    Network.

Community Day Charter School
190 Hampshire St, Lawrence, MA 01840
Sheila Balboni, 508-682-6628
Type: charter
140–180 students, K–6th grade
Affiliation: MA Executive Office of Ed
Parental ESL and literacy training.

Presentation of Mary
209 Lawrence St, Methuen, MA 01844-3884
Type: Montessori

Andover School of Montessori (1975)
180 Main St, N Andover, MA 01845
Michelle B. DuBois, 508-688-1086
Tuition: $2,420/4,760/yr
4 teachers, 4 assistants, 75 students, ages 3–6
Affiliations: AMS, MSM, ISAM
Governance by board, administrator
Life skills; childcare; suburban location; interns accepted.

Lowell Charter School
11 Kearney Square, Lowell, MA 01852
Richard Howe, 508-454-9167
Type: charter
400 students, K–4th grade
Affiliation: MA Executive Office of Ed
Edison Project school; expanding to K–12; groups of 100 stu-
    dents will work with teams of 4 teachers; extended day
    and year.

Lowell Middlesex Academy Charter School
33 Kearney Square, Lowell, MA 01852
Karen Saberi-Moore, 508-656-3286
Type: charter
100 students, ages 16–22, senior high
Affiliation: MA Executive Office of Ed
Remediation program for drop-outs; traditional curriculum
    integrated with community activities; 2+2 program with
    Middlesex CC.

Greater Boston Home Educators
16 Hawthorne St, Wakefield, MA 01880
617-246-2059

Kitchen School Group
PO Box 96, W Boxford, MA 01885
617-352-2023
Type: home-based

Massachusetts Homeschool Organization of Parent
    Educators
15 Ohio St, Wilmington, MA 01887
508-658-8970

Children's Own School, Inc
86 Main St, Winchester, MA 01890-3928
Type: Montessori

Cape Ann Waldorf School
668 Hale St, Beverly Farms, MA 01915
Elizabeth Trocki

The Harborlight Montessori
243 Essex St, Beverly, MA 01915-1958
Susan McDonough

North Shore Homeschool Support Group
62 Matthies St, Beverly, MA 01915-2448
Marci Anthony, 508-927-8383

Danvers Alternative High School (1978)
57 Conant St, Danvers, MA 01923
Dane Hamilton, Dir, 508-887-9567
Type: public at-risk
5 teachers, 25 students, mainly at-risk, ages 14–18, 9–12th
    grade
Governance by teachers, principal, democratic school
    meeting
Teacher qualifications: certification in moderate special needs
Therapeutic milieu; extensive field trips; multi-aged classes;
    no letter grades; non-compulsory class attendance; subur-
    ban location; interns accepted.

Cape Ann Homeschoolers (1992)
6 Emily La, Magnolia, MA 01930
Judith A. Humbert, Dir, 508-525-3061
Non-profit
12 teachers, 25 students, ages 5–12, K–6th grade
Governance by parent cooperative
Monthly meetings; non-sectarian; suburban location.

Gloucester Alternative School (1983)
48 Magnolia Ave, Magnolia, MA 01930
Cynthia Smith, Team Chair, 508-525-3572
Type: public at-risk
5 teachers, 24 students, ages 14–19, HS
Governance by teachers and principal
Teacher qualifications: SE certification
Multi-aged classes; suburban location; interns accepted.

Ipswich Montessori (1976)
PO Box 612, Ipswich, MA 01938
Jame Brissette, 508-356-5698
Tuition: $1,575/3,500/yr
2 teachers, 2 assistants, 35 students, ages 3–6
Governance by administrator
Extensive nature studies in woods.

Children's Montessori School
PO Box 681, Ipswich, MA 01938-0681

Don Bosco, Sacred Heart
RR 1 A, Ipswich, MA 01938-9801
Type: Montessori

Newburyport Montessori School
23 Pleasant St, Newburyport, MA 01950-2622

Salem Montessori School, Inc
4 Holly St, Salem, MA 01970-4611

Notre Dame Children's Class
74 Grapevine Rd, Wenham, MA 01984-1712
Type: Montessori

Bellingham Alternative Jr/Sr High School
387 Hartford Ave; mailing: 60 Harpin St, Bellingham, MA 02019
John Bonin, Dir, 508-966-1622, FAX: 508-966-4050
Type: public at-risk; tuition: $10,000 out of district
4 teachers, 33 students, ages 12–19, 7–12th grade
Governance by teachers, principal
Teacher qualifications: SE certification
Problem solving; mainstream re-entry; multi-aged classes;
    suburban location; transportation; interns accepted.

Blue Hill Montessori School
163 Turnpike St, Canton, MA 02021-1300
Patricia Lukos

Dover Montessori School (1969)
16 Sherbrooke Dr, Dover, MA 02030
Terry Brown or Debbie Egan, 508-785-1387
Tuition: $2,795-5,200/yr
2 teachers, 5 assistants, 75 students, ages 3-6
Affiliations: NAMTA, NAEYC, BAEYC, AMI, AMS; accreditation:
    SNMC
Governance by administrator
Small group lessons in Spanish and science; large playground
    facility; special needs training; childcare; suburban location;
    interns accepted.

King's Wood Montessori (1968)
12 Gilmore St, Foxboro, MA 02035
Kathleen Dunn, 508-543-6391
Non-profit; tuition: $1,960-3,120/yr
2 teachers, 3 assistants, 58 students, ages 3-6
Affiliation: MSMA
Governance by administrator, parent cooperative
Childcare; suburban location; interns accepted.

Benjamin Franklin Classical Charter School
390 Oakland Pkwy, Franklin, MA 02038
Timothy Casey, 617-849-1800 x4204
Type: charter
270 students, K-8th grade
Affiliation: MA Executive Office of Ed
Core Knowledge curriculum; parents as primary educators;
    goal of achieving 10% higher levels than traditional public
    schools.

South Shore Charter School
390 Oakland Pkwy, Franklin, MA 02038
Timothy Anderson, 617-849-1800 x4204
Type: charter
150-400 students, K-1 & 11-12th grade
Affiliation: MA Executive Office of Ed
Environmental service corps emphasis; plans to become a
    family learning resource center.

**Seacoast Center Montessori Teacher Education
    Program**
PO Box 185, Scituate, MA 02040
Gary Davidson

Old Colony Montessori School
20 Derby St, Hingham, MA 02043-3707

Woodside Montessori School (1985)
350 Village St, Millis, MA 02054
Raui Kaur Khalsa, 508-376-5320
Tuition: $1,800-5,650/yr
4 teachers, 3 assistants, 72 students, ages 3-9
Governance by administrator
Low-ropes course built to scale; special needs accomodated;
    childcare; suburban location; interns accepted.

Harborside Montessori, Inc (1988)
188 First Parish Rd, Scituate, MA 02066
Shirley Carpenter, Adm/Dir, 617-545-2626
Tuition: $2,600/yr
1 teacher, 1 assistant, 24 students, ages 3-6
Affiliations: NAMTA, MSMA
Governance by administrator
French-speaking assistant; Kodaly music; professional gym-
    nastics; after-school French, recorder, piano for fee;
    childcare.

The Montessori Community School (1973)
136 Cornet Stetson Rd, Scituate, MA 02066
Charles Terranova, Head, 617-545-5544, FAX: 612-545-6522
Non-profit; tuition: $4,150-7,050/yr
10 teachers, 186 students, ages infant-12

Affiliations: AMS, MSMA
Governance by board
Childcare; suburban location; interns accepted.

Jewish Home Educator's Network (1991)
2 Webb Rd, Sharon, MA 02067
Marc Ernstoff, Treasurer, 617-784-9091

Transition Demonstration Programs
43 Mt Vernon St, Boston, MA 02108
David Robinson, EdD, Dir of Research, 617-227-2280
Type: public choice
K-3rd grade
Developmentally-appropriate; family, health services.

Boston Renaissance Charter School (1995)
Horace Mann Foundation
21 Custom House, Boston, MA 02110
John Schindler, 671-469-6843
Type: charter
700 students
Affiliations: MA Executive Office of Ed, Horace Mann
    Foundation
Edison Project school; every student will have a home
    computer.

Boston University Charter School
775 Commonwealth Ave, Boston, MA 02115
Rear Admiral W. Norman Johnson, USN (Ret.), 617-353-4126
Type: at-risk charter, boarding
150-180 students, 7-12th grade
Affiliation: MA Executive Office of Ed
Uses military realignment for teachers and other resources.

Kingsley Montessori School (1986)
30 Fairfield St, Boston, MA 02116
Carole Forbes, Head, 617-536-5984, FAX: 617-536-7507
Non-profit; tuition: $2,470/6,370/yr
8 teachers, 7 assistants, 108 students, mainly international,
    ages infant-12
Affiliation: AMS; accreditation: AISNE
Governance by administrator, board of trustees
Childcare; urban location; interns accepted.

National Coalition of Advocates For Stududents
(See Resource Section)

YouthBuild Boston Charter School
173a Norfolk Ave, Roxbury, MA 02119
Jackie Gelb, 617-445-8887
Type: at-risk charter
50 students, senior high
Affiliation: MA Executive Office of Ed
Voc targets construction; students renovate abandoned
    buildings for homeless.

Martin Luther King Middle School
77 Lawrence Ave, Dorchester, MA 02121
Steven Leonard, 617-445-4120
Type: magnet
6-8th grade
Communication; writing; arts.

Dorchester Youth Alternative School (1983)
1514A Dorchester Ave, Dorchester, MA 02122
Mary Lou O'Neill, Ed Dir, 617-288-1748, FAX: -2136
Type: public at-risk
3 teachers, 18 students, ages 12-16, 6-10th grade
Affiliation: Dept of Social Services/BPS
Governance by faculty, student reps, board
Individualized; flexible; accommodates different learning
    styles; multi-aged classes; extensive field trips; urban loca-
    tion; transportation; interns accepted.

The Log School (1975)
225 Bowdoin St, Dorchester, MA 02122
Gilbert Waytes, Dir, 617-288-6683

Type: public at-risk
3 teachers, 35 students, ages 12-15, 6-8th grade
Affiliation: Boston Public Schools
Governance by principal
Teacher qualifications: state certification
Extensive field trips; urban location.

Dorchester High School
9 Peacevale Rd, Dorchester, MA 02124
Christopher Lane, 617-436-2065
Type: magnet
9-12th grade
Public service.

Neighborhood House Charter School
232 Centre St, Dorchester, MA 02124
Kristin McCormack, 617-282-5034
Type: at-risk charter
45-135 students
Affiliation: MA Executive Office of Ed
Settlement house model; 1:10 ratio; Family Cooperative
membership required; social services, GED, ESL, etc.

Notre Dame Montessori School
263/265 Mt Vernon St, Dorchester, MA 02125
Sr Elizabeth Calcagni

Julie's Children's House
230 W 6th St, South Boston, MA 02127-2635
Type: Montessori

Fenway II Charter School
Fenway College Middle HS
250 Rutherford Ave, Charlestown, MA 02129
Linda Nathan, 617-635-9911
Type: charter
420 students, 79% minority, all at-risk, 6-12th grade
Affiliations: CES, MA Executive Office of Ed
Conversion from 10-yr old school.

Creative Building Association Inc
54 Kenrick St, Brighton, MA 02135
Brad Harson
Type: Montessori

Pilot School
459 Broadway, Cambridge, MA 02138
617-349-6674
Type: public choice

Educator's Publishing Service (EPS)
(See Resource Section)

Cambridge Montessori School
161 Garden St, Cambridge, MA 02138-1240

Lesley College
29 Everett St, Cambridge, MA 02138-2790
Gives credit support to Audubon Exploration Institute, other
alternative programs.

Graham and Parks Alternative Public School (1972)
15 Upton St, Cambridge, MA 02139
Len Solo, principal, 617-349-6613, FAX: -6615
Type: public choice
19 teachers, 370 students, ages 4.5-14, K-8th grade
Governance by parent and staff shared decision-making
Teacher qualifications: certified, experienced in urban ed,
curriculum developer, high energy
Self-contained, multi-graded, open classrooms in K-6; flexible, student-centered program for grades 7-8; teacher
developed, multi-cultural curriculum; extensive parent
involvement; no letter grades; multi-aged classes; urban
location; interns accepted.

National Center for Fair and Open Testing (FairTest)
(See Resource Section)

Cambridge Friends School (1961)
5 Cadbury Rd, Cambridge, MA 02140
Mary L. Johnson, Head, 617-354-3880, FAX: 876-1815
Type: Quaker, non-profit; tuition: $8,180-8,980/yr,
scholarships
22 teachers, 200 students, ages 5-14, K-8th grade
Affiliations: FCOE, NAIS
Governance by principal, teachers, and board
Teacher qualifications: experience, agreement with mission
Multi-cultural, anti-racist, anti-homophobic curr; no letter
grades; multi-aged classes; urban location; interns
accepted.

Growing Without Schooling
(See Resource Section)

Holt Associates
(See Resource Section)

Full Circle High School
165 Broadway, Somerville, MA 02145
Type: independent

City on a Hill Charter School
39 Jordan Rd, Brookline, MA 02146
Sarah Kass, 617-566-3037
Type: charter
60 students, 9-10th grade
Affiliation: MA Executive Office of Ed
Expanding to 7-12; emphasis on civic ed, community service,
internships.

School Within a School (1970)
115 Greenough St, Brookline, MA 02146
Ellen Kaplovitz, Coord, 617-730-2747
Type: public choice
4 teachers, 100 students, ages 14-18, 10-12th grade
Teacher qualifications: state certification
Democratic school with town meeting; student-directed
activities; suburban location.

The Apple Orchard School (1971)
282D Newton St, Brookline, MA 02146
Lee Albright, Dir, 617-731-6463
Type: independent
80 students, ages 3-6
Located in renovated barn on farm; fields; woods; ponds;
animals; environmental emphasis.

Hatsoff! Development Corp
42 Greenleaf St, Walden, MA 02148
Paul DuPont
Type: Montessori

Waltham Transition High School
100 Summer St, Waltham, MA 02154
William A Nolan, Prin, 617-647-0309, FAX: 617-647-9316
Type: public at-risk
6 teachers, 30 students, ages 14-18, 8-12th grade
Affiliation: Waltham Public Schools
Governance by teachers, principal
Teacher qualifications: state certification, Academic and
Occupational
Living & learning skills; health/PE; career exploration
sequence; multi-aged classes; suburban location.

Walnut Park Montessori School
47 Walnut Park, Newton, MA 02158-1442

Montessori Educare Inc
80 Crescent Ave, Newton, MA 02159-2102

Homeschoolers of Massachusetts Education Club
60 Parkway Rd, Newton, MA 02160
617-489-3275

Winthrop House at Brookline High School (1983)
490 Heath St, Brookline, MA 02167
Cathy Heller, Dir, 617-730-2507
Type: public at-risk
2 teachers, 1 assistant, 20 students, ages 14-22, 9-12th
    grade
Governance by teachers, director, administrators
Teacher qualifications: SE certification
Cooperative; hands-on; life skills; conflict resolution; thera-
    peutic intervention; multi-aged classes; suburban location;
    transportation.

Lexington Montessori School
130 Pleasant St, Lexington, MA 02173-8257
Peter Burleigh

Learning Things, Inc
(See Resource Section)

Waldorf School (1971)
739 Massachusetts Ave, Lexington, MA 02174
Susan Morris, Adms Coord, 617-863-1062
Non-profit; tuition: $4,500-6,700/yr, scholarships
30 teachers, 210 students, ages 3.5-14, pre K-8th grade
Affiliations: AWSNA, AISNE
Governance by faculty committee
Teacher qualifications: college degree, Waldorf certification
Special subject teachers; suburban location; interns accepted.

Wellesley Montessori School
79 Denton Rd, Wellesley, MA 02181-6404
Ida Friedman

Program at Braintree High School
128 Town St, Braintree, MA 02184
David M Swanton, Coord, 617-848-4000
Type: public at-risk
4 teachers, 30 students, ages 14-21, 9-12th grade
Governance by teachers, prin, coord, democratic school
    meeting
Teacher qualifications: special ed or social sciences
    certification
School within a school; team teaching; counseling; behavior
    management system; daily group meetings; graduation
    credit; job training; multi-aged classes; extensive field trips;
    suburban location; interns accepted.

Thacher Montessori School
1425 Blue Hill Ave, Milton, MA 02186-2349
Maureen Coughlin

Institute for Responsive Education
(See Resource Section)

Munchkin Montessori Inc
145 Loring St, Duxbury, MA 02332-4823
Pam Malbouf

Pinewood Montessori
Federal Furnace Rd, Plymouth, MA 02360

South Shore Home Schoolers
163 Hingham St, Rockland, MA 02370

READS Academy
70 Howard St, W Bridgewater, MA 02379
Deirdre Dowd-Pizzuto, LICSW, 508-587-6862
Type: public at-risk
4 teachers, 4 assistants, 25-40 students, ages 5-22, K-12th
    grade
Governance by board
Teacher qualifications: certification in moderate special needs
Basic interpersonal, social skills; counseling; behavior man-
    agement; multi-aged classes; rural location; interns
    accepted.

Small World Children's House (1976)
395 West St, West Bridgewater, MA 02379-1014
Helena Bolster Marcotte, 508-584-0222
Type: Montessori; tuition: $355/mo
2 teachers, 6 assistants, 40 students, mainly international,
    ages 3-6
Affiliations: MSMA, NAEYC; accreditation: MA
Governance by administrator
Many student observers from nearby Bridgewater State and
    Stonehill Colleges; childcare.

South Shore Homeschoolers
87 Snell Av, Brockton, MA 02402
508-588-1529

Waldorf School of Cape Cod (1984)
85 Cotuit Rd, PO Box 3212, Bourne, MA 02532
Susan Joslin, Dev Dir, 508-759-7499
Non-profit; tuition: $2,400-5,250/yr, scholarships
14 teachers, 98 students, ages 3-13, nursery-8th grade
Affiliation: AWSNA
Governance by faculty and board of directors
Teacher qualifications: Waldorf cert preferred
Values-based; suburban location; interns accepted.

Center of Independent Learning, Inc (1989)
Box 619, 5 Depot Rd, Cataumet, MA 02534
Linda M. Zuern, Dir, 508-564-4875
Type: independent, non-profit; tuition: $140/session
1 teacher, 10-20 students, ages 5-13, K-8th grade
Governance by board; dir
Teacher qualifications: BS or MS in Education
Small group classes; students, parents help set goals for each
    session; rural location.

Barnstable Montessori School
PO Box 832, East Sandwich, MA 02537-0832

Children's House of Nantucket
Pheasant Way, Nantucket, MA 02554
Type: Montessori

Nantucket New School
45 Surfside Rd, Nantucket, MA 02554
Linda Zola, Dir, 508-228-8569
Type: independent, non-profit; tuition: $0-5,000/yr, tuition-
    replacement jobs available
2 teachers, 21 students, ages 4-13, pre K-7th grade
Governance by teachers, principal
Equal emphasis on left and right brain functions; behavior
    modification; quiet classes; broad socioeconomic range;
    high CAT scores; 4-5 yr olds read and write; multi-aged
    classes; art; drama; suburban location.

Vineyard Montessori School
Main & Tashmoo Sts, PO Box 994, Vineyard Haven, MA 02568-
    0994
Debra Polucci

Abbington Academy (1983)
Box 330, Wareham, MA 02571-3303
Kristen Heisler, School Liaison, 508-291-1229
Type: home-based, non-profit; cost: $300/yr/family,
    scholarships
25 students, ages 6-18, 1-12th grade
Governance by parent cooperative
Self-directed, community, and home-based learning; strong
    parental involvement in planning and activities; descriptive
    assessments and portfolios; apprenticeships, community
    service; no letter grades; multi-aged classes; extensive field
    trips; non-compulsory class attendance; suburban
    location.

Country Day Montessori School
1643 Hyannis Rd, Barnstable, MA 02630
Lynn Heslinga

Barnstable Country Day School
240 Flint St, Marstons Mills, MA 02648
Type: Montessori

Cape Cod Lighthouse Charter School
PO Box 968, South Orleans, MA 02662
Don Krohn, 508-255-6399
Type: charter
100-130 students, 6-8th grade
Affiliation: MA Executive Office of Ed
May expand to 6-12; community-based.

Montessori School of the Angels
PO Box 360, Fall River, MA 02724-0360

St Joseph Montessori School
2501 S Main St, Fall River, MA 02724-2015

West Side Jr/Sr High School
181 Hillman St, New Bedford, MA 02740
508-997-4511 x2372
Type: public at-risk
11 teachers, 60 students, ages 14-20, 7-12th grade
Governance by principal
Teacher qualifications: state certification
Culinary, woodwork, art, pottery, photography shops; CCP computer lab; student operated restaurant; multi-aged classes; extensive field trips; urban location; transportation; interns accepted.

Michigan

Novi Worthville Montessori
6561 Tamerlane, Novi, MI 18375
Geetha Rao, Adm, 313-348-3033
Tuition: $200/336
3 teachers, 8 assistants, 77 students, mainly international, ages 3-6
Affiliation: Social Services
Governance by administrator
Highly academic and structured program includes music, gym, and art; childcare; suburban location.

Birmingham Community Montessori (1979)
2225 Fourteen Mile Rd, Birmingham, MI 48009
Arlene Ross, Administrator, 313-646-1535
Tuition: $2,260/yr
2 teachers, 2 assistants, 44 students, ages 3-6
Affiliation: MIMS
Governance by administrator, democratic school meeting
Weekly music; suburban location; interns accepted.

Gateway Montessori School
32605 W Bellvine Tr, Bervery Hills, MI 48025
Mary Jo Meagher

Novi Northville Montessori (1984)
6561 Tamerlane, W Bloomfield, MI 48033
Geetha Rao, Adm, 810-348-3033
Tuition: $200/365/wk
3 teachers, 8 assistants, 70 students, mainly international, ages 3-6
Accreditation: AMS
Governance by an administrator and democratic school meeting
Language; math; geography; science; music; art; French; childcare; interns accepted.

Montessori Stepping Stones
19 Byron Ct, Mount Clemens, MI 48043-5518

Upland Hills School (1971)
2575 Indian Lake Road, Oxford, MI 48051
Phillip Moore, Director, 313-693-2878, FAX:-1021
Type: independent, non-profit; tuition: $4,020
9 teachers, 75 students, ages 4-14, K-8th grade
Governance by teachers and principal, board
Developing tools of self-awareness; celebrating nature; emphasis on the arts; to promote, foster, nurture and defend childhood; multi-aged classes; extensive field trips; rural location; interns accepted.

Enterprise High School (1983)
175 Croswell, Romeo, MI 48065
Mary Tewksbury, Coord, 810-752-0312, FAX: -0228

Type: public choice
4 teachers, 50 students, mainly former drop-outs, ages 16-21
Governance by teachers, principal
Teacher qualifications: certification
Classes run like small businesses; students decide on products, prices, profits; multi-aged classes

Romeo Montessori Center (1977)
PO Box 414, Romeo, MI 48065
Susan Parker, 313-752-4411
Tuition: $165-385/mo
4 teachers, 4 assistants, 80 students, ages 3-6
Affiliations: AMS, MI MS
Childcare; interns accepted.

Holy Innocents
226200 Ridgemont, Roseville, MI 48066
Type: Montessori

Montessori Children's Center
18720 E 13 Mile Rd, Roseville, MI 48066-1326

Little Learners' Montessori Center
814 N Campbell Rd, Royal Oak, MI 48067-2125

Montessori School of St Clair
955 Fred Moore Hywy, St Clair, MI 48079
Diane Judson

Little Learners Montessori
22418 Grove Pointe St, St Clair Shores, MI 48081-1626

REACH (1983)
28500 Alden St, Madison Hts, MI 48083
Ruth Turner, Coord, 313-545-5585, FAX: -0112
Type: public at-risk
4 teachers, 70-80 students, ages 16-20, 10-12th grade
Governance by teachers, principal
Teacher qualifications: certification
Community service agencies networking; team-building; cooperative learning; problem-solving activities; initiatives course; camping experience; multi-aged classes; interns accepted.

Troy Montessori
3950 Livernois Rd, Troy, MI 48083-5036

Maria Montessori Center
3813 Finch Rd, Troy, MI 48084-1670

Montessori Children's Learning Center
4141 Laurence, Allen Park, MI 48101
Jeannette B Vickery, 313-382-2777
7 teachers, 16 assistants, 165 students, ages 3-9

Affiliations: AMS, MI MS
Governance by administrator
Basic skills; art; music; gym; Spanish; choir; private and group music lessons available; childcare; interns accepted.

Bach Open Elementary
600 W Jefferson, Ann Arbor, MI 48103
JoAnn Okey, Prin
Type: public choice
K-5th grade

Middle Years Alternative
1655 Newport Rd, Ann Arbor, MI 48103
Patrick O'Neill, Prin
Type: public choice

Rudolf Steiner School of Ann Arbor (1980)
2775 Newport Rd, Ann Arbor, MI 48103
Sha W. Buikema, Adm, 313-995-4141
Type: Waldorf, non-profit; tuition: $4,500-4,600/yr, scholarships
30 teachers; student ages 4-14, pre K-8th grade
Affiliations: AWSNA, AIMS
Governance by faculty, administrators, parents, community members board
Teacher qualifications: college degree, Waldorf training
Global understanding; suburban location; interns accepted.

Peach Tree Montessori Preschool Workshop
319 N Ashley St, Ann Arbor, MI 48103-3305

Clonlara School (1967)
1289 Jewett St, Ann Arbor, MI 48104
Barb Maling, Coord, 313-769-4511, FAX: -9629
Type: independent, non-profit; tuition: $3,000/yr
4 teachers, 40 students, ages 4-19, pre K-12th grade
Affiliations: NCACS, Clonlara HBEP
Governance by democratic school meeting
Teacher qualifications: love of young people; willingness to work on self; creative.
Classes are formed by mutual agreement among equal parties; teachers as models, resources; community built among free, autonomous individuals; no letter grades; non-compulsory class attendance; multi-aged classes; extensive field trips; urban location; interns accepted.

Clonlara School Home Based Education Program
(See Resource Section)

Community High School (1992)
401 N Division St, Ann Arbor, MI 48104
Robert A. Galardi, Dean, 313-994-2021, FAX: -0042
Type: public choice
30 teachers, 388 students, ages 14-18, 9-12th grade
Governance by principal
Creative curriculum; community-based; student support; student input; extensive field trips; multi-aged classe; interns accepted.

Gay-Jay Montessori School
1128 White St, Ann Arbor, MI 48104-3741

Michelle Norris Montessori School
1122-1128 White St, Ann Arbor, MI 48104-3741

Law Montessori School
1150 Rosewood St, Ann Arbor, MI 48104-6227

Daycroft Montessori
100 Oakbrook Dr, Ann Arbor, MI 48104-6703

Go Like the Wind! Montessori School (1987)
3540 Dixboro Ln, Ann Arbor, MI 48105
Karl W. Young, Prin, 313-747-7422
Tuition: $2,185-3,795/yr
4 teachers, 3 assistants, 90 students, ages 3-12
Accreditation: AMS
Governance by administrator

Custom designed Montessori CAI; one computer/3 students; moral environment; childcare; rural location; transportation; interns accepted.

Oak Trails School and Children's House (1956)
6561 Warren Rd, Ann Arbor, MI 48105
Kathryn Cote, Adm Asst, 313-662-8016
Type: Montessori, non-profit
3 teachers, 57 students, ages 2.5-13, pre K-8th grade
Affiliation: AMS
Teacher qualifications: Montessori or state certification
44 acres of old-growth hardwood; weekly field trips to YM/YWCA for swimming; suburban location; transportation; interns accepted.

Modern Montessori & Nursery School
2250-60 Nixon Rd, Ann Arbor, MI 48105-1418

Aristoplay, Ltd
(See Resource Section)

Livingston Montessori Center
1381 S Old US 23, Brighton, MI 48116

Brighton Montessori School
1385 S Old US 23, Brighton, MI 48116-7608
Marge Arnott

Dearborn Heights Montessori Center (1972)
4950 Madison, Dearborn Heights, MI 48125
Kay Neff, Adm, 313-291-3200, FAX: 313-562-2239
Non-profit; tuition: $2,325-4,500/yr
9 teachers, 20 assistants, 250 students, ages 3-12
Affiliation: AMS
Governance by teachers and administrators
Classic Montessori approach; French; music; art; PE; childcare; suburban location; interns accepted.

Montessori Center of Our Lady
36800 Schoolcraft Rd, Livonia, MI 48150-1115

Oasis
20155 Middlebelt, Livonia, MI 48152
Rose Govig, Cont Ed Mgr, 313-473-8933, FAX: -8932
Type: public choice
4 teachers, 40 students, mainly at-risk, ages 16-20, 9-12th grade
Governance by teachers, principal
Teacher qualifications: certified, experienced
Self-paced; individualized; team teaching; behavioral and academic contract; multi-aged classes

Livonia Montessori Center (1972)
32765 Lyndon St, Livonia, MI 48154
Kay Neff, Adm, 313-427-8255, FAX: 313-562-2239
Non-profit; tuition: $2,325-4,250/yr
3 teachers, 6 assistants, 90 students, ages 2.5-6
Affiliation: AMS
Governance by teachers and administrators
Classic Montessori approach; French, music specialists; childcare; suburban location; interns accepted.

Jefferson Schools
2400 N Dixie Hwy, Monroe, MI 48161
T Fitzpatrick, Asst Supt
Type: Montessori

Meadow Montessori School
502 W Elm Ave, Monroe, MI 48161-2833
Meg Fedorowicz

Montessori Children's House
PO Box 155, Monroe, MI 48166

Hines Park Montessori School
45801 W Ann Arbor Rd, Plymouth, MI 48170

New Morning School (1973)
14501 Haggerty Rd, Plymouth, MI 48170
Elaine Yagiela, Exec Dir, 313-420-3331
Type: independent, non-profit
10 teachers, 108 students, ages 3-14, pre K-8th grade
Governance by parent cooperative and Exec Dir
Teacher qualifications: state certification
Student-centered; responsibility, self esteem, positive relationships; learning to evaluate information, problem-solve, set and attain goals; multi-aged classes; suburban location; interns accepted.

Northville Montessori Center
15709 Haggerty Rd, Plymouth, MI 48170
Lynn Gall, Adm, 313-420-0924
4 teachers, 79 students, ages 3-12
Affiliations: MIMS, AMS
Governance by administrator
Large campus; nature study; Japanese; childcare; suburban location; interns accepted.

West Middle School
44401 W Ann Arbor Trail, Plymouth, MI 48170
Renee Eley, 313-451-6573

Michigan Montessori Society, c/o Northville Montessori Center
15709 N Haggerty Rd, Plymouth, MI 48170-4861
Anne Carson

Cory Elementary
35200 Smith Rd, Romulus, MI 48174-1604
Type: Montessori

Plymouth Canton Montessori School
45245 Joy Rd, Canton, MI 48187-1772

Montessori Children's Learning Center
17188 Fordline St, Riverview, MI 48192-7543

Creative Montessori Center
15500 Howard St, Southgate, MI 48195-1610

Montessori Center of Downriver
14151 Trenton Rd, Southgate, MI 48195-1936

Roberto Clemente Student Development Center (1974)
4377 Textile Rd, Ypsilanti, MI 48197
Joseph Dulin, Prin, 313-434-4611
Type: public at-risk
7 teachers, 60-80 students, ages 14-19, 8-12th grade
Affiliation: Ann Arbor Public Schools
Teacher qualifications: MI certification
Weekly rap sessions; teacher visits home; breakfast daily; six mandatory classes; no letter grades; multi-aged classes; interns accepted.

Spencer Home Learning Center
1717 Gregory, Ypsilanti, MI 48197
313-485-3548
Student ages 4-10
Certified teacher; consulting; informal assessments; private tutoring; resource center; program planning; suburban location.

Wayne State University School
Metropolitan Center for High Technology
2727 Second Ave, Detroit, MI 48201
Tom Watkins, 313-577-5971
Type: charter
340 students, many poverty-level, junior high
Affiliation: Wayne State U
University faculty supervisory board
Full integration with U programs; urban location.

New Center Montessori School
8007 2nd Ave, Detroit, MI 48202-2403

Montessori Children's House of Martyrs of Uganda County
4317 Blaine St, Detroit, MI 48204-2301

Childhood Center, Inc
20210 Schoenherr St, Detroit, MI 48205-1108
Type: Montessori

Friends School in Detroit
1100 S Aubin Blvd, Detroit, MI 48207
Gail Thomas, Head, 313-259-6722, FAX: 313-259-8066
Type: Quaker, non-profit; tuition: $5,000/yr, scholarships
18 teachers, 125 students, ages 4-14, pre K-8th grade
Affiliation: Quaker
Governance by principal
Teacher qualifications: MI certification
Whole language; experiential; thematic studies; cooperation and peaceful conflict resolution; no letter grades; interns accepted.

Greater Detroit Montessori Center
900 North Ave, Detroit, MI 48207

Sunshine Montessori School
1519 Martin Luther King Jr Blvd, Detroit, MI 48208-2867

Rose Open School
5830 Field, Detroit, MI 48213
Joan Nagrant, 313-245-3673
Type: magnet
Pre K-5th grade
Open School.

Area E Open Magnet Middle School
2301 Van Dyke, Detroit, MI 48214
Michael Bartley, 313-245-3932
6-8th grade

Bates Academy
Detroit, MI 48214
Beverly Gibson, 313-494-7000
Type: magnet
Pre K-8th grade
Gifted and talented.

Detroit Waldorf School
2555 Burns Ave, Detroit, MI 48214
Francina Graef

Casa Maria Academy (1989)
1500 Trumbull, Detroit, MI 48216
Rosaana Pardo, 313-962-4230
Type: at-risk, charter pending
34 students
Affiliation: Central MI U

Detroit Open School
24601 Frisbee, Detroit, MI 48219
Laurajean Milligan, 313-533-1525
Type: magnet
K-8th grade

Ferndale Montessori Center
400 W Marshall St, Ferndale, MI 48220-2419

Giving Tree Montessori School
4351 Marseilles St, Detroit, MI 48224-1481

The Macomb Academy
16901 Cranford Ln, Grosse Pointe, MI 48230
Gaile Rice, 313-884-4384
Type: charter
Affiliation: Macomb Intermediate SD

Greater Grace Education Center
18940 Schaefer Hwy, Detroit, MI 48235-1763
Type: Montessori

Grosse Pointe Academy, Early and Lower Schools
171 Lake Shore Rd, Grosse Pointe Farms, MI 48236-3793
Camille DeMario
Type: Montessori

Deror Montessori Center
24061 Coolidge Hwy, Oak Park, MI 48237-1654

Aishu Shule/ W. E. B. DuBois Prep Public School
10711 Puritan, Detroit, MI 48238
Imani Humphrey, 313-345-6050
Type: charter
K-12th grade
Affiliation: Detroit BE
Conversion of two private Afrocentric schools.

Acadia Montessori (1980)
1515 S Woodward, Bloomfield Hills, MI 48302
Delvita DiMichele, Adm, 335-7070
Tuition: $1,900-3,975/yr
64 students, ages Infant-9
Accreditation: AMS
Governance by administrator
Music; gymnastics; French; computers; childcare; urban location; interns accepted.

Oakland Steiner School (1989)
1050 Square Lake Rd, Bloomfield Hills, MI 48304
Noemi Schaffa, Adm, 313-646-2540, FAX: 313-643-8316
Type: Waldorf, non-profit; tuition: $5,075/yr, scholarships
8 teachers, 84 students, ages 3-12, pre K-6th grade
Affiliation: AWSNA
Governance by faculty and board
Teacher qualifications: MI, Waldorf certification or equivalent
Suburban location; interns accepted.

Kensington Academy Montessori Program
1020 E Square Lake Rd, Bloomfield Hills, MI 48304-1957
Sherry Bass

Bloomfield Hills Montessori Center (1972)
2101 Opdyke Rd, Bloomfield Hills, MI 48304-2216
Dot Feaheny, Laura Plotchan, Adm, 313-338-1166
Tuition: $2,991-4,882/yr
5 teachers, 9 assistants, 65 students, ages infant-12
Affiliation: AMS
Governance by administrator
Childcare; suburban location; interns accepted.

Avon Montessori Center
596 Willard Ave, Rochester Hills, MI 48307-2360

Daffodils Montessori & Day Care
879 W Auburn Rd, Rochester Hills, MI 48307-4901

Meadowbrook Montessori Center
151 Grosse Pines Dr, Rochester, MI 48309-1829

Messmore Education Center
8742 Dill Dr, Sterling Heights, MI 48312-1235
Ms Stacherski
Type: Montessori

Walsh Elementary School
38901 Dodge Park Rd, Sterling Heights, MI 48312-1323
Type: Montessori

Utica Montessori Program
53800 Mound Rd, Utica, MI 48316-1727

Ward Homeschool Fellowship
6734 Edinborough, W Bloomfield, MI 48322
Gene & Robin Newman, 313-626-8431

Bloomfield Maples Montessori
6201 W Maple Rd, West Bloomfield, MI 48322-2171
Usha Mangrulkar

Brookfield Academy
2965 Walnut Lake Rd, West Bloomfield, MI 48323-3757
Judith Scott
Type: Montessori

Mrs Mary's Montessori School
6350 Commerce Rd, West Bloomfield, MI 48324-2710

Discovery 21 (1989)
1415 Crescent Lake Rd, Waterford, MI 48327
Wayne Malin, Prin, 313-673-1241
Type: public choice
4 teachers, 75-100 students, ages 17-21, 9-12th grade
Governance by teachers and principal
Teacher qualifications: MI certification
HS completion; internships with local businesses; self-esteem; teen parenting; student-operated store.

Laurel Montessori School
2490 Airport Rd, Waterford, MI 48327-1210

Montessori Center of Farmington Hills
29001 W 13 Mile Rd, Farmington, MI 48334-2504

STRIVE Alternative High School (1983)
5275 Maybee Rd, Clarkston, MI 48346
Kathryn Larkin, CSW, 810-674-0993
Type: public choice/at-risk
6 teachers, 100 students, mainly at-risk, ages 16-19, 10-12th grade
Governance by teachers and principal
Teacher qualifications: certification
Suburban location.

Oxford Montessori Center
775 E Drahner Rd #167, Oxford, MI 48371-5315

Highland Montessori School
4501 Highland Rd, Milford, MI 48380
Lee Johnson

Milford Montessori School
2700 W Commerce Rd, Milford, MI 48380-3208

Lakes Area Montessori
8605 Richardson Rd, Walled Lake, MI 48390-1362

Clio's BEST (1988)
430 N Mill St, Clio, MI 48420
Brenda S. May, Supervisor, 810-687-8198
Type: public at-risk
9 teachers, 70 students, mainly teen parents, ages 13-19, 9-12th grade
Governance by teachers, principal, parent cooperative
Teacher qualifications: MI certification
Applied math for industries; journalism class produces bi-monthly newsletter, yearbook; prom; community service requirement; fund raiser; multi-aged classes; extensive field trips; childcare; interns accepted.

Montessori Academy
PO Box 52, Davison, MI 48423-0052

Owosso (1990)
120 Michigan Ave, Owosso, MI 48429
Shirley McNier, Coord, ?-723-5598
Type: public choice, boarding
7 teachers, 65 students, mainly at-risk, ages 16-18
Affiliation: MAEO
Governance by principal, faculty, student reps, board
Teacher qualifications: secondary certification
Electives; Glasser's control theory; reality therapy for behavior control; hands-on projects; volunteer work; suburban location; interns accepted.

Mid-Michigan Homeschoolers
6109 Pebbleshire, Grand Blanc, MI 48439
313-695-0904

Heritage Home Educators (1989)
c/o Kander, 2122 Houser Rd, Holly, MI 48442
Lisa Hodge-Kander, Newsletter Editor, 313-634-4337
Non-profit
Parent meetings; family enrichment activities; children's programs; newsletter.

Montessori Children's Center
1100 W Newark Rd, Lapeer, MI 48446-9449

Montrose Alternative (1989)
300 Nanita Dr, Montrose, MI 48457
Mark W. Sands, 313-639-6131, FAX: 313-238-3864
Type: public at-risk
2 teachers, 25 students, ages 16-20, 9-12th grade
Governance by teachers and principal
Teacher qualifications: Certification, experience
Flexible block schedule; multi-aged classes; rural location.

Sanilac Alternative for Education
147 Aitken, Peck, MI 48466
Juanita Clark, Coord, ?-648-4700
Type: public choice
2 teachers, 14 students, ages 16-20, 9-12th grade
Governance by board and Community Ed Dir
Multi-aged classes; rural location.

Alpha Montessori School
701 Church St, Flint, MI 48502-1107

Montessori Children's House
1805 W Court St, Flint, MI 48503-3577
Ms Pitts

Forest Hill Montessori
2200 Forest Hill, Flint, MI 48504

Charity Day Care Center & Montessori School
4601 Clio Rd, Flint, MI 48504-1885

Weston Early Childhood Education Center
2499 Cashin St, Burton, MI 48509-1123
Type: Montessori

Success Express (1987)
820 Vine St, Chesaning, MI 48616
Thomas Tihof, Comm Ed Dir, 517-845-7020, FAX: -3722
Type: public at-risk
5 teachers, 43 students, ages 15-20, 9-12th grade
Governance by teachers, principal
Teacher qualifications: MI certification
Interns accepted.

Northlane Math and Science Academy (1991)
8045 N River Rd, Freeland, MI 48623
Ronald Helmer, 517-695-9909
Type: charter
32 students
Affiliation: Central MI U

Windover High School
32 S Homer Rd, Midland, MI 48640
517-832-0852
Type: charter
Affiliation: Midland Intermediate SD

Midland Montessori School
5709 Eastman Ave, Midland, MI 48640-2516

Montessori Children's House
5200 Jefferson Ave, Midland, MI 48640-2907

Bay City Homeschooling Support Group
401 W Jenny, Bay City, MI 48706
517-893-7608

Alternative Choices in Education (1981)
300 Republic Ave, Alma, MI 48801
Jan Gooding, Prin, 517-463-2488
Type: public at-risk; tuition: $4,000/yr

4 teachers, 55 students, ages 15-22, 9-12th grade
Affiliation: MAEO
Governance by faculty and student representatives
Teacher qualifications: state certification
School-operated silk screening business; multi-aged classes; rural location; transportation; interns accepted.

East Lansing High School (1905)
509 Burcham Dr, E Lansing, MI 48823
Celeste M. Crouch, Reading Consultant, 517-332-2545
Type: public choice
75 teachers, 1150 students, ages 13-18, 9-12th grade
Governance by teachers, principal
Teacher qualifications: MI certification
On-going monitoring of interpersonal skills; individual, group and teacher evaluations; evening classes; team teaching; collaborative learning; multi-aged classes; interns accepted.

The Montessori Center (1982)
469 N Hagadorn Rd, E Lansing, MI 48823
Loraine Friedl, Adm, 517-337-0674
Non-profit; tuition: $1,610/2,345/yr
2 teachers, 3 assistants, 55 students, mainly international, ages 3-6
Affiliation: MIMS
Governance by administrator and board of trustees
Childcare; suburban location; interns accepted.

Haslett (1982)
6157 Rutherford, East Lansing, MI 48823
Susan Doneson, Supervisor, 517-337-1722
Type: public choice
8 teachers, 50 students, ages 14-19, 9-12th grade
Governance by district community ed component
Teacher qualifications: MI certification
Teen parent support group; community referrals and networking; multi-aged classes; extensive field trips; childcare.

Holt (1982)
2169 N Cedar, Holt, MI 48842
J R Rauschert, 517-694-5780
4 teachers, 60 students, ages 15-19, 9-12th grade
Affiliation: MAEO
Governance by teachers and support staff with student input
Involves parents, community organizations, state agencies; small class size; contracts; suburban location.

Mason Alternative High School (1985)
1001 S Barnes St, Mason, MI 48854
Joe Kelly, 517-676-6498
Type: public choice
2 teachers, 20 students, mainly at-risk, ages 15-19, 9-12th grade
Governance by faculty and student representatives
Teacher qualifications: MI certification
Suburban location.

Saginaw Chippewa Academy
7070 E Broadway, Mount Pleasant, MI 48858
517-773-5858
Type: charter, Montessori (ES)
40 elem & 20 teen students, ages 5-8 & 13-17
Affiliation: Central MI U

Oasis High School (1986)
310 W Michigan, Mt Pleasant, MI 48858
Carol Meixner, 517-773-1383
Type: public at-risk
6 teachers, 160 students, ages 15-22, 9-12th grade
Governance by faculty and student representatives
Teacher qualifications: certification at secondary level
Personalized, family atmosphere; competency-based credit every 3-wks; independent study; job shadowing/experience; interdisciplinary units; team teaching; mentorships; non-compulsory class attendance; multi-aged classes; urban location; interns accepted.

Odyssey High School (1988)
3441 S Wise Rd, Mt Pleasant, MI 48858
Raymond Yaklin, Lead Tch, 773-9473
Non-profit
5 teachers, 60 students, partly at-risk, ages 12-20, 7-12th
grade
Affiliation: Shepherd PS
Teacher qualifications: MI certification
80 acres; multi-aged classes; extensive field trips; childcare;
interns accepted.

Binoojiinh Montessori
7070 E Broadway Rd, Mount Pleasant, MI 48858-8970
Leanne Barton

Okemos Montessori
2745 E Mount Hope, Okemos, MI 48864
Susan Cavanaugh

Michigan Montessori Internationale
2745 Mount Hope Rd, Okemos, MI 48864-2418

School Within A School
765 E North St, Owosso, MI 48867
Roger Elford, 517-723-8231

Saranac (1986)
150 Pleasant St, Saranac, MI 48881
Susan Dunfee, Comm Ed Coord, ?-642-9232, FAX: -6850
Type: public choice/at-risk
1 teacher, 18 students, mainly at-risk, ages 16-21, 9-12th
grade
Governance by teachers and principal
Teacher qualifications: secondary education certified
Social, personal, academic rehab; multi-aged classes; rural
location; interns accepted.

Six Lakes Discovery Program
107 E Vota PO Box 148, Six Lakes, MI 48886
Terry Evanish, Dir, 517-365-3887, FAX: -3845
Type: public at-risk
4 teachers, 62 students, ages 12-18, 7-12th grade
Affiliation: MAEO
Governance by principal
Teacher qualifications: majors in subject area
Skill development; self-esteem; motivation; rural location;
transportation; interns accepted.

Noah Webster Academy
PO Box 80824, Lansing, MI 48908
David Kallman, 517-444-0693
Type: home-based
1500-2000 students, K-12th grade
Affiliations: Berlin Township School Board, Ionia County
Each student receives a computer and resource teacher
support; extra funds placed in trust for post secondary
education.

Michigan Early Childhood Center (1984)
727 N Jenison, Lansing, MI 48915
Kathryn Cole, 517-372-0038
Type: charter
25 students, K-3rd grade
Affiliation: Central MI U

Montessori Children's House of Lansing
2100 W St Joseph, Lansing, MI 48915
Suzanne M Husband

Portage Alternative High School (1986)
1010 W Milham, Portage, MI 49002
Sarah Sult, 616-381-0393
Type: public choice
30 teachers, 250 students, ages 16-19, 9-12th grade
Governance by teachers, principal, faculty and student reps
Teacher qualifications: MI certification
Critical thinking; parenting classes; "C" lowest grade assigned;
multi-aged classes; extensive field trips; interns accepted.

Shamrock Montessori Center
7025 Rockford St, Portage, MI 49002-4119

The Montessori School (1972)
750 Howard St, Kalamazoo, MI 49008
Pamela Boudreau, Head, 616-349-3248
Non-profit; tuition: $2,333-3,612/yr
6 teachers, 14 assistants, 144 students, ages 3-12
Affiliations: MAC, NAMTA, MIMS; accreditations: MIDSS, MIDE, MSS
Governance by administrator, board
Urban location; interns accepted.

Vine Street Alternative High School (1983)
604 W Vine St, Kalamazoo, MI 49008
Robert Horton, Prin, 616-337-0760
Type: public at-risk
13 teachers, 180 students, ages 14-18, 7-12th grade
Affiliation: MAEO
Governance by teachers and principal
Multi-aged classes; urban location; transportation; interns
accepted.

Kazoo School
1401 Cherry St, Kalamazoo, MI 49008-2278
616-345-3239
Type: public choice

Montessori Children's House
2424 Glenwood Dr, Kalamazoo, MI 49008-2406
Gertrude Palm Girr

South Ward School (1981)
550 Fifth St, Allegan, MI 49010
Ken Ebersole, Dir, 616-673-5433
Type: public choice
7 teachers, 75-100 students, mainly at-risk, ages 14+, 9-12th
grade
Governance by teachers, principal
Teacher qualifications: MI certification
"Essential" school philosophy; performance exhibitions;
interns accepted.

Bangor Alternative High School (1986)
309 S Walnut, Bangor, MI 49013
Patrick J. Conroy, Coord, 616-427-6861, FAX: 616-427-8274
Type: public at-risk
8 teachers, 110 students, 9-12th grade
Affiliation: MI Alt Ed Org
Governance by teachers, principal
Teacher qualification: MI certification
Emphasis on student preferences, teamwork, self-help; inte-
grated alternative and adult HS; specialized classes;
women's issues group; Aikido; computer, science lab;
interns accepted.

Boynton Montessori School
1700 E Britain Ave, Benton Harbor, MI 49022-1604

**Benton Harbor Area Schools Montessori Magnet
Program**
636 Pipestone St, Benton Harbor, MI 49022-4152

Brookview School
501 Zollar Dr, Benton Harbor, MI 49022-6429
Type: Montessori

LaPetite Learning Center
86 S Clay St, Coldwater, MI 49036-1853
Matilda Hindbaugh
Type: Montessori

Dowagiac Schools (1986)
206 Main St, Dowagiac, MI 49047
Max Sala, Dir, 616-782-4470, FAX: 616-782-9748
Type: public at-risk
3 teachers, 15 students, ages 14-18, 9-12th grade
Governance by teachers and principal
Teacher qualifications: MI Certification
Multi-aged classes; rural location.

St Joseph (1989)
2521 Stadium Dr, St Joseph, MI 49085
Marjorie Camelet, 982-4622 x40
Type: public at-risk
2 teachers, 1 assistant, 26 students, ages 14-19, 9-12th grade
Affiliation: MI Assn Ed Options
Governance by teachers; principal
Re-designed each semester to meet students' needs; intra/
    interpersonal skills; multi-aged classes

South Haven (1978)
600 Elkenburg St, South Haven, MI 49090
Scott Raue or Cindy Liscow, Instructors, 616-637-0591
Type: public at-risk
2 teachers, 25 students, ages 14-19, 9-12th grade
Governance by teachers and principal
Teacher qualifications: certification in core curriculum offered
Self-contained classroom; contracts; independent study;
    team teaching; multi-aged classes; rural location; trans-
    portation; interns accepted.

Cooperative Learning Center (1989)
216 Vinewood, Sturgis, MI 49091
Lance Goodlock, Tch/Coord, 616-659-1586
Type: public at-risk
3 teachers, 30 students, ages 14-19, 9-12th grade
Governance by teachers and principal
Rural location; transportation; interns accepted.

Bridgman Elementary School
3891 Lake St, Bridgman, MI 49106-9709
C Garbuschewski
Type: Montessori

Cedar Lane (1989)
2301 Niles-Buchanan Rd, Niles, MI 49120
Jeneen Conway, Dir, 616-684-9554
Type: public choice, at-risk
4 teachers, 100 students, mainly at-risk, ages 14-19, 9-12th
    grade
Affiliation: Niles Community Schools
Governance by board
Teacher qualifications: certification
Self-esteem; goals; problem solving; development of socially
    acceptable behavior; cooperative learning; discipline with
    dignity; multi-aged classes; extensive field trip; interns
    accepted.

The Home School Manual, from Gazelle Publications
(See Resource Section)

Jackson Alternative School (1971)
766 Park Rd, Jackson, MI 49203
Donald R. Tassie, Prin, 517-784-3144
Type: public at-risk
10 teachers, 180 students, ages 12-20, 7-12th grade
Governance by teachers and principal
Highly structured; clear expectations; multi-aged classes;
    urban location.

Montessori Children's House
1267 E Siena Heights Dr, Adrian, MI 49221-1755
Linda Salenbien

Exceptional Training System
9960 Matthews Hwy, Tecumseh, MI 49286
Judy Edwards, 517-423-5982
Consulting to alternative schools.

Caledonia Options High School (1987)
330 Johnson, Caledonia, MI 49316
Jon Swets, Dir/Head Tch, ?-891-0236
Type: public choice/at-risk
3 teachers, 70 students, ages 14-20, 9-12th grade
Affiliation: MAEO
Governance by teachers and principal
Teacher qualifications: college, experience

Variety of learning styles; student-run restaurant; technol-
    ogy; languages; sports; field trips; suburban location;
    transportation; interns accepted.

Loomis High School (1981)
360 S Mill St, Newaygo, MI 49337
Dick Smith, Prin, 616-652-6333
Type: public at-risk
6 teachers, 60-70 students, ages 14-21, 8-12th grade
Governance by faculty and student reps
Teacher qualifications: MI certificate
Utilizes area natural resources; mastery concept; interns
    accepted.

Hansen Montessori Child Development Center
5511 130th Ave, Fennville, MI 49408-9477

Phoenix/Goals Alternative Schools (1980)
96 W 15th St, Holland, MI 49423
Jan Dalman, Assoc Dir/Adult Ed, 616-393-7600, FAX: -7615
Type: public choice/at-risk
4 teachers, 75 students, mainly at-risk, ages 16-18, 9-12th
    grade
Governance by teachers and principal
Teacher qualifications: MI Certification, affective skills
Outcome-based; teen parenting; childcare; problem solving;
    caring for self/others; urban location; interns accepted.

Learning Tree Montessori School
370 Country Club Rd, Holland, MI 49423-7447

Holland Homeschool Group
17217 Riley, Holland, MI 49424
Sarah Aitken

Lakeside Montessori (1993)
411 Butternut, Holland, MI 49424
Ronan Young, 616-392-7009
Tuition: $2,700/yr
1 teacher, 20 students, ages 5-8
Governance by democratic school meeting
Multi-aged classes; urban location; interns accepted.

Michigan Dunes Montessori (1981)
5248 Henry St, Muskegon, MI 49441
Claire Chiasson, Adm, 616-798-7293
Non-profit; tuition: $1,850-4,000/yr
5 teachers, 15 assistants, 145 students, ages infant-12
Affiliations: AMS, MIMS, NAEYC
Governance by administrator
French instruction at all levels; nature trail constructed and
    maintained by 6-12 year-olds; childcare; suburban location;
    interns accepted.

Blue Lake Fine Arts Camp
RR 2, Twin Lake, MI 49457
Type: Montessori

Vandenberg Creative Arts Academy
406 Lafayette SE, Grand Rapids, MI 49503
Sharon Altena, 616-456-4900
Type: magnet
Student ages 4+,-6th grade

Stepping Stones Montessori
1110 College Ave NE, Grand Rapids, MI 49503-1123

Grand Rapids Elementary School
143 Bostwick Ave NE, Grand Rapids, MI 49503-3201
Type: Montessori

Excalibur Prep (1992)
1138 Pine NW, Grand Rapids, MI 49504
Janet Van Deusen, Prin, 616-771-2702
Type: public at-risk
8 teachers, 150 students, ages 13-18, 8-12th grade
Affiliation: Grand Rapids Public Schools
Governance by teachers, principal
Teacher qualifications: MI teaching license

Special trips and activities; community volunteer activities; accomodates SE and special needs students; multi-aged classes; interns accepted.

Information Network for Christian Homes
4150 Ambrose NE, Grand Rapids, MI 49505
616-364-4438

Wellerwood Montessori Academy
800 Wellerwood Ave, Grand Rapids, MI 49505
Carol Davis, 616-364-6763
Type: Montessori magnet
Student ages 4+,-K

Greenhouse Montessori (1989)
2023 E Fulton, Grand Rapids, MI 49506
Susan K. Brondyk, Adm, 459-3923
Non-profit; tuition: $1,800/yr
2 teachers, 1 assistant, 40 students, ages 3-6
Affiliations: AMS, MIMS
Governance by board
Children in Worship; urban location; interns accepted.

Congress Park Montessori Academy
940 Baldwin St SE, Grand Rapids, MI 49506-1429
Gordon Griffen

Ottawa Montessori
1515 Fisk Rd SE, Grand Rapids, MI 49506-6545

Climbing Tree School (1971)
256 Alger SE, Grand Rapids, MI 49507
Hildi Paulson, Director, 616-243-4763
Type: independent, non-profit; tuition: $2,400/yr, scholarships
6 teachers, 85 students, ages 3-11, pre K-5th grade
Governance by board
Teacher qualifications: experience in similar program
Multi-cultural and environmental ed; parent participation required; hands-on; conflict resolution; Spanish; no letter grades; multi-aged classes; extensive field trips; urban location; transportation; interns accepted.

New Branches School (1971)
256 Alger SE, Grand Rapids, MI 49507
Dave Frederick, 616-243-6221
Type: charter
65 students, ages 5-11
Affiliation: Central MI U
Formerly the Climbing Tree School.

Horizons High School (1978)
2550 Rogers Lane SW, Lansing, MI 49509
Dan Diedrich, 616-530-7535
Type: charter
140 students
Affiliation: Central MI U
Conversion.

Wyoming Community Education
4334 Byron Ctr SW, Wyoming, MI 49509
Dan Diedrich, 616-530-7535
Type: public choice

West Michigan Academy of Environmental Science
PO Box 140561, Grand Rapids, MI 49514
Dave Lehman, 616-771-3466
Type: charter
100 students, K-7th grade
Affiliation: Kent Intermediate SD

Discovery High School (1979)
173 54th St SW, Wyoming, MI 49548
Sandra Wilkinson, Coordinator, 616-531-7433
Type: public at-risk; tuition: for students under 16 yrs
6 teachers, 120 students, ages 15-18, 9-12th grade
Affiliation: Southkent Comm Ed; Godfrey-Lee PS
Governance by principal, faculty, and student representatives
Teacher qualifications: subject area certification, experience with adolescents

Teacher serves as academic advisor/advocate; student board; fund-raising for yearly senior trip; cooperative learning; independent study; suburban location.

Pathfinders High School (1989)
3333 S Division, Wyoming, MI 49548
Susan Meyer, Dir of Adult & Comm Ed; Ila Dillinger, Program Supervisor, 616-241-2661, FAX: 616-241-2664
Type: public at-risk
4 teachers, 90 students, ages 16-21, 9-12th grade
Governance by board
Teacher qualifications: state certification
For immigrant/refugee students; ESL; basic skills; HS completion courses; suburban location; transportation; interns accepted.

Benzie Home Educators
PO Box 208, Benzonia, MI 49616

Reed City (1990)
202 W Slosson, Reed City, MI 49677
Louis Stieg, Dir, ?-832-5517
Type: public at-risk
2 teachers, 24 students, ages 14-19, 8-12th grade
Governance by teachers and principal
Community service; self-paced; outcome-based; no fail; job-readiness; behavior mod; self-esteem; multi-aged classes; outdoor adventure; rural location; interns accepted.

Montessori Children's House
PO Box 54, Suttons Bay, MI 49682
Gretchen Modrall, Adm, 616-271-3291
Non-profit; tuition: $2,350-3,100/yr
6 teachers, 6 assistants, 113 students, ages infant-6
Affiliations: NAMTA, MAC, AMI
Wooded setting; trout stream; gardens; wildlife; childcare; urban location; interns accepted.

Montessori Indian Preschool
1200 Ramsdell Rd, Traverse City, MI 49684-1451

Montessori Children's Center
6105 Center Rd, Traverse City, MI 49684-1923

Bay Mills Academy
MI 49715
Robert VanAlstine, 906-632-6809
Type: charter
Affiliation: Bay Mills CC
Native American.

Cheboygan Montessori East Elementary
PO Box 100, Cheboygan, MI 49721-0100

Presque Isle Children's House
719 N Bradley Hwy, Rogers City, MI 49779-1512
Type: Montessori

James R. Fitz Harris High School (1979)
408 N 9th St, Gladstone, MI 49837
R Bruce Carlson, Dir, 906-428-3146, FAX: 786-9318
Type: public at-risk
6 teachers, 50-63 students, ages 15-21, 9-12th grade
Affiliation: MAEO; accreditation: NCASC
Governance by teachers, principal, democratic school meeting, board.
Teacher qualifications: MI Certification
Multi-aged classes; outcome-based; student input to curriculum; placement testing; rural location; interns accepted.

Learning Tree Resource Center
S Superior Rd RR 1 Box 80-B, Atlantic Mine, MI 49905
906-482-6393
Type: home-based

Sunnyridge Alternative Learning Center
HCO 1 Box 134, Pelkie, MI 49958
Type: home-based

Minnesota

Home-Based Educators Accrediting Association
Rt 1 Box 381, Cambridge, MN 55008

Montessori School of Cottage Grove
8177 S Hillside Tr, Cottage Grove, MN 55016

Forest Lake Alternative Learning Center
6101 Scandia Trail N, Forest Lake, MN 55025
Dr Janet Palmer, 612-464-9343
Type: public at-risk

Minnesota Home School Network
9669 E 123rd, Hastings, MN 55033
612-437-3049

Montessori School of Hastings
1314 W 15th St, Hastings, MN 55033

Homeward
(See Resource Section)

Forest Lake Montessori School
17126 Manning Tr, Marine on St Croix, MN 55047
Jane Norbin

Country Haven Montessori School
14878 Saint Croix Trail N, Marine on St Croix, MN 55047-9791

Intermediate School
320 Main St, North Branch, MN 55056
Lyle Koski, 612-674-7001
Type: magnet
4-5th grade
Creative arts; global studies; environment.

Primary School
1108 1st, North Branch, MN 55056
Janice Fisher, 612-674-5270
Type: magnet
K-3rd grade
Creative arts; global studies; environment.

Prairie Creek Community School (1983)
27695 Denmark Ave, Northfield, MN 55057
Joanne Esser, teacher, 507-645-9640
Type: independent, non-profit
6 teachers, 100 students, ages 5-11, K-5th grade
Governance by teachers and principal, board
Teacher qualifications: strong foundation in child
  development
Thematic curr; coop learning; whole language; holistic assessment, including portfolios; strong parental participation
  through consensus model; no letter grades; multi-aged
  classes; extensive field trips; rural location; transportation;
  interns accepted.

St Mary's Montessori Center
122 E McKinley St, Owatonna, MN 55060-3326

Goodhue County DAC
1618 W 3rd, Red Wing, MN 55066
Type: Montessori

Montessori Preschool
240 Mississippi Ave, Red Wing, MN 55066

Dakota County Area Learning Center (1989)
1400 E 145th St, Rosemount, MN 55068
Karen O'Brien, Dir, 612-423-8210, FAX: 612-423-1179
Type: public choice/at-risk
10 teachers, 92 students, ages 15-21, 10-12th grade
Governance by board
Experiential; small classes; field trips; integration of voca-
  tional; multi-aged classes; rural location; interns accepted.

Prairie Island Dakota Community
1158 Island Blvd, Welch, MN 55069
Ramona Jones, 612-385-0083
Type: charter pending

South St Paul Area Learning Center
201 N Concord Exchange, South St Paul, MN 55075
Bill Zimniewicz, 612-450-9966
Type: public at-risk
Individualized; middle level program: support services; youth
  service; personal, social skills.

Providence School
785 17th Ave N, S St Paul, MN 55075-1429
Type: Montessori

New Heights Schools, Inc (1993)
614 W Mulberry St, Stillwater, MN 55082
Karen Garley, 612-439-1962
Type: charter
200 students, ages 16-20, K-12th grade

City Academy
958 Jesse St, St. Paul, MN 55101
Milo Cutter, 612-298-4624
Type: charter
35 teachers; student ages 13-21
Affiliation: MN BE
First charter school in US; students participated in design of
  proposal; year-round.

Downtown Kindergarten Magnet School
Pioneer Building, 336 Robert, St Paul, MN 55101
Anne Rosten, 612-290-8372
Student ages 4+,-K
Work-place magnet.

Metro Deaf
289 East 5th St, St. Paul, MN 55101
Kristen Stolte, 612-224-3995
Type: charter
Affiliation: MN BE
Instruction in ASL.

Saturn School of Tomorrow
65 E Kellogg, St Paul, MN 55101
Paul Leverenty, 612-290-8354
Type: magnet
4-8th grade
Technology-based; personal groth; ungraded; community.

Jefferson Alternative
90 S Western Ave, St Paul, MN 55102
Don Sonsaela
Type: public choice

Cathedral Montessori
328 6th St W, Saint Paul, MN 55102-1997

MacDonald Montessori Childcare Center
175 Western Ave S, Saint Paul, MN 55102-2997

AGAPE
360 Colborne, St Paul, MN 55102-3299
612-228-7746
Career exploration; health and counseling services; vocational
  experience; personal skills; childcare.

Adams Montessori Magnet School
615 Chatsworth St S, Saint Paul, MN 55102-4038

Capital Hill Magnet School
560 Condordia Ave, St Paul, MN 55103
Robert Miller, 612-293-5918
1-8th grade
Gifted and talented.

Jackson Preparatory Magnet School
437 Edmund Ave, St Paul, MN 55103
Louis Mariucri, 612-293-8650
K-6th grade
Life Long Learning.

Red School House
643 Virginia St, St Paul, MN 55103
Anne R. Mitchell, 612-488-6626
Students mainly Native American, all ages
Culture-based curriculum.

Designs for Learning
(See Resource Section)

EXPO Middle School
631 N Albert St, St Paul, MN 55104
Joan Sorenson, 612-293-5970
Type: magnet
6-8th grade
Learning theatre; ungraded.

Longfellow Humanities Magnet School
318 Moore St, St Paul, MN 55104
Juanita Morgan, 612-293-8725
K-6th grade
Humanities.

St Paul Expo Schools
449 Desnoyer, St Paul, MN 55104
Joan Sorenson, 612-644-2805

J. J. Hill Montessori Magnet (1986-87)
998 Selby Ave, St. Paul, MN 55104-6532
Dr Maria Calderon, Prin, 612-293-8720
Type: public
18 teachers, 6 assistants, 465 students, partly at-risk, ages
   3-12
Affiliations: AMS, AMI, NAMTA
Governance by teachers and administrators, democratic
   school meeting
Urban location; transportation; interns accepted.

A Children's Place
1820 St Clair Ave, St Paul, MN 55105
Type: Montessori

Open School
1023 Osceola Ave, St Paul, MN 55105
Brad Manor, 612-293-8670
Type: magnet
K-12th grade
Open education.

Ramsey Junior High School
1700 Summit, St Paul, MN 55105
Dorothy LeGault, 612-293-8860
Type: magnet
7-8th grade
Gifted and talented; humanities.

St Catherine's Montessori (1931)
2004 Randolph Ave, St Paul, MN 55105
Cindy Scalia, Adm, 612-690-6608
Non-profit
Student ages 3-6
Affiliation: AMS
Governance by administrator
Complete Montessori materials; 1:20 ratio; lab school; parents
   welcome; childcare; urban location; interns accepted

Sunny Hollow Montessori (1981)
225 Cleveland Ave S, St. Paul, MN 55105
Jeanette Meyer, Dir, 612-690-2307
Non-profit; tuition: $190-455/mo
3 teachers, 3 assistants, 70 students, ages 3-6
Affiliation: NAMTA
Governance by administrator, board
Childcare.

American Indian Magnet School
1075 E 3rd St, St Paul, MN 55106
Cornel Pewewardy, 612-293-5938
K-8th grade
Native American Culture.

Cleveland Quality School
1000 Walsh St, St Paul, MN 55106
Larry Gallatin, 612-293-8880
Type: magnet
6-8th grade
Work with parents and students; success for all.

Cherokee Heights Pangea Ed Comm
694 Charlton St, St Paul, MN 55107
Christopher Canelake, 612-293-8610
Type: magnet
4-6th grade
PANGEA Educational Community.

Guadalupe Area Project
381 E Robie St, St. Paul, MN 55107
Allen Selinski, 612-222-0757
Students mainly at-risk, HS
Multi-cultural; individualized.

Panger Educational Community School
160 E Isabel St, St Paul, MN 55107
Joan Rourke, 612-293-8655
Type: magnet
K-3rd grade
Part of cluster.

Riverview Panger Educational Center
271 E Belvidere, St Paul, MN 55107
Joan Schlen, 612-293-8665
Type: magnet
K-1st grade
PANGEA Educational Community.

Transition Plus
251 Starkey St, St Paul, MN 55107
Vernon Schultz, 612-293-5420
Students mainly SE, ages 18-21
Case managers; individualized plans focus on home living,
   community participation, leisure, world of work, post secondary exploration.

622 Alternative High School (1972)
1945 Manton St, Maplewood, MN 55109
William R. Postiglione, Coord, 612-770-4745, FAX: 612-779-
   5845
Type: public choice
11 teachers, 120 students, mainly at-risk, ages 16-21
Governance by board
Teacher qualifications: MN certification
Career counseling; no letter grades; interns accepted.

Growing Room
2555 Hazelwood, Maplewood, MN 55109
Type: Montessori

Little School of Montessori
1390 Larpenteur Ave E, St Paul, MN 55109-4524

LaPepiniere Montessori School, Inc
PO Box 11245, St Paul, MN 55111

Catholic Home School Newsletter
(See Resource Section)

Harbon Montessori School
2349 NW 15th St, New Brighton, MN 55112

Minnesota Waldorf School (1981)
2129 Fairview Ave N, Roseville, MN 55113
Carol-Jean Swanson; Jean Nelson, PR Coords, 612-636-6577
Non-profit; tuition: $3,770-4,990/yr, scholarships

21 teachers; student ages 4-14, K-8th grade
Affiliation: AWSNA
Governance by faculty, parent council, board
Teacher qualifications: BA and 2-yr Waldorf training
Suburban location; interns accepted.

Kinderhaus Montessori School
3115 Victoria St N, Roseville, MN 55113-1935

States Educational Alternatives League (SEAL)
(See Resource Section)

Expo Excellence Magnet School
540 Warwick St, St Paul, MN 55116
Diana Swanson, 612-290-8384
K-6th grade
Ungraded; family; theatres of learning.

Highland Park Montessori School
1287 Ford Pkwy, St Paul, MN 55116-2259

Mississippi Creative Arts Magnet
1575 L'Orient St, St Paul, MN 55117
612-293-8840
K-6th grade
Creative Arts.

Twin Pines Montessori School
1919 Knob Rd, Mendota Heights, MN 55118

Mississippi Valley Montessori
1575 Charlton, St Paul, MN 55118

Creative Playhouse
1588 S Victoria Rd, Mendota Heights, MN 55118-3658
Type: Montessori

Families Nurturing Lifelong Learners
2452 Southcrest Av, Maplewood, MN 55119
Type: home-based

Woodbury Montessori School, Inc
1220 McKnight Rd, Maplewood, MN 55119

Boys Totem Town
398 Totem Rd, St Paul, MN 55119
Dave Ardoff, 612-292-6295
Boarding
Career exploration; work experience; year-round.

East Side Montessori
2019 Case Ave, St Paul, MN 55119

Nokomis Montessori/Developmental
985 Ruth St, St Paul, MN 55119
Elnore Battle, 612-293-8857
Type: magnet
Student ages 4+,-3rd grade
Childcare.

Highwood Hills School
2188 Londin Ln, Saint Paul, MN 55119-5393
Type: Montessori

Convent of the Vistation Montessori
2455 Visitation Dr, Mendota Heights, MN 55120-1696

Eagan Montessori & Child Care Center
1250 Lone Oak Rd, Saint Paul, MN 55121-2103

Cedar Alternative Center (1987)
2140 Diffley Rd, Eagan, MN 55122
Beverly Brucciani, Coord, 612-895-7429, FAX: 612-895-7297
Type: public choice/at-risk
7 teachers, 84 students, mainly at-risk, ages 16-21, 10-12th
grade
Affiliation: ISD #191
Governance by faculty and student representatives, site
council

Teacher qualifications: secondary certification
Informal setting; parenting program; results-oriented; small
group instruction; diploma program; suburban location.

Lanka Trading
9129 Sequoia Bay, Woodbury, MN 55125
Bart Ratnayake
Type: Montessori

Woodview Terrace Montessori
6255 Upper Afton Rd, Woodbury, MN 55125

Independence Montessori
850 South St, Anoka, MN 55303
Carol Landkamer, Adm; Charlotte Cushman, Dir, 612-427-3976
Tuition: $160/mo
1 teacher, 1 assistant, 50 students, ages 3-6
Accreditations: AMI, AMS
Suburban location; interns accepted.

Minnesota Association of Christian Home Educators
PO Box 188, Anoka, MN 55303
612-753-2370

Parents Allied with Children and Teachers
600 E Main St, Anoka, MN 55303
Dr Joseph Abeler, 612-421-3722
Type: charter
84 students
Affiliation: MN BE
Parents tutor guided independent study; multi-aged classes.

Northern Lights School
3450 152nd Ln NW, Andover, MN 55304-3003
Type: Montessori

Jonathon Montessori House of Children, Inc. (1968)
112050 Hundertmark Rd, Chaska, MN 55318
Randi Shapiro, Dir, 612-448-5232
Non-profit; tuition: $220-437/mo
3 teachers, 4 assistants, 48 students, ages 3-6
Governance by administrator, board
3 acres in semi-rural area; nature trails; committed parents
and staff; childcare; interns accepted.

Hopkins Montessori
3500 Willison Rd, Minnetonka, MN 55343

Prairie Center Alternative (PCA)
250 Prairie Center Dr, Suite 100, Eden Prairie, MN 55344
Doug Andrus, 612-941-7860
Student ages 16+
Independent study; extended year; community resources.

High Point Montessori
9051 High Point Circle, Eden Priarie, MN 55344

Ombudsman Educational Services, Ltd
6585 Edenvale Blvd #170, Eden Prairie, MN 55346
Laura Hauler, Director, 612-934-9791

Activities for Learning
(See Resource Section)

Minnesota Homeschool Alliance
PO Box 281, Maple Plain, MN 55359
612-491-2828

Student on a Rebound (SOAR) (1985)
317 2nd Ave NW, Osseo, MN 55369
LeRoy Putman, Prog Coord, 612-425-2323, FAX: -2702
Type: public at-risk
9 teachers, 60 students, ages 16-21, 10-12th grade
Affiliation: MN DE
Governance by teachers and principal
Teacher qualifications: BA/BS degree
No letter grades; childcare; multi-aged classes; suburban
location; interns accepted.

Dorothy's Daily Discoveries
1035 Bluff Ave E, Shakopee, MN 55379
Type: Montessori

Spring Hill Waldorf School
865 N Ferndale Rd, Wayzata, MN 55391
Brenda Fleisher, Tch, 612-473-2262
Non-profit; tuition: $1,120-2,500/yr
2 teachers, 20 students, ages 3-6
Governance by parent cooperative and board.
Natural and handmade play materials; storytelling; nature
    activities; sewing; cooking; gardening; outdoor adventures;
    suburban location.

Deephaven Montessori School
18325 Minnetonka Blvd, Wayzata, MN 55391-3231

Katahdin
337 Oak Grove St, Minneapolis, MN 55403
Mia Olsen, 612-872-4701
35 students, mainly at-risk, ages 12-18
Accreditation: yes
Individualized; counseling; social, recreational activities; inde-
    pendent living, employment skills; reintegration into home
    school.

Loring Nicollet Alternative School
1925 Nicollet Ave, Minneapolis, MN 55403
Marin Peplinski, 612-871-2031
45 students, mainly at-risk, HS
10-12 students/class.

Skills for Tomorrow
52 10th Street S, Minneapolis, MN 55403
Tony Scallon, 612-962-4535
Type: charter
Affiliations: MN BE, Teamsters Service Bureau and the MN
    Business Partnership
Voc/tech; internships.

Urban League Street Academy
1911 Nicollet Ave S, Minneapolis, MN 55403
Marge Freeman or Richard Dillard, 612-874-9667
70 students, mainly at-risk, ages 16-21
HS diploma; computer programming; health; teen parenting;
    PE; urban location.

Child Garden Total Environment Montessori
1900 Nicollet Ave, Minneapolis, MN 55403-3746

Bryant Glenwood Montessori
4300 Bryant Ave N, Minneapolis, MN 55404

Center School, Inc
2421 Bloomington Ave S, Minneapolis, MN 55404
Paul Hegre, 612-721-1655
7-12th grade
Accreditation: yes
Small classes; counseling: individual, family, chemical depen-
    dency, career; student leadership; urban location.

Minneapolis Education & Employment Resource Center
2539 Pleasant Ave S, Minneapolis, MN 55404
Tyria Taylor Cobb, 612-872-8811
Max 45 students, mainly at-risk, ages 15-21
Accreditation: yes
Emphasis on job-related skills, maintaining employment.

Cedar-Riverside Community School
12 Oliver Ave S, Minneapolis, MN 55405
Barbara Schmidt, 612-377-8109
Type: charter
85 students, K-8th grade
Affiliation: MN BE
In low-income, multi-cultural area.

Minneapolis Community Learning Center
1800 Glenwood Ave N, Minneapolis, MN 55405

Robert Distad, 612-374-1532
Type: charter
Affiliation: MN BE

Harrison Open School
1500 4th Ave N, Minneapolis, MN 55405-1105
Type: Montessori

Jefferson Elementary
1200 W 26th St, Minneapolis, MN 55405-3541
Type: Montessori

Dowling School School
3900 W River Pkwy, Minneapolis, MN 55406
Jeffrey Ralson, 612-627-2732
Type: magnet
K-6th grade
Urban environment.

Minnesota Alliance of Montessorians
914 Franklin Ter, Minneapolis, MN 55406
Cameron Gordon

Seward Montessori School
2309 28th Ave S, Minneapolis, MN 55406-1397

Friends School of Minnesota (1988)
3244 34th Ave S, Minneapolis, MN 55406-2185
Mark Niedermier, Dir, 612-722-2046
Type: Quaker, non-profit; tuition: $4,050/yr, scholarships
11 teachers, 73 students, ages 5-13, K-6th grade
Affiliation: FCOE
Governance by board
Hands-on, integrated curr; global, environmental, multi-
    cultural topics; conflict resolution; anti-sexist, racist, and
    homophobic; no letter grades; multi-aged classes; urban
    location; transportation; interns accepted.

Northrap Elementary
1611 E 46th St, Minneapolis, MN 55407
Sylvia Adams, 612-627-2810
Type: magnet
K-6th grade
Urban environment.

South High School
3131 19th Ave S, Minneapolis, MN 55407
Hubert Denny, 612-627-2508
Type: magnet
9-12th grade
Liberal arts; open; all Native American nations.

Public School Montessorian
(See Resource Section)

Montessori Day Care Center
2608 Blaisdell, Minneapolis, MN 55408

Southside Family School (1972)
2740 1st Ave S, Minneapolis, MN 55408
Flo Golod, 612-872-8322
Type: independent, non-profit
6 teachers, 52 students, ages 5-13, K-6th grade
Governance by board
Social justice; individualized; volunteer service; student advo-
    cacy; model for area educators; no letter grades; multi-
    aged classes; extensive field trips; interns accepted.

Superlearning
3028 Emerson Ave S, Minneapolis, MN 55408
Libyan Labiosa, 612-827-4856
Type: independent

Center for Public Montessori Programs
(See Resource Section)

Little Red Hen Montessori School
4225 3rd Ave S, Minneapolis, MN 55409

Ramsey International Fine Arts Center
1 W 49th St, Minneapolis, MN 55409
Doris Zachary, 612-627-2540
Type: magnet
K-8th grade
International Studies/Fine Arts.

Lake Country School
3755 Pleasant Ave, Minneapolis, MN 55409-1282
Larry Shafer
Type: Montessori

Lake Harriet Montessori
4501 Colfax Ave S, Minneapolis, MN 55409-1736

WOLF School (1994)
c/o 5535 Richmond Curve, Minneapolis, MN 55410
Karen Locke, Co-Founder, 612-925-9819
Type: home-based, non-profit
7+ students, ages 4-14, K-12th grade
Governance by democratic school meeting.
Student-centered and directed; urban location.

North High School
1500 James Ave N, Minneapolis, MN 55411
Harlan Anderson, 612-627-2778
Type: magnet
9-12th grade
Arts; communications.

Bethune Elementary School
919 Emerson Ave N, Minneapolis, MN 55411-4199
Type: Montessori

City School-Northside/Southside
1315 12th Ave N / 1545 E Lake St, Minneapolis, MN
55411/55407
Bobby Hickman or Ron Simmons / Terry Tendle, 612-377-
7559, 724-3689
Students mainly inner city at-risk, 7-12th grade
Affiliations: The City, Inc; accreditation: yes
Employment; recreation; individual, family counseling; childcare; urban location.

Afrocentric Educational Academy
1015 Olson Memorial Hwy, Minneapolis, MN 55412
Nell Collier or Birch Jones, 612-377-1556
Student ages 11-15
History; language arts; tutoring; mentoring; small classes;
outcome-based; coop learning; multi-media technology.

Minneapolis Junior High Alternative School
1006 W Lake St, Minneapolis, MN 55412
Harvey Winston or R. C. Johnson, 612-627-2850
Student ages 12-15
Transitional; support services; career exploration; parent
support groups; summer program.

New Visions School
3820 Emerson Ave N, Minneapolis, MN 55412
Bob DeBoer, 612-521-2266
1-6th grade
Developmental problems; whole brain; whole language;
optometric services; physical movement.

New Visions School
3820 Emerson Ave N, Minneapolis, MN 55412
Paul McClusky, 612-521-2266
Type: charter
Affiliation: MN BE

Pregnant Adolescent Continuing Education ()
1201 Hennepin, Minneapolis, MN 55412
Lois Gehrman or Barbara Bellair, 612-339-6712
Student ages 12-20
Individualized; SE assessments; health screening; prenatal
education; crisis counseling; career planning.

Heart of the Earth Survival School
1209 4th St SE, Minneapolis, MN 55414
Edward Benton-Benai or Mark Aquash, 612-331-8862,
FAX:-1747
55 teachers, 250 students, mainly Native American, K-12th
grade
Native American culture-based; parent, community support.

Marcy Open School (1971)
415 4th Ave SE, Minneapolis, MN 55414
Jay Scoggin, Tch/Leadership Council Co-Chair, 612-627-7474
Type: public choice
27 teachers, 630 students, ages 5-14, K-8th grade
Governance by teacher, administration, community, student
leadership council
Family, community involvement; self-directed; student-
centered; environmental education; volunteer program;
Higher Order Thinking Skills; no letter grades; multi-aged
classes; extensive field trips; interns accepted.

Peace Academy/Holos Foundation
601 13th Ave SE, Minneapolis, MN 55414
Barbara Schmidt, 612-377-8109
Type: public choice
Holistic, interdisciplinary; competency-based; credit by self/
staff evaluation; multi-aged classes; urban location.

Second Foundation School
1219 University Ave SE, Minneapolis, MN 55414
Bob Vincent, Director, 612-378-1014
Type: independent, non-profit; tuition: $20-500/mo, sliding
scale
4 teachers, 32 students, ages 5-18, K-12th grade
Governance by democratic school meeting
Based on idea that people have good inner motivation,
unique styles; students follow natural interests, work at
their own pace; cooperation between students fostered;
no letter grades; non-compulsory class attendance; multi-
aged classes; urban location; transportation.

Children's Village Child Care Center
2812 University Ave SE, Minneapolis, MN 55414-3212
Type: Montessori

Operation deNovo
251 Portland Ave S, Minneapolis, MN 55415
Ralph Davies, 612-348-4805
Education contract; monthly evaluation by student, staff,
probation officer, parent/guardian; failure results in correctional facility placement; urban location.

Discoveries for Children
4100 Vernon Ave S, Saint Louis Park, MN 55416-3199
Heidi Dorfmeister
Type: Montessori

Menlo Park Alternative School
1929 2nd St NE, Minneapolis, MN 55418
Patricia A. Lobash, 612-781-6011
1:10 ratio; teen parent workers; violence/abuse education;
youth work; computer; urban location.

Kenny Elementary School
57th & Emerson, Minneapolis, MN 55419
Type: Montessori

Mrs Liiste's Montessori School
8036 Lyndale Ave S, Bloomington, MN 55420

Raamalynn Montessori Academy
9600 3rd Ave S, Bloomington, MN 55420

Rainbow Montessori
8736 Nicollet Ave, Bloomington, MN 55420

Marianna Montessori Day Care
8000 Portland Ave, Minneapolis, MN 55420

Little Voyageurs Montessori School
1515 44th Ave NE, Columbia Heights, MN 55421

Breck Montessori
123 Ottawa Ave N, Golden Valley, MN 55422

Minnesota High School for the Arts
6125 Olson Memorial Hwy, Golden Valley, MN 55422
Jim Undercofler, 612-591-4700
Type: public choice

TEACH Institute
4350 Lakeland Ave N, N Robbinsdale, MN 55422
Type: state home-based
Accrediting association for Christian home educators; consulting services available nationwide.

Minnesota Homeschoolers Alliance (1990)
Box 23072, Richfield, MN 55423
Tara Tieso-Battis, 612-491-2828
Non-profit
Nine member elected board
Inclusive; Grapevine newsletter; annual conference; workshops, special events; interns accepted.

Edina Montessori School
5701 Normandale, Edina, MN 55424
Sunil Aiyadurai

City of Lakes Waldorf School (1989)
3450 Irving Ave S, Minneapolis, MN 55426
Carol Jean Swanson, Adms Coord, 612-822-1092
Non-profit; tuition: $4,740/yr, scholarships
20 teachers, 165 students, ages 3-14, pre K-8th grade
Affiliation: AWSNA
Governance by faculty and student representatives, board
Teacher qualifications: college, Waldorf training or equivalent
Urban location; transportation; interns accepted.

Knollwood Montessori
8115 Hwy 7, Minneapolis, MN 55426

Learning Through Music
3503 Sumter Ave S, St Louis Park, MN 55426
Hestia Abeyesekera
Type: Montessori

70,001 Golden Valley Montessori School
PO Box 27321, Golden Valley, MN 55427-0321

Brookdale Montessori School
5827 Humboldt Ave N, Minneapolis, MN 55430-2637

Mariana Montessori
2501 W 84th St, Bloomington, MN 55431
Marie Dias

Ramalynn Montessori Academy
8800 Queen Ave S, Bloomington, MN 55431

Interaction Book Company
(See Resource Section)

La Pepiniere Montessori School
6515 Barrie Rd, Edina, MN 55435-2305

ABC/International Montessori Academy, Inc (1974)
10801 Normandale Blvd S, Bloomington, MN 55437
Dr Vijay B Gupta, Dir, 612-881-1717
Non-profit; tuition: $300-450/mo
12 teachers, 6 assistants, 143 students, mainly international,
ages 3-15
Affiliations: AMI, MF MN; accreditation: MF MN
Governed by administrator
Modern Montessori building; ballet; Spanish; theatre; piano;
cosmic curriculum; childcare; urban location.

New Vistas School
2701 4th Ave S, Minneapolis, MN 55440

Gladys Randle, 612-870-6219
10-12th grade
Affiliation: Honeywell
Outcome-based; CAI; coop learning; inductive thinking; mentoring; work experience; vocational courses; childcare,
health, social services; urban location; transportation.

Armstrong HS, Alternative Program
10635 36th Ave N, Plymouth, MN 55441
John Lloyd, 612-546-3266
Type: public choice

Montessori School of Wayzata Bay
13501 Cty Rd 15, Plymouth, MN 55441

College of St Catherine
St Mary's Campus (1985)
2500 S 6th St, Minneapolis, MN 55454
Michael Dorer, Prog Dir, 612-690-7779, FAX: 612-690-7849
Type: Montessori teacher education
10-18 teachers, 33 students, ages infant-12/adult
Accreditations: AMS, MACTE
Governance by administrator
Urban location.

Anwatin Middle School
256 Upton Ave S, Minneapolis, MN 55455
612-627-3150
Type: public choice
6-8th grade
Affiliations: Dain Bosworth, Inc
Governance by principal, council
Student council; community service; computers; A/V; conflict
mediation training; environmental learning center; Pre-IB
Magnet Program; multi-aged classes; parent center.

Bethune Public School Academy
919 Emerson Ave N, Minneapolis, MN 55455
612-627-2685
Type: public choice
K-6th grade
Governance by teachers, principal
1:14 ratio; cooperative learning; parent involvement; in-class
telephones, answering machines; partnership with General
Mills.

Chiron Middle School
25 N 16th St, Minneapolis, MN 55455
612-627-3250
Type: public choice
6-8th grade
Governance by parents, staff, students
Hands-on, cooperative learning; whole language; arts, government, science, technology; mentorships; community
service; multi-aged classes; annual August festivities.

Downtown Open
730 2nd Ave S, Minneapolis, MN 55455
612-627-7145
Type: public choice
K-4th grade
Affiliations: NSP, IDS, Augsburg College
Governance by principal
Student-centered; cooperative learning; community interaction; individualized; whole language; Spanish-English bilingual; non-competitive evaluations; tutors; multi-aged
classes; childcare; interns accepted.

Emerson Spanish Immersion Learning Center
1421 Spruce Place, Minneapolis, MN 55455
612-627-7452
Type: public choice
K-8th grade
Governance by parents, teachers, principal
Teacher qualifications: ESL specialty
Technology instruction; choir; band; computer lab; stage.

Four Winds Native American and French Language School
2300 Chicago Ave, Minneapolis, MN 55455
612-627-7160
Type: public choice
K-8th grade
Governance by principal
Cooperative learning; French immersion for grades 1-5; Dakota, Ojibwe language; community service; parent involvement; tutors; drum and dance group; community ed; preschool; childcare.

Franklin Middle School
1501 Aldrich Ave N, Minneapolis, MN 55455
612-627-2869
Type: magnet
6-8th grade
Governance by principal
Math/science/tech; small classes; computers; A/V; piano lab; cooperative learning; team teaching; interdisciplinary; parent involvement; peer groups; support services.

Hall Montessori School
1601 Aldrich Ave N, Minneapolis, MN 55455
612-627-2339
K-6th grade
Governance by principal
Teacher qualifications: Montessori training
Continue with same teacher for consecutive years; emphasis on global interrelatedness; practical life experiences; environmental and peace education; multi-aged classes.

Mill City Montessori
219 S 4th St, Minneapolis, MN 55455
612-338-5765
Type: public choice
K-5th grade
Governance by teachers, principal, parents
Teacher qualifications: Montessori, MN Certification
Student-centered; cooperative learning; computers; multi-aged classes; childcare.

Native American Program at Andersen Open School
1098 Andersen Ln, Minneapolis, MN 55455
612-627-2295
Type: public choice
K-8th grade
Governance by teachers and principal
Self-directed; student-centered; Student Leadership Councils; individual projects; thematic instruction; tutoring; team teaching; elder on staff; parent involvement; Ojibway language; multi-aged classes; childcare; multi-cultural gender fair and disability-aware lab demo site.

Northeast Middle School
2955 Hayes St NE, Minneapolis, MN 55455
612-627-3042
Type: public choice
6-8th grade
Governance by principal
Cooperative learning; mentorships; integrated curriculum; computers; peer tutoring, coaching; conflict mgmt; artist in residence; pre-IB; career exploration; multi-aged classes; parent involvement.

Pillsbury Math/Science/Technology School
2250 Garfield St NE, Minneapolis, MN 55455
612-627-2822
Type: public choice
K-6th grade
Governance by principal
School-wide theme projects; cooperative learning; parent involvement; computers; mentors; preschool and early childhood SE; multi-aged classes; childcare.

Sanford Middle School
3524 42nd Ave S, Minneapolis, MN 55455

612-627-2720
Type: public choice
6-8th grade
Governance by principal
Cooperative learning; interdisciplinary; environmental science; social skills; parent involvement.

Sheridan International/Fine Arts
1201 University Ave NE, Minneapolis, MN 55455
612-627-2348
Type: public choice
K-6th grade
Governance by principal
Individualized; whole language; Math Their Way; cooperative learning; learning centers; thematic instruction; parent involvement; weekly classroom newsletter; string instruments; Russian language, culture.

Shingle Creek Urban Environmental Center
5034 Oliver Ave N, Minneapolis, MN 55455
612-627-2673
Type: public choice
K-6th grade
Governance by principal
Individualized; along creek banks, adjacent to park; parent involvement.

Webster Open School
425 5th St NE, Minneapolis, MN 55455
612-627-2312
K-8th grade
Community, parent involvement; self-directed; Spanish; arts specialist; CAI; thematic learning; multi-cultural.

Willard Math/Science/Technology Magnet
1615 Queen Ave N, Minneapolis, MN 55455
612-627-2529
K-6th grade
Governance by council
Cooperative, experiential learning; whole language; role models; CAI; A/V; parent involvement; take-home family science kits; partnerships with Cray Research and Augsburg College; extensive field trips; yearly camping trip.

Northshore Children's House
PO Box 535, Grand Marais, MN 55604-0535
Type: Montessori

Toivola Meadowlands
7705 Western Ave, Meadowlands, MN 55765
Tim Robison, 218-722-3371
Type: charter
190 students, K-12th grade
Affiliation: MN BE
Multi-aged classes; outcome-based.

New Moon Publishing
(See Resource Section)

Montessori School of Duluth, Inc
1215 Rice Lake Rd, Duluth, MN 55811-2160

Rochester Montessori School
400 5th Ave SW, Rochester, MN 55903
Chace Anderson, RMS

Franklin School
1801 SE 9th Ave, Rochester, MN 55904
Robert Funk
Type: Montessori

Austin Area Learning Center
301 3rd St NW, Austin, MN 55912
Royce R Helmbrecht, 507-433-0408
Student ages 12+
Open entry/exit; support services; parent involvement; youth service; personal/social skills; teen parenting; competency-based; childcare.

Bluffview Montessori (1988)
101 E Wabasha St, Winona, MN 55987
Haine Crown, Adm Asst, 507-452-2807
Type: Montessori charter, non-profit; tuition: $150/250 for
ages 3–6
4 teachers, 4 assistants, 99 students, ages 3–12
Affiliations: AMI/USA, NAMTA
Governance by administration and staff
MN's first charter school; nation's first Montessori charter
school; childcare; suburban/rural location; transportation;
interns accepted.

Montessori School of Winona
PO Box 991, Winonaa, MN 55987

Bluffview Montessori School
101 E 7th St, Winona, MN 55987-3594

Good Counsel Montessori School
512 Mulberry St, Mankato, MN 56001

Albert Lea Area Learning Center
504 W Clark St, Albert Lea, MN 56007
Rob Esse, 507-377-6540
90–110 students
Evening classes; middle level program at SW JHS, Brookside
MS: support services; parent involvement; youth service,
personal/social skills; individualized.

Minnesota New Country School
115 1/2 N 5th St, Suite 200, LeSueur, MN 56058
Nancy Miller, 612-665-4033
Type: charter
7–12th grade
Affiliation: MN BE
CES CAI.

Worthington Montessori School (1971)
Box 434, Worthington, MN 56187
Sally-Anne Benson, Dir, 507-376-3669
Non-profit; tuition: $110/mo
1 teacher, 1 assistant, 20 students, ages 3–6
Accreditations: AMS, MN DHS
Governance by parent-run board
Childcare.

Benson Area Learning Center
1400 Montana Ave, Benson, MN 56215
Doug Manzke or Gary Williams, 612-843-2710
Type: public at-risk

Dakota/Open Charter School
7 Lower Sioux Trail W; PO Box 129, Morton, MN 56270-0129
Dennis McLaughlin, 507-697-6372
Type: charter
7–12th grade
Affiliation: MN BE

Montessori School of St Cloud (1968)
302 S 5th Ave, St Cloud, MN 56301
Mary Theresa Anderson, Prin, 612-253-4719
Tuition: $195/390/mo
4 teachers, 7 assistants, 75 students, ages 3–6
Governance by administrator
Christian; non-denominational; language development; child-
care; urban location; interns accepted.

Learning Day Montessori School
3124 Southway Dr, Saint Cloud, MN 56301-9589

Runestone Regional Learning Center
1224 N Nokomis, Alexandria, MN 56308
Katy Mohabir, 612-762-0627
Life skills; evening classes; middle level program: holistic;
support services; parent involvement; youth service.

W. C. Camphill Village MN
Rt 3, Box 249, Sauk Centre, MN 56378
Debbie Leighton, 612-732-6365
Type: Waldorf

Brainerd Area Education Center
1102 Willow St, Brainerd, MN 56401
Arlo Renschler, 218-829-2915
Independent study; CAI; mentorships; middle level program
at ALC, Franklin JHS, Washington MS: support services;
youth service; personal/social skills; technology.

Minnesota Association of Alternative Programs (MAAP)
Area Education Center
(See Resource Section)

Emily Community Learning Center
HC 2, Box 46, Emily, MN 56447
Lorraine Gaulke, 218-763-3400
Type: charter

Detroit Lakes Alternative Learning Center
1301 Rosevelt Ave, Detroit Lakes, MN 56501
Robert Soukup, 218-847-4491
Type: home-based
100+ students, ages 16+
100% independent study; multi-aged classes.

Fargo-Moorehead Homeschool Association
1909-8th St S, Moorehead, MN 56560

Perham Alternative Learning Program
200 5th St NE, Perham, MN 56573
Jan Turgeon, 218-346-6502
Students mainly out-of-school, ages 16+
Home ec; PE; teen parenting; career planning.

Bemidji Area Learning Center
201 15th St NW, Bemidji, MN 56601
Dave Bucher, 218-759-3119
Experiential learning; individualized; life, job skills; middle
level program: support services; parent involvement;
youth service; personal/social skills; self-directed.

Riverside Schoolhouse
(See Resource Section)

Bagley Alternative High School
202 Bagley Ave NW, Bagley, MN 56621
Gary Bratvold, 218-694-6184
Type: public at-risk

Montessori PreSchool
518 10th Ave W, International Falls, MN 56649-2238

Mississippi

Clarksdale City School
301 Washington St, Clarksdale, MS 38614
Bueford O. Spain, Prin, 601-627-8573
Type: public at-risk
6 teachers, 20 students, ages 14-18, 9-11th grade
Governance by principal
Teacher qualifications: certification
Urban location; interns accepted.

Tate County Alternative School (1990)
PO Box CC, Coldwater, MS 38618
William Kelvin Knox, Dir, 601-622-0130
Type: public choice/at-risk
7 teachers; students mainly at-risk, ages 13+, 7-12th grade
Governance by board
Teacher qualifications: certification
Part-time retired academics teachers; SE; counselor; enrichment teacher; no letter grades; multi-aged classes; suburban location.

Center of Attention
2047 Clifton Rd, Hernando, MS 38632
Type: Montessori

Cadet Child Care Center
PO Box 610, Holly Springs, MS 38635
Type: Montessori

Olive Branch Elementary School
9459 Pigeon Roost Rd, Olive Branch, MS 38654-2608
Type: Montessori

The Children's House of Tupelo
2225 W Main St, Tupelo, MS 38801-3143
Type: Montessori

NE Mississippi Regional Co-op (1993)
PO Box 247, Booneville, MS 38829
Lisa Wigginton, Dir, 601-728-7144, FAX: -7104
Type: public at-risk
6 teachers, 71 students, ages 10-21, 5-12th grade
Governance by board
Teacher qualifications: must meet MTAI guidelines
4 counties; for repeatedly suspended, expelled students; social, academic skills; behavior mod; multi-aged classes; interns accepted.

The Children's House, Inc
1710 Magnolia Rd, Corinth, MS 38834
Type: Montessori

Debbie Walker
RR 1, Plantersville, MS 38862-9801
Type: Montessori

T.Y. Fleming Alternative School (1993)
1901 Highway 82 W, Greenwood, MS 38930
Irvin L. Whittaker, Supt, 601-453-8566, FAX: 459-7250
Type: public at-risk
3 teachers, 30 students, ages 12-18, 6-12th grade
Governance by teachers, principal, security officials
Social science; life, job skills; multi-aged classes; rural location; transportation.

The Learning Tree
211 W Pres Ave, Greenwood, MS 38930-3545
Type: Montessori

Alternative Learning Center of Montgomery County (1993)
PO Box 687, Winona, MS 38967
W.P. Williamson, Coord, 601-283-1696
Type: public choice

1 teacher, 10-12 students, mainly at-risk, ages 13-17, 7-10th grade
Governance by ALC committee, teacher, coord, superintendent
Multi-aged classes

Cotton Boll Learning Center (1993)
301 Fairground St, Winona, MS 38967
Eddie Hamilton, 601-283-1244, FAX: 601-283-1003
Type: public at-risk
3 teachers, 15 students, ages 11-18, 5-12th grade
Governance by teachers and principal
Teacher qualifications: elementary and secondary qualifications
GED; multi-aged classes; urban location; transportation; interns accepted.

Yazoo County High School Alternative Program (1993)
PO Box 288, Benton, MS 39039
John P. Smith, Prin, 601-673-9777
Type: public at-risk
4 teachers, 12 students, ages 15-20, 9-12th grade
Governance by principal
Teacher qualifications: certification
No letter grades; rural location; transportation.

Simpson County Schools (1993)
101 Court St, Mendenhall, MS 39114
Lillie L. Hardy, Asst Supt, 601-847-1890, FAX: -8003
Type: public at-risk
1 teacher, 15 students, ages 12-20, 6-12th grade
Governance by teachers and principal
Teacher qualifications: certification
No letter grades; multi-aged classes; transportation.

Natchez Adams School District
1089 Commerce St, Natchez, MS 39120
Etta Mae Swalm
Type: Montessori

Home Educators of Central Mississippi
c/o McDonald, 109 W Willow Ct, Ridgeland, MS 39157
601-366-9218

Center for Alternative Programs (1992)
102 Army-Nary Dr, Vicksburg, MS 39182
Noah Johnson, Dir, 601-631-2910
Type: public choice/at-risk
61 students, mainly at-risk, ages 8-17, 1-9th grade
Governance by teachers, principal, board
Day treatment; joint effort of SD, mental health agency; counseling; social skills; multi-aged classes; urban location; interns accepted.

Davis Magnet School
750 N Congress St, Jackson, MS 39202
Paula Keller, 601-960-5333
K-5th grade
Open education with emphasis on arts.

APEC at Chastain Middle School
4650 Manhattan Rd, Jackson, MS 39206
Jack Rice, 601-987-3550
Type: magnet
6-8th grade
Fine and performing arts.

APEC at Murrah High School
1120 Riverside Dr, Jackson, MS 39206
Linda Dick, 601-960-5380
Type: magnet
9-12th grade
Fine and performing arts.

APEC at Power Elementary
1120 Riverside Dr, Jackson, MS 39206
Linda Dick, 601-960-5387
Type: magnet
K-5th grade
Fine and performing arts.

Children's House Montessori School
PO Box 16011, Jackson, MS 39206

Educational Services Center (1993)
475 Parkway Drive; PO Box 5750, Pearl, MS 39208
Betty B. Wilson, Dir, 601-933-2461, FAX: 601-933-2462
Type: public at-risk
4 teachers, 20 students, ages 10–16, 3-8th grade
Governance by teachers and principal
Teacher qualifications: MS Certification
One behavior targeted per student; incentives; positive
    reductive techniques; modified report cards; field trips;
    multi-aged classes; suburban location; transportation;
    interns accepted.

APEC at Powell Middle School
3655 Livingston Rd, Jackson, MS 39213
John Wicks, 601-987-3580
Type: magnet
6-8th grade
Fine and performing arts.

The Children's House Montessori School
2700 Davis St, Meridian, MS 39301-5707

Noxubee County Alternative School (1993)
PO Box 540, Macon, MS 39341
Murphy R. Greer, Head Adm, 601-726-4288, FAX: -2800
Type: public at-risk
4 teachers, 60 students, ages 13–21, 6-12th grade
Governance by board
Multi-aged classes; rural location; transportation; interns
    accepted.

Hattiesburg Montessori Children's House (1982)
323 S 23rd Ave, Hattiesburg, MS 39401
Erlene Welden, Owner/Dir, 601-545-1944
Tuition: $155-225/mo
3 teachers, 4 assistants, 52 students, ages infant-9
Accreditation: MSMA
Governance by administrator
Modern dance; ballet; Spanish; private piano; childcare;
    transportation.

Mississippi Home Educators Association
Rt 9, Box 350, Laurel, MS 39440
601-649-6432

Pine Belt Education Service Center (1990)
923-B Sawmill Rd; PO Box 6441, Laurel, MS 39441
Dewey Blackledge, 601-649-4141, FAX: 601-649-4150
Type: public at-risk
12 teachers, 177 students, ages 13–21, 5-12th grade
Governance by board, Supt, teachers and principal
Teacher qualifications: MS Certification
Serves 8 districts; pilot for alt ed designated by MS DE; behav-
    ioral modification; rural location; transportation.

First Baptist Church Daycare
2105 14th St, Gulfport, MS 39501-2004
Type: Montessori

The Learning Center (1993)
1215 Church St, Gulfport, MS 39507
Charlotte Taylor, Building Prin, 601-897-6045
Type: public at-risk
8 teachers, 52 students, ages 12–18, 7-12th grade
Affiliation: MAAAE
Governance by board
Teacher qualifications: MS Certification

No textbooks; hands-on activities; computers; self-esteem;
    multi-aged classes; extensive field trips; urban location;
    interns accepted.

Westminister Academy
5003 Lawson Ave, Gulfport, MS 39507-4498
Type: Montessori

Project New Start (1993)
750 Blue Meadow Rd, Bay St Louis, MS 39520
Jo-Dell Beckham, Alt Tch, 601-467-6611
Type: public at-risk
1 teacher, 19 students, ages 13–18, 7-12th grade
Governance by principal
Teacher qualifications: certified, with at risk experience
Vocational skills; behavior modification; community, work
    ethics; in-school suspension program; drug education;
    multi-aged classes; urban location.

Kinderlearn
310 Delrays Ave, Biloxi, MS 39530
Type: Montessori

Kessler AFB Montessori/Thelma Miller
1299 Kensington Dr, Biloxi, MS 39530-1623

Creative Learning Center
2140 Pass Rd, Biloxi, MS 39531-4002
Type: Montessori

Holy Angels
PO Box 523, Biloxi, MS 39533-0523
Type: Montessori

Montessori Special Preschool (1969)
Keesler AFB, Biloxi, MS 39534
Thelma Miller, Dir, 601-432-5109
Non-profit; tuition: Variable
1 teacher, 5 assistants, 40 students, ages 3–6
Governance by administrator
Urban location.

Loving Care Learning Center
644 E RailRd St, Long Beach, MS 39560
Type: Montessori

St Thomas School
712 E Beach Blvd, Long Beach, MS 39560-6298
Type: Montessori

Moss Point Alternative School (1986)
4924 Church St, Moss Point, MS 39563
Burton W. Hoitt, Coord, 601-769-1309
Type: public at-risk
5 teachers, 2 assistants, 40 students, ages 13–21, 7-12th
    grade
Governance by principal
Teacher qualifications: certification
Behavior modification; Glasser's Quality School; central theory
    taught and practiced; computer; multi-aged classes; urban
    location; transportation; interns accepted.

St Martin Elementary
Rose Farm Rd, Ocean Springs, MS 39564
Type: Montessori

Children's House Montessori
PO Box 668, Ocean Springs, MS 39564-0668

Alpha Montessori School
PO Box 698, Ocean Springs, MS 39564-0698

Montessori Schools & Day Care
2221 Government St, Ocean Springs, MS 39564-3957

Jackson County Alternative Program (1993)
PO Box 5069, Vancleave, MS 39565-5069
Ernest L. Rivers, Asst Supt, 601-826-1757, FAX: -1765
Type: public at-risk

4 teachers, 18 students, ages 12-18, 7-12th grade
Governance by board
Teacher qualifications: MS Certification
Alternative to expulsion; rural location.

Hancock County School for Success (1993)
6069 Cueras Town Rd, Pass Christian, MS 39571
Elaine Lizana, Prin, 601-255-6626
Type: public at-risk
3 teachers, 30 students, mainly at-risk, ages 13-19, 9-12th grade
Governance by teachers, principal, board.
CYBIS computer-based system; no letter grades; multi-aged classes; rural location; transportation.

Pineville School
5192 Menge Ave, Pass Christian, MS 39571
Type: Montessori

Program of Amite County (1990)
PO Box 378, Liberty, MS 39645
Dale Bailey, Dir of Psych Serv, 601-657-4361, FAX: -4291

Type: public choice
15 teachers, 68 students, partly at-risk, ages 12-20, 8-12th grade
Governance by director and principal
Teacher qualifications: BA
Field trips; rural location; interns accepted.

Columbus Alternative (1993)
2217 7th St N, Columbus, MS 39701
Donnie E. Gross, Prin, 601-243-7601
Type: public at-risk
6 teachers, 51 students, mainly at-risk, ages 6-17, 1-12th grade
Governance by teachers and principal
Teacher qualifications: certification
Separate facilities from regular students; multi-aged classes; transportation.

The Children's House Montessori School
923 6th Ave N, Columbus, MS 39701-4621

Missouri

Free State Montessori (1980)
2018 Rock Spring Rd, Forest Hill, MO 21050
Claire J Salkowski, Head, 410-879-2132
Non-profit
3 teachers, 60 students
Affiliation: AMS
Elementary camping; school-wide community service; suburban location; interns accepted.

Linda Vista Catholic School
1633 Kehrs Mill Rd, Chesterfield, MO 63005-4310
Type: Montessori

Hope Montessori West
48 Strecker Rd, Ellisville, MO 63011-1904
Serena Shelton-Dodge

Montessori Children's House (1981)
14000 Ladue Rd, Chesterfield, MO 63017
Anita Chastain
Tuition: $3,852-7,704/yr
6 teachers, 8 assistants, 91 students, ages infant-9
Affiliation: AMI
Governance by administrator
Classic Montessori; student-centered; self-paced; childcare; suburban location; interns accepted.

Chesterfield Day School (1963)
1100 White Rd, Chesterfield, MO 63021
Dr Barbara Fulton, Head, 314-469-6622, FAX: 314-469-7889
Type: Montessori, non-profit
22 teachers, 5 assistants, 274 students, ages infant-12
Affiliations: NAIS, AMS; accreditation: ISACS
Governance by board
Traditional approach in grades 2-3; accelerated, departmentalized program in grades 4-6; parental involvement; childcare; suburban location; interns accepted.

Progressive Results
(See Resource Section)

Practical Homeschooling
(See Resource Section)

Midwest Montessori School
13775 New Halls Ferry Rd #A, Florissant, MO 63033-3028

Children of Promise Christian Montessori (1984)
11339 St Charles Rock Rd, Bridgetown, MO 63043
314-878-1534
Tuition: $50-200/mo
2 teachers, 3 assistants, 36 students, mainly international, ages Infant-6
Affiliation: MMA; accreditation: AMI
Governance by administrator
German.

Washington Montessori School (1978)
53 Durham Dr, Washington, MO 63090
Nancy Schwartz, Owner/Adm, 314-239-5144
Non-profit
2 teachers, 2 assistants, 25 students, ages 3-6
Accreditation: AMS
Governance by administrator

Humbolt Visual & Performing Arts
2516 S 9th St, St Louis, MO 63104
James Strughold, 314-772-3164
Type: magnet
6-8th grade

A Growing Place Montessori School (1975)
6800 Wydown Blvd, St Louis, MO 63105
Laurie H. Kleen, Owner/Dir, 314-863-9493
Tuition: $200-300/mo
3 teachers, 2 assistants, 27 students, mainly international, ages 3-6
Affiliation: NAMTA; accreditations: MMA, SNMC
Governance by administrator
Enclosed courtyard; adjoining woods; ecological classroom; urban location.

Ames Visual & Performing Arts School
2900 Hadley, St Louis, MO 63107
David Bird, 314-241-7165
Type: magnet
Student ages 4+,-5th grade

Central Visual & Performing Arts
3616 N Garrison Ave, St Louis, MO 63107
Carl Landis, 314-371-1046
Type: magnet
9-12th grade

Marquette Visual & Performing Art
4015 McPherson Ave, St Louis, MO 63108
Alice Roach, 314-531-6233
Type: magnet
6-8th grade

Enright Classical Junior Academy
5351 Enright Ave, St Louis, MO 63112
Mary Beth Purdy, 314-367-0555
Type: magnet
6-8th grade
Gifted education.

Nursery Foundation of St Louis
1916 N Euclid Ave, Saint Louis, MO 63113-1701
Type: Montessori

Euclid Montessori School
1131 N Euclid Ave, St Louis, MO 63113-2009
Bessy Mosley

Visitation Holy Ghost
4515 Evans Ave, Saint Louis, MO 63113-2390
Type: Montessori

Christy Park Academy Montessori
5800 Christy Blvd, Saint Louis, MO 63116-2211

A.B. Green Middle School (1992)
1313 Boland, Richmond Heights, MO 63117
Arline Kalishman, Prin, 314-644-4406
Type: public choice
19 teachers, 207 students, ages 11-16, 7-8th grade
Governance by teachers and principal
Teacher qualifications: state certification
Only US school to combine philosophy of Ted Sizer's CES and
   Henry Levin's Accelerated Schools Project; no D or F
   grades; 8 block schedule (4 85-min classes one day, 4
   others next day); suburban location; transportation;
   interns accepted.

Society for Utopian Studies
(See Resource Section)

Kirkwood High Alternative
801 W Essex, Kirkwood, MO 63122
Deborah Coco, Assoc Prin, 314-984-4407
Type: public at-risk
110 teachers, 1500 students, ages 14-19, HS
Governance by board
Teacher qualifications: MO Certification
Independent study; small groups; language arts; pre-
   vocational skills; special services; GED; teaming; sometimes
   no letter grades; multi-aged classes; suburban location;
   transportation; interns accepted.

Villa di Maria Montessori Center
1280 Simmons Ave, Saint Louis, MO 63122-1113

Kirkwood Children's House
11232 Big Bend Blvd, Saint Louis, MO 63122-5719
Type: Montessori

Home Schooling Network
47 Clermont Ln, St Louis, MO 63124

Montessori Learning Center
3612 Union Rd, Saint Louis, MO 63125-4315

South County Montessori School
12016 Tesson Ferry Rd, St Louis, MO 63128-1727

Casa Cia Montessori Teacher Training
610 Kinswood Ln, St Louis, MO 63129
Type: Montessori teacher education

Child of Nazareth Lutheran School (1975)
1401 N Hanley Rd, St Louis, MO 63130
Ruth Hummel, Dir, 314-863-0520

Type: Montessori; tuition: $300/350/mo
2 teachers, 3 assistants, 52 students, ages infant-6
Affiliation: Lutheran School System
Governance by administrator, board
Mainstreams deaf students in both classes; childcare; subur-
   ban location; interns accepted.

Montessori Institute for the Deaf (1990)
1417 Anna Ave, St Louis, MO 63130
Emilie McArthur, 314-863-0520
Non-profit; tuition: $208/340/430/mo
2 teachers, 1 assistant, 14 students, mainly at-risk, ages 3-9
Governance by administrator
Sign language and speech taught; childcare; transportation.

Des Peres Montessori School
11155 Clayton Rd, St Louis, MO 63131

Sherwood Montessori School
12292 Clayton Rd, St Louis, MO 63131

The Principia
13201 Clayton Rd, St. Louis, MO 63131
Type: independent

Academy of the Visitation Montessori School
3020 N Ballas Rd, Saint Louis, MO 63131-2316

Ferguson-Florissant Education Center (1972)
6038 Caroline, Berkeley, MO 63134
Jeffrey Spiegel, Adm, 314-522-0867
Type: public at-risk
25 teachers, 525 students, all ages, K-12th grade
Governance by teachers and principal
Teacher qualifications: MO certification
Aggression replacement training; drug ed; contracts; social,
   SE, psychological, support services; adult ed; ESL; multi-
   aged classes; parenting; childcare; senior citizens' center

L'Académie Montessori
9859 Halls Ferry Rd, Saint Louis, MO 63136-4048

Kennard Classical Junior Academy
5031 Potomac, St Louis, MO 63139
Frances Gooden, 314-353-8875
Type: magnet
Student ages 4+,-5th grade
Gifted education.

Shaw Visual & Performing Arts School
5329 Columbia, St Louis, MO 63139
Robert Lewis, 314-776-5091
Type: magnet
K-5th grade

Fern Ridge High School (1992)
13157 N Olive Spur Rd, Creve Coeur, MO 63141
Beth Plunkett, Prin, 542-0042, FAX: 542-0695
Type: public choice
9 teachers, 100 students, mainly at-risk, ages 15-19, 9–12th
   grade
Governance by principal
Teacher qualifications: MO certification

Countryside Montessori School (1964)
12226 Ladue Rd, St Louis, MO 63141
Rita Zimny, Dir, 314-434-2821
Tuition: $255-495/mo
2 teachers, 6 assistants, 90 students, ages 2.5-6
Affiliation: AMS
Governance by administrator
Art; French; spacious playground; vegetable garden; wooded
   valley for nature walks, study; two resident ponies; child-
   care; suburban location; interns accepted.

Hope Montessori Academy-Central
900 Mason Rd N, Creve Coeur, MO 63141-6308
Susan Shelton-Dodge

Saint Charles Montessori Academy
1250 Hawks Nest Dr, Saint Charles, MO 63303-3670

Eastern Jackson County Alternative High School (1988)
205 NW 16th St, Blue Springs, MO 64015
Dr Glenn A. Berry, Prin, 816-224-4388, FAX: 224-1374
Type: public at-risk
4 teachers, 120 students, ages 14-20, 9-12th grade
Governance by teachers, principal, board
Science weather station; garden; newspaper; yearbook;
  hands-on projects; multi-aged classes; suburban location;
  transportation; interns accepted.

Families for Home Education
4400 Woods Rd, Sibley, MO 64088

Woodland Elementary
711 Woodland, Kansas City, MO 64106
Marcella Clay, 816-871-7950
Type: magnet
K-5th grade
Classical Greek.

Phillips Elementary
1619 E 24th Terrace, Kansas City, MO 64108
Marilyn Cowthran, 816-871-1660
Type: magnet
K-5th grade
Visual and performing arts.

De La Salle Education Center (1971)
3740 Forest, Kansas City, MO 64109
Jim Dougherty, Exec Dir, 816-561-3312, FAX: -6106
Type: independent, non-profit
34 teachers, 530 students, mainly at-risk, ages 13-21, HS
Governance by board
Teacher qualifications: certification
Nationally recognized; comprehensive; individualized; voca-
  tional instruction; intensive counseling; no letter grades;
  interns accepted.

Discovery Montessori School
5603 Nieman Rd, Kansas City, MO 64109

Faxon Montessori School
1320 E 32nd Terrace, Kansas City, MO 64109
Frank Vincent, 816-871-6450
Type: magnet
Student ages 3+,-5th grade
Montessori.

Longfellow Elementary
2830 Holmes, Kansas City, MO 64109
Gayle Bradshaw, 816-871-7050
Type: magnet
K-5th grade
Visual and performing arts.

Notre Dame DeSion Grande
3823 Locust St, Kansas City, MO 64109-2697
Type: Montessori

KC Middle School of the Arts
4848 Woodland, Kansas City, MO 64110
Roger Williams, 816-871-0550
Type: magnet
6-8th grade

Paseo Academy
4747 Flora, Kansas City, MO 64110
Patti Bippus, 816-871-0500
Type: magnet
9-12th grade
Fine and performing arts.

Forest Jones & Company
3130 Broadway, Kansas City, MO 64111
G Jan Pacey
Type: Montessori

St Paul's Episcopal School
4005 Main St, Kansas City, MO 64111-2312
Type: Montessori

Global Montessori Academy (1984)
707 W 47th St, Kansas City, MO 64112
Ellen Hamilton, Exec Dir, 816-561-4533
Non-profit; tuition: $264-323/mo
4 teachers, 5 assistants, 62 students, ages infant-9
Accreditation: MIA
Governance by parent cooperative
Robert Muller's Global Peace Curriculum; Lessons in Living:
  values, character development, self-esteem; childcare;
  urban location; interns accepted.

The Belmont Schools
6900 Ward Pky, Kansas City, MO 64113-2018
Type: Montessori

Hartman Elementary
8111 Oak, Kansas City, MO 64114
Elinor Etterling, 816-871-4950
Type: Montessori magnet
K-1st grade

St Peter's Episcopal School
100 E Red Bridge Rd, Kansas City, MO 64114-5499
Type: Montessori

Kansas City Center Montessori Education
5026 N Brighton Ave, Kansas City, MO 64119
Type: Montessori teacher education

Civic Center Children's House
Holmes at 13th, Kansas City, MO 64120-1089
Type: Montessori

Gladstone Academy
335 N Elmwood, Kansas City, MO 64123
Diana Kolen, 816-871-6800
Type: magnet
K-5th grade
Visual and performing arts; science and math.

Northeast Middle School
4904 Independence Ave, Kansas City, MO 64124
Lloyd Seales, 816-871-6830
Type: magnet
6-8th grade
Global studies.

Oliver Montessori School
4206 E 9th St, Kansas City, MO 64124-2822

Paul Robeson Middle School
4610 E 24th St, Kansas City, MO 64127
Cleo Washington, 816-871-6950
Type: magnet
6-8th grade
Classical Greek.

Central High School
3211 Indiana, Kansas City, MO 64128
Emmerson Payne, 816-871-8900
Type: magnet
9-12th grade
Computers Unlimited; classical Greek.

Genesis School Inc (1975)
3831 E 43rd St, Kansas City, MO 64130
Mamie Isler, Dir, 816-921-0775, FAX: 921-6248
Type: public/independent at-risk
7 teachers, 85 students, mainly at-risk, ages 11-21, 6-11th
  grade
Governance by faculty and student reps, parent cooperative,
  board
Teacher qualifications: MO certification
Holistic approach; multi-ethnic curriculum; counseling; community outreach; multi-aged classes; urban location;
  interns accepted.

Harold Holliday Montessori School
5015 Garfield, Kansas City, MO 64130
Douglas Becker, 816-871-0200
Type: magnet
Student ages 3+,-2nd grade

Meservey Elementary
4210 E 45th St, Kansas City, MO 64130
Carole Ladd, 816-871-0240
Type: magnet
K-5th grade
Visual and performing arts.

Bishop Helmsing Early Childhood Center
1221 E Meyer Blvd, Kansas City, MO 64131
Type: Montessori

Satchel Paige Elementary
3301 E 75th St, Kansas City, MO 64132
Herman Gant, 816-871-5320
Type: magnet
K-5th grade
Classical Greek.

Little Red School House
10029 E 63rd Terr, Kansas City, MO 64133
Type: Montessori

Pitcher Elementary
9915 E 38th Tr, Kansas City, MO 64133
Deborah Kelly, 816-871-0400
Type: magnet
K-5th grade
Classical Greek.

Bright Beginnings, Inc. (1983)
9812 E 66 St, Raytown, MO 64133
Mary Catalano, Owner/Dir, 816-356-3514
Type: Montessori; tuition: $10/14/day
3 teachers, 7 assistants, 60 students, ages infant-6
Affiliation: AEYC-GKC & MO. Vol. Accreditation
Governance by administrator
Language, math, cultural arts, social studies, science, Spanish;
    childcare; interns accepted.

Small World Montessori
5301 Blue Ridge Blvd, Raytown, MO 64133-3062

The Children's Center
11327 Hickman Mills Dr, Kansas City, MO 64134-4206
Type: Montessori

Children's Center
325 E Gundell, Kansas City, MO 64141
Type: Montessori

Highlands Montessori School
8050 Mission Blvd, Kansas City, MO 64141

Avila Montessori School
11901 Wornall Rd, Kansas City, MO 64145
Carol Frevert, 816-942-8400 x2268
Tuition: $90-195/mo
2 teachers, 1 assistant, 45 students, ages 3-6
Affiliation: NAEYC; accreditation: MIA
Governance by teachers, administrators
Teacher qualifications: BS in Ed, Montessori certification
Computers; childcare; suburban location; interns accepted.

Academy Montessori Internationals
12501 State Line Rd, Kansas City, MO 64145-1149

L'Ecole Montessori
3 Woodbridge Ln, Kansas City, MO 64145-1325

Clay Platte Children's House
5901 NW Waukomis Dr, Kansas City, MO 64151
Larry Merriman, Owner/Adm, 816-741-6940
Type: Montessori; tuition: $165-340/mo

21 teachers, 5 assistants, 211 students, ages infant-12
Affiliation: MIA
Governance by administrator
10-acre campus; childcare; suburban location; interns
    accepted.

Montessori Institute of America
(See Resource Section)

Satellite Alternative School
2nd & School Sts, Joplin, MO 64801
417-625-5293
Type: public choice

Neosho Evening Alternative School (1987)
511 Neosho Blvd, Neosho, MO 64850
Robin D. Montz, Coord, 417-451-8662, FAX: -8694
Type: public at-risk
12 teachers, 36 students, ages 15-20, 9-12th grade
Governance by teachers and principal
Teacher qualifications: MO certification
Parenting education; self-esteem; vocational; multi-aged
    classes; variable credit; rural location.

Eldon Montessori Children's House
Rt Box 361, Eldon, MO 65026

Jefferson City Children's House
1212 East High, Jefferson City, MO 65101
Type: Montessori

Scholastic Book Clubs, Inc
(See Resource Section)

Children's House Montessori
524 Schumate Chapel Rd, Jefferson City, MO 65109-4915

Children's House of Columbia, Inc (1972)
915 Maryland Ave, Columbia, MO 65201
Mary-Angela Johnson, 314-443-2825, FAX: 442-4134
Type: Montessori, non-profit; tuition: $250-380/mo
4 teachers, 5 assistants; student ages 2-8
Affiliation: AMS; accreditation: NAEYC
Governance by board
Straightforward, assertive, non-violent conflict resolution;
    independent study; cooperative; urban location.

Missouri Association of Teaching Christian Homes
307 E Ash St #146, Columbia, MO 65201
314-443-8217

Golden Moment Montessori Center
300 Saint James St, Columbia, MO 65201-4952

Columbia Montessori School (1967)
3 Anderson Ave, Columbia, MO 65203
Rebecca Melton, Dir, 314-449-5418
Non-profit; tuition: $270-460/mo
4 teachers, 16 assistants, 101 students, mainly international,
    ages infant-9
Accreditations: MIA, MO DFS
Governance by administrator
Multi-cultural; inclusive; childcare; suburban location.

Phoenix International School for Peace
Box 336, Birch Tree, MO 65438
John Staniloiu, Dir, 314-292-3880
Type: independent, boarding
Student ages 8-16
320 acres; animals; rivers; caves; hands-on experiences.

Little Piney Schoolhouse
Rt 1, Box 20, Newburg, MO 65550
314-762-2036
Type: independent

Ozark Lore Society (LORE) (1990)
c/o Resource Center, Brixey, MO 65618
Debra Eisenmann, Founder/Organizer, 417-679-4773,-3391

Homeschooling support network founded on principles of bioregionalism; newsletter; bioregional programs.

East Wind Community
Rfd 682, Tecumseh, MO 65761
Type: independent
Affiliation: Federation of Egalitarian Communities

Bailey Education Center (1987)
501 W Central, Springfield, MO 65802
Dr Gloria Creed, Prin, 417-831-0979
Type: public at-risk

7 teachers, 100 students, ages 14-20, 9-12th grade
Governance by teachers and principal
Teacher qualifications: MO Certification
Interdisciplinary; thematic; teaming; cooperative learning; community service; nursery; multi-aged classes; urban location; interns accepted.

Children's House Montessori
1461 E Seminole, Springfield, MO 65804

Springfield Area Homeschoolers
1730 W Winchester Rd, Springfield, MO 65807-4487

Montana

Gardiner's Homeschoolers
PO Box 201, Gardiner, MT 59030
406-848-7226

Crazy Mountains Montessori
PO Box E, Harlowton, MT 59036-0905

Pan American Montessori
PO Box A, Corwin Springs, MT 59047
Mary Ellen Mautz

Billings Montessori School
2316 Rehberg Ln, Billings, MT 59102-2044
Nancy Jo McElroy

New Child Montessori School
1241 Crawford Dr, Billings, MT 59102-2442

Great Falls Montessori School
1521 1st Ave N, Great Falls, MT 59401-3206
Sally Heard

Little Flower Montessori
1625 Central Ave, Great Falls, MT 59401-3837

Shining Mountain Elementary
423 W Montana, Leviston, MT 59457

Helena Area Christian Home Educators
1263 Bighorn Rd, Helena, MT 59601
406-442-9510

Valley Montessori
1041 Leslie, Helena, MT 59601
Michele Webster, Dir, 406-449-3726
Tuition: $150/275
1 teacher, 2 assistants, 20 students, ages 3-6
Affiliation: AMI
Governance by administrator
Director is AMI trained; childcare; rural location.

Central Elementary
402 N Warren St, Helena, MT 59601-4047
Type: Montessori

Rocky Mountain Montessori Neighborhood Center
201 S Main St, Helena, MT 59601-4136

Bryant School
1529 Boulder Ave, Helena, MT 59624

Homeschoolers of Montana
PO Box 654, Helena, MT 59624-0654
406-443-5826

Butte Home Education Association
2950 Bayard, Butte, MT 59701
Melda Freeman, 406-494-7949

Silver Bow Montessori School
1416 W Gold St, Butte, MT 59701-2114

Headwaters
216 W Wallace Ave, Bozeman, MT 59715
TimTate, 406-586-8158

Headwaters Academy (1990)
418 W Garfield St, Box 7258, Bozeman, MT 59715
Jill King, Off Mgr, 406-585-9997
Type: independent, boarding, non-profit; tuition: $4,950/yr, scholarships
10 teachers, 40 students, ages 11-18, ungraded
Affiliation: PNAIS
Governance by board
Teacher qualifications: credential or advanced degree
Cooperative; integrated; community study; travel to Baja, Spain, Guatamala; multi-aged classes; rural location.

The Learning Circle Montessori
516 W Cleveland, Bozeman, MT 59715
Nancy Characklis, Dir, 406-587-2672
Tuition: $250-310/mo
7 teachers, 50 students, ages 3-8
Affiliations: AMS, ECEA
Governance by administrator
No letter grades; multi-aged classes; urban location; interns accepted.

Learning Circle
516 W Cleveland St, Bozeman, MT 59715-5122
Type: Montessori

Great Beginnings Montessori (1986)
PO Box 1794, Bozeman, MT 59771
Phyllis White, Adm, 406-587-0132
Non-profit; tuition: $200/360/mo
3 teachers, 1 assistant, 35 students, ages 3-6
Affiliations: AMS, AMI, NAEYC
Governance by board of directors elected by current parent-owners
Childcare; suburban location; interns accepted.

Sussex School
1800 S 2nd West, Missoula, MT 59801
Beth Loehnen, 406-721-1696
Type: independent
66 students, K-8th grade

Swann Beckwith Montessori
715 E Beckwith Ave, Missoula, MT 59801-4420

Clark Fork School (1983)
432 E Pine, Missoula, MT 59802
Ann Ford, Administrator, 406-728-3395
Type: independent, non-profit; tuition: $1,000-4,000/yr, scholarships

8 teachers, 2 assistants, 44 students, ages 3-10, pre K-3rd grade
Governance by parent cooperative
Teacher qualifications: creativity and respect for students; formal requirements
Themes; environmental emphasis; no letter grades; non-compulsory class attendance; multi-aged classes; extensive field trips; urban location; interns accepted.

Avalon School (1989)
Box 5676, Missoula, MT 59806
Dr. Louise Bell, Administrator, 406-543-1976
Type: independent, non-profit; tuition: $125-220/mo, scholarships
3 teachers, 17 students, ages 3-10, pre K-6th grade
Governance by board
Teacher qualifications: teacher certification
Process approach to writing; literature-based reading; computer programs; hands-on approach to science; no letter grades; multi-aged classes; extensive field trips; urban location.

Missoula Homeschoolers Association
PO Box 3228, Missoula, MT 59806
Pascal & Mona Redfern, 406-273-2430
Other contacts: Lyle & Debbie Kline, 406-721-1714; Kevin Rognstad, 406-542-1222.

Primrose Montessori
600 S Ave E/PO Box 3354, Missoula, MT 59806
Nancy Deskins

Shining Mountain School (1989)
Box 4402, Missoula, MT 59806
406-721-6303
Type: independent, non-profit

Mission Mountain School
Guest Ranch Rd, Condon, MT 59862

Homeschool Information
PO Box 960, Seeley Lake, MT 59868

The Grapevine (Montana Homeschool News)
(See Resource Section)

Kalispell Montessori School (1977)
5 Park Hill Rd, Kalispell, MT 59901
Sally Black Welder, Adm, 406-755-3824
Non-profit; tuition: $150-240/mo
8 teachers, 10 assistants, 130 students, ages 3-12
Affiliation: AMS
Governance by administrator, teachers, board
Strong bond with community; childcare; interns accepted.

Garden
985 N Meridan Rd, Kalispel, MT 59903

Sugar N Spice
255 Summit Ridge Dr, Kalispel, MT 59903

Flathead Homeschool Association
360 One Way, Columbia Falls, MT 59912
406-892-4052

Nebraska

Cony High Alternative Program for Students (CHAPS) (1986)
104 Cony St, Augusta, NE 04330
Nancy Ruark, 402-626-2460
Type: public choice
4 teachers, 45 students, mainly at-risk, ages 14-19, HS
Governance by principal
Teacher qualifications: ME Certification
Employment for credit; point reward system; opportunities to explore areas of special interest; work portfolios; urban location.

Nebraska Home School Contact
1208 Robin Dr, Bellevue, NE 68005
Doug and Cindy Nurss, 402-292-0962

Alternative Learning Center (1974)
957 N Pierce, Fremont, NE 68025
Cindy Diers, Head Tch, 402-727-3180
Type: public choice/at-risk
4 teachers, 50 students, mainly at-risk, ages 13-21, 7-12th grade
Governance by teachers and principal
Graduation or exit to home school; contracts; voc, social skills; multi-aged classes; rural location; transportation.

Nebraska Home School Contact
Rt 1 Box 7, Herman, NE 68029
Nancy Boswell, 402-456-7692,-7733

Montessori Children's Room
5405 Franklin St, Omaha, NE 68104
Mary Boden

Child's World
7101 Mercy Rd, Omaha, NE 68106-2619
Type: Montessori

Druid Hill Math & Computer Center
3030 Spaulding St, Omaha, NE 68111
Elmer Crumbley, 402-554-6084
Type: magnet
4-6th grade
Communications; arts.

Westside Alternative School
1414 Robertson Dr, Omaha, NE 68114
Suzann Morin, Dir, 402-390-8214
Type: public choice
100 students, mainly at-risk, 10-12th grade
Individualized; social skills; vocational.

Montessori School of Omaha
PO Box 24211, Omaha, NE 68124

Father Flanagan High School (1983)
2606 Hamilton, Omaha, NE 68131
Dave Patten, 402-494-3038
Type: independent
27 teachers, 300 students, mainly at-risk, ages 14-21, 8-12th grade
Affiliation: Boys Town
Governance by principal
Teacher qualifications: NE Certification
Success-oriented; social services; self-paced; voc, group, individual counseling; religion; sports; plays; yearbook; newspaper; social skills; multi-aged classes; childcare.

Omaha Magnet Center
3230 Burt St, Omaha, NE 68131
402-554-6738

Montessori Parent's Co-Op for Children
3869 Webster St, Omaha, NE 68131-1809

House of Montessori
400 S 39th St, Omaha, NE 68131-3711

Montessori Academy for Children (1983)
7828 MapleSt, Omaha, NE 68134
Peggy A. Klausen, Dir, 402-393-2035
Tuition: $303/mo
2 teachers, 1 assistant, 22 students, mainly international,
ages 3-6
Affiliations: AMS, NAEYC
Governance by administrator
Fully equipped Montessori environment fosters individual ini-
tiative and growth; suburban location.

Sandor Elementary
5959 Oak Hills Dr, Omaha, NE 68137-3319
Type: Montessori

Montclair Elementary School
2405 S 138th St, Omaha, NE 68144-2498
Barbara Junes
Type: Montessori

OPEN
7930 Raven Oaks Dr, Omaha, NE 68152
402-572-8515
Type: home-based

Great Plains Montessori
12610 Pacific, Omaha, NE 68154

Millard Public Schools
1010 S 144th St, Omaha, NE 68154
Dr Tom Nenneman
Type: Montessori

Montessori Educational Centers
12504 Pacific St, Omaha, NE 68154-3599
Lavonne Plambeck

Nebraska Home School Contact
Rt 1 Box 115, Firth, NE 68358
Bonnie Paschold, 402-791-5717

Nebraska Home School Contact
RR 1, Johson, NE 68378
Nancy Baltensperger, 402-868-6765

Nebraska Home School Contact
Rt 2 Box 129A, Milford, NE 68405
Arlyn and Cindy Hanseling, 402-761-2225

Nebraska Home School Contact
Rt 3 Box 222, Nebraska City, NE 68410
Mike and Garcia Binder, 402-873-4627

Prairie Hill Learning Center
RR 1 Box 17, Roca, NE 68430-9708
Type: Montessori

Howard Dougherty Learning Center at Epworth Village
21st & Divion Ave, York, NE 68467
George Young, 402-362-3353
Type: independent
Students mainly at-risk, K-12th grade
Holistic treatment; work experience; small groups;
individualized.

The Villare Pre-School
1328 Plum St, Lincoln, NE 68502-2342
Type: Montessori

LEARN
7741 E Avon Ln, Lincoln, NE 68505
402-488-7741
Type: home-based

Nebraska Christian Home Educators Association
Box 57041, Lincoln, NE 68505

Children's Circle Montessori
121 Skyway Rd, Lincoln, NE 68505-2627

Montessori School for Young Children (1977)
4727 A St, Lincoln, NE 68506
Debbie Nugara, Suzanne Wolford or Chris Dregalla, 402-489-
4366
Non-profit; tuition: $170-185/wk
2 teachers, 4 assistants; students mainly international, ages
infant-6
Affiliations: AMS, AMI
Governance by teachers, administrators, parent cooperative;
urban location; interns accepted.

Nebraska Independent Homeschoolers Network
8010 Lillibridge St, Lincoln, NE 68506

Nebraska Home School Contact
2610 Winchester S, Lincoln, NE 68512
Kathleen Lenzen, 402-423-4297

Lincoln Independent Study High School
University of Nebraska (1929)
269 NCCE, Lincoln, NE 68583-9800
James E. Schiefelbein, EdD, Prin, 402-472-1926, FAX: 404-472-
1901
Type: independent, non-profit; tuition: $81/course
12 teachers, 4,000 students, ages 13-19, HS
Accreditation: NCACS; NE
Governance by principal
Teacher qualifications: NE Certification
Complete college prep; urban location

Nebraska Home School Contact
1601 Clark St, Norfolk, NE 68701
Walt and Kathy Steinke, 402-371-8089

Nebraska Home School Contact
PO Box 576, Dakota, NE 68731
Ed Reising, 402-987-3827

The Children's Place
504 W 10th St, Grand Island, NE 68801-4045
Type: Montessori

Nebraska Home School Contact
Rt 3 Box 238, Kearney, NE 68847
Bill and Robin Phipps, 308-237-3783

Nebraska Home School Contact
Rt 1 Box 116, Merna, NE 68856
Martin and Karen Bredthauer, 308-643-2591

Nebraska Home School Contact
Rt 3 Box 73, Ord, NE 68862
Duane and Kathy Lange, 308-728-3217

Nebraska Home School Contact
1323 7th Ave, Holdrege, NE 68949
Linda Rodenbaugh, 308-995-2485

Nebraska Home School Contact
212 Water Ave, Holdrege, NE 68949
Lee and Carol Sanders, 308-995-6933

Nebraska Home School Contact
RR1 Box 23, Oxford, NE 68967
Robert and Martha Bergquist, 308-824-3452

Nebraska Home School Contact
R1 Box 159, Indianola, NE 69034
Jim and Marilyn Gaster, 308-364-2528

Nebraska Home School Contact
1404 Burlington, North Platte, NE 69101
Walt and Jolene Catlett, 308-728-3217

Haskell Hill Montessori
1600 Ash St, Sidney, NE 69162-1122
Wendy Lou Jacons

Nebraska Home School Contact
Rt 2 Box 210, Miniature, NE 69359
Rod and Lori McCoy, 308-783-2208

Nevada

Clark County Program
1941 Jefferson St, N Las Vegas, NV 89030
Bill Rohnkohl
Type: public

Montessori Academy of Southern Nevada
6000 W Oakey Blvd, Las Vegas, NV 89102-1253
Connie Mormon

Clark Cty
2201 E St. Louis Ave, Las Vegas, NV 89104
Steve Mudery
Type: public choice

Christian Home Educators of Nevada
1576 Del Almo Dr, Las Vegas, NV 89104-5009
Joleen Hatfield

Our Lady of Las Vegas Montessori School
3036 Alta Dr, Las Vegas, NV 89107-3202

Home Education and Righteous Training
Box 42264, Las Vegas, NV 89116-0264
702-593-4927

Home Schools United/Vegas Valley
PO Box 93564, Las Vegas, NV 89121
702-870-9566

Trinity Montessori School
PO Box 2246, Reno, NV 89505-2246

Cambridge School
1330 Foster Dr #A, Reno, NV 89509-1200
Type: Montessori

Nevada Home Schools, Inc
PO Box 21323, Reno, NV 89515
702-972-4126

New Hampshire

New Hampshire Home Education Association
9 Mizoras Dr, Nashua, NH

Souhegan High School
Boston Post Rd, Amherst, NH 03031
Dr Robert McKin, Prin, 603-673-9940
Type: public; tuition: $7,200/yr
60 teachers, 675 students, ages 14-18, HS
Affiliation: CES
Governance by school-based community council, board,
    faculty and student reps
Teacher qualifications: NH Certification
Interdisciplinary; team structures; outcomes-based; exit exhi-
    bitions, portfolios; inclusive; rural location; interns
    accepted.

Derry Montessori School (1982)
65 E Broadway, Derry, NH 03038
Donna J. Ouellette, Adm, 603-432-8345
Tuition: $2,200-2,700/yr
5 teachers, 2 assistants, 50 students, ages 3-6
Affiliation: AMS
Governance by administrator, board
Music; computer programs; summer program includes arts,
    swim instruction, science; childcare; interns accepted.

New England Montessori Teacher Education Center
    (1977)
30 Moose Club Rd, Goffstown, NH 03045
Bonne LaMothe, 603-641-5156, FAX:-1339
Type: Montessori higher education
Affiliation: AMS; accreditation: MALTE

Wild Quest! Wilderness Adventures
1372 Valley Rd, Mason, NH 03048
Chris Balch, Dir, 603-878-2175
Type: independent

Clearway Alternative High School (1977)
40 Arlington St, Nashua, NH 03060
Keith Howard, Prin, 603-598-8303, FAX: 603-882-0069
Type: independent, non-profit; tuition: $7,558/yr
8 teachers, 60 students, mainly at-risk, ages 15-19
Governance by principal, teachers

Teacher qualifications: Learning disabilities, emotional handi-
    caps, subject certification
Improvisational theater; 160+ performances nationwide; no
    letter grades; non-compulsory class attendance; multi-
    aged classes; interns accepted.

Materials Company of Boston
(See Resource Section)

New England Montessori Children's Center
223 Main St, Salem, NH 03079

Geocommons College (1991)
RR 2 Box 793 Derbyshire Farm, Temple, NH 03084
Bruce Kantner, Dir, 603-654-6705
Boarding, non-profit; tuition: variable, scholarships
4 teachers, 5-15 students
Affiliations: UNH, Gaia Educational Outreach Institute
Governance by consensus
Teacher qualifications: background, skills, goals in harmony
    with program
Sustainable community; ecological literacy; bioregional, world
    studies; compassionate, mindful living; visits exemplary
    communities in USA, Europe, India; partial UNH credit;
    interns accepted.

High Mowing School (1942)
PO Box 850, Abbot Hill Rd, Wilton, NH 03086
Virginia R. Buhr, Adms Dir, 603-654-2391
Type: Waldorf, boarding, non-profit; tuition: $9,950-10,500
    day, $16,250-18,000 boarding/yr, scholarships
20 teachers, 85 students, ages 13-19, 9-12th grade
Affiliations: NEASC, NAIS, ISANNE, AWSNA, SATB
Governance by faculty
Teacher qualifications: BA, Waldorf interest/training, love
    teenagers
College prep; extensive arts; social responsibility; interna-
    tional community; multi-aged classes; rural location;
    interns accepted.

Pine Hill Waldorf School (1972)
PO Box 668, Abbot Hill Rd, Wilton, NH 03086
Catherine Weld, Adm, 603-654-6003, FAX: 603-654-2662
Non-profit; tuition: $5,000/yr, scholarships

215 students, ages 4.5–14, K-8th grade
Affiliation: NAWS
Governance by teachers, principal, board
Teacher qualifications: Waldorf certification
Extensive field trips; rural location; interns accepted.

New Hampshire Alliance for Home Education
16 Winter Circle #RFD3, Manchester, NH 03103-1008

Christian Home Educators of New Hampshire
PO Box 961, Manchester, NH 03105
603-647-1463

Bedford Montessori School (1984)
24 Tirrell Hill Rd, Bedford, NH 03110-5208
Gail R. Bannon, Adm, 603-627-9545
Tuition: $2,200/yr
5 teachers, 4 assistants, 65 students, ages 3–6
Affiliations: AMS, NAMTA, NAEYC
Governance by administrator
Foreign language; private and group music lessons; gymnastics; interns accepted.

Montessori Learning Center (1977)
389 Pembroke St, Pembroke, NH 03275
Myrta Bergevin, Adm, 603-485-8550
Non-profit; tuition: $4,100-4,200/yr
3 teachers, 3 assistants, 59 students, ages 3–12
Governance by democratic school meeting, board
Childcare; rural location; interns accepted.

Second Start (1979)
19 Knight St, Concord, NH 03301
Jim Snodgrass, Caroline Durr, 603-225-3318
Type: public at-risk
4 teachers, 40 students, ages 14–19, 8–12th grade
Governance by principal, board
Some students identified as having learning or emotional handicaps; structured, highly individualized program; no letter grades; multi-aged classes; also located at 450 N State St.; interns accepted.

New Hampshire Homeschooling Coalition
PO Box 2224, Concord, NH 03302
Abbey Lawrence, Coord, 603-539-7233
$15/yr membership fee; bi-monthly newsletter; guidebook.

Monadnock Waldorf School (1976)
98 S Lincoln St, Keene, NH 03431
Hanneke Van Riel, Admission Dir, 603-357-4442, FAX: -2955
Non-profit; tuition: $2,500-4,850/yr, scholarships
20 teachers, 150 students, ages 3.5–14, pre K-8th grade
Affiliation: AWSNA
Governance by college of teachers and board
Teacher qualifications: Waldorf training, experience
Largest independent ES in region; 2 sites; student experiences self as musician, painter, craftsperson, scholar, actor, writer, citizen; urban & rural location; interns accepted.

Montessori Schoolhouse of Cheshire County
259 Summit Rd, Keene, NH 03431-1581

Keene Montessori School
91 West St, Keene, NH 03431-3374
Diane Lucas Plotczyk

Antioch New England Graduate School (1964)
40 Avon St, Keene, NH 03431-3516
Torin Finser, Dir, Waldorf; David Sobel, Heidi Watts, Ed Dept, 603-357-3122, FAX: -0718
Type: Waldorf higher education; tuition: Waldorf cert $7,725 masters $12,300, scholarships
Governance by board
Fully accredited MA, MEd, MHSA, MS programs; integrated day, science and env ed, counseling psychology, dance, administration; Waldorf Program limited to 20 new students/yr; the arts and internship are essential parts of program; no letter grades.

The Well School
360 Middle Hancock Rd, Peterboro, NH 03458
Jay Garland, 603-924-6908
Type: independent

Cobblestone Publishing
(See Resource Section)

The Meeting School (1957)
Thomas Rd, Rindge, NH 03461-9781
Ed Miller, Admissions Director, 603-899-3366
Type: independent, boarding, non-profit; tuition: $15,000, scholarships
12 teachers, 27 students, ages 13–19, 9–12th grade
Affiliations: NCACS, ISEANNE
Governance by faculty consensus for some decisions; whole community or board for some
Student/faculty co-op households; 4-hr work study: farm, childcare, office; 4-week intersession project/travel; apprenticeships, peace studies; student-run radio station; no letter grades; multi-aged classes; extensive field trips; rural location; interns accepted.

Montessori Childcare Center
58 South St, Littleton, NH 03561-1818

The Children's House
30 Bronson St, Littleton, NH 03561-1826
Type: Montessori

Claremont Kindergarten Center
10 Vine St, Claremont, NH 03743
Peg Lyon
Type: Montessori

Dartmouth College Area Montessori School
10 Barrett Rd, Hanover, NH 03755-2421
Moira Ripley

Boynton School (1964)
RR 1, Box 31B, Orford, NH 03777
Arthur Boynton Jr, Director, 603-353-4874
Type: independent, boarding; tuition: $5,000
2 teachers; 7–12+
Governance by cooperative
Individualized help with languages, music, athletics; multi-aged classes; no letter grades; rural location; interns accepted.

Heinemann Educational Books
(See Resource Section)

Lancaster Children's House
RFD 1 Box 156, Conway, NH 03818
Type: Montessori

Green Fields Montessori School
PO Box 259, Dover, NH 03820-0259

Montessori School of Exeter (1979)
2 Newfields Rd, Exeter, NH 03833
603-772-5558
Tuition: $3,500-4,600/yr
78 students, ages infant-9
Affiliations: AMI, AMS
Governance by administrator

Montessori School for the Arts and Sciences
13 School St, Exeter, NH 03833-3207

Rockingham County Montessori School, Inc (1983)
144 East Rd, Hampstead, NH 03841-2230
Sara A. Covell, Owner/Adm, 603-329-8041
Tuition: $1,250/1,975/4,100/yr
3 teachers, 4 assistants, 77 students, ages infant-9
Affiliations: AMS, NHDE
Governance by administrator
Drama; arts; childcare; suburban location; interns accepted.

Support Alternative Family Education (SAFE) (1992)
PO Box 15, Plaistow, NH 03865
Sandra Maida, 603-382-3839
Non-profit
Non-sectarian; monthly meetings; weekly gatherings for children.

The Children's House Montessori School (1988)
80 Sagamore Rd, Rye, NH 03870-2025
Rebecca Varner, 603-436-5074
Tuition: $2,314-4,819/yr
3 teachers, 4 assistants, 80 students, ages infant-6
Affiliations: NAMTA, NAEYC
Governance by administrator
French; music; childcare; suburban location; interns accepted.

Community School (1989)
Perkins Farm Rd Box B, S Tamworth, NH 03883
Martha Carlson, Dir, 603-323-7000
Type: independent, non-profit; tuition: $4,300/yr, scholarships
4 teachers, 7 assistants, 28 students, ages 12-18, 6-12th grade

Governance by democratic school meeting, board, faculty and student representatives
Non-competitive atmosphere; traditional academics; community service; hands-on problem solving; environmental education; no letter grades; multi-aged classes; extensive field trips; rural location; interns accepted.

The Cornerstone School (1985)
146 High St, Stratham, NH 03885
Margaret Rice, Adm, 603-772-4349
Type: Montessori, non-profit
14 teachers, 125 students, ages 3-15
Affiliation: AMS
Governance by administrator, board
In pilot program by MAS for NAIS; childcare; rural location; interns accepted.

The Book Cellar
(See Resource Section)

Children's House/Children's World Magazines
(See Resource Section)

New Jersey

Children's House
437 Pompton Ave, Cedar Grove, NJ 07009-1802
Type: Montessori

Small World Montessori School
777 Anderson Ave, Cliffside Park, NJ 07010-2121

Rainbow Montessori School
43 Clifton Ave, Clifton, NJ 07011

Project Rebound at Clifton High School
333 Colfax Ave, Clifton, NJ 07013
Bill Cannici, Vice Prin, 201-470-2455
5 teachers, 21 students, mainly at-risk
Volunteer staff, students.

Montessori School of Cranford
110 Eastman St, Cranford, NJ 07016-2122

Apple Montessori
8 Adelaide Pl, Edgewater, NJ 07020
R. Bailey

Fort Lee Preschool
449 Anderson Ave, Fort Lee, NJ 07024
Type: Montessori

Early Education Centre
326 Guntzer St, Fort Lee, NJ 07024-4709
Type: Montessori

St Anthony Montessori School
672 Passaic Ave, Kearny, NJ 07032
Sr Bernadette

Project ASPIRE (1989)
Monmouth Court Community Center, Livingston, NJ 07039
Rosemary McGuinness, Dir, 201-535-8179
Type: public choice
5 teachers, 40 students, 10-12th grade
Tutorial; cooperative; small groups; flexible schedule; contracts; CAI; interdisciplinary; independent study; team teaching; field trips.

Montessori School of Millburn
19 Main St, Millburn, NJ 07041-1301

Edgemont Elementary
20 Edgemont Rd, Montclair, NJ 07042
Adunni Anderson, 201-509-4162
Type: magnet
Student ages 4+,-5th grade
Montessori.

Glenfield Middle School
25 Maple Ave, Montclair, NJ 07042
David Gidich, 201-509-4171
Type: magnet
6-8th grade
Gifted and talented; performing arts.

Montclair Cooperative School
65 Chestnut St, Montclair, NJ 07042
Lauretta Freeman
Type: independent

Montclair High School Alternative Programs
Rand Bldg, 176 N Fullerton Ave, Montclair, NJ 07042
Frank Rennie, Prin, 201-783-8957
35 students, mainly at-risk
Separate facility on campus; community service; guidance; work study.

Nishuane Primary
32 Cedar Ave, Montclair, NJ 07042
Frank Alvarez, 201-509-4222
Type: magnet
Student ages 4+,-2nd grade
Gifted and talented.

Maria Montessori Early Learning
90 Christopher St, Montclair, NJ 07042-4228

George Innes Annex
141 Park St, Montclair, NJ 07043
Roger Scales, 201-509-4004
Type: magnet
9-12th grade
Performing arts.

Montclair High School
1000 Chestnut St, Montclair, NJ 07043
Roger Scales, 201-509-4100

Type: magnet
9-12th grade
Performing arts.

Montessori Pre-School
43 Watchung Ave, Montclair, NJ 07043-1337

The Children's House, Inc
26 Montrose Ave, Verona, NJ 07044-1813
Type: Montessori

Mustard Seed Montessori
PO Box 261, Montville, NJ 07045-0261

St Elizabeth's Montessori
499 Park Rd, Parsippany, NJ 07054-1736
Sr Anna Maria

Children's Place
PO Box 1272, Plainfield, NJ 07061-1272
Type: Montessori

Rutherford Alternative Program
56 Passaic Ave, Rutherford, NJ 07070
Marilyn Gillio, Dir, 201-933-2671
10 students, mainly at-risk, 7-8th grade
Community experiences; individualized; interest-based.

Phoenix School
144 Boiling Springs, East Rutherford, NJ 07073
Melinda Miller
Type: Montessori

The Christopher Academy (1986)
1390 Terrill Rd, Scotch Plains, NJ 07076
Amelia McTamaney, Evelyn Hagman, 908-322-4652, FAX: 908-322-4616
Type: Montessori, non-profit; tuition: $1,430-5,940/yr
100 students, ages infant-6
Affiliations: AMS, NJAC, NAEYC
Governance by administrator and board of trustees
On-site teacher training program associated with SNMC; workshop site for SNMC correspondence students; summer camp with swimming; childcare; suburban location; interns accepted.

L'Academy Montessori
1171 Terrill Rd, Scotch Plains, NJ 07076-2227

South Orange Country Day School
461 Vose Ave, South Orange, NJ 07079-3018
Type: Montessori

Children's Academy of Springfield (1977)
37 Church Mall, Springfield, NJ 07081
Susan Weller, Dir/Owner, 201-379-3524
Type: Montessori; tuition: $2,350-5,600/yr
6 teachers, 1 assistant, 120 students, ages toddler-6
Governance by administrator
Computer; French; dance; piano; storytelling and book signings by well-known children's authors; suburban location.

Union City Student Awareness of Substance Abuse Program
3912 Bergen Tpk, Union City, NJ 07087
Tom Kelly, Dir, 201-392-3642
K-12th grade
City-wide programs; Here's Looking at You-2000; peer groups;counseling; linked with Project Fresh and UCPD Dare Program.

The Christopher Academy (1963)
510 Hillcrest Ave, Westfield, NJ 07090
Amelia McTamaney or Cathy Maravetz, Dir, 908-233-7414, FAX: 908-322-4616
Type: Montessori
4 teachers, 6 assistants, 100 students, ages infant-6
Affiliations: AMS, NJMAC; accreditations: SNMC, NAEEC

Governance by administrator
Teacher training program associated with SNMC; workshop site for SNMC correspondence students; summer program; childcare; suburban location; interns accepted.

Arts High School
550 Dr Martin L. King Blvd, Newark, NJ 07102
Eleta J. Caldwell, Prin, 201-733-6757
Type: public choice
500 students, 9-12th grade

University High School
55 Clinton Pl, Newark, NJ 07108
Doris Culver, 201-374-3190
Type: magnet
9-12th grade
Humanities.

Frank H. Morrell
1253 Clinton Ave, Irvington, NJ 07111
Anthony Pilone, 201-399-6893
Type: magnet
9-12th grade
Musically and artistically talented.

Madison Ave School
163 Madison Ave, Irvington, NJ 07111
Franklin Saunders, 201-399-6871
Type: magnet
K-6th grade
Gifted.

Mt Vernon Ave School
36 Mt Wernon Ave, Irvington, NJ 07111
Priscella Butts, 201-399-6875
Type: magnet
K-8th grade
Gifted.

Union Ave School
427 Union Ave, Irvington, NJ 07111
Walter Rusak, 201-399-6885
Type: magnet
K-8th grade
Musically and artistically talented.

Mont-Vail Day Care Center
871 Sanford Ave, Irvington, NJ 07111-1511
Type: Montessori

Apple Montessori
104 Boonton Ave, Kennelong, NJ 07405

Kinnelon Montessori School
Maple Ln, Kinnelon, NJ 07405

Pride Alternative School at Fairlawn High School
Berdan Ave, Fair Lawn, NJ 07410
Peter J. Natale, Dir, 794-5457
15-45 students, mainly at-risk
Off-campus facility.

Young World Day School (1972)
585 Wyckoff Ave, Mahwah, NJ 07430
Janet D. Jaarsma, 201-327-3888
Type: Montessori, non-profit; tuition: $810-6,000/yr
17 teachers, 7 assistants, 230 students, ages infant-12
Affiliations: AMS, NCCAA; accreditation: NAEYC
Governance by administrator
Ungraded classrooms; max 2:18 ratio/class; traditional Montessori preschool, K; childcare; suburban location; transportation; interns accepted.

Friends' Neighborhood School (1953)
224 Highwood Ave, Ridgewood, NJ 07450
Penny Dalto, Dir, 201-445-0681
Type: public/independent choice; scholarships
6 teachers, 55-63 students, partly at-risk, ages 2.5-5, pre-K

Governance by board
Teacher qualifications: BA in early childhood
Developmentally-appropriate; conflict resolution; problem solving; no letter grades; suburban location; interns accepted.

Montessori Learning Center
169 Fairmont Rd, Ridgewood, NJ 07450
Patricia Janson

Ridgewood Friends Neighborhood Nursery
224 Highwood, Ridgewood, NJ 07450
Penny Dalto
Type: Quaker

Ridgwood Montessori School (1989)
52 Passaic St, Ridgewood, NJ 07450
Evelyn Moshier, Dir, 201-447-5989
Tuition: $175-575/mo
3 teachers, 3 assistants, 52 students, ages infant-6
Affiliation: AMS
Governance by administrator
Computer ed; drama; art; childcare; suburban location; transportation; interns accepted.

The Village School for Children (1977)
660 E Glen Ave, Ridgewood, NJ 07450
Marilyn Larkin, 201-445-6160
Type: Montessori, non-profit; tuition: $3,024-7,100/yr
10 teachers, 7 assistants, 138 students, ages infant-9
Affiliation: AMS
Governance by board of trustees
Childcare; suburban location; interns accepted.

Lakeland Regional High School Alternative Program
205 Conklintown Rd, Wanaque, NJ 07465
Ann Badia, Dir, 201-835-1900
20-30 students, mainly emotionally disturbed, 7-12th grade
Departmentalized curriculum; counseling; work study; behavior modification system; computers.

Apple Montessori
Church Ln, Wayne, NJ 07470

Rainbow Montessori Schools
970 Black Oak Ridge Rd, Wayne, NJ 07470
Cheryl Trutt

New World Montessori School
165 Burton Ave, Hasbrouck Heights, NJ 07604-1923
Susan Fleming

Maywood Montessori Learning Center (1981)
39 E Pleasant Ave, Maywood, NJ 07607
Barbara Pilipie, Dir, 201-843-4466
Tuition: $2,600-4,000/yr
4 teachers, 3 assistants, 75 students, mainly international, ages 3-6
Affiliations: AMS, NCCA, NAMTA,NEA, NJMAC, NJAEYC, NJCCA
Governance by administrator
Inclusive; flexibility for working parents; computer program; convenient location; childcare; rural location; interns accepted.

Center for Design Studies
154 St Nicholas Ave, Englewood, NJ 07631
Michael J Shannon, Dir, 201-568-5528, FAX: 201-568-9341
Non-profit
Interdisciplinary; hands-on; project and community-based.

Institute of General Semantics
(See Resource Section)

Bede School
255 Walnut, Englewood, NJ 07631-3104
D Lilly
Type: Montessori

The Spring School (1970)
276 Haworth Ave, Haworth, NJ 07641
Dr Deborah Knapp, Dir, 201-384-2444, FAX: -0590
Type: Montessori, non-profit; tuition: $1,800-5,700/yr
4 teachers, 4 assistants, 47-92 students, ages infant-12
Affiliation: AMS; accreditations: AMS, NJ
Governance by administrator, board of trustees
History of science curriculum includes experiments; whole language; phonics; suburban location; interns accepted.

North Jersey Home Schoolers Association (1987)
c/o 44 Oak St, Hillsdale, NJ 07642
Christa Grajcar, New Member Coord, 666-6025
Non-profit
Student ages 4-18, pre K-12th grade
Christian; classes; special events; newsletter; bi-annual kids' newsletter; all faiths, backgrounds supported.

Creative Learning, Inc
465 Westminister Pl, Lodi, NJ 07644
Donna Jemas
Type: Montessori

Paramus Community School Transitional Class
145 Spring Valley Rd, Paramus, NJ 07652
Richard Piazza, Dir, 201-261-7800
18 students, mainly at-risk, 9-12th grade

Montessori Learning Center (1974)
65 Pascack Rd, Park Ridge, NJ 07656
Helen M. O'Brien, Adm, 201-573-0898
Tuition: $1,750-$6,000/yr
4 teachers, 2 assistants, 41 students, ages infant-6
Affiliations: AMS, NJMAC, MI
Governance by administrator
Teacher qualifications: average 13 yrs Montessori experience
Music; PE; computers; suburban location; interns accepted.

Teaneck High School Alternative II
100 Elizabeth Ave, Teaneck, NJ 07666
Carl Emerick, Head Teacher, 201-833-5440,-5436
3 teachers, 1 assistant, 50-70 students, mainly at-risk, 9-12th grade

Early Learning Center
1234 Teaneck Rd, Teaneck, NJ 07666-4929
Type: Montessori

Chrismont Academy (1986)
701 D St, Belmar, NJ 07719
Patricia Fosdick, Dir, 908-681-2572
Type: Montessori; tuition: $2,000/yr
1 teacher, 1 assistant, 40 students, ages 3-6
Affiliations: NAMTA, NJMAC
Governance by administrator
French; dance/movement; suburban location.

Wall Township Educational Improvement Program
PO Box 1199, Wall, NJ 07719
Raymond Steelman, Dir, 201-449-3070, 681-9772
20 students, mainly at-risk, 9-12th grade
Individualized; Lifeskills curriculum.

New Jersey Unschoolers
2 Smith Rd, Farmingdale, NJ 07727
Nancy Plent, 908-938-2473
Type: state home-based

Montessori Enrichment Center (1979)
29 Newbury Rd, Howell, NJ 07731
Joanne Lister or Maureene Peruzzi, Co-Dirs, 908-364-2244
Tuition: $150-300/mo
5 teachers, 5 assistants, 150 students, ages infant-6
Affiliations: NAMPTA, NJMAC; accreditation: AMS
Governance by board
New building; intro to French; childcare; suburban location; interns accepted.

The New School of Monmouth County (1969)
301 Middle Rd, Holmdel, NJ 07733
Jay Smith, Dir, 201-787-7900
50 students, K-8th grade
Based on philosophies of Dewey, Piaget, British Integrated
Day; family involvement; individualized; ungraded;
student-centered; Spanish; drama; piano; music.

A Child's Place (1974)
1409 W Front St, Lincroft, NJ 07738
Alba DiBello, Dir, 908-474-0141, FAX: 842-9599
Student ages 3-7, pre K-1st grade
Affiliations: NAEYC, OMEP, ACEI
Learning empowerment; creative self-expression; 2 acres,
new custom building; multi-aged classes.

Vincent S. Mastro Montessori
36 Birch Ave, Little Silver, NJ 07739-1194

Education Network of Christian Homeschoolers of NJ
(ENOCH)
65 Middlesex Rd, Matawan, NJ 07747-3030
908-583-7128

Montessori Academy of New Jersey
3504 Asbury Ave, Neptune, NJ 07753-2504
Chari Torello

Roots and Wings
8 Landing Trl, Denville, NJ 07834-1004
Type: home-based

Deer Path Montessori School
24 Main St, Flanders, NJ 07836-9112
Cindy Meyer

Rockaway Township Board of Education
School Rd, Hibernia, NJ 07842
Dr Fanning
Type: Montessori

Hilltop Montessori School
32 Lafayette Rd, Sparta, NJ 07871-3599
Laraine Kensicki

Eisenhower Middle School Alternative Program
47 Eyland Ave, Succasunna, NJ 07876
Owen Toale or Penny Sharp, 201-584-2973
8-12 students, mainly at-risk, 8th grade

New Jersey Family Schools Association
RD 3 Box 208, Washington, NJ 07882
Type: state home-based

Project Excel
PO Box 451, Washington, NJ 07882
Robert Fluck, Dir, 201-689-2193, 689-2199
40-45 students, mainly at-risk, 9-12th grade
Small classes; inter-agency support; pre-employment skills;
on-the-job experience.

The Albrook School (1979)
PO Box 352, 361A Somerville Rd, Basking Ridge, NJ 07920
Anita Albers, Dir, 908-580-0661, FAX: 908-580-0785
Type: Montessori, non-profit; tuition: $1,675-6,750/yr
12 teachers, 3 assistants, 207 students, ages toddler-12
Affiliations: AMS, NJMAC, NAEYC
Governance by administrator
6.5 acres; heated pool; summer program; art; music; foreign
language; childcare; rural location; interns accepted.

Somerset Montessori School
173 Madisonville Rd, Basking Ridge, NJ 07920-0109
Anneliese Gliese

Albrook School
PO Box 352, Basking Ridge, NJ 07920-0352
Type: Montessori

Montessori School
190 Lord Stirling Rd, Basking Ridge, NJ 07920-1329

Sprout House
200 Main St, Chatham, NJ 07928
Joanne Lockwood-White, 201-635-9658
Type: independent, non-profit; tuition: $350/mo, scholarships
4 teachers, 38 students, ages 5-12, ungraded
Affiliation: NAEYC
Governance by teachers and principal
Teacher qualifications: certification
Younger students focus on science and children's literature,
older students on social studies; family-type closeness;
natural food; strong environmental committment; no
letter grades; extensive field trips; suburban location;
interns accepted.

Madison Montessori School (1981)
19 Green Ave, Madison, NJ 07940
Teresa A Armstrong or Kathy Jenco, 201-966-9544
Non-profit; tuition: $2,400-3,275/yr
7 teachers, 4 assistants, 68 students, ages infant-6
Affiliation: AMS
Year-long study of one country; small classes; suburban loca-
tion; interns accepted.

Rainbow Montessori
53 Central Ave, Madison, NJ 07940-1848

Westmont Montessori School (1964)
577 Rte 24, Mendham, NJ 07945
Enid Lattner, 908-879-6355, FAX: -8127
Non-profit; tuition: $2,400-4,500/yr
6 teachers, 6 assistants, 144 students, ages infant-6
Affiliation: AMS
Governance by administrator, board
Interns accepted.

Montessori Children's House of Morristown (1965)
21 Cutler St, Morristown, NJ 07960
Brenda Mizel, Exec Dir, 201-539-7853, FAX: 201-539-5182
Non-profit; tuition: $3,250-5,600/yr
9 teachers, 5 assistants, 146 students, ages 3-12
Affiliations: NAMPTA, NJAIS; accreditations: AMS, MSA, NAEYC
Governance by board
Hands-on workshops, forums in visual, music, performing
arts at Children's Cultural Arts Center; childcare; suburban
location; interns accepted.

Environmental Montessori School
40 St Joseph Dr, Stirling, NJ 07980
Ms Walsh

Montessori Ceneter for Early Learning
304 Berkshire Ave, Cherry Hill, NJ 08002
Eydie Cohen

Montessori Children's House (1970)
1825 Garden Ave, Cherry Hill, NJ 08003-2303
Caryl Founds, Director, 609-424-0077
Tuition: $2,600/3,800/yr
4 teachers, 7 assistants, 107 students, mainly international,
ages 2.5-6
Governance by administrator
Gymnastics, music and Tiny Tumbles optional; suburban location; transportation; interns accepted.

Unschoolers Support Group for Central NJ
150 Folwell Station Rd, Jobstown, NJ 08041
Karen Mende-Fridkis
Type: home-based
Weekly activities; writers workshop; science; music; field trips;
art; play; suburban location.

LaHara Steele Productions
705 Downing Ct, Willingboro, NJ 08046
Joe Steele, Dir, 609-871-3318
Write, produce, perform music about dangers of substance
abuse.

Montessori Child Development Center
PO Box 231, Marlton, NJ 08053

Naudain Academy
RD 1 School Ln, Marlton, NJ 08053
Leddy Naudain
Type: Montessori

Moorestown Friends School
110 E Main St, Moorestown, NJ 08057
Alan Craig, Head, 609-235-2900
Type: Quaker

Burlington County Special Services School District
PO Box 775, Woodlane Rd, Mt Holly, NJ 08060
Dr Carmine DeSopo, Supt, 609-261-5600
800 students, ages–21
For multiply-handicapped, trainable mentally retarded and
    emotionally disturbed students.

Friends School (1969)
15 High St; Box 488, Mullica Hill, NJ 08062
Hanshi Deshbandhu, Tch/Adm, 609-478-2908, FAX: -0263
Type: Quaker, non-profit; tuition: $5,550-6,250/yr,
    scholarships
23 teachers, 218 students, ages 4-14, pre K-8th grade
Affiliation: FCOE-MS Ac. S
Governance by head of school
Teacher qualifications: college degree
Ethnically diverse; languages; sports; word processing; com-
    munity service; extensive field trips; childcare.

Rancocas Friends School
1 E Main St, Rancocas, NJ 08073
Constance Beetle, 609-267-8198
Type: Quaker

Infanta Montessori School
Conrow Rd, Delran, NJ 08075
Accreditation: AMI

Montessori Academy
Conrow Rd, Delran, NJ 08075
Ellen Fox Tronco, 609-461-2121
Non-profit; tuition: $2,955-6,030/yr
3 teachers, 3 assistants, 35 students, ages infant-12
Accreditations: AMI, MTA, AMS
Governance by administrator
Childcare.

Project ADVANCE
172 Salem-Woodstown Rd, Salem, NJ 08079
Raymond J. Bielicki, Dir, 609-935-7363
24 students, mainly severely emotionally disturbed, ages 11-21
Behavior mod; individualized; (pre)vocational training.

Homeschoolers of South Jersey
Rt 2 Burnt House Rd, Vincentown, NJ 08088

Children's Montessori Schoolhouse (1986)
730 Barlow Ave, Woodbury, NJ 08096
Ritamarie Akins, Owner/Adm, 609-848-0922, FAX: 609-848-
    1623
Tuition: $1,695-2,730/yr
2 teachers, 2 assistants, 40 students, ages 3-6
Governance by administrator
Custom designed facility; 4 large child-height windows/class-
    room; yearly nature camp; weekly enrichment in science/
    nature study; creative movement/music; theatre; dance;
    art; childcare; suburban location; interns accepted.

Atlantic County New School
1021 South Main St, Pleasantville, NJ 08232
Type: independent

II (Pregnant Adolescents Continuing Education)
115 W Decatur Ave, Pleasantville, NJ 08232
Sherry Spence, 609-383-6809

9-12th grade
Childbirth, nutrition, parenting classes; counseling;
    adaptive PE.

Atlantic County Alternative High School
Atlantic CC, 5100 Black Horse Pike, Mays Landing, NJ 08330
John Kellmayer, Prin, 609-343-5004
Type: public choice
80 students, mainly at-risk, 10-12th grade
County-wide; behavior mod; job skills; access to college
    resources; counseling; learning contracts.

Millville Alternative High School
200 Wade Blvd, Millville, NJ 08332
Charles J. Brett, Jr, Prin, 609-825-2341
9 teachers, 110 students, mainly at-risk, 8-12th grade
Small, evening classes; counseling.

The Tutor (1989)
1239 Whitaker Ave, Millville, NJ 08332
Rose Sias, Dir, 609-327-1224
Type: home-based
1 teacher, 4 students, ages 4-14, pre K-12th grade
Supplies textbooks; extensive field trips; suburban location

Upper Freehold Regional Alternative School
27 High St, Allentown, NJ 08501
Joe Jakubowski, Dir, 609-259-0300
Max 20 students, mainly at-risk, 9-12th grade
Off-campus; individualized; small groups.

Project RISE at Hopewell Valley Central High School
Pennington-Titusville Rd, Pennington, NJ 08534
Diane Paul, Dir, 609-737-1411
19 students, mainly at-risk, 9-10th grade
Individualized; parent contracts; counseling specialists.

Pennington Montessori School
102 W Franklin Ave, Pennington, NJ 08534-1483
Maria O'Connell

Lakeside Montessori Center
39 Magnolia Ln, Princeton, NJ 08540

Princeton Friends School (1987)
470 Quaker Rd, Princeton, NJ 08540
Bonnie Benbow, Adm Coord, 609-683-1194, FAX: 292-0686
Type: Quaker, non-profit; tuition: $3-6,700/yr, scholarships
14 teachers, 80 students, ages 4-14, pre K-8th grade
Affiliations: RSF, NAYS
Governance by teachers and principal
Community service; integrated curriculum; foreign language;
    art; music; dance; exchange with Katzenback School for
    the Deaf; weekly worship; suburban location.

Princeton Montessori School (1968)
487 Cherry Valley Rd, Princeton, NJ 08540
Anita Corzano, Admissions Dir, 609-924-4591, FAX: 609-924-
    2216
Non-profit
315 students, ages infant-15
Affiliations: AMS, NAIS, NJAIS; accreditation: MSA
Governance by board of trustees
Serves as lab school for Princeton Center for Teacher Educa-
    tion; childcare; suburban location; interns accepted.

Waldorf School of Princeton (1983)
1062 Cherry Hill Rd, Princeton, NJ 08540
Patricia Cuyler, Adm, 609-466-1970
Non-profit; tuition: $6,300/yr, scholarships
27 teachers, 180 students, ages 3.5-14, pre K-8th grade
Affiliations: AWSNA, NJAIS
Governance by board, college of teachers and administrative
    staff
Teacher qualifications: Waldorf certificate or Masters in
    Waldorf ed
Historic farmstead on 20 acres; field studies; rural location;
    interns accepted.

Holland Middle School
1001 W State St, Trenton, NJ 08618
Morris Kimble, 609-989-2730
Type: magnet
6-8th grade
Fine and performing arts.

LIFT, Inc
225 N Warren St, Trenton, NJ 08618
Alma J. Hill, Exec Dir, 609-392-8688
Students mainly pregnant
GED prep; counseling; emergency assistance.

Hedgepeth/Williams Middle School
301 Gladstone Ave, Trenton, NJ 08629
Michael Rothstein, 609-989-2780
Type: magnet
6-8th grade
Fine and performing arts.

Independence Montessori
2157 Pennington Rd, Trenton, NJ 08638-1429

Pathways at Laurelton School
1819 Rt 88, Brick, NJ 08724
Jane Kohlrenken, 477-2800 x304
Students mainly emotionally disturbed, ages 8-18
Counseling; educational services.

Seeds of Learning (1988)
1138 Concord Dr, Brick, NJ 08724-1015
Maria Hidaldo Dolan, Esq, Founder, 908-458-5435
Type: home-based, non-profit
1 teacher, 2 students, ages 1-5, pre K
Governance by parent cooperative
Teacher qualifications: parent
No letter grades; non-compulsory class attendance; multi-
   aged classes; extensive field trips; multi-cultural.

Woodmansee at Lacey High School
PO Box 206, Haines St, Lanopa Harbor, NJ 08734
William Kaskow, 609-971-1391
9-16 students, mainly classified ED, 9-12th grade
Vocational; life skills; behavior mod model; counseling; bi-
   weekly parent conferences; parent workshops.

Toms River Alternative Learning Center
1 Drake Ln S, Toms River, NJ 08757
Stephen Finkelstein, Dir, 908-505-5770, FAX: 908-341-1853
70-80 students, mainly at-risk, 8-10th grade

Twilight Program
PO Box 6350; N Bridge St & Vogt Dr, Bridgewater, NJ 08807

Sherman Harris, Dir, 201-526-8900
60 students, ages 14-21
Vocational training; career counseling; job orientation.

Dunellen High School Pupil Improvement Program (PIP)
1st St & Lincoln Ave, Dunellen, NJ 08812
John A. Feldman, EdD, Prin, Marybeth Connolly or Cota Kania,
   908-968-0885
1 teacher, 30-35 students, mainly at-risk, 7-12th grade
Social worker on staff.

Unitarian Montessori (1985)
176 Tices La, East Brunswick, NJ 08816
Mary Ann Keller, Dir, 908-246-0606
Non-profit; tuition: $400
2 teachers, 5 assistants, 50 students, ages 3-6
Affiliation: AMS
Governance by an administrator and a committee of parents
   and Unitarian Society members
Near Rutgers U; childcare; suburban location; interns
   accepted.

Acorn Montessori School (1984)
1222 Route 31, Lebanon, NJ 08833
Beverly Peutz, 908-730-8986
Non-profit; tuition: $2,525-5,100/yr
3 teachers, 4 assistants; student ages 3-6
Affiliation: AMS
Governance by administrator, board
Childcare; rural location; interns accepted.

Peppermint Tree Child Care
165 Fieldcrest Ave, Edison, NJ 08837-3622
Type: Montessori

Montessori Children's House of Kendall Park
N Main & E Church St, Milltown, NJ 08850

Raritan Valley Montessori
880 S Branch River Rd, Somerville, NJ 08876-4047
Leslie Meldrum

Charlotte Mason Research & Supply
(See Resource Section)

Children's House Montessori School
115 Commercial Ave, New Brunswick, NJ 08901-2748
Sandra Murgall

Lipman-Stern
341-C Crowell's Rd, Highland Park, NJ 08904
Type: home-based
Rituals for Solstice, Rosh Hoshanah, Kwanza, etc.

New Mexico

Montessori Learning Center
PO Box 2720, Corrales, NM 87048
Woodcock

Albuquerque Friends School (1992)
1600 5th St NW, Albuquerque, NM 87102-1302
Beverly Booth McCauley, Head, 505-242-8092
Type: Quaker, non-profit; tuition: $4,500/yr; scholarships
2 teachers, 7 students, ages 5-8, K-3rd grade
Affiliation: Friends Council on Education
Governance by board
Teacher qualifications: share values, competent, creative,
   energetic
Whole-child approach; multiple intelligences; conflict resolu-
   tion skills; strong in Spanish; no letter grades; multi-aged
   classes; extensive field trips; urban location.

Escuela Del Sol Montessori (1968)
1315 Mountain Rd NW, Albuquerque, NM 87104
Friedje van Gils, Head, 505-242-9817
Non-profit; tuition: $1,617-4,000/yr, scholarships
8 teachers, 6 assistants, 111 students, ages 3-12
Affiliation: AMS
Governance by administrator, faculty/student representatives, board of trustees
Modern approach to Montessori; parental involvement;
   multi-cultural; childcare; multi-aged classes; suburban
   location; interns accepted.

Albuquerque Family School (1989)
3211 Monte Vista Blvd NE, Albuquerque, NM 87106
Gael Keyes, Co-ord, 505-268-0252
Non-profit

8 teachers, 160 students, ages 6–13, 1–8th grade
Governance by teachers, principal, parent cooperative
Half-day public school, half-day home school; parent-taught
  class once a week; no letter grades; interns accepted.

Adobe Rose Montessori
333 Osuna NW, Albuquerque, NM 87107

The Montessori School
3821 Singer Blvd NE, Albuquerque, NM 87109-5804
Dan Herrick

New Futures School (1973)
5400 Cutler NE, Albuquerque, NM 87110
Dr. Sandy Dixon, Prin, 505-883-5680, FAX: 880-3977
Type: public at-risk
30 teachers, 380 students, ages 12–20, 7–12th grade
Governance by principal
Teacher qualifications: state certification
Works with community health and social services; prenatal
  and child health clinics; infant day care; mentorships; comprehensive counseling; parent support groups; multi-aged
  classes; urban location; transportation; interns accepted.

Montessori of the Southwest
3111 Eubank NE, Albuquerque, NM 87111
Roxanne Checchini

Sunset Mesa Schools
3020 Morris St NE, Albuquerque, NM 87111-4900
Type: Montessori

Academy Montessori School
11216 Phoenix NE, Albuquerque, NM 87112
Indu Kaushal

Albuquerque Montessori School
1334 Wyoming NE, Albuquerque, NM 87112

Sandia Montessori
2433 Chelwood NE, Albuquerque, NM 87112
Mindy Montes, 505-293-6614

New Mexico Christian Home Education
5749 Paradise NW, Albuquerque, NM 87114
505-897-1772

New Mexico Family Educators
PO Box 92276, Albuquerque, NM 87199-2276
Type: state home-based

Aztec Montessori
PO Box 3103, Gallup, NM 87301
Sherry Haskins, Dir, 505-863-4430

Rocky Mountain High Academy
PO Box 418, Flora Vista, NM 87415
Type: home-based

Shiprock Alternative School
PO Box 1799, Shiprock, NM 87420
Karen Bates, Exec Dir, 505-368-4904
Type: public choice

Devon's Montessori
844 Old Santa Fe Tr, Santa Fe, NM 87501
Devon Stokhof de Jong

Nizhoni School for Global Consciousness
1304 Old Pecos Trail, Santa Fe, NM 87501
Alex Petofi, 505-982-8293
Type: independent; tuition: $15,000/yr, scholarships
40 students, ages 14–21
Spirituality classes; world travel; diplomas and certificates in
  arts, ecology, business; students from 12 countries; 2 one-
  month trips abroad.

Camel Tracks Montessori
10 E Wildflower Dr, Santa Fe, NM 87501-8501

Little Earth School (1978)
321 West Zia Rd, Santa Fe, NM 87505
Ellen Souberman, Administrator, 505-988-1968
Type: independent, non-profit; tuition: $4,300-4,700,
  scholarships
10 teachers, 52 students, ages 4–8, pre K–3rd grade
Governance by teachers and principal, board
Teacher qualifications: state certification
Integrated, multi-cultural, hands-on, developmentally-
  appropriate; story telling, music, Spanish, visual and performing arts; co-op learning; diverse student body and
  staff; large outdoor learning environment; no letter
  grades; multi-aged classes; extensive field trips; rural location; interns accepted.

Odyssey Montessori
2638 Via Caballero del Norte, Santa Fe, NM 87505
Shelly Bailey

Santa Fe Learning Cooperative
2463 Camino Capitan, Santa Fe, NM 87505
Type: home-based

Santa Fe Waldorf School (1983)
Rt 9, PO Box 50-B3, Santa Fe, NM 87505
Marline Marquez Scally, Dev & Events Coord, 505-983-9727,
  FAX: -0486
Non-profit; tuition: $4,900+/yr, scholarships
22 teachers, 183 students, ages 4–13, K–8th grade
Governance by faculty committees, college, and board
Teacher qualifications: Waldorf training
Spanish; German; instrumental & choral music; fall & spring
  camping/study trips; spring theater presentations; subur-
  ban location; interns accepted.

A Voice For Children
(See Resource Section)

Monte Vista Montessori School
1001 Avenida Vista Grande, Santa Fe, NM 87505-8796
Teresa Seamster

National Coalition of Alternative Community Schools
(See Resource Section)

Chamisa Mesa High School
PO Box 220, El Prado, NM 87529
Maritza Vega, Adm, 505-751-0943
Type: independent, non-profit; tuition: $3,200/yr, 10 $1,000
  scholarships
8 teachers, 50 students, ages 14–18, 9–12th grade
Governance by faculty board
Teacher qualifications: MA, credential or unique subject
  qualification
Classical liberal arts program; evaluation by demonstration;
  emphasis on critical thinking and problem solving; college
  type schedule; coached seminars; interns accepted.

Glorieta Family Educators
Star Rt 1 Box 404, Glorieta, NM 87535
Type: home-based

Canyoncito Montessori
PO Box 1261, 2525 Canyon Rd, Los Alamos, NM 87544
Mary Ann Schnedler, 505-662-2910

Los Alamos Montessori
2400 Canyon Rd, Los Alamos, NM 87544

Sage Montessori School (1972)
304 Rover Blvd, Los Alamos, NM 87544
Connie Hayden, Owner, 505-672-3189, FAX: 505-672-9218
Tuition: $431/445/mo
130 students, ages 3–10
Affiliation: NCME
Governance by principal
Complete Montessori curriculum; no letter grades; multi-
  aged classes; suburban location; interns accepted.

School of the North Star
627 North Star Route, Questa, NM 87556
Connie Long, Pres, 505-586-0112; 586-1392
Type: independent, non-profit
6 students, ages 5–14
Individualized; group experience, cooperation; creative problem solving; artistic, creative expression encouraged.

Vista Grande Preparatory School (1978)
PO Box 1656, Taos, NM 87571
Carolyn Lake, Dir, 505-758-9306
Type: independent; tuition: $250/mo, scholarships
55 students, K–6th grade
Accreditations: Rio Grande Ed Assn, NM Assn of Non-Public Schools
Low ratio; parent involvement.

Armand Hammer United World College (1982)
Box 248, Montezuma, NM 87731
Dan Tyson, Adms Dir, 505-454-4248, FAX: -4274
Type: independent, boarding, non-profit; tuition: $16,500/yr, scholarships
24 teachers, 200 students, ages 16–19
Governance by teachers; principal
Teacher qualifications: Masters in teaching field, international experience
IB curriculum, 6th form; equivalent to grades 12–13; students enter into UK 3-yr undergraduate programs or as sophomores in the US; extensive field trips; community service; rural location; transportation; interns accepted.

Mesilla Valley Montessori
1809 El Paseo St, Las Cruces, NM 88001-6009
Carolann Staley

Mount Cristo Rey Challenge High School (1991)
PO Drawer 899, Santa Teresa, NM 88008
Russell E. Phipps, Administrator, 505-589-5350
Type: public at-risk
8 teachers, 180 students, ages 16–27, 9–12th grade
Governance by teachers, principal, board
Teacher qualifications: BS, state certification
Day care; drug/alcohol intervention; mastery learning; no letter grades; non-compulsory class attendance; multi-aged classes; rural location; transportation; interns accepted.

Animas Elementary School
PO Box 85, Animas, NM 88020-0085
Type: Montessori

National Homeschool Service
(See Resource Section)

Down to Earth School (1988)
112 E 11th St, Silver City, NM 88061
Linda Egge, Dir, 505-388-2902
Type: independent; tuition: $160/mo, scholarships

16 teachers, 33 students, ages 11–19, 7–12th grade
Governance by co-directors
Teacher qualifications: student acceptance, knowledge of subject
Specialist teachers from community; overnight camping trips; Latin; German; Spanish; mechanics; mountain biking; student-created electives; multi-aged classes; urban location; interns accepted.

Guadalupe Montessori School (1979)
1731 N Alabama St, Silver City, NM 88061
Kathy Dahl-Bredine, 505-388-3343
Tuition: $1,380-1,836/yr, scholarships
4 teachers, 4 assistants, 91 students, ages 3–12
Accreditation: AMI
Governance by administrator
Spanish bilingual program; Catechesis of the Good Shepherd; parent involvement; family diversity; childcare.

Broad Horizons Educational Center (1992)
1034 Community Way, Portales, NM 88130
Betty Johnson, Project Dir, 505-356-4254, FAX: -4303
Type: public at-risk
100 students, mainly at-risk, ages 15–50, 8–12th grade
Outcome-based; social services; work-study; open entry/open exit; self-paced; learning style assessment; multi-aged classes; no letter grades; rural location; interns accepted.

CHAPS Alternative Junior High School (1989)
1401 College Ave, Alamogordo, NM 88310
505-439-3350, FAX: 505-439-3354
Type: public choice
4 teachers, 60 students, mainly at-risk, ages 12–15
Governance by teachers and coordinator
Cooperative learning; integrated instruction; extended day; natural-logical consequences discipline; field trips; rural location; interns accepted.

Montessori Learning Center/Alamogordo Montessori Academy
1012 Cuba Ave, Alamogordo, NM 88310
Laurie A. Roth, Dir; Cindy Crouch, Asst Dir, 505-437-0993
Tuition: $190/320/mo
65 students, mainly international, ages 1–12
Affiliation: AMS
Governance by teachers and principal
Manipulative materials for all ages in all academic areas; extensive field trips; non-compulsory class attendance; no letter grades; suburban location; transportation; interns accepted.

Montessori's Little Red School House
PO Box 1977, Ruidoso, NM 88345-1977
Kortney Lee Hall, 505-258-4945

Starlite Montessori School
407 Mechem Dr, Ruidoso, NM 88345-6811

New York

A+ Discount Distributors and Educational Warehouse
(See Resource Section)

Institute for Secondary Education (1993)
127 E 22 St, New York, NY 10001
John Pettinato, Dir, 212-475-7972
Type: public choice
6 teachers, 75 students, ages 12–15, 7–9th grade
Affiliation: CES
Governance by director, teachers, parents, students
Teacher qualifications: Masters- min 12 ed credits

For college bound; cultivates college collaborations; transportation; interns accepted.

Phoenix Learning Resources
12 W 31st St, New York, NY 10001
Nancy Woodruff
Type: Montessori

Eugene Lang College
65 W 11th St, NY, NY 10001
Jenifer Gill Fondiller, Admissions, 212-229-5665

350 students
Seminar approach; max 15/class; emphasis on discussion and participation; no texts or core curriculum; interdisciplinary; internships.

West Chelsea Learning Center
330 W 28th St, New York, NY 10001-4722
Type: Montessori

Auxiliary Services for High Schools (1969)
198 Forsyth St, New York, NY 10002
Margaret Bing-Wade, Dir, IA, 212-673-8254, FAX: 260-2617
Type: public at-risk
300 teachers, 14,500 students, mainly GED, ages 16+, 9-12th grade
Affiliation: NYC BE
Governance by principal, school-based planning committee
Teacher qualifications: NYC BE License
92 sites throughout NYC; GED prep; career services, counseling; individual, whole group, collaborative self-paced instruction in 7 languages; community-based job training; day and evening classes; open-entry, exit; multi-cultural; student-centered; ongoing personalized assessment; extensive field trips; multi-aged classes; interns accepted.

Florence Nightingale Elementary
285 Delancey St, New York, NY 10002
Alex Tare, 718-674-2690
Type: magnet
Student ages 4+,-6th grade
Gifted and talented.

John Burroughs Elementary
442 E Houston St, New York, NY 10002
George Fener, 718-677-5710
Type: magnet
Student ages 4+,-6th grade
Communication; arts.

Lower East Side Preparatory School (1970)
145 Stanton St, 4th Floor, NY, NY 10002
John W Lee, Prin, 212-505-6366
Type: public choice
575 students, 9-12th grade
Full academic program; serves emotional, socio-economic, and academic needs of students.

East Manhattan School for Bright and Gifted Children (1968)
208 E 18th St, New York, NY 10003
Irina Pigott, MA, 212-475-8671
Non-profit; tuition: $6,000-8,000/yr
113 students, ages infant-12
Affiliations: NAEYC, Parents League; accreditation: NY HD
Governance by board
Based on premise that giftedness depends on early stimulation and encouragement; childcare; transportation; interns accepted.

Friends Seminary (1786)
222 E 16 St, New York, NY 10003
Richard Eldridge, 212-979-5030, FAX: -5035
Type: Quaker, non-profit; tuition: $12,000/yr, scholarships
7 teachers, 570 students, ages 5-18, K-12th grade
Affiliations: FCOE, NAIS
Governance by board
Teacher qualifications: BA
Community service required; daily meeting for worship; wilderness program; integrated curr; no letter grades for K-8; multi-aged classes; extensive field trips; interns accepted.

New York U Montessori Teacher Education Center
200 E Building, Washington Sq, New York, NY 10003
Marleen Barron

PS 40 Professional Development Lab
319 E 19th St, New York, NY 10003
Bea Ramirez-Epstein, 212-475-5500

Type: magnet
K-6th grade
Integrated multi-cultural.

Village Montessori School
7 E 14th St, New York, NY 10003
Dr Ruth Selman

Manhattan Comprehensive Night and Day HS (1989)
240 2nd Ave, NY, NY 10003
Stanley L Gordon, Dir Community Affairs, 212-353-2010
Type: public choice
500 students, ages 17-21, 9-12th grade
Certified, accredited night and day HS; diploma program; emphasis on nurturing and flexibility; services students with adult responsibilities and new immigrants.

New York City Home Educators Alliance (1988)
341 E 5th St #1R, NY, NY 10003
Theresa Morris, 212-505-9884
Library; newsletter.

Independence School at PS 234
292 Greenwich St, New York, NY 10007
Anne Switzer, Prin, 212-233-6034
Type: public choice
ES
Affiliations: NYC Public School, Center for Collaborative Education
Governance by staff and parents
Collaboratively designed building; social studies core of integrated curriculum; interactive learning; urban location.

Satellite Academy High School (1972)
51 Chambers St, New York City, NY 10007
Alan Dichter, Prin, 212-349-5350, FAX: 964-5587
Type: public at-risk
60 teachers, 800 students, ages 15-21, 9-12th grade
Affiliation: Coalition of Essential Schools
Governance by staff with student/parent input
Portfolios; interns accepted.

The Odysseus Group
(See Resource Section)

East Side Community High School
420 E 12th St, NY, NY 10009
Jill Herman, Director

Lower East Side School (LESS)
333 E 4th, NY, NY 10009
Barbara Goldman, 212-982-0682
Type: public choice
7 teachers, 100 students, ages 4-12, pre K-6th grade
Affiliation: CCE
Governance by democratic meeting, with parents having decision making power.
Started by parents; small classes; student-centered, developmentally-appropriate, individualized program; whole language approach; arts enrichment; multi-cultural population and curriculum.

Escuela Hispana Montessori
12 Ave D, New York, NY 10009-7011

Institute for Democracy In Eastern Europe
(See Resource Section)

American Montessori Society
150 Fifth Ave #203, New York, NY 10011
Michael Eanes

Career Education Center (1986)
250 W 18th St, New York, NY 10011
212-727-7720
Type: public choice
HS

Affiliation: NYC Schools
Transitional programs for students in temporary housing; GED prep; counseling; computers; small classes; CAI; vocational.

City and Country (1914)
146 W 13th St, New York, NY 10011
Zoe Hauser, Adms, 212-242-7802, FAX: -7996
Type: independent, non-profit; tuition: $7,300-10,500/yr, scholarships
14 teachers, 12 assistants, 195 students, ages 2-13
Governance by board, teachers and principal
Relevant; developmentally-appropriate; job program; school store, 100-yr-old print shop; creative block building; no letter grades; extensive field trips.

Clinton School
320 W 21st St, New York, NY 10011
Jill Myers, 212-255-8860
Type: magnet
6-8th grade
Visual arts.

Corlears School (1968)
324 W 15 St, New York, NY 10011
Marion Greenwood, Head, 212-741-2800, FAX: 807-1550
Type: independent, non-profit; tuition: $7,400-10,400/yr, scholarships
35 teachers, 115 students, ages 2.5-9
Affiliations: NYSAIS, NYAEC, NAIS
Governance by board
Teacher qualifications: BA/MA in Ed
Real experiences; manipulative materials; parents and community involvement; no letter grades; multi-aged classes; extensive field trips; interns accepted.

New York Foundlings
590 Ave of Americas, New York, NY 10011
Type: Montessori

NYC Lab School for Gifted Education (1989)
333 W 17 St, New York, NY 10011
Sheila Breslaw, Rob Menken, Co-Dirs, 212-691-6119, FAX: -6219
Type: public choice
16 teachers, 305 students, partly MISI SE, 6-9th grade
Governance by teachers and principal
Interdisciplinary planning, study; strong student govt; weekly community service; co-op learning; electives; peer tutoring in math; chess team; computers, video, CD-ROM; interns accepted.

Project BLEND: Building Learning Experiences in New Directions (1990)
351 W 18th St, New York, NY 10011
212-206-0570
Type: public choice
HS
Affiliation: NYC Schools
Multi-sited; interdisciplinary; supportive; vocational; SE; student leadership; small classes; support services; family groups.

PS 11 Chelsea Primary
320 W 21st St, New York, NY 10011
Leslie Gordon, 212-929-1743
Type: magnet
Pre K-6th grade
School for peace; literacy curriculum.

School for the Physical City
333 W 17th St, New York, NY 10011
Mark Weiss
Type: magnet
6-12th grade
Urban Studies.

The American Montessori Society
(See Resource Section)

Nazareth Nursery Montessori School (1901)
216 W 15th St, NY, NY 10011
Sister Lucy Sabatini, 212-243-1881
55 students, ages 2-6
Montessori philosophy, methods, and materials.

The Urban Academy (1986)
High School of the Humanities, 351 W 18th St, NY, NY 10011
Ann Cook or Herb Mack, Co-Directors, 212-220-6397
Type: public choice
100 students, HS
An outgrowth of "Inquiry Demonstration Project"; inquiry-based curriculum; independent research; external learning experiences.

Vanguard High School
14th St Armory, 125 W 14th St, 3rd fl, NY, NY 10011
Louis Delgado, 212-337-4445

Greenwich Village Neighborhood School
219 Sullivan St, New York, NY 10012
Type: Montessori

New York Open Center
83 Spring St, NY, NY 10012
212-219-2527
Type: higher education

Unity Alternative High School at The Door Youth Agency (1990)
555 Broome St, New York, NY 10013
212-941-9090
Type: public choice
Affiliations: NYC Schools, Citibank
Interdisciplinary; thematic; college prep; mentorships.

City-As-School High School (1971)
16 Clarkson St, New York, NY 10014
Robert Hubetsky, Prin, 212-691-7801, FAX: 212-675-2858
Type: public choice
70 teachers, 750 students, mainly at-risk, ages 16-19, 9-12th grade
Affiliation: NYC BE
Governance by SMB/SOM
Teacher qualifications: NYC or NY certification
Community learning experiences; student-centered Learning Experience Activities Packets; multi-aged classes; no letter grade; interns accepted.

Executive Internship Program (1980)
16 Clarkson St, New York, NY 10014
212-691-7801
Type: public choice, HS
Affiliation: NYC Schools
Government, politics, community agencies, business and industry; weekly seminars; transportation.

PS3 Charrette School
490 Hudson St, New York, NY 10014
Donna Connelly, 212-691-1183
Type: magnet
K-6th grade
Open classroom; whole language.

School of Culture and Communication (1993)
490 Hudson St, New York, NY 10014
Kathy McCullagh, Dir, 212-647-9275
Type: public choice
3 teachers, 53 students, ages 11-14, 6-8th grade
Affiliation: Center for Collaborative Ed
Governance by advisory council of administrators, parents and teachers
Teacher qualifications: experience with diverse urban pop. and integrated cur development, enjoy adolescents
Anthropological emphasis; photography; video; community service; integrated curr; advisory program; co-ed, multi-aged, cooperative groups; assessment by portfolio; extensive field trips; non-compulsory class attendance; interns accepted.

The 15th Street School Foundation
(See Resource Section)

The School of the Future
210 East 33rd St, New York, NY 10016
Gwen Solomon, Dir, 212-679-0328
Type: public choice
7-8th grade
Affiliations: NYC Public Schools, Center for Collaborative
    Education
Integration of technology into all aspects of school life; inter-
    disciplinary studies; diverse.

Family School (1975)
323 E 47th St, NY, NY 10017
Lesley Nan Haberman, Head, 212-688-5950
Type: Montessori
100 students, pre K-6th grade
Multi-cultural/socio-economic environment; individualized;
    eclectic classroom approach.

Landmark High School (1993)
220 W 58 St, New York, NY 10019
Sylvia Rabiner, Dir, 212-866-4450, FAX: 289-4195
Type: public choice
8 teachers, 85 students, ages 14-16, 9th grade
Affiliation: CES
Governance by teachers and principal
Teacher qualifications: extensive interview process
Small, heterogeneous classes; active/cooperative learning;
    advisory classes; individualized; graduation by demonstra-
    tion/performance; no letter grades; extensive field trips;
    urban location; interns accepted.

Public School Repertory Company at Park West HS (1991)
525 W 50th St, New York, NY 10019
212-262-5860 x289
Type: public choice
Affiliation: NYC Schools
Performing arts; small classes; interdisciplinary.

East Side Middle School
1458 York Ave, New York, NY 10021
Ann Hochman, 212-439-6278
Type: magnet
6-8th grade
Interdisciplinary.

Rudolf Steiner School (1928)
15 E 79 St, New York, NY 10021
Lucy Schneider, Fac Chair, 212-535-2130, FAX: 861-1378
Type: Waldorf, non-profit; tuition: $7,250-10,500, scholarships
24 ft, 7 pt teachers, 235 students, ages 3-18, pre K-12th
    grade
Affiliations: NYSAIS, NAIS, ISAAGNY, Guild of Ind. Schools NYC,
    AWSNA, Ind. Schools Athletic League
Governance by faculty and non-faculty board members
Teacher qualifications: pre-school: MA; primary: BA; sec-
    ondary: MA min, PhD desirable
Block system allows focused concentration, multiple
    approaches; same teacher for 8 yrs; professional music/art
    faculty; extensive field trips; interns accepted.

Caedmon School (1962)
416 E 80th St, NY, NY 10021
Carol G Devine, 212-879-2296
Type: Montessori
190 students, ages 2.5-10, pre K-5th grade
Modified approach; mixed age groups, family environment;
    group work encouraged.

Resurrection Episcopal Day School (1990)
119 E 74th St, NY, NY 10021
Ruth Wiltshire, 212-535-9666
Type: Montessori
30 students, ages 2.6-6
Formerly Vera Gander School.

PS 59 United Nations Public School
228 E 57th St, New York, NY 10022
Galen Guberman, 212-722-2998
Type: magnet
K-6th grade
Interdisciplinary science and art program.

Manhattan Montessori School of NY
347 E 55th St, NY, NY 10022
Miss Lina, 212-223-4630
80 students, ages 2.5-14
Branches in Brooklyn and Queens.

Beacon School, c/o Fordham U (1993)
1213 W 60th St, New York, NY 10023
718-974-6096
Computer science; educational, cultural, community services;
    performance-based; shared decision-making.

Center School
270 W 70 St, New York, NY 10023
Elaine Schwartz, 212-678-2729
Type: magnet
5-8th grade
Drama.

PS 191
210 W 61 St, New York, NY 10023
Elena Nasereddin, 212-678-2810
Type: magnet
Pre K-5th grade
Media.

PS 44 W. Sherman Humanities School
160 W 78th St, New York, NY 10023
Jane Hind, 212-678-2826
Type: magnet
K-5th grade
Humanities.

Integrative Studies
242 W 76th St, NY, NY 10023
Dr. Fern Crowell, 212-838-5122
Type: independent

Beacon School (1993)
113 W 60 St, Room 1024, New York, NY 10024
212 636-7811, FAX: 636-7113
Computer science; educational, cultural, community services;
    performance-based; shared decision-making.

IS 44
100 W 77 St, New York, NY 10024
William Colavito, 212-678-2817
Type: magnet
6-8th grade
Science; art.

PS 166
132 W 89th St, New York, NY 10024
Jack Regan, 212-678-2829
Type: magnet
Pre K-5th grade
Arts.

DOME Project (1973)
486 Amsterdam Ave, NY, NY 10024
Joe Flax, 212-724-1780
Type: public at-risk
40 students, 6-8th grade
Small classes; part of 1200 student recreation and education
    agency; summer, college prep, prep school placement,
    after school and dance programs; community garden;
    juvenile justice assistance; truancy prevention services.

Crossroads School (1990)
234 West 109th St, New York, NY 10025
Ann F.Wiener, Dir, 212-316-5256

Type: public choice
6 teachers, 125 students, ages 10–14, 6-8th grade
Governance by teachers and principal
Active parent involvement; small classes; diverse; teachers
write curriculum; community service; writing and writing
technologies; multi-aged classes; no letter grades; extensive field trips; interns accepted.

MS 54
103 W 107 St, New York, NY 10025
Jules Linden, 212-678-2902
Type: magnet
6-8th grade
Global education.

PS 145 Bloomingdale School
150 W 105th St, New York, NY 10025
Ann Budd, 212-678-2857
Type: magnet
Student ages 4+,-6th grade
Performing and creative arts.

PS 163
163 W 97 St, New York, NY 10025
Jorge Izquierdo, 212-678-2854
Type: magnet
Pre K-5th grade
Community ventures.

PS 84
32 W 92 St, New York, NY 10025
Sidney Morison, 212-678-2823
Type: magnet
Pre K-5th grade
Environmental arts and science.

West Side Montessori School (1963)
309 W 92nd St, New York, NY 10025
Marlene Barron, Head, 212-662-8000, FAX: -8323
Non-profit; tuition: $5,350-9,710/yr
15 teachers, 19 assistants, 200 students, ages 3-6
Affiliations: AMS, NYSAIS, ISAAGNY, ERB
Governance by board
Multi-cultural; family involvement; interns accepted.

Bank Street College
610 W 112th St, NY, NY 10025
Happy Byers
Affiliated with Little Red Schoolhouse.

Holy Name School (1905)
202 W 97th St, NY, NY 10025
Deborah L Hurd, Asst Prin, 212-749-1240
Type: independent
600 students, pre K-8th grade
Multi-cultural student body; Montessori early childhood;
computer technology; IBM writing to read; after school
program.

Morningside Montessori School
251 W 100th St, NY, NY 10025
212-316-1555

St Michael's Montessori School
225 W 99th St, NY, NY 10025
Ramani Dealwis, 212-663-0555

West Side Alternative High School (1972)
140 W 102nd St, NY, NY 10025
Ed Reynolds, Prin, 212-865-3522
Type: public at-risk
650 students, ages 15-21, 9-12th grade
Governance by school-based management team
Family groups; day care; health clinic; court liaison; job coun-
selor; 9 social workers; SE; night school; adult ed.

National Center for Restructuring Education (NCREST)
(See Resource Section)

**Central Harlem Montessori School/Champ Morningside
Children's Center** (1968)
160 W 129th St, NY, NY 10027
Roslyn Williams, 212-864-0400
176 students, pre K-6th grade
Multi-cultural; parents help with some classes.

Manhattan New School
311 E 82nd St, New York, NY 10028
Shelley Harwayne, 212-734-7127
Type: magnet
K-6th grade
Student-centered; collaborative; multi-cultural; language.

Upper Lab
311 E 82nd St, New York, NY 10028
Shiela Brewslaw, 212-570-6880
Type: magnet
6-12th grade
Interdisciplinary; gifted.

East Harlem Performing Arts School
433 E 100 St, New York, NY 10029
Randy Soderman, 212-860-5958
Type: magnet
5-9th grade

Harbor Performing Arts Junior High School
240 E 109 St, New York, NY 10029
Victor Lopez, 212-860-8947
Type: magnet
7-9th grade

Manhattan West Center For Humanities
19 E 103rd St, New York, NY 10029
Karen Marino, 212-860-7953
Type: magnet
7-8th grade

Central Park East I/JHS 113 (1974)
1573 Madison Ave, NY, NY 10029
Lucy Matos, 212-860-5821
Type: public choice
18 teachers, 265 students, ages 4-12, pre K-6th grade
Governance by democratic school meeting
Informal, personalized program; model-making, scientific
experimentation, sculpture, drama, and library research;
no workbooks; close family-school relationship required;
no letter grades; extensive field trips.

Central Park East II
215 E 99th St, NY, NY 10029
Kyle Haver, Director, 212-860-6010
Type: public choice
K-6th grade
"Hands-on" program; integrated curricular themes; two years
with same teacher; close parent-student-teacher team-
work; field trips; visiting professionals; individual research.

Central Park East Secondary School (1985)
1573 Madison Avenue, NY, NY 10029
Deborah Meier, Prin; Paul Schwartz, Co-Director, 212 860-5871
Type: public choice
450 students, 7-12th grade
Affiliation: National Coalition of Essential Schools
Governance by principal and teachers
Grew out of success of CPE Alternative School; emphasizes
learning how to learn, reason, work collaboratively; internships; mentorships; community service; demonstration-
based diploma.

College for Human Services Junior High/PS 21
232 E 103 St, NY, NY 10029
Linda Hill, Director, 212-860-6044
Type: public choice
30 students, 7-8th grade
Combines academic learning with life experience in a service
setting; internships at schools, day care and senior settings, community offices.

Park East High School (1970)
230 E 105th St, NY, NY 10029
Jacqueline E Beverly, 212-831-1517
Type: public choice
400 students, HS
Founded by coalition of community groups; business education; college and career advisement; active student government; off site vocational training; computer literacy.

River East
116th St & FDR Dr, NY, NY 10029
Leslie Alexander, Director, 212-860-6033
Type: public choice
Pre k-6th grade
Part of Manhattan Center for Science and Math; same
teacher for 2-3 years; interest-based.

The Bridge School (1977)
141 E 111th St, NY, NY 10029
Michael Friedman, Director, 212-860-5890
Type: public choice
230 students, 6-9th grade
Emphasizes mutual respect and responsibility; criminal
justice, human relations, consumer and career ed;
overnight trips to Washington, Boston, etc.

Center for Collaborative Education
1573 Madison Ave, Room 201, NY, NY 10029-3988
Heather Lewis, Priscilla Ellington, Co-Directors, 212-348-7821
Type: public choice
Joint project with 18 NYC public schools; focuses on thinking
skills, personalizing teaching and learning, student participation, parental input, and evaluation based on
performance.

Salome Urena Middle Academics
4600 Broadway, New York, NY 10034
Mark Kavakshy, 212-567-2322
Type: magnet
6-8th grade
Business studies; community service; technology; fine and
performing arts.

Borough Academies (1992)
2005 Madison Ave, New York, NY 10035
212-423-0251
Type: public choice
HS
Affiliation: NYC Public Schools
Extended day; CAI; community service; enriched arts; creative
conflict resolution; guidance; credit for continuous
progress.

Children's Storefront Support Corporation (1966)
57 E 129th St, NY, NY 10035
Ned O'Gorman, 212-427-7900
Type: independent
115 students, ages 2.5-14, pre K-8th grade
Governance by director and staff
Non-tuition, private school in Harlem, with traditional academic program; goal is to heal, liberate, and teach the
oppressed child.

Choir Academy of Harlem
2005 Madison Ave, NY, NY 10035
212-289-6227
Type: public choice
Affiliation: NY BE
Based at the Boys' Choir of Harlem; vocal training; college
preparatory program; multi-cultural focus; concert
performances.

Coalition School For Social Change (1993)
2005 Madison Ave, NY, NY 10035
Charlene Jordan, Director, 212-860-0212
Type: public choice
10 teachers, 92 students, ages 14-15, 9th grade

Affiliation: CES
Governance by teachers and principal
Essential school philosophy; project-based assessment; inter-
disciplinary; urban location; interns accepted.

Northview Technical Junior High School
319 E 117th St, NY, NY 10035
Maria Bonet, Director, 212-860-7952
Type: public choice
130 students, 7-9th grade
Affiliation: Youth Alliance Program
Family-oriented, mentoring program; computers; internships
in other schools.

Urban Peace Academy
2351 First Ave, NY, NY 10035
212-987-1906

Midtown West
328 W 48th St, New York, NY 10036
Saudhi Vargas, 212-247-0208
Type: magnet
K-5th grade
Student-centered; multi-cultural.

Professional Performing Arts School (1990)
328 West 48 St, New York, NY 10036
Claudia DiSalvo, Dir, 212-247-8652, 246-7576, FAX: -7514
Type: public choice
25 teachers, 340 students, ages 10-18, 6-11th grade
Governance by director
On-location academics program for students wherever they
are in US or overseas.

Manhattan International High School
PS 126, 80 Catherine St, NY, NY 10038
212-964-2286

Community Service Academy (1992)
4600 Broadway, NY, NY 10040
Lydia Bassett, Asst Prin, 212-567-2589
18 teachers, 350 students, ages 11-15, 6-8th grade
Affiliations: CCE, Bank St College, NCSL
Governance by teachers and principal
Teacher qualifications: NYC Bd of Ed License, community
involvement
Builds on natural instincts of early adolescents to make the
world a better place; school-community collaboration:
teacher works with student advisory group and community organization to design service learning project.;
interns accepted.

Enterprise Foundation
888 7th Ave #402, New York, NY 10106
Margarita R Reynes
Type: Montessori

Cooperative Tech (1986)
321 E 96th St, New York, NY 10128
212-369-8800
Type: public choice
Student ages 16+, 11-12th grade
Affiliation: NYC Schools
Advanced, specialized training in 10 voc-tech areas; ESL
support services; building construction/repair; day care;
job placement; occupational skills; transportation.

Lower Lab
1700 Third Ave, New York, NY 10128
Denise Levine, 212-427-2798
Type: magnet
K-6th grade
Inquiry-based; intergrated; gifted.

Partnership School
1763 First Ave, New York, NY 10128
Carole Mulligan, 212-876-7248
Type: magnet

K-6th grade
Multi-cultural whole language curriculum.

Primary Effective Program
1700 Third Ave, New York, NY 10128
Nancy Rodriguez, 212-427-6489
Type: magnet
K-6th grade
Multi-cultural creative arts curriculum.

PS 198 Multicultural School
1700 Third Ave, New York, NY 10128
Goria Buckery, 212-289-3702
Type: magnet
Pre K-6th grade
Whole language; literature-based curriculum.

The Dalton School
108 E 89th St, New York, NY 10128
Catherine Evedon
Type: Montessori

Manhattan Country School
7 E 96th St, NY, NY 10128
Gus Trowbridge, 212-348-0952
Type: independent; tuition: sliding scale, income dependent
50% white, 50% minority by design.

Seton Day Care Center
1675 3rd Ave #93RD, New York, NY 10128-3702
Maria Gravel
Type: Montessori

St Vartan Playgroup (1992)
PO Box 1073, NY, NY 10156-0604
Ellen Ellis, President, 212-447-6035
Type: public choice; tuition: $550
10 students, ages 2-5
Governance by parent cooperative
Extension of homeschooling; multi-aged classes; urban
location.

Building Blocks Montessori School (1972)
55 Forest Ave, Staten Island, NY 10301
Gloria Friedman, Dir, 718-448-2992
Tuition: $2,400-4,800/yr
7 teachers, 13 assistants, 150 students, ages infant-12
Accreditations: NYS, NYC
Governance by board
Multi-cultural curriculum; Spanish education; childcare; trans-
portation; interns accepted.

Children's Harbor Preschool
1000 Richmond Terr, Staten Island, NY 10301
Leanne Bernacki, Dir, 718-442-6112
Non-profit; tuition: $1,170-4,160/yr
3 teachers, 4 assistants, 60 students, ages infant-6
Accreditation: AMS
Governance by board
Art-based; at Snug Harbor Cultural Center; parent co-op;
childcare; suburban location; transportation; interns
accepted.

Tanglewood School (1983)
15 Tanglewood Dr, Staten Island, NY 10308
Fay Taranto, 718-967-2424
Type: Montessori
275 students, ages 2.5-6
Extensive materials.

Staten Island Montessori (1966)
500 Butler Blvd, Staten Island, NY 10309
Stephanie Whalen, 718-356-7833
150 students, pre K-5th grade

Hostos-Lincoln Academy of Science (1986)
475 Grand Concourse, Bronx, NY 10451
Dr Michele Cataldi, Prin, 718-518-4333

Type: public at-risk
300 students, ages 14-18, 9-12th grade
Governance by principal, democratic school meeting
Internships; independent study; college courses in partnership with Hostos Community College; designed to improve
basic skills, reduce absenteeism and dropping out.

Youth Options Unlimited (YOU) (1987)
470 E 172nd St, Bronx, NY 10452
718-993-5350 x209,210
Type: public at-risk
JH
Affiliation: NYC Schools
Peer group counseling; parental involvement; career explo-
ration; small classes; individualized; open entrance.

University Heights High School at Bronx Community
College
University Ave & W 181st St, Bronx, NY 10456
Deborah L Harris, 212-220-6397
Type: public choice
375 students, ages 16+
Smaller, personalized program with support services to help
students prepare for college/career.

Pace Academy Middle School 118 (1972)
577 E 179 St, Bronx, NY 10457
Joseph Landes, 718-584-2568
Type: public choice

Riverdale Academy (1982)
3333 Independence Ave, Bronx, NY 10463
Joseph F Sasiela, 212-796-8630
Type: public choice
186 students, 7-9th grade
Atmosphere of a small private school, but diversity of services of a comprehensive junior high school.

The Bronx New School
3200 Jerome Ave, Bronx, NY 10468
Esther Forrest, Prin, 212-584-8772
Type: public choice
225 students, K-6th grade

C S 152 School
1007 Evergreen Ave, Bronx, NY 10472
Ms Eidlin, 718-822-5029
Type: magnet
4-6th grade
Fine and performing arts.

Northeast Academy (1978)
750 Baychester Ave, Bronx, NY 10475
Harry Reiss, 212-671-7700
Type: public choice

Ardsley Alternative High School (1992)
300 Farm Rd, Ardsley, NY 10502
Jay Shaplou, Dir, 914-693-6300 x231, FAX: 914-693-0892
Type: public choice
1 teacher, 20 students, mainly at-risk, ages 15-18, 10-12th
grade
Governance by democratic school meeting
First community-as-school in county; business partnerships;
whole language; required evening parent meetings every 8
weeks; multi-aged classes; suburban location.

Alcott School (1968)
700 Ashford Ave/Crane Rd at Woodlands Pl, Ardsley/Scars-
dale, NY 10502/10583
A. Donegan, 914-472-4404
Type: Montessori, non-profit; tuition: $2,575-7,000/yr
6 teachers, 18 assistants, 300 students, mainly international,
ages infant-6
Affiliation: AMS; accreditation: NAEYC
Governance by board
SE for ages 1.5-5; ESL; science; art; music; childcare; suburban
location; interns accepted.

Montessori Children's Room (1970)
67 Old Route 22, Armonk, NY 10504
914-273-3291
Tuition: $430-935/mo
7 teachers, 5 assistants, 72 students, ages infant-6
Affiliation: AMI
Governance by administrator
Childcare.

Academic Community for Educational Success (1977)
200 Railroad Ave, Bedford Hills, NY 10507
Joan E. Barickman, Tch/Dir, 914-666-5983
Non-profit
2 teachers, 25 students, partly at-risk, ages 14-21, 9-12th
   grade
Affiliation: Bedford Central Schools
Governance by democratic school meeting
Teacher qualifications: certification
Intensive core courses; adventure-based counseling; PE; gov-
   ernment course; multi-aged classes; extensive field trips

Haldane Alternate Program (1982)
Craigside Dr, Cold Spring, NY 10516
Dennis Cairl, Tch, 914-265-9254 x18
Type: public choice
1 teacher, 24 students, mainly at-risk, ages 14-18, 9-12th
   grade
Governance by principal, teachers, board
Teacher qualifications: certification in secondary English and
   Social Studies
Success-oriented curriculum; structured; multi-aged classes;
   rural location.

Croton Montessori School (1968)
Box 84, Croton-on-Hudson, NY 10520
Elizabeth Terpoorton, 914-271-6580
Tuition: $2,100/4,000
2 teachers, 3 assistants, 50 students, mainly international,
   ages 3-6
Affiliations: AMS, AMT
Governance by administrator
Music, art, foreign languages; suburban location; interns
   accepted.

Berjan School (1984)
145 New St, Mamaroneck, NY 10543
Jane Marsella Schumer, 914-698-4002
Type: Montessori; tuition: $2,550-6,200/yr
90 students, ages 2-7
Small classes; self-paced, wholistic curriculum.

Westchester Day School
856 Orienta Ave, Mamaroneck, NY 10543
Zeev Aviezer, 914-698-8900
Type: independent
370 students, pre K-8th grade
Pre-school is Montessori; combines English and Judaic
   studies.

Fox Lane Middle School
Route 172, Mount Kisko, NY 10549
Dennis Mcgrath, 914-241-6118
Type: public choice

Bronxville Montessori School (1977)
101 Pondfield Rd W, Bronxville, NY 10550
Jean Nelson, 914-793-2083, FAX: 914-793-2360
Non-profit; tuition: $3,075-6,500/yr
4 teachers, 10 assistants, 144 students, mainly international,
   ages infant-6
Affiliation: NAEYC; accreditations: AMS, NY DSS
Governance by administrator, board
Multi-cultural; movement; music; ESL; psychotherapist; large
   gym; play areas; childcare; suburban location; interns
   accepted.

The Fleetwood Montessori School (1969)
199 North Columbus Ave, Mount Vernon, NY 10553-1101
William B. Adams, Director, 914-668-5570
Tuition: $1,680/2,800/yr
1 teacher, 3 assistants, 35 students, ages infant-6
Affiliations: AMI, WAEYC
Governance by administrator
Suburban location.

PASS-Peekskill Alternative Secondary School (1986)
1432 Park St, Peekskill, NY 10566
Delores Jones, Dir; Sheldon Levine, Prin, 914-737-2088, FAX: -
   3912
Type: public at-risk
4 teachers, 64 students, ages 14-19, 9-12th grade
Governance by director and principal
Teacher qualifications: NY Certification
Total inclusion classes; investigating a curriculum; multi-aged
   classes; urban location.

Program at Pleasantville HS (1985)
Romer Ave, Pleasantville, NY 10570
Vivian Owowski, 914-769-8102
Type: public choice

Resurrection School
116 Milton Rd, Rye, NY 10580
Alice Sweeney
Type: Montessori

Choice Program at Scarsdale Junior High School (1974)
Mamaroneck Rd, Scardsdale, NY 10583
Susan Taylor, 914-472-3478
Type: public choice
49 students, 7-8th grade
Governance by teachers and principal
Some ungraded classes; model United Nations; community
   meeting.

Our Lady of Fatima School
963 Scarsdale Rd, Scarsdale, NY 10583
Type: Montessori

Scarsdale Alternative School (1972)
45 Wayside Ln, Scarsdale, NY 10583
Tony Arenella, Dir, 914-721-2590
Type: public choice
5 teachers, 75 students, ages 14-18, 10-12th grade
Affiliation: CES
Governance by democratic school meeting
Teacher qualifications: NY Certification
"Just Community"; 1-month community service internship;
   Senior Project; no letter grades; multi-aged classes; subur-
   ban location; interns accepted.

Scarsdale Friends Nursery School (1954)
133 Popham Rd, Scarsdale, NY 10583
Jeanette Livoti, Dir, 914-472-6550
Type: Quaker, non-profit; tuition: $1,300/yr, scholarships
3 teachers, 20 students
Governance by teachers, parents, Quaker board
Teacher qualifications: certification for director
Suburban location.

Lakeland Alternative High School (1982)
Rt 132, Shrub Oak, NY 10588
Marc Gessin, Prin, 914-245-3382, FAX: 914-245-4391
Type: public at-risk
5 teachers, 40 students, mainly at-risk, ages 15-21, 10-12th
   grade
Governance by board
Teacher qualifications: state SE certification
Thematic instruction; cooperative learning; team teaching;
   Glasser's Ten-Step Approach to Discipline; parent support
   group; non-traditional counseling; work experience;
   project adventure challenge program; multi-aged classes;
   suburban location; transportation; interns accepted.

Phoenix Academy
PO Box 458 Stoney St, Shrub Oak, NY 10588
Joan Ahern, 914-962-2402
Type: public at-risk

Putnam-Westchester BOCES Alternative High School
(1977)
Fox Meadow Rd, Yorktown, NY 10598
Robert Kelderhouse, 914-245-2700
Type: public choice

Our Montessori School (1972)
PO Box 72, Yorktown Heights, NY 10598
Werner H. Hengst, Adm, 914-962-9466, FAX: same
Tuition: $3,750-7,500/yr
11 teachers, 20 assistants, 204 students, ages infant-12
Governance by administrator
Individualized; music; dance; computer; French; Montessori
     teacher training course; childcare; suburban location;
     interns accepted.

Bright Beginnings Pre-school Learning Center
1974 Commerce St, Yorktown Hts, NY 10598
Mara Ziedins, 914-962-2929
Type: Montessori
100 students, ages 18 mo-5
Three locations: Yorktown, Amawalk, Granite Springs;
     summer programs.

The Walkabout (1977)
Pinesbridge Rd, Yorktown Hts, NY 10598
Eugene Lebwohl, 914-245-2700
Type: public choice
Affiliation: Putnam-Westchester BOCES

Caroline Montessori School
52 N Broadway, White Plains, NY 10603

Regional Alternative High School
666 Old Orchard St, N White Plains, NY 10604
David Chura
Type: public choice

Montessori Children's Center at Burke (1991)
785 Mamaroneck Ave, White Plains, NY 10605
Carole Wolfe Korngold, Exec Dir, 914-948-2501, FAX: 421-0779
Tuition: $8,923/10,437
7 teachers, 8 assistants, 50 students, ages infant-6
Affiliation: AMS
Governance by administrator
Park-like site; toddler, infant, early childhood classrooms;
     childcare; suburban location; interns accepted.

Community School (1972)
228 Fisher Ave, White Plains, NY 10606
John P Garcia, 914-997-2420
Type: public choice

Enrico Fermi School for Performing Arts
27 Poplar St, Yonkers, NY 10701
Edward DeFino, 914-376-8460
Type: magnet
Pre K-6th grade
Computers; Montessori.

Museum School of the Arts & Sciences
579 Warburton Ave, Yonkers, NY 10701
Robert Torp, 914-376-8450
Type: magnet
Pre K-6th grade

School 32
1 Montclair Pl, Yonkers, NY 10701
Jennifer Schulman, 914-376-8595
Type: magnet
Pre K-6th grade
Family school.

Emerson Junior High School
160 Bolmer Ave, Yonkers, NY 10703
Charles Whelan, 914-376-8300
Type: magnet
7-8th grade
Computer science; arts; scenery and display.

School 22
1408 Nepperhan, Yonkers, NY 10703
Marvin Feldberg, 914-376-8440
Type: magnet
K-6th grade
FLAME: foreign language and multi-cultural education.

School 9
53 Fairview St, Yonkers, NY 10703
Jacques Weaver, 914-376-8325
Type: magnet
K-6th grade
Humanities.

Mark Twain Junior High
160 Woodland Ave, Yonkers, NY 10704
Ivan Toper, 914-376-8540
Type: magnet
7-8th grade
Health related studies; humanities.

Montessori, Humanities and Creative Arts Magnet
132 Valentine Ln, Yonkers, NY 10704
Kathleen P. MacSweeney, 914-376-8455
Type: public choice
Pre K-K

Burroughs Junior High School
150 Roackland Ave, Yonkers, NY 10705
Mary Lou Macdonald, 914-376-8200
Type: magnet
7-8th grade
Computers; business; human services; international studies.

Montessori at School 27 (1986)
132 Valentine Ln, Yonkers, NY 10705
Kathleen P. MacSweeney, 914-376-8455
Type: Public choice Montessori
16 teachers, 16 assistants, 364 students, ages 3-12
Affiliation: AMS
Governance by administrator
Italian; greenhouse studies; transportation.

Pearls Elementary
348 Hawthorne Ave, Yonkers, NY 10705
Sara Butler, 914-376-8253
Type: magnet
Pre K-6th grade
Gifted and talented.

School 21
100 Lee Ave, Yonkers, NY 10705
E. Cardona-Zuckerman, 914-376-8435
Type: magnet
K-6th grade
FLAME: foreign language and multi-cultural education.

Westchester Home Learners (1989)
190 Hollywood Ave, Crestwood, NY 10707
Beryl Polin, 914-337-5825
15-20 students, ages 2-13
Lending library.

Roosevelt High School
631 Tuckahee Rd, Yonkers, NY 10710
Michael Yarzulo, 914-376-8519
Type: magnet
9-12th grade
Commercial illustration, photography; fine arts.

New Rochelle Prep (1978)
116 Guion Pl, New Rochelle, NY 10801
Helen McLaughlin, 914-235-2969
Type: public choice

Brain-Compatible Information
(See Resource Section)

Transitional Learning Center
19 2nd Ave, Pelham, NY 10803-1417
Type: Montessori

Hudson Country Montessori School (1972)
340 Quaker Ridge Rd, New Rochelle, NY 10804
Musya Meyer, Dir, 914-636-6202, FAX: 914-636-5139
Non-profit; tuition: $3,065-8,470/yr
14 teachers, 23 assistants, 315 students, ages infant-9
Affiliation: SNMC; accreditations: NAEYC, DSS
Governance by administrator, board
Also Hudson Institute for Teacher Education; childcare; sub-
　urban location; transportation; interns accepted.

New Rochelle Academy
80 Mount Tom Rd, New Rochelle, NY 10805
Type: Montessori

Suffern Montessori School (1984)
3 Church Rd, Suffern, NY 10901
Martha Hyams, 914-357-1410
30 students, ages 3-6, pre K-1st grade
Multi-aged classes.

Sugar Loaf Union Free School (1991)
PO Box 530, Gibson Hill Rd, Chester, NY 10918
Stephen Janove, 914-469-2136
Type: public choice
30 students

Thevenet Montessori School (1972)
Country Rd 105, Highland Hills, NY 10930
Sr Loretta Knapp, 914 -928-2213
120 students, pre K-1st grade
Student-centered approach.

Middletown Alternative High School (1994)
Gardner Ave Ext, Middletown, NY 10940
914-341-5318
Type: public choice
4 teachers, 30 students, mainly at-risk, ages 15-18, 9-12th
　grade
Governance by teachers and principal.
Multi-aged classes; extensive field trips; individualized; subur-
　ban location.

Stepping Stones Montessori School (1984)
66 Bennett St, Middletown, NY 10940
Rose Moskowitz, 914-343-5774
64 students, ages 2.6-7, pre K-2nd grade

**STTAR (Saunders Trades and Technical Academic
　Response)** (1993)
181 Palmer Rd, Yonkers, NY 10956
Bernard Pierorazio, Prin, 914-376-8150, FAX: -8154
Type: public at-risk
3 teachers, 30 students, ages 14-18, 9th grade
Governance by teachers and principal
Individualized and cooperative learning; research, film, slide,
　video and computer work culminate in portfolios; multi-
　aged classes; suburban location; transportation.

Montessori Center of Nyack
77 Marion St, Nyack, NY 10960-2035

Rockland Learning Center (1971)
130 Concklin Rd, Pomona, NY 10970
Freyda Michelson, Dir, 914-354-5253
Non-profit; tuition: $243/486/mo
2 teachers, 1 assistant, 40 students, mainly international,
　ages 3-9

Accreditation: NY Chartered pre k-6
Governance by administrator, democratic school meeting,
　board
Teacher qualifications: taught together 22 years
Monthly units in science; music; childcare; suburban location;
　transportation; interns accepted.

Green Meadow Waldorf School (1950)
Hungry Hollow Rd, Chestnut Ridge, NY 10977
David Sloan, High School Chair, FAX: 914-356-2921
Non-profit; tuition: $4,225-7,110/yr, scholarships
418 students, ages 3-18, nursery, K-12th grade
Affiliations: NYSAIS, AWSNA
Governance by faculty
Teacher qualifications: college, Waldorf training
Exchange program with Waldorf in Europe, Australia, New
　Zealand; suburban location; transportation; interns
　accepted.

Waldorf Institute of Sunbridge College (1967)
260 Hungry Hollow Rd, Chestnut Ridge, NY 10977
Jonathan Hilton, Reg, 914-425-0055, FAX: 425-1413
Type: Waldorf higher education, non-profit; tuition: variable,
　scholarships
30 teachers, 125 adult students
Affiliations: AWSNA, Assn of Anthroposophical Colleges
Governance by faculty and board
Teacher qualifications: MSEd in early childhood, elem ed
Lectures; workshops; seasonal, special events; suburban
　location.

Tri-County Homeschoolers
130 Blanchard Rd, Stoneypoint, NY 10980
914-429-5156

**Grade 9 Alternative Program at North Rockland High
　School** (1985)
Hammond Rd, Thiells, NY 10984
George F Jochum, 914-942-2700
Type: public choice

Blue Rock School (1987)
110 Demarest Mill Rd, W Nyack, NY 10994
Mary Guthrie, Administrator, 914-627-0234
Type: independent, non-profit; tuition: $3,392-6,254,
　scholarships
K-6th grade
Non-sectarian; whole language; philosophy: when student is
　wholly engaged, her/his work is her/his own.

Gemini (1987)
Demarest Mill Rd, W Nyack, NY 10994
Anne Gusmano, English Teacher, 914-624-3480
Type: home-based public at-risk
4 teachers, 50 students, mainly at-risk, ages 15-18, 10-12th
　grade
Governance by teachers and principal
Teacher qualifications: MA degree
Teachers serve as mentors/informal counselors; interdiscipli-
　nary projects; contracts; suburban location; interns
　accepted.

Rockland County BOCES City As School Program (1993)
61 Parrot Rd, W Nyack, NY 10994
Ron Tullock, Adm, 914-627-4794, FAX: 914-627-6124
Type: public choice
2 students

Spirit of January
(See Resource Section)

Village School (1971)
614 Middle Neck Rd, Great Neck, NY 11023
Charles Piemonte, PhD, Dir, 516-773-1705
Type: public choice
6 teachers, 40 students, mainly at-risk, ages 14-18, 9-12th
　grade
Governance by teachers, principal

Student-directed; advisory system; Exhibition Studies; portfolio assessment; multi-aged classes; extensive field trips; interns accepted.

Our Lady of Grace Montessori (1968)
29 Shelter Rock Rd, Manhasset, NY 11030
Sr Dorothy Kibler, Prin, 516-365-9832, FAX: 516-365-9329
Non-profit; tuition: $2,025-2,925/yr
8 teachers, 5 assistants, 190 students, ages 3-6
Affiliation: NCEA; accreditations: AMS, MSA
Governance by administrator
Suburban location; interns accepted.

Happy Montessori School (1970)
40 Pleasant Ave, Port Washington, NY 11050
Amrit Sethi, Dir, 516-883-1131
55 students, nursery-K

International High School at LaGuardia CC (1985)
31-10 Thomson Ave, Long Island City, NY 11101
Eric Nadelstern, Prin, 718-482-5455
Type: public choice/at-risk
35 teachers, 460 students, mainly at-risk, ages 14-21
Affiliations: CUNY, NYC BE
Governance by teachers and principal
Teacher qualifications: NYC License
Multi-lingual/cultural; interdisciplinary; experiential; collaborative; multi-aged classes; urban location; interns accepted.

Les Enfants Montessori
2921 Newtown Ave, Long Island City, NY 11102-2128

Institute for the Arts and Technology
31-51 21st St, Astoria, NY 11106
Terry Borne, Co-Director, 718-349-4009

Brooklyn Friends School (1867)
375 Pearl St, Brooklyn, NY 11201
718-852-1029, FAX: 718-643-4868
Type: Quaker, non-profit; tuition: $11,000/yr, scholarships
55 teachers, 440 students, ages toddler-18, pre K-12th grade
Affiliations: NAIS, NYSAIS
Governance by principal
Teacher qualifications: MA
Video-making; ceramics; wood shop; art studies; computer labs; strong science dept; community service; racially diverse; no letter grades; extensive field trips; interns accepted.

Brooklyn Heights Montessori School (1965)
185 Court St, Brooklyn, NY 11201
Marcia Gardere, Dir, 718-858-5100, FAX: 243-0261
Non-profit; tuition: $5,550-8,975/yr
12 teachers, 1 assistant, 156 students, ages 3-9
Affiliations: AMS, NAEYC, ASCD, AECI
Governance by administrator, board
The Little Room, preschool SE program; childcare; transportation; interns accepted.

Mary McDowell Center For Learning (1984)
110 Schermerhorn St, Brooklyn, NY 11201
Debbie Zlotowitz, Head, 718-625-3939
Type: Quaker, non-profit; tuition: $15,600/yr, scholarships
8 teachers, 32 students, mainly at-risk, ages 5-11, ungraded
Affiliation: FCOE
Governance by principal, board
Teacher qualifications: head teacher: MA Special Ed; asst teacher: BA/BS
Responsibility, recognition of individual worth; individualized; multi-aged classes; interns accepted.

The New Program at PS 261 (1988)
314 Pacific St, Brooklyn, NY 11201
Arthur Foresta, Prin or Ann Powers, Dir, 718-330-9275
Type: public choice
Affiliations: NYC Public Schools, Center for Collaborative Education

Open classrooms; hands-on experience; individual work; small groups; developmentally-based social studies; includes thematic units; active parent participation.

IS 285
5909 Beverly Rd, Brooklyn, NY 11203
Anthony Raziano, 718-451-2200
Type: magnet
6-8th grade
Careers in the performing arts.

P 235
525 Lenox Rd, Brooklyn, NY 11203
Mitchel Levine, 718-773-4869
Type: magnet
Pre K-5th grade
Gifted students; early learning center.

Mercy Montessori School
1397 Brooklyn Ave, Brooklyn, NY 11203-5518
Sr Mary Harvey

Mapleton School
6015 18th Ave, Brooklyn, NY 11204
Joseph Maiello, 718-232-3880
Type: magnet
K-5th grade
Visions: community activists and ambassadors.

PS 192
4715 18th Ave, Brooklyn, NY 11204
Gennaro DeMarco, 718-633-3061
Type: magnet
K-5th grade
Environmental arts.

East New York Family Academy (1993)
2057 Linden Blvd, Brooklyn, NY 11207
718-927-0012
Type: public choice
HS
Affiliation: NYC Schools
College prep; vocational; internships; community service; personalized.

IS 296
125 Covert St, Brooklyn, NY 11207
N. Letow, 718-574-0288
Type: magnet
6-8th grade
Business careers; theater technology.

Brooklyn College Academy (1986)
1311 James Hall, 2900 Bedford Ave, Brooklyn, NY 11210
Madeline Lumachi, 718-951-9541
Type: public choice, at-risk
HS
Uses college facilities; interest-related internships; college prep; taught by college professors; HS, college credit.

Midwood Montessori
2825 Bedford Ave, Brooklyn, NY 11210
Harriet Safran

High School Redirection (1969)
226 Bristol St, Brooklyn, NY 11212
Sharyn Wetjen, Prin, 718-498-2605
Type: public choice
35 teachers, 500 students, mainly at-risk, ages 17-21
Governance by teachers, principal
Teacher qualifications: NYC credential
Intense guidance; no letter grades; multi-aged classes.

IS 281
8787 24th Ave, Brooklyn, NY 11214
Rose Molinelli, 718-996-6706
Type: magnet
6-8th grade
Media and communication arts.

Brooklyn New School (1987)
330 18th Street, Brooklyn, NY 11215
Mary Ellen Bosch, Director, 718 330-9288
Type: public choice
15 teachers, 250 students, ages 5–12, K–6th grade
Affiliations: Center for Collaborative Education, Coalition of
    Essential Schools
Governance by staff, parents and director
Teacher qualifications: NY License
Created by parents and teachers; hands-on curriculum for
    racially mixed population; no letter grades; multi-aged
    classes; extensive field trips; transportation; interns
    accepted.

The Children's House of Park Slope (1977)
421 7th St, Brooklyn, NY 11215
Gretchen Courage, Dir, 718-499-5667
Type: Montessori; tuition: $5,350-7,500/yr
3 teachers, 3 assistants, 48 students, ages 3–6
Affiliation: AMS
Governance by administrator
Childcare; urban location; interns accepted.

Carroll Street School
712 Carroll St, Brooklyn, NY 11215-2101
Angela Apuzzi
Type: Montessori

Frederick Douglass Literacy Center (1982)
832 Marcy Ave, New York, NY 11216
Lois Rekosh, 718-636-5770, FAX: 398-4476
Type: public at-risk
10 teachers, 180 students, ages 17–21, 10th grade
Affiliation: NYC Board of Ed
Governance by shared decision making
Literacy classes; computer lab; free meals available; trans-
    portation; interns accepted.

Street Academy High School (1971)
832 Marcy Ave, New York, NY 11216
718-622-4310
Type: public at-risk
250 students, 9–12th grade
Family program; career development; external learning expe-
    riences; keyboarding and computer tech.

Metropolitan Corporate Academy (1990)
362 Schermerhorn St, Brooklyn, NY 11217
212-935-5911
Type: public choice
9–12th grade
Affiliations: NYC BE, Goldman Sachs Inc
Interdisciplinary; school-based mgmt; internships; business
    ed; portfolio assessment; social services; college prep;
    parental involvement.

The Berkeley Caroll School
181 Lincoln Pl, Brooklyn, NY 11217
Joan Martin, 718-965-4166
Type: Montessori
635 students, pre K–12th grade
Three locations; lower school has Montessori approach.

YMCA Montessori Day School
30 3rd Ave, Brooklyn, NY 11217-1822

Peaceable School Montessori
33 7th Ave, Brooklyn, NY 11217-3439

New York City Vocational Training Center (1987)
1171 65th Street, Brooklyn, NY 11219
Alan Werner, Prin, 718-236-1661, FAX: -4340
Type: public/independent
60 teachers, 2000 students, mainly at-risk, ages 17–21,
    ungraded
Affiliation: NYC BE
Governance by principal

Teacher qualifications: NYC License
Industrial work experience; on-site academic and voc train-
    ing; diploma/GED; multi-aged classes; no letter grades.

Bay Ridge Montessori School
6301 12th Ave, Brooklyn, NY 11219-5213
June Grancio

J 126 School
424 Leanard, Brooklyn, NY 11222
Dr Toback, 718-782-2527
Type: magnet
7–9th grade
Creative arts.

PS 215
415 Ave S, Brooklyn, NY 11223
Gail Feuer, 718-339-2464
Type: magnet
K–1st grade
Gifted and talented.

PS 95
345 Van Sicklen St, Brooklyn, NY 11223
James Filatro, 718-449-5050
Type: magnet
K–5th grade
Multi-grade primary; open door.

IS 239
2401 Neptune Ave, Brooklyn, NY 11224
Gary Goldstein, 718-266-0814
Type: magnet
6–8th grade
Gifted and talented.

PS 188
3314 Neptune Ave, Brooklyn, NY 11224
Augusto Martinez, 718-266-6380
Type: magnet
K–5th grade
Gifted and talented.

PS 329
2929 W 30th St, Brooklyn, NY 11224
Stephen Levy, 718-996-3800
Type: magnet
K–5th grade
Gifted and talented.

Hawthorne Corners Preschool (1965)
1950 Bedford Ave, Brooklyn, NY 11225
Patricia Oduba, 718-282-7200
Type: Montessori
61 students, ages 3–6
Located in East Flatbush; population is mainly from the
    Caribbean and USA.

Lefferts Gardens Montessori (1982)
559 Rogers Ave, Brooklyn, NY 11225
Lenore Briggs, 718-773-0287
45 students, ages 2.5–8
Two locations.

Rosa Weatherless Alternative Middle School
797 Bushwick Ave, Brooklyn, NY 11227
S. Callari, 718-574-0148
Type: magnet
6–8th grade

Lefferts Park School
7115 15th Ave, Brooklyn, NY 11228
Alex Poehlemann, 718-232-0685
Type: magnet
K–5th grade
Global studies through literature, performing arts and media.

Windmill Montessori School
1317 Ave T, Brooklyn, NY 11229-3397
Liza Herzberg, Dir, 718-375-4277
Tuition: $3,200-5,800/yr
8 teachers, 8 assistants, 151 students, ages infant–15
Affiliation: AMS; accreditation: BH; NYS
Governance by administrator
Outer-bound JHS; upper elementary is part of Newsday programs; urban location; interns accepted.

PS 99
1120 E 10th St, Brooklyn, NY 11230
Louis Galinsky, 718-338-9201
Type: magnet
K–7th grade
Gifted and talented.

The Alternative Program at PS 27 (1987)
Hicks St & Nelson St, Brooklyn, NY 11231
Paul Schwarz, 718-330-9345
Type: public choice

East Brooklyn Congregations High School for Public Service-Bushwick, East New York (1993)
1495 Herkimer St, Brooklyn, NY 11233
718-385-6071
Type: public choice
HS
Affiliation: NYC Public Schools
Mentorships; internships; inquiry-based; student-centered.

Montessori School of Mill Basin
6311 Avenue N, Brooklyn, NY 11234
Joan Indovino, Dir, 718-444-3200
Also has annex at 6301 Ave N, Brooklyn, 11234.

Montessori School of Mill Beach
6311 Ave N, Main Bldg, Brooklyn, NY 11234

P 276
1070 E 83 St, Brooklyn, NY 11236
Eileene Leibowitz, 718-241-5757
Type: magnet
Pre K–5th grade
Gifted and talented.

IS 162
1390 Willoughby Ave, Brooklyn, NY 11237
Aida Rivera, 718-821-4860
Type: magnet
6–8th grade
Bio-medical; performing arts.

IS 291
231 Palmetto St, Brooklyn, NY 11237
A. Bryan, 718-574-0361
Type: magnet
6–8th grade
Video technology; bilingual.

IS 383
1300 Greene Ave, Brooklyn, NY 11237
Mildred Boyce, 718-574-0390
Type: magnet
6–8th grade
Gifted and talented.

Barbara Taylor School (1986)
627 Vanderbilt Ave, Brooklyn, NY 11238
Dr Lois Holzman, Dir, 718-638-6255
Type: independent, non-profit; tuition: $3,000, one scholarship
3 teachers, 17 students, mainly at-risk, ages 4-13, K–8th grade
Affiliation: East Side Inst for Short Term Psychotherapy
Governance by staff, students, parents

Vygotsky approach; like infants, everyone goes "beyond themselves"; no letter grades; non-compulsory class attendance; multi-aged classes; extensive field trips; urban location; interns accepted.

Tree of Life Montessori
810 Classen Ave, Brooklyn, NY 11238

Flushing Montessori School (1982)
147-08 Bayside Ave, Flushing, NY 11354
Mrs H Lucas, Director, 718-353-5544
30 students, ages 3–5, nursery-K
Governance by principal
2, 3 and 5-day schedules; environmental awareness in outdoor, parklike setting.

The House for Bright and Gifted Children (1989)
33-15 154th St, Flushing, NY 11354
718-461-6464
Type: independent
28 students, nursery-K
Everyone is gifted;"playing is learning, learning is playing"; stress on English.

PS 29 School of Theater Arts
125-10 23 Ave, College Point, NY 11356
Theresa Harris, 718-886-5111
Type: magnet
K–6th grade

PS 193
152-20 11th Ave, Whitestone, NY 11357
Marc Rosenberg, 718-767-8810
Type: magnet
1–6th grade
Discovery.

Early Education Program at St Mary's Hospital for Children (1991)
29-01 216th St, Bayside, NY 11360
Sondra Friedman, Dir, 718-281-8841, FAX: 718-428-0531
Type: Montessori, non-profit
2 teachers, 3 assistants, 16 students, ages infant–5
Accreditation: AMS
Suburban location; interns accepted.

Linda Tagliaferro
(See Resource Section)

MS 67
51-60 Marathon Pkwy, Little Neck, NY 11362
Mae Fong, 718-423-8138
Type: magnet
6–9th grade
Inquiry-based.

PS 162
201-02 53rd Ave, Bayside, NY 11364
Georgina Durando, 718-423-8621
Type: magnet
3–4th grade
Inquiry-based.

Parsons Junior High School 168
157-40 76th Rd, Flushing, NY 11366
Nat Blaivas, 718-591-9000
Type: magnet
7–9th grade
Performing arts.

PS 154
75-02 162 St, Flushing, NY 11366
Marjorie Richardson, 718-591-1500
Type: magnet
7–9th grade
Art and design.

IS 250
144-39 D Gravett Rd, Flushing, NY 11367
Jeffrey Ratner, 718-544-6912
Type: magnet
7-9th grade
Community campus school.

PS 164 School of Visual, Performing & Literary Arts
138-01 77 Ave, Flushing, NY 11367
Barbara Brown, 718-544-1083
Type: magnet
K-6th grade

PS 164 The Queens Valley
138-01 77th Ave, Flushing, NY 11367
Barbara Brown, 718-544-1083
Type: magnet
1-6th grade
Visual, performing and literary arts.

Kew Resources
(See Resource Section)

Rainbow Montessori School
15030 Union Tpke, Flushing, NY 11367-3977

Apple Montessori School
5938 Xenia St, Rego Park, NY 11368-3926

PS 92
99-01 34th Ave, Corona, NY 11370
Kathleen Murphy, 718-458-4580
Type: magnet
K-5th grade
Music; multi-cultural.

JHS 141
37-11 21st Ave, Long Island, NY 11370
Carl Tomaselli, 718-278-6547
Type: magnet
7-9th grade
Humanities.

PS 112
35-05 37th Ave, Long Island, NY 11370
Daisy Martin, 718-784-5250
Type: magnet
K-6th grade
Social studies; multi-cultural.

PS 126
31-51 21st St, Long Island, NY 11370
Barbara Embriano, 718-274-8316
Type: magnet
6-9th grade
Visual and performing arts.

PS 171
14-14 29th Ave, Long Island, NY 11370
Anne Bussell, 718-932-0909
Type: magnet
K-5th grade
Media and telecommunications.

Montessori Progressive Learning
195-09 Linden Blvd, St Albans, NY 11412

Wise Memorial Montessori Learning Center
195-05 Linden Blvd, St Albans, NY 11412

PS 178
189-10 Radnor Rd, Jamaica, NY 11423
Joan Weingarten, 718-464-5763
Type: magnet
4-5th grade
Inquiry-based.

Ideal Montessori School (1982)
87-41 165th St, Jamaica, NY 11432
K P Chandu, Prin, 718-523-6237

140 students, ages 3-14, K-8th grade
Governance by principal
SE.

Montessori Tutoring & Pre-School
9001 Merrick Blvd, Jamaica, NY 11432-5244

Dover Publications, Inc
(See Resource Section)

Jack & Jill Montessori School
23 Front St, E Rockaway, NY 11518

Kid's Place of Choice, South Nassau HS Resource Room
(1992)
186 E Ave, Freeport, NY 11520
Devorah Weinmann, 516-868-5766, FAX: 516-379-8435
Type: home-based, non-profit
15 students, ages 3-16
Governance by parent cooperative
Supervision by parents on rotating basis; member-generated
activities

Long Island Growing at Home (LIGHT) (1990)
186 E Ave, Freeport, NY 11520
Devorah Weinmann, 516-868-5766, FAX: 516-379-8435
Governance by parent cooperative
Homeschool support group for Suffolk, Nassau, Queens;
monthly meetings; 2-3 field trips/mo.

P S International Montessori School
228 S Ocean Ave, Freeport, NY 11520-4446
516-623-0716
Pre K-6th grade

The Waldorf School of Garden City (1947)
Cambridge Ave, Garden City, NY 11530
Marilyn Ruppart, Faculty Chair, 516-742-3434
Non-profit; tuition: $1,650-8,200/yr, scholarships
37 teachers, 270 students, ages 3-18, nursery-12th grade
Governance by teachers and principal
Teacher qualifications: BA, Waldorf mentoring
1-wk/yr at New Hampshire campus; suburban location.

Program of Alternative Comprehensive Education
(PACE)
195 Brookville Rd, Brookville, NY 11545
Yvette Villegas, Adm, 615-626-1022
Type: public at-risk
47 students, ages 14+, 9-12th grade
Affiliation: BOCES
For able but disaffected youth; not for special ed; campus
located at Brookville Outdoor Ed Ctr; placement made
through local school district which provides transportation;
interdisciplinary; access to occupational education programs; can meet all requirements for high school diploma;
almost all go on to higher ed.

Another Way at North Shore High School (1990)
450 Glen Cove Ave, Glen Head, NY 11545
Jay Emmer, Coordinator, 516-671-5500
Type: public at-risk
2 teachers, 15 students, ages 14-18, 9-12th grade
Governance by teachers and principal
Teacher qualifications: state certification
Team teaching; narrative assessments; interdisciplinary;
multi-aged classes; suburban location.

City As School Program at Hempstead High School
(1993)
185 Peninsula Blvd, Hempstead, NY 11550
Lisa Harris, 516-292-7052
Type: public choice
25 students

New Frontier Montessori School (1970)
35 Fulton St, Hempstead, NY 11550
Leona Budin, 516-678-2983

93 students, ages 2.5-11, pre K-6th grade
Affiliation: AMS

City As School Program at Long Beach High School
(1993)
233 Lagoon Drive West, Lido Beach, NY 11561
Robert Dodes, 516-897-2036
Type: public choice
10 students

Progressive School of Long Island (1985)
1425 Merrick Ave, Merrick, NY 11566
Eric Jacobson, Director, 516-868-6835
Type: independent, non-profit; tuition: $3,750, scholarships
17 teachers, 105 students, ages 5-12, K-6th grade
Governance by teachers and principal, board
Philosophy of "neo-humanism," which embraces oneness of
    all things; 2 teachers per class; varied learning styles; yoga,
    computer, drama, social awareness, other electives; subur-
    ban location; transportation; interns accepted.

SWS (School Within A School) c/o The Wheatley School
(1972)
11 Bacon Rd, Old Westbury, NY 11568
Bob Bernstein, Coordinator, 516-876-4700
Type: public choice
4 teachers, 76 students, ages 15-18, 10-12th grade
Governance by democratic school meeting
Academically rigorous; honesty, integrity, and trust; student
    accepts responsibility for own education; constitution;
    supreme court; elected moderator; multi-aged classes;
    suburban location; interns accepted.

Ann Frank Montessori School
430 DeMott Ave, Rockville Centre, NY 11570
Carolyn Larcy, 516-678-5955
75 students, ages 3-8
Affiliation: AMI
Individualized program; advanced students transfer to Maria
    Montessori School in Levitown.

Greenhouse Alternative at South Side High School (1974)
Shepherd St, Rockville Centre, NY 11570
Richard Zodda, Coord, 516-255-8962
Type: public at-risk
3 teachers, 30 students, ages 15-18, 10-12th grade
Governance by democratic school meeting
Comprehensive; career awareness; community resources;
    basic social skills; extensive field trips; multi-aged classes;
    suburban location; interns accepted.

Southside High School City As School Program (1993)
140 Shepherd St, Rockville Centre, NY 11570
Robin Calitri, 516-255-8947
Type: public choice
34 students

Merle Avenue Program (1985)
Merle Ave School, Oceanside, NY 11572
Ira Sarison, 516-678-1200
Type: public choice

Extended Support Program (1986)
Roslyn High School, Roslyn, NY 11577
Dr Pat James Jordan, 516-625-6379
Type: public choice
2 teachers, 25 students, mainly at-risk, ages 14-19
Governance by board
School-within-a-school; counseling; course work; behavior
    modification; suburban location.

Alternative Education Resource Organization (AERO)
(See Resource Section)

Valley Street Central High School (1987)
One Kent Rd, Valley Stream, NY 11582
Henry Cram, 516-561-7910
Type: public choice

Alternative School
W Tresper Clarke HS, Westbury, NY 11590
William J. Schaub, Asst Prin, 516-876-7416
Type: public at-risk
3 teachers, 30 students, ages 15-21, 10-12th grade
Governance by teachers and principal
For potential drop-outs; suburban location; transportation;
    interns accepted.

North Babylon Alternative High School (1985)
1 Phelps Ln, North Babylon, NY 11703
Carl A. Torrillo, Coord, 516-321-3279
Type: public at-risk
18 teachers, 50 students, ages 15-19, 10-12th grade
Governance by principal
Teacher qualifications: NY Certification, experience
Diploma; contract; strict attendance policy; no letter grades;
    multi-aged classes; suburban location.

John F. Kennedy Elementary
175 Brookvale Ave, W Babylon, NY 11704
Emanuel Campisi, 516-321-3053
Type: magnet
4-5th grade
Cognitively gifted.

South Bay Elementary
160 Great E Neck Rd, W Babylon, NY 11704
Patricia Farrell, 516-321-3145
Type: magnet
3rd grade
Cognitively gifted.

Tooker Ave Elementary
855 Tooker Ave, W Babylon, NY 11704
Gary Loker, 516-321-3136
Type: magnet
K-5th grade
Cognitively gifted.

Bethpage Alternative for Success Curriculum (BASC)
(1986)
Cherry Ave, Bethpage, NY 11714
Ira J. Kahn, Asst Prin, 516-733-3750
Type: public choice
9 teachers, 28 students, ages 14-17, 9-11th grade
Governance by board
Teacher qualifications: NY certification
Regents level education.

Grasso Homeschool (1993)
332 Brentwood Parkway, Brentwood, NY 11717
Alicia Grasso, 516-434-1117
1 teacher, 1 student, age 8, 4th grade
Works with 2 PTAs, Council of PTAs, school improvement
    team, Brentwood Bd of Ed, to improve education for all
    children; suburban location.

Bellport PM High School (1985)
Beaver Dam Rd, Brookhaven, NY 11719
Bette E Errig, 516-286-4363
Type: public choice

Middle Country Performing Arts School (1985)
Unity Drive School, Centereach, NY 11720
Arthur Dermer, 516-588-1029
Type: public choice

American Open University (1955)
211 Carlton Ave, Central Islip, NY 11722
Dr Norma Talley, 516-348-3300
Tuition: $90/credit hour
Non-residential arm of NY Institute of Technology; courses by
    computer teleconferencing; credit for previous experi-
    ence; mentors.

Central Islip Alternative High School (1989)
Wheeler Rd, Central Islip, NY 11722
D. Meehan, Prin, 516-348-5065

Type: public at-risk
4 teachers, 25-60 students, ages 15-21, 9-12th grade
Governance by teachers, principal, and board
Daily counseling; suburban location; transportation; interns accepted.

Operation: Setauket Approach to Interage Learning (OP-SAIL) at Setauket ES (1976)
134 Main St, E Setauket, NY 11733
Dr Thomas DeBello, Prin, 516-474-7690
Type: public choice
3 teachers, 70 students, ages 9-12, 4-6th grade
Governance by principal, teachers, parent cooperative, board, democratic school meeting, faculty and student reps
Interns accepted.

Theatre Arts Option (1981)
134 Main St, Setauket, NY 11733-2867
Joseph Baldino, 516-474-7690, FAX: 516-474-7692
Type: public choice
2 teachers, 50 students, ages 9-12, 5-6th grade
Teacher qualifications: certification
Interns accepted.

PAGE at Farmingdale Senior High School (1983)
Lincoln & Midwood, Farmingdale, NY 11735
Eugene McSweeney, Coord, 516-752-6624
Type: public at-risk
5 teachers, 50-60 students, mainly at-risk, ages 15-18, 10-12th grade
Governance by teachers and principal
Building self-confidence; peer counseling; student council; yearbook; holiday dinners; fund raisers; suburban location; interns accepted.

The North Suffolk Montessori School (1965)
PO Box 525, Huntington, NY 11743
Patricia St Jean, Director, 516-449-0988, 516-331-5113
Non-profit; tuition: $2,200-5,400, scholarships
150 students, ages 2-12, pre K-6th grade
Governance by principal and teachers
Multisensory; multi-cultural; computer-aided, hands-on learning; teaching teams; small classes; after school enrichment; summer sessions; student internship; 2 locations: North Huntington, Commack.

West Hills Montessori School (1968)
21 Sweet Hollow Rd, Huntington, NY 11743-6530
Sheldon Thompson, Director, 516-385-3342
Tuition: $1,895 pre-K, 2250 K, 2800 Extended, scholarships
150 students, ages 3-9, pre K-3rd grade
Affiliation: AMS
Governance by teachers and principal
Full range of Montessori materials.

Center for the Study of Educational Alternatives (1977)
Hofstra University, Hempstead, NY 11746
Dr Mary Anne Raywid, Director, 516-463-5766, 516-271-0661
Type: higher education, non-profit
Undertakes research and evaluations related to alternative schools; clearinghouse, consulting.

South Huntington Alternative High School (1988)
301 W Hills Rd, Huntington Station, NY 11746
Daniel Kalina, Dir, 516-673-1772
Type: public at-risk
6 teachers, 24 students, ages 16-19, 11-12th grade
Governance by principal
Teacher qualifications: NY certification
Small classes; life skills; academic prep; suburban location.

Early Childhood Center (1985)
Craig Gariepy Ave, Islip Terrace, NY 11752
Margaret Harper, 516-581-1600, FAX: 516-581-1617
Type: Montessori
2 teachers, 1 assistant, 60 students, ages 3-6
Governance by administrator

Ameliorates entering kindergarteners' learning difficulties; childcare; suburban location.

East Islip Public Schools-Montessori Preschool
Craig B Gariepy Ave, Islip Terrace, NY 11752
Barbara Mead

Maria Montessori School (1964)
11 Laurel Lane, Levitown, NY 11756
Carolyn Larcy, 516-520-0301
100 students, ages 3-14
Affiliation: AMI
Four levels: 3-6, 6-9, 9-12, junior high; students ready for Regents by 8th grade.

Levittown Schools Alternative Program (1988)
Division Avenue HS, Division Ave, Levittown, NY 11756
Daniel K. Provost, 516-520-5719
Type: public at-risk
1 teacher, 14 students, mainly at-risk, ages 15-21, HS
Governance by teachers, principal, and building chairman
Teacher qualifications: SE certification, experience with ED population
Half-day; contract-based; voc; GED prep; multi-aged classes; suburban location.

Lindenhurst Alternative Learning Center (1986)
350 Daniel St, Lindenhurst, NY 11757
James Connolly, Asst Prin, 516-226-6562
Type: public at-risk
4 teachers, 70 students, ages 13-19, 9-12th grade
Affiliation: Lindenhurst HS
Governance by teachers and principal
Teacher qualifications: patience and resourcefulness
Academic and social behavior modification; multi-aged classes; extensive field trips; suburban location; transportation.

Montessori School of Lindenhurst (1971)
1755 11th St, Lindenhurst, NY 11757-4509
Maryellen Clark, Owner/Administrator, 516-226-3066
Affiliation: AMS

Alternative Learning Program at Plainedge HS (1986)
Wyngate Dr, Massapequa, NY 11758
Frank Caramanica, Team Coord, 516-797-4428
Type: public at-risk
2 teachers, 20 students, ages 14-20, 9-12th grade
Governance by team of teachers with student input
Teacher qualifications: certification
Breakfast program; daily school meeting; multi-aged classes; suburban location; interns accepted.

Montessori Children's School, Inc (1966)
Box 422, Central & Jerusalem Aves, Massapequa, NY 11758
Charlene Sherwin, 516-541-6365
120 students, ages 2 yrs 9 mo-8 yrs, pre K-3rd grade
Affiliation: AMS
Didactic materials used in all areas of curriculum.

Long Island Home Schoolers Association
4 Seville Pl, Massapequa Park, NY 11762
Lynn Rudin, 516-795-5554
12+ students
Non-sectarian; field trips.

Step by Step Early Learing Center
138 Radio Ave, Miller Place, NY 11764-3412
Type: Montessori

LMC Montessori Teacher Centre
Nantucket Way, Mt Sinai, Long Island, NY 11766
Type: Montessori teacher education

Environment Team, Northport High School
Laurel Hill Rd, Northport, NY 11768
Bob Benner, 516-261-9000
Type: public choice

3 teachers, 60 students, 11-12th grade
Program within a school; science, social studies and art projects; camping; community involvement.

Sachem (1978)
Sachem North HS, 212 Smith Rd, Lake Ronkonkoma, NY 11779
William Schmidt, Supervisor; John Heslin, Asst Supervisor, 516-476-0417
Type: public at-risk
15 teachers, 40 students, mainly at-risk, ages 14-21, 9-12+
Governance by teachers and principal
Teacher qualifications: certifications
Student, parent sign an educational contract; low ratio; secure, structured classroom environment; counselors, psychologist address behavior, life problems; no letter grades; multi-aged classes; suburban location; interns accepted.

Suffolk Lutheran School-Montessori Program
Moriches & Woodlawn, St James, NY 11780

Children's Montessori Center
7 Flowerfield #32, Saint James, NY 11780-1514

Maria Montessori School
2025 Washington Ave, Seaford, NY 11783
Carolyn Larcy, 516-785-0372
Tuition: $2,600-5,000
120 students, K-8th grade
Experiential learning; extended field trips.

Montessori School of Selden (1976)
38 Adirondack Dr, PO Box 1028, Selden, NY 11784
Linda Beeccroft, Director, 516-736-2246
Tuition: $139-414/mo
72 students, ages 2.75-6, pre K-6th grade
Governance by principal
BOCES II.

North Shore Montessori School
218 Christian Ave, Stony Brook, NY 11790
Barbara Ende, 516-689-8273
Creative movement; drama; Spanish twice a week; library; music.

Wyandanch Memorial High School (1973)
32 St & Brooklyn Ave, Wyandanch, NY 11798
Anthony Fusco, 516-491-1022
Type: public choice

Hampton Day School (1966)
Butter Lane, Bridgehampton, NY 11932
Claud Okin, 516-537-1240
Type: independent; tuition: $2,150-6,500, scholarships
26 teachers, 164 students, pre K-8th grade
No letter grades; thematic approach; child-driven curriculum.

William Floyd HS Equivalent Attendance Program (1985)
240 Mastic Beach Rd, Mastic Beach, NY 11951
Jean Thoden, 516-281-3020
Type: public choice
40 students, ages 16-17, 9-12th grade
GED prep; work credit given.

Southampton Montessori School (1983)
135 St. Andrews Rd, Southampton, NY 11968
Irene Hope Gazza, Dir, 516-283-2223
Tuition: $3,400/yr
4 teachers; student ages 3-6
Accreditations: AMS, NY Charter
Governance by administrator, teachers, democratic school meeting
Suburban location; interns accepted.

Friends World Program of Long Island University (1965)
Southampton Campus, Southampton, NY 11968
Lewis Greenstein, Director, 516-287-8464, FAX: 283-4081

Type: Quaker higher education, boarding, non-profit; tuition: $11,000, scholarships
23 teachers, 130 students, ages 17+
Governance by democratic school meeting
Teacher qualifications: PhD, MA/MS
Fully accredited BA program; experiential model; students study at eight centers in China, India, Costa Rica, England, Israel, Japan, Kenya and US; internships; ind study; no letter grades.

Rensselaer Columbia Greene Boces High School (1984)
1550 Schuurman Rd, Castleton, NY 12033
Diane Keating, 518-477-8771
Type: public choice

The Alternative Learning Center (1991)
c/o Barnett-Mulligan, 143 Hudson Ave, Chatham, NY 12037
Wendy Barnett-Mulligan
Type: independent, non-profit; tuition: $25/half-year session
Governance by parent cooperative
Children/parent group; skills, interest sharing; workshops; field trips; rural location.

Schoharie County Area Home Educators
RD 2, Box 759, Cobleskill, NY 12043
Amy G White

Montessori Center
75 Jordan Blvd, Delmar, NY 12054
Kathleen Hutter

Blossoms Montessori Learning Program
56 Hudson Ave, PO Box 223/56, Delmar, NY 12054-0121
Gaston Cadieux

ALLPIE: The Alliance for Parental Involvement in Education
(See Resource Section)

Alternative Program
Luther Road, East Greenbush, NY 12061
Gerald Elliott, Asst Prin, 518-477-4138
Type: public at-risk
30 students, mainly at-risk, ages 13-20, 9-12th grade
Governance by principal and board
Teacher qualifications: NYS certification in subject area
Small classes; extra counseling; some older students exit to mainstream; suburban location.

Hawthorne Valley School (1973)
Rd 2 Box 225, Ghent, NY 12075
Patrick Stolfo, College Chair, 518-672-7120, FAX: -0181
Type: Waldorf, non-profit; tuition: $5,300-5,800, scholarships
32 teachers, 305 students, ages 4-18, pre K-12th grade
Affiliation: R. Steiner Ed & Farming Assn
Governance by college faculty with mandated committees
Teacher qualifications: college degree, prefer Waldorf training
Specialist teachers; near working farm; rural location; transportation; interns accepted.

GALLAH (Green/Albany Learning At Home) (1991)
Rte 54, Hanacroix, NY 12087
Charlotte Carter, Sally Bogardus, 518-756-6120
20+ students, K-6th grade
Governance by parent cooperative
Peer workshops; newsletter.

Johnstown Alternative and Continuing Education (1991)
501 Glebe St, Johnstown, NY 12095
Laurie Bargstedt, Community Educator, 518-762-4769
Type: public choice
Student ages 16-60
GED, diploma and ESL programs; computer literacy; Adkins Life Skills; conflict management; career development; apprenticeships; personal interest courses; parenting and financial education; counseling.

Montessori School of Albany
PO Box 245, Rensselaer, NY 12144-0245
Bernadine Starrs

Capital District Home Educators
Rd 2, Box 6A, Schaghticoke, NY 12154
Rebecca MacKenzie

Robert C Parker School (1991)
141 Main Ave, Wyantskill, NY 12198
Susan Merrett, Director, 518-286-3449
Type: independent; tuition: $5,600, scholarships
50 students, ages 8-13, 4-8th grade
Governance by principal
Self-paced, individualized curriculum; cooperative, hands-on
    learning; small classes.

Montessori Magnet School, Albany Public Schools
75 Park Ave, Albany, NY 12202
Kathleen Mrozak or Maggie Fuller, 518-462-7140

The Free School (1971)
8 Elm St, Albany, NY 12202
Mary Leue, Dir Emeritus, 518-434-3072, FAX: 432-8984
Type: independent, non-profit; tuition: sliding scale
10 teachers, 42 students, ages 3 mo-14, ungraded
Affiliation: NCACS
Governance by democratic school meeting, board; teachers
    do long-range planning.
Staff counseling training; forest land in Taconic Mts; no letter
    grades; non-compulsory class attendance; extensive field
    trips; childcare; urban location; interns accepted.

SKOLE
(See Resource Section)

St Catherine's Center for Children
40 N Main Ave, Albany, NY 12203
Sr Dorothy Copson
Type: Montessori

Pine Hills Montessori Day Care
715 Morris St, Albany, NY 12208
Jean Dearstyne

Loving Education At Home
Box 12846, Albany, NY 12212-2846

Assistant Commissioner for Non-Public Schools
State Education Department, Albany, NY 12234
Rachel Smith, 518-474-3879
Type: state home-based
NY state does not require parents to be certified; individual-
    ized home instruction plan, quarterly progress reports,
    annual assessment are submitted to local superintendent;
    testing required in alternate years in grades 4-8 and every
    year 9-12.

Albany Area Home Schoolers (1992)
46 Pershing Ave, Scotia, NY 12302
Jon or Sheila Stone, 518-346-3413, FAX: 518-399-3277
Governance by board
Newsletter; support.

Graduation Achievement Program (1989)
2072 Curry Rd, Rotterdam, NY 12303
Niel Tebbano, Prin; Rosemarie Devoe, Tch/Coord, 518-356-
    5010, FAX: 518-356-1518
Type: public choice
1 teacher, 1 assistant, 25-30 students, mainly at-risk, ages
    16-20, 10-12th grade
Governance by teachers and principal
Teacher qualifications: secondary certification
Self-motivation is an essential goal; 3-hour academic ses-
    sions; independent study; no letter grades; 100% parental
    involvement; suburban location; transportation.

Shalmont High School (1993)
1 Sabre Dr, Schenectady, NY 12306
Peter Rings, 518-355-6110
Type: independent, non-profit
1 teacher, 8 students, ages 15-19, 9-12th grade
Governance by board
No letter grades; rural location.

Linton Ace Program (1985)
The Plaza Linton High School, Schenectady, NY 12308
Albert Aldi, 518-370-8190
Type: public choice

The Montessori School (1991)
2117 Union St, Niskayuna, NY 12309
Pam Slotsky, Dir/Tch, 518-374-4764
24 students, ages 3-6
Affiliations: AMS, NAMTA
Governance by administrator
12/class max; traditional Montessori program; cooking; sign
    language; Spanish; multi-aged classes; suburban location.

Open School at Howe School (1971)
Baker Ave, Schenectady, NY 12309
Jack D Hickey, 518-370-8295
Type: public choice

Villa Fusco Montessori School
955 Balltown Rd, Schenectady, NY 12309-6532

Woodstock Support Group
PO Box 34, Lake Hill, NY 12448
Mary Pustilnik
Type: home-based

Port Ewen Ed Ctr
Rt 9W, Box 1176, Port Ewen, NY 12466
Nancy Plummer, 914-339-8710
Type: public at-risk

Ulster County BOCES Alternative School (1985)
PO Box 1176, Port Ewen, NY 12466
Nancy Plumer, 914-339-8718
Type: public at-risk
110 students, 7-12th grade
Teen parent, GED, vocational and diploma programs; focus on
    integration of arts in curriculum.

High Meadow School (1984)
PO Box 552, Stone Ridge, NY 12484
Hope S. Wootan, Adm, 914-681-4855
Type: independent, non-profit
14 teachers, 51 students, ages 4-12, K-7th grade
Governance by teachers, principal, democratic school
    meeting, parent cooperative, board
Student-centered; self-directed; cooperative spirit; wholistic;
    self-esteem; conflict resolution; no letter grades; multi-
    aged classes; extensive field trips; rural location; trans-
    portation; interns accepted.

Mountain Laurel Waldorf (1978)
PO Box 208, Tillson, NY 12486-0208
Julia Roig, Administrator, 914-658-3740
Tuition: $4,500, scholarships
92 students, ages 4-14, K-7th grade
Affiliation: AWSNA
Governance by board/faculty with parent involvement

Wise Woman Center (1982)
PO Box 64, Woodstock, NY 12498
Susun S. Weed, 914-246-8081, FAX: same
Type: higher education, boarding
Mainly for women only
Workshops and apprenticeships in herbal medicine and
    Goddess spirituality; program calendar available.

Woodstock Montessori School
Rt 212, Woodstock, NY 12498

City As School Program at Cornwall Central High School
(1992)
122 Main St, Cornwall, NY 12518
Robert Maher, Prin, 914-534-8908
Type: public choice
25 students

HELP Resource Center
RR1 Box 60-B, Elizaville, NY 12523
Barbara S. Calabrese, 914-756-3902
Type: home-based

Anthroposophic Press
(See Resource Section)

R-C-G BOCES (1985)
61 Union Tpk, Hudson, NY 12534
Fred Root, 518-828-4157, FAX: 518-828-0084
Type: public at-risk; tuition: $8,000/yr, scholarships
7 teachers, 98 students, ages 13–21, 7-12th grade
Governance by teachers and principal
Teacher qualifications: NYS certification in subject area
Emphasis on affective education; thematic curriculum; coop-
erative learning design; "Project Adventure" activities; rural
location; transportation; interns accepted.

Haviland Junior High School Program (1983)
20 Haviland Rd, Hyde Park, NY 12538
Richard Kuralt, 914-229-2181
Type: public choice

Children's House (1982)
RD 1 Galle Lane, La Grangeville, NY 12540
Cathy Billone, 914-223-3783
Type: Montessori
50 students, ages 2–6
Three-year age groupings; student-centered environment;
individual instruction.

Duane Lake Academy (1983)
PO Box 372, Millbrook, NY 12545
Gail Holly, Adm, 914-677-6845
Type: independent, home-based, non-profit; cost: $3,000
20 students, ages 4–20
Governance by parent cooperative, board
Teacher qualifications: must love children, be a good
communicator
Classes on Monday and Wednesday; students home study
other days; parents teach at school; progressive mastery
learning; students can operate at different grade levels at
once; multi-aged classes; rural location; interns accepted.

Valley Central High School City As School Program (1992)
1175 Route 17K, Montgomery, NY 12549-2210
Don Crispell, Asst Prin, 914-457-3122
Type: public choice
34 students

Fostertown ETC
216 Fostertown Rd, Newburgh, NY 12550
Peter Copeletti, 914-563-7337
Type: magnet
K–6th grade
Education through creativity.

Horizons-on-the-Hudson
137 Montgomery St, Newburgh, NY 12550
Mary Ann Joyce, 914-563-7373
Type: magnet
K–6th grade
Gifted; talented.

Meadow Hill GEM
50 Meadow Hill Rd, Newburgh, NY 12550
William Castellane, 914-563-7600
Type: magnet
K–6th grade
Global explorations.

Newburgh Middle School
191 Washington St, Newburgh, NY 12550
Louis Tullo, 914-563-7744
Type: magnet
6–8th grade
Interdisciplinary; black rock forest.

West Street Community
39 W St, Newburgh, NY 12550
Joan Goudy-Crosson, 914-563-7777
Type: magnet
K–6th grade
Micro community.

Creamery Kids Adventure Group
173 Huguenot St, New Paltz, NY 12561
Michelle Riddell, 914-255-5482
Type: home-based

New Paltz Area Home Educators Collective (1993)
415 Springtown Rd, New Paltz, NY 12561
Joanne Clark, 914-255-5032
Non-profit
40 students, ages 1–15, K-12th grade
Governance by parent cooperative
Weekly meetings; students may participate in planned activities or create their own; outdoor play; suburban location;
interns accepted.

The Threefold Review
(See Resource Section)

Omega Institute for Holistic Studies (1977)
260 Lake Dr, Rhinebeck, NY 12572
Kathleen Jespersen, Marketing Asst, 914-266-4444, FAX: 914-
266-4828
Type: independent, non-profit; tuition: $130–350/course,
scholarships
250–300 teachers, 10,000 students, ages 8+
Workshops; conferences; health, psychology, multi-cultural
arts, spirituality; winter traveling programs.

National Coalition of Educational Activists (NCEA)
(See Resource Section)

Montessori School of Dutchess
Bradley Court, Poughkeepsie, NY 12601

Oakwood School (1976)
515 South Rd, Poughkeepsie, NY 12601
Dexter S. Lewis, 914-462-4200
Type: Quaker
120 students, 9–12+
Governance by consensus of students and teachers
Boarding and day; 60-acre campus; strong emphasis on
visual and performing arts; advanced placement courses;
competitive sports.

Dutchess County Homeschoolers
24 Cramer Rd, Poughkeepsie, NY 12603
Tracey Covell

Frost Valley Environmental Education (1968)
2000 Frost Valley Rd, Claryville, NY 12725
John Haskin, Dir, 914-985-2291, FAX: 914-985-0056
Type: independent, non-profit; tuition: variable, scholarships
25 teachers, 11,800 students, K-adult ages
Affiliation: International YMCAs
Governance by teachers, principal and board
Teacher qualifications: BS
Resident program; discovery-based; urban location; interns
accepted.

Homestead School
326 Hollow Rd, Glen Spey, NY 12737
Type: Montessori

Saratoga Independent School
Box 112, Gansevoort, NY 12831-0112
Julie Van Deusen, 518-583-0841
Type: independent, non-profit
3 teachers, 30 students, ages 5-8, K-3rd grade
Governance by board
Teacher qualifications: certification
Open classroom; developmental program, by needs, not age; hand-on, manipulative work; tutorials; no letter grades; non-compulsory class attendance; extensive field trips; rural location.

Saratoga Springs Alternative at Saratoga Springs JHS (1979)
W Circular St, Saratoga Springs, NY 12866
J Michael Gonroff, 518-584-7510
Type: public choice

Spring Hill School (1981)
62-66 York Ave, Saratoga Springs, NY 12866
Virginia W Reamer, Office Coord, 518-584-7643
Type: Waldorf, non-profit; tuition: $675-4350; scholarships
119 students, ages 3-11, pre K-6th grade
Governance by faculty
Waldorf-trained staff; integration of material into rhythms of human growth and development; wholistic curriculum includes moral, artistic and intellectual aspects.

Schuyler Academy on the Hudson
Clarks Mill Rd, Schuylerville, NY 12871
Type: Montessori

Infant & Child Developmental Center
8 Coastland Dr, Plattsburgh, NY 12901-9504
Type: Montessori

North Country School (1938)
Box 187, Lake Placid, NY 12946
Christine Lefevre, Adms Dir, 518-523-9329, FAX: -4858
Type: independent, boarding, non-profit; tuition: $22,000/yr, scholarships
30 teachers, 55 students, ages 9-14, 4-8th grade
Affiliation: Camp Treetops
Governance by board
Teacher qualifications: BA/BS and interest/experience
School-as-village model; outdoor ed; art; work program; greenhouse; organic gardens; farm animals; maple-sugaring; no letter grades; transportation; interns accepted.

Raymond Street Preschool
26 Raymond St, Malone, NY 12953-1626
Type: Montessori

Tri-Lakes Community Home Educators (1990)
PO Box 270, Raybrook, NY 12977
Lynn Waickman, 518-891-5657
Rural location.

Prevocational Alt Ed Student System, Adirondack Educational Center (1986)
RD 1 Box 7A, Saranac Lake, NY 12983
Nancy Montevago, 518-891-1330
Type: public at-risk

West Genesee Step Program (1968)
Sanderson Rd, Camillus, NY 13031
Marvin A Bodley, 315-487-4601
Type: public choice
9-12th grade

The Eidos In-School Program (1975)
Town & County Plaza, Cazanovia, NY 13035-0455
Brian W. Burns, Exec Dir, 315-655-2704
Type: public at-risk
12-20 students, ages 12-19, 7-12th grade
Affiliation: The Idyllic Foundation

Governance by staff and student body cooperative
Counseling/education program for Madison Cty youth experiencing home, community, school and employment problems; internships; community service and entrepreneurial projects; diploma, GED prep.

Families for Home Education (1991)
3219 Coulter Rd, Cazenovia, NY 13035-9461
Brynda Filkins, Coord, 315-655-3238
Non-profit
Pre K-8th grade
Governance by parent cooperative
Group lessons; play groups; 20 families; suburban & rural.

Discovery Montessori School
241 Seneca St, Chittenango, NY 13037-1638

Parents Instructing Challenged Children (PICC) (1987)
615 Utica St, Fulton, NY 13069-1954
Allen and Barb Mulvey, 315-592-7257
Type: state home-based
100+ members.

The Academy (1990)
4 Burkle St, Oswego, NY 13126
Warren Shaw, Dir, 315-341-5992
Type: public at-risk
9 teachers, 80 students, ages 13-21, 7-12th grade
Governance by teachers and principal
Teacher qualifications: NY Certification
Mastery learning; technology, mentorships; students assigned to family groups; performance-based; multi-aged classes; childcare; suburban location; transportation; interns accepted.

Homer/Cortland Home Educators
4211 Cuyler Rd, Truxton, NY 13158
Priscilla Colletto

The New School (1988)
1103 Burnet Ave, Syracuse, NY 13203
Lisa Saile, 315-475-6453
Type: independent
16 students, ages 5-11
Governance by parents' board.
Individualized curriculum; non-graded; team-teaching; students work independently on agreed contracts.

Occupational Learning Center at Fowler High School (1986)
227 Magnolia St, Syracuse, NY 13204
Linda Cimusz, 315-425-4376
Type: public choice

Loving Education at Home (LEAH) (1983)
PO Box 332, Syracuse, NY 13205
315-468-2225
Christian; 1,900 member families in 105 local chapters; quarterly newsletter; seminars; legislative info.

William R. Beard Alternative (1978)
220 W Kennedy St, Syracuse, NY 13205
Dr Joe D. Woods, Dir, 315-435-5855
Type: public at-risk
21 teachers, 300 students, mainly at-risk, ages 11-21, 4-12th grade
Governance by teachers, principal, democratic school meeting, and Supt designee
Teacher qualifications: state certification
Individual and group counseling; no diplomas; no letter grades; transportation; interns accepted.

Qualifying School at Henninger High School (1986)
600 Robinson St, Syracuse, NY 13206
Peter Kavanagh, 315-425-4343
Type: public choice

Syracuse City As School Program (1993)
725 Harrison St, Syracuse, NY 13210
Richard List, 315-435-5842
Type: public choice
70 students

The Learning Co-op
522 Nottingham Rd, Syracuse, NY 13210
Barb Irvine
Type: home-based
Small group of homeschooling families who meet one
    morning a week to coordinate cooperative activities.

Upstate Homeschoolers
Rd 2, Box 104A, Earlville, NY 13332
Jim Goldstein

EIDOS Program (1985)
221 Broad St, Oneida LC, Oneida, NY 13421
Krista Raineri, Site Coordinator, 315-363-4073
Type: independent at-risk, non-profit
30 students, mainly at-risk, ages 16–21
GED, job, lifeskills education; work experience, counseling,
    and support available.

Conkling Futures Academy
1115 Mohawk St, Utica, NY 13501
Karen Kunkel, 315-792-2180
Type: magnet
K–6th grade
Futures.

Watson Williams
107 Elmwood Place, Utica, NY 13501
John Scriber, 315-792-2167
Type: magnet
K–6th grade
Performing arts.

St Lawrence County Group
Christian Fellowship Academy, Box 5, Madrid, NY 13660
Debbie Marr
Type: home-based

Norwood-Norfolk ELP (1993)
Rt 56; Norwood Rd, Norwood, NY 13668
Jane S. Mott, 315-353-6631
Type: public at-risk
4 teachers, 10 students, ages 14–17, 9–11th grade
Governance by board
Teacher qualifications: BS in Education

St. Lawrence-Lewis BOCES Comprehensive Youth (1985)
PO Box 236, Rt 56, Norwood, NY 13668
Bill Short, Prog Specialist; April Bender, Sr Prog Ldr, 315-353-
    6693, FAX: -8875
Type: public at-risk
15 teachers, 200 students, mainly at-risk, ages 16–20
Governance by faculty and student representatives
Teacher qualifications: NY certification in any K–12 area
Custom mix of basic, life and voc ed; support services; voc
    cert program; paid work experience and/or community
    service; ind study; team learning life skills; no letter grades;
    multi-aged classes; extensive field trips; rural location;
    transportation; interns accepted.

The Opportunity Centers (1984)
c/o Pinewood Box 225, Norwood, NY 13668
David Lansford, 315-353-6643
Type: public choice

Akwesasne Freedom School (1979)
Box 290, Rooseveltown, NY 13683
James Ransom, Parent Committee, 518-358-2073
Type: independent, non-profit; tuition: $500
6 teachers, 46 students, mainly Mohawk, ages 5–13, pre
    K–7th grade
Governance by parent cooperative
Teacher qualifications: fluent in Mohawk language
Traditionalist school taught in the Mohawk language; designed
    to help preserve language and culture; curriculum reflects
    Iroquoian environmental philosophy; encourages coopera-
    tion rather than competitiveness; rural location.

Broome-Chenango Alternative High School (1986)
Cumber Rd, Harpursville, NY 13787
Dr Joyce O. Knapp, Prin, 607-693-3110
Type: public at-risk; tuition: $4,591/yr
5 teachers, 105 students, ages 12–21, 7–12th grade
Affiliation: Broome-Tioga BOCES
Teacher qualifications: NY secondary certification
Work experience; apprenticeship; self-esteem; rural location.

Day Care Center of Owego
228 Main St, Owego, NY 13827-1683
Type: Montessori

Christian Homesteading Movement (1961)
RD #2-G, Oxford, NY 13830-1580
Richard Fahey
Non-profit; tuition: $200/wk
5 teachers, 15 students
Governance by dir
Basic, intense study of farm animals, gardening, fruit trees,
    forestry, herbs, midwifery, hand tools, log building, Christ-
    ian celebration and spirituality; rural location.

Evergreen (1983)
201 Main St, Vestal, NY 13850
Alice Heier, Program Coord, 607-785-8216, FAX: -8218
Type: public at-risk
4 teachers, 47 students, ages 16–21, 9–12th grade
Governance by teachers and principal
Independent study; community-based; performance-based;
    cooperative learning; town meetings; counseling; subur-
    ban location; transportation.

Home Education Exchange of the Southern Tier (1991)
59 Grippen Hill Rd, Vestal, NY 13850
Allison Mesnard, 607-754-9456
Nonsectarian; support.

9 East Aurora Montessori (1975)
591 Porterville Rd, East Aurora, NY 14052
Mary Jane Wesoloski or Sharon Lewis, 716-668-8211
Tuition: $1,220-2,120/yr
2 teachers, 2 assistants, 40 students, ages 3–6
Affiliation: NAMTA
Governance by administrators
Suburban location.

School to Employment Program (STEP) (1986)
Fredonia Central School, Fredonia, NY 14063
Terry Redman, District Prin, 679-1581
Type: public choice; tuition: $1,600/yr
5 teachers, 20 students, mainly at-risk, ages 15–16, 9–10th
    grade
Governance by teachers and principal
All students go to paying jobs in afternoon; multi-aged
    classes; rural location; interns accepted.

Western NY Homeschooling Network
53 Maple Ave, Fredonia, NY 14063
Wendy Westwood

Montessori Early Childhood Education Center
Cattaraugus Reservation, Irving, NY 14081

Southtown's Children's Creative Center
6006 Old Lake Shore Rd, Lakeview, NY 14085-9525
Type: Montessori

Harrison/BOCES Coop Program (1985)
3181 Saunders Settlement Rd, Sanborn, NY 14132
Art Polychronis, Coord, 716-625-6811

Type: public choice
Student ages 15–18, 11–12th grade
Alternately work as apprentices for 2 weeks and attend
school for 2 weeks; accelerated subjects; emphasis on
science and math

Stella Niagara Education Park
4421 Lower River Rd, Stella Niagara, NY 14144-1001
Type: Montessori

Kaleidoscope Montessori Center
1216 E Quaker St, East Aurora, NY 14152

Aurora Waldorf School
525 W Falls Rd, West Falls, NY 14170
Jeff Tunkey

City-As-School Satellite at D'Youville College (1992)
320 Porter Ave, Buffalo, NY 14201
716-888-7185
Type: public choice
50 students

Academic Challenge Center (1977)
S Division & Hickory Sts, Buffalo, NY 14204
Bernice T. Richardson, Prin, 716-851-3767, FAX: 716-851-3770
Type: public choice
72 teachers; student ages 4–15, pre K–8th grade
Governance by board
Personalized; Project Advance; whole language; Push-Excel,
motivates and supports student; interns accepted.

Bennett Park Montessori School
342 Clinton St, Buffalo, NY 14204

Buffalo Montessori Teacher Education Program
453 Parker Ave, Buffalo, NY 14216
Eileen Buermann

7 St Andrew's Country Day Montessori School
1545 Sheridan Dr, Kenmore, NY 14217-1211

Maplemere Elementary (1958)
236 E Maplemere Rd, Amherst, NY 14221
Michelle Kavanaugh, Prin, 716-634-6260
Type: public choice
35 teachers, 435 students, ages 4–12, K–5th grade
Governance by school leadership team, values education
committee
Partnership with U of Buffalo, Public Library; Geologo;
authors, artists in residence; literary, cultural awareness;
Creative Empowerment Model; cross-age peer partnering;
parent involvement; no letter grade; interns accepted.

Nardin Academy
135 Cleveland Ave, Buffalo, NY 14222-1699
Type: Montessori

Pine Hill Middle School (1980)
1635 E Delavan Ave, Cheektowaga, NY 14225
Frank A Cantie, 716-892-1033
Type: public choice

Union East Elementary School (1968)
3550 Union Rd, Cheektowaga, NY 14225
William E Koepf, 716-686-3620
Type: public choice

Alternate 7/8 Program at Albion Middle School (1985)
254 East Ave, Albion, NY 14411
Robert E Huyck, 716-589-7033
Type: public choice

Brockport Montessori School
472 West Ave, Brockport, NY 14420

Canandaigua Montessori School
11 Gibson St, Canandaigua, NY 14424-1309

Churchville Chili Central School (1986)
5786 Buffalo Rd, Churchville, NY 14428
William J O'Connell, 716-293-1800
Type: public choice

Trinity Montessori (1967)
501 S Garfield St, East Rochester, NY 14445
Sr Clare Francis Mogenhan, Adm, 716-586-1044
Non-profit; tuition: $920-2,840/yr
6 teachers, 5 assistants, 92 students, ages infant-7
Affiliation: AMS; accreditation: NYDE
Governance by administrator, board
Teacher qualifications: Montessori certification
Complete Montessori materials; childcare; suburban location;
interns accepted.

Geneva Middle School (1993)
63 Pultney St, Geneva, NY 14456
Marlene Simizon, 716-781-0404
Type: public choice
1 teacher, 16-20 students, ages 12-16, 7-8th grade
Governance by teachers, principal, board
Teacher qualifications: New York certified, experience
Organizational skills; stress reduction; cooperation; community involvement; volunteer projects; how to say "no" to
negative peer pressure; extensive field trips; multi-aged
classes; interns accepted.

WAS (Work and Study Academy) (1985)
625 Peirson Ave, Newark, NY 14513
P. David Caccamise, Dir, 315-331-5150, FAX: 332-3567
Type: public at-risk
4 teachers, 6 students, mainly at-risk, ages 16-18, 9-12th
grade
Governance by teachers and principal
Teacher qualifications: state certification
No letter grades; suburban location.

Penn Yan Academy Alternative (1985)
305 Court St, Penn Yan, NY 14527
Linda G Shail, Coordinator, 315-536-4408
Type: public at-risk
10-16 students, ages 12-14, 7-9th grade
Goal is to break cycle of truancy and failure and return stu-
dents to mainstream; uses Project Adventure and New
Games; social skills program; high success rate.

Cobblestone School (1983)
10 Prince St, Rochester, NY 14607
Jon Greenbaum, 716-271-2320
Type: independent, non-profit; tuition: $4,385, scholarships
15 teachers, 175 students, ages 4-12, ungraded
Governance by two co-directors and parent board, weekly
student meeting
Integrated, thematic; student-centered; progressive, open
classroom tradition enables students to become independent and cooperative learners; no letter grades; multi-
aged classes; extensive field trips; rural & urban location;
transportation; interns accepted.

School of the Arts
494 Averill Ave, Rochester, NY 14607
David Silver, 716-325-7594
Type: magnet
7-12th grade

Frederick Douglass Middle School
940 Fernwood Park, Rochester, NY 14609
Bert Alexander, 716-482-2000
Type: magnet
6-8th grade

Morgan Home School (1991)
1851 E Main St, Rochester, NY 14609
Linda Morgan, PhD, 716-654-9153
1 teacher, 1 student, age 18, 12th grade
Governance by democratic school meeting

Have homeschooled two boys (age 18 and 19) for a total of 9 years; work-study (co-op); urban location.

Rochester Area Homeschoolers Association (1980)
275 Yarmouth Rd, Rochester, NY 14610
Amy Berkley Mantell, 716-482-8592
Child-led activities and clubs; extensive field trips; multi-aged activities; inclusive.

Lincoln Park School #44
820 Chili Ave, Rochester, NY 14611
Joan Miller, 716-328-5272
Type: magnet
2-6th grade
Multi-cultural studies.

Association Montessori Internationale
(See Resource Section)

School Without Walls (1971)
480 Broadway, Rochester, NY 14617
Dan Drmacich, 716-546-6732
Type: public choice
175 students, ages 13-19, 9-12th grade
Affiliation: Coalition of Essential Schools
Governance by democratic school meeting, principal and teachers, school-based planning team
Teacher qualifications: support of school philosophy
Internships; ind study; creative problem solving; time management; authentic assessment by portfolio; community service; evaluation as a learning experience; learner-centered curriculum; senior project; multi-aged classes; extensive field trips.

Brighton Montessori House of Children
2131 Elmwood Ave, Rochester, NY 14618-1021

Rochester Children's House
175 Allens Creek Rd, Rochester, NY 14618-3229
Type: Montessori

Lewis H. Morgan School #37
353 Congress Ave, Rochester, NY 14619
Miriam Vazques, 716-328-0037
Type: magnet
K-6th grade
Intercultural studies; PAL.

James P.B. Duffy School #12
999 S Ave, Rochester, NY 14620
Barbara Wagner, 716-461-3240
Type: magnet
K-6th grade
Inter-cultural studies center.

Pinnacle School #35
194 Field St, Rochester, NY 14620
Charles Moscato, 716-271-4583
Type: magnet
K-6th grade
Communication through performing arts; bilingual; multi-cultural.

Webster Montessori School (1967)
260 Embury Rd, Rochester, NY 14625
David F Boneham, Prin, 716-671-9269
Non-profit; tuition: $2,300-2,900/yr
2 teachers, 2 assistants, 60 students, mainly international, ages 3-6
Affiliations: AMI, NAMTA
Governance by administrator, board of trustees
Traditional; child care; suburban location; transportation by local school district for 5 & 6 yr olds.

Greece Montessori School
200 Alcott Rd, Rochester, NY 14626-2424

Alternative Learning Program at South Western Central (1972)
600 Hunt Rd, Jamestown, NY 14701
D. Clifton Bowman, 716-664-6273
Type: public at-risk
1 teacher, 25 students, mainly at-risk, ages 14-18, HS
Governance by principal
Self-examination and development of a personal value system; goal-setting, decision-making, vocational and survival skills; cooperative learning; relaxed and supportive atmosphere; no letter grades; multi-aged classes; extensive field trips; suburban location; transportation.

Montessori Children House
120 Chandler, Jamestown, NY 14701

Montessori Children' s House of Olean
1020 Reed St, Olean, NY 14760-2221
Brenda Snyder

Salamanca Alternative High School (1991)
50 Iroquois Dr, Salamanca, NY 14779
Paula Kenneson, Coord, 716-945-2405 x527, FAX: -5736
Type: public at-risk
6 teachers, 35 students, partly at-risk, ages 13-18
Governance by teachers, principal, board
Teacher qualifications: certification
Work experience; School & Business Alliance and JTPA provide career experiences, skill training; outcome-based; rural location; interns accepted.

Seneca Nation of Indians Montessori
PO Box 231, Salamanca, NY 14779-0231

Alfred Montessori School
Openhym Dorm, Alfred Univ, Alfred, NY 14802

Steuben-Allegany BOCES (1985)
RD 1, Bath, NY 14810
Michael Bracy, 607-776-7631
Type: public choice

Valley Montessori (1976)
PO Box 198, Winters Rd, Big Flatts, NY 14814
Cynthia Raj, Administrator, 607-562-8754
Non-profit; tuition: $1,600-3,400
7 teachers, 6 assistants, 130 students, ages 2-12, pre K-6th grade
Governance by parent cooperative
On wooded acreage; Italian classes for students 6-12 years.

Southern Tier Unschoolers
8033 Van Amburg Rd, Hammondsport, NY 14840
Lisa Treichler
Type: home-based

Alternative Community School (1974)
111 Chestnut St, Ithaca, NY 14850
Dave Lehman, Prin, 607-274-2183,-2263
Type: public choice
260 students, ages 11-19, 6-12th grade
Affiliations: CES, NYS Compact Partnership
Governance by democratic school meeting, teachers, principal
Internships; community & independent studies; small family groups; some services for homeschoolers; interdisciplinary; integrated studies.

Democratic School of the Finger Lakes (1994)
206 Muriel St, Ithaca, NY 14850
Kay Slentz Milling, Organizer, 607-257-4769
Type: independent, non-profit
Student ages 5-19
Governance by democratic school meeting
Sudbury Valley School model; no letter grades; non-compulsory class attendance; multi-aged classes; extensive field trips; rural location; interns accepted.

Fingerlakes Unschoolers Network (1988)
249 Coddington Rd, Ithaca, NY 14850
Linda Holzbaur, Coord, 607-277-6300, FAX: 607-277-6300
Type: home-based
Directory; newsletter; workshops; field trips; referrals.

Hillside Children's Garden (1978)
26 Quarry St, Ithaca, NY 14850
Kundry Willwerth, Director, 607-277-6371
Type: Waldorf; tuition: $2,620
25 students, ages 3-6, pre K-K
Affiliation: WKANA
Governance by teachers and principal
Stresses development through play and artistic activities,
    rather than academic learning, in the early years.

Montessori School of Ithaca (1979)
120 E King Rd, Ithaca, NY 14850
Andrea B. Coby, Adm, 607-277-7335
Non-profit; tuition: $2,875-4,235/yr
7 teachers, 3 assistants, 99 students, mainly international,
    ages 3-12
Accreditations: AMS, NY
Governance by administrator, board
Childcare; rural location; interns accepted.

T-S-T Community School (1986)
555 Warren Rd, Ithaca, NY 14850

Dr Gerry Friedman, Prin, 607-273-9015, FAX: 275-9702
Type: public at-risk
7 teachers, 100 students, ages 12-21, 6-12th grade
Governance by democratic school meeting, teachers, and
    principal
Program for pregnant/parenting teens in supportive yet
    demanding democratic community; life skills; apprentice-
    ships; family groups; childcare; multi-aged classes; exten-
    sive field trips; urban location; transportation; interns
    accepted.

Waldorf School of the Finger Lakes (1982)
855 Five Mile Dr, Ithaca, NY 14850
Maureen C. McKenna, Dir Adms, Dev, 607-273-4088
Non-profit; tuition: $2,400-4,600/yr, scholarships
17 teachers, 98 students, ages 3.5-15, pre K-8th grade
Affiliation: AWSNA
Governance by board, faculty, parent council
Teacher qualifications: Waldorf training
Two sites; French; strings; before, after school care; trans-
    portation; interns accepted.

The Children's Room
Box 147, Van Etten, NY 14889
Type: Montessori

North Carolina

Heart of Carolina
1523 Cellwood Rd, Raleigh, NC
Janice and Lewis McKenzie, 919-787-3482
Type: home-based

Petree Middle School
3815 Old Greensboro Rd, Winston-Salem, NC 27101
Ben Henderson or Ron A. Caviness, 919-761-0868
Type: public at-risk
13 teachers, 145 students, 6-8th grade
Governance by teachers, principal, board
Teacher qualifications: certification
Behavior management; banking; school store; academic indi-
    vidualization; Adler's Paideia approach; urban location;
    interns accepted.

Winston-Salem/Forsyth Elementary Alternative
    Program
Box 2513, Winston-Salem, NC 27102
C. Douglas Carter, 919-727-2816

Montessori Children's Center
3908 Old Vineyard Rd #3904, Winston-Salem, NC 27104-4740

Forsyth Montessori School
407 Petree Rd, Winston Salem, NC 27106-3502

Reynolds Montessori School
2130 Brookfield Dr, Winston Salem, NC 27106-5813

Montessori School
23 Banner Ave, Winston-Salem, NC 27107

The Jefferson Academy
PO Box 7383 Reynolds Sta, Winston-Salem, NC 27109
Type: Montessori

Magnum Opus Developmental Education Laboratory
    (MODEL) (1987)
607 S Park St, Asheboro, NC 27203

Gary L. Cameron, 919-625-1656
Type: home-based
6 students, ages 2-12
Governance by parent cooperative
Focus on developing the family; no letter grades; suburban
    location; interns accepted.

Randolph County Christian Home Educators
637 Allred St, Asheboro, NC 27203
Brenda Yelverton, 910-626-2751

High Point Area Home Educators
610 Monlieu Ave, High Point, NC 27262
Amy Gies, 919-882-4339

Our Greenhouse (1986)
610 Montlieu Ave, High Point, NC 27262
Amy Gies, Mother, 910-882-4339
Type: home-based, non-profit
1 teacher, 2 students, age 10 & 12, 5, 8th grade
Affiliation: Christian Home
Governance by parents under non-public school state office
Teacher qualifications: HS diploma or degree
History unit approach; extensive use of local library; multi-
    aged classes; no letter grades; urban location.

Brookside Montessori School (1981)
736 Piney Grove Rd, Kernsville, NC 27284
Marjorie Carson, Adm, 910-996-5351
Non-profit; tuition: $212/470/mo
2 teachers, 1 assistant, 30 students, ages 3-12
Affiliations: AMS, Montessori Assn. of the Carolinas
Governance by administrator
Childcare; suburban location; interns accepted.

A Discovery Place
PO Box 1471, Sanford, NC 27331-1471
Paula Rowland
Type: Montessori

Thomasville Home Educators
324 Walker St, Thomasville, NC 27360
Christi Crane, 919-643-7088

EDU*CARE Montessori School
40 Archie Rd, West End, NC 27376

Dudley High School
1200 Lincoln St, Greensboro, NC 27401
Lenwood Edwards, 919-370-8130
Type: magnet
9-12th grade
Science, math, technology; open education.

Peeler Elementary
2200 Randall St, Greensboro, NC 27401
Martha Hudson, 919-370-8270
Type: magnet
K-5th grade
Open education.

Greensboro Home Educators
PO Box 4213, Greensboro, NC 27404
910-548-5111

Erwin Elementary
3012 E Bessemer Ave, Greensboro, NC 27405
Dan Jones, 919-370-8150
Type: magnet
K-5th grade
Open education.

Jones Elementary
502 S St, Greensboro, NC 27406
Edward Allred, 919-370-8230
Type: magnet
K-5th grade
Cultural arts; foreign language.

Global Studies Year Round School
1215 Westover Tr, Greensboro, NC 27408
Phillip Mobley, 919-370-8228
Type: magnet
K-4th grade
Global studies.

Hester's Creative Schools
2715 Pinedale Rd, Greensboro, NC 27408-4713
Type: Montessori

Greensboro Montessori
2856 Horse Pen Creek Rd, Greensboro, NC 27410
919-668-0119
12 teachers, 8 assistants; student ages infant-15
Affiliations: AMS, SACS
Governance by board
Childcare; suburban location; interns accepted.

New Garden Friends School (1971)
1128 New Garden Rd, Greensboro, NC 27410
David R. Tomlin, Co-Head, 919-299-0964
Type: Quaker, non-profit; tuition: $3,700/yr, scholarships
15 teachers, 110 students, ages 3-15, pre K-8th grade
Affiliation: FCOE
Governance by board
Whole language; integrated studies; community service; narrative evaluations; contracts; team teaching; cooperative learning; independent study; craft design tech; multi-aged classes; extensive field trips; no letter grades; suburban location; interns accepted.

Randolph County Home Educators
3606 Birchwood Ln, Greensboro, NC 27410-2802
Susan Pratt, 919-241-2399

International Alliance for Invitational Education
(See Resource Section)

Apex Elementary
700 Tingen Rd, Apex, NC 27502
Claude Willie III, 919-387-2150
Type: magnet
K-5th grade
Gifted; talented.

Christian Home Education Association of Greater Durham
PO Box 3293, Durham, NC 27512-3293

Sas Institute Daycare Center
1 Sas Cir, Bldg K, Box 8000, Cary, NC 27512-8000
Type: Montessori

Chapel Hill Homeschoolers (1989)
PO Box 269, Chapel Hill, NC 27514
Dale Pratt-Wilson, 919-942-3300, FAX: -0700
Non-profit
65 teachers
Governance by board
Field trips; special classes, events; clubs.

Montessori Day School
1165 Weaver Dairy Rd, Chapel Hill, NC 27514-1576

Lincoln-Heights Elementary
307 Bridge St, Fuquary-Varina, NC 27526
Marge Ronco, 919-557-2588
Type: magnet
K-5th grade
Gifted; talented.

Pathfinders
5400 Lafayette Dr, Fuquay-Varina, NC 27526
Lucinda and Sharles Estill, 919-552-0578
Type: home-based

Wayne Christian Home Educators
607 Prince St, Goldsboro, NC 27530
Pat Wright, 919-734-4441

Wayne Montessori School
PO Box 10646, Goldsboro, NC 27532-0646

Cary Montessori School (1989)
201 High House Rd, Cary, NC 27573-4204
Andrea Uzzell, Dir, 919-469-9406
Tuition: $55-150/wk
8 teachers, 12 assistants, 144 students, ages infant-9
Affiliation: AMS
Governance by board of trustees
47 wks/yr; childcare; suburban location; interns accepted.

Wake Forest Elementary
136 W Sycamore St, Wake Forest, NC 27587
C.W. Fisher, 919-554-8655
Type: magnet
K-5th grade
Gifted; talented.

Carver Elementary
1 Morphus Bridge Rd, Box 769, Wendell, NC 27591
Alex Taylor, 919-365-2680
Type: magnet
K-1st grade
Gifted; talented.

Wendell Elementary
212 W Wilson Ave Box 727, Wendell, NC 27591
Elizabeth Rountree, 919-365-2660
Type: magnet
2-5th grade
Gifted; talented.

New Beginnings
Rt 3, Box 114-D, Zebulon, NC 27597
Evelyn and William Wesson, 919-269-6165
Type: home-based

Zebulon Elementary
700 Proctor St, Zebulon, NC 27597
Lewis Liles, 919-269-3680
Type: magnet
K-5th grade
Gifted; talented.

Hunter Elementary
1018 E Davie St, Raleigh, NC 27601
Ceclia Lindsey, 919-856-7676
Type: magnet
K-5th grade
Gifted; talented.

Washington Elementary
1000 Fayetteville St, Raleigh, NC 27601
Del Burns, 919-856-7960
Type: magnet
K-5th grade
Gifted; talented.

North Carolinians for Home Education (1984)
419 N Boylan Ave, Raleigh, NC 27603-1211
Susan Van Dyke, Exec Adm, 919-834-6243, FAX: 919-834-6241
Non-profit
Governance by board
1,500 members; supported by contributions; newsletter;
    large annual conference and book fair.

Conn Elementary
1221 Brookside Ave, Raleigh, NC 27604
Lois Hart, 919-856-7637
Type: magnet
K-5th grade
Gifted; talented.

The "Y" Group
1012 Oberlin Rd, Raleigh, NC 27605
Beth Stevenson, 919-828-3205
Type: home-based

Martin Middle School
1701 Ridge Rd, Raleigh, NC 27607
David C. Coley, 919-881-4970
Type: magnet
6-8th grade
Gifted; talented.

Joyner Elementary
2300 Noble Rd, Raleigh, NC 27608
George L. Risinger, 919-856-7650
Type: magnet
K-5th grade
Language arts; communications; extended day.

New School Montessori Center for Children
1810 White Oak Rd, Raleigh, NC 27608
Ceres Schroer York

Underwood Elementary
1614 Glenwood Ave, Raleigh, NC 27608
Anne Doman, 919-856-7663
Type: magnet
K-5th grade
Gifted; talented.

National Society For Internships
(See Resource Section)

St Timothy's School
4523 Six Forks Rd, Raleigh, NC 27609-5759
Type: Montessori

Carnage Middle School
1425 Carnage Dr, Raleigh, NC 27610
William Crockett, Jr, 919-856-7600
Type: magnet
6-8th grade
Gifted; talented.

Enloe High School
128 Clarendon Crescent, Raleigh, NC 27610
Calvin Dobbins, 919-856-7860
Type: magnet
9-12th grade
Gifted; talented.

Fuller Elementary
806 Calloway Dr, Raliegh, NC 27610
Marlee Ray, 919-856-7625
Type: magnet
K-5th grade
Gifted; talented.

Powell Elementary
1130 Marlborough Rd, Raliegh, NC 27610
Joyce Faulkner, 919-856-7737
Type: magnet
K-5th grade
Gifted; talented.

Wake County Schools
3600 Wake Forest Rd, Raleigh, NC 27611
Pat Kinlaw, Magnets Dir
Type: Montessori

TEACH of NC
7804 Hemlock Ct, Raleigh, NC 27615
Sherry and Blake Talbott, 919-846-2556
Type: home-based

Montessori School of Raleigh
7005 Lead Mine Rd, Raleigh, NC 27615-5905
William Friday, Exec Dir

Duke UniversityTalent Identification Program
(See Resource Section)

Carolina Friends School
4809 Friends School Rd, Durham, NC 27705
John Baird, Prin, 919-383-6602
Type: Quaker

Home Education Association
2934 Ridge Rd, Durham, NC 27705
Sarah Howe or Susan Dunathan, 919-490-6304

Montessori Community School (1980)
4512 Pope Rd, Durham, NC 27707
Barbara Crockett, Adm, 919-493-8541
Non-profit; tuition: $3,320-4,250/yr
6 teachers, 7 assistants, 132 students, ages 3-9
Affiliation: AMS
Governance by board; administrator
9 wooded acres; serves Chapel Hill, Durham, Raleigh; child-
    care; suburban location; interns accepted.

Montessori Children's House of Durham
2400 University Dr, Durham, NC 27707-2150

Park Montessori School
PO Box 12363, Research Triangle Park, NC 27709-2363

**CHARM: Christian Homeschool Association of Rocky
    Mount**
296 Creekridge Dr, Rocky Mount, NC 27804
Susan Stone, Pres, 919-937-8540
Cost: $10/yr
Inclusive membership, Christian leadership; about 55 families.

Families Learning Together (1989)
Rt 1, Box 219, Chocowinity, NC 27817
Jocelyn Butler or Feryl Masters, Membership Co-ords
Inclusive; non-sectarian; family directory; bi-annual meeting.

Down East Homeschoolers
717 W 2nd St, Washington, NC 27889
Jocelyn Butler, 919-975-2020

Profile
404 W Main St, Elizabeth City, NC 27909
Gladys Racette, 919-338-5905
Type: home-based

PATH
Rt 1 Box 25A, Manteo, NC 27954
Pat Rouckle, Co-Chair, 919-473-1301
Homeschoolers support group.

Stanly/Montgomery
2222 Monza Dr, Albemarle, NC 28001
Karen McAlister, 704-983-1559
Type: home-based

Children's House Montessori School
PO Box 1326, Bessemer City, NC 28016-1326

Montessori Community School of Bessemer City
119 W Pennsylvania Ave #A, Bessemer City, NC 28016-2635

Gaston County Homeschool Network
2107 Twin Ave, Gastonia, NC 28052
Becky Kendrick, 704-864-8097

Mooresville Optional Year Round Program (1990)
160 S Magnolia St, Mooresville, NC 28115
Carol Carroll, Prin, 704-664-9520, FAX: 704-663-3005
Type: public choice
47 teachers, 1,040 students, ages 5-14, K-8th grade
Governance by teachers and principal
Teacher qualifications: NC Certification
Remediation; enrichment; childcare; transportation; interns
    accepted.

Countryside Montessori School
PO Box 427, Newell, NC 28126

Rowan County Homeschoolers
333 Montrose Rd, Salisbury, NC 28146
Pam Ribelin, 704-633-0325

Irwin Avenue Open School
329 N Irwin, Charlotte, NC 28202
Type: public choice

Piedmont Open School
6000 Rose Valley Dr, Charlotte, NC 28210
Dan Faris
Type: public choice

Charlotte Montessori School (1971)
212 Boyce Rd, Charlotte, NC 28211
Maura Leahy-Tucker, Head, 704-366-5994
Tuition: $3,600-4,050/yr
12 teachers, 8 assistants, 189 students, ages toddler-12
Affiliation: London Montessori; accreditations: AMS, NC non-
    public schools
Governance by administrator
6 acres; new custom designed buildings; childcare; suburban
    location; interns accepted.

Imagination Times
(See Resource Section)

Concord Montessori School
7324 Cedarbrook Dr, Charlotte, NC 28215
Suzann Herrington

Brisbane Academy
5901 Statesville Rd, Charlotte, NC 28269
Geraldine Brisbane-White, 704-598-5208, FAX: same, call first
Type: Montessori; tuition: $2,500/yr
27 students, ages 3-12
Governance by administrator
Teacher qualifications: NC certification
Fosters love of self and the learning process; childcare;
    interns accepted.

Charlotte Home Educators Association
8600 Duck's Bill Dr, Charlotte, NC 28277
Debbie Mason, 704-541-5145

Omni Montessori (1984)
9536 Blakeney-Heath Rd, Charlotte, NC 28277
Cindy Boucherle, 704-541-1326
Tuition: $250-405/mo
6 teachers, 5 assistants, 101 students, ages 3-12
Accreditation: AMI
Governance by teachers, administrators, board
Parent participation encouraged; parent education program;
    childcare; rural location; interns accepted.

Montessori School of Fayetteville
1201 Cape Ct, Fayetteville, NC 28304-4404
Kerry Lydon

Home Offering Meaningful Education
2606 Phoenician Dr, Fayetteville, NC 28306
Dale Kozikowski, 919-323-0539

Sandhills Montessori School
205 S Pinehurst St, Aberdeen, NC 28315-2010

Children's House by Edu-Care
3150 McIntyre Rd Sta, Pinehurst, NC 28374
Type: Montessori

Wilmington Homeschool Organization
Box 6011, Hanover Center, Wilmington, NC 28403
Marty Grist, 919-251-9444

Home Educators of Carteret
Rt 3 Box 241, Beaufort, NC 28516
Frances Arrington, 919-728-2809

New Bern Homeschoolers
PO Box 125, Ernul, NC 28527
Joan Cowell, 919-244-1912

Greenville Montessori School
21 Baywood Dr, Winterville, NC 28590-9615

Creekside School-A Montessori Middle School
Route 2, Box 545A, Boone, NC 28607
Elizabeth Howell

Mountain Pathways School
Route 5, Box 593 A, Boone, NC 28607
Cheryl M. Smith, Director, 704-262-5787
Type: Montessori; tuition: $2,950, scholarships
5 teachers, 40 students, ages 3-9, pre K-3rd grade
Governance by board
Teacher qualifications: NC teaching certificate, Montessori
    training
No letter grades; multi-aged classes; rural location; interns
    accepted.

SHARE
305 Maplewood Dr, Morganton, NC 28655
Bonnie Perkins, 704-437-1210
Type: home-based

The Children's School
105 W Concord St, Morganton, NC 28655
Joanna Young, 704-438-8835
Type: independent

Montessori Learning Center of Wilkes, Inc
601 Boston Ave, N Wilkesboro, NC 28659
Elizabeth Aversa, 919-667-4032
Non-profit; tuition: $320/mo
2 teachers, 3 assistants, 30 students, ages 3-6
Affiliations: AMS, NAMTA
Governance by administrator
Rural location; interns accepted.

Iredell County Home Educators
Rt 18, Box 227, Statesville, NC 28677
Donna and Roger Hames, 704-876-6516

Montessori Children's House
111 Hartness Rd, Statesville, NC 28677-3209

Fellowship & Instruction to Home Educators
1808 Chestnut Ave, Charlotte, NC 28705
Catheryn Pell, 704-376-5093

Camp Elliot Therapeutic Wilderness Program (1987)
601 Camp Elliot Rd, Black, NC 28711
Catherine Buie or Linda Tatsapaugh, 704-669-8639, FAX: -2521
Type: independent, non-profit
2 teachers, 14–20 students, mainly at-risk boys, ages 12–17
Governance by exec committee, head staff
Teacher qualifications: special education
Construct and maintain buildings; SE; multi-aged classes;
   interns accepted.

Arthur Morgan School (1962)
1901 Hannah Branch Rd, Burnsville, NC 28714
Johno Zakelj & Joy Montagano, Co-clerks, 704-675-4262
Type: Quaker, boarding, non-profit; tuition: $5,150-10,500,
   scholarships
12 teachers, 24 students, ages 12–15, 7-9th grade
Affiliations: NCACS, NAMTA, FEAA
Governance by staff, staff and student all-school meeting
Rare junior high boarding school, geared to meet their specific needs; challenging outdoor experiences; community
   service; daily work projects; caring community environment; based on Montessori's Erkinder model; no letter
   grades; multi-aged classes; extensive field trips; rural location; interns accepted.

CELO Community
816 Grindstaff Rd, Burnsville, NC 28714
Barbara Stuehling, 704-675-9590
Type: home-based

The Hampton School
PO Box 546, Cashiers, NC 28717-0546
Type: Montessori

Blue Ridge Waldorf Community
Rt 2, Box 2972, Columbus, NC 28722
Beth Love, 704-863-2775
Waldorf study group; play groups, festivals; children's learn-
   ing days.

Carolina Superschoolers
Rt 2, PO Box 2972, Columbus, NC 28722
704-863-2775
Type: home-based

Cullowhee Montessori
Rt 66, Box 73-B, Cullowhee, NC 28723

Christian Home Education Association of Franklin
141 Harrison Ave, Franklin, NC 28734
Catherine Wright, 704-524-2208

ED-venturous Learning Families
68 Lakey Creek, Franklin, NC 28734
Trish Severin or Doug Woodward, 704-369-6491
Type: home-based

Montessori Center of Hendersonville
1306 Valmont Dr, Hendersonville, NC 28739

Statesville Montessori School, Inc (1989)
1012 Harmony Dr/ 111 Hartness Rd, Statesville, NC 28766-
   6080
Julia Sutton, Dir, 704-873-1092
Tuition: $1,950-3,650/yr
13 teachers, 5 assistants, 123 students, ages 3–12
Affiliation: AMS

Governance by administrator
Childcare; urban location; interns accepted.

Carolina Mountain Montessori
28 Ridgeway St, Sylva, NC 28779-2946

Haywood County Home Educators
506 Oak St, Waynesville, NC 28786

Union Acres Alternative School
Rt 1, Box 61J, Whittier, NC 28789
Margaret Haun, 704-497-4964
Type: home-based

Claxton Elementary
241 Merrimon Ave, Asheville, NC 28801
Charles Cutshall, 201-255-5367
Type: magnet
K-5th grade
Arts; multi-cultural; humanities.

Issac Dickson Elementary
125 Hill St, Asheville, NC 28801
Bob McGrattan, 201-255-5376
Type: magnet
K-5th grade
Fox Fire School; experiential; continuous program.

Randoff Elementary
90 Montford Ave, Asheville, NC 28801
Barbara Lewis, 201-255-5359
Type: magnet
4-5th grade
Gifted and talented.

Ashville Montessori School
23 Congress St, Asheville, NC 28801-4342

St Genevieve-Biggons Hall School, Inc
103 Victoria Rd, Asheville, NC 28801-4811
Type: Montessori

The Robert Muller School
1875 Hendersonville Rd, Asheville, NC 28803
Barbara Darden, 704-274-0283

Jones Primary
544 Kimberly Ave, Asheville, NC 28804
Sue Harris, 201-255-5366
Type: magnet
K-3rd grade
Gifted and talented.

Children's Grammar School
10 Kidstown Rd, Asheville, NC 28806
Type: independent

Rainbow Mountain School
574 Haywood Rd, Asheville, NC 28806
Type: independent

Warren Wilson College (1984)
PO Box 9000, Asheville, NC 28815
Tom Weede, Dean of Admission, 704-298-3325, FAX: 704-299-
   3326
Boarding, non-profit; tuition: $12,917/yr, scholarships
47 teachers, 500 students, ages 18–25
Governance by democratic school meeting and board
Diverse; all students work 15 hrs/wk for College, do 20 hrs/yr
   community service; rural location.

Ligon Middle School
706 E Lenoir St, Raleigh, NC 62701
Dan Bowers, 919-856-7929
Type: magnet
6-8th grade
Gifted and talented.

North Dakota

Community High school
315 N University, Fargo, ND 58102
Jerry Hasche, Prin, 701-241-4856

Woodrow Wilson (1971)
315 N University Dr, Fargo, ND 58102
Jerry Hasche, Prin, 701 241-4889
Type: public at-risk
7 teachers, 200 students, mainly at-risk, ages 16–19, 9–12th
   grade
Affiliation: Fargo Public Schools
Governance by teachers, principal, board
Urban location; interns accepted.

Academy for Children
20 S 8th St, Fargo, ND 58103-1805
701-232-7787
Type: Montessori; tuition: $145–340/mo
4 teachers, 3 assistants, 81 students, ages infant-9
Affiliation: NAEYC
Governance by administrator
French and music for all ages; childcare; urban location;
   interns accepted.

Dakota Montessori School
1620 16th Ave S, Fargo, ND 58103-4055
Elizabeth Boyer

Community High School
911 Cottonwood St, Grand Forks, ND 58201
William O'Toole, Prin, 701-746-2425

Little Scholarship
1420 24th Ave S, Grand Forks, ND 58201-6735
Type: Montessori

Kinderhaus Montessori
PO Box 1284, Jamestown, ND 58402-1284

Missouri Valley Montessori School
2600 Gateway Ave, Bismarck, ND 58501-0568
Laurie Langeliers

North Dakota Home School Association
PO Box 486, Mandan, ND 58554
701-663-2868

Ohio

Delaware Montessori
117 Eaton St, Delaware, OH 43015

Dublin Montessori Academy (1987)
6055 Glick Rd, Powell, OH 43065
Mary Jill Roshon, Owner, 614-761-2020
Tuition: $1,800-4,392/yr
2 teachers, 2 assistants, 72 students, ages 3-6
Affiliation: AMS
Governance by administrator
Childcare; suburban location; interns accepted.

Shamrock Montessori Academy
PO Box 605, Powell, OH 43065-0605

Reynoldsburg High School
6699 E Livingston Ave, Reynoldsburg, OH 43068
Dan Hoffman, Prin, 614-866-6397, FAX: 614-575-3098
Type: public choice
65 teachers, 1100 students, 10–12th grade
Affiliation: CES
Governance by teachers and principal
Employs CES research: reorganizes time, curriculum and the
   assignment of students to teachers; interdisciplinary work;
   double-blocked classes; inclusion strategies; suburban
   location; interns accepted.

Johnny Appleseed Montessori
PO Box 189, Urbana, OH 43078-0189

Lancaster Montessori Center
PO Box 52, Lancaster, OH 43130-0052

**Fifth Ave Alternative Elementary for International
   Studies**
1300 Forsythe Ave, Columbus, OH 43201
614-365-5564, FAX: 614-365-5564
Type: public choice
K–5th grade

Multi-age grouping; team teaching; whole language; literature-based; integrated; open space/informal; flexible;
   culture studies; camping trips; educational tours.

Indianola Elementary
140 E 16th Ave, Columbus, OH 43201
614-365-5579
Type: public choice
K–5th grade
Self-directed; individualized.

Champion Middle School
1270 Hawthorne Ave, Columbus, OH 43203
Andrew Meilton, 614-365-6082
Type: magnet
6–8th grade

Hilltonia Alternative Middle School
2345 W Mound St, Columbus, OH 43204
Robert Jones, 614-365-5937
Type: magnet
6–8th grade

**Westgate/Windsor Schools of Academic and Physical
   Excellence**
3080 Wicklow Rd/1219 E 12th Ave, Columbus, OH
   43204/43211
614-365-5971/365-5906
Type: public choice
K–5th grade
Fitness; nutrition; critical thinking; healthy lifestyles.

Open Space at Douglas Elementary
43 S Douglas St, Columbus, OH 43205
614-365-6087
Type: public choice
K–5th grade
Incorporates city institutions, activities; flexible scheduling;
   multi-age grouping; cooperative teaching.

ICE (Individually Guided Education)
Fairwood/Linden Park Elementaries
726 Fairwood Ave/1400 Myrtle Ave, Columbus, OH 43205/43211
614-365-6111/365-6037
Type: public choice
K–5th grade

Project Adventure at Cedarwood/Devonshire Elementaries
775 Bartfield Dr/6286 Ambleside Dr, Columbus, OH 43207/43229
614-365-5421/365-5335
Type: public choice
K–5th grade
Holistic; experiential.

Spanish Immersion at Gladstone Elementary
1965 Gladstone Ave, Columbus, OH 43211
614-365-5565
Type: public choice
K–5th grade

Columbus Montessori Center
5412 Malibu Dr, Columbus, OH 43213
Anne McCarrick, SND
Type: Montessori teacher education

Home Education League of Parents (HELP)
Columbus Chapter (1992)
PO Box 14296, Columbus, OH 43214
Laurie Clark or Janet Attanasio, 614-268-5363
Non-profit
Student ages infant–18
Governance by parent cooperative
Inclusive; newsletter.

Mohawk Alternative Middle School
300 E Livingston Ave, Columbus, OH 43215
Lorenzo Hunt, 614-365-6517
Type: magnet
6–8th grade

St Joseph Montessori School
300 E Main St, Columbus, OH 43215

Literature Based/Language Arts
Franklinton/Olde Orchard Elementaries
617 W State St/800 McNaughten Rd, Columbus, OH 43215/43213
614-365-6525/365-5388
Type: public choice
K–5th grade
Magazines; newspapers; young authors' promotions.

Christian Home Educators of Ohio
PO Box 262, Columbus, OH 43216
800-274-2436

Brentnell Montessori School
1270 Brentnell Ave, Columbus, OH 43219
614-365-6079
Type: public choice
K–5th grade

Duxbury Park Elementary
1779 E Maynard Ave, Columbus, OH 43219
William Dwyer, 614-365-6023
Type: magnet
K–5th grade
Fine and performing arts.

St Mary of the Springs Montessori School (1962)
2320 Airport Dr, Columbus, OH 43219
Sr Marietta Miller, OP, Adm, 614-258-0024
Tuition: $215-375/mo
3 teachers, 4 assistants, 72 students, ages 3–6
Affiliation: AMS; accreditation: OHDHS
Governance by board

Spirituality of natural environment; foreign language; multi-cultural; newspaper; enrichment; parent participation; summer program; childcare; suburban location; interns accepted.

IMPACT (Interdisciplinary Model Program in the Arts for Children and Teachers) at Duxberry Park/Fair Elementaries
1779 E Maynard Ave/1395 Fair Ave, Columbus, OH 43219/43205
614-365-6023/365-6107
Type: public choice
K–5th grade

French Immersion at Kenwood Elementary
3770 Shattuck Ave, Columbus, OH 43220
614-365-5502
Type: public choice
K–5th grade

Columbus Montessori Education Center
979 S James Rd, Columbus, OH 43227
Dottie Feldman, Mary Lee
Type: Montessori teacher education

Science/Math/Environmental Studies
Georgian Heights Elementary
784 Georgian Dr, Columbus, OH 43228
614-365-5931
Type: public choice
K–5th grade
Experiential; math integrated into other subjects; other sites: Hamilton, 2047 Hamilton Ave, 43211, 365-5568; Cassady, 2500 N Cassady Ave, 43219, 365-5456; Berwick, 2595 Scottwood Rd, 43209, 365-6140 (lottery only).

Growing Together (1988)
1676 Tendril Ct, Columbus, OH 43229
Nancy McKibben, 614-890-3141
Type: home-based
Non-sectarian; bi-monthly learning co-op; newsletter; participates in events such as National Geography Bee.

Montessori School of Bowling Green, Inc (1980)
630 S Maple St, Bowling Green, OH 43402
Dr Charlotte Scherer, Dir, 419-352-4203
Tuition: $1,365-3,100/yr
6 teachers, 4 assistants, 31+ students, ages 3–12
Affiliation: AMS; accreditation: OH Charter
Governance by board of trustees
2.5 wooded acres; outdoor ed; transportation for ages 3–6; childcare; rural location; interns accepted.

Wood County Juvenile Detention, In-School and Out-of-School Youth Programs
Courthouse Square, Bowling Green, OH 43402
Polli Balie/Deb Doup Bailey/Christy C. Spontelli, 419-354-9010
Job seeking and placement assistance; career counseling; financial assistance for support services.

Nazarene Montessori School
1291 Conneaut Ave, Bowling Green, OH 43402-2125

The Defiance College
701 N Clinton, Defiance, OH 43512
Philip A Griswold, Ed D
Type: Montessori

Henry County Alternate Learning Center
PO Box 345, Haley St; 660 N Perry St, McClure, OH 43534
John Wilhelm, Co Supt or Rick Bailin, Dir, 419-592-1861, 748-8102
Serves handicapped, emotionally disturbed, severely behaviorally handicapped students.

Montessori Children's House
840 Ashbury Dr, Perrysburg, OH 43551
Barbara Kaiser, 419-874-7030

Tuition: $2,000/4,000/yr
1 teacher, 3 assistants, 34 students, mainly international, ages 3-6
Affiliation: AMS
Governance by administrator
French; cooking; baking; music; piano; language; parent study; Dreikurs Series discipline; childcare; suburban location; interns accepted.

Home Education League of Parents
PO Box 98, Perrysburg, OH 43552-0098
419-874-2148

West Side Montessori Center
2105 N McCord Rd, Toledo, OH 43615-3001
Lynn Fisher

RSM Creative Services Inc
(See Resource Section)

Olney Friends School (1837)
61830 Sandy Ridge Rd, Barnesville, OH 43713
Bonnie Irwin, Asst Head, 614-425-3655
Type: Quaker, boarding, non-profit; tuition: $13,230/yr, scholarships
12 teachers, 49 students, ages 13-19, 9-12th grade
Affiliations: ISACS, NAIS, FCOE
Teacher qualifications: BS with a major in subject to be taught
Whole-person approach; college prep; multi-aged classes; rural location; interns accepted.

Sandstone Montessori
582 Church St, Amherst, OH 44001-2203
Kristine Huffman, 216-984-2729
Non-profit; tuition: $100/mo, 2700/yr
1 teacher, 4 assistants, 49 students, ages infant-6
Affiliation: AMS
Governance by democratic school meeting and a committee of teachers and parents
Childcare; suburban location; interns accepted.

Ohio Home Educators Network (Cleaveland-Akron area)
PO Box 23054, Chagrin Falls, OH 44023-0054
216-543-5644, 216-562-5173

Notre Dame Montessori
13000 Auburn Rd, Chardon, OH 44024-9331
Sr Mary Doloretta Coyne

Faith Montessori School
8665 Prescott Dr, Chesterland, OH 44026

Golden Crescent Montessori (1982)
266 Washington Ave, Elyria, OH 44035
Evelyn L. Miller, Adm, 216-323-6925
Non-profit; tuition: $990-1,550/yr
2 teachers, 2 assistants, 49 students, ages infant-6
Affiliation: AMS; accreditation: NAEYC
Governance by administrator, board
Suburban location; interns accepted.

Gilmour Academy Montessori School
34001 Cedar Rd, Gates Mills, OH 44040-9732
Sr Loretta May

Washington Continous Progress Academy
2700 Washington Ave, Lorain, OH 44052
Sam Coleman, 216-246-2187
Type: magnet
K-3rd grade
Continuous progress; fine arts.

Lorain City Schools Montessori Program
1020 W 7th St, Lorain, OH 44052-1459
Doug Mathews

Montessori Child Enrichment Center
3840 Kolbe Rd, Lorain, OH 44053

Lincoln Academy
E 31st St & Vine Ave, Lorain, OH 44055
Tim Dortch, 216-277-8188
Type: Montessori magnet
K-6th grade

Palm Academy
3330 Palm Ave, Lorain, OH 44055
Sylvia Cooper, 216-277-9226
Type: Montessori magnet
K-3rd grade

HELP-Northern Ohio (1993)
10915 Pyle-S Amherst Rd, Oberlin, OH 44074
Gina McKay Lodge, Coord, 216-774-2720, FAX: 775-1368
Type: home-based, non-profit
Resources; support; participation in adult work; field trips; suburban location.

Hershey Montessori School, Inc (1978)
10229 Prouty Rd, Concord Township, OH 44077
Michael Bagiackas, Head, 216-357-0918, FAX: 216-357-1505
Non-profit
7 teachers, 135 students, ages 1-12
Governance by board of trustees
Custom designed building; parent-child program; 11+ acres; land lab; developing farmstead; integration of indoor and outdoor learning environments; no letter grades; multi-aged classes; suburban location.

Ohio Coalition of Educational Alternatives Now (OCEAN)
PO Box 94, Thompson, OH 44086
Type: state home-based

Willoughby Montessori Dayschool
5543 Som Center Rd, Willoughby, OH 44094-4281

Max S Hayes Vocational High School
4600 Detroit Ave, Cleveland, OH 44102
Theodis Fipps, Prin, 216-631-1528
Type: public choice
HS
Autobody, diesel technician; construction; textiles; welding cutting; manufacturing; placement assistance.

Thomas Jefferson CompuTech Center
3145 W 46th St, Cleveland, OH 44102
Joseph Mueller, Prin, 216-631-5962
Type: public choice
6-8th grade
Instruction supported by electronic technology.

West Technical High School
2201 W 93rd St, Cleveland, OH 44102
Bobby McDowell, Prin, 216-281-9100
Type: public choice, HS
School of manufacturing, automotive and related technologies; childcare; commercial art; drafting/graphics; construction; electronics; landscape; Project Smart apprenticeship program.

Marotta Montessori School
11450 Franklin Blvd, Cleveland, OH 44102-2310
Alcillia Clifford

East High Academy of Finance and Vocational Magnet
1349 E 79th St, Cleveland, OH 44103
Mary Stokes, Prin, 216-431-5361
Type: public choice
Childcare; commercial art; drafting/graphics; construction; cosmetology; electronics; landscape; small animal care.

Martin Luther King Jr Law and Public Service High School
1651 E 71st St, Cleveland, OH 44103
Melvin Jones, Prin, 216-431-6858
Type: public choice, HS
Mediation and conflict management.

Alfred A Benesch Primary Achievement Program
5393 Quincy Ave, Cleveland, OH 44104
Allene Warren, Prin, 216-431-4132
Type: public choice
K–3rd grade
Ungraded; self-paced.

Anton Gardina Primary Achievement Program
3050 E 77th, Cleveland, OH 44104
Inez Powell, Prin, 216-641-7477
Type: public choice
K–3rd grade
Ungraded; self-paced.

Dike Montessori Center
2501 E 61st St, Cleveland, OH 44104
Carolyn Bridges-Graves, Prin, 216-361-0708
Type: public choice
K–4th grade
Cooperative learning; multi-aged classes.

East Technical High School Engineering/Technician Program and Vocational Magnet
2439 E 55th St, Cleveland, OH 44104
Terry Butler, Prin, 216-431-2626
HS
Childcare; commercial art; computer-aided drafting, graphics; electronics; food service.

Harvey Rice Primary Achievement Program
11529 Buckeye Rd, Cleveland, OH 44104
Elizabeth Ward, Prin, 216-231-2411
Type: public choice
1–3rd grade
Ungraded; self-paced.

Corlett Primary Achievement Program
13013 Corlett Ave, Cleveland, OH 44105
David Keilin, Prin, 216-295-2590
Type: public choice
1–3rd grade
Ungraded; self-paced.

John Adams Classical Academy
3817 Martin Luther King Jr Dr, Cleveland, OH 44105
Darryl Smith, Prin, 216-561-2200
Type: public choice
HS
College prep.

Robert H Jamison CompuTech Center
13905 Harvard Ave, Cleveland, OH 44105
George J. Billingsley, Prin, 216-295-0655
Type: public choice
K–5th grade
Keyboarding; WP; computer programming.

South High School
Sports and Health Management Program and Vocational Magnet
7415 Broadway Ave, Cleveland, OH 44105
Jerry T. Mitchell, Prin, 216-641-0410
Type: public choice
Childcare; commercial art; drafting/graphics; construction; cosmetology; electronics; landscape; small animal care.

Bolton Primary Achievement Program
9803 Quebec Ave, Cleveland, OH 44106
William Lodwick, Prin, 216-231-2585
Type: public choice
K–3rd grade
Ungraded; self-paced.

Cleveland School of the Arts
2064 Stearns Rd, Cleveland, OH 44106
Anthony Vitanza, Prin, 216-791-2496
Type: public choice

5–12th grade
Opportunities with Cleveland Inst of Music, Cleveland Inst of Art, Cleveland Ballet, Music School Settlement.

John Hay Medical/Biological Program
2075 E 107th St, Cleveland, OH 44106
Leroy L. Melton, Prin, 216-421-7700
Type: public choice
HS

North American Montessori Teachers' Association
(See Resource Section)

Forest Hill Montessori School
2419 Euclid Heights Blvd, Cleveland Heights, OH 44106-2707

Montessori Neighborhood School
2555 Euclid Hts Blvd, Cleveland Heights, OH 44106-2709

AMI Montessori Learning Center
12900 Lake Ave #1116, Cleveland, OH 44107-1552

Empire CompuTech Center
9113 Parmelee Ave, Cleveland, OH 44108
Lincoln Haughton, Prin, 216-268-6350
Type: public choice
K–5th grade
Keyboarding; WP; computer programming.

Glenville Vocational Magnet Program
650 E 113th St, Cleveland, OH 44108
Elbert Cobbs, Jr, Prin, 216-851-9400
Type: public choice
HS
Childcare; commercial art; drafting/graphics; construction; cosmetology; electronics; landscape; small animal care.

Louis Pasteur Primary Achievement Program
815 Linn Dr, Cleveland, OH 44108
Norma J. Murray, Prin, 216-541-5727
Type: public choice
1–3rd grade
Ungraded; self-paced.

Miles Standish Primary Achievement
1000 E 92nd St, Cleveland, OH 44108
James Eland, 216-451-7013
Type: magnet
1–3rd grade
Non-graded; continuous progress; individualized; Montessori.

Wm. C. Bryant Primary Achievement
3121 Oak Park Ave, Cleveland, OH 44109
Marilyn Kurnath, 216-351-6343
Type: magnet
1–3rd grade
Non-graded; continuous progress; individualized; Montessori.

East Clark Primary Achievement Program
885 E 146th St, Cleveland, OH 44110
Peggie Brown, Prin, 216-451-4973
Type: public choice
K–3rd grade
Ungraded; self-paced.

Margaret Spellacy CompuTech Center
655 E 162nd St, Cleveland, OH 44110
Henry Orr, Prin, 216-531-2872
Type: public choice
6–8th grade
Instruction supported by electronic technology.

Teaching Professions at Collinwood High School
15210 St Clair Ave, Cleveland, OH 44110
William Martin, Prin, 216-451-8782
Type: public choice

Garfield CompuTech Center
3800 W 140th St, Cleveland, OH 44111
Barbara Clark, Prin, 216-251-3876
Type: public choice
3-6th grade
Keyboarding; WP; computer programming.

Louis Agassiz
3595 Bosworth Rd, Cleveland, OH 44111
Kathleen Freilino, Prin, 216-251-7747
Type: public choice
1-3rd grade

Newton D Baker School of the Arts
3690 W 159th St, Cleveland, OH 44111
Marion E. Aguilera, Prin, 216-252-2131
Type: public choice
K-4th grade
Activities with various cultural institutions.

Garrett Morgan Cleveland School of Science
4016 Woodbine Ave, Cleveland, OH 44113
Patricia Oster, Prin, 216-281-6188
Type: public choice
6-12th grade
Experiential; computers.

Hicks Montessori School
2409 Bridge Ave, Cleveland, OH 44113
H. Barbara Booker, Prin, 216-621-2616
Type: public choice
K-4th grade
Cooperative learning; multi-aged classes.

Lincoln Contemporary Academy
1701 Castle Ave, Cleveland, OH 44113
James Joyner, Prin, 216-241-7440
Type: public choice
6-8th grade
Learning styles inventory; individualized.

Aviation High School
4101 N Marginal Rd, Cleveland, OH 44114
Joseph Takacs, Prin, 216-621-1357
Type: public choice
Aircraft maintenance; avionics; marketing; air traffic control;
   ground support equipment; FAA certification test.

Health Careers Center
1740 E 32nd St, Cleveland, OH 44114
Robert J. Black III, Prin, 216-579-9984
Type: public choice
HS
Dental/lab, medical/lab, OR, optical lab assistants; senior com-
   munity health technician; mentorships.

Jane Addams Business Careers Center
2373 E 30th St, Cleveland, OH 44115
Gwendolyn Lynton, Prin, 216-621-2131
Type: public choice
11-12th grade
Computer business systems; finance/credit; legal, medical
   secretary; merchandising; computer repair; food service.

Ruffing Montessori School of Rocky River
1285 Orchard Park Dr, Rocky River, OH 44116
Tim Duax

Westshore Montessori Association
1101 Morewood Pky, Rocky River, OH 44116-1499

Montessori School of University Heights
2441 Fenwick Rd, Cleveland, OH 44118

Westshore Montessori
3249 E Monmouth Rd, Cleveland Heights, OH 44118
Ro Eugene

Lafayette Contemporary Academy
12416 Signet Ave, Cleveland, OH 44120
John Nairus, Prin, 216-561-2561
Type: public choice
K-5th grade
Individualized; learning kits.

Rainbow Bridge Montessori
3875 Monticello Blvd, Cleveland, OH 44121

Lillian Ratner Montessori School
4900 Anderson Rd, Lyndhurst, OH 44124-1000
Linda Shapiro

Emile B. deSauze Contemporary Academy
4747 E 176th St, Cleveland, OH 44128
Patricia Faulkner, Prin, 216-587-2133
Type: public choice
K-5th grade
Individualized; learning kits.

**John F Kennedy Communications and Technology
   Program**
17100 Harvard Ave, Cleveland, OH 44128
Wally Caleb, Prin, 216-921-1450
Type: public choice, HS

Moses Cleveland Primary Achievement
4092 E 146th St, Cleveland, OH 44128
Cynthia Evans, 216-295-3508
Type: magnet
1-3rd grade
Non-graded; continuous progress; individualized;
   Montessori.

Foreign Languages/International Studies Program
Robinson G Jones Elementary
4550 W 150th St, Cleveland, OH 44135
Shirley McNair-Robinson, Prin, 216-267-6464
Type: public choice
K-5th grade
Foreign language, world cultures, heritage studies.

Valley View Community School
17200 Valley View Ave, Cleveland, OH 44135
Angela Zaccardelli, Prin, 216-251-5873
Type: public choice
K-5th grade
Radio station WCTC: We Celebrate the Children.

Berea Area Montessori School
19543 Lunn Rd, Cleveland, OH 44136-4915

Solon Creative Playrooms Montessori School
32800 Solon Rd, Solon, OH 44139

Bay Village Montessori
493 Forestview Rd, Bay Village, OH 44140-2757
Karen Cunningham

South Suburban Montessori School
23 Public Sq, Cleveland, OH 44141-1801

Westlake Montessori & Child Development Center
26830 Detroit Rd, Westlake, OH 44145-2368

Decker Family Development Center
633 Brady Ave, Barberton, OH 44203
Mary Frances Ahern, Dir; Dee Siegferth, Literacy Coord, 216-
   848-4264
Student ages infant-7
Educational, social and health services.

Hudson Montessori School
7545 Darrow Rd, Hudson, OH 44236-1399

Medina Children's House
425 Ridge Dr, Medina, OH 44256
Type: Montessori

Spring Garden Waldorf School (1981)
2141 Pickle Rd, Akron, OH 44312
Jennell A. Woodard, Coord, 216-644-1160
Non-profit; tuition: $3,000/yr
16 teachers, 111 students, ages 4-14, pre K-8th grade
Affiliation: AWSNA; accreditation: State certified
Governance by faculty and board
Teacher qualifications: degree
Suburban location.

Margaret Park School
1413 Manchester, Akron, OH 44314
Barbara Nelson
Type: Montessori

Erie Island School
1532 Peckham Ave, Akron, OH 44320
Johnnette Curry
Type: Montessori

Lisbon Montessori School
P O Box 87, Lisbon, OH 44432

Childhood Manor Montessori School
North Rd, Warren, OH 44483

Blossom Montessori, Inc
2138 E Market St, Warren, OH 44483-6104

Natural Beginnings Preschool
1145 Turin Ave, Youngstown, OH 44510
Type: Montessori

St Anthony's Montessori School
1145 Turin St, Youngstown, OH 44510-1198

Montessori School of Mahoning Valley
2008 Lynn Ave, Youngstown, OH 44514-1123
216-788-4622
Non-profit
5 teachers, 3 assistants, 81 students, ages 3-12
Affiliations: AMS, IMS; accreditation: AMS
Governance by administrator
Wooded setting; nature studies; childcare; sub/urban location; interns accepted.

Children's House Montessori (1984)
637 College Ave, Wooster, OH 44691
Marge Thomas, Head, 216-264-5222, FAX: 216-262-6295
Non-profit; tuition: $1,800/2,650/yr
1 teacher, 1 assistant, 21 students, ages 3-6
Affiliations: AMS, NAEYC
Governance by board of trustees
Low enrollment fosters teacher-parent-student relationships; kindergarten participates in archaeological dig; rural location; interns accepted.

Canton Montessori School
125 15th St NW, Canton, OH 44703-3207

La Escuela de Las Madras y Los Ninos
3500 Cleveland Ave NW, Canton, OH 44709-2749
Type: Montessori

Ashland University Montessori Preschool (1981)
Jacobs Hall, Ashland, OH 44805
Sarah Telego, Dir, 419-289-5699
Tuition: $1,125-2,831/yr
1 teacher, 4 assistants, 50 students, ages 3-6
Affiliation: AMS; accreditations: NAEYC, OHDS
Governance by board
Swimming; university students read to, interact with students, conduct gym class; childcare; rural location; interns accepted.

Home Ed League of Parents/HELP Unlimited
Box 93, Ashland, OH 44805
419-869-7916

Montessori Child Enrichment Center
710 Cleveland Rd E, Huron, OH 44839-1871
Mary Helen Kay

Home Educator's Resource Organization (1991)
4 Erie St, Norwalk, OH 44857
Jane Janovyak, Support Group Leader, 419-668-6480
Non-profit

St Peter's Montessori Pre-School
63 Mulberry St S, Mansfield, OH 44902-1909
Tina Siegfried

Project Renew at the D Russell Lee Career Center
3603 Hamilton-Middletown Rd, Hamilton, OH 45011
Antoinette Lipscomb, 513-868-6300
Assists drop-out re-entry, GED or job training.

St Julie Billiart School
1206 Shuler Ave, Hamilton, OH 45011
Type: Montessori

St Mary School
610 High St, Hamilton, OH 45011
Type: Montessori

Homeschool Network of Greater Cincinnati
3470 Greenfield Ct, Maineville, OH 45039-9517
513-732-6455
Issues-oriented; contact for info on new Association of OH Homeschoolers

The Child's Place- A Montessori Preschool, Inc (1987)
4936 Irwin-Simpson Rd, Mason, OH 45040-5004
Patricia M. Elder, Dir/Owner, 513-793-0569, 398-7773
Tuition: $2,225/yr
3 teachers, 2 assistants, 70 students, ages 3-6
Affiliation: AMS
Governance by administrator
Custom designed facility; large outdoor area; geography/cultural program enriched by multi-ethnic student body; childcare; suburban location; interns accepted.

Children's Meeting House Montessori School (1972)
931 O'Bannonville Rd, Loveland, OH 45140
Barbara W. Collins, Director, 513-683-4757
Non-profit; tuition: $2,480/3,500/yr
7 teachers, 112 students, ages 3-12
Affiliation: AMS; accreditation: State of Ohio
Governance by administrator, board
5-acre eco-learning lab: pond, orchard, vegetable and flower gardens, pine forest and nature trail; suburban location; interns accepted.

Children's House
5878 Cook Rd, Milford, OH 45150-1506
Type: Montessori

Montessori Center East
2505 Eastern Ave, Cincinnati, OH 45202-1815

Total Learning Center for Children
205 W 4th St, Cincinnati, OH 45202-2628
Jennifer Hartman
Type: Montessori

Downtown Montessori
318 E 4th St, Cincinnati, OH 45202-4202

Montessori School of Western Cincinnati (1987)
4431 Glenway Ave, Cincinnati, OH 45205
Eileen Hof, Dir, 513-471-6792
Non-profit; tuition: $1,475/yr
2 teachers, 1 assistant, 60 students, ages 3-6
Affiliation: Cincinnati MS; accreditation: AMS
Governance by board
Extensive science program; suburban location; interns accepted.

Western Hills Montessori
4125 St William Ave, Cincinnati, OH 45205

Union Institute (1964)
440 E McMillan St, Cincinatti, OH 45206
Anu M. Mitra, Communications Dir, 513-861-6400, FAX: -0779
Type: higher education, non-profit; tuition: $2,175-2,484/qrtr,
  scholarships
105 teachers, 1600 students
Governance by board of trustees
BA, BS, PhD; fully accredited; home-study; interdisciplinary;
  tutorials; no letter grades.

Walnut Hills Montessori Child Care Center
813 Beecher St, Cincinnati, OH 45206-1513

Mercy Montessori Center
2335 Grandview Ave, Cincinnati, OH 45206-2219
Sr Mary Jacinta Shay

**Xavier University Montessori Teacher Education
  Program**
3800 Victory Pkwy, Cincinnati, OH 45207-7341
Elizabeth L Bronsil

Summit Country Day School
2161 Grandin Rd, Cincinnati, OH 45208-3300
Phyllis Schueler
Type: Montessori

Parents & Children
34 Green St, Cincinnati, OH 45210-1252
Type: Montessori

Montessori Discoveries International
3756 Carson Ave, Cincinnati, OH 45211-4610

Cincinnati Waldorf School (1973)
5411 Moeller Ave, Norwood, OH 45212
Brenda Roberts, Adm Coord, 513-531-5135
Non-profit; tuition: $1,500-3,840/yr, scholarships
10 teachers, 53 students, ages 3-8, pre K-2nd grade
Affiliation: AWSNA
Governance by faculty and parent representatives
Teacher qualifications: commitment to anthroposophy,
  Waldorf training, college degree
Foundation program in Anthroposophical Studies for adults;
  weekend and summer programs for students; urban loca-
  tion; interns accepted.

Kennedy Heights Montessori Center
6065 Red Bank Rd, Cincinnati, OH 45213
513-631-8135
Non-profit; tuition: $150/375/mo
4 teachers, 4 assistants, 96 students, ages 3-6
Affiliations: AMI, AMS
Governance by board of trustees
Suburban location.

Sands Montessori (1975)
940 Poplar St, Cincinnati, OH 45214
Rita Swegman, Prin, 357-4330, FAX: 357-4333
Type: public choice; tuition: $1,395
29 teachers, 27 assistants, 707 students, ages 3-12
Affiliation: AMS
Governance by administrator
Unique playground and auditorium; over 30 specialized pro-
  grams; teacher trainers on staff; nation's first public
  Montessori school; childcare; urban location; transporta-
  tion; interns accepted.

Montessori Creative Portfolio
PO Box 15132-L, Cincinnati, OH 45215
Judith A Berger

Montessori Matters
701 E Columbia Ave, Cincinnati, OH 45215
Sr Helen Denise Somers

Reading Hilltop Community School (1967)
2236 Bolser Dr, Reading, OH 45215
Arnol Elam, Prin, 513-733-4322
Type: Montessori; tuition: $800/yr
1 teacher, 1 assistant, 41 students, ages 3-6
Affiliation: AMS
Governance by administrator
Suburban location; interns accepted.

Terry's Montessori School
209 Wyoming Ave, Cincinnati, OH 45215-4307

National Homeschool Association
PO Box 157290, Cincinnati, OH 45215-7290
Sydney Mathis, Office Coord, 513-772-9580, FAX: same: call
  first
Non-profit
Annual conference; Homeschoolers Travel Network.

Clifton Montessori Center
351 Volkert Ave, Cincinnati, OH 45219-1138

Montessori Learning Center
2147 Auburn Ave, Cincinnati, OH 45219-2906

Cincinnati Montessori Society
395 Terrace, Cincinnati, OH 45220
Rita Hoppert

Clifton Multi-Age Elementary
3645 Clifton Ave, Cincinnati, OH 45220
Jay Parks, 513-861-7640
Type: magnet
K-6th grade
Multi-Age.

St Mary Lisa Steigerwald
1768 Cedar Ave, Cincinnati, OH 45224-2802
Type: Montessori

Lotspeich Montessori Center
5400 Red Bank Rd, Cincinnati, OH 45227-1122

North Avandale Montessori School
615 Clinton Springs Ave, Cincinnati, OH 45229
Thomas Rothwell, 513-221-3478
Type: magnet
K-6th grade
Montessori.

The New School (1970)
3 Burton Woods Ln, Cincinnati, OH 45229
Robyn Breiman, Dir, 413-281-7999
Type: Montessori, non-profit
11 teachers, 4 assistants, 133 students, ages 3-12
Affiliations: AMS, OHAIS; accreditation: OH
Governance by board
In 101-year-old stone mansion; national historic site; child-
  care; urban location; interns accepted.

Apple Hill Montessori School
1009 Nimitz Ln, Cincinnati, OH 45230-3648

Children's Way Montessori School
8779 Winton Rd, Cincinnati, OH 45231-4821

Children's Montessori Center
7000 Hamilton Ave, Cincinnati, OH 45231-5240

McKie Montessori School
124 Zinn Pl, Cincinnati, OH 45233-1227

Bond Hill Child Development Center
1600 Carolina Ave, Cincinnati, OH 45237
Type: Montessori

Dayspring Children's Center
6831 Colerain Ave, Cincinnati, OH 45239
Type: Montessori

Child's Place, A Montessori Preschool
7745 Trailwind Dr, Cincinnati, OH 45242-5004

Cincinnati Country Day School
6905 Given Rd, Cincinnati, OH 45243-2898
Type: Montessori

Maple Knoll Child Center (1977)
11070 Springfield Pike, Springdale, OH 45246
Nancy Drobish Lloyd, Dir, 513-782-2450
Type: Montessori, non-profit; tuition: $3,744/1,953
5 teachers, 55 students
Affiliation: AMS
Located in retirement village; suburban location; interns
accepted.

Garden Montessori School
8108 Beechmont Ave, Cincinnati, OH 45255-3154

Fifth & Walnut Montessori
600 Walnut St, Greenville, OH 45331-1944
Nancy Dean

Miami County Juvenile Court Program
201 W Main St, Troy, OH 45373
Diane Cline, Adm, 513-332-6993
1 teacher
Teacher qualifications: OH Certification
Serves probation or parole youths suspended or expelled
from school; operates 3 hrs/day.

Miami Montessori School
86 Troy Town Rd, Troy, OH 45373-2328

Antioch School (1921)
1160 Corry St, Box 242, Yellow Springs, OH 45387
Gilah Rittenhouse, School Manager, 513-767-7642
Type: independent, non-profit; tuition: $3,275
5 teachers, 75 students, ages 3.5-11, pre K-6th grade
Governance by faculty and board of parents, community
members
Teacher qualifications: certification
All students learn to ride unicycles; school-wide art/science
program; borders on 1000-acre nature preserve; founded
by Arthur Morgan, who was President of Antioch University; no letter grades; multi-aged classes; suburban
location.

Antioch University
Admissions, Yellow Springs, OH 45387
Jimmy Williams, Dean of Adms, 800-543-9436
Tuition: $17,500/yr, scholarships
675 students
Pioneer in co-op ed, with six experience-based programs
across US and abroad; scholarships for environmental and
social action; no letter grades.

Community Service, Inc
(See Resource Section)

Home Education League of Parents (HELP)
Miami Valley Chapter (1993)
PO Box 63, Yellow Springs, OH 45387
Leslie Baynes, Coord, 513-767-2346
Non-profit
Inclusive; interest-based.

Montessori Nature School
1045 E Hyde Rd, Yellow Springs, OH 45387-9756

Lutheran School of Dayton
239 Wayne Ave, Dayton, OH 45402-2939
Type: Montessori

Stivers Middle School
1313 E Fifth St, Dayton, OH 45403
Timothy Nealon, 513-223-3175
Type: magnet
7-8th grade
Visual and performing arts.

Wilbur Wright Middle School
1361 Huffman Ave, Dayton, OH 45403
Dale Frederick, 513-253-2343
Type: magnet
7-8th grade
Individualized.

Franklin Montessori School (1989)
2617 E 5th St, Dayton, OH 45403-2696
Judith O'Ryan, 513-253-2138
Type: public choice
21 teachers, 19 assistants, 465 students, ages 3-12
Affiliation: AMS; accreditation: MACTE
Governance by teachers and administrators
Peace education; character education; cultural programs;
extensive field trips; urban location; transportation; interns
accepted.

Horace Mann Montessori (1979)
715 Krebs Ave, Dayton, OH 45403-2696
Theolauda Harewood, 278-0966
342 students, ages 3-12
Affiliation: AMS
Governance by teachers and administrators
Transportation; interns accepted.

Charles H. Loos Elementary
45 Wampler Ave, Dayton, OH 45405
Winifred Lee, 513-278-0785
Type: magnet
1-6th grade
Environmental studies; museum studies.

Colonel White High School
501 Niagara Ave, Dayton, OH 45405
Craig William, 513-276-2107
Type: magnet
9-12th grade
Visual and performing arts.

E. J. Brown Elementary
48 W Parkwood Dr, Dayton, OH 45405
Jane Rafal, 513-276-2144
Type: magnet
K-6th grade
Individualized.

Van Cleve Elementary
45 W Helena St, Dayton, OH 45405
Lillian Walker, 513-228-4153
Type: magnet
1-6th grade
Visual and performing arts.

Jefferson Montessori, Campus 1
1231 N Euclid Ave, Dayton, OH 45407
Therman Sampson, 513-276-2147
Type: magnet
K-2nd grade
Montessori.

Lincoln Elementary School
401 Nassau St, Dayton, OH 45410
Grayee Toles, 513-252-9915
Type: magnet
K-6th grade
Individualized.

Gloria Dei Montessori School (1962)
615 Shiloh Dr, Dayton, OH 45415
Virginia Varga, Adm, 513-274-7195
Non-profit; tuition: $230-349/mo
7 teachers, 7 assistants, 118 students, ages infant-12
Affiliation: AMS; accreditation: OH DE
Governance by board
Childcare.

Dayton Public Schools
2013 W 3rd St #158, Dayton, OH 45417
Diane Sherman, Dir of Elem Ed
Type: Montessori

Jackson Elementary
3201 McCall St, Dayton, OH 45417
Kenneth Dixon, 513-268-6791
Type: magnet
1-6th grade
Environmental studies; museum studies.

Cleveland Elementary
1102 Pursell Ave, Dayton, OH 45420
Darlene Borgert, 513-253-2175
Type: magnet
1-6th grade
Visual and performing arts.

Alexandria Montessori School
2900 Acosta, Kettering, OH 45420
Carol Schwob

Montessori Children's Center (1978)
4369 Valley Pike, Dayton, OH 45424
Dianne Remmers, Head, 513-236-6805
Tuition: $145-250/mo
2 teachers, 3 assistants, 65 students, ages 3-9
Affiliation: NAMTA; accreditation: Chartered
Governance by administrator
Childcare; suburban location; interns accepted.

Cassidy and Nells
(See Resource Section)

Beavercreek Montessori School
2262 N Tulane Dr, Beavercreek, OH 45431

Discovery House Montessori School
2525 Obetz Dr, Beaver Creek, OH 45434-6956
Ardyce Powell

Effica School of Montessori
71 Marco Ln, Centerville, OH 45458-3818

Montessori School of Centerville (1977)
16 E Elmwood Dr, Centerville, OH 45459
Wende Delre, Dir, 513-435-4572
Non-profit; tuition: $1,750/3,800/yr
1 teacher, 2 assistants, 40 students, ages 3-6
Accreditations: AMS, OH DE
Governance by administrator, board
Student-centered curriculum; practical life skills; interper-

sonal skills; emphasis on independence and self-
confidence; suburban location; interns accepted.

Nightingale Montessori School
1106 E High St, Springfield, OH 45505
Nancy Schwab

Ohio Organization
(See Resource Section)

Andis Center and
Drift Creek Farm for Youth
2204 SR 217, Kitts Hill, OH 45645
Earl Hutchinson, Dir, 614-532-8882,-9068
Boarding
81 acres; voc; natural resources, agri. prod, work & family; lab
work in forestry, soil conservation, hydroponic horticulture, food prep, nutrition; CAI.

Special Friends
Box 457, Winchester, OH 45647-0457
Ann Vanorio
Type: home-based

Institute for Democracy in Education
(See Resource Section)

River Valley Community School (1982)
8075 State Route 56, Athens, OH 45701-9206
Claudia Shultz, Director, 614-698-6154
Type: independent, non-profit
4 teachers, 67 students, ages 3-12, pre K-6th grade
Affiliations: NAEYC, IDE
Governance by board
Developmentally-appropriate; integrated, theme-based; conflict resolution, foreign languages, fine arts, movement; no
letter grades; multi-aged classes; extensive field trips; rural
location; interns accepted.

Attention Alternate Learning Program
1850 Spenceville Rd, Lima, OH 45805
Sandra J Monfort, Dir, 419-227-5531
Type: public at-risk
6-12th grade
Affiliation: Allen Cty Juvenile Ct's Unruly Dept
Multi-aged classes; books and assignments from respective
schools; urban location.

Ohio Association
49 E College Ave, Springfield, OH 54404
Nadine Koogler, State & Fed Prgms
Type: Montessori

Oklahoma

Project Connect (1989)
6505 E Highway 66, El Reno, OK 73036
Clark McCaskill, Dir, 405-422-2200, FAX: 405-422-2299
Type: public at-risk
3 teachers, 2 assistants, 60 students, ages 15-19, 9-12th
grade
Affiliation: Canadian Valley Vo-Tech
Governance by teachers, principal, advisory committee
Teacher qualifications: OK certification
Learning packets; vocational; counseling; adaptive PE; com-
munity service; no letter grades; multi-aged classes; subur-
ban location; transportation.

Guthrie Job Corps Center
PO Box 978, Guthrie, OK 73044-0978
Type: Montessori

Children's House of Norman (1971)
606 S Santa Fe, Norman, OK 73069
Marilyn Hammond, Adm, 405-321-1275
Type: Montessori, non-profit; tuition: $125/250/mo
3 teachers, 4 assistants, 80 students, ages 3-6
Affiliation: AMS
Governance by teachers and administrators
Teacher qualifications: Montessori certification
Student-centered environment; developmentally-
appropriate; childcare; suburban location; interns
accepted.

Home Educators Resource Organization (1993)
475 College, Norman, OK 73069
Lynne M. Keller, Coord, 405-321-6423
Non-profit

12 teachers, 26 students, ages infant-17, pre K-12th grade
Student newspaper; resource center; field trips; urban
location.

Saxon Publishers, Inc
(See Resource Section)

Southwind Montessori, Inc (1982)
1601 Imhoff, Norman, OK 73072
Carol Zerboni, Owner/Prin, 405-364-2772
3 teachers, 4 assistants, 50 students, ages 3-6
Governance by administrator

Pathways Child Development Center
1901 N Douglas Ave, Oklahoma City, OK 73106-4263
Mary Ann Heard
Type: Montessori

Southwest Montessori Early Learn
5419 S Western Ave, Oklahoma City, OK 73109-4506

The Rainbow Fleet
4305 Meadow Oak, Oklahoma City, OK 73110
Alfreda Little
Type: Montessori

Westminster Day School
4400 N Shartel Ave, Oklahoma City, OK 73118-6400
Type: Montessori

Northwest Montessori Preschool
13417 Inverness Ave, Oklahoma City, OK 73120-8512

OK Central Home Educators Consociation
PO Box 270601, OKC, OK 73137

Casaday School-Primary Division
PO Box 20390, Oklahoma City, OK 73156-0390
Type: Montessori

Oak Hall Montessori (1971)
401 3rd St NW, Ardmore, OK 73401
Bettye Brown, Vicki Smith or Ginny Little, 405-223-1244
Non-profit; tuition: $120/mo
3 teachers, 3 assistants, 52 students, ages 3-9
Affiliation: Episcopal Diocese of OK; accreditation: AMS
Governance by administrator, board of trustees
In-depth geography study; art; cooking; childcare; urban
location; interns accepted.

Take Two-AES (Services) (1993)
2600 Harris, PO Box 1709, Ardmore, OK 73401
Bob Haynes, Director, 405-226-7680
Type: public at-risk
5 teachers, 36 students, ages 16-21, 9-12th grade
Affiliation: PS I-19
Governance by teachers, principal, board
Teacher qualifications: state certification
Contracts; intensive core curriculum; multi-aged classes;
interns accepted.

Montessori School of Ardmore
401 3rd Ave NW, Ardmore, OK 73401-6106

Cimarron School
419 W Maple, Enid, OK 73701
Amy Cromwell
Type: Montessori

Springwater Children's House
4619 W Randolph Ave, Enid, OK 73703-3442
Type: Montessori

Montessori Academy
127 S Chickasaw Ave, Bartlesville, OK 74003-2810

Bartlesville Alternative High School
PO Box 1357, Bartlesville, OK 74005
Beverly Teague

Cornerstone
PO Box 2472, Broken Arrow, OK 74013-2472
Paulet Garrett, 918-481-6248
Type: home-based
Everyone welcome.

Bartlett Alternative School
1 S Mission St, Sapulpa, OK 74066-4633
Susan Wheeler, Prin, 918-224-7958, FAX: 227-3287
Type: public choice
4 teachers, 30 students, ages 14-21, 9-12th grade
Governance by board
Teacher qualifications: certification
Basic skills; emphasis on self-esteem, study skills, socially-
appropriate problem solving, conflict resolution; behavior
management; extensive field trips; multi-aged classes;
interns accepted.

Booker T. Washington High School
1631 E Woodrow Place, Tulsa, OK 74106
James Furch, 918-428-6000
Type: magnet
9-12th grade
Multi-cultural; IB.

Carver Middle School
624 E Oklahoma Place, Tulsa, OK 74106
Bobbie Johnson, 918-587-5583
Type: magnet
6-8th grade
Multi-cultural; multi-age grouping.

Emerson Elementary
909 N Boston, Tulsa, OK 74106
Catherine Frederick, 918-583-5808
Type: Montessori magnet
K-5th grade
Open classroom; non-graded; individualized.

Street School
1135 S Yale, Tulsa, OK 74112
Mitch Dittus, 918-834-4300
Type: independent; tuition: none
90 students, mainly at-risk, ages 13-19
Goal setting behavior modification; drug/alcohol prevention;
life skills program.

Cornerstone
1148 S Owasso Av, Tulsa, OK 74120
Type: home-based

Margaret Hudson Program (1968)
1205 W Newton, Tulsa, OK 74127
Jan L. Figart, Exec Dir, 918-585-8163, FAX: 592-2368
Type: public at-risk
13 teachers, 400 students, ages 11-21, 6-12th grade
Governance by board
Teacher qualifications: OK Certification
Health, social services; 3 sites: Tulsa, Broken Arrow, Owano;
multi-aged classes; interns accepted.

Project 12 (1970)
1205 W Newton, Tulsa, OK 74127
Farryl Stokes, Coord, 918-587-8133
Type: public choice
8 teachers, 150 students, ages 16-21, 9-12th grade
Governance by teachers and principal
Teacher qualifications: OK Certification
HS diploma program for returning students; urban location;
transportation; interns accepted.

Montessori Academy
4018 S Oswego Ave, Tulsa, OK 74135-2431
Judith Billings

Undercroft Montessori School (1964)
3745 S Huds, Tulsa, OK 74135-5604
M. LeAnn Huxall, Adm, 918-622-2890

Non-profit; tuition: $1,880-3,660/yr
6 teachers, 5 assistants, 111 students, ages 3-12
Affiliation: AMS
Governance by administrator, board
Fine arts; located near major expressway; childcare; urban location; interns accepted.

STAR (Student Training and Reentry) Program (1988)
3420 S Memorial, Tulsa, OK 74145
Dr Leslie Hale, Coord, 918-627-7200, FAX: -9499
Type: public at-risk
1 teacher, 150 students, ages 14-21

Affiliation: Tulsa Technology Center
Governance by principal
Teacher qualifications: MA, certification, experience
Follow up for 5 years; scholarships for vocational training; multi-aged classes; urban location; interns accepted.

Oklahoma Christian Home Educators Association
PO Box 471032, Tulsa, OK 74147-1032

Learning All Ways
(See Resource Section)

Oregon

SAGE School (1992)
19701 S Beavercreek Rd, Oregon City, OR 97004
Barbara Markwell or Ron McMurry, Tchs, 503-650-6600
Type: public at-risk
2 teachers, 60 students, ages 14-21, 9-12th grade
Affiliation: Oregon City District
Governance by faculty
Diploma; GED; outcome-based; portfolios; contracts for interdisciplinary projects; non-compulsory class attendance; multi-aged classes; suburban location; interns accepted.

Oregon Home Education Network (1991)
4470 SW Hall Blvd #286, Beaverton, OR 97005
Ann Lahrson, Coord, 503-321-5166

LUNO (Learning Unlimited Network of Oregon) (1985)
31960 SE Chin St, Boring, OR 97009
Gene Lehman, 503-663-5153
Type: independent
Inclusive; Phonetic Fun for Everyone; non-compulsory ungoverned class attendance.

Alternative Choices in Education (1988)
721 SW 4th, Canby, OR 97013
Jim Gadberry, Prin or Marcia Parker, 503-266-7861
Type: public choice
1 teacher, 45-50 students, mainly at-risk, ages 14-18, 9-12th grade
Tutorial; study skills; self-esteem; rewards for grades and attendance.

Sunnyside Montessori Center
12011 SE Sunnyside Rd, Clackamas, OR 97015-9312
Durward Gurusinghe

Colton Regional Learning Center (1993)
30205 S Wall St, Colton, OR 97017
Pat Gentry, Coord, 503-824-4495
Type: public choice; tuition: variable, scholarships
1 teacher, 35 students, ages 14+, 8th grade-college
Governance by input from all parties
Work experience; home study; credit options; multi-aged classes; non-compulsory class attendance; rural location; interns accepted.

Mt Hood Academy (1985)
PO Box 189, Government Camp, OR 97028
Mary M. Gunesch, 503-272-3503
Type: independent, non-profit
4 teachers, 23 students, ages 14-18, 9-12th grade
College-prep for nationally-ranked ski racers; student-athletes travel 4-6 weeks each winter.

Hall School Montessori (1984)
2505 NE 23rd, Gresham, OR 97030
Debra Clark, Doug Shivers and Diane Ingle, Teachers, 503-661-6330
Type: public choice
3 teachers, 100 students, ages 3-9
Affiliations: NEA, OEA
Governance by teachers and administrators
Suburban location; interns accepted.

Morningstar Montessori House
PO Box 401, Gresham, OR 97030-0075

Lakeridge HS Alternative Program (1975)
PO Box 739, Lake Oswego, OR 97034
Jack DePue, Coord, 503-635-0319, FAX: 503-635-9495
Type: public choice
1 teacher, 30 students, mainly at-risk, ages 15-21, 10-12th grade
Governance by principal, teachers
Teacher qualifications: OR certification
Democratic classroom; student-initiated; self-motivation

Alternative Programs Department
Clackamas Community College (1981)
19600 S Molalla Ave, Oregon City, OR 97045
Mary Craren, Dept Chair, 503-657-6958, FAX: 650-6659
Type: public at-risk
11 teachers, 150 students, ages 15-19
Governance by teachers, department chair, administration
Teacher qualifications: MA or BA, experience
Suburban location.

Crossroads Alternative School (1971)
724 Molalla Ave; PO Box 348, Oregon City, OR 97045
Jacy Zarosinski, 503-655-2755
Type: public choice
3 teachers, 35 students, 7-12th grade
Basic skills; self-esteem; problem solving; critical thinking; counseling.

Parrott Creek School/Canby Union Annex (1971)
22518 S Parrott Creek Rd, Oregon City, OR 97045
Bill Shapiro or Lonnie Shumaker, 503-655-9144
Type: independent, non-profit
1 teacher, 21 students, mainly at-risk, ages 14-18, 8-12th grade
Tutorial; GED prep.

Vocational Options Program (1985)
701 John Adams, Oregon City, OR 97045
Michael Watkins, Instructor, 503-655-8220
Type: public choice
3 teachers, 1 assistant, 40 students, ages 16-21, HS
Governance by Clackamas CC
Work experience; job placement.

Youth Adventures, Inc (1990)
15544 S Clackamas River Dr, Oregon City, OR 97045
Marcia McClocklin, Exec Dir, 503-656-8005
Non-profit
1 teacher, 10 students, mainly at-risk, ages 13–18, 7–12th
   grade
Accreditation: OR Alliance of Children
Intensive day treatment program.

Montessori Institute NW (1979)
PO Box 771, Oregon City, OR 97045-0052
M. Shannon Helfrich, Exec Dir, 206-260-0360
Type: Montessori teacher education, non-profit
2 teachers
Affiliations: AMI, AMI/USA, NAMTA, NAEYC
Governance by board of trustees
Urban location.

Sun Garden Montessori Center (1981)
2284 Long St, Westlinn, OR 97068
David Cannon, Adm, 508-655-2609
Non-profit; tuition: $240-360/mo
4 teachers, 2 assistants, 95 students, ages 3–9
Accreditation: AMI
Governance by administrator and board
Suburban location; interns accepted.

North Marion Alternative High School (1993)
120 E Lincoln, Woodburn, OR 97071
Mr MacDonald, Tch/Supervisor, 503-981-5331
Type: independent, non-profit
2 teachers, 29 students, mainly at-risk, ages 16–19, 10–12th
   grade
Affiliation: Chemeketa College
Governance by Chemeketa College, districts.
Teacher qualifications: bilingual, certification, experience with
   at-risk students
Open entry; independent study; diploma; urban location.

Parents Education Association
PO Box 1482, Beaverton, OR 97075
503-693-0724
Type: home-based

Fire Mountain School (1983)
Box 96, 6505 Elk Flat Rd, Arch Cape, OR 97102
Barbara McLaughlin, Board President, 503-436-2610
Type: independent, non-profit; tuition: $3,000, scholarships
3 teachers, 27 students, ages 5–12, K–6th grade
Governance by parent cooperative, board
Cooperative community setting; high priority on self-esteem,
   love of learning; integrated approach to all subjects; multi-
   aged classes; no letter grades; rural location.

Tongue Point Job Corps (1972)
Hwy 30, Astoria, OR 97103
Carol Puls, Academic Progs Mgr, 503-325-2131, FAX: -5365
29 teachers, 530 students, mainly at-risk, ages 16–24
Teacher qualifications: state certification
Voc, ed, GED, and diploma programs; no letter grades; rural
   location; interns accepted.

Forestry Education Assistance Program
Oregon Department of Forestry
(See Resource Section)

**CHOICES: Challenging Holistic Opportunities
Individualized in a Cooperative Environment for
Success** (1992)
800 E 2nd St, McMinnville, OR 97128
Sandy Cameli, Instructor, 503-434-4358, FAX: 472-8778
Type: public at-risk
1 teacher, 30 students, ages 11–14, 6–8th grade
Governance by board, Educational Services District
Teacher qualifications: Experience with at-risk adolescents
Cooperative learning; heterogeneous grouping; multi-
   assessment; interdisciplinary; no letter grades; multi-aged
   classes; rural location; transportation; interns accepted.

Windson Learning Center
1101 Brooks, McMinnville, OR 97128
Karin Schockley, 503-472-4876
Type: public choice
Also, homeschooler support.

McMinnville Montessori School
PO Box 372, McMinnville, OR 97128-0372

Tillamook Program
2605 12th St, Tillamook, OR 97141
Julie Widder, Alt Ed Tch, 503-842-2566
Type: public choice
2 teachers, 40 students, ages 14–19, 9–12th grade
Governance by principal
Multi-subject classes; voluntary mentoring program; multi-
   aged classes; rural location.

Italic Handwriting Series
Portland State University
(See Resource Section)

North Willamette Homeschoolers
6501 SW Macadam, Portland, OR 97202
503-291-8493

New Deal at Roosevelt High School
6941 N Central, Portland, OR 97203
Diane Green, Coordinator, 503-280-5260
Type: public at-risk
15 students, ages 15–18, 9–12th grade
Affiliation: Portland Public Schools
Governance by teachers, principal
Teacher qualifications: extensive experience in alternative
   education environments
Students stay in same group for all classes; modified curricu-
   lum; urban location.

Open Meadow Learning Center (1971)
7654 N Crawford, Portland, OR 97203
Carole Smith, Dir, 503-285-0508
Type: independent, non-profit; tuition: by contracts
11 teachers, 84 students, mainly at-risk, ages 13–18, 7–12th
   grade
Governance by teachers, principal, board
Teacher qualifications: state certification & 4 yrs experience
   with high risk population
No letter grades; multi-aged classes; urban location.

Northwest Earth Institute (1993)
921 W Morrison, Suite 532, Portland, OR 97205
Jennifer West, Development Dir, 503-227-2807, FAX: -2917
Type: resource, non-profit
Study groups in deep ecology, voluntary simplicity in the
   home or workplace; special focus on youth; "EarthMatters"
   newsletter; Lawyers for Env Responsibility.

Greenhouse Alternative High School (1990)
820 SW Oak, Portland, OR 97205
Jay Harris, Prin, 503-239-1247
Type: independent, non-profit
4 teachers, 200 students, mainly at-risk, ages 13–21, 7–12th
   grade
Affiliations: Portland Public Schools, Salvation Army
Governance by faculty and student reps
Teacher qualifications: lots of patience and big heart
GED; diploma; emotional, employment skills; Freire, Ilyich,
   Bruner learning methodologies; youth crisis support:
   counseling, food, clothing; non-compulsory class atten-
   dance; multi-aged classes; extensive field trips; urban loca-
   tion; transportation; interns accepted.

Montessori School of Portland
6148 SE Holgate Blvd, Portland, OR 97206-4739

Metropolitan Learning Center
2033 NW Glisan St, Portland, OR 97209
Patrick Burk, 503-280-5737
Type: magnet
K–12th grade

Childpeace Montessori School
105 NW Park Ave, Portland, OR 97209-3315
Sue Pritzker

Oregon Christian Home Educators Association Network (OCEAN)
2515 NE 37th St, Portland, OR 97212
503-288-1285

Montessori Education Center of Oregon
4370 NE Halsey #218, Portland, OR 97213
Type: Montessori teacher education

Portland Waldorf School
109 NE 50th Ave, Portland, OR 97213
John Miles, Administrator, 503-234-9660, FAX: -6206
Non-profit; tuition: $4,620/yr, scholarships
25 teachers, 234 students, ages 3–15, pre K–8th grade
Affiliation: AWSNA; OFIS
Governance by college of teachers
Teacher qualifications: Waldorf training
Community enrichment courses; extensive field trips; urban location; interns accepted.

Providence Montessori School
830 NE 47th Ave, Portland, OR 97213-2212

Buckman Elementary
320 SE 16th Ave, Portland, OR 97214
Candice Beck, 503-280-6230
Type: magnet
K–5th grade
Arts.

Sunnyside Mennonite Montessori
1312 SE 35th Ave, Portland, OR 97214-4236

V.I.P. Learning Community (1994)
2368 SE 58 Ave, Portland, OR 97215
Don Berg, Tch, 503-423-5816, 235-1297
Type: independent
Student ages 5+
Contract-based; consensus; life-skills; flex schedule; non-discrimination; student-directed; non-graded; community-based.

Jefferson High School
5210 N Kerby Ave, Portland, OR 97217
Alcena Boozer, 503-280-5180
Type: magnet
9–12th grade
Performing arts; TV production.

Child's View Montessori (1988)
4729 SW Taylors Ferry Rd, Portland, OR 97219
Tamara Lacey, 503-293-9422
Tuition: $210-415/mo
3 teachers, 3 assistants, 49 students, ages 3–6
Affiliations: NAEYC, NAMTA, OFIS, OMA
Governance by administrator
Strong emphasis on peace, acceptance/respect, caring for the world, and building self-esteem; suburban location; interns accepted.

West Hills Montessori School
4920 SW Vermont St, Portland, OR 97219
Anne Blickenstaff

Portland Community College
PO Box 19000, Portland, OR 97219-0990
Cathy Howard, Counselor/Advisor, 503-244-6111, FAX: 452-4947

Mainly at-risk, ages 16+
Governance by college
Teacher qualifications: college degree, preferably Masters
Concurrent college, HS credits; students pay college tuition; multi-aged classes; suburban location.

The Teaching Home
(See Resource Section)

Raleigh Hills Montessori
4909 SW Shattuck Rd, Portland, OR 97221-2945

Cascade Valley School
13515 A SE Rusk Rd, Portland, OR 97222-3230
Cary Brown, staff member, 503-653-8128
Type: independent, non-profit; tuition: $3,500/yr, $2,700, $1,500 subsequent
7 teachers, 24 students, ages 4–18, ungraded
Sudbury Valley School approach.

Montessori School of Beaverton (1977)
PO Box 25021, Portland, OR 97225
Peter Davidson, Adm, 503-645-5247
Non-profit; tuition: $2,100-3,650/yr
6 teachers, 6 assistants, 145 students, ages 3–12
Affiliations: ORMA, ORFIS; accreditation: AMI
Governance by board of trustees
Environmental ed includes nature studies, conservation of daily resources, recycling, composting, student-led fundraising for old-growth forest preservation; suburban location; interns accepted.

Franciscan Montessori Earth School (1977)
14030 NE Sacramento St, Portland, OR 97230
M. Cardew
Tuition: $2,210-4,493/yr
22 teachers, 15 assistants, 366 students, ages 3–18
Affiliations: AMI, FISA, ORDE; accreditation: AMI
Governance by administrator
Childcare; urban location; interns accepted.

Centennial Learning Center
14750 SE Clinton, Portland, OR 97236
Darrel Dyer, 503-251-2202, FAX: -7990
Type: public at-risk

Enthusiasm for Learning Foundation
(See Resource Section)

AIM High School (1976)
10822 SE Bush, Portland, OR 97266
Dr Don E O'Neill, Dir, 503-256-6530, 252-2900 x530
Type: public at-risk; tuition: $15, or $601 out of district
12 teachers, 253 students, ages 13–20, 8–12th grade
Governance by teachers, principal
Teacher qualifications: state certification
Family approach; vocational; extensive sports; outdoor work experience; diploma; multi-aged classes; extensive field trips; suburban location; transportation.

Oliver P Lent Elementary School
5105 SE 97th Ave, Portland, OR 97266-3799
Type: Montessori

Owen Sabin Occupational Skills Center (1982)
14211 SE Johnson Rd, Milwaukie, OR 97267
Ron Dextor, Dir, 503-653-3812
Type: public choice
2 teachers, 45 students, ages 16–18, 9–10th grade
GED; AIM; CAI.

Putnam High School-SAIL Program (1981)
4950 SE Roethe, MIlwaukie, OR 97267
David Ware, 503-653-3794
Type: public at-risk
15–20 students, ages 14–19, 9–12th grade
Weekly goal setting and evaluation; daily group sessions; counseling.

Homeschooling in Oregon, the Handbook
(See Resource Section)

People Assisting the Challenge of Home-Study
PO Box 82415, Portland, OR 97282

Montessori Children's House
600 State St, Salem, OR 97301-3848

National Home Education Research Institute
(See Resource Section)

HELP-Salem
2850 Vibbert St S, Salem, OR 97302
503-370-9534

The Downtown Learning Center (1987)
360 Commercial St, Salem, OR 97302
Jim Hindman, Mgr, 503-399-3421, FAX: 503-399-3407
Type: public at-risk
10 teachers, 250 students, ages 16+
Governance by board
Teacher qualifications: state certification
Partnership between public school system, CC, JTPA; HS
   credit; GED; multi-aged classes; urban location.

Waldo Helping Everyone Experience Learning (WHEEL)
at Waldo MS
2805 Lansing Ave NE, Salem, OR 97303
Anthony Stamper, Tch, 503-399-3215
Type: public choice
58 teachers, 1000+ students, ages 12-15, 7-8th grade
Independent study skills; service learning projects; tutoring;
   camp cleanup; cooperative community activities

MECCA at McKay High School (1992)
2440 Lancaster Dr, Salem, OR 97305
John Neal, Asst Prin, 503-399-3080
Type: public choice
1 teacher, 37 students, mainly at-risk, ages 16-20, 11-12th
   grade
Governance by teachers, principal
Teacher qualifications: state certification
Self-paced; career research/job shadowing; no letter grades;
   urban location; transportation.

SERVE at McKay High School (1992)
2440 Lancaster Dr, Salem, OR 97305
John Neal, Asst Prin, 503-399-3080
Type: public choice
1 teacher, 20 students, mainly at-risk, ages 14-16, 9-10th
   grade
Governance by teachers, principal
Teacher qualifications: state certification
Self-paced; community service; no letter grades; extensive
   field trips; urban location; transportation.

Albany Montessori School
PO Box 1844, Albany, OR 97321-0502

Philomath Montessori School (1984)
1123 Main St, Philomath, OR 97324
Pauline Tanaka, Adm, 503-929-2672
Tuition: $1,500-1,850/yr
1 teacher, 1 assistant, 24 students, ages 3-6
Affiliations: AMI, NAMTA, OR MA
Governance by administrator
Rural location; interns accepted.

Cooperative Work Experience, Parenteen, Options in
Education (1990)
836 NW 11th St, Corvallis, OR 97330
Cherie Baker, Facilitator, 503-757-5871
Type: public choice/at-risk
12 students, ages 14-20, 9-12th grade
Affiliation: Corvallis HS
Supportive problem-solving; vocational exploration; parent-
   ing; community agency access; decision making; commu-
   nication skills; stress management; work experience.

Corvallis Montessori School
1240 NW 27th St, Corvallis, OR 97330
Cathryn Kasper

Aleph Montessori Children's House
437 NW 6th St, Corvallis, OR 97330-6424

OPTIONS (1981)
316 Main St, Dallas, OR 97338
Fred R Ott, Dir/Tch, 503-623-7889
Type: public at-risk
1 teacher, 50 students, ages 13-21, 7-12th grade
Governance by teachers, principal, board
Teacher qualifications: prefer Master's (SE)
HS credits; GED; life, job hunting skills; counseling; multi-aged
   classes; urban location; transportation.

Lincoln City Montessori School
4094 NE Hwy 101, Lincoln City, OR 97367-5069

West Valley Academy
PO Box 127, Sheridan, OR 97378
Jan Davidson, Exec Dir, 503-843-4123, FAX: 503-843-2080
Type: public at-risk; tuition: $4,000/yr, scholarships
18 teachers, 85 students, partly at-risk, ages 5-19, K-12th
   grade
Affiliations: OR DE, OR Mental Health Dept
Governance by teachers, principal
Teacher qualifications: Master's in specialized areas
Intervention; diversion; remediation; diagnostic testing;
   counseling; workshop; written evaluations; Intelligence
   Education Training; active parental participation; multi-
   aged classes; extensive field trips; rural location; trans-
   portation; interns accepted.

Santiam Montessori
171 W Locust St, Stayton, OR 97383-1667

Leonardo da Vinci Middle School (1987)
850 Howard Ave, Eugene, OR 97401
Michael Caley, Jill Heyerly or Tim Whitely, 503-687-3224
Type: public choice
6 teachers, 168 students, ages 11-14, 6-8th grade
Governance by teachers, principal
Teacher qualifications: state certification
Educational technology; committed to success of all; subur-
   ban location.

Looking Glass Educational Services
44 W Broadway Suite 501, Eugene, OR 97401
Galen Phipps, Dir, 503-686-2688
Type: independent
4 teachers, mainly at-risk, ages 11-18, 5-12th grade
Governance by teachers, principal
Teacher qualifications: state certification
Basic academics, psychology, sex ed and life skills; no letter
   grades; multi-aged classes; urban location; interns
   accepted.

Eugene Montessori School
2255 Oakmont Way, Eugene, OR 97401-5554
Ethel Barclay

Lane School
1200 Hwy 99 N, Eugene, OR 97402
Dr Michael George, Supervisor, 503-334-4796, FAX: 503-688-
   4015
Type: public at-risk
3 teachers, 28 students, ages 12-17, 6-12th grade
Governance by teachers, principal
Teacher qualifications: state certification (HLE)
Short-term; remedial; educational-behavioral model for
   teaching pro-social behaviors; urban location; interns
   accepted.

Patterson Family School
1510 W 15th, Eugene, OR 97402
Kay Mehas, 503-687-3406
Type: magnet, K-5th grade

Alternative Kindergarten
1150 E 29th Ave, Eugene, OR 97403
George Wilhelmr, 503-687-3286
Type: magnet
K

Pioneer Montessori Children's House
1639 E 19th Ave, Eugene, OR 97403-1902

Corridor Elementary Alternative School
250 Silver Ln, Eugene, OR 97404
Judy Sobba, Prin, 503-687-3165
Type: public choice
12 teachers, 240 students, ages 5-11, K-5th grade
Governance by teachers, principal
Teacher qualifications: state certification
Team planning; thematic units; large group performance in
community (drama, music, juggling); staff with special skill
areas; parental involvement; multi-aged classes; suburban
location; interns accepted.

Drinking Gourd Elementary School (1991)
2809 Shirley St, Eugene, OR 97404
Tricia Whitney, Dir, 503-461-4570
Type: independent; tuition: $300/mo, 2 half scholarships for
minorities
1 teacher, 10 students, ages 5-8, ungraded
Director runs business and decides curriculum; students
decide social concerns in consensus class meetings;
success-based curriculum; anti-bias approach; conflict resolution skills; cooperative learning; no letter grades; multi-
aged classes; suburban location; interns accepted.

Traditional Alternative School
950 W 22nd Ave, Eugene, OR 97404
Penny McDonlad, 503-687-3475
Type: magnet
K-5th grade

Eastside Alternative School
2855 Lincoln St, Eugene, OR 97405
Ted Calhoun, 503-687-3375
Type: magnet
1-5th grade
Non-graded; continuous progress.

Eugene Waldorf School (1980)
1350 McLean Blvd, Eugene, OR 97405
Holly Tracy, Business Mgr, 503-683-6951
Non-profit; tuition: $2,850-3,900/yr, scholarships
33 teachers, 253 students, ages 4-17, K-12th grade
Governance by college of teachers
Teacher qualifications: 2-yr Waldorf training
Suburban location; interns accepted.

Magnet Arts Alternative School
1620 W 22nd Ave, Eugene, OR 97405
Bob Bolden, 503-687-3331
K-5th grade

Willamette Homeschoolers (early 80s)
245 W 27th Ave, Eugene, OR 97405
Jill Hubbard, 503-344-4956
Student ages infant-18
40 families; inclusive; activities; park days.

Children's House
585 Douglas Ave Box 1214, Bandon, OR 97411
Donna Leveridge-Campbell
Type: Montessori

Camas Valley
PO Box 57, Camas Valley, OR 97416
Robert E. Kloss, 503-445-2131
Type: public choice
6 teachers, 25 students, ages 18-21, HS
Accreditation: NW Assn
ND DE correspondence courses.

Eugene International High School (1984)
400 E 19th, Eugene, OR 97419
Jon Doornink, Head Tch, 503-687-3115
Type: public choice
25 teachers, 952 students, ages 14-18, 9-12th grade
Affiliation: IB
Governance by site-based policy council
Teacher qualifications: state certification
School within a school; interdisciplinary; based on Socratic
method; global perspective; option to earn IB; multi-aged
classes; urban location; interns accepted.

Psychology of Success at Marshfield High School
10th & Ingersoll, Coos Bay, OR 97420
Les Engle, 503-267-3104 x265
Type: public choice
1 teacher, 102 students, ages 14-19, HS
Accreditation: NW Assn
Required elective class; making choices; positive attitudes;
self-esteem; personal power.

The Upstairs School
Alternative Youth Activities, Inc (1981)
575 S Main St, Coos Bay, OR 97420
Norman A. Welch, 503-888-2543
Type: independent, non-profit
5 teachers, 2 assistants, 105 students, mainly at-risk, ages
12-18, 7-12th grade
Counseling; self-paced; tutoring; life skills; nutrition instruction for young parents.

Aprovecho Research Center (1978)
80574 Hazelton Rd, Cottage Grove, OR 97424
503-942-8198
Type: higher education, non-profit; tuition: $300/mo,
scholarships
5 teachers, 6 students
Governance by board
Teacher qualifications: Experts in their field
Internships in appropriate technology, sustainable forestry,
organic farming.

Willamette Valley Montessori School
PO Box 11470, Eugene, OR 97440-3670

Wolf Creek Job Corps (1965)
2010 Opportunity Ln, Glide, OR 97443
John Voltz, Prin, 503-496-3507
Type: public choice
15 teachers, 250 students, ages 16-22
Accreditation: NW Assn
Vocational training, union programs, and basic education for
disadvantaged youth.

SOCRATES (1989)
PO Box 1485, Gold Beach, OR 97444
Rick Foertsch, 503-247-4140, 469-2650, 469-0873
Type: independent, non-profit
2 teachers, 75-100 students, mainly at-risk, ages 14-21, HS
3 sites; open-entry; self-paced; occupational skills; parenting.

The Opportunity Center
Myrtle Creek, OR 97457
Carol Hildebrand, Dir, 503-863-5846, FAX: 863-5486
Type: public at-risk; scholarships
1 teacher, 30 students, ages 16-21, 11-12th grade
Affiliation: S Umpqua HS
Governance by principal and board
Teacher qualifications: experience
GED; self-paced; classes and childcare for teen parents; career
and employment planning and training; community con-
nection; individualized; rural location; interns accepted.

Pacific Child Center, Inc (1972)
PO Box 987, North Bend, OR 97459
Dr Dale Helland, Dir, 503-756-2516
Type: independent, non-profit

1 teacher, 1 assistant, 12 students, ages 5-13, K-6th grade
Accreditation: NW Association
Pacific Student Center program; resource room at Roosevelt
    ES.

Douglas County Homeschoolers Connection
4053 Hanna St, Roseburg, OR 97470

Umpqua Community College (1963)
PO Box 967, Roseburg, OR 97470
Doris A Johnson, Dir, 503-440-4603, FAX: same
Non-profit; tuition: $20/term, scholarships
25 teachers, 1,800 students, ages 16-72, ungraded
Governance by board
Teacher qualifications: BA in Ed or equivalent
Progressive software for cognitive rehabilitation; individual-
    ized learning labs; transition classes; developmental
    studies; disability services; tutoring; GED Plus; no letter
    grades; multi-aged classes; non-compulsory class atten-
    dance; rural location.

Woolley Center (1955)
PO Box 967, Roseburg, OR 97470
Doris Johnson, 503-440-4603
Type: public choice/session
3 teachers, 75 students, ages 16+
Accreditation: NW Assn
Governance by Umpqua CC
GED prep; individualized learning labs; group work; lectures;
    computers.

The Learning Network (1985)
91913 Marcola Rd, Springfield, OR 97478
Bruce Gates, Prin, 503-933-2034
Type: home-based; cost: $25/mo, scholarships
5 teachers; student ages infant-18
Affiliation: NCACS/NALSAS
Governance by democratic school meeting; board
Music; art; philosophy; language; human relations, potentials;
    creative movement; majic; non-compulsory class atten-
    dance; rural location; interns accepted.

Scotts Valley Alternative School
290 5th St, Yoncalla, OR 97499
Sharon, Director, 503-849-2175
Type: public at-risk
1 teacher, 15 students, ages 16+, 9-12th grade
Governance by teachers and principal
GED/diploma; teen parenting; rural location.

Medford Center (1992)
W 4th & Oakdale, Medford, OR 97501
Ginna Neufeld, 503-770-5339
Type: public choice
36 students, ages 16+
ESL; ABE; GED/HS completion.

Youthworks Educational Services (1988)
1032 W Main, Medford, OR 97501
Michael Warner, 503-770-1270
Type: independent, non-profit
3 teachers, 40 students, mainly at-risk, ages 14-20, 7-12th
    grade
Service center model; life skills; counseling; cooperative work
    experience; medical services; case management; childcare;
    transportation

Alternative Program at Crater High School (1987)
4410 N Rogue Valley Blvd, Central Point, OR 97502
Dave Gardner, Prin, 503-664-6611
Type: public choice
2 teachers, 40 students, mainly at-risk, ages 14-19, HS
Accreditation: NW Assn
Self-paced; tutoring.

Early Years Montessori School
3347 Old Stage Rd, Central Point, OR 97502-1132

Crossroads (1988)
1150 Knutsen #6, Medford, OR 97504
Michael Warner, Dir, 503-770-1270, FAX: 503-779-3317
Type: public at-risk
6 teachers, 60 students, mainly at-risk, ages 14-21, 7-12th
    grade
Affiliation: Youthworks
Teacher qualifications: certification (any state)
CAI; outcome-based; GED; HS diploma; cooperative work
    experience; small groups; life skills; childcare; parenting;
    on-site clinic; no letter grades; multi-aged classes; exten-
    sive field trips; non-compulsory class attendance; subur-
    ban location; transportation; interns accepted.

Lithia Springs School (1987)
540 YMCA Way, Ashland, OR 97520
Doug Shipley, Prin, 503-482-5818
Type: independent, non-profit
3 teachers, 22 students, mainly at-risk, ages 14-18, 9-12th
    grade
Affiliations: OAAE, NWASC
Governance by teachers, principal
Computer lab; vocational setting; multi-aged classes; exten-
    sive field trips; suburban location; transportation.

Rogue Community College, Ashland Center (1978)
455 Walker St, Ashland, OR 97520
Linda Renfro, 503-482-3868
Type: public choice
476 students, ages 16+
ABE; GED/HS completion.

The Waldorf School of the Rogue Valley (1979)
78 4th St, Ashland, OR 97520
Clista Perlle-Tworek, Co-Office Mgr, 503-482-9825
Non-profit; tuition: $3,500/yr
8 teachers, 150 students, ages 3+, pre K-8th grade
Affiliation: AWSNA
Governance by faculty and board
Teacher qualifications: BA, Waldorf training
Extensive field trips; rural location; interns accepted.

The Dome School (1976)
9367 Takilma Rd, Cave Junction, OR 97523
Oshana Emerald, 503-592-3911
Type: independent, non-profit; tuition: $50-135/mo,
    scholarships
6 teachers, 55 students, ages 3-11, pre K-5th grade
Governance by parent co-op, board
Teacher qualifications: experience, willing to work in coopera-
    tive environment.
Low ratios; team teaching; multi-cultural; mainstream enroll-
    ment for multi-handicapped community children; no
    letter grades; multi-aged classes; rural location; interns
    accepted.

Eagle Point Junior High School Nova Program
PO Box 218, Eagle Point, OR 97524
Deborah Dorn, Tch, 503-479-3001
Type: public at-risk
1 teacher, 18 students, ages 12-15, 7-8th grade
Governance by teachers, principal
Integrated; based on token system for rewards; rural
    location.

Education Exchange at Grants Pass High School
522 NE Olive St, Grants Pass, Or 97526
Dave Currie, Vice Prin, 503-474-5710
Type: public choice
1 teacher, 30 students, ages 14-16, 9-10th grade
Accreditation: NW Assn

The Learning Connection
PO Box 1091 #196, Grants Pass, OR 97526
503-476-5686
Type: home-based

Josephine County Alternative Center
415 Murphy Creek Rd, Grants Pass, OR 97527
Jan Bonn, Dir, 503-862-2517
Type: independent
4 teachers, 30 students, mainly at-risk, ages 13–19, 7–12th grade
Teacher qualifications: credential and/or experience with at-risk teens
Democratic governance; students decide attendance and discipline; small/large groups or individual instruction; multi-aged classes; rural location.

North Valley Alternative Center (1992)
6781 Monument Dr, Grants Pass, OR 97527
Stephen H Calkins, 503-476-8252
Type: public at-risk
1 teacher, 20–25 students, partly at-risk, ages 13–21, 7–12th grade
Governance by teachers, principal, faculty, student reps, district personnel
Teacher qualifications: state certification
Life-skills-oriented; cooperative; independent study contracts; multi-aged classes; rural location; transportation; interns accepted.

Children's House Montessori
2175 Williams Hwy, Grants Pass, OR 97527-5686

Rogue Community College, Rogue River Center
Rogue River High School, Rogue River, OR 97537
Vickie Reese
Type: public choice
Student ages 16+, HS
Accreditation: NW Assn
Basic skills; ABE; GED/HS completion.

Horizon School (1981)
1960 E Fork Rd, Williams, OR 97544
503-846-6944
Type: independent, non-profit; scholarships
4 teachers, 24–30 students, ages 4–11, pre K–5th grade
Governance by parent-teacher cooperative
Teacher qualifications: credential, first aid/cpr
Parents actively involved; nearby creek, pond, fields, woods are extensions of classroom; cooperative games; 4-day wk; multi-cultural curriculum; no letter grades; non-compulsory class attendance; multi-aged classes; extensive field trips; rural location; interns accepted.

Klamath Institute (1987)
3810 S 6th, Klamath Falls, OR 97603
Martha F. Christensen, Head Teacher, 503-883-4719
Type: public at-risk; tuition: if out of district
500 students, ages 14+, 9–12th grade
Affiliation: Rogue CC
Governance by staff
Teacher qualifications: state certification
Self-paced; academic work follows regular school; open entry, open exit; independent study; rural location.

Lake County Learning Center (1986)
8 N "F" St, Lakeview, OR 97630
Joyce Thayer, Learning Mgr, 503-947-4883
Type: independent
1 teacher, 5–12 students, mainly at-risk, ages 14+
Affiliations: JTPA, FSA "Jobs"
Governance by learning manager
Teacher qualifications: state certification (Secondary Ed)
Self-paced; comprehensive; competency-based; job readiness training; diploma; GED; computer literacy; open entry/exit; multi-aged classes; rural location.

Hands On Schools (1993)
1072 NW Union, Bend, OR 97701
Glenn Young, Owner, 503-389-9238
Type: independent; tuition: $300/mo
1 teacher, 12 students, mainly at-risk, ages 10–15

Governance by owner
Teacher qualifications: empathy, business and occupational skills
Self-esteem; group cooperation; math; music; students develop business-for-profit activities, share in earned profits; no letter grades; multi-aged classes; rural location; interns accepted.

Nomadic Tipi Makers
17671 Snow Creek Rd, Bend, OR 97701
Jeb Barton
Type: Montessori

Oregon Association of Alternatives in Education
(See Resource Section)

Westside Learning Center High School (1989)
1010 NW 14th St, Bend, OR 97701
Jan Hughes, E.S.C., 503-388-9019
Type: public choice
1 teacher, 30 students, mainly at-risk, ages 14–18, HS
Self-paced packet system.

Montessori Children's House of Bend
520 NW Wall St # 212, Bend, OR 97701-2608

Central Oregon Community College (1949)
2600 NW College Way, Bend, OR 97701-5998
Dianne Dean, 503-383-7277
Tuition: variable
4 teachers; student ages 16–18, HS
HS completion; study skills.

Westsider Alternative at Cascade Middle School (1990)
19740 SW Century Dr, Bend, OR 97702
Tom Achterman, 503-388-5477
10 students, mainly at-risk, ages 11–14, 6–8th grade
Self-esteem; social skills.

Bend Homeschoolers
PO Box 9306, Bend, OR 97708
503-382-1547

COIC Skills Lab (1987)
411 W Third, Prineville, OR 97754
Ann Thomas; Meredith Junge; D. Tillinghast, 503-548-8163, 447-3119
Type: public choice; scholarships
1 teacher, 88 students, ages 14+, HS
One of 4 sites; open to economically disadvantaged, dislocated, unemployed; Youth Conservation Corp for drop-outs; diploma or skill improvement for adults.

Program at Obsidian Junior High School (1991)
1335 SW Obsidian, Redmond, OR 97756
Margaret Goodman, AE Coord/Tch, 503-923-4900
Type: public at-risk
1 teacher, 17 students, ages 12–15, 7–8th grade
Governance by teachers, principal
Teacher qualifications: BA Elem Ed, Ed M Reading
Interest-based; students tutor daily in elementary classrooms; visits to businesses and job sites; adopted city park; multi-aged classes; weekly grades; rural location.

Blue Mountain Community College (1988)
PO Box 575, Condon, OR 97823
Candy Barnett, 503-384-6221
Type: public choice
15 students, ages 19+, HS
Accreditation: NW Assn
GED prep; adult HS completion; ESL; other location in Grant County at: S Canyon Blvd, John Day, OR, 97845, contact Cindy Kimble at 503-575-1799.

Condon High School
PO Box 575, Condon, OR 97823
Rita Rattray, 503-384-2441
Type: public choice

Student ages 14-18
Accreditation: NW Assn
Independent and/or guided instruction.

Grant Union High School (1989)
PO Box 129, John Day, OR 97845
Dorothy Piazza; Carl Lino, 503-575-1799
Type: public choice
1 teacher, 60 students, ages 15-30+, HS
Accreditation: NW Assn
Evenings; tutorial; GED prep; slower paced; makeup credit;
    work experience; independent study.

Union Alternative School
10100 N McAlister Rd, Island City, OR 97850
Lyle Mann, Dir, 503-963-4106, FAX: 503-963-7256
Type: public at-risk
4 teachers, 300 students, ages 14+, 9-12th grade

Governance by board
Teacher qualifications: BA or BS
Self-paced; competency-based; non-compulsory class atten-
    dance; rural location; interns accepted.

Harmony Lane School (1993)
932 Harmony Ln, Ashland, OR 99520
Peter Spring, Head, 503-482-6536
Type: independent, non-profit; tuition: $200/mo,
    scholarships
2 teachers, 8 students, ages 6-16
Governance by democratic school meeting
Emphasis on music; headmaster is former professional musi-
    cian, flute-maker, piano tuner; students' rock band; no
    letter grades; non-compulsory class attendance; multi-
    aged classes; extensive field trips; suburban location;
    interns accepted.

Pennsylvania

Franklin Elementary School
Cheltenham & Rising Sun, Philadelphia, PA 10120
Type: Montessori

Beaver Montessori School
855 2nd St, Beaver, PA 15009-2600

St Agatha Montessori School
220 Station St, Bridgeville, PA 15017-1897

MonValley Montessori Preschool &K
550 Isabella Ave, Charleroi, PA 15022-2337

Monessen Catholic Montessori Preschool
7th & Schnmaker Ave, Monessen, PA 15062

Southwestern Pennsylvania Home Education Network
Rd 3, PO Box 256 B, Tarentrum, PA 15084
412-922-8344

Northern Area Alternative High School (1978)
9600 Babcock Blvd, Allison Park, PA 15101
Dr Victor T. Zakowski, Prin, 412-366-2800, FAX: 412-366-9600
Type: public at-risk
7 teachers, 76 students, ages 15-19, 9-12th grade
Governance by teachers and principal
Teacher qualifications: PA Certification
Vocational education; multi-aged classes; transportation.

Western PA Montessori School (1965)
2379 Wyland Ave, Allison Park, PA 15101
Carol Miskell, Adm, 487-2700
Non-profit; tuition: $1,990-4,240/yr
6 teachers, 5 assistants, 106 students, ages 3-6
Affiliation: PAEYC; accreditation: AMS
Governance by administrator, board
Childcare; suburban location; interns accepted.

Montessori Childhood Center
5303 Madison Ave, Bethel Park, PA 15102-3631

Franklin Street Montessori
400 Franklin St, East Pittsburgh, PA 15112-1019

Montessori Centre Academy
1014 Wm Flynn Hwy, Glenshaw, PA 15116
Yolanda Glasso or Yolanda Sweenie

Glen Montessori School
RR 2, Sewickley, PA 15143-9802

East Suburban Montessori School
500 Laurel Dr, Monroeville, PA 15146-1136

Secondary Options Center
City As School Program (1993)
Washington Education Bldg, 169 40th St, Pittsburgh, PA
    15201
Georgia Vassilakis, Adm, 412-622-3490, FAX: 622-3489
Type: public choice
10 students

St Francis Montessori (1989)
45th St, Pittsburgh, PA 15201
Sister Mary Meyer, Director, 412-622-7128
Non-profit; tuition: $18/day
1 teacher, 2 assistants, 37 students, ages 3-6
Affiliation: Greater Pittsburgh M
Governance by administrator
In-hospital setting lets students see facility in action; child-
    care; urban location; interns accepted.

The Village Montessori School
10 Walnut St, Pittsburgh, PA 15202-1541
John Crawford

Rogers Creative & Performing Arts School
5525 Columbo St, Pittsburgh, PA 15206
Neal Huguley, 412-665-2000
Type: magnet
6-12th grade

Pittsburgh Creative & Performing Arts
925 Brushton Ave, Pittsburgh, PA 15208
Harry Clark, 412-247-7860
Type: magnet
9-12th grade

Homewood Montessori (1980)
Hamilton and Lang St, Pittsburgh, PA 15208-1829
Dr Johnson Martin, 412-247-7855
Type: public choice
15 teachers, 2 assistants, 124 students, ages 3-9
Accreditation: MSA
Governance by teachers and administrators, parent coopera-
    tive, school board

Carlow Campus Montessori (1975)
3333 5th Ave, Pittsburgh, PA 15213
Billie Girard, Adms Dir, 412-578-6075

Non-profit; tuition: $3,550/5,000/yr
2 teachers, 2 assistants, 40 students, ages 3–6
Affiliation: AMS; accreditation: MSA
Governance by administrator
French; swimming; art; computer ed; librarian; transportation for K students; childcare; interns accepted.

Project Succeed at Keystone Oaks High School (1990)
1000 Kelton Ave, Pittsburgh, PA 15216
Joel Vanucci, Dir, 412-571-6066, FAX: 571-6006
Type: public at-risk
5 teachers, 14 students, ages 19–55
Governance by director/Teachers
Teacher qualifications: PA certification
Night classes; HS diploma; community service required.

Camalt Elementary
1583 Breining St, Pittsburgh, PA 15226
Elmer Parks, 412-885-7760
Type: magnet
1–5th grade
Open space.

Laural Learning Centers, Inc
2720 Custer Ave, Pittsburgh, PA 15227-2153
Type: Montessori

Mt. Lebanon Montessori School (1976)
550 Sleepy Hollow Rd, Mt Lebanon, PA 15228
Barbara Popchak, Dir, 412-563-2858
Non-profit; tuition: $600/2500
5 teachers, 7 assistants, 124 students, partly international, ages infant–9
Affiliations: AMS, AMI, NAMTA
Governance by administrator and board of trustees
Music; Orff & Kodaly philosophies; involved parent body; play area blends indoor, outdoor environments; gardening; childcare; suburban location; transportation; interns accepted.

Maria Montessori PreSchool
957 Connor Rd, Pittsburgh, PA 15234-1003
Bianca Nardei

Pittsburgh East Suburban Homeschoolers
238 1/2 Evaline St, Pittsburgh, PA 15235
Debbie Jackson, 412-247-4497

Montessori Early Childhood
407 Southvue Dr, Pittsburgh, PA 15236-2030

Holiday Farms Country Day School
1907 O'Block Rd, Pittsburgh, PA 15239-2333
Dorothy Lamuth
Type: Montessori

Washington County Alternative School (1988)
524 E Beau St, Washington, PA 15301
Herman J. Ross, Dir, 412-225-5505
Type: public at-risk
4 teachers, 55 students, ages 15–21, 9–12th grade
Governance by board
Teacher qualifications: state certification
Drug, alcohol counseling; life skills; work exploration; community service; GED prep; open-ended courses; suburban location; transportation.

Elizabeth Seton Montessori School
RR 7 Box 268, Greensburg, PA 15601-9569
Anita Schulte

Verna Montessori School
RD 2, Box 348, Mt Pleasant, PA 15666
Sr Margherita Ferrero

Keys Montessori School, Inc
695 School St, Indiana, PA 15701-3076

AYS Day Treatment (1991)
115 S Marion St, Ebensburg, PA 15931
Thomas Prout, Exec Dir, 814-472-7874, FAX: -7920
Type: independent, boarding, non-profit
8 teachers, 40 students, mainly at-risk, ages 11–18, 4–12th grade
Governance by board
Very structured.

Central Area Pennsylvania Home Education Network
PO Box 191, Summerhill, PA 15958
Karen Leventry, 814-495-5651

Montessori Pre-School (1989)
One Benbrooke Pl, Butler, PA 16001
Maryanne Herbert Pribis, 412-482-4200
1 teacher, 3 assistants, 34 students, ages infant–6
Affiliation: WMS of Pittsburgh; accreditations: AMI, PDOE
Governance by teachers and administrators
Rolling hills and valley; summer nature camp; childcare; rural location; interns accepted.

Montessori Day Academy
321A Benbrook Rd, Butler, PA 16001-7301

Butler Area Homeschoolers
145 Brose Rd, Marwood, PA 16023
412-352-2639

Sunflower School
Box 3732 Rd 3, Grove City, PA 16127
Joe Jenkins
Type: home-based

Pennsylvania Homeschoolers
RD 2 Box 117, Kittanning, PA 16201
Susan Richman, 412-783-6512

Armstrong County Area Homeschoolers
Rd 1, PO Box 221A, Templeton, PA 16259
Sandy Houston, 412-868-2331

Lakeland Home Educators (1986)
285 Allegheny St, Meadville, PA 16335
Jean Bartlett, Vicki Bocan, Brendra Van Matre, 814-333-2852
Field trips; social activities; bi-monthly newsletter; phone tree.

Pennsylvania Home Education Network
285 Allegheny St, Meadville, PA 16335
Diana Baseman, 412-265-2734
Non-profit; cost: $15/yr
Inclusive; newsletter.

Erie County Homeschoolers
9129 State Rd, Cranesville, PA 16410
Janet Preston, 814-774-8598

Homeworks
10730 Rt 98, Edinboro, PA 16412
Laurea Polo, 814-734-7180

Montessori Day School
1372 W 6th St, Erie, PA 16505-2596

Montessori School of Erie County
2910 Sterrettania Rd, Erie, PA 16506-2646
Martin Maly

Children's House of Erie Montessori School, Inc (1981)
4701 Old French Rd, Erie, PA 16509
S. Daniel Magoc, Exec Dir, 814-868-0615
Non-profit; tuition: $1,500/2,100/yr
2 teachers, 3 assistants, 53 students, ages 3–6
Affiliation: NAMTA
Governance by board
Teacher qualifications: AMI credential
Childcare; suburban location; interns accepted.

Pennsylvania Montessori Academy
439 Lotz Ave-Lakemont, Altoona, PA 16602-5643
Michelle Hartye

Parent-Child Press
(See Resource Section)

Delta Program (1973)
411 S Fraser St, State College, PA 16801
Kathy Kelly, Dir, 814-231-1000, FAX: -4103
Type: public choice; tuition: $6,000/yr for non-residents
12 teachers, 120 students, ages 11–21, 7–12th grade
Governance by shared decision making
Teacher qualifications: PA certification
Team planning; goal achievement support; no letter grades;
    extensive field trips; multi-aged classes; interns accepted.

State College Alternative Program
4011 S Fraser St, State College, PA 16801
Type: public choice

State College Friends School (1980)
611 E Prospect Ave, State College, PA 16801
Lee Quinby, Head, 814-237-8386
Type: Quaker, non-profit; tuition: $3,700/yr
10 teachers, 90 students, ages 5–12, K–6th grade
Affiliation: Friends Meeting
Governance by teachers, principal
Parent involvement; non-violent conflict resolution; thematic
    studies; no letter grades; multi-aged classes; interns
    accepted.

STS Program, Penn State U
133 Willard, University Park, PA 16802
Lee Hoinacki

Park Forest Montessori School
1833 Park Forest Ave, State College, PA 16803-1403
Rose Park or Janet Dargitz

Our Children's Center
Corner of Mary & Mulberry Sts, Lemont, PA 16851
Martha Torrence
Type: Montessori

United Methodist Childrens Center
PO Box 531, Wellsboro, PA 16901-0531
Type: Montessori

Endless Mountains Homeschoolers
c/o Kellogg, RD 3 Box 80, Columbia Cross Rds, PA 16914
717-549-8179

Circle School (1984)
210 Oakleigh Ave, Harrisburg, PA 17111
Beth Stone, Comm Chair, 717-564-6700, FAX: 938-0190
Type: independent, non-profit; tuition: $2,900/yr,
    scholarships
9 teachers, 36 students, ages 3–16
Governed by democratic school meeting; students manage
    their own time; no letter grades; non-compulsory class
    attendance; multi-aged classes; extensive field trips; urban
    location; transportation; interns accepted.

Manito Inc (1979)
7564 Browns Mill Rd, Chambersburg, PA 17201
Robert C. Whitmore, EdD, Exec Dir, 717-375-4733, FAX: -4336
Type: public at-risk
14 teachers, 110 students, ages 12–18, 7–12th grade
Governance by board
Teacher qualifications: BS or MS
Integration of counseling, educational services; conflict reso-
    lution skills; 3 locations, urban and rural; transportation;
    interns accepted.

Montessori School of Chambersburg
2011 Scotland Ave, Chambersburg, PA 17201-1451
Mary Jane Bittle

Lancaster Home Educators Association
c/o RR 6 Box 3335, Red Lion, PA 17356-9557
Kim Huber, 717-246-0188

Circle of Children Co-op, Cornucopia Enterprises (1993)
PO Box 67, Shrewsbury, PA 17361
Eileen Stein, Pres, 717-993-3603
Type: home-based; cost: $500-1,500/yr
2 teachers; student ages infant–18, pre K–12th grade
Affiliation: NCACS
Governance by parent co-op and staff under guidance of
    pres
Teacher qualifications: 4 yr college degree or in process of
    acquiring; regard for children, humanity, nature
Holistic; Kids in Business; Creative Solutions for teens; parent
    co-op ECE; low ratio; real-life activities; extensive field trips;
    rural location; transportation; interns accepted.

Christian Homeschool Association of Pennsylvania
Box 3603, York, PA 17402-0603
717-661-2185

Montessori Children's House of York
3417 E Market St, York, PA 17402-2623
Movair Chami

York County High School (1990)
W Manchester Mall; Box 8042, York, PA 17404
Donald Bohr, Dir, 717-767-4863, FAX: 717-767-4336
Type: public at-risk
6 teachers, 100 students, ages 16–45, 9–12th grade
Governance by director, counselor, teachers
Teacher qualifications: PA Certification
Self-paced; competency-based; multi-aged classes; urban
    location.

Montessori Academy
PO Box 177, East Petersburg, PA 17520

Susquehanna Waldorf School (1987)
15 W Walnut St, Marietta, PA 17547
Diana Ingraham, Faculty Chair, 717-426-4026
Non-profit; tuition: $2,616-3,228/yr, scholarships
8 teachers, 105 students, ages 3.5–12, nursery-6th grade
Affiliation: AWSNA
Suburban location; interns accepted.

Alternative Program at Willow St Vo-Tech (1988)
1730 Han Herr Dr, Willow St 1, PA 17584
Daniel Burkholder, 717-464-2771
Type: public at-risk
3 teachers, 45 students, ages 15–20, 8–12th grade
Affiliation: Intermediate Unit #13
Governance by teachers and principal
Support groups; community-based; extensive field trips;
    multi-aged classes; suburban location; transportation;
    interns accepted.

Montessori Academy of Lancaster (1982)
1460 Eden Rd, Lancaster, PA 17601
Mary E. Gerhart, Dir, 717-397-4617
Non-profit; tuition: $1,600-3,950/yr
5 teachers, 5 assistants, 70 students, ages toddler–9
Affiliation: MTA-PA; accreditation: AMS
Governance by board of trustees
Weekly classes in Spanish, fine arts, music, PE, and library;
    childcare; suburban location; interns accepted.

Montessori Learning Center
700 Pleasure Rd, Lancaster, PA 17601-4438

The New School of Lancaster (1990)
2312 Marietta Ave, Lancaster, PA 17603
Beth M. Crosby, Dir, 717-397-7655
Type: Montessori, non-profit; tuition: $1,200-3,850/yr
7 teachers, 6 assistants, 141 students, ages infant–9

Accreditation: PA State Board of Private Academic Schools; day care license
Governance by board of trustees
Searching for new building to expand and include ages 9-16; childcare; suburban location; interns accepted.

West Branch School (1970)
755 Moore Ave, Williamsport, PA 17701
Carolyn Erickson, Coordinator, 717-323-5498
Type: independent; tuition: $2,200/yr, scholarships
50 students, K-6th grade
Uses basic skills as tools; real experiences in solving problems, accepting responsibilities, making decisions.

Montessori School
320 Valley Rd, Bloomsburg, PA 17815-8441

Greenwood Friends School
PO Box 438, Millville, PA 17846
Sheila Lunger, Dir, 717-458-5532
Type: Quaker, non-profit; need-based scholarships
6 teachers, 50 students, ages 3-12, pre 6th grade
Affiliation: Friends Council on Education
Governance by board
Community of families and friends; student-centered; no letter grades; multi-aged classes; extensive field trips; rural location; transportation; interns accepted.

TASHKA Directives/Alcott Montessori School
PO Box 148, Bethlehem, PA 18016

Datzyk Montessori School
3300 Broadway, Allentown, PA 18104-5927
Ruth Datzyk

Childrens Learning Center
PO Box 253, Hazleton, PA 18201-0253
Type: Montessori

Preschool House —Rush Elementary School
RD #2 Meadow Ave, Tamaqua, PA 18252
Type: Montessori

Crossroads Day Treatment (1994)
PO Box 1191, Broadheadsville, PA 18322
Betty Jeanne Segear, Dir, 717-992-1473, FAX: -7490
Type: independent at-risk, non-profit
2 teachers, 1 assistant, 24 students, mainly at-risk, ES-HS
Governance by multi-disciplinary team
Teacher qualifications: SE Degree
SE; socially/emotionally disturbed; LD; tutoring.

Growing Concern
515 Hemlock Dr, Mt Bethel, PA 18342
Type: Montessori

Montessori Childrens House of the Poconos
PO Box 667, Stroudsburg, PA 18360-0667
Stuart Scharf

Harmony Home Educators
Rd 3 Waverly Rd, Dalton, PA 18414
Charlene Radman, 717-563-2368

Hamlin Elementary Center
Matthews & Ferraro, Hamlin, PA 18427
Type: Montessori

Montessori Elementary School of Scranton
134 School St, Scranton, PA 18508-2766

Children's Cornerstone (1986)
1759 Sanderson Ave, Scranton, PA 18509
Barbara Holzman, Owner/Director, 717-347-4450
Type: Montessori; tuition: $1,500/2,600/yr
1 teacher, 1 assistant, 30 students, ages 3-6
Affiliation: AMS
Converted old Victorian home; located in progressive city near the Poconos; interns accepted.

Early Learning Center Marywood College
2300 Adams Ave, Scranton, PA 18509
Sr Regina Barrett
Type: Montessori

Himalayan Institute Children's School
RR 1 Box 400, Honsdale, PA 18531
Irene Avlonitis
Type: Montessori

Wyoming Valley Montessori
851 W Market St, Kingston, PA 18704
Jean Warrington, Adm, 717-288-3708
Non-profit
7 teachers, 8 assistants, 177 students, ages infant-12
Affiliation: AMS
Governance by board
Urban location; transportation; interns accepted.

Barclay Friends School
RD 1, Box 167-B, Towanda, PA 18848
Kathy White, Head Tch, 717-265-9620
Type: Quaker

Northern Tier Regional Planning & Development Commission (1983)
507 Main St, Towanda, PA 18848
James W. Gregory, Dir, 717-265-9103, FAX: 265-7585
Students mainly at-risk
Governance by board
Administers JTPA and Economic Dislocated Worker Assistance Act; serves Bradford, Sullivan, Susquehanna, Tioga, Wyoming; rural location.

Newton Friends School
Newtown Langhorne Rd, Newton, PA 18904
Type: Quaker

Creative Education Network (1993)
Star Route, Mechanicsville Rd, Carversville, PA 18913
Mary Lounsbury, 215-297-0642
Type: home-based, non-profit
Governance by parent cooperative
Workshops; 30 family membership; rural location.

Buckingham Friends School (1974)
Box 158, Lahaska, PA 18931
Peter Pearson, Prin, 215-794-7491, FAX: 215-794-7955
Type: Quaker, non-profit; tuition: $7,200/yr, scholarships
22 teachers, 176 students, ages 5-15, K-8th grade
Affiliation: Society of Friends
Governance by principal, board
Sense of community; meeting for worship; extensive field trips; rural location; interns accepted.

TLC Montessori Educational Preschool
5179 New Hope Rd, New Hope, PA 18938-5408

George School (1893)
Box 4000, Newtown, PA 18940
Karen S. Hallowell, Adms Dir, 215-579-6500, FAX: -6549
Type: Quaker, boarding, non-profit; tuition: res:$17,900/yr day:$11,650/yr, scholarships
70 teachers, 525 students, ages 13-18, 9-12th grade
Affiliation: Religious Society of Friends
Governance by consensus
Teacher qualifications: college degree
65 hours community service; work camps in developing countries; IB; suburban location.

Newtown Friends School
PO Box 978, Newtown, PA 18940
Joel Schmidt, Head, 215-968-2225
Type: Quaker

Wrightstown Friends Nursery School
Box 293, Penns Park, PA 18943
Martha Severn, 215-968-9900
Type: Quaker

Waldorf School Association of the Delaware River Valley (1991)
PO Box 112, Bridge Two Lane, Pt. Pleasant, PA 18950
Leslie Torkelson, Dev Coord, 215-297-5713, FAX: -8863
Non-profit
2 teachers, 20 students, ages 3.5-6, pre K-1st grade
Governance by board of parents, teachers, community
Rural location; interns accepted.

Country Gardens
4126 Axehandle Rd, Quakertown, PA 18951
Arlene Albright, 215-536-2703
Type: independent

United Friends School (1983)
20 S 10th St, Quakertown, PA 18951
Betty Sue Zellner, Head, 215-538-1733
Type: Quaker, non-profit; tuition: $3,900/yr, scholarships
10 teachers, 80 students, ages 5-12, K-6th grade
Affiliation: RSF
Governance by board
Teacher qualifications: college degree
Whole language; manipulative math; hands-on-science; extensive field trips; no letter grades; urban location.

Childtowne Montessori School
348 Coldspring Rd, Southampton, PA 18966-3530

Middle Earth, Inc
299 Jacksonville Rd, Warminster, PA 18974
Elizabeth A Quigley, Ed Prog Dir, 215-443-0280, FAX: -0245
Type: independent, non-profit; tuition: per diem
7 teachers, 60 students, mainly at-risk, ages 13-18, 9-12th grade
Governance by teachers and principal
Teacher qualifications: background in education, psychology, social work, or criminal justice
Democratic; tutorials; therapeutic community; suburban location; interns accepted.

Abington Children's House
2350 Easton Rd, Roslyn, PA 19001
Type: Montessori

Bala House (1969)
PO Box 91/Conshohocket and St Asaphs Rd, Bala Cynwyd, PA 19004
Debbie Eastwood, 215-664-6767
Non-profit; tuition: $6,200/yr, scholarships
3 teachers, 3 assistants, 65 students, ages 3-6
Affiliations: AMS, NAEYC, DVAEYC
Governance by board
Right outside Philadelphia; multi-cultural; suburban location; interns accepted.

Montgomery Montessori School
1620 Pine Rd, Huntingdon Valley, PA 19006-7938

Delaware Valley Friends School (1987)
PO Box 71, Bryn Mawr, PA 19010
Irene McHenry, Head, 215-526-9595, FAX: 526-2756
Type: Quaker, non-profit; tuition: $13,200/yr, scholarships
29 teachers, 102 students, ages 12-19, 7-12th grade
Affiliation: RSF
Governance by board
Teacher qualifications: college degree, prefer certification
Multi-sensory; Orton-Gillingham approach; organizational, study skills; computer writing lab; adventure-based; effort grades; extensive field trips; suburban location; interns accepted.

Family Resource Center
312 Bryn Mawr Ave, Bryn Mawr, PA 19010
Peter Bergson, 215-527-1504, 527-4982
Type: home-based

Media Childrens House
24 Radio Park Ln, Brookhaven, PA 19015
Type: Montessori

Ted DiRenzo Montessori School
709 Bartram Ave, Collingdale, PA 19023-3508

Children's House of Bucks County
840 Trenton Rd, Fairless Hills, PA 19030-2598
Virgina Cannon
Type: Montessori

Montessori Children's House
200 Camp Hill Rd, Fort Washington, PA 19034

New Horizons Montessori School
PO Box 408; Madison & Prospect Aves, Fort Washington, PA 19034
Maggi Funchiow

Whitemarsh Montessori
7215 Sheaff Ln, Ft Washington, PA 19034

The Gladwyne Montessori School (1962)
920 Youngs Pond Rd, Gladwyne, PA 19035
Annmarie R. Torres, Head, 215-649-1761, FAX: 215-649-7178
Non-profit; tuition: $3,675-6,495/yr
10 teachers, 15 assistants; student ages infant-12
Affiliations: NAMTA, MTA; accreditation: PAPAS
Governance by board of trustees
Summer and after-school programs in art, music, drama, French and nature study; childcare; suburban location; interns accepted.

The Wetherill School
1321 Beaumont Dr, Gladwyne, PA 19035-1392
Type: Montessori

InPrint for Children
(See Resource Section)

The Quaker School at Horsham (1982)
318 Meetinghouse Rd, Horsham, PA 19044
William S. Hallowell, Head, 215-674-2875
Type: Quaker, non-profit; tuition: $11,200/yr, scholarships
15 teachers, 50 students, mainly at-risk, ages 6-13, 1-7th grade
Governance by teachers, principal, board
Teacher qualifications: Masters in Special Ed
Auditory skills; speech therapy; study skills; woodshop; individualized, hands-on; multi-aged classes; no letter grades; suburban location; transportation; interns accepted.

Abington Friends School
575 Washington Ln, Jenkintown, PA 19046
Bruce Stewart, Head, 215-886-4350
Type: Quaker

Meadowlane Montessori (1961)
616 Meetinghouse Rd, Jenkintown, PA 19046
JoAnne Hartsough, 215-887-1222
Non-profit; tuition: $298-616/mo
6 teachers, 3 assistants, 45 students, ages infant-6
Affiliations: MTA, AMS; accreditation: AMS
Governance by administrator
Childcare; interns accepted.

Neshaminy Valley Montessori School
4951 Central Ave, Trevose, PA 19047

Lansdowne Friends School
110 N Lansdowne Ave, Lansdowne, PA 19050
Paul Seaton, Head, 215-623-2548
Type: Quaker

Bucks County Alternative School (1976)
280 Red Cedar Dr, Levittown, PA 19055
Dr Charles Miller, Supervisor, 215-547-0962
Type: public at-risk

4 teachers, 36 students, mainly SE, ages 12-19, 7-12th grade
Teacher qualifications: state SE certification
Credit-earning coop ed (work exp) for age 16+; suburban location; transportation; interns accepted.

Media Providence Friends School
125 W 3rd St, Media, PA 19063
Stewart Bartow, Head, 215-565-1960
Type: Quaker

The School in Rose Valley (1929)
20 School Ln, Moylan, PA 19065
Paul Lindenmaier, Prin, 215-566-1088, FAX: -4640
Type: independent, non-profit; tuition: $6,375-6,750, scholarships
14 teachers, 100 students, ages 3-12, pre K-6th grade
Governance by principal
Several unique buildings; safe environmental setting; wood shop, art room, multi-purpose dome, music room, science room, library, kitchen, projects building; whole child approach; no letter grades; multi-aged classes; suburban location; interns accepted.

Mercy Montessori Center
513 Montgomery Ave, Merion, PA 19066-1214
Sr Mary Christella

Springton Lake Montessori School
3090 S Newtown St Rd, Newtown Square, PA 19073-3913

The Walden School (1967)
100 College Ave, Swarthmore, PA 19081
Cynthia K. Wein, 544-8970
Type: Montessori, non-profit; tuition: $2,175-3,885/yr
148 students, ages 3-15
Affiliations: MTA-PA, ESR, ASCD
Governance by administrator, board
Environmental, peace education; literature enrichment; childcare; suburban location.

Stratford Friends School (1976)
5 Llandillo Rd, Havertown, PA 19083
215-446-3144
Type: Quaker, non-profit; tuition: $11,450/yr, scholarships
63 students, mainly SE, LD, ages 5-12
Affiliation: Papas
Enriched thematic curriculum; SE Masters Core Program in Multisensory Teaching; no letter grades; multi-aged classes; camping trip; Orton-Gillingham reading/writing for dyslexics; interns accepted.

Pendle Hill
338 Plush Rd, Wallingford, PA 19086
Daniel Seeger, Exec Sec, 215-742-3150, FAX: 566-4507
Type: Quaker higher education

Springfield Children's House
2 Chester Rd, Wallingford, PA 19086-6606
Type: Montessori

Montessori Children's House
600 Walker Rd, Wayne, PA 19087-1420
Mary Jane Chapman

Armenian Sisters Academy
440 Upper Gulph Rd, Radnor, PA 19087-4699
Type: Montessori

Lakeside School (1976)
Box L, Willow Grove, PA 19090
Brian Dager, Dir, 215-542-7737, FAX: 657-3593
Type: independent, non-profit; tuition: $51-61/day
41 teachers, 150 students, mainly at-risk, ages 10-21, 6-12th grade
Affiliation: local SD funding
Governance by board
Integrated systematic approach; 40-acre campus; intensive individual and group therapy; vo-tech; behavior manage-ments by reward, recognition, problem resolution; suburban location; interns accepted.

Vantage Program (1992)
PO Box L, Willow Grove, PA 19090
Kathy Van Horn, Alt Ed Dir, 215-542-7737, FAX: 657-3593
Type: independent, non-profit; paid by district
7-10 teachers, 25-35 students, mainly At-risk, ages 12-21, 7-12th grade
Affiliation: Lakeside Youth Service
Governance by board
Teacher qualifications: PA certification
Involves family, community; intensive counseling; conflict resolution, social skills; 8-12 students/class; transition to district classes; suburban location; interns accepted.

Friends Central School
1101 City Ave, Wynnewood, PA 19096
David Felsen, Head, 215-642-7575
Type: independent

Lane Montessori School
630 Clothier Rd, Wynnewood, PA 19096-2214

Friends Council on Education
(See Resource Section)

Center City Homeschoolers (1989)
2203 Spruce St, Philadelphia, PA 19103
Marion Cohen; Kitty Anderson, 215-732-7723, 482-7933
Non-profit

Friends Select School
17th & the Parkway, Philadelphia, PA 19103
Donald Billingsley, 215-561-5900
Type: Quaker

Greene Towne School
2013 Appletree St, Philadelphia, PA 19103-1409
Regina Delaney
Type: Montessori

Montessori Genesis II
631 N 39th St, Philadelphia, PA 19104

Schuylkill City Child Development
PO Box 302, Philadelphia, PA 19105-0302
Type: Montessori

Wyndmoor Montessori School/AERCO Montessori Teacher Ed Program
1400 E Willow Grove Ave, Philadelphia, PA 19118-1652
Barbara Pimental

Chestnut Hill College Montessori TEP
Germantown & Northwestern, Philadelphia, PA 19118-2695
Roseann Quinn, SSJ
Type: Montessori teacher education

Norwood-Fontbonne Academy
8891 Germantown Ave, Philadelphia, PA 19118-2777
Sr Roseann Quinn
Type: Montessori

Project Learn School (1969)
6525 Germantown Ave, Philadelphia, PA 19119
Robin Ann Ingram, Educational Coordinator, 215-438-3623
Type: independent, non-profit; tuition: $3,900/yr
8 teachers, 80 students, ages 5-14
Governance by parent cooperative
Staff/parent and student consensus decision-making; student narrative self-evaluation; extensive parent participation and teaching; no letter grades; multi-aged classes; extensive field trips; interns accepted.

Germantown Montessori School
6767 Germantown Ave, Philadelphia, PA 19119-2111

William Dick Head Start Program
2500 W Diamond St, Philadelphia, PA 19121-1202
Type: Montessori

Philadephia Schools Pre-K Head Start
Stevens Bldg, 13th & Spring Garden #301, Philadephia, PA 19123
David Silberman, Asst Dir of Pre K Headstart
Type: Montessori

Frankford Friends School
1500 Orthodox St, Philadelphia, PA 19124
J.Terrrence Farley, Prin, 215-533-5368
Type: Quaker

Young Horizons Learning Center
5024 Penn St, Philadelphia, PA 19124-2628
Type: Montessori

Bambino Gesu Nursery
1624 W 16th St, Philadelphia, PA 19130
Type: Montessori

New Path Montessori School
4953 N 10th St, Philadelphia, PA 19141
Ilona Shafer or Richard Chapman

Manna Head Start
4830 N 11th St, Philadelphia, PA 19141-3404
Type: Montessori

Morton School
63rd & Elmwood, Philadelphia, PA 19142
Type: Montessori

Philadelphia Community School
4625 Baltimore St, Philadelphia, PA 19143

Germantown Friends School
31 W Coulter St, Philadelphia, PA 19144
Richard Goldman, 215-951-2300
Type: Quaker

Greene Street Friends School
5511 Greene St, Philadelphia, PA 19144
Norma Vogel, Prin, 215-438-7545
Type: Quaker

William Penn Charter School
3000 W School House Ln, Philadelphia, PA 19144
Earl Ball, 215-844-3460
Type: independent

Aquarian Research Foundation
(See Resource Section)

Philadelphia School (1972)
2501 Lombard St, Philadelphia, PA 19146
Sandra Dean, Prin, 215-545-5323, FAX: 546-1798
Type: independent, non-profit; scholarships
27 teachers, 239 students, ages 5-14, K-8th grade
Affiliations: PAPAS, NAIS
Governance by board
Interdisciplinary; thematic; empasis on environmental ed, urban studies and the arts; Spanish; team teaching; no letter grades; multi-aged classes; extensive field trips; interns accepted.

Creative and Performing Arts
11th and Catherine Sts, Philadelphia, PA 19147
Ellen Savitz, 215-351-7140
Type: magnet
9-12th grade

Homeschool Resource Center
7318 Castor Ave, Philadeophia, PA 19152

School of Living
(See Resource Section)

Concord Friends Nursery School (1963)
Box 23, Concordville, PA 19331
Noreen Gaynor, Dir
Type: Quaker, non-profit; tuition: $1,400/yr, scholarships
3 teachers, 17 students, ages 4-5, pre K
Affiliation: Quaker
Governance by principal, board
Teacher qualifications: early childhood, elementary certification
Hands-on approach; environment and nature study.

Chester County Homeschoolers (1985)
226 Llandovery Dr, Exton, PA 19341
Don & Claudia Joye; Pres, Secretary/Editor, 215-524-0296
Large group; newsletter; meetings; classes; workshops; clubs; field trips; project fairs.

NCACS Teacher Education Program (1991)
429 Greenridge Rd, Glenmoore, PA 19343
Sandra M. Hurst, Dir, 215-458-5138
Type: higher education
Individually designed mentorships; seminars; research or project; alternative month placement; certification.

Upattinas School (1971)
429 Greenridge Rd, Glenmoore, PA 19343
Sandra Hurst, Dir, 215-458-5138
Type: independent, home-based, boarding, non-profit
11 teachers, 80 students, ages 5-19, K-12th grade
Governance by democratic school meeting
Teacher qualifications: individually decided by school
Enrollment, materials, support for homeschooling; international student placement; I-20 authorization; exchanges, part time programs; HS diploma for in-school and ind study; no letter grades; non-compulsory class attendance; multi-aged classes; extensive field trips; rural location; interns accepted.

Allshouse
88 E Thomas Ctd, Kennett Square, PA 19348-1852
Sara T Allshouse
Type: Montessori

Willistown Country Day School
Paoli Pike, Malvern, PA 19355
Marilyn Reeves
Type: Montessori

Fairville Early Learning Center
Box 189, Mendenhall, PA 19357
Barbara Rowe, 215-388-1268
Type: independent

Goshen Friends School (1959)
814 N Chester Rd, West Chester, PA 19380
Linda H. Traver-Neeld, Head, 215-696-8869
Type: Quaker, non-profit; tuition: $910-4300/yr, scholarships
15 teachers, 172 students, ages 3-10, pre K-5th grade
Affiliation: Society of Friends
Governance by school committee, Goshen Friends Meeting
Teacher qualifications: college degree, experience, ability to create programs
Eclectic approach; thematic; stresses community building; conflict resolution; suburban location.

West Chester Friends School
415 N High St, West Chester, PA 19380
Leslie Spangler, Dir of Adms, 610-696-293, FAX: 610-431-1457
Type: independent, non-profit; tuition: $5,600-5,900/yr, scholarships
24 teachers, 161 students, ages 5-12, K-6th grade
Affiliation: Religious Society of Friends

Governance by principal, board
On-site intergenerational service in adjacent boarding home for elderly; extensive field trips; suburban location; transportation; interns accepted.

Geode Educational Options
(See Resource Section)

Brandy Wine Children's House
4121 Ciderknoll Way, West Chester, PA 19382
Type: Montessori

Montessori Requisites-USA
(See Resource Section)

Shelter Educational Program
Montgomery County Youth Center (1988)
540 Port Indian Rd, Norristown, PA 19403
Kevin Gentilcore, Lead Tch, 215-631-1893, FAX: -5394
Type: public at-risk
2 teachers, 12 students, ages 12-17, 6-12th grade
Governance by lead teacher and exec dir
Teacher qualifications: PA Certification, 3 years experience
Law related curriculum; teens and tots program; guest speakers; field trips; art; multi-aged classes; suburban location; interns accepted.

Centre Square Montessori School
1775 Skippack Pike, Centre Square, PA 19422-1314
Patricia McNicholas

Gwynedd Friends Preschool (1943)
Rt 202 & Sumneytown Pke, Box 142, Gwynedd, PA 19436
Pam Callentine, Dir, 215-699-3055
Type: Quaker, non-profit; tuition: $580-1,260/mo, scholarships
9 teachers, 100 students, ages 2.5-5
Affiliation: Religious Society of Friends
Governance by principal, board
Teacher qualifications: education degree preferred
Wholistic; suburban location.

Kimberton Waldorf School
W Seven Star Rd, Kimberton, PA 19442
Andy Dill

Learning Tree Montessori School
500 W Main St, Lansdale, PA 19446

Miquon School
Harts Lane, Miquon, PA 19452
Greg Williams, 215-828-1231
Type: independent

Plymouth Meeting Friends School
2150 Butler Pile, Plymouth Meeting, PA 19462
Anne Javsicas, Head, 215-828-2288
Type: Quaker

Children's House of Northern Chester County (1978)
RD #2 Old Rt 23, Pottstown, PA 19464
Caryl Ann Cooper, 215-469-0742
Type: Montessori, non-profit
1 teacher, 1 assistant, 30 students, ages 3-6
Governance by administrator
Music; aerobics; kinder-gym; one-way observation mirrors; parent volunteers accepted for various activities; childcare; suburban location.

Collegeville Montessori Academy
952 Bethel Church Rd, Spring City, PA 19475
Alisa Dooley

Montessori Academy of Pennsylvania
645 South Reading Ave, Boyertown, PA 19512-2017
Robin John

Alsace Montessori Day Care
RR 3 Box 3221, Fleetwood, PA 19522-9323

Montessori Childrens House
RR 2 Box 2403, Fleetwood, PA 19522-9422

Winston Hall
2249 Fairview Ave, Reading, PA 19606-1823
Elaine Macey
Type: Montessori

Alvernia Montessori School
Mt Alvernia, Reading, PA 19607

Montessori Country Day School
2200 State Hill Rd, Wyomissing, PA 19610
Cindy Rusnak

Puerto Rico

Escuela Montessori del Caribe
PO Box 8607, Huaco, PR 00661

Christian Home Educators of the Caribbean
Palmas Del Mar Mail Service, Box 888-Suite 273, Humacao, PR 00791
809-852-5284

Puerto Rico Homeschooling Association
503 Barbe St, Santurce, PR 00912

Centro Pre-Escolar Montessori
622 Andalucia Ave, Puerto Nuevo, PR 00920

Centro de Estudios Montessori
Apartado 34155-Estación San Fernando,Calle Paraná, Río Piedras, PR 00926-4155
Type: Montessori teacher education

Escuela Montessori Mercedes Morales
Calle Eugenia 6A #1, Guaynabo, PR 00966
Mercedes Morales

Rhode Island

Rhode Island Guild of Home Teachers
97 Robin Hollow Rd, W. Greenwich, RI 02817

Frenchtown Learning Center
PO Box 252, East Greenwich, RI 02818-0252
Type: Montessori

Merlyn's Pen
(See Resource Section)

Parent Educators of Rhode Island
PO Box 782, Glendale, RI 02826
Type: state home-based

South County Montessori School
1239 Tower Hill Rd, N Kingstown, RI 02852
Marika Moosbrugger, 401-294-3575, FAX: 401-295-8444
Non-profit
6 teachers, 14 assistants, 98 students, mainly international,
    ages 3-6
Affiliation: NAEYC; accreditations: RI DE, DCYF
Governance by administrator, board
Childcare; rural location; interns accepted.

Community School at South Kingston HS
215 Columbia St, Wakefield, RI 02879
Type: public choice

Rhode Island Guild of Home Teachers
272 Pequot Av, Warwick, RI 02886
401-737-2265

Meadowbrook Waldorf School (1988)
PO Box 508, West Kingston, RI 02892
Patricia McGauran, Secretary, 401-782-1312
Non-profit; tuition: $2,780-4,050/yr, scholarships
14 teachers, 117 students, ages 4-11, K-5th grade
Affiliations: AWSNA, AEC, Waldorf Kindergarten Assn
Governance by faculty and staff
Teacher qualifications: college degree, Waldorf certificate
Rural location; interns accepted.

E. W. Flynn Elementary
220 Blackstone St, Providence, RI 02905
Robert Britto, 401-456-9373
Type: magnet
K-5th grade
Critical thinking; gifted.

Mary E. Fogarty Elementary
199 Oxford St, Providence, RI 02905
Lummer Jennings, 401-456-9381
Type: magnet
K-5th grade
Computers; multi-media; gifted.

Roger Williams Middle School
278 Thurbers Ave, Providence, RI 02905
Joseph Maguire, 401-456-9355
Type: magnet
6-8th grade
Science; visual, performing arts.

Wellspring Community School (1993)
155 Gordon Ave, Providence, RI 02905
Maria Sperduti, Dir, 401-941-3114

Type: independent; tuition: $4,200/yr, scholarships
2 teachers, 12 students, ages 5-7, K-3rd grade
Governance by teachers, principal, board
Experiential; multi-disciplinary; encourages independent and
    cooperative work; empathy and respect; active and fun; no
    letter grades; multi-aged classes; extensive field trips;
    urban location.

Hope High School
424 Hope St, Providence, RI 02906
John Short, 401-456-9161
Type: magnet
9-12th grade
Arts; communications.

Lincoln School (1984)
301 Butler Ave, Providence, RI 02906
Hallie Sammartino, Marketing/PR Dir, 401-331-9696, FAX: 751-
    6670
Type: Quaker, non-profit; tuition: $4,600-9,500/yr,
    scholarships
58 teachers, 305 students, ages 5-18, pre K-12th grade
Governance by administrative council, board
College prep; honors sections; AP courses; extensive field
    trips; interns accepted.

Moses Brown School
250 Lloyd Ave, Providence, RI 02906
David C.Burnham, Head
Type: independent

School One
75 John St, Providence, RI 02906
Type: independent

NEECA Childcare Program
343 Morris Ave, Providence, RI 02906-2610
Nancy Rose
Type: Montessori

Montessori Children's House
518 Lloyd Ave, Providence, RI 02906-5429

Educational Resource Center of Rhode Island
50 Rounds Avenue, Providence, RI 02907
Maria Sperduti, 401-941-4114
Type: home-based, non-profit

The Alternate Learning Project
582 Elmwood Ave, Providence, RI 02907
Anne Colannino, Coord, 401-456-9194
Type: public choice
HS

Curriculum Resource Center, Rhode Island College
600 Mt Pleasant Ave, Providence, RI 02908
Dr David C Woolman
Type: Montessori

Coalition of Essential Scholls
(See Resource Section)

Montessori School, Inc
160 Orchard St, E Providence, RI 02914

South Carolina

Montessori Learning Center (1978)
190 Battleship Rd, Camden, SC 29020
Sheryl M. Sweet, Adm Dir, 803-432-6828
Non-profit; tuition: $1,650-2,650/yr
5 teachers, 5 assistants, 67 students, mainly international,
　ages infant-12
Accreditation: MIA
Governance by administrator, board
Childcare; suburban location; interns accepted.

Institute for Guided Studies, Montessori Unlimited (1990)
PO Box 13, Lugoff, SC 29020
Sheryl M. Sweet, Course Dir, 803-438-1797
Type: Montessori teacher education
Students mainly international
Affiliation: MIA
Governance by administrator
Seminars; workshops; consultants; on-site programs.

**South Carolina Association of Independent
　Homeschools**
PO Box 2104, Irmo, SC 29063
803-551-1003

South Carolina Home Educators Association
PO Box 612, Lexington, SC 29071
803-951-8960

College of Early Learning
PO Box 711, Columbia, SC 29202
Kathy Macedon, 803-772-3317
Type: Montessori
Student ages 2-14

Crystal Montessori Elementary School of Columbia
3949 Kenilworth Rd, Columbia, SC 29205-1503

Montessori Child Development Center
611 Holly St, Columbia, SC 29205-2513

Montessori Middle School of Columbia, Inc. (1989)
4020 Rosewood Dr, Columbia, SC 29205-3561
Diane Buchanan, Dir, 803-254-6646
Non-profit; tuition: $2,650/yr.
1 teacher, 15 students, ages 12-15
Affiliation: AMS
Governance by board of trustees
Focus on full personal development.

Montessori Elementary School of Columbia (1983)
2807 Oleola St, Columbia, SC 29205-3846
Nathan M. Crystal, Treasurer, 803-256-2823
Non-profit; tuition: $2,600/yr
2 teachers, 1 assistant, 39 students, ages 6-12
Accreditation: AMS
Governance by board
Spanish; arts; interns accepted.

Montessori Early Learning Center, Inc
1101 Balsam Rd, Columbia, SC 29210-7914

Wil Lou Gray Opportunity School (1921)
PO Drawer 280128, Columbia, SC 29228
Dr Mary Catherine Norwood, Superintendent, 803-822-5480,
　FAX: -8146
Type: public at-risk, boarding; scholarships
23 teachers, 170 students, ages 15+, 9-12th grade
Governance by board
Case management teams; outdoor education; vocational
　training; college residential setting; individualized; subur-
　ban location; interns accepted.

Hidden Vista Montessori
7500 Hwy 9, Inman, SC 29349-8030

Montessori Fountainhead School
PO Box 729, Bryn Athyn, SC 29401

Burke Academic High School
244 President St, Charleston, SC 29403
Leckyler Gaillard, 803-724-7290
Type: magnet
9-12th grade
School within school.

Ashlye River Elementary
1871 Wallace School Rd, Charleston, SC 29407
Rose Maree Myers, 803-723-1555
Type: magnet
K-5th grade
Arts-at-Heart.

Charles Towne Montessori School
56 Leinbach Dr, Charleston, SC 29407-6988
Esta Drr

Montessori School of Charleston
95 Folly Rd Blvd, Charleston, SC 29407-7532

Montessori Community School (1989)
2120 Wood Ave, Charleston, SC 29414
Eva Abbate, Dir, 803-763-8506, FAX: 803-763-5827 x51
Non-profit; tuition: $220-285/mo
3 teachers, 3 assistants, 39 students, ages 3-12
Affiliation: AMI
Governance by board
Childcare; suburban location; interns accepted.

Montessori School of Mount Pleasant
414 Whilden St, Mount Pleasant, SC 29464-5341

Compu-Educare BBS
(See Resource Section)

Montessori School of Florence
619 Gregg Ave, Florence, SC 29501
B. J. Warner

Pawleys Island Montessori
Hwy 17 S, PO Box 426, Pawleys Island, SC 29585
Pamela Mills

Bob Jones University Press
(See Resource Section)

Montessori School of Greenville
305 Pelham Rd, Greenville, SC 29615-3110

Montessori School of Anderson (1973)
280 Sam McGee Rd, Anderson, SC 29621
Karen R. Holt, Adm, 803-226-5344
Non-profit; tuition: $200-335/mo
6 teachers, 6 assistants, 175 students, ages infant-15
Affiliation: AMI; accreditation: AMS
Governance by administrator, board
Community outreach projects for grades 5-8; multi-cultural;
　childcare; rural location; interns accepted.

Clemson Montessori School (1976)
207 Pendleton Rd, Clemson, SC 29631
Gail Paul, Dir, 654-4483
Tuition: $1,300-3,350/yr
8 teachers, 4 assistants, 102 students, mainly international,
　ages infant-12
Governance by administrator
Emphasis on science and art; childcare; rural location; interns
　accepted.

Alpha Montessori School
211 Pendleton Rd, Clemson, SC 29631-2262

National Dropout Prevention Center
(See Resource Section)

Todd's Montessori School
109 Blakely St, Mauldin, SC 29662

Montessori Children's House
PO Box 743, Mauldin, SC 29662-0743
Mallika Vejay

Robins Nest
POB 1558, Lancaster, SC 29721
803-286-9990
Type: home-based

Aiken Montessori Center
15 Hills Woodland Ln SW, Aiken, SC 29801-3383
Ellen Snyder

Aiken Area Home Educators
758 Sommer Ave, Aiken, SC 29803
Also serving Edgefield County.

Walden Hall Christian Montessori
1896 Knobcone Ave, North Augusta, SC 29841-6027

E. C. Montessori School (1973)
PO Box 1438, Beaufort, SC 29901
Jeni C. Feeser, Adm Dir, 803-525-1141
Non-profit; tuition: $1,710-2,385/ 9mo
5 teachers, 4 assistants, 15 students, ages infant-12
Affiliations: AMS, AMI
Governance by board
Urban location; interns accepted.

Eleanor Christensen Montessori
PO Box 1438, Beaufort, SC 29901
Ellen Taylor

Sea Pines Montessori School (1968)
9 Fox Grape Rd, Hilton Head Island, SC 29928
Maxine, 803-785-2534, FAX: 803-785-9537
Non-profit; tuition: $950-2,990/yr
9 teachers, 17 assistants, 270 students, ages infant-6
Affiliations: AMS, SCAEYC
Governance by board
Teacher qualifications: AMS Certification
Cited by Ford Foundation as one of top 10 US preschools.;
    interns accepted.

South Dakota

Aspire High
1109 W Cedar, Beresford, SD 57004
Dean Lindstrom, Dir

STRIVE High Alternative School (1989)
513 E 8th St, Dell Rapids, SD 57022
Barb Resick, Coord, 605-428-5231
Type: public at-risk
2 teachers, 24 students, ages 14-21, 9-12th grade
Affiliation: DL&E
Governance by board, coordinator, staff, district
Teacher qualifications: certification
Training program; required attendance; students must have
    part-time job, work one subject at a time; rural location;
    interns accepted.

South Dakota Homeschool Association
PO Box 882, Sioux Falls, SD 57101

Montessori Center of Aberdeen
117 12th Ave NE, Aberdeen, SD 57401

Gutzon Borglum Alternative (1990)
2000 Mulberry, Yankton, SD 57580
Elaine Kauer, Coord, 605-665-1416, FAX: 605-665-8369
Type: public at-risk
3 teachers, 25 students, ages 16-21, 10-12th grade
Governance by teachers and principal
Teacher qualifications: SD Certification
Urban location.

Western Dakota Christian Home Schools
Box 528, Black Hawk, SD 57718
605-787-4153

Red Cloud Indian School
Holy Rosary Mission, Pine Ridge, SD 57770
Type: Montessori

Tennessee

Overton High School
1770 Lanier, Memphis, TN 33117
Clark White, 901-684-2136
Type: magnet
9-12th grade
Creative and performing arts.

Hawkins County Alternative (1992)
Hwy 11 W, Surgoinsville, TN 33117
Gena Venable, 615-345-3506
Type: public at-risk
3 teachers, 50 students, ages 14-18, HS
Governance by principal
Multi-aged classes.

Montessori Academy (1967)
6021 Cloverland Dr, Brentwood, TN 37027
Eileen Bernstorf, 615-833-3610
Non-profit; tuition: $180-380/mo
11 teachers, 8 assistants, 240 students, ages 3-12
Affiliation: AMS
Governance by administrator
24 acres; French; PE; music; extras include Suzuki violin and
    piano, drama, Montessori singers; childcare; suburban
    location; interns accepted.

Montessori School
121 Circle Hill Dr, Clarksville, TN 37042-6438

Harpeth Academy
150 Franklin Rd, Franklin, TN 37064-2216
Type: Montessori

Ithaka Montessori
1261 Columbia Ave, Franklin, TN 37064-3639
Merrie B King

Greenleaf Press
(See Resource Section)

Family Christian Academy
(See Resource Section)

Murfreesboro Montessori School
324 E College St, Murfreesboro, TN 37130-3825

Abintra Montessori School (1980)
914 Davidson Dr, Nashville, TN 37205
Francie Beard, Dir, 615-352-4317, FAX: 615-352-1529
Non-profit; tuition: $3,675-4,150/yr
6 teachers, 4 assistants, 100 students, ages 3-12
Affiliation: AMS; TNDHS License
Governance by board of trustees
4 wooded acres in residential area; visual arts, music and
    drama artist in residence program; whole language, anti-
    bias, multi-cultural specialist; childcare; interns accepted.

Overbrook School
4210 Harding Rd, Nashville, TN 37205-2088
Type: Montessori

Academy for Kiddies
1007 21st Ave N, Nashville, TN 37208-2911
Type: Montessori

Home Education Association of Tennessee (HEAT)
3677 Richbriar Ct, Nashville, TN 37211
615-834-3529

Mercy Montessori School
2008 24th Ave S, Nashville, TN 37212-4202

HOT
3135 Lakeland Dr, Nashville, TN 37214-3312
Jacki Willard
Type: home-based

Children's House of Nashville
3404 Belmont Blvd, Nashville, TN 37215-1642
Type: Montessori

Montessori Centre (1967)
4608 Granny White Pike, Nashville, TN 37220
Harriette Derryberry, Owner/Dir, 615-373-0897
Tuition: $407-500/mo
3 teachers, 3 assistants, 64 students, ages infant-6
Affiliation: AMS
Governance by owner
Twelve month, full day; on 4 acres; urban location; interns
    accepted.

North Cleveland Alternative School (1991)
PO Box 399, Cleveland, TN 37364
John Driver, 2ndary Supervisor, 615-476-0620, FAX: -0485
Type: public at-risk
3 teachers, 25 students, ages 6-18, 1-12th grade
Governance by board
Teacher qualifications: state license
SE, SED, BD, LD; urban location; interns accepted.

Montessori Children's House
302 Signal Mountain Blvd, Signal Mountain, TN 37377-1831

Alternative Classroom (1990)
Grundy County High School, Tracy City, TN 37387
Marshall Gilliam, Tch, 615-592-5741, FAX: 615-692-2188
Type: public at-risk
1 teacher, 10 students, ages 11-18, 7-12th grade

Governance by teachers, principal, parent coop, board
Teacher qualifications: TN Certification
Rural location; transportation; interns accepted.

Ray's Montessori School
101 Bragg Circle, Tullahoma, TN 37388-2975

School Training At-Risk Students (STARS) (1988)
College St, Winchester, TN 37398
Juanita Syler, Attendance Supervisor, 615-967-5317, FAX: -
    7832
Type: public at-risk
2 teachers; students mainly at-risk, ages 12+, 7-12th grade
Governance by Disciplinary Hearing Authority
Teacher qualifications: bachelor's degree/vocational skills
Mission: place students in the world of work, with skills for
    getting a job; emphasis on survival skills; rural location.

Training Learning Center (TLC) (1988)
Franklin County BE, PO Box 129, Winchester, TN 37398
Juanita Syler, Attendance Supervisor, 615-967-2574, FAX: 615-
    967-7832
Type: public choice/at-risk
1 teacher; students mainly at-risk, ages 12-17, 6-12th grade
Governance by board and Disciplinary Hearing Authority
Teacher qualifications: bachelor's degree/special ed
Mission: prepare students to return to regular classes to get
    regular or special diploma; emphasis on behavioral skills;
    individual attention; multi-aged classes; rural location.

Red Bank Middle and Central High (1990)
201 Broad St, Chattanooga, TN 37401-1089
Don Upton, 2ndary Ed Dir, 615-757-1730, FAX:-1777
Type: public at-risk
10 teachers, 40 students, ages 12-21
Governance by teachers and principal
Teacher qualifications: TN certification
Suburban location.

Montessori World of Children (1981)
1080 McCallie Ave, Chattanooga, TN 37404
Bobbe Spink, Dir, 615-622-6366
Tuition: $225-350/mo
5 teachers, 5 assistants, 105 students, ages infant-12
Governance by teachers and administrators
French (ages 5-12); computer programming (ages 6-12); girl
    and boy scouts (age 6-12); childcare; urban location.

Henry L. Barger School
4808 Brainerd Rd, Chattanooga, TN 37411
Christine Hicks
Type: Montessori

CSTHEA: Chattanooga Southeast Tennessee Home
    Education Association
2316 Jennifer Dr, Chattanooga, TN 37421
Ann Ritterbush, 615-855-9899
Annual curriculum fair.

Johnson City Montessori School
1208 Timberlake Rd, Johnson City, TN 37601

Ashley Academy
816 Lacy St, Johnson City, TN 37604-3767
Type: Montessori

Johnson Academy (1993)
John Exum Pkwy, Johnson City, TN 37605
Frank Hill, Dir, 615-434-5570
Type: public at-risk
7 teachers, 125 students, Pre-K, 6-12th grade
Governance by principal and democratic school meeting
Multiple-handicapped preschoolers; suburban location;
    interns accepted.

Tennessee Homeschool Families
888 Shadden Rd, Gray, TN 37615
Margie Lesch

YMCA Children's House
400 Edgemont Ave, Bristol, TN 37620-2360
Type: Montessori

Kingsport Montessori School
1705 Orchard Ct, Kingsport, TN 37660-4521

Alcon City Schools
524 Faraday St, Alcon, TN 37701
Bill Symon, 615-989-0531, FAX: 615-984-5830
Non-profit
1500 students, ages 5-20
Governance by principal
Multi-aged classes; extensive field trips; suburban location; interns accepted.

Maryville Montessori School
1833 Wright Rd, Alcon, TN 37701

Alternative Vocational Program (1980)
Rt 4 Box 445, Harriman, TN 37748
Chester Silvers, 615-882-6815
Type: public at-risk
3 teachers, 20 students, ages 14-18, 9-12th grade
Governance by faculty and student representatives
Glasser control theory; no letter grades; rural location.

Educational Choices
Rt 2, Box 224X, Harriman, TN 37748
Susan Thatcher
Type: home-based

New Horizon Montessori School (1978)
913 Cumberland Dr, Louisville, TN 37777
Aleta Ledendecker, 615-970-4322
Tuition: $225-310/mo
4 teachers, 2 assistants, 64 students, ages 3-15
Affiliations: NAMTA, AMI, TN; accreditation: MEI
Governance by administrator
Nursing home visits; student-directed Shakespearean and original plays; childcare; suburban location; interns accepted.

Montessori Center of Oak Ridge (1976)
100 Adams Ln, Suite C, Oak Ridge, TN 37830-4903
Susan Tull, Administrator, 615-482-5036
Non-profit; tuition: $200/260/mo
2 teachers, 2 assistants, 50 students, ages 3-6
Affiliations: AMS, AMI
Governance by administrator, board
Childcare; urban location.

Homeschooling Families
214 Park Ln, Oliver Springs, TN 37840

Oneida Special School District (1915)
PO Box 4819, Oneida, TN 37841
L. Mayfield Brown, Supt, 615-569-8912, FAX: 569-2201
Type: public choice
82 teachers, 1180 students, ages 4-22, pre K-12th grade
Governance by school board, Supt
Teacher qualifications: certification
Flexible scheduling; mini-courses; low ratio; fine arts; whole language; manipulatives; cooperative learning; multi-aged classes; interns accepted.

Sevier County PS City As School Program (1993)
1150 Dolly Parton Pkwy, Sevierville, TN 37862
Scott Borah, 615-453-1077
Type: public choice
25 students

The Elijah Company
(See Resource Section)

Laurel High School
1539 Laurel Ave, Knoxville, TN 37914
Mary Oliver, 615-525-3885

Type: independent; tuition: $3,478/yr, scholarships
5 teachers, 30 students
Governance by board, democratic school meeting
Wide range of classes and independent projects; considers that education goes on all the time and gives recognition for any constructive activity, in or out of school; non-compulsory class attendance; multi-aged classes; extensive field trips; urban location.

Nature's Way Montessori School
3225 Garden Dr, Knoxville, TN 37918
Mary Smith

Giving Tree Montessori School
4311 Kingston Pike, Knoxville, TN 37919-4077

Smoky Mountain Chapter, Tennessee Home Education Association
925 View Harbor, Knoxville, TN 37922
615-675-3073

Crockett County Alternative School (1988)
Conley Rd, Rte 2, Alamo, TN 38001
Charles Williamson, Dir, 901-696-4778
Type: public at-risk
2 teachers, 5-15 students, ages 12-18, 5-12th grade
Teacher qualifications: BS, TN license
Rural location; transportation.

Volunteer State Academy
PO Box 143, Brownsville, TN 38012
Type: Montessori

Lauderdale County Alternative High School (1989)
PO Box 350, Ripley, TN 38063
Louis Wheatley, 901-635-2941, FAX: 901-635-7985
Type: public at-risk
1 teacher, 15 students, ages 14-18, 7-12th grade
Governance by principal and board
Teacher qualifications: state certification
Rural location; interns accepted.

Idlewild Elementary
1950 Linden, Memphis, TN 38104
Dr James Luckey, 901-733-3440
Type: magnet
1-6th grade
Individualized.

Cendrillion Montessori School
1642 Poplar Ave, Memphis, TN 38104-2510

St Peter's Day Care
1805 Poplar Ave, Memphis, TN 38104-2650
Type: Montessori

First Class Montessori School
1336 Peabody Ave, Memphis, TN 38104-3500

Greater Community Day Care
PO Box 7271, Memphis, TN 38107
Type: Montessori

Vollentine Elementary
1682 Vollentine, Memphis, TN 38107
Nettye Hassan, 901-722-4632
Type: magnet
1-6th grade
Individualized.

Springdale/Memphis Magnet School
880 N Hollywood, Memphis, TN 38108
Mamie Foster, 901-325-3488
1-6th grade
Open education.

Double Tree Elementary
4500 Double Tree, Memphis, TN 38109
Dora Purdy, 901-789-8144

Type: magnet
K-6th grade
Montessori.

Center of Attention
150 Hayden Pl, Memphis, TN 38111-3506
Type: Montessori

Threshold-A Montessori School
581 Ellsworth St, Memphis, TN 38111-4331

Lipman Montessori School
3771 Poplar Ave, Memphis, TN 38111-6020

Optional Schools Project
2597 Avery Ave, Room 106, Memphis, TN 38112
Marilyn Simmons, 901-454-5200
Type: public choice

Roselle Elementary
993 Roland, Memphis, TN 38112
Charlene Turner, 901-722-4612
Type: magnet
1-6th grade
Creative and performing arts.

Lamplighter (1967)
1021 Mosby Rd, Memphis, TN 38116
Kathy Roemer, Assoc Head, 901-332-7500
Type: Montessori; tuition: $2,808-5,643/yr
6 teachers, 3 assistants, 155 students, ages infant-12
Affiliation: Memphis Ind. Schools; accreditations: AMS, SACS
Governance by board
Field trips to area museums; History of the Universe; foreign
   languages; computers; childcare; sub/urban location;
   interns accepted.

First Montessori Mid-South School
1864 Janis Dr, Memphis, TN 38116-2008

The Frady School
951 McClure Rd, Memphis, TN 38116-7715
Type: Montessori

Colonial Junior High School
4778 Sea Isle Rd, Memphis, TN 38117
Donna Essary, 901-761-8980
Type: magnet
7-9th grade
Creative and performing arts.

LaPapillon Montessori School
3246 Raines Rd E, Memphis, TN 38118

Israel Preschool
1376 East Massey, Memphis, TN 38120
Type: Montessori

Lausanne Montessori School
1381 W Massey Rd, Memphis, TN 38120-3298

Maria Montessori School at St Michael
3848 Forrest Ave, Memphis, TN 38122-3808

Memphis Montessori School
2619 Tricia Dr #2, Memphis, TN 38127

St Elizabeth Montessori School
4780 Yale Rd, Memphis, TN 38128

Montessori School
7623 US Highway 64, Memphis, TN 38133-3905

Raleigh-Bartlett Montessori
6050 Hwy 70, Bartlett, TN 38134

Olivia's Montessori School (1990)
2755 Appling, Memphis, TN 38134
Olivia Flasdick, 901-377-3081

Non-profit; tuition: $300/mo
1 teacher, 2 assistants, 20 students, ages 3-6
Affiliations: AMS, NAEYC
Governance by an administrator and democratic school
   meeting
Non-sexist, non-racist; ASL; Orff music; childcare; suburban
   location; interns accepted.

Play Care Montessori
6634 US Hwy 70, Bartlett, TN 38134-4741

Middle College High School at Shelby State CC (1987)
737 Union Ave E-102, Memphis, TN 38174-0568
Joyce C. Mitchell, Prin, 901-544-5360, FAX: -5368
Non-profit
21 teachers, 300 students, mainly at-risk, ages 15-20,
   10-12th grade
Affiliations: Memphis City Schools, SACS/TBR
Governance by faculty, principal, parents, students
Interdisciplinary; dual credit/enrollment; internships; teacher-
   counselor concept; activities; community outreach; interns
   accepted.

Parkview Elementary (1992)
905 E Chester St, Jackson, TN 38301
Charles I. Mercer, Prin, 401-422-3116
Type: Public choice Montessori
6 teachers, 6 assistants, 136 students, ages 3-9
Affiliation: AMS
Governance by administrator

University School of Jackson (1970)
1981 Hollywood Dr, Jackson, TN 38305
Sherry Tignor, Admissions Dir, 668-0444;664-0812, FAX: 668-
   6910
Type: Montessori, non-profit; tuition: $2,190-3,660/yr
8 teachers, 8 assistants, 805 students, ages 3-18
Affiliations: NAMTA, TNMA, NAEYC, TNAEYC, NAIS, TNAIS; accreditation: SACS
Governance by board
20 acres; nature studies; student-centered approach; childcare; rural location; transportation.

Montessori Center of Jackson
2732 N Highland Ave, Jackson, TN 38305-1764

Montessori Kinder Care
502 S High St, Trenton, TN 38382-2032

The Farm School
50 The Farm, Summertown, TN 38483
615-964-2325
Type: home-based, non-profit
20 students, ages 5-12
Serves community and some outside students.

Dry Valley Alternative School (1979)
3860 Phifer Mtn Rd, Cookeville, TN 38501
Marcus Durley, Prin, 615-528-1847, FAX: 372-0382
Type: public at-risk
4 teachers, 40 students, ages 10-17, 5-12th grade
Governance by principal, board
Teacher qualifications: BA or BS
Multi-aged classes; individualized; suburban location; trans-
   portation; interns accepted.

Montessori Children's House
122 E 12th St, Cookeville, TN 38501-1303

Early School Materials
(See Resource Section)

Southeast Educational Materials
(See Resource Section)

Texas

Pebblebrook Academy
612 Pebblebrook, Allen, TX 75002
Type: Montessori

Contemporary Montessori Education
PO Box 1036, Allen, TX 75002-1036
Carmen Sexton

Carrollton Montessori at Midway (1988)
3225 Belmeade, Carrollton, TX 75006-2341
214-380-2395
Tuition: $325/435/mo
4 teachers, 8 assistants, 110 students, ages 3–6
Affiliations: MACTE, NAMTA; accreditation: MIA
Governance by administrator
Breakfast and lunch served; childcare; suburban location;
    transportation; interns accepted.

A Child's Garden Montessori
1935 Old Denton Rd, Carrollton, TX 75006-3756
Patricia Bradford

West Plano Montessori School
3425 Ashington Ln, Plano, TX 75023-3930

Preston Meadow Montessori School
6912 Ohio Dr, Plano, TX 75024-2515

DeGroot Learning Centers, Inc (1968)
PO Box 260765, Plano, TX 75026
Patricia De Groot-Cowles, Pres, 214-422-2414, FAX: 214-732-
    0678
Type: Montessori
10 teachers, 16 assistants, 206 students, ages infant-12
Affiliation: NAEYC
Governance by administrator
Mortensen math; childcare; suburban location; interns
    accepted.

Sing and Learn Curriculum Supplies
(See Resource Section)

The Helping Hand
(See Resource Section)

Westchester Montessori
290 Westchester Pkwy, Grand Prairie, TX 75052

Agape School
151 W Purnell St, Lewisville, TX 75057-3917
Pat Bottalico
Type: Montessori

Amberwood Montessori Academy
804 W Pioneer Dr, Irving, TX 75061-7434

Montessori of Las Colinas School & Training Center (1988)
4961 N O'Connor Blvd, Irving, TX 75062
Gale Keppler, Exec Dir, 214-717-0417
Type: Montessori higher education; tuition: $350-505/mo
8 teachers, 12 assistants, 134 students, ages infant-6/adult
Accreditations: MIA, MACTE
Governance by administrator
Full certification; evening and weekend classes; childcare;
    urban location; interns accepted.

Redeemer Montessori School (1978)
120 E Rochelle Rd, Irving, TX 75062
Donna Hatter, 214-257-3517
Tuition: $270-360/mo
4 teachers, 3 assistants, 65 students, ages 3–9
Affiliation: AMS
Culturally diverse area; Spanish; art; music; PE; intern site for

AMS; staff development; strong parent group; childcare;
    suburban location; interns accepted.

North Texas Self Educators (1991)
150 Forest Ln, Double Oak, TX 75067
Sarah Jordan, 817-430-4835, FAX: -4311
Non-profit
Inclusive; John Holt's student-led approach; workshops.

Montessori Learning Center
1319 Monaco Dr, Lewisville, TX 75067-5613

MORE: Metroplex Middle of the Road Home Educators
1702 S Hwy 121, Ste 607-110, Lewisville, TX 75067-8946
Dorian Karthauser
Cost: $18/yr
Inclusive; co-op classes; park days; mother's night out;
    preschool activities; teacher ed workshops; resources
    database.

Holy Nativity Montessori
2200 18th St Box 467, Plano, TX 75074

Montessori: New Beginnings Academy
1301 Custer Rd #703, Plano, TX 75075-7486
Laurann Sutton

Highland Academy (1981)
1231 W Belt Line Rd, Richardson, TX 75080
Faye E. Handlogten, Dir, 214-238-7568
Type: independent; tuition: $7,000/yr, scholarships
14 teachers, 65 students, mainly at-risk, ages 5–14
Governance by principal, teachers, democratic school
    meeting
Teacher qualifications: Academic Language Therapy
    certification
No letter grades; interns accepted.

Weise Memorial Academy (1991)
801 Canyon Creek Sq, Richardson, TX 75080
Rita Weise, Dir, 214-497-9667, FAX: 497-9667
Type: independent, non-profit; tuition: $6,500/yr,
    scholarships
8 teachers, 35 students, mainly at-risk, ages 12–19, 7–12th
    grade
Governance by board, director
Teacher qualifications: degree, certification
Close personal relationship between student and teacher;
    small groups; interns accepted.

Alexander School (1975)
409 Richardson Pkwy, Richardson, TX 75081
David B. Bowlin, Exec Dir, 214-690-9210, FAX: -9284
Type: independent; tuition: $12,000/yr
21 teachers, 50 students, ages 13–19
Affiliation: SACS
Governance by teachers and principal
Teacher qualifications: degree, min 24 semester hrs in field
One to one teaching; supervised study time; electives in small
    groups; free tutoring; science lab; urban location.

Dallas Learning Center (1990)
301 S Sherman, Suite 116, Richardson, TX 75081
Kathleen Herrin-Kinard, Dir, 231-3723
Type: independent; tuition: $7,000/yr
4 teachers, 20 students, mainly at-risk, ages 14–20, 9–12th
    grade
Governance by teachers, principal
Teacher qualifications: TX certification and/or Master's
Self-paced; tutorials; accelerated programs; credit make up;
    no letter grades; multi-aged classes; extensive field trips;
    interns accepted.

KONOS
(See Resource Section)

Kinderhaus
203 Woodpark Ln, Rockwall, TX 75087
Judith A Head
Type: Montessori

Ridge Road Montessori School
2306 Ridge Rd, Rockwall, TX 75087

Creative Learning Center
704 Ridgeview Dr, Rockwall, TX 75087-4137
Type: Montessori

Belden Street Montessori School
618 W Belden St, Sherman, TX 75090-3711
Scottie Johnson

Pace School (1993)
815 Fairlawn Dr, Duncanville, TX 75116
Ruth Richey, Prin, 214-298-9661, FAX: 298-9698
Type: public at-risk
4 teachers, 27 students, mainly at-risk, ages 16-19, 10-12th
   grade
Governance by faculty and student representatives
Teacher qualifications: state certification
Self-paced; individualized; flexible scheduling; suburban loca-
   tion; transportation.

Lancaster ISD
1105 Westridge, Lancaster, TX 75146
Kathlyn Williams
Type: Montessori

B.T. Washington High School
2501 Flora, Dallas, TX 75201
Robert Watkins, 214-720-7300
Type: magnet
9-12th grade
Visual and performing arts.

School Community Guidance Center (1986)
912 S Ervay, Dallas, TX 75201
Maurice E. Walker, Prin, 214-746-2650, FAX: 746-2655
Type: public at-risk
10 teachers, 125 students, ages 12-17, 7-12th grade
Affiliation: TX EA
Governance by principal
Teacher qualifications: TEA certification
Intensive management system; focus on appropriate behav-
   ior; multi-aged classes; urban location.

St Christopher's Montessori School
2600 Westminster Ave, Dallas, TX 75205-1503

White Rock Montessori School (1975)
3204 Skillman St, Dallas, TX 75206-5999
Sue Henry, Dir, 214-827-3220, FAX: 214-327-3229
Non-profit; tuition: $2,048-3,616/yr
7 teachers, 3 assistants, 94 students, ages 3-12
Affiliations: AMS, NAMTA
Governance by administrator and board of trustees
Cultural studies; Spanish; cooking; music; art; drama; com-
   puter; PE; plant and animal care; after-school drama, violin,
   piano; childcare; urban location; interns accepted.

Sidney Lanier Expressive Arts Vang.
1400 Walmsley, Dallas, TX 75208
Miriam Kelley, 214-746-2670
Type: magnet
4-6th grade
Expressive Arts.

Montessori School Park Cities
4011 Inwood Rd, Dallas, TX 75209-5711
Cathy Rutherford

Amelia Earhart Montessori Vanguard School
3531 N Westmoreland Rd, Dallas, TX 75212-2358

Branch Schools
6144 Prospect Ave, Dallas, TX 75214
Hart Robinson
Type: Montessori

Texas Home School Coalition
PO Box 140944, Dallas, TX 75214
214-227-0333

Education & Social Services
1738 Gano, Dallas, TX 75215
Ruth Woodward, 214-565-6570
Type: magnet
9-12th grade

Lincoln Humanities/Communications
2826 Hatcher, Dallas, TX 75215
Napoleon Lewis, 214-421-7121
Type: magnet
9-12th grade

Harry Stone Elementary
4747 Veterans Dr, Dallas, TX 75216
Myrtle Walker, 214-302-2180
Type: magnet
Student ages 4+,-6th grade
Montessori.

White Rock Montessori School of the Good Samaritan
1522 Highland Rd, Dallas, TX 75218-4420

Sam Houston Elementary School
2827 Throckmorton St, Dallas, TX 75219-3447
Type: Montessori

Lakemont Academy (1976)
3993 W Northwest Hwy, Dallas, TX 75220
Edward Fidellow, Headmaster, 214-351-6404, FAX: 214-358-
   4510
Type: Montessori, non-profit; tuition: $3,960-5,880/yr
9 teachers, 3 assistants, 121 students, ages infant-18
Affiliations: CMF; ACSI, TX ANS; accreditation: SACS
Governance by board
Renaissance curriculum; formal dining room; etiquette; farm
   animals; garden; greenhouse; travel; sports; entrepreneur-
   ship; childcare; urban location; interns accepted.

East Dallas Community School
924 Wayne St, Dallas, TX 75223
Type: independent

Windsong Montessori School (1992)
4331 Allencrest Ln, Dallas, TX 75224
Mr or Ms Albanese, Dirs, 214-239-0537, FAX: 214-490-0427
Tuition: $4,000/4,500/yr
2 teachers, 3 assistants, 35 students, ages 6-12
Affiliations: AMITOT, CME
Governance by administrator
Teacher qualifications: Directors: 20+ yrs experience
Suburban location; interns accepted.

Montessori Sunshine High School
11215 Ferguson Rd, Dallas, TX 75228-1953

Dallas Montessori Academy
7979 E R L Thornton Fwy, Dallas, TX 75228-6950
Dina Paulik

Meadowbrook School
5414 N W Highway, Dallas, TX 75229
Type: Montessori

Ursuline Montessori School
4900 Walnut Hill Ln, Dallas, TX 75229

Montessori Center of Light
6525 Forest Ln, Dallas, TX 75230

St Alcuin Montessori School (1964)
6144 Churchill Way, Dallas, TX 75230
Ron Ackerman, Dir, 214-239-1745, FAX: 214-934-8727
Non-profit; tuition: $2,975-6,235/yr
19 teachers, 18 assistants, 437 students, ages infant-15
Affiliations: NAMTA, AMITOT; accreditation: AMI/USA
Governance by board of trustees
Childcare; suburban location; interns accepted.

The Robert Muller School, Whole Kids
5707 Caladeium, Dallas, TX 75230
Angie Levy, 214-987-1546

L.L. Hotchkiss Montessori Academy
6929 Town N Dr, Dallas, TX 75231
Torance Vandygriff, 214-553-4430
Type: magnet
7-8th grade
Montessori.

North Texas Montessori Center
6929 Town North Dr, Dallas, TX 75231
Marge Farmer
Type: Montessori teacher education

Montessori Children's House
7335 Abrams Rd, Dallas, TX 75231-4703

Dean Memorial Learning Center
8800 N Central Expy #300, Dallas, TX 75231-6421
Type: Montessori

Williams Montessori School
1030 Oak Park Dr, Dallas, TX 75232-1238

Advent Montessori School
6697 S Hampton Rd, Dallas, TX 75232-2917

St James Montessori School
9845 McCree Rd, Dallas, TX 75238-3444
Marie Maneley

Hillcrest Academy Foundation
6930 Alpha Rd, Dallas, TX 75240-3602
Type: Montessori

Carillon Montessori
6411 LBJ Freeway, Dallas, TX 75240-6406

Bending Oaks High School (1985)
13777 N Central Expwy, Dallas, TX 75243
Dr Robert Costello, Prin, 214-669-0000, FAX: 669-8149
Type: independent; tuition: $8,000/yr
15 teachers, 70 students, ages 14-18, 9-12th grade
Governance by teachers and principal
Teacher qualifications: TX Certification or MA
College schedule; open campus; extensive field trips.

Westwood Montessori School (1983)
13618 Gamma Rd, Dallas, TX 75244
Pamela A. Butler, Adm, 214-239-8598, FAX: 214-239-1028
Tuition: $2,450-4,750/yr
4 teachers, 1 assistant, 54 students, ages 3-12
Affiliation: NAEYC; accreditation: AMITOT
Governance by administrator
Kumon math; science-by-mail; computer programming; ACP
    curriculum; transportation available to and from school,
    and to music, athletics, and art classes; childcare; urban
    location; interns accepted.

Montessori School of North Dallas
18303 Davenport Rd, Dallas, TX 75252-5454

Basic Education
PO Box 610589, D/FW Airport, TX 75261
214-462-1909
Type: home-based

Summit Christian Academy
(See Resource Section)

The Children's House Montessori School of Commerce
1722 Park St, Commerce, TX 75428

Carver Children's House
2300 Preston St, Texarkana, TX 75502-5762
Type: Montessori

Donna Hatter Three Candles School
c/o St Lukes Methodist, 3500 Main St, Texarkana, TX 75503
Type: Montessori

Cullen, Olympia Outdoor Centers
Trinity, TX 75862
Carol King, Tom Cosper, 800-659-2733, 800-729-6291
Type: magnet
5th grade

Rapid Advancement Program (1978)
1523 E Main St, Nacogdoches, TX 75961
Vicki Stephens, Exec Dir, 409-564-1222
Type: independent, non-profit; tuition: $200/mo,
    scholarships
5 teachers, 40-60 students, infant-8th grade
Governance by parent cooperative
Teacher qualifications: BS in Ed, teaching certificate
Extensive phonics training; humane education; summer
    enrichment; no letter grades; multi-aged classes; extensive
    field trips; urban location; interns accepted.

Arlington Country Day School
1100 Roosevelt St, Arlington, TX 76011
Lenny Young
Type: Montessori

Children's House of Arlington Montessori
1400 S Cooper St, Arlington, TX 76013-2752
Pamela Watson and Bobbie Nelson

Arlington Cooperative Montessori School
2217 Michigan Ave #A, Arlington, TX 76013-5916

Montessori Academy
2111 Roosevelt Dr, Arlington, TX 76013-5920
Gail Corley
Also at 5 Kingston Ct, Bedford

Robert Muller School (1979)
6005 Royaloak Dr, Arlington, TX 76016
Gloria Crook, 817-654-1028
Type: independent, non-profit
8 teachers, 17 students, ages 2-17, Pre K-12th grade
Accreditation: Southern Association of Colleges and Schools
Governance by pupils, teachers, and parents
Teacher qualifications: certification or college degree
World Core Curriculum: our planetary home and place in the
    universe, our place in time, the family, the miracle of life;
    no letter grades; non-compulsory class attendance; multi-
    aged classes; extensive field trips; suburban location;
    interns accepted.

Barbara Gordon Montessori (1971)
1513 Hall Johnson Road, Colleyville, TX 76034
Rosemarie Blais, 817-354-6670
Non-profit; tuition: $2,950/4,485
6 teachers, 6 assistants, 144 students, ages infant-9
Affiliation: AMI
Governance by board of trustees
Well-equipped; supportive parents; Spanish, music, art, PE;
    after-school classes; summers; childcare; suburban loca-
    tion; interns accepted.

North Texas Self-Educators
3013 Hickory Hill, Colleyville, TX 76034
Barb Lundgren, 817-354-4305
Type: home-based
Monthly one-day workshop for beginners; unstructured,
    child-led approaches emphasized.

Happy Hill Farm Academy/Home
Star Route, Box 56, Grandbury, TX 76048

McGuffey Academy
2213 Spur Trail, Grapevine, TX 76051
Arlon A. Widder, PhD, Adm, 817-481-7008
Type: independent
3 teachers, 400 students, ages 5–19
Complete correspondence school; variety of curricula; diagnostic, achievement testing.

NAM Enterprises
(See Resource Section)

Highland Meadow Montessori Academy (1980)
1060 Highland St, Southlake, TX 76092
Pat McCormick, Adm, 817-488-2138
Non-profit; tuition: $1,800-4,400/yr
8 teachers, 4 assistants, 74 students, ages infant–12
Accreditation: AMS
Governance by administrator, board of trustees
Childcare; interns accepted.

Clariden School
1325 N White Chapel Blvd, Grapevine, TX 76092-9017
Type: Montessori

Carroll Peak Elementary
1212 Elmwood Ave, Fort Worth, TX 76104-5733
Type: Montessori

Morningside Elementary
2601 Evans Ave, Fort Worth, TX 76104-6898
Type: Montessori

Metro Opportunity School (1979)
215 NE 14th St, Fort Worth, TX 76106
Gladys Pettid, Prin, 817-740-5550, FAX: -5566
Type: public at-risk
11 teachers, 124 students, ages 14–21, HS
Governance by prin and site-based decision-making team
Independent study; mentor program; career day; volunteer tutors assigned for TAAS prep; multi-aged classes; community service; drama group; urban location; interns accepted.

Como Montessori Elementary
4001 Littlepage St, Fort Worth, TX 76107
Robert Vick, 817-377-7379
Type: Montessori magnet
K-6th grade

Ft Worth Montessori School
1801 Ashland Ave, Fort Worth, TX 76107-3809
Denise Pulido

South Hi Mount
4101 Birchman Ave, Fort Worth, TX 76107-4396
Type: Montessori

Trinity Episcopal
3401 Bellaire Dr S, Fort Worth, TX 76109-2199
Type: Montessori

B.H. Carroll/New Lives
3908 McCart, Fort Worth, TX 76110
Jody Wycoff, 817-922-6840
Type: public at-risk

Daggett Middle School (1983)
1108 Carlock, Fort Worth, TX 76110
Attn: Adm Coord, 817-922-6550
Type: Montessori; tuition: none
9 teachers, 1 assistant, 180 students, mainly international
Affiliations: AMS, NAMTA, MSA, MSTX
Governance by administrator and democratic school meeting
Two years/same staff; environmental activites; childcare; urban location; transportation; interns accepted.

Essential Program at R.L. Paschal High School (1984)
3001 Forest Park Blvd, Fort Worth, TX 76110
Larry B. Barnes, Coord, 817-922-6600, FAX: 817-922-6661
Type: public
15 teachers, 375 students, ages 12–18, HS
Governance by board
Collaborative; interdisciplinary; cross disciplinary; multi-aged classes; interns accepted.

New Lives School
3908 McCart, Fort Worth, TX 76110
Jody Wyckoff, 817-922-6840
Type: public at-risk

Daggett Elementary Montessori School
958 Page, Fort Worth, TX 76110-2627
Judy Seymour

Worth Heights Montessori
519 E Butler St, Fort Worth, TX 76110-5598

Montessori Children's House
3420 Clayton Rd E, Fort Worth, TX 76116-7342
Joy Sheffield

Glen Park Elementary (1983)
3601 Pecos St, Ft Worth, TX 76119
Dr Pat Coemes, Prin, 531-6380
Type: public choice
3 teachers, 1 assistant, 66 students, ages 3–9
Affiliation: AMS
Governance by teachers and administrators
Urban location.

A.M. Pate Elementary School
3800 Anglin Dr, Fort Worth, TX 76119-2126
Type: Montessori

Event Montessori School
PO Box 921001, Fort Worth, TX 76121-0001

Sycamore School, Inc
3400 Charleston Ave, Fort Worth, TX 76123
817-292-3434

Benbrook Elementary
800 Mercedes St, Benbrook, TX 76126-2594
Type: Montessori

Fort Worth Montessori School (1984)
6605 Dan Danciger Rd/ 1801 Ashland St, Ft Worth, TX 76133/76107
817-732-4276, 294-9850, FAX: 817-732-6502
Tuition: $164-293/mo
7 teachers, 7 assistants, 80 students, mainly international, ages infant-6
Governance by administrator
Two campuses; childcare; suburban location; interns accepted.

Azlann Montessori School (1986)
2301 Hinkle Dr, Denton, TX 76201
Beverly Morey, 817-565-9330
Tuition: $2,600-3,600/yr
6 teachers, 2 assistants, students mainly international, ages 2.5–11
Affiliations: AMS, AMI, NAMTA
Governance by administrator
Most staff are adjunct professors; childcare; suburban location; interns accepted.

Community School (1991)
2046 Scripture, Denton, TX 76201
Linda Lavendar, 817-387-0995
Type: independent, non-profit; tuition: $3,250
4 teachers, 2 assistants, 50 students
Governance by teachers and owners
Suburban location; interns accepted.

Evenhorn School
2301 Hinkle, Denton, TX 76201
Type: Montessori

R.E. Lee Elementary School
800 Mack Dr, Denton, TX 76201-6314
Type: Montessori

Selwyn School–Lower School
3333 W University Dr, Denton, TX 76201-7495
Alan Gibby
Type: Montessori

Borman Elementary School
1201 Parvin St, Denton, TX 76205-6799
Type: Montessori

Bright Ideas School (1985)
2507 Central Frwy E, Wichita Falls, TX 76302
Linda Plummer, Prin, 817-767-1561
Type: independent, non-profit
5 teachers, 28 students, ages 3–15, pre K–11th grade
Governance by teachers and principal
Interdisciplinary projects; history-based curriculum; gifted
education approach; encourages responsibility and self-
direction; multi-aged classes; extensive field trips; urban
location; interns accepted.

Notre Dame Elementary
4060 York, Wichita Falls, TX 76309
Dr Bronte Gonsalzes
Type: Montessori

Harrell Alternative Learning Center (1992)
3115 5th St, Wichita Falls, TX 76310
R.J. Stone, Prin, 817-720-3144, FAX: 817-720-3228
Type: public at-risk
17 teachers, 192 students, ages 17–21
Governance by teachers, principal, board
Open entry/exit; computers; work experience, job-search; no
letter grades; multi-aged classes; suburban location;
interns accepted.

Montessori Children's House
3119 Commerce Dr, Killeen, TX 76543-4012

Waco Montessori School (1976)
1300 Austin Ave, Waco, TX 76701
Judy Schmeltekopf, Dir, 817-754-3966
Non-profit; tuition: $167-260/mo
5 teachers, 5 assistants, 88 students, ages infant-9
Affiliation: AMS
Governance by board
New facility; childcare; urban location; interns accepted.

Hillcrest Professional Development School
4225 Pine, Waco, TX 76703
Ronald McIntire, 817-772-4286
Type: magnet
Pre K–5th grade
Multi age; interdisciplinary.

J.H. Hines Elementary
1102 Paul Quinn St, Waco, TX 76704
Renee Garrett
Type: Montessori

Options Learning Center (1991)
2100 Fir, McAllen, TX 76850
Rosalinda S. Gonzalez, Prin, 210-632-3222
Type: public at-risk
13 teachers, 162 students, 9–12th grade
Governance by principal
Teacher qualifications: certification
Cross-age tutoring; work/study; self-paced; contracts; self-
esteem; community involvement; counseling; transporta-
tion; interns accepted.

First Baptist Church Child Development Center
37 E Harris Ave, San Angelo, TX 76903-5821
Type: Montessori

Cathedral House Montessori School
1100 Prairie St, Houston, TX 77002-3119

Dominican Montessori School
3617 Milam St, Houston, TX 77002-9535

Dodson Elementary
1808 Sampson, Houston, TX 77003
O. D. Curtis, 713-225-5624
Type: magnet
K–5th grade
Montessori.

Born to Explore, Inc (1992)
2625 San Jacinto St, Houston, TX 77004
Rosalba Ortiz Dow, Pres, 713-659-2425
Type: Montessori; tuition: $350-400/mo
2 teachers, 4 assistants, 45 students, ages infant-6
Affiliation: HAAEYC
Governance by administrator
Bilingual; Hooked on Phonics; Spanish classes for ages 5-10
on Saturdays; childcare.

Ryan Middle School
2610 Elgin, Houston, TX 77004
Anita Ellis, 713-528-0922
Type: magnet
6–8th grade
Gifted and talented.

Turner Elementary
3200 Rosedale, Houston, TX 77004
Alma Allen, 713-523-3265
Type: magnet
People place center.

Montessori School of Downtown
4701 San Jacinto St, Houston, TX 77004-5045

The Sheridan School
5116 Caroline St, Houston, TX 77004-5802
Type: Montessori

St Mary's School
3002 Rosedale St, Houston, TX 77004-6128
Type: Montessori

Palmer Dev Center
5310 Greenbriar, Houston, TX 77005
Type: Montessori

Village Montessori School
2329 Bissonnet St, Houston, TX 77005-1511

Southampton Montessori School
5012 Morningside Dr, Houston, TX 77005-2592

Avalon Academy
1616 Indiana, Houston, TX 77006
Roseanne Sands, 713-524-1174

Montessori Country Day School
30 Oakdale St, Houston, TX 77006-6522
Marge Ellison

St Peter Pre-Kindergarten
1501 Houston Ave, Houston, TX 77007-4135
Type: Montessori

Hamilton Middle School
139 E 20th St, Houston, TX 77008
Diana Mulet, 713-861-9478
Type: magnet
6–8th grade
Gifted and talented.

Heights Montessori School (1981)
2028 Harvard St, Houston, TX 77008
Jennifer Bennett, Owner/Dir, 713-862-3792
Tuition: $255-460/mo
4 teachers, 7 assistants, 55 students, ages infant-6
Affiliation: AMS
Governance by administrator
Homey environment in historic area; urban location; interns
accepted.

Travis Elementary
3311 Beauchamp, Houston, TX 77009
Helen Clingan, 713-862-1796
Type: magnet
K-3rd grade
Gifted and talented.

DeZavala Elementary
7521 Ave H, Houston, TX 77012
Mwerva Perez, 713-923-8669
Type: magnet
3-5th grade
Gifted and talented.

Northwood Montessori School
14901 Welcome Ln, Houston, TX 77014-1405

New Beginnings Montessori
335 Audrey Ln, Houston, TX 77015-2209

St Christopher School
8134 Park Place Blvd, Houston, TX 77017
Susan E Sanchez
Type: Montessori

Oak Forest Elementary
1401 W 43rd St, Houston, TX 77018
Sharon Koonce, 713-613-2536
Type: magnet
K-5th grade
Gifted and talented.

River Oaks Elementary
2008 Kirby Dr, Houston, TX 77019
Michele Pola, 713-528-7319
Type: magnet
K-5th grade
Gifted and talented.

Montessori Society of Houston
1800 Huldy St, Houston, TX 77019-5725

Whidby Elementary
7625 Springhill, Houston, TX 77021
Vivian Harrison, 713-747-1233
Type: magnet
K-5th grade
Montessori.

Burbank Middle School
315 Berry Rd, Houston, TX 77022
Glenda Alvarez, 713-694-2813
Type: magnet
6-8th grade
Gifted and talented.

Burrus Elementary
701 E 33rd St, Houston, TX 77022
Flossie Sylvester, 713-861-6938
Type: magnet
K-5th grade
Arts.

Roosevelt Elementary
6700 Fulton, Houston, TX 77022
Charlotte Parker, 713-695-2772
Type: magnet
K-5th grade
Gifted and talented.

Houston Montessori Center (1973)
9601 Katy Freeway, Suite 170, Houston, TX 77024
Elisabeth Coe, PhD, 713-465-7670
Type: Montessori higher education, non-profit; tuition:
$1,475-3,250/yr
26 teachers, 1 assistant; students mainly international
Affiliation: AMS; accreditations: MACTE, TX Ed Agency
Governance by administrator, board
Speakers and consultants for institutions across country;
urban location; interns accepted.

Montessori Morning Glory School
737 Bunker Hill Rd, Houston, TX 77024-4405

Fleming Middle School
4910 Collingsworth, Houston, TX 77026
Chester Smith, 713-674-3415
Type: magnet
6-8th grade
Arts; physical development.

The Briarwood School
4811 San Felipe, Houston, TX 77027
Type: Montessori

The Wilhelm Schole
4242 Richmond, Houston, TX 77027
713-626-2532

River Oaks Baptist School
2300 Willowick Rd, Houston, TX 77027-3996
Type: Montessori

Holland Middle School
1600 Gellhorn, Houston, TX 77029
Adele Rogers, 713-675-3538
Type: magnet
6-8th grade
Gifted and talented.

Pleasantville Elementary
1431 Gellhorn, Houston, TX 77029
Linda Whitley, 713-673-2726
Type: magnet
K-5th grade
Gifted and talented.

Children's Hour Montessori
2227 Dorrington, Houston, TX 77030
Carolyn Mullen

Wildlife Discovery (Houston Zoo)
1513 Outer Belt Dr, Houston, TX 77030
Karyl Watz, 713-520-3265
Type: magnet
3rd grade

Jones High School
7414 St Louis, Houston, TX 77033
Arthur Pace, 713-733-1111
Type: magnet
9-12th grade
Gifted and talented.

Little Red Schoolhouse (1960)
611 Westbury Sq, Houston, TX 77035
Sheila Finch, Head, 713-723-2877
Type: Montessori; tuition: $2,000-3,730/yr
21 teachers, 4 assistants, 244 students, ages infant-15
Affiliation: AMS
Governance by administrator
Computer lab; computers in every classroom; grades 6-8
edit, format documents, use data base; childcare; subur-
ban location; interns accepted.

Montessori Vistas
12138 Fondren Rd, Houston, TX 77035-4002

Southwest Teacher
7497 S W Frwy, Houston, TX 77036
Type: Montessori

Montessori Conservatory
10001 Westheimer Rd, Houston, TX 77042-3132

Sherwood Forest Montessori School
1331 Sherwood Forest St, Houston, TX 77043-4637

Magnet Schools of America
(See Resource Section)

Awty International School
7455 Awty School Ln, Houston, TX 77055
713 686 4830
Type: independent

School of the Woods (1962)
1321 Wirt, Houston, TX 77055
Sherry Herron, Dir, 713-686-8811, FAX: 713-686-1936
Type: Montessori, non-profit; tuition: $240-470/mo
17 teachers, 8 assistants, 295 students, ages 3-15
Affiliations: AMS, NAEYC, TXAEYC
Governance by board of trustees
5-acre wooded site; cultivates respect, uniqueness and life-long learning; childcare; suburban location; interns accepted.

T. H. Rogers Middle School
5840 San Felipe, Houston, TX 77057
Meredith Wedin, 713-783-6220
Type: magnet
6-8th grade
Gifted and talented.

Clear Lake Montessori (1973)
16300 Sealark Rd, Houston, TX 77062
Cheryl Cook, Prin, 713-486-4416, FAX: 713-486-7167
Tuition: $2,520-2,900/yr
11 teachers, 291 students, ages infant-12
Affiliations: SNMTA, NAMTA, MACTE; accreditation: SNMC
Governance by administrator
Extensive math materials; childcare; interns accepted.

Montessori & Day Care School
8644 Richmond Ave, Houston, TX 77063-5629

Montessori Child Development
11707 Huffmeister, Houston, TX 77065

Learn 'n Play- Montessori
11707 Huffmeister Rd, Houston, TX 77065-1047

Greystone House
6731 Apple Valley Ln, Houston, TX 77069
Brenda Berleith
Type: Montessori

Southeast Texas Homeschool Association
5620 FM 191960 W, PO Box 354, Houston, TX 77069
713-370-8787

Montessori Vistas Inc
7910 Deer Meadow Dr, Houston, TX 77071-2713

Martin Elementary School
11718 Hendon, Houston, TX 77072
Diane Stanky
Type: Montessori

Montessori Learning Institute
5701 Beechnut, Houston, TX 77074
Myle Yo

Askew Elementary
11200 Woodlodge, Houston, TX 77077
Elaine Allen, 713-497-5450
Type: magnet

3-5th grade
Gifted and talented.

Westside Montessori School, Inc
1570 S Dairy Ashford, Houston, TX 77077-3862

Wingate Montessori
14130 Westheimer Rd, Houston, TX 77077-5363

Smaller Scholars Montessori School
12280 Westheimer Rd #50, Houston, TX 77077-6050
Dot Ahuja

American Montessori School (1986)
14434 Bellaire Blvd, Houston, TX 77083
Mrs Trehan or Mrs Weiser, Dirs, 713-498-6000, FAX: 713-265-3147
Tuition: $215/405
5 teachers, 7 assistants, 82 students, ages 2.5-8
Governance by administrator
Suburban location.

Windsor Village Elementary
14440 Polo, Houston, TX 77085
Sandra Satterwhite, 713-726-3542
Type: magnet
K-5th grade
Gifted and talented.

Penelope Vanderwerth-Carter
6308 Spindle, Houston, TX 77086
Type: Montessori

Montessori Children's Cottage/Inwood
4646 Victory Dr, Houston, TX 77088-7238

Montessori Adventure, Inc
10904 Scarsdale #256, Houston, TX 77089
Laura C Trellue

Brookwoods Montessori Elementary School
4107 Sherwood Ln, Houston, TX 77092
Cynthia Foster, Admissions Director, 713-686-5427, FAX: 713-686-8780
Tuition: $420/435/mo
5 teachers, 4 assistants, 97 students, ages 3-9
Affiliation: AMS
Governance by administrator
French daily; separate classroom for studies/experiments in nature, science, and art; greenhouse; 3+ acres; indoor pool; summer program; childcare; suburban location; interns accepted.

Montessori Children's Cottage/Copperfield (1970)
15703 Longenbaugh, Houston, TX 77092
Cynthia Foster, Admissions Coordinator, 713-550-1191, FAX: 713-686-8780
Tuition: $280-585/mo
5 teachers, 8 assistants, 100 students
Affiliation: AMS
Governance by administrator
French lesson daily for students over 3 years; PE; dance; tumbling; piano; separate classroom for science, nature, and geography studies/experiments; summer program; childcare; suburban location; interns accepted.

Janice Newsum Montessori Preschool
6111 Del Rio, Houston, TX 77095

West Montessori School of Copperfield
15810 Longenbaugh Dr, Houston, TX 77095-1606

Cottage School System
7142 Cherry Park Dr, Houston, TX 77095-2713
Type: Montessori

Herod Elementary
5627 Jason, Houston, TX 77096
Nancy Nichols, 713-774-6972

Type: magnet
K–3rd grade
Gifted and talented.

United Orthodox Montessori
9001 Greenwillow St, Houston, TX 77096-3599
Hetty Perl

Lanier Middle School
2600 Woodhead, Houston, TX 77098
Brenda Lanclos, 713-529-5451
Type: magnet
6–8th grade
Gifted and talented.

St Stephen's Episcopal School
1805 Alabama, Houston, TX 77098
Type: Montessori

Children's Garden Montessori
2144 Kipling St, Houston, TX 77098-2304

Alief Westwood Montessori (1971)
11959 Bissonnet (at Kirkwood), Houston, TX 77099
Ms Selby, Dir, 713-933-6808
Tuition: $235-375/mo
3 teachers, 4 assistants, 53 students, ages infant–9
Governance by administrator
Individualized; childcare; interns accepted.

Southwest Montessori Center
12222 Bissonnet St #3, Houston, TX 77099-1439

St Catherine's Montessori
PO Box 20728, Houston, TX 77225-0728

Montessori Children's House
200 Ave J, Conroe, TX 77301-3779

The Pines Montessori
3059 Woodland Hills, Kingwood, TX 77339

Pines Montessori School
3535 Cedar Knolls Dr, Kingwood, TX 77339-2468
Maureen Peterson

Rustic Woods Montessori
3923 Rustic Woods Dr, Kingwood, TX 77339-2611

Kingwood Day School
Loop 494 at Memorial Dr, Porter, TX 77365
Type: Montessori

Northwest Montessori School
301 S Cherry St, Tomball, TX 77375-6614

Woodlands Montessori Schools
1201 Many Pines, Woodlands, TX 77380
Joni McEuen

Post Oak School (1963)
4600 Bissonnet, Houston, TX 77401
Suzanne Pugin, 912-661-6688, FAX: 912-661-4959
Type: Montessori; tuition: $4,100-7,00/yr
15 teachers, 15 assistants, 166 students, ages infant–15
Affiliations: NAMTA, AMITOT; accreditation: AMI
Governance by administrator
Enrichment classes, specialists; art; music; PE; computers;
    dance; childcare; urban location; interns accepted.

Nature Discovery Center (1979)
PO Box 777, Bellaire, TX 77402
Melissa Geis, Dir, 713-667-6550, FAX: same
Type: Montessori, non-profit
1 teacher, 5 assistants
Accreditation: TX Ed Agency
Governance by board
Ecology approach; urban location.

Alief Children's House
4215 H St, PO Box 702, Alief, TX 77411
Type: Montessori

Cy-Fair Montessori (1980)
12815 Huffmeister Rd, Cypress, TX 77429
Rebecca Huebner, Dir, 713-890-3937
Non-profit; tuition: $160-290/mo
3 teachers, 2 assistants, 75 students, ages infant–6
Affiliation: Corporate Hands Network; accreditation: AMI
Governance by administrator, parent cooperative
4 wooded acres; childcare; rural location.

Houston Alliance
12811 Ivy Forest Dr, Cypress, TX 77429
Kay Crowley
Type: home-based

Montessori Child Development Center
11103 Mills Rd, Cypress, TX 77429-3008

Katy Montessori School
2437 N Fry Rd, Katy, TX 77449-6220

The Cottage School
20201 Kingsland Blvd, Katy, TX 77450-3008
Niroo Somaya
Type: Montessori

Great Expectations Montessori Center
3420 Cartwright Rd, Missouri City, TX 77459-2434

Children's World Montessori Center
4010 Ave N, Rosenberg, TX 77471-4802

First Colony Montessori
2229 Settlers Way Blvd, Sugar Land, TX 77478-5231
Ruean Ulesee

Riverbend Montessori School (1976)
4225 Elkins St, Sugar Land, TX 77479
Barbara Crawford, Adm, 713-980-4123, FAX: 980-0120
Tuition: $235-385/mo
6 teachers, 7 assistants, 140 students, mainly international,
    ages infant–12
Affiliation: AMS
Governance by board of trustees
Childcare; suburban location; interns accepted.

Cedarwood School, Inc
311 Present St, Missouri City, TX 77489-1145
Type: Montessori

Montessori School of Pasadena
1033 Fairmont Pkwy, Pasadena, TX 77504
Joseph Manjos

ASSETS Learning Center (1993)
605 W House, Alvin, TX 77511
Sherry Goen, 713-388-1130
Type: public at-risk
5 teachers, 60-75 students, ages 14–16, 7–8th grade
Governance by faculty and student representatives
Teacher qualifications: state certification
Boys Town social skills curriculum; cooperative learning;
    adventure-based counseling; community service; town
    and parent meetings; mentor and advisory programs;
    computer lab; multi-aged classes; extensive field trips;
    suburban location.

Holy Comforter Episcopal School
227 S Chenango St, Angleton, TX 77515-6001
Type: Montessori

Montessori Pre-School
7 Flounder Circle, Freeport, TX 77541-8910

Montessori School & Day Care
809 S Friendswood Dr, Friendswood, TX 77546-4556

Clear Creek Montessori School
1903 Carriage Creek Ln, Friendswood, TX 77546-5133

Island Montessori School
1520 Market St, Galveston, TX 77550

Montessori Unlimited
10122 Carlow Ln, La Porte, TX 77571
Gail Morgan

South Shore Montessori School
201 S Shore Blvd, League City, TX 77573-4389

School of Montessori
1503 S 16th St, Nederland, TX 77627-4427

Central Catholic School
3611 Gulfway Dr, Port Arthur, TX 77642-3675
Type: Montessori

Children's House Montessori School
2510 N 11th St, Beaumont, TX 77703

Montessori School House (1979)
2509 Roundtree Dr, Bryan, TX 77801
Lydia Cumings, Owner, 409-822-5192
Tuition: $155-355/mo
3 teachers, 1 assistant, 68 students, ages 3-6
Affiliation: NAMTA; accreditation: AMI
Governance by administrator

Aggieland Country School
1701 Brook Hollow Dr, Bryan, TX 77802-1122
Type: Montessori

Keystone Montessori School
2320 E Villa Maria Rd, Bryan, TX 77802-2549
Kim Oehme

Brenham Montessori School
1500 S Baylor, Brenham, TX 77833-4969

Alternative Academic Program (1993)
1812 Welsh St, College Station, TX 77840
Claude Cunningham, 2ndary Dir, 409-764-5481, FAX: -5492
Type: public at-risk
2 teachers, 15 students, ages 17-20, 9-12th grade
Teacher qualifications: Texas Certification
Self-paced; self-directed; career/technology credit; no letter grades; multi-aged classes; suburban location.

Dudley Elementary
3307 Callis St, Victoria, TX 77901
Armando Villarreal, 512-575-3477
Type: magnet
Pre K-5th grade
Gifted and talented.

Hill Country Montessori School, Inc (1981)
606 S School St, Boerne, TX 78006
Peggy Wallace, Financial Adm, 210-816-3819
Non-profit; tuition: $275-340/mo
4 teachers, 4 assistants, 57 students, ages infant-9
Affiliations: AMI, NAMTA; accreditation: AMITOT
Governance by teachers and administrators
Natural lighting; integrates indoors and outdoors; secure surrounding; childcare; suburban location.

Montessori Pre-School
517 B Wigham, Kerrville, TX 78028

The Circle School (1965)
217 Pershing, San Antonio, TX 78209
Mary Barton, Co-op Pres, 210-822-0461
Type: independent, non-profit; tuition: $300/mo
6 teachers, 50 students, ages 2.5-12, pre K-5th grade
Governance by parent cooperative
Teacher qualifications: long-term experience in alternative teaching, open-mindedness

Curriculum integrates Montessori, Waldorf, peace studies, Native American learning, oral traditions; story-telling used daily; no letter grades; non-compulsory class attendance; multi-aged classes; extensive field trips; urban location; interns accepted.

Kriterion Montessori School (1965)
611 W Ashby Pl, San Antonio, TX 78212
Andreas Laven, Business Mgr, 210-735-9778
Tuition: $380/400/mo
8 teachers, 4 assistants, 120 students, ages 3-15
Affiliations: AMS, AMI, NCME, IMS, NMSA
Governance by administrator
Childcare; urban location.

The Judson Montessori School (1974)
705 Trafalgar, San Antonio, TX 78216
James J. Judson, Dir, 210-344-3117, FAX: 210-344-1223
Non-profit; tuition: $3,735-5,400/yr
24 teachers, 8 assistants, 201 students, ages 3-15
Affiliations: COE, TAN; accreditation: AMITOT
Governance by administrator, board
Junior Great Books; communications and debate; computers; science; library resource center; Orff & Kodaly music; Spanish; after-school sports and arts; chess; childcare; suburban location; interns accepted.

Mount Sacred Heart Montessori Society
619 Mount Sacred Heart Rd, San Antonio, TX 78216-6695
Pam Snow

St Mary's Hall Montessori (1968)
9401 Starcrest Dr, San Antonio, TX 78217
Vicki S. Raney, 210-655-7721, FAX: 210-655-6276
Non-profit; tuition: $3,320/4,735/yr
7 teachers, 7 assistants, 139 students, ages 3-6
Affiliation: AMS; accreditation: ISASW
Governance by administrator and board of trustees
Wooded 54-acre campus; feeds into traditional college prep, coed school, grades 1-12; students from TX, SW states, other countries; suburban location.

Children's House & Montessori School
4927 Evers Rd, San Antonio, TX 78228-2148

Bilingual Montessori School
3703 John Alden Ave, San Antonio, TX 78230-3203
Stephen Jackson

San Antonio Country Day School
4194 Jung Rd, San Antonio, TX 78247-2711
Type: Montessori

Open the Door to a Different Approach to Learning
(1991)
PO Box 871, Kingsville, TX 78363
Mary Ann Colin, Dir, 512-592-3368
Type: public choice; scholarships
5 teachers, 100 students, mainly at-risk, ages 16-21, 9-12th grade
Governance by teachers, principal
Teacher qualifications: BS
Open entry/exit; outcome-based; mastery learning; integrated instruction; career, technology training; support services; cooperative education; multi-aged classes; extensive field trips; childcare; interns accepted.

The Montessori School of Corpus Christi
2205 16th St, Corpus Christi, TX 78404

Incarnate Word Montessori
450 Chamberlain St, Corpus Christi, TX 78404-2442
Sr M Christina Bradley

Windsor Park Elementary
4525 S Alameda St, Corpus Christi, TX 78412
Ginger Harris, 512-994-3664
Type: magnet

1-5th grade
Gifted and talented.

The Living Classroom
2526 Flour Bluff Dr, Corpus Christi, TX 78418
Type: Montessori

McAllen Montessori School
2917 W US Hwy 83 #250, McAllen, TX 78501

Discovery School
4601 N 2nd St, McAllen, TX 78504-2927
Ann Chambers and Patricia Deeren
Type: Montessori

Bowie School
Box 2514, Alamo, TX 78516
Type: Montessori

Franklin School
900 Brich St, Alamo, TX 78516
Type: Montessori

Kenmont —The Montessori School (1972)
2734 N Coria St, Brownsville, TX 78520
Donald G. Massey, Dir, 210-542-0500
Tuition: $1,950-2,730/yr
7 teachers, 6 assistants, 172 students, ages infant-12
Accreditation: AMITOT
Governance by administrator
Childcare; suburban location.

Home Montessori School
925 E Los Ebanos Blvd, Brownsville, TX 78520-8726

Gonzalez Elementary School
4450 Coffee Port, Brownsville, TX 78521
Janet R Schooley
Type: Montessori

Claire's House for Children
RR 4 Box 823, Edinburg, TX 78539-9418
Claire van der Put
Type: Montessori

Montessori Academy of Harlingen
1806 Laurel, Harlingen, TX 78550
Ann Hall

Henry Ford Elementary School
PO Box JJ, Pharr, TX 78577-1236
Type: Montessori

Longoria School
400 E Rendon St, Pharr, TX 78577-1859
Type: Montessori

Napper School
903 N Flag St, Pharr, TX 78577-2999
Type: Montessori

Buell School
218 E Juarez St, Pharr, TX 78577-3990
Type: Montessori

Carnahan School
317 W Gore St, Pharr, TX 78577-5331
Type: Montessori

Palmer School
703 E Sam Houston St, Pharr, TX 78577-5599
Type: Montessori

Clover School
N San Juan Rd, San Juan, TX 78589
Type: Montessori

Garza-Pena Primary School
E Gasline Rd PO Box 1270, San Juan, TX 78589
Type: Montessori

Sorensen School
715 S Standard Ave, San Juan, TX 78589-2446
Type: Montessori

Greenbriar School (1969)
Box 466, Elgin, TX 78621
Jose & Maria Garcia, 512-285-2661
Type: independent
25 students
Located on 171 acres of woodland; evolved into collective
  homeschooling in a cooperative intentional community;
  community members are volunteer staff; many are self
  employed craftsmen, etc, and involve students with work.

Kindernest Montessori (1990)
113 E San Antonio, Fredericksburg, TX 78624
Linda Muegge, Dir, 210-997-8939
Non-profit; tuition: $173/205
2 teachers, 2 assistants, 48 students, ages 3-9
Affiliation: NAMTA
Governance by board of trustees
Music, art, aerobics, German; childcare; suburban location;
  interns accepted.

Old Town Elementary School
2001 Old Settlers Blvd, Round Rock, TX 78681-2160
Type: Montessori

Govalle Elementary School
3801 Govalle Ave, Austin, TX 78702
Type: Montessori

Casa Montessori Child Development Center
2201 W 1st St, Austin, TX 78703-4619

Town & Country Montessori House of Children
3801 Keats Dr, Austin, TX 78704

Montessori Center
605 Academy Dr, Austin, TX 78704-1816

Montessori House of Children of Austin
1601 Brackenridge, Austin, TX 78704-6741
Ginger Logan

Austin Children's House
8512 F M 969, Austin, TX 78724-5719
Type: Montessori

Jollyville Learning Center
13401 Pond Springs, Austin, TX 78729
Mike Mirelez, 513-331-5270

Case Montessori Child Development Centers
4025 Tealwood Dr, Austin, TX 78731

The Children's School, Inc (1979)
2825 Hancock Dr, Austin, TX 78731
Clay Wallin, Adm, 512-453-1126
Type: Montessori; tuition: $200-295/mo
6 teachers, 9 assistants, 130 students, ages infant-9
Affiliation: AMS; accreditation: AMITOT
Governance by administrator
Childcare; urban location; interns accepted.

Austin Waldorf School (1980)
8702 Southview Rd, Austin, TX 78737
Betsy Hanelius, Faculty Chair, 512-288-5942, FAX: -9578
Non-profit; tuition: $4,000/yr, scholarships
18 teachers, 135 students, ages 4-12, K-6th grade
Affiliation: AWSNA
Governance by teachers and board of trustees
Teacher qualifications: college, Waldorf training
Suburban location; interns accepted.

Austin Montessori School (1967)
5014 Sunset Trail, Austin, TX 78745
Donald C. Goertz, PhD, Exec Dir, 512-892-0253
Tuition: $2,100-3,700/yr

11 teachers, 11 assistants, 270 students, ages 3–12
Affiliation: NAMTA; accreditations: AMI, AMITOT
Governance by administrator, board
Classical curriculum; alternative methodology; emphasis on personal responsibility; childcare; rural location; transportation; interns accepted.

Bay Area Montessori House
PO Box 891083, Austin, TX 78745

White Bird Montessori School
6305 Manchaca Rd, Austin, TX 78745-4945

The Montessori Center (1983)
4108 Ave H, Austin, TX 78751-4725
Jessica Salinas, Dir, 512-451-5081
Tuition: $255/370/mo
4 teachers, 5 assistants, 49 students, ages infant-6
Affiliation: AMS; accreditation: NAECP
Governance by teachers and administrators
Warm, loving, respectful environment fostered in school and at home; childcare; suburban location; interns accepted.

Duane Lake Academy
2700 W Anderson Ln, Suite 415, Austin, TX 78757
Neil D. Lubart, Dir, 512-454-2260, FAX: same
Type: independent, non-profit; tuition: $3,000, scholarships
5 teachers, 20 students, ages 5-18, ungraded
Governance by teachers and principal.
Teacher qualifications: Certified, student centered
Multi-aged classes; 2 days/wk; parents participate daily; continuous progress through mastery learning; extensive field trips; urban location; interns accepted.

A Bar Z Pondersoa
Alief-Westwood, Austin, TX 78758
Type: Montessori

HOPE: Home-Oriented Private Education for Texas
PO Box 17755, Austin, TX 78760-7755
512-280-HOPE

Gibko
808 Saunders, Round Rock, TX 78864
Type: Montessori

Children's Montessori House of Canyon
2523 5th Ave, Canyon, TX 79015
Martha Johnson

St Mary's Montessori Preschool
1200 S Washington St, Amarillo, TX 79102-1645

Amarillo Montessori Academy
3806 Bowie St, Amarillo, TX 79110-1235

Post Elementary School
200 W 8th St, Post, TX 79356-3217
Type: Montessori

Iles Elementary
2401 Date Ave, Lubbock, TX 79404
Suzanne Christopher, 806-766-1755
Type: magnet
K-6th grade
Creative and expressive arts.

Williams Elementary
4812 58th St, Lubbock, TX 79414
Carolyn Solomon, 806-766-0988
Type: magnet

K-6th grade
Self-esteem; cooperative learning.

Montessori School of the Plains
4600 48th St, Lubbock, TX 79414-3502

Texas Homeschool Coalition
Box 6982, Lubbock, TX 79493
806-797-4927

Hobbs Accelerated Education Co-op
Rt 1 Box 1086, Rotan, TX 79546
Dr Frank Cockrell, 915-735-2850

PASS: Project for Academic Success and Skills (1986)
342 Cockerell Dr, Abilene, TX 79601
Don Eiland, Prin, 915-672-6456
Type: public at-risk
8 teachers, 113 students, ages 13-17, 6-8th grade
Governance by teachers and principal
Teacher qualifications: selected from AISD
Accelerated option (two yrs in one); multi-aged classes; suburban location; interns accepted.

Viola M. Coleman High School
1600 E Golf Course Rd, Midland, TX 79701
Helen B. Lackey, Prin, 915-689-5000, FAX: 689-5016
Type: public at-risk
10 teachers, 300 students, ages 15-21, 9-12th grade
Teacher qualifications: certification
Computers; non-compulsory class attendance; childcare; urban location; transportation.

Milam Magnet Elementary
815 S Dixie, Odessa, TX 79761
Cindy Abel, 915-337-1561
K-6th grade
Visual and performing arts.

Alpine Montessori School (1988)
Box 664 Marfa Hwy, Alpine, TX 79831
Liz Sibley, Bd Pres, 915-837-2173
Non-profit; tuition: $175-265/mo, scholarships
1 teacher, 4 assistants; students mainly Hispanic, ages 3-9
Governance by board
Near Big Bend Nat'l Park; bilingual teaching in preschool; Spanish; childcare; rural location; interns accepted.

The Xinachtli Project (1989)
8404 N Loop D4, El Paso, TX 79907
Carlos Aceves, 915-594-8683
Type: independent
3 teachers; students mainly Chicano, ages 5-18
Integrates MesoAmerican culture with holistic approaches; workshop presentations.

Wm Beaumont Army Medical Center
PO Box 70537, El Passo, TX 79920
Type: Montessori

Jardin de Ninos Montessori School
10476 Seawood Dr, El Paso, TX 79925
Erma Chandler

East Montessori Learning Center
3510 N Yarbrough Dr, El Paso, TX 79925-1626

El Paso Homeschoolers Association
PO Box 371676, El Paso, TX 79937
Mare Hohholt, 915-857-3487

U.S. Virgin Islands

Virgin Islands Montessori School
6936 Vessup Ln, St Thomas, USVI 00802
Shournagh McWeeney

The Manor School
4236 La Grande Princesse, Christiansted, St Croix, USVI 00820-
4449
Type: Montessori

Rattan Montessori School
3B Est Rattan/Box 1798, Kingshill, USVI 00851
Jane Little

Utah

American Montessori Academy
215 N Center St, American Fork, UT 84003-1629

Gingerbread House Pre-School
867 W 3800 S, Bountiful, UT 84010-8433
Type: Montessori

Great Basin High School
PO Box 1388, Clearfield, UT 84016
Mary DeLaRosa, Prin, 801-774-4000
100 students
Accreditation: NWASC
Residential, vocational ed.

Montessori Learning Center
538 Monterey Dr, Orem, UT 84057-3926

Valley High School
11020 S State, Sandy, UT 84070
Clyde Melberg, Prin or Michele Hendrickson, 801-565-7574
19 teachers, 600 students, 10-12th grade
Accreditation: NWASC
Evening classes; teen mothers program.

Ashley Valley High School (1989)
650 N Vernal Ave, Vernal, UT 84078
Dr A. J. Pease, Prin, 801-781-3125, FAX: 801-781-3128
Type: public choice/at-risk
4 teachers, 145 students, ages 13+, 9-12th grade
Affiliation: NASC
Governance by faculty, student reps, democratic school
meeting, board
Teacher qualifications: UT Certification
Application worth 1/2 credit; mentor/advisor for every
student; Glasser's control theory; reality therapy; non-
compulsory class attendance; multi-aged classes; rural
location; interns accepted.

Montessori Children's House
1303 S 11th E, Salt Lake City, UT 84105-2420

Bonnyview High School
4984 S 300 W, Murray, UT 84107
Shauna Ballou, Prin, 801-264-7470
6 teachers, 150 students, 7-12th grade
Accreditation: NWASC
Night classes; home study.

Mount Vernon Academy
184 Vine St, Murray, UT 84107
Type: home-based

Hawthorne University
2965 East, 3435 South, Salt Lake City, UT 84109

Dr Alfred Munzert, 801-485-1801, FAX:-1563
100 students
HS/concurrent college program.

Utah Christian Homeschoolers
Box 3942, Salt Lake City, UT 84110
801-394-4156

Central High School (1973)
3031 S 200 E, Salt Lake City, UT 84115
Edward Campos, Prin, 801-481-7100, FAX: 801-481-7104
Type: public at-risk
18 teachers, 700 students, ages 13-19, 7-12th grade
Governance by principal, teachers
Teacher qualifications: UT Certification
Home study; intensive learning; high expectation in acade-
mics, behavior; urban location; interns accepted.

Granite District Coordinator for
340 E 3545 S, Salt Lake City, UT 84115
Shelley Iverson, Coord, 801-268-8560, 481-7105
Programs in each junior, senior high school.

Brighton Montessori Early Learning Center
2887 E 7000 S, Salt Lake City, UT 84121-3444

American Home Academy/
Latter Day Saints Home Educators' Association
(See Resource Section)

National Association of Mormon Home Educators
2770 S 1000 W, Perry, UT 84302

Logan Alternative Programs
83 S 100 W, Logan, UT 84321
Larry Petersen, Dir, 801-755-2395
Cache District Young Mothers Program: 2 teachers, 24 stu-
dents; Logan North Campus: 42 students; Logan South
Campus, 347 S 300 W, Logan, UT: 65 students.

Valley Montessori Preschool
1240 N 225 E, Logan, UT 84321

Weber Basin High School
RFD #6, Ogden, UT 84405
Vern Brown, Prin, 801-479-9806
Type: public at-risk

Canyon Country Homeschoolers
1605 W. Highland Dr, Moab, UT 84532
Donna Grah, 801-259-5864

HELP-Four Corners
Castle Valley Star Route, PO Box 1901, Moab, UT 84532
801-259-6968

FCLA Utah Spice Group
1510 W 500 N, Provo, UT 84601
801-377-4728
Type: home-based

Brigham Young U- Dept of Independent Study
(See Resource Section)

Utah Home Education Association
PO Box 50565, Provo, UT 84605
Karl Pearson, Pres, 801-342-4027, 535-1533
Convention; newsletter; bookstore; testing.

Home School Supply House
(See Resource Section)

Cedar Ridge High School
50 N 650 W, Richfield, UT 84701
Randall E. Brown, Prin, 801-896-9464
5 teachers, 125+ students, ages 14+
Accreditation: NWASC
Night classes; home study.

Vermont

Montessori School of the Upper Valley, Inc (1973)
PO Box 368 Main St, Norwich, VT 05055
Joyce Dion, Head Teacher, 802-649-2827
Non-profit; tuition: $2,350/yr
1 teacher, 1 assistant, 31 students, ages 3-6
Governance by board
Rural location; interns accepted.

Upper Valley Waldorf School (1991)
PO Box 15, Norwich, VT 05074
Phebe McCosker, Coord, 802-649-5729
Tuition: $2,500-3,250/yr, scholarships
5 teachers, 32 students, ages 4-9, K-2nd grade
Affiliation: AWSNA
Governance by board
Teacher qualifications: college degree and Waldorf training
Rural location.

Open Fields School
Academy Rd, Thetford, VT 05074
Jean Aull, 802-785-2077
Type: independent

Mtn. School Program of Milton Academy
RFD Box 123-F, Vershire, VT 05079
David Grant, 802-685-4520
Type: independent

at Windsor High School (1993)
Union St, Windsor, VT 05089
Martin Tewksbury, Tch/Coord
Type: public choice
1 teacher, 7 students, ages 12-16, 7-10th grade
Governance by principal
Teacher qualifications: VT certification
Opportunity to design course work, schedule and work expe-
    rience wtih staff guidance, support; positive relationship
    development with peers, staff, public and home; multi-
    aged classes; interns accepted.

Gifted and Talented Program
Bellows Falls Union High School, Bellows Falls, VT 05101
Mark Kennedy, 802-463-3944
Type: public choice
HS
Newsletter; inclusive; self-selective; decompartmentalized.

Global Alliance for Transforming Education
(See Resource Section)

West River Montessori School
Box 171, South Londonderry, VT 05155
Kim Merrow

Bennington Program (1970)
Mount Anthony UHSD, Bennington, VT 05201

Ralph Wright, 802-442-2811
Type: public at-risk
7-12th grade
School/community partnerships; early intervention; voca-
    tional training; job placement; work transition; wilderness
    experience; HS diploma.

Bennington School, Inc
19 Fairview St, Bennington, VT 05201
Jeffrey La Bonte, 802-447-1557
Type: independent
Students mainly at-risk

Hiland Hall School (1991)
RR 2 Box 1700, Bennington, VT 05201
Jessica Howard, Prin, 802-442-3868
Type: independent, non-profit; tuition: $1,500-5,500/yr,
    scholarships
2 teachers, 28 students, ages 5-14
Governance by principal, board
Teacher qualifications: Bachelor's, experience
Low ratio; individual attention; self-understanding; critical
    thinking; communication; skills mastery; no letter grades;
    multi-aged classes; extensive field trips; interns accepted.

Central Vermont Homeschool Group
RR1, PO Box 2980, Manchester Center, VT 05255
802-362-4337

Southshire Community School
Box 634, N Bennington, VT 05257
Susan Lambert, Adm Asst, 802-442-4601
Type: independent, non-profit; tuition: $2,875/yr,
    scholarships
3 teachers, 30 students, ages 4.5-12, K-6th grade
Governance primarily by parents
Located in a small village; family-oriented; child's inner world
    is recognized, valued, guided; self-directed; no letter
    grades; multi-aged classes; interns accepted.

Hilltop Montessori School
118 Maple St, Brattleboro, VT 05301
Tonia LWheeler, 802-257-0500

School for International Training
Kipling Rd, Brattleboro, VT 05301
Bill Huff, 802-257-7751, 800-451-4465
Type: higher education; tuition: variable, scholarships
250 students, under/graduate
Study abroad; language teaching.

The Neighborhood Schoolhouse (1980)
Box 119, Brattleboro, VT 05302
Norma Willingham, Prin, 802-257-5544
Type: independent, non-profit; tuition: $3,880, scholarships
68 students, ages 3-12, ungraded

Affiliations: NCACS, NAEYC, VISA
Governance by consensus of principal/staff or board
Developmentally-appropriate; experiential; student need and interest-based; no letter grades; multi-aged classes; rural location; interns accepted.

Marlboro College (1946)
PO Box A, Marlboro, VT 05344
Wayne R. Wood, Adms Dir, 802-257-4333, FAX: -4154
Boarding, non-profit; tuition: $17,175/yr, scholarships
36 teachers, 270 students, ages 17-40
Governance by faculty and student reps
Self-designed; tutorials; small classes.

Grammar School (1960)
RR4 Box 195, Hickory Ridge Rd, Putney, VT 05346
Marcia Leader, Adms Dir, 802-387-5364
Type: independent, non-profit; tuition: $5,540-7,500/yr, scholarships
15 teachers, 99 students, ages 5-14, K-8th grade
Affiliations: NEASC, NAIS, AISNE, VISA, ERB
Governance by board
Science fairs; 9 yr French program; skiing; running; computer literacy; visual, performing arts; poetry; rural location; interns accepted.

Windham County Homeschool Group
RR 2, PO Box 1332, Putney, VT 05346
Julie Tamler, 802-387-5285

Rutland County Homeschoolers
PO Box 161, Pittsford, VT 05352
Liz Swift, 802-483-6296

Burlington College (1972)
95 North Ave, Burlington, VT 05401
Nancy Wilson, Adms Dir, 802-862-9616, FAX: 658-0071
Non-profit; tuition: $250/cr, scholarships
75 teachers, 230 students
Governance by faculty and student reps
Accredited degrees in psychology, humanities, human services, feminist studies, fine arts or individualized major; external degree program; no letter grades; urban location.

Learning Materials Workshop
274 N Winiski Ave, Burlington, VT 05401
Karen Hewitt
Type: Montessori

ONTOP
14 S Williams, Burlington, VT 05401
Rick Ebel
Type: public at-risk

Rock Point School
Institute Rd, Burlington, VT 05401
Russell Ellis
Type: independent, boarding
Students mainly at-risk, HS
Low ratio; counseling; tutoring; self-image/motivation; substance abuse counseling; 24 hr/day supportive environment; positive peer culture.

Schoolhouse
99 Proctor Ave Ext, S Burlington, VT 05403
Joni Avritic, 802-658-4164
Type: independent, non-profit; tuition: $2,850/yr, scholarships
4 teachers, 39 students, ages 5-12, K-6th grade
Governance by parent cooperative
Teacher qualifications: VT license or degree and related experience
Thematic units; art; yearly all school play based on cultural study; peer conflict resolution; parent-taught mini-courses; no letter grades; multi-aged classes; suburban location; interns accepted.

Red Cedar School (1989)
PO Box 393, Bristol, VT 05443
Jackie Werner Gavrin, 802-453-5213
Type: independent; tuition: $3,600/yr, scholarships
2 teachers, 17 students, ages 4-12
Affiliation: Sudbury Valley School
Governance by weekly democratic school meeting
Teacher qualifications: interest and ability to work with young people; commitment to philosophy of school.
Self-directed; no letter grades; multi-aged classes; extensive field trips; rural location; interns accepted.

Vermont Homeschoolers Association
Rd 2, PO Box 4440, Bristol, VT 05443

West Wind Montessori School
West Wind Farm, Charlotte, VT 05445

ACE: Alternative Center for Education
Essex Junction Ed Center, Essex Junction, VT 05452
Lars Baris, 802-878-1392
Type: public at-risk
Work experience; group activities; field trips; parent involvement; community partnerships; adventure-based counseling; pregnant, teen parenting support.

Life Program
Champlain Valley High School, Hinesburg, VT 05461
Thomas Hart, 802-482-2109
Type: public at-risk
School/community partnerships; family involvement; support, transition to work, return to school; GED; vocational training; job placement.

Saxon Hill School Inc
PO Box 68, Jericho, VT 05465
Ann Manning, 802-899-3832
Type: independent

Lake Champlain Waldorf School (1983)
27 Harbor Rd, Shelborne, VT 05482
Pam Graham, Adm, 802-985-2827
Non-profit; tuition: $3,600-4,320/yr, scholarships
14 teachers, 116 students, ages 3-12, pre K-6th grade
Affiliation: AWSNA
Governance by faculty
Teacher qualifications: Waldorf certification
Suburban location; interns accepted.

Heartworks School
PO Box 835, Shelburne, VT 05482
Diane Rooney, 802-985-2153

Resource Center for Redesigning Education
(See Resource Section)

Addison County Homeschool Group
Rd 2, PO Box 2850, Vergennes, VT 05491
802-877-3959

Homeschool Representative
RD 1, PO Box 1265, Belvidere, VT 05492
Denise Starkey, 802-644-2606

Bellweather School and Family resource Center (1995)
120 S. Borwnell Rd, Williston, VT 05495
Ron Miller, 802-865-9752
Tuition: $4500, scholarships
3 teachers, 25 students, ages 3-10
Ungraded; democratic meeting; ecological focus; holistic curriculum; services for homeschoolers

Pine Ridge School
1075 Williston Rd, Williston, VT 05495
Mary Jean Thielen, 802-434-2161
Type: independent
Students mainly at-risk

The Montpelier Waldorf Child's Garden (1991)
280 Main St, Montpelier, VT 05602
Susan Darrah, 802-223-5346
Non-profit; tuition: variable
Student ages 4-5
Governance by parent cooperative
Honor dignity, joy of nurturing, sustaining life; cooking,
crafts, gardening, watercolors, ample play.

U 32 Jr-Sr High School
RR2 Box 3315, Gallison Hill Rd, Montpelier, VT 05602
Ann Burns, 802-229-0322, FAX: 802-229-2761
Type: public choice

Vermont Home Schoolers
c/o Vermont Dept of Ed, Montpelier, VT 05620
Sue Lafavre, Sec or Natalie Casco, Dir, 802-828-3352
Also contact DeWes Guarnaccia, VT Homeschoolers Assn, 207-
777-0077; interns accepted.

Christian Home Educators of Vermont
2 Webster Ave, Barre, VT 05641
802-476-8821

Home School Coordination—At Risk Youth
Spaulding High School, Barre, VT 05641
Linda Mailly, 802-476-6411
Type: public at-risk
6-12th grade
Career, academic counseling; first Inter-Agency Collaboration
Group in VT; behavioral, disciplinary modification; sub-
stance abuse counseling; pregnant teen/young parent
support.

Laraway School
Box 618, Johnson, VT 05656
Scott Johnson, 802-635-7212
Type: independent
Students mainly at-risk

Upward Bound
Johnson State College, Johnson, VT 05656
Sally Ballin
Type: independent

Lamoille County Homeschool Group
RR2, PO Box 3344, Morrisville, VT 05661
Dena Keith, 802-888-3574

The Regional Alternative Program-Aim High (1990)
PO Box 340, Morrisville, VT 05661
Richard F. Kovacs, Director, 802-888-6586
Type: public at-risk
3 teachers, 20 students, ages 14-18, 9-12th grade
Affiliation: Lamoille South Supervisory Union
Governance by teachers and principal
Teacher qualifications: alt ed experience
Project-oriented; theme-based; hands-on; forestry, conser-
vation and agriculture; extensive field trips; rural location;
transportation; interns accepted.

Goddard College
Plainfield, VT 05667
Peter Burns, Admissions Director, 802-434-8311
Boarding, non-profit
450 students
Governance by collaborative models involving staff, faculty,
students, administration
Experiential, Dewey approach; student-designed BA, MA, MFA;
on old farm estate; for independent, creative individuals
who write well, read extensively; on and off-campus programs; no letter grades.

Maplehilll Community School
POBox 248, Plainfield, VT 05667
Karen Heath, 802-454-7747
Type: independent
Students mainly at-risk

New School,Inc
PO Box 378, Plainfield, VT 05667
Susan Remington, 802-454-8534
Type: independent

Green Mount Valley School
RR1 Box 166, Waitsfield, VT 05673
Cavid Gavett, 802-496-2150
Type: independent

Vermont Home Schoolers (1985)
RD 2 Box 1775, Plainfield, VT 05677
Mary Harris, Secretary/Treasurer, 802-454-8555
Assists in writing education plans, dealing with VT DE hear-
ings; interns accepted.

Washington County Homeschool Group
PO Box 111, Waterbury Center, VT 05677
Anne Marie Parker, 802-244-5351

Green Mountain Waldorf School (1982)
RR 1 Box 4885, Wolcott, VT 05680
Karen Case Talbert, Adm, 802-888-2828
Non-profit; tuition: $2,755/yr, scholarships
9 teachers, 76 students, ages 3-12, pre K-6th grade
Affiliation: AWSNA
Governance by faculty, board, administrator
Environment; oral tradition; extensive field trips; multi-aged
classes; rural location; transportation.

Mountain View Community School
PO Box 202, Rutland, VT 05702
Teresa Miele, 802-775-4067
Type: independent; tuition: $2,100/yr, scholarships
40 students, pre K-2nd grade
Developmentally-appropriate; childcare; multi-aged classes.

Holistic Education Press
(See Resource Section)

Smokey House Project (1974)
RFD Box 292, Danby, VT 05739
Lynn Bondurant, 802-293-5121
Type: independent
Students mainly at-risk, ages 14-19
Natural resource mgmt; trained adult crew leaders in
forestry, agriculture; work experience; community partner-
ships; Benchmarking; work transition.

Eckerd Wilderness
RR 2 Box 6800, Fair Haven, VT 05743-9112
Mike Kydd, 802-537-4101
Type: independent
Students mainly at-risk

Bridge School
PO Box 27, Midddlebury, VT 05753
Gerry Loney, 802-388-3498
Type: independent

Atrium Society
(See Resource Section)

Gailer School
19 Shannon St, Middlebury, VT 05753
Harry Chaucer, 802-388-0830
Type: independent

Middlebury Union High School AEP (1982)
Charles Ave, Middlebury, VT 05753
Rodney Morris, 802-388-4460
Type: public at-risk
4 teachers, 25 students, ages 12-18, 9-12th grade
Governance by principal and board
Voc; job placement; case mgmt; comprehensive planning;
work/study; multi-aged classes; extensive field trips.

Vermont Homeschool Association
RR 1, Box 6680, Middletown Springs, VT 05757
Debbie Kniffin

North Hollow School
PO Box 358, Rochester, VT 05767
Judy Geller, 802-767-3580
Type: independent

Addison County Home Schoolers
RD 1, PO Box 150, Salisbury, VT 05769
Leigh Harder, 802-388-2005

Project Rediscovery
25 Western Ave, St Johnsbury, VT 05819
D. James King or Howard Crawford, 802-748-8912, 748-8171
Type: public choice
JH
Career awareness; vocational; family involvement; behavior management; school/community partnerships; comprehensive planning process.

School of Human Service (1978)
PO Box 66 Emerson Falls Rd, St Johnsbury, VT 05819
800-444-1812, FAX: 802-748-5719

Type: higher education, non-profit; tuition: $6,000/yr, scholarships
12 teachers, 70 students, partly at-risk
Affiliation: Springfield College
Teacher qualifications: MA/MS or equivalent
Work related; portfolio-based; rural location; interns accepted.

Northeast Kingdom Homeschool Group
RD 1, PO Box 37, Irasburg, VT 05845
802-754-8780

Caledonia County Homeschool Group
PO Box 55, Lyndon Center, VT 05850
Colleen LaRiviere, 802-626-9503

Creative Beginnings/Creative Beginnings Too
2180 Sidewinder/1800 Prospector Ave, Park City, VT 84060
802-645-7315, FAX: 649-4097
Type: Montessori; tuition: $250-500/mo
1 teacher, 10 assistants, 111 students, ages infant-6
Affiliation: AMI
Governance by administrator
Childcare; transportation.

Virginia

Montessori School of Northern Virginia (1962)
6820 Pacific Ln, Annandale, VA 22003
Betsy Mitchell, 703-256-9577
Non-profit; tuition: $2,440-4,585/yr
5 teachers, 5 assistants, 129 students, mainly international, ages infant-9
Affiliation: AMS
Governance by administrator, board of trustees
Custom built; in secluded area surrounded by parkland; childcare; suburban location; transportation; interns accepted.

Hope Montessori School
4614 Ravensworth Rd, Annandale, VA 22003-5641

Linton Hall
9535 Linton Hall Rd, Bristow, VA 22013
Glenna Smith
Type: Montessori

New School of Northern Virginia (1989)
9431 Silver King Court, Fairfax, VA 22031
John Potter, 703-691-3041
Type: independent, non-profit; tuition: $7,700/yr, scholarships
9 teachers, 70 students, ages 5-18, K-12th grade
Affiliation: NCACS
Governance by Head, staff, students.
Self-directed; community issues, Socratic, experiential; many Summerhillian values; uses H. Gardner's multiple intelligences; no letter grades; multi-aged classes; extensive field; trips; non-compulsory class attendance; suburban location; interns accepted.

Montessori School of Cedar Lane
3035 Cedar Ln, Fairfax, VA 22031-2100
Lance Gilbert

Montessori School of Holmes Run (1973)
3527 Gallows Road, Falls Church, VA 22042
Judith W. Clarke, Head, 703-573-7652
4 teachers, 2 assistants, 76 students, ages 3-12
Affiliation: AMS

Governance by principal
Strong parent participation; suburban location; interns accepted.

Falls Church Children's House of Montessori
3335 Annandale Rd, Falls Church, VA 22042-3721

Montessori Children's Center
6103 Arlington Blvd, Falls Church, VA 22044

Montessori Country School (1971)
621 Alabama Dr, Herndon, VA 22070
Pat Kretsch, Adm, 703-437-8285
Non-profit; tuition: $2,290/3,120/yr
8 teachers, 4 assistants, 115 students, mainly international, ages 3-6
Governance by board
Suburban location; interns accepted.

The Learning Community Inc
PO Box 5177, Herndon, VA 22070
Type: home-based

Montessori School of Herndon (1984)
840 Dranesville Rd, Herndon, VA 22070-3019
Nasim Mallick Khan, Dir, 703-437-8229
Tuition: Variable
8 teachers, 12 assistants; student ages 3-12
Affiliations: AMS, NAEYC
Governance by administrator and democratic school meeting
4-acres; computers in each class; daily French; after school clubs, music, dance, karate; strong PTA; childcare; suburban location.

Douglass Community School
407 E Market St, Leesburg, VA 22075
Laurraine G. Landolt, Prin

Reston Montessori School (1987)
1928 Isaac Newton Sq W, Reston, VA 22090
Kathleen Lanfear, Dir, 703-481-2922
Tuition: $300-840/mo
8 teachers, 150 students, ages 2.5-9

Affiliations: AMS, NAEYC, VAMA
Governance by administrator
Kindermusik/Orff; French for ages 2.5-6; French bilingual for ages 6-9; childcare; suburban location; interns accepted.

Montessori School of McLean (1973)
1711 Kirby Rd, McLean, VA 22101
Dorothy P. DiDio, Head, 703-790-1049, FAX: 703-790-1962
Non-profit; tuition: $3,400-4,100/yr
7 teachers, 7 assistants, 165 students, mainly international, ages 3-9
Affiliation: AMS
Governance by board
Professional art program for ages 5+; near Washington, DC; suburban location; interns accepted.

National-Louis University's Northern Virginia/ Washington, DC Center (1986)
8000 Westpart Dr Suite 125, McLean, VA 22101
Dr Robert Skenes, Assoc Prof, 703-749-3000
Non-profit; scholarships
Students mainly employed, ages 22+
Governance by faculty and student reps
15 students/class; practical, applied learning; BS, Master's degrees; suburban location.

The Brooksfield School (1987)
1830 Kirby Rd, McLean, VA 22101
Mary Anne Duthis, 703-356-5437, FAX: same
Type: Montessori, non-profit; tuition: $3,900-15,500/yr
5 teachers, 4 assistants, 73 students, mainly international, ages 3-9
Affiliations: AMS, NAYEC
Governance by administrator
Cultural studies; individualized; emphasis on language and arts; childcare; suburban location; interns accepted.

Ridgemont Montessori School
6519 Georgetown Pike, Mc Lean, VA 22101-2223
Mary Beth Humen

Center (1991)
8220 Conner Dr, Manassas, VA 22110
Dr. Ed Doyle, Prin, 703-361-9808, FAX: 703-361-2864
Type: public at-risk
70 students, ages 13-18, 7-12th grade
Partnership with George Mason U; mobile classroom; community outreach; suburban location; interns accepted.

Elementary Montessori School of Oakton
PO Box 412, Oakton, VA 22124-0412

Montessori School of Oakton
12113 Vale Rd, Oakton, VA 22124-2222

Home School Legal Defense Association
(See Resource Section)

St Mark's Montessori School (1968)
5800 Backlick Rd, Springfield, VA 22150
Judith Carter-Sanford, Dir, 703-451-4470
Non-profit; tuition: $180/220/mo
3 teachers, 3 assistants, 71 students, mainly international, ages 3-6
Affiliation: AMI
Governance by administrator and board of trustees
Childcare; suburban location.

The Springs School
5407 Backlick Rd, Springfield, VA 22151-3915
Cathy Shields
Type: Montessori

Home Instruction Support Group
217 Willow Terr, Sterling, VA 22170

Green Hedges School
415 Windover Ave NW, Vienna, VA 22180-4232
Type: Montessori

LEARN/Northern Virginia Homeschoolers
2520 Rocky Branch Rd, Vienna, VA 22181
Marta Krause

Cardinal Montessori (1992)
1424 G St, Woodbridge, VA 22191
Leneale A. Gallegos, Dir, 703-491-3810
Tuition: $2,250/3,500/yr
3 teachers, 1 assistant, 40 students, ages 3-9
Affiliation: AMS
Governance by administrator
Childcare; suburban location; interns accepted.

Richard M. Milburn School (1975)
14416 Jefferson Davis Hwy Suite 12, Woodbridge, VA 22191
Robert H. Crosby, Pres
Type: independent at-risk
Corporation runs 7 alt HS's in VA and two in MA under contract with public schools; 90% of students stay in school or graduate

Edelen's Montessori Learning Center
1337 Horner Rd, Woodbridge, VA 22191-1722

Francis Scott Key School
2300 Key Blvd, Arlington, VA 22201-3415
Type: Montessori

Montessori Children's Creative Center, Inc
3809 Washington Blvd, Arlington, VA 22201-4514

Hoffman-Boston Public School
1415 S Queen St, Arlington, VA 22204-4739
Type: Montessori

Drew Model School (1971)
3500 S 24th St, Arlington, VA 22206
Dr Michael Grinder, Prin, 703-358-5825
Type: Public choice Montessori
20 teachers, 410 students, ages 3-11, pre K-5th grade
Governance by teachers, principal
Teacher qualifications: VA certification
Cooperative learning; no letter grades; multi-aged classes; interns accepted.

Chesterbrook Montessori School
3455 N Glebe Rd, Arlington, VA 22207
Judy Balcazar-Mercill, 703-241-8271
Tuition: $2,600/3,000/yr
3 teachers, 2 assistants, 60 students, mainly international, ages 3-6
Affiliation: AMS
Governance by administrator
Emphasis on music, singing; Spanish; suburban location; interns accepted.

H. B. Woodlawn High School
City As School Program (1987)
4100 Vacation Lane, Arlington, VA 22207
Deneen Snow, 703-358-6376
Type: public choice
10 students

H-B Woodlawn Program (1971)
4100 N Vacation Lane, Arlington, VA 22207
Ray Anderson, Prin, 703-358-6363, FAX: 703-358-6383
Type: public choice
41 teachers, 522 students, 6-12th grade
Governance by democratic school meeting
Students primarily responsible for use of time, behavior, goal setting, school governanc; interns accepted.

Key Elementary School-Partial Immersion
2300 Key Blvd, Arlington, VA 22207
Katharine G. Panfel, Prin, 703-358-4210
Type: public choice
58 teachers, 703 students, ages 3-12
Affiliation: SACS

Governance by staff
Teacher qualifications: VA certification, bilingual
Spanish bilingual; extensive field trips; multi-aged classes;
   interns accepted.

Montessori Chesterbrook School
3455 N Glebe Rd, Arlington, VA 22207

Glebe School
1770 N Glebe Rd, Arlington, VA 22207-2098
Type: Montessori

Aquinas Montessori School
8334 Mount Vernon Hwy, Alexandria, VA 22309-1998
Kathleen H Futrell

Gyldenlove School
3709 Colonial Ave, Alexandria, VA 22309-2546
Type: Montessori

Montessori School of Alexandria, Inc (1969)
6300 Florence Ln, Alexandria, VA 22310-2200
Jean Adolphi, Administrator, 703-960-3498, FAX: same
Non-profit; tuition: $3,150/4,250/4,995/yr
4 teachers, 4 assistants, 108 students, ages infant-12
Governance by board
Emphasis on students' independence, joy of learning, and
   choosing appropriate work; childcare.

Institute for Alternative Futures
(See Resource Section)

Old Town Montessori School
115 S Washington St, Alexandria, VA 22314-3028

Home Educators Network
3320 Waverly Dr, Fredericksburg, VA 22401

Fredericksburg Montessori
312 Sophia St, Fredericksburg, VA 22401-6057

School Within a School at Stafford High School (1989)
33 Stafford Indian Ln, Falmouth, VA 22405
Walt Breede, 703-371-7200, FAX: -2389
Type: public at-risk
4 teachers
Contracts; max 15/class; guest speakers; team teaching;
   motivational games; mini-courses.

Winchester Montessori School
1905 Henry Ave, Winchester, VA 22601-6309

Seton Home Study School (1975)
1350 Progress Dr, Front Royal, VA 22630
Dr Mary Kay Clark, 703-636-9990, FAX:-1602
Cost: $500/yr, scholarships
35 teachers, 6300 students, K-12th grade
Governance by board
Catholic curriculum in all subject areas.

Home Educators Association of Virginia
PO Box 1810, Front Royal, VA 22630-1810
703-635-9322

Children's Center Montessori
PO Box 184, Strasburg, VA 22657-0184

Core Knowledge Foundation
(See Resource Section)

Elementary Montessori
RR 13 Box 53, Charlottesville, VA 22901

Montessori Community School (1982)
Rt 13, PO Box 53, Charlottesville, VA 22901
Laurie Curtin, Adm, 804-979-8886
Non-profit
4 teachers, 3 assistants, 54 students, ages 3-12
Governance by teachers, administrators and a board of
   trustees
Rural location; interns accepted.

Montessori School of Charlottesville
631 Cutler Ln, Charlottesville, VA 22901-3901
Lindsey Schwab

Living Education Center for Ecology and the Arts (1993)
PO Box 2612, Charlottesville, VA 22902
Ernie & Sue Reed, Dirs, 804-971-1647
Type: home-based, non-profit; cost: variable
2 teachers, 15 students, ages 13–18
Affiliation: Oak Meadow School
Governance by directors
Individualized; student/parent responsibility for education
   emphasized; community resources; non-compulsory class
   attendance; multi-aged classes; urban location.

Children's Montessori School
109 E Jefferson St, Charlottesville, VA 22902-5103
Bliss Abbot or Penny Gorman

Elementary Montessori School of Charlottesville
1901 Thomson Rd, Charlottesville, VA 22903
Dan Roell

University Montessori School (1978)
322 Monte Vista Ave, Charlottesville, VA 22903
Michele Mattioli, Dir, 804-977-0583
4 teachers, 3 assistants, 36 students, mainly international,
   ages infant-6
Affiliations: AMS, NAEYC
Governance by administrator
Actiive community of students, parents, teachers; childcare;
   suburban location; interns accepted.

Elementary School of Charlottesville
401 Alderman Rd, Charlottesville, VA 22903-2403
Type: Montessori

**BRANCH: Blue Ridge Area Network for Congenial
   Homeschoolers** (1991)
Rt 3, PO Box 602, Afton, VA 22920
Joan Cichon, Founder/Coordinator, 703-456-9822
Reconciling religious and secular groups; newsletter; 4-H;
   drama; writer's club; languages; arts and crafts; camping;
   no letter grades; multi-aged classes; extensive field trips;
   rural location.

North Branch School (1983)
Rt 1, Box 386, Afton, VA 22920
Charlotte Zinsser Booth, Head teacher, 703-456-8450
Type: independent, non-profit; tuition: $20-320/mo,
   scholarships
11 teachers, 95 students, ages 3-14, nursery-8th grade
Governance by teachers and principal, board; all students and
   parents are polled per issues, discuss solutions.
Teacher qualifications: flexible, prefer alternative ed
   experience
11-acre site, woods, meadows, stream, mountain views;
   strong music, movement, drama; board works toward
   diversity of student body; extended-family context; no
   letter grades; multi-aged classes; extensive field trips; rural
   location.

Crossroads Waldorf School (1982)
Rt 3 Box 189, Crozet, VA 22932
Priscilla Friedberg, Coord, 804-823-6800
Non-profit; tuition: $2,810-4,350/yr
21 teachers, 185 students, ages 3-13, pre K-7th grade
Governance by teachers, principal, and board
Teacher qualifications: certification, higher ed degree,
   Waldorf training, experience
Rural location; interns accepted.

Waynesboro High School Alternative Program
Blue Ridge Community College
Wayne Hills Center, Waynesboro, VA 22980
George Buzzard
Type: public choice

Gloucester Montessori School
Business Rt 17, Gloucester, VA 23061-1506
Patricia Landau

To Kids-For Kids-By Kids Newsletter
(See Resource Section)

Sunrise Montessori
856-A Longhill Rd, Williamsburg, VA 23185

Williamsburg Montessori School (1982)
4214 Longhill Rd, Williamsburg, VA 23188
Carlotta P. Cundari, Adm, 804-565-0977
Non-profit; tuition: $2,550-5,472/yr
7 teachers, 4 assistants, 67 students, ages infant-6
Accreditation: AMS
Governance by administrator, board
Childcare; rural location; interns accepted.

Open Senior High School
600 S Pine St, Richmond, VA 23220
Brenda Drew, 804-780-4661
Type: magnet
9-12th grade
Community-based.

The Governor's School for International Studies (1991)
4100 W Grace St, Richmond, VA 23221
Dr Steven E. Ballowe, Dir, 510-780-6155, FAX: -6043
Type: public choice
47 teachers, 400 students, ages 11-17, 9-12th grade
Governance by principal
Teacher qualifications: Master's, PhD, or in progress
Interdisciplinary; multi-aged classes; extensive field trips;
interns accepted.

George Wythe High School
4314 Crutchfield St, Richmond, VA 23225
James Bynum, 904-780-5037
Type: magnet
9-12th grade
Visual and performing arts.

Southside Montessori School
7833 Brentford, Richmond, VA 23225
Pamela Ranson

Richmond Community High School
5800 Patterson Ave, Richmond, VA 23226
Pamela Trotter-Cornell

Thomas H. Henderson Model School
4319 Old Brook Rd, Richmond, VA 23227
Harold Fitrer, 804-780-8288
Type: magnet
6-8th grade
School within a school.

Richmond Montessori School
499 Parham Rd, Richmond, VA 23229-7217
Nelda Nutter

Burger King Academy at Meadowbrook High School
4901 Cogbill Rd, Richmond, VA 23234
Jamie Accashian, Site Coord, 804-743-3675 x42
Type: public at-risk
3 teachers, 54 students, ages 14-20, 9-12th grade
Affiliations: Burger King, City in Schools
Governance by site coord, principal, faculty and student reps
Teacher qualifications: current degree
Computers; degree program at night; extensive field trips;
suburban location; transportation.

Virginia Commonwealth University TEP
School of Education, Richmond, VA 23284
Type: Montessori teacher education

The Robert Muller School
905 Clear Springs Ct, Chesapeake, VA 23320
Dr Catherine K Clark, 804-548-9030

Montessori School of Learning
2004 Dock Landing Rd, Chesapeake, VA 23321

Montessori Preparatory School
4032 Maple Dr, Chesapeake, VA 23321-1915
Marilyn Jennings

Montessori Harmony School
2100 Christopher Dr, Chesapeake, VA 23321-2004

Chesapeake Alternative (1975)
920 Minuteman Rd, Chesapeake, VA 23323
J.E. Thompkins, Prin, 804-494-7620
Type: public at-risk
17 teachers, 120 students, mainly at-risk, ages 12-18, 7-10th
grade
Governance by principal
Individualized; clearly defined limits; strictly enforced consequences for inappropriate behavior; urban location; transportation; interns accepted.

Home Free
PO Box 562, Virginia Beach, VA 23451
JR DuBois

Virginia Beach Friends School
1537 Laskin Rd, Virginia Beach, VA 23451
Phyllis Sullivan, Head, 804-428-7534
Type: Quaker

Bayshore Learning Center
1608 Pleasure House Rd #112, Virginia Beach, VA 23455
Kinney Glascock
Type: Montessori

St Nicholas Montessori
4425 Monmouth Castle Rd, Virginia Beach, VA 23455
Nancy Guarnieri

Open Campus High School
4400 Virginia Beach Blvd, Virginia Beach, VA 23462
Lillian J. Donnally, Prin

Montessori Children's House
700 Hillingdon Ct, Virginia Beach, VA 23462-6455

**Beach Educators Association for Creative
Homeschooling (BEACH)**
1305 White Marlin Ln, Virginia Beach, VA 23464
804-474-0389

Summit School and Montessori Center
1100 Indian Lakes Blvd, Virginia Beach, VA 23464-6012
Louise Becerra

Ghent Montessori School (1978)
610 Mowbray Arch, Norfolk, VA 23507
Sarah Frost, Owner, 804-622-8174
Tuition: $1,625-4,220/yr
8 teachers, 6 assistants, 119 students, ages infant-12
Accreditation: AMS
Governance by administrator
Childcare; urban location; interns accepted.

Virginia Montessori School
818 Jacinth Cir, Newport News, VA 23602-3526

Hampton Roads Montessori School (1991)
12749 Nettles Dr, Newport News, VA 23606-1870
Carol Frieden, Business Dir, 804-930-9545
Non-profit
3 teachers, 3 assistants, 75 students, mainly international,
ages 3-6
Affiliation: VAMA; accreditation: AMI
Governance by teachers and administrators, board
Childcare; interns accepted.

Peninsula Montessori School
372 Hiden Blvd, Newport News, VA 23606-2934
Mary McIntosh

Beachside Alternative School (1983)
710 Buckroe Ave, Hampton, VA 23664
Benjamin C. Rich, Prin, 804-850-5068, FAX: -5072
Type: public at-risk
23 teachers, 301 students, mainly at-risk, ages 13-18, 8-12th
  grade
Affiliations: Hampton Univ, Thomas Nelson CC
Governance by teachers and principal
Teacher qualifications: state certification
Five programs; multi-aged classes; urban location;
  transportation.

Montessori Harmony School
PO Box 3505, Portsmouth, VA 23701

Montessori School of Learning
PO Box 6102, Portsmouth, VA 23703-0102

Portsmouth Public Schools
3651 Hartford St, Portsmouth, VA 23707
Daisy Murphy
Type: Montessori

Center (1992)
PO Box 190, Boydton, VA 23917
E.A. Lyons, Asst Supt or M.G. Walker, Dir of Student Support,
  738-6111, FAX: -6679
Type: public at-risk
3 teachers, 42 students, ages 11-21, 6-12th grade
Governance by teachers, principal, board
GED prep; multi-aged classes; rural location; transportation.

Highland Park Learning Center
1212 Fifth St SW, Roanoke, VA 24016
John Lensch, 703-981-2963
Type: magnet
K-5th grade
Continuous progress; experiential.

Forest Park New American School
2730 Melrose Ave NW, Roanoke, VA 24017
Judith Gorham, 703-981-2923
Type: magnet
K-5th grade
Cultures; commununications; problem solving.

Westside Elementary of Performing Arts
1441 Westside Blvd NW, Roanoke, VA 24017
Linda Wright, 703-981-2697
Type: magnet
K-5th grade

The Children's House
4515 Brandleton Rd, Roanoke, VA 24018
Judith Larson
Type: Montessori

Community School (1971)
7815 Williamson Rd, Roanoke, VA 24019
Tina Dawson, Director, 703-563-5036
Type: independent, home-based, non-profit; cost: $2,750-
  3,200, scholarships
20 teachers, 140 students, ages 3-14
Affiliation: NCACS
Governance by board
Builds on child's natural curiosity; teachers monitor mastery
  skills; relaxed atmosphere; diverse population; earth ed
  program with organic farm; community ecological systems
  study; internships; no letter grades; multi-aged classes;
  extensive field trips; suburban location; interns accepted.

Blacksburg New School
1660 Whipple Dr, Blacksburg, VA 24060
Type: independent

Montessori Children's House of Blacksburg
703 Tall Oaks Dr, Blacksburg, VA 24060-4400

Oak Meadow School (1975)
PO Box 712, Blacksburg, VA 24063
Lawrence T. Williams, EdD, Dir, 703-552-3263, FAX: 703-552-
  9474
scholarships
30 teachers, 1,000 students, ages 5-18, K-12th grade
Governance by teachers and Prin
Teacher qualifications: BS or BA; completion of teacher training program
Home study only: curr materials, diploma programs; Waldorf
  inspired; telecommunications program for grades 5-12;
  interns accepted.

Blacksburg Montessori School
PO Box 684, Blacksburg, VA 24063-0684
Lynne Knox

Schwartz-Gralla Homeschool (1981)
Rt 1 Box 43, Check, VA 24072
Randye Schwartz, 703-651-3971
Non-profit
2 teachers, 2 students, ages 9-12
Governance by democratic school meeting
Teacher qualifications: certification
Small homestead in Blue Ridge Mtns; family works on raising
  food, repairing and building projects, community service,
  travel; no letter grades.

Pulaski County High School Alternative Program
5414 Cougar Trail Rd, Dublin, VA 24084
Kelly Fitzpatrick, Coordinator, 703-674-8659
Type: public at-risk
6 teachers, 40 students, ages 13-17, 9-10th grade
Governance by teachers and principal
Teacher qualifications: state certification
Contracts; cooperative learning; volunteer college student
  tutor-assistants; rural location; transportation.

Blue Mountain School (1981)
Rt 3, Box 211, Floyd, VA 24091
Chrys Bason, Administrator, 703-745-4234
Type: independent, non-profit; tuition: $125/mo, scholarships
3 teachers, 22 students, ages 3-12, pre K-7th grade
Governance by parent cooperative, council
On 8 wooded acres near town; no letter grades; rural loca-
  tion; interns accepted.

YES Program at G.W. Carver Middle School (1987)
Rt 4 Box 800, Martinsville, VA 24112
Fredrick Lockhart, Instructor, 703-957-2226
Type: public at-risk
50 teachers, 460 students, ages 11-13, 6-8th grade
Governance by principal
Teacher qualifications: VA Certification
Basic life skills; incentives; rural location; transportation.

Children's Circle (1986)
Rt 1, Box 132A, Mouth of Wilson, VA 24363
Deborah Greif, 703-579-4252
Type: home-based, non-profit
8 teachers; student ages 2-13
Governance by parent cooperative
Crafts, drama, puppets, science, nature projects; games;
  rural location.

Staunton Montessori School
Box 722, Staunton, VA 24402
Linda Grogan, Dir, 703-885-4301
Non-profit; tuition: $1,800/2,200/yr
1 teacher, 1 assistant, 28 students, ages 3-6
Affiliation: NAMTA; accreditation: AMI
Governance by board
Teacher qualifications: 21 years AMI experience
In historic Italianate house on Stuart Hall campus; rural loca-
  tion; interns accepted.

Regional Alternative Program (1993)
Rt 3 Boyshome, Covington, VA 24426
Dwayne Ross, Dir, 703-965-1118, FAX: 703-965-3445
Type: public at-risk
7 teachers, 22 students, ages 17–19, 9–12th grade
Governance by teachers and principal
GED prep; unstructured; hands-on; no letter grades; extensive field trips; multi-aged classes; transportation.

Bear Mountain Outdoor School (1987)
Hightown, VA 24444
Thomas Brody, Owner/Dir, 703-468-2700
Type: higher education, boarding
560-acre farm; workshops in appropriate tech, ecology, sustainable ag, homebuilding.

Montessori Center for Children (1992)
2 Dold Pl, Lexington, VA 24450
Shirley Ziegler, Dir, 703-463-6461, FAX: 703-463-1141
Non-profit; tuition: $2,000/2,700/yr
1 teacher, 1 assistant, 25 students, ages 3–6
Affiliations: AMI, AMS, NAMTA
Governance by administrator and board of trustees
Rural location; interns accepted.

Shenendoah Country Day School (1993)
Route 5 Box 394, Lexington, VA 24450
Tom McNalley, 703-463-7246
Type: independent
2 teachers, 15 students, ages 6–11
Integrated curriculum; French, German, musical instruments, hands-on science; whole language; no letter grades; non-compulsary class attendance; extensive field trips; multi-aged classes.

Snakefoot School (1989)
PO Box 189, Lexington, VA 24450
Lenna Ojure, Board Member, 703-463-9645
Type: home-based, non-profit; cost: 1,125/yr, scholarships
2 teachers, 14 students, ages 6–14, 1–7th grade
Governance by parent cooperative, board
Teacher qualifications: state certification, experience, compatible philosophy
3 days/wk on-site; no letter grades; multi-aged classes; rural location; interns accepted.

National Consortium of Specialized Secondary Schools of Mathematics, Science and Technology
Governor's School, 3020 Ward's Ferry Rd, Lynchburg, VA 24502
Cheryl Lindeman, Pres, 804-582-1104
National group of several dozen schools.

Lynchburg Montessori School
PO Box 3061, Lynchburg, VA 24503-0061

Legacy
Rte 4 Box 265-MT, Bedford, VA 24523
Type: Montessori

Cherry Hill Montessori School
PO Box 2722, Danville, VA 24541-0722
Grace Thomas

Blue Ridge Montessori School (1982)
Rt 4 Box 47, Forest, VA 24551
Tom Taylor, Dir, 804-525-0061
Tuition: $1,450-1,800/yr
1 teacher, 1 assistant, 30 students, ages 3–6
Affiliation: AMS
Governance by administrator
Suburban location; interns accepted.

Program; Halifax-S Boston (1977)
PO Box 1849, Halifax, VA 24558
Charles C. Edwards, Jr, Coord, 804-476-3114, FAX:-1858
Type: public at-risk
9 teachers, 100 students, ages 14–21, 7–12th grade
Governance by teachers, principal, board
Teacher qualifications: Master of Ed, experience
Evenings; transferable credits; computers; low ratio; rural location; interns accepted.

VA Association
(See Resource Section)

National Institute for Christian Home Education
(See Resource Section)

Washington

Auburn Alternative Junior High School (1974)
615 15th St SW, Auburn, WA 98001
Dr Largo Wales, Adm, 206-931-4992
Type: public choice
2 teachers, 40 students, ages 12–15
Self-paced.

Creative Montessori
14904 Juanita Dr, Bothell, WA 98001
Alice B Evans

St Nicholas Montessori School
31015 Military Rd S, Auburn, WA 98001-3218
Susan Ennaro

West Auburn Senior High (1971)
401 W Main St, Auburn, WA 98002
Bob Wiley, Prin, 206-931-4990
10 teachers, 250 students, ages 14–21, 9–12th grade
Social responsibility; vocational; contract night school; day care/teen parenting combination; self-paced JH class; Reading Lab.

Contract Based Education (1981)
31455 28th Ave S, Federal Way, WA 98003
Bob Kohn, Coord, 206-941-8237,-9417
Type: public at-risk

Spring Valley Montessori School
36605 Pacific Hwy S, Federal Way, WA 98003-7499
Gulsevin Kayihan

Bellevue Montessori School
2411-112th NE, Bellevue, WA 98004

Montessori Teacher College Northwest
2411 112th Ave NE, Bellevue, WA 98004
Type: Montessori teacher education

Puget Sound Community School
1715 112th Ave NE, Bellevue, WA 98004
Andy Smallman, 206-455-7617
Type: home-based
1 teacher, 10 students
Resource teacher; field trips; computer networking.

The Little School (1959)
2812 116th St NE, Bellevue, WA 98004
Lorna Greene, Director, 206-927-8708
Type: independent, non-profit
14 teachers, 170 students, ages 3-12, ungraded
Affiliations: NAIS, PNAIS, NAEYC
Governance by board with input from faculty and parents
Teacher qualifications: WA credential, experience
11-acre site; self contained classroom developmental groups; emergent curriculum; whole language; multi-ethnic awareness; required parental observation; narrative evaluations. Teacher education program affiliated with Pacific Oaks College; no letter grades; multi-aged classes; suburban location.

Cougar Mountain Montessori (1978)
4442 158th Ave, SE, Bellevue, WA 98006
Eileen Peterson, 206-747-5029
Tuition: $285/450/mo
4 teachers, 4 assistants, 37 students, ages infant-6
Accreditation: AMS
Governance by administrator
Large playground adjacent to woods; bunnies, gerbils, fish, birds, cat and goat; childcare; suburban location; interns accepted.

Off Campus High School (1970)
14200 SE 13th Pl, Bellevue, WA 98007
Phil Barber, 206-455-6183
Type: public choice
17 teachers, 255 students, ages 14-21, 9-12th grade
Student-centered; individualized; competency-based; student input; self-paced; flexible schedule; year-round; open exit/entry; tutorials; teen parenting.

Absorbent Mind Montessori
15653 NE 6th, Bellevue, WA 98008
Henrietta Walker

Eton School (1978)
2701 Bel-Red Rd, Bellevue, WA 98008
Dr Patricia Feltin, 206-881-4230
Type: Montessori; tuition: $2,700-6,800/yr
16 teachers, 12 assistants, 324 students, ages 3-15
Affiliations: AMS, PNAIS, PNMA
Governance by administrator
National Blue Ribbon Award Winner, '91-92; Montessori Timeline approach; childcare; suburban location; interns accepted.

Olympus Northwest (1974)
16247 NE 24th St, Bellevue, WA 98008
Jan Fluter, Head Tch, 206-455-6152
Type: public choice
5 teachers, 110 students, ages 11-14, 6-8th grade
Governance by council of students, parents, staff
Teacher qualifications: K-8 or 6-8 Certification
Non-traditional; liberal arts; home groups integral to process; no letter grades; multi-aged classes; extensive field trips; suburban location; interns accepted.

Lake Hills Montessori
114 157th Ave NE, Bellevue, WA 98008-4336

The International School (1991)
301 151st Pl NE, Bellevue, WA 98009-9010
Terry LaRussa Banton, 206-455-6266
Type: public choice
6 teachers, 400 students, ages 11-18, 6-12th grade
Inclusive; interdisciplinary; team efforts; cooperative learning; independent study; mentorships; year-round; Bellevue Children's Theater; extensive field trips.

Evergreen Academy (1977)
16017 118th Pl NE, Bothell, WA 98011
Krista McKee, Head, 206-488-8000, FAX: 206-488-0994
Type: Montessori; tuition: $2,000-3,950/yr

4 teachers, 5 assistants, 75 students, ages 3-6
Affiliation: PNAIS; accreditations: NAEYC, NASC
Governance by administrator
French; computers; childcare; suburban location; transportation.

Homeschoolers Organized for Meaningful Education (HOME)
10352 NE 141st St, Bothell, WA 98011

Duvall Montessori School
217 Main St, Duvall, WA 98019

SnoValley Homeschool Association
PO Box 1244, Duvall, WA 98019
Connie Douvier, 206-788-0149

Madrona Elementary School (1985)
9300 236th SW, Edmonds, WA 98020
Joe Rice, Prin, 206-670-7980
Type: public choice
11 teachers, 280 students, ages 5-13
Students stay in multi-aged units for three year periods with same teacher; competency-based; foreign language; school-based management; parent involvement.

Pacific Montessori Learning Center
23700 104th Ave W, Edmonds, WA 98020
Nancy Kesteek

Washington Homeschool Organization (WHO) (1986)
18130 Midvale Ave N Suite C, Seattle, WA 98020
206-546-9483, 298-8942, FAX: 206-546-1810
Non-profit
Inclusive; convention.

Edmonds Horizon Montessori School (1982)
700 Main St, Edmonds, WA 98020-3032
Rick Schleicher, Administrator, 206-742-0344
Tuition: $140/mo
3 teachers, 48 students, ages 3-6
Affiliation: UMA; accreditation: WFIS
Governance by administrator
Ballet, gymnastics, tai kwan do and music enhancement optional (at Cultural Center); urban location; interns accepted.

Whole Earth Montessori
2930 228th St SE, Bothell, WA 98021-8927

Tower Montessori School
1606 SW Dash Point Rd, Federal Way, WA 98023-4530

Issaquah Montessori School
22601 SE 56th St, Issaquah, WA 98027
Conleth Grotob

Sequoia Montessori School
24611 SE Mirrormont Dr, Issaquah, WA 98027
Meg Wade

Tiger Mountain High School (1975)
565 NW Holly St, Issaquah, WA 98027
Jeanne Hanson, Prin, 206-392-0840
Type: public choice
17 teachers, 95 students, ages 14-21
12-14 students/class; optional activities; pass/fail; computerized on network; community involvement; mini-courses; integrated SE; teen parenting; extensive field trips.

Clark Elementary School (1976)
565 NW Holly St, PO Box 7003, Issaquah, WA 98027-7003
Randy Fortenberry, Prin, 206-392-0813
Type: public choice
28 teachers, 425 students, ages 5-11, K-5th grade
Parents commit min 40 hrs/student/yr, participate in curriculum development; computer literacy; cooperative learning; mathematical problem solving; integrated curriculum.

Big Sky Montessori
14800 245th Ave SE, Issaquah, WA 98027-7322
Maggie Worrix-Hosking

Montessori Plus School (1971)
3410 S 272nd St, Kent, WA 98032-7802
Sharlet J. McClurkin, Dir, 206-859-2262, FAX: 206-859-1737
Non-profit; tuition: $180/mo
3 teachers, 5 assistants, 50 students, ages 3-6
Affiliation: PNMA; accreditation: MIA
Governance by board of trustees
International interns, primarily from Taiwan and Korea; suburban location; interns accepted.

Community Elementary (1960)
11133 NE 65th, Kirkland, WA 98033
Lynn Shebilske, Prin, 206-827-0735
Type: public choice
3 teachers, 78 students, 1-6th grade
Parents as instructional partners; multi-disciplinary; enriched discovery-type environment; whole child approach; split grades; fluid transition between grades; whole-school multi-age instruction and environment projects; partnership projects with JH and HS.

Blue Gables Montessori
11410 NE 124th St #349, Kirkland, WA 98034-4399

Montessori School
13446 NE 132nd St, Kirkland, WA 98034-5608

Brier Montessori Preschool & Kindergarten
24016 29 A West, Brier, WA 98036

Scriber Lake High School (1969)
19400 56th Ave W, Lynnwood, WA 98036
Karol L. Gadwa, Prin, 206-670-7270
Type: public choice
16 teachers, 250 students, ages 14-19
CAI; self-paced; teen parenting integrated with day care; mini-courses; Resource Room; career center; support groups; GED prep; fire service training; carpentry; ESL.

WALA, CLIP I-V (Contracted Learning for Individual Pacing) (1984)
3800 196th SW, Lynnwood, WA 98036
Karol Gadwa, Coord, 206-670-7270
8 teachers, 150 students, ages 14-20, 9-12th grade
Individualized; self-paced; flexible scheduling; competency-based; mentorships; community service; experiential learning; independent study; tutorials; seminars.

Teaching Parents Association
14004 Jefferson Way, Lynnwood, WA 98037
Mary Ehrmin, 206-742-7033
Type: home-based

Homeschoolers in FOCUS
17105 36th Ave W, Lynwood, WA 98037
Deane Schrader, 206-742-2521

Homeschoolers Support Association (1985)
PO Box 413, Maple Valley, WA 98038
Janice M. Hedin, 206-432-9805
Non-profit
Governance by board

Lake Wilderness Elementary School
24216 Witte Rd SE, Maple Valley, WA 98038-6827
Type: Montessori

Crest Learning Center (1971)
4150 86th Ave SE, Mercer Island, WA 98040
Michael Hagen, Head Tch, 206-236-3390
Type: public choice
5 teachers, 2 assistants, 115 students, ages 14-21, 9-12th grade

Northwest Montessori-Mercer Island
4545 Island Crest Way, Mercer Island, WA 98040-4443

Snoqualmie Valley Homeschoolers Co-op
42512 SE 170th Ct, North Bend, WA 98045
Melode Brewer, 206-888-0461

Parent Cooperative Elementary Program (1983)
PO Box 1602, Lynnwood, WA 98046
Pam Hurst; Teresa Henrichs, 206-670-7086
8 teachers, 180 students, ages 5-12
Required monthly meeting; min 90 hrs in-class time/yr/student; mini-courses; fund raising; voluntary pledge system; Math Their Way; Weekly Readers; computers; French; Spanish; ASL; extensive field trips.

Builder Books
(See Resource Section)

Cascadia Montessori School (1977)
4239 162nd Ave NE, Redmond, WA 98052
Marilyn Franklin, Dir, 206-881-1026
1 teacher, 2 assistants, 27 students, ages 6-9
Accreditations: AMS, WA BE
Governance by administrator
Teacher-parent communication; childcare; suburban location.

Marymoor Montessori
4244 Bel Red Rd, Redmond, WA 98052

Sammamish Montessori School (1977)
17411 NE Union Hill Rd #150, Redmond, WA 98052
Joan M Starling, Dir, 206-869-0804
Tuition: $209-418/mo
7 teachers, 20 assistants, 275 students, ages 3-6
Affiliations: NAMTA, NCME, MWEI
Governance by administrator
Childcare; interns accepted.

Cedar River School
15828 SE Jones Rd, Renton, WA 98058
Melissa Baker, Business Dir, 206-271-9614, FAX: same
Type: Montessori, non-profit; tuition: $270/495/mo
8 teachers, 4 assistants, 75 students, ages 3-15
Affiliation: NAMTA
Governance by board
16-acre farm with animals, garden; heated outdoor swimming pool; 12-mo program; childcare; rural location; interns accepted.

Teaching Parents Association
16109 NE 169th Pl, Woodinville, WA 98072
Type: home-based

Under the Apple Tree Magazine
Apple Tree Press
(See Resource Section)

Woodinville Montessori
13965 NE 166th St, Woodinville, WA 98072-9085

The Drinking Gourd, Harambee
(See Resource Section)

Pacific First Montessori Children's Center
1420 5th Ave, Seattle, WA 98101-2333

American Indian Heritage School (1969)
1330 N 90th St, Seattle, WA 98103
Robert Eaglestaff, Prin, 206-298-7801
Type: public choice
6 teachers, 109 students, ages 10-20, 6-12th grade
Indian Heritage values and traditions; sports based on traditional Indian sports: cross-country, basketball, track & field, Indian Dancing.

B.F. Day Elementary School
3921 Linden Ave N, Seattle, WA 98103
Carole Williams, 206-281-6340

Type: magnet
K–5th grade
World culture center.

Small Planet Montessori (1988)
2125 N 51st St, Seattle, WA 98103
Lucie Ury, Dir, 206-632-3434
Tuition: $185/mo
2 teachers, 2 assistants, 24 students, ages 3–6
Affiliations: AMS, NAMTA
Governance by administrator
Urban location; interns accepted.

Pacific Crest Montessori School
5555 Phinney Ave N, Seattle, WA 98103-5853

Northwest Montessori-Woodland Park
4910 Phinney Ave N, Seattle, WA 98103-6347

Highland Park Elementary
1012 SW Trenton St, Seattle, WA 98106
Venus Place-Barber, 206-281-6480
Type: magnet
K–5th grade
World culture center.

Rainbow Way Homeschool Group
5004 20th Av NW, Seattle, WA 98107
206-782-3071,-9076
Holt oriented.

Concord Elementary
723 S Concord St, Seattle, WA 98108
Toby Gonzales, 206-281-6320
Type: magnet
K–5th grade
World culture center.

Maple Elementary
4925 Corson Ave S, Seattle, WA 98108
Lynn Fuller, 206-281-6960
Type: magnet
K–5th grade
World culture center.

New Option Middle School (1990)
411 Boston, Seattle, WA 98109
Barbara Kuznetz, 206-281-6226
Type: public choice
5 teachers, 11 students, ages 12–18, 6–9th grade
Central theme is "Global Citizenship"; individual support;
     mutual trust; multi-cultural; parent participation.

Montessori Country School (1992)
10994 Arrow Pt Dr, Bainbridge Island, WA 98110
Patricia Christensen, Director, 842-4966
Non-profit; tuition: $800-3,750/yr
7 teachers, 95 students, ages infant-9
Affiliations: NAEYC, NW MA, NAMTA
Governance by board
2.5 acres; 35 minute ferry from Seattle; parent support;
     interns accepted.

Children's Montessori School on Bainbridge
PO Box 11127, Bainbridge Is, WA 98110-5127

II
1222 41st Ave E, Seattle, WA 98112

Minimax Montessori School
946 17th Ave E, Seattle, WA 98112

Montessori School of Seattle
720 18th E, Seattle, WA 98112
Steffani Mott, 206-325-0497
Tuition: $250-500/mo
3 teachers, 3 assistants, 70 students, ages 3–6
Affiliation: NAMTA

Governance by administrator
Within large parochial school; dance; Spanish; music; interns
     accepted.

Montessori School
720 18th Ave E, Seattle, WA 98112-3928

Bryant Elementary
3311 NE 60th, Seattle, WA 98115
Terry Acena, 206-281-6290
Type: magnet
K–5th grade
World culture center.

Children's World Montessori
7711 43rd NE, Seattle, WA 98115
Suzanne Haggard

New Horizons For Learning
(See Resource Section)

Northwest Montessori School (1965)
7400 25th Ave NE, Seattle, WA 98115
Jan Thorslund, Dir, 524-4244
Non-profit; tuition: $2,422-3,753/yr
11 teachers, 14 assistants, 195 students, mainly International,
     ages 3–12
Affiliation: NAMTA; accreditation: AMI
Governance by board
Spanish; 'going out' opportunities for elementary; childcare;
     sub/urban location; interns accepted.

Ballard Homeschoolers
7037 22nd Ave NW, Seattle, WA 98117
Marcy Ray, 206-789-1721

Cinquegranelli Montessori (1989)
3316 NW 68, Seattle, WA 98117
Gail Longo, 206-789-2942
Tuition: $250/390/mo
2 teachers, 22 students, ages 3–6
Affiliations: AMS, NAMTA, MIA
Governance by administrator
Italian language, culture; outdoor ed; urban location; interns
     accepted.

Shine Bright Montessori School
8350 14th Ave NW, Seattle, WA 98117-4232

The Niche
1412 NW 67th St, Seattle, WA 98117-5240
Type: Montessori

Brighton Elementary
4425 S Holly St, Seattle, WA 98118
Beverly Raines, 206-281-6270
Type: magnet
K–5th grade
Global studies.

Cornerstone Montessori Academy
6027 S Roxbury, Seattle, WA 98118

Graham Hill Montessori (1990)
5149 S Graham St, Seattle, WA 98118
Gloria Etcheson, 206-281-6430
Type: public choice; tuition: $0-140/mo sliding scale
4 teachers, 2 assistants, 102 students, ages 3–12
Affiliation: PNMA
Inclusive; plans for expansion; childcare; urban location;
     transportation; interns accepted.

Jesse's Corner
5200 Wilson Ave S, Seattle, WA 98118
Susan Lenihan
Type: Montessori

ORCA at Columbia Elementary (1972)
3528 S Ferdinand St, Seattle, WA 98118
Larry Jacobs, Prin, 206-281-6310
Type: public choice
18 teachers, 240 students, ages 5–11, K–5th grade
Arts, dance, and environmental science; ethnically balanced
    community of staff and parents; team teaching; parent
    participation; multi-disciplinary; artists-in-residence; art
    resource teacher; computer lab; greenhouse; multi-aged
    classes; extensive field trips.

Sunnyside Montessori
3939 S Americus St, Seattle, WA 98118-1639

Montessori South Pre-School
4602 43rd Ave S, Seattle, WA 98118-1802

Children's House Montessori
6027 S Roxbury St, Seattle, WA 98118-5944
Andrea Skeel

Nova (1968)
2410 E Cherry, Seattle, WA 98122
Elaine S. Packard, Program Mgr, 206-281-6363
Type: public choice
5 teachers, 130 students, ages 14–21, 9–12th grade

The Learning Tree Montessori Childcare (1979)
1721 15th Ave, Seattle, WA 98122-2614
Laurie Ross, Director, 206-324-4788
Non-profit; tuition: $485/mo, scholarships
3 teachers, 5 assistants, 50 students, mainly international,
    ages 3–6
Affiliations: AMS, PNMA, NCME; accreditation: NAEYC
Governance by administrator
Multi-ethnic population; staff 1/2 male; very active parent
    involvement; childcare; urban location; interns accepted.

**Montessori Education Institute of the Pacific
    Northwest**
Seattle University, Seattle, WA 98122-4460
John Chattin-McNichols, PhD or Dora Lange
Type: Montessori teacher education

Alternative School #1 (1969)
11530 12th Ave NE, Seattle, WA 98125
Ron Snyder, Prin, 206-281-6970
Type: public choice
10 teachers, 158 students, ages 5–14, K–8th grade
Affiliation: Seattle Public Schools
Governance by principal, council of staff, parents, students
Teacher qualifications: WA certification, alternative
    endorsement
Experiential kinesthetic and visual teaching-learning center;
    extensive field trips; no letter grades; multi-aged classes;
    interns accepted.

SUMMIT K-12 (1978)
11051 34th Ave NE, Seattle, WA 98125
Catherine Hayes, Prin, 206-281-6880
Type: public choice
47 teachers, 606 students, ages 5–18, K–12th grade
District's only K–12 school; conflict resolution; multi-cultural;
    cross-age tutoring; cooperative problem-solving; artists-in-
    residence; family-oriented; extensive arts experiences;
    widespread use of community resources; multi-aged
    classes.

West Seattle Montessori School
4536 38th Ave SW, Seattle, WA 98126-2725

Montessori for Kids (1986)
14410 Greenwood Ave N, Seattle, WA 98133
Mary Louise Ellsworth, 206-361-2264
Tuition: $280/425/mo
6 teachers, 50 students, ages 3–6
Affiliation: PN MA; accreditations: MIA, AMI

Governance by administrator
Spanish; movement; computer; art; urban location; interns
    accepted.

Franklin High School
3013 S Mt Baker Blvd, Seattle, WA 98144
Sharon Green, 206-281-6030
Type: magnet
9–12th grade
Literary, visual and performing arts.

Montessori in Seattle Public Schools
3308 19th Ave S, Seattle, WA 98144
Frederica Merrell

Satellite Alternative High School (1969)
440 S 186th St, Seattle, WA 98148
Barbara Birch, Prin, 206-433-2574
Type: public choice
27 teachers, 384 students, mainly at-risk, ages 12–20
Short-term intervention; tutorials; work experience; evening
    classes; individualized; GED prep; teen parenting; childcare.

Alta Vista Curriculum (1983)
PO Box 55535, Seattle, WA 98155
Susan Talbot, Curriculum Coordinator, 206-771-7740, 800-
    544-1397, FAX: 206-771-6861
Pre K–9th grade
Affiliation: Alta Vista College
Bible-based; hands-on approach to all activities including
    student texts and worksheets.

Lake Forest Park Montessori
19935 19th Ave NE, Seattle, WA 98155
Connie Falconer

Room Nine Program
Meridian Park Elementary (1974)
17077 Meridian Ave N, Seattle, WA 98155
Wendy Borton, Tch, 206-368-4127
Type: public choice
3 teachers, 72 students, ages 5–12, K–6th grade
Governance by teachers, principal, democratic school
    meeting, parent cooperative
Hands-on curriculum; problem solving; arts; student self-
    assessment; multi-aged classes; extensive field trips;
    interns accepted.

Shorecrest Program
15343 25th Ave NE, Seattle, WA 98155
David Paul
Type: public choice

Shoreline Homeschoolers Co-op
1131 NE 187th, Seattle, WA 98155
Lyn Baxter, 206-367-4680

Family Academy (1982)
146 SW 153rd #290, Seattle, WA 98166
Candice Oneschak, Adm, 206-246-9227, FAX: 785-4995
Type: independent, non-profit; tuition: $600-1,700/yr
40 teachers, 45 students, ages 5+, K–12th grade
Governance by board
Teacher qualifications: certification
Weekly learning activities for homeschoolers with local
    teacher; no letter grades; multi-aged classes; extensive
    field trips.

Burien Rainbow Montessori School
1005 SW 152nd St, Seattle, WA 98166-1845

Seattle Homeschool Group
1221 NW Norcross Way, Seattle, WA 98177
206-367-9440

Seattle Waldorf School (1980)
2728 NE 100th, Seattle, WA 98177
Elena Leonard, Office Mgr, 206-524-5320

Non-profit; tuition: $3,830-5,300/yr, scholarships
18 teachers, 194 students, ages 4-14, pre K-8th grade
Affiliation: AWSNA
Governance by parent/faculty, board of trustees, and college
  of teachers
Teacher qualifications: Waldorf training
7 specialist teachers; urban location; interns accepted.

Renton Alternative High School (1969)
7800 S 132nd St, Seattle, WA 98178
John Rogers, Prin, 206-235-2272
Type: public at-risk

Valley View Alternative Elementary (1979)
17622 46th Ave S, Seattle, WA 98188
Janice E. Tietz, 206-433-2377
Type: public choice
30 teachers, 258 students, ages 5-12
Open concept building; team teaching; challenge program.

Discovery Montessori School (1983)
2836 34th Ave W, Seattle, WA 98199
Dee Hirsch, Dir, 206-282-3848
Non-profit; tuition: $210/270/mo
4-5 teachers, 1-2 assistants, 48 students, ages infant-6
Affiliations: NAMTA, PNMA, St Nicholas NCME
Governance by administrator
Science room; outdoor activity area; urban location; interns
  accepted.

Tuscany Montessori School
6801 Stanton Pl NW, Seattle, WA 98199
Stacia Kostuik

Contract Learning Opportunities Program (1991)
3516 Rucker Ave, Everett, WA 98201
Roy E. Morris, Jr, Prin, 206-339-4320
Type: public choice
15 teachers, 30 students, ages 14-21, 9-12th grade
Self-paced; conferences; seminars; flexible schedule; teen
  parenting; counseling; evening class.

Everett Alternatives (1979)
3516 Rucker Ave, Everett, WA 98201
Roy E. Morris, Jr, Prin, 206-339-4320
Type: public choice
25 teachers, 400 students, ages 14-20, 9-12th grade
Variable start times; vocational training; contracts; individualized; small classes; accelerated credit achievement; teen
  parenting; childcare.

Middle College at Everett Community College (1991)
801 Wetmore Ave, Everett, WA 98203
Roy E. Morris, Jr; Karla Wilson, 206-338-9245
Type: public choice
2 teachers, 40 students, ages 16-21, 9-12th grade
Self-paced; HS and/or college credit; counseling; support;
  teen parenting; childcare.

Montessori Schools
1804 Puget Dr, Everett, WA 98203-6600

Trestle Homeschoolers
5305 131st SE, Everett, WA 98208
Bev Wendt, 206-337-0530

Our Children's House
1308 7th St, Anacortes, WA 98221-1811
Type: Montessori

Arlington Alternative School (1984)
18722 59th Ave NE, Arlington, WA 98223
Deborah Borgens, Dir, 206-435-8375
Type: public choice
5 teachers, 115 students, ages 14-20, 9-12th grade
Monthly Celebrations of Achievement; required participation
  in staff-facilitated discussion groups; contracts; extracurriculars; vocational; teen parenting; childcare.

The Home School
(See Resource Section)

Bellingham Cooperative School
2710 McKenzie, Bellingham, WA 98225
Scott Stodola, 206-733-1024
Type: independent

Fairhaven College (1967)
Western Washington U, Bellingham, WA 98225-9118
Marie Eaton, Dean, 206-650-3680, FAX: 206-650-3677
Tuition: $660-2,316/qtr, scholarships
15 teachers, 380 students, ages 17+
Governance by faculty, students, dean
Students may design their majors; no letter grades; extensive
  field trips; urban location.

Whatcom Hills Waldorf School (1986)
941 Austin St, Bellingham, WA 98226
Pam Went, Adm, 206-671-1035
Non-profit; tuition: $2,100-4,100/yr, scholarships
10 teachers, 100 students, ages 4-14, K-8th grade
Governance by faculty, board, administrator
Teacher qualifications: Waldorf, WA certification
Botany, zoology, history, physics, physiology, chemistry,
  geography; suburban location; interns accepted.

Whatcom Homeschool Association
3851 Britton Rd, Bellingham, WA 98226
206-671-3689

Burlington Little School
207 S Gardener Rd, Burlington, WA 98233
Roberta Nelson, 206-757-8257
Type: independent

Whidbey Island Waldorf School
Box 469, Clinton, WA 98236
Kendall Hubbard

Garden Isle Montessori School
207 NW Cloveland Box 1305, Coupeville, WA 98239
Darrellyn Currier

Orcas Homeschoolers
Rt 1, Box 10-G, Eastsound, WA 98245
Cheryl Dankin, 206-376-5396

Everson Homeschool Support Group
7107 Goodwin Rd, Everson, WA 98247
Rose Anne Featherston, 206-966-5005

Mt Pilchuck Homeschoolers
PO Box 1097, Granite Falls, WA 98252
Karen Rieger, 206-691-6066

South Whidbey Homeschool Support Group
5410 S Coles Rd, Langley, WA 98260
206-321-6477

Lynden Home Learners
9856 Van Buren Rd, Lynden, WA 98264
Mark and Kathy Iblings, 206-988-4038

Children's House Montessori
202 S 9th, Mt Vernon, WA 98273
Arlene Forsyth

Skagit Alternative High School
2121 E College Way, PO Box 217, Mt Vernon, WA 98273
Pam Church, Coord, 206-428-4818
Type: independent, non-profit
5 teachers, 65-70 students, mainly at-risk, ages 13-21
Independent study; self-paced; contract-based home study;
  teen parenting.

Skagit Valley Homeschool Association
1198 Farm to Market Rd, Mt Vernon, WA 98273
Mr or Mrs Peterson, 206-757-4170

Homeschoolers On Whidbey
1348 Western Dr, Oak Harbor, WA 98277
M. Mattson, 206-679-3150

Der Kinderhuis Inc
5096 50th St NW, Oak Harbor, WA 98277-4024
Jeanan Richter
Type: Montessori

Valley View Middle School (1994)
14308 Broadway Ave, Snohomish, WA 98290
Ken Knautz, Prin, 206-568-0671
Type: public at-risk
650 students, ages 12-14, 7-8th grade

Crown Hill Montessori School
13801 235th St SE, Snohomish, WA 98290-7871

Sky County Home Educators
31931 116th St SE, Sultan, WA 98294
Peggy Tuttle, 206-793-2445

TEAM School (1987)
5550 Tracyton Blvd NW, Bremerton, WA 98310
Marian Turgeon, 206-692-3137
Type: public choice
4 teachers, 100 students, ages 6-12, 1-6th grade
Inclusive; parent involvement; competency-based.

Montessori Country Schools
1547 Sheridan Rd, Bremerton, WA 98310-3423

Lakeside Montessori
7730 NW Wildcat Lake Rd, Bremerton, WA 98312
Lee Ann Powers, 206-830-4568
Tuition: $1,450/yr
2 teachers, 2 assistants, 38 students, ages 3-6
Governance by administrator
Fully equipped; rural location; interns accepted.

Central Kitsap Montessori Program
6200 Dowell Rd, Bremerton, WA 98312-1895

Eatonville Area Homeschool Association
PO Box 430, Eatonville, WA 98328
Michelle Wilbur, 206-832-4568

Forks Alternative High School (1987)
PO Box 60, Forks, WA 98331
Linda Wells, Dir, 206-374-2475
Type: public choice
90 students, ages 12-21, 7-12th grade

Greater Gig Harbor Homeschool Support Group
PO Box 2041, Gig Harbor, WA 98335
206-265-8210

HALL Program (1992)
PO Box 2253, Gig Harbor, WA 98335
Tom Schneider, Liaison, 206-858-5574
Type: public choice, home-based
2 teachers, 175 students, ages 5-18, K-12th grade
Affiliation: Peninsula PSD
Overseen by administrator with parent input.
Extensive software for CAI; official transcripts, diploma;
   parent-taught subjects; non-compulsory class attendance;
   multi-aged classes; extensive field trips; suburban location.

Harbor Montessori
5414 68th St Ct NW, Gig Harbor, WA 98335

Graham Homeschool Fellowship
13915 240th L St E, Graham, WA 98339
Nowl Orton, 206-893-5392

Spectrum Community School (1984)
8998 NE West Kingston Rd, Kingston, WA 98346
Chris Wendelyn, Dir, 206-297-2132
Type: public choice

7 teachers, 100 students, ages 15-21, 9-12th grade
Daily classes & independent study; counseling; vocational;
   parenting classes; men's and women's groups; electives in
   art, media, music, computer graphics, and foreign languages; school-wide projects in human rights advocacy;
   foreign student exchanges.

**National Challenged Homeschoolers Associated
   Network**
5383 Alpine Rd SE, Olalla, WA 98359
Tom or Sherry Bushnell, 206-857-4257
Newsletter; family directory; lending library.

Choice High School
216 E 24th St, Port Angeles, WA 98362
Michelle Reid, 206-452-7602
Type: magnet
9-12th grade
Drop-out retrieval.

Franklin Elementary (1980)
2505 S Washington St, Port Angeles, WA 98362
Ron Bellamy, Prin, 206-457-9111
Type: public choice
4 teachers, 100 students, ages 5-11, K-5th grade
Numerous volunteers and supportive parents; independent
   learners; flexible groupings/room arrangements; weekly/
   daily contracts; multi-aged classes.

HOPE: Homeschooling and Other Parents Encouraged
7017 Knight Dr SE, Pt Orchard, WA 98366
Karen Jogerst, 206-871-7249

OPEPO (Optional Education Program) (1977)
1919 Blaine St, Port Townsend, WA 98368
Bob DeWeese, parent, 206-385-2124
Type: public choice
3 teachers, 60 students, ages 6-12, 1-6th grade
Multi-aged classes; self-paced, interest-directed learning;
   integrated curriculum emphasizing cooperative problem
   solving; group/individual projects; parent participation; 3-
   day camping trip.

Port Townsend Migrant Education Program (1978)
450 Fir St, Port Townsend, WA 98368
Penny Kelley, Coord, 206-385-5737
Type: home-based public choice
1 teacher, 41 students, ages 5-18, K-12th grade
Correspondence; individualized; parents act as Home
   Teachers.

Washington Alternative Learning Assn (WALA)
(See Resource Section)

The Montessori Farm
17197 Clear Creek Rd, Poulsbo, WA 98370
Barbara Rhoe or Marie Cable

Puyallup Homeschool Fellowship
13023 126th Ave E, Puyallup, WA 98374
206-840-3834

Christian Home Educators
111 Bon Jon View Way, Sequim, WA 98382
Bonnie Baisotti, 206-683-8625

Homeschoolers in Sequim
178 Kirner Rd, Sequim, WA 98382
Diana Hay, 206-683-6731

North Olympic Homeschool Association
72 W Quail Ln, Sequim, WA 98382
Rose Marshall

Silverwood School
8551 Dickey Pl NW, Silverdale, WA 98383
Jane Van Buecken
Type: Montessori

Brownsville Montessori School
PO Box 3510, Silverdale, WA 98383-0733
Diana Zegers

Olympic View Montessori
PO Box 733, Silverdale, WA 98383-0733

Challenger High School, Graham Campus (1990)
7311 Eustus Hunt Rd, Spanawax, WA 98387
Ande Chapman; John Zurfluh, 206-847-4768
Type: public choice
2 teachers, 50 students, ages 15-21, 9-12th grade
In renovated farmhouse; small groups; life skills; health professions; career exploration; teen parenting; childcare; rural location.

Challenger High School (1974)
18020 E "B" St, Spanaway, WA 98387
Gary Mesick, Prin, 206-846-9734
Type: public choice
15 teachers, 205 students, mainly at-risk, ages 16+, 10-12th grade
Daily discussion groups for skills development, career planning; self-developed contracts; drug/alcohol counselor; social worker; teen parenting; multi-aged classes.

Explorer Elementary (1989)
18020 E "B" St, Spanaway, WA 98387
Gary Mesick, Prin, 206-846-9734
Type: public choice
3-4 teachers, 30 students, ages 6-12, 1-6th grade
Hands-on education; parent involvement required; independent learning; multi-aged classes.

Voyager Junior High (1984)
18020 E "B" St, Spanaway, WA 98387
Gary Mesick, Coord, 206-846-9734
Type: public choice
3 teachers, 36 students, ages 13-15
Modified contract system; peer tutoring; cooperative learning; teen parenting; drug/alcohol counselor; social worker; support groups.

Bonney Homeschool Support Group
5521 175th Ave Ct E, Sumner, WA 98390
Terri McCoy, 206-863-7266

Suquamish Options in Education (1990)
18950 Park Ave NE, Suquamish, WA 98392
Bruce Colley, Prin, 206-598-4219,-4164
Type: public choice
2 teachers, 50 students, ages 6-12, 1-6th grade
Multi-age groups; class meetings; parent involvement; field trips; family atmosphere.

St Patrick Montessori
1112 N G St, Tacoma, WA 98403-2518

Lister Elementary
2106 E 44th St, Tacoma, WA 98404
Leonoa Schmit, 206-596-2066
Type: magnet
K-5th grade
Arts; multi-cultural; humanities.

Tacoma Homeschool Fellowship
2017 E 35th St, Tacoma, WA 98404
Cheryl Hulsizer, 206-272-1498

Parent Assisted Learning Services (1992)
3110 S 43rd St, Tacoma, WA 98408
Dr Wanda Buckner, 206-596-1875
Type: home-based public choice
1 teacher, 40 students, ages 6-14, 1-8th grade
Support for homeschoolers; certified teacher consults in establishing learning objectives, designing lessons, and documenting progress.

Homeschool Support for Military Families
6380 Olive Way, Ft Lewis, WA 98433
Janet De Villars, 206-964-0572

Homeschool Support Association
9024 24th L Ave E, Tacoma, WA 98445
Barbara Atchison, 206-537-7192

Larchmont Elementary
8601 East B, Tacoma, WA 98445
Richard Klumpar, 206-596-2096
Type: magnet
K-5th grade
Technology; world cultures.

Montessori School of Tacoma
7727 40th St W, Tacoma, WA 98466-3146
Charlene Moffet

Lakewood Christian Home Educators
6305 78th St W, Tacoma, WA 98467
Joan Kozelman, 206-582-1751

Lincoln Elementary/Options (1984)
213 E 21st St, Olympia, WA 98501
Doug Gall, Prin, 206-753-8967
Type: public choice
7 teachers, 144 students, ages 5-12, K-5th grade
Classrooms contain up to 3 grade levels each; required parent participation; individualized; community is part of the school.

Adventures in Montessori
2010-A Blacklake Blvd SW, Olympia, WA 98502
Dixie Matthews

Olympia Home School Support Group
1616 Brawne Ave NE, Olympia, WA 98502
James Hall, 206-754-0375

Cathedral of Praise Home Education Support
5204 Brentwood Dr SE, Lacey, WA 98503
Cathleen Lamb, 206-456-4617

New Century High School (1989)
6120 Mullen Rd SE, Lacey, WA 98503
Gail McBride, Prin, 206-493-2992
Type: public choice
15 teachers, 140 students, ages 16-19, 10-12th grade
High-tech: data bases, word processing, and on-line searches; focus on building leadership and creating a link between school and community.

Schools for the 21st Century
(See Resource Section)

Evergreen State College
Olympia, WA 98505
Doug Skinner, 206-866-6824

Capital Montessori
3604 Surrey Dr NE, Olympia, WA 98506
Mergene Noble

Grays Harbor Christian Homeschool Parent Support Group
PO Box 1163, Aberdeen, WA 98520
Linda Edwards, 206-533-6418

Olympia Waldorf School (1983)
8126 Normandy St SE; PO Box 638, E Olympia, WA 98540
Kathy Kelly, Board; Julie Barrett, Faculty Chair, 206-493-0906
Non-profit; tuition: $3,500-3,950/yr, scholarships
11 teachers, 90 students, ages 4-12, K-5th grade
Governance by board, faculty, parent council.
Teacher qualifications: Waldorf training
In circa 1914 wooden schoolhouse; all students learn knitting, crochet, wooden flute/lyre playing, singing, watercolor, ceramics, woodwork; ethnic dinners; Yuletide craft fairs; Maypole dancing; seasonal celebrations; multi-aged classes; rural location; interns accepted.

CLOC: Community Learning Opportunity Center (1990)
303 4th St, Raymond, WA 98577
Nina Jeffre, Prog Dir, 206-942-9721
Type: public at-risk
1 teacher, 45 students, mainly at-risk, ages 16-20, 9-12th
  grade
Governance by teachers and principal
Teacher qualifications: state certification
Community service required; independent study; CAI; teen
  parent ed; environmental ed; community volunteers teach
  special interest subjects; student government; non-
  compulsory class attendance; multi-aged classes; extensive
  field trips; integrated curriculum; rural location.

Willapa Community School (1987)
656 Barnhart St, Raymond, WA 98577
Karen Good, Dir, 206-942-3212
Type: independent, non-profit
1 teacher, 8 students, ages 5-15, K-8th grade
Governance by faculty and student representatives
Teacher qualifications: MA
Highly experiential; holistic; independent study; thematic curriculum; in former church building adjacent to woods;
  music; art; pottery; computer; no letter grades; non-
  compulsory class attendance; multi-aged classes; extensive
  field trips; rural location; interns accepted.

Timberdoodle
(See Resource Section)

Battle Ground District Alternative Learning Program
  (1990)
11104 NE 149 St/ 204 W Main, Brush Prairie, WA 98604
Vynnette Rettenmaier; Warren Reeves, 206-260-5331
5 teachers, 300 students, ages 14-21, 7-12th grade
Contracts; individualized.

Moore Academy
(See Resource Section)

New World Montessori Children's House
4035 Rosewood, Longview, WA 98632
DeAnne Lightfoot

Family Centered Learning Alternatives
HCR 63 Box 713, Naselle, WA 98638
206-484-3252
Type: home-based

South Pacific County Homeschoolers
27010 U St, Ocean Park, WA 98640
Ariel Campbell, 206-665-6698

Lewis River Home Educators
33112 NW Lancaster Rd, Ridgefield, WA 98642
206-887-8050

Skinner School
400 E Evergreen Blvd, Vancouver, WA 98660-3263
Type: Montessori

Vancouver Montessori School
10316 NE 14th St, Vancouver, WA 98664-4304
Audreen Williams

Hazel Dell Montessori
76207 NE Hazel Dell Ave, Vancouver, WA 98665
Robin Matson

Clark County Christian Home Educators (1988)
PO Box 5941, Vancouver, WA 98668

Evergreen Alternative Learning Center (1976)
PO Box 8910, Vancouver, WA 98668-8910
Jeffrey Evans, Coord, 206-256-6015
Type: public choice
22 teachers, 180 students, ages 14-21, 9-12th grade
6 programs: Quest: academically committed students;

Bridge: grade 9; Recovery Transition: after drug/alcohol
  treatment; Independent Study/Contract; Teen Parenting;
  Credit Recovery; childcare.

Hewitt Research Foundation
(See Resource Section)

View Point Alternative School (1986)
2349 "B" St, Washougal, WA 98671
Tom Hays, Tch, 206-835-8766
Type: public at-risk

Woodland Homeschool Support Group
189 Dee Creek Rd, Woodland, WA 98674
Jim & Veronica Stult, 206-225-6173

Family Advocates in Teaching Homes
PO Box 326, Yacolt, WA 98675
Darlene Beatty

Valley Home Educators
209 Stull Ct, E Wenatchee, WA 98802
Kim Bartel, 509-884-7635

Children's Gate Montessori School
PO Box 4025, Wenatchee, WA 98807-4025

Grant County Home Educators Association
730 Rd V NW, Quincy, WA 98848
Harriet Weber, 509-787-3757

Home Education Press
(See Resource Section)

Little Star School-Montessori (1982)
PO Box 608, Winthrop, WA 98862
Rayma Hayes, Dir, 509-996-2797, FAX: 509-996-2889
Non-profit; tuition: $1,800-2,900/yr
4 teachers, 6 assistants, 65 students, ages infant-9
Affiliations: AMS, NCME, AMI, PNMA
Governance by teachers, administrators, democratic school
  meeting, board
Childcare; rural location.

Adams Elementary (1990)
723 S 8th St, Yakima, WA 98901
Marcia McGill, Co-ord, 509-575-3448
Type: public choice
14 teachers, 14 assistants, 350 students, mainly at-risk &
  international, ages 3-9
Accreditation: AMS
Governance by administrator
Childcare; urban location; transportation; interns accepted.

Children's House Montessori
905 S 48th Ave, Yakima, WA 98907
Esther Closner

Montessori Society of Yakima (1928)
511 N 44th Ave, Yakima, WA 98908
Bonnie Eglin, Adm, 509-966-2768
Tuition: $150/260/mo
4 teachers, 4 assistants, 76 students, ages 3-6
Affiliations: NAMTA, OMA, PNMA
Urban location; interns accepted.

Ellensburg High School Program (1979)
Hogue Tech, Rm 197, Central WA U, Ellensburg, WA 98926
Jim Ayer, Coord, 509-925-6185
3 teachers, 25-35 students, ages 14-20, 9-12th grade
Individualized; films; swimming; extensive field trips; re-entry
  into regular program

Ellensburg Homeschool Support Group
11 Frontier Rd, Ellensburg, WA 98926

Kittitas Valley Homeschool Association (1988)
PO Box 1492, Ellensburg, WA 98926

Debbie Williams, Communications Chair, 509-925-4033, FAX: same
50 teachers, 200 students, ages 5-15, K-9th grade
Governance by parent cooperative
Teacher qualifications: 45 college credit-hours
Interns accepted.

REACH at Lincoln Elementary (1982)
200 S Sampson, Ellensburg, WA 98926
Rod Goosman, Prin, 509-925-9831
Type: public choice
5 teachers, 125 students, ages 6-11, 1-5th grade
Parent support team; arts; competency-based; team teaching.

Rainbow Valley School
1510 Freimuth Rd, Selah, WA 98942-9732
Marcia Williams
Type: Montessori

Zillah Homeschoolers
PO Box 1277, Zillah, WA 98953
William J. & Rebecca Schenker

Cheney High School Parallel Education (1985)
460 N 6th St, Cheney, WA 99004
Roy A. Schmidt, Asst Prin, 509-235-9510
2 teachers, 84 students, ages 15-21, 9-12th grade
Educational planning; CAI; GED prep.

Woodinville Montessori School (1983)
13965 NE 166th St, Woodinville, WA 99072
Mary Schneider or Sheri Nick, 206-481-2300
Tuition: $1,750-4,000/yr
7 teachers, 9 assistants, 60 students, ages 6-12
Affiliations: AMS, NAEYC, PNMA; accreditation: WA
Governance by administrator
In open valley with horses; traditional Montessori program with innovative touches; childcare; rural location; interns accepted.

Homeschooling on the Palouse
SE 405 Hill, Pullman, WA 99163
Susan McMinn Seefeldt, 509-332-8127
Nonsectarian family support group; also based in Idaho.

Montessori School of Pullman (1968)
NW 115 State St, Pullman, WA 99163
Tanya Carper, Adm, 509-334-4114
Non-profit; tuition: $125/mo, scholarships
4 teachers, 4 assistants, 70 students, ages 3-6, pre K, K
Affiliations: AMI, AMS, NAMTA, PNMA
Governance by parent-executive committee, non-profit board
Teacher qualifications: Montessori Certification
Daily French class; music; movement; daily circle activities, outdoor play; multi-aged classes; suburban location; interns accepted.

St Aloysius School
611 E Mission Ave, Spokane, WA 99202-1917
Susan Boughton
Type: Montessori

Little Way Montessori Services
2213 29th, Spokane, WA 99203
Barbara Templin

Montessori Central
S 2900 Bernard, Spokane, WA 99203
Beverley Burger

Montessori Schools of Washington
E 2213 29th Ave, Spokane, WA 99203
Brian Templin

Jefferson Elementary School
3612 S Grand Blvd, Spokane, WA 99203-2693
Type: Montessori

Spokane Montessori West
4040 W Wright Ave, Spokane, WA 99204
Hope Caprye-Boos

Woodland Montessori School
3404 W Woodland Blvd, Spokane, WA 99204-2240

Montessori Central Preschool, Inc
W 2421 Garland Ave, Spokane, WA 99205
Beverly Burger

Spokane Montessori Schools
W 1904 Glass Ave, Spokane, WA 99205

4 Learning Opportunity Center (1988)
S 123 Bowdish, Spokane, WA 99206
Bob Shill, Dir, 509-927-1100
2 teachers, 80 students, ages 12-20, 7-12th grade
Individualized; self-paced; competency-based; A/V; CAI; 15-20 students/class; immediate feedback; life skills.

S (Student Parent Alternative Classroom Experience) at South Pines Elementary (1988)
E 12021 24th Ave, Spokane, WA 99206
Ralph Larsen, Prin, 509-922-6760
Type: public choice
14 teachers, 62 students, ages 6-12, 1-6th grade
Individualized; competency-based; attempts made to balance boys and girls, and home school and non-home school students; multi-aged classes.

Family Learning Center
Box 7256, Spokane, WA 99207-0256
Kathleen McCurdy, 509-467-2552
Type: home-based

SPICE at Seth Woodward Elementary (1985)
E 8508 Uprive Dr, Spokane, WA 99212
Sherri Wagemann, Tch, 509-921-2160
Type: public choice
3 teachers, 73 students, ages 5-11, 1-5th grade
Student-centered; multi-aged; emphasizes parent, teacher, student, community interaction; intense parent participation; variety of instructional strategies.

Spokane Valley High School (1981)
E 8920 Valleyway, Spokane, WA 99212
Doug Grace, Prin, 509-922-5475
7 teachers, 140-150 students, mainly at-risk, ages 14-20
Individualized; self-paced; small class size; SE; teen parenting; community activities; career/counseling center; hot lunches; childcare; transportation.

Washington Association of Teaching Christian Homes
N 2904 Dora Rd, Spokane, WA 99212
509-922-4811

Valley Montessori
13900 E Mission Ave, Spokane, WA 99216-1932
Gwen Melcher

Tri-Cities Homeschool Support Group
4355 Kahlotus Rd, Pasco, WA 99301
Kay Hayes, 509-547-6623

Wee Kare Korner
927 W Henry, Pasco, WA 99301
Terri Allen
Type: Montessori

Lower Valley Homeschool Support Group
PO Box 157, Bickleton, WA 99322
Kathy Juris, 509-896-2315

House of Children
6510 W Arrowhead, Kennewick, WA 99336
Lorretta Levno
Type: Montessori

St Joseph's Montessori
901 W 4th, Kennewick, WA 99337
Cherie Moll

Cathedral Montessori School
325 W Gage Blvd, Richland, WA 99352-9603
Shawna Boolen

Blue Mountain Homeschool Association
PO Box 13631, Walla Walla, WA 99362
509-525-2860

The Educational Opportunity Center (1993)
PO Box 665, Clarkston, WA 99403
Elece Lockridge, Dir, 509-758-5591
Type: public at-risk
2 teachers, 2 assistants, 70 students, ages 14-21
Individualized; CCP; independent contract; GED prep; GRADS;
   self esteem; community support, involvement.

Washington DC

Benjamin Banneker Academic High School
800 Euclid St NW, Washington, DC 20001
Linette M. Adams, Prin, 202-673-7322
Type: public choice
9-12th grade
Rigorous; 270 hrs community service required.

M. M. Washington Career Senior High School
27 "O" St, NW, Washington, DC 20001
Alethia Spraggins, Prin, 202-673-7224
Type: public choice
10-12th grade
Health care; business-medical fields; culinary arts.

Pre-Engineering Program at Dunbar Senior High School
1301 New Jersey Ave, NW, Washington, DC 20001
Eva R. Rousseau, Prin, 202-673-7239
Type: public choice
10-12th grade

Midtown Montessori School
33 K St, NW, Washington, DC 20001-1369
Cheryl Harris

**Academy of Integrated Media Studies (AIM), Public
   Safety Program at McKinley/Penn SHS**
2nd & T Sts, NE, Washington, DC 20002
James Greene, Prin, 202-576-6011
Type: public choice
9-12th grade
AIM: management, journalism, advertising/marketing, photography, publishing, broadcast engineering; PSP: law
   enforcement, fire fighting, corrections; cadets earn hourly
   wage; post-grad employment options.

Institute for Independent Education
(See Resource Section)

Marsh Montessori School
300 G St NE, Washington, DC 20002

Phelps Career Senior High School
26th St & Benning Rd, NE, Washington, DC 20002
Earnest Johnson, Prin, 202-724-4516
Type: public choice
10-12th grade
Floriculture; agri-business; construction; transportation; post
   grad apprenticeships; Integrated Design and Electronics
   Acad: UDC-prep for JROTC students.

Chamberlain Career Development Center
14th St & Potomac Ave, SE, Washington, DC 20003
Waverly Jones, Prin, 202-724-4648
Type: public choice
10-12th grade

Health and Human Services Academy at Eastern SHS
17th & E Capitol Sts, NE, Washington, DC 20003
Ralph Neal, Prin, 202-724-4805,-8737
Type: public choice
9-12th grade

Watkins Elementary School
12th & E Sts, SE, Washington, DC 20003
Helen Flagg, Prin, 202-724-4714
Type: Public choice Montessori
Pre K-4th grade

Capitol Hill Montessori School
701 5th St SE, Washington, DC 20003-4210
Brenda Neal

High School/College Internship Program
Guidance and Counseling Office, Rm 906
415- 12th St NW, Washington, DC 20004
Dr Dorothy Jenkins, Dir, 202-724-4185
Type: public choice
12th grade
College courses for HS credit.

Ellington School of the Arts
35th & R Sts, NW, Washington, DC 20007
Carolyn Wilson, Acting Prin, 202-282-0123
Type: public choice
9-12th grade

Georgetown Montessori School
1301 35th St, NW, Washington, DC 20007
Lee Allard

Montessori School of Washington
1556 Wisconsin Ave NW, Washington, DC 20007

Second Renaissance Montessori School
3526 Garfield St, NW, Washington, DC 20007
Margaret Bethea Abourezk

The Children's House of Washington
3133 Dumbarton St, NW, Washington, DC 20007-3309
Patti Harburger
Type: Montessori

Academic Preparation Centers of Transemantics Inc
4301 Connecticut Ave NW, Washington, DC 20008
Type: Montessori

Mater Amoris Montessori School
3600 Ellicott St, NW, Washington, DC 20008
Charlottee Kovach

School For Friends
2121 Decatur Pl NW, Washington, DC 20008
James Clay, Director, 202-328-1789
Type: independent

Washington Montessori Institute
2119 "S" St NW, Washington, DC 20008
Type: Montessori teacher education

Home Study Directory/National Home Study Council
(See Resource Section)

TransTech Academy at Cardozo Senior High School
13th & Clifton Sts, NW, Washington, DC 20009
Bernard Lucas, Acting Prin, 202-673-7385
Type: public choice
10-12th grade
Transportation technology.

Mt Pleasant Montessori School
PO Box 21362, Washington, DC 20009-0862

Language Development, Career Specializations, and 2+2 Tech-Prep at Bell Multicultural SHS
3145 Hiatt Pl, NW, Washington, DC 20010
Maria Tukeva, Prin, 202-673-7314
Type: public choice

Lincoln Multicultural Middle School
16th & Irving Sts, NW, Washington, DC 20010
Roberto R. Butler, Prin, 202-673-7345
Type: public choice
6-8th grade
Stresses 5 geo-cultures of student population from over 35 ethnic groups.

Burdick Career Development Center
1300 Allison St, NW, Washington, DC 20011
Ruth Clauselle, Prin, 202-576-6241
Type: public choice
10-12th grade
Computer repair, cosmetology, hair and child care.

Coolidge High School for the Teaching Professions Program (1988)
5th & Tuckerman Sts, NW, Washington, DC 20011
Christine Easterling, 202-722-1656, 576-6143
Type: public choice
Students mainly African-American, 9-12th grade
Foreign language, government, physics, calculus, English, communication skills; professional practicum; work-study.

Parkmont School
4842 16th St NW, Washington, DC 20011
202-726-0740
Type: independent

Travel and Tourism Program at Roosevelt SHS
13th & Upshur Sts, NW, Washington, DC 20011
Robert Gill, Acting Prin, 202-576-6130
Type: public choice
9-12th grade
Hotel and convention management.

Aiden Montessori School (1961)
3100 Military Rd NW, Washington, DC 20015
Jane Scheuermann, Admissions; Marsha Donnelly, Adm, 202-966-0360, FAX: 202-966-1878
Non-profit; tuition: $2,061-6,670/yr
8 teachers, 5 assistants, 120 students
Affiliations: NAMTA, AISGW, MAC/USA; accreditation: AMI
Governance by board of trustees
Childcare; urban location.

Montessori School of Chevy Chase
5312 Connecticut Ave, NW, Washington, DC 20015-1804
Donna Tambornino

International Studies Program at W. Wilson SHS
Nebraska Ave & Chesapeake St, NW, Washington, DC 20016
Sherri Furlott, Coord, 202-282-0120
Type: public choice
9-12th grade
Social studies, languages; work-study; foreign exchange.

Math, Science and Technology Magnet
Backus Middle School
S Dakota Ave & Hamilton St, NE, Washington, DC 20017
Ann Hilliard, Acting Prin, 202-576-6110
Type: public choice
6-8th grade

Trinity College School of Professional Studies
125 Michigan Ave, NE, Washington, DC 20017-1094
Type: Montessori teacher education

Fort Lincoln Elementary School
Fort Lincoln & Barney Drs, NE, Washington, DC 20018
Barbara Colston, Prin, 202-576-6900
Type: Public choice Montessori
Pre K-7th grade

John Burroughs Montessori Program
18th & Monroe St NE, Washington, DC 20018

Montessori Avalon School
2814 Franklin NE, Washington, DC 20018

Montessori Memories
3137 24th St NE, Washington, DC 20018
Pam Bellino

Woodridge Elementary School
Carlton & Central Aves, NE, Washington, DC 20018
Claudia Thompson, Prin, 202-576-6042
Type: Public choice Montessori
Pre K-6th grade

Business and Finance Program at H. D. Woodson SHS
55th & Eads Sts, NE, Washington, DC 20019
Lucile E. Christian, Prin, 202-724-4512
Type: public choice
10-12th grade

Kimball Elementary School
Minnesota Ave & Ely Pl, SE, Washington, DC 20019
Isaac Jackson, Acting Prin, 202-767-7011
Type: Public choice Montessori
Pre K-6th grade

Math, Science and Technology Magnet
Roper Middle School
4800 Meade St, NE, Washington, DC 20019
Helena N. Jones, Acting Prin, 202-724-4632
Type: public choice
6-8th grade

Merritt Elementary School
50th & Hayes Sts, NE, Washington, DC 20019
Nancy Shannon, Prin, 202-724-4618
Type: Public choice Montessori
Pre K-7th grade

Nalle Elementary School
50th & C Sts, SE, Washington, DC 20019
Shirley Williams, Prin, 202-767-7029
Type: Public choice Montessori
Pre K-6th grade

Public Service Academy at Anacostia Senior High School
16th & R Sts, SE, Washington, DC 20020
Zavolia D. Willis, Prin, 202-767-7041, 7040
Type: public choice
9-12th grade

Douglass Junior High School
Douglas & Stanton Rds, SE, Washington, DC 20032
Louise Buckner, Prin, 202-767-7190
Type: public choice
7-9th grade
Focus on self-esteem and leadership.

School of Mathematics and Science
Ballou Senior High School
4th & Trenton St, SE, Washington, DC 20032
Richard Washington, Prin, 202-767-7071
Type: public choice
Educational partnerships with NASA, Naval Research Lab,
    Westinghouse, Smithsonian, etc.

Network of Educators on the Americas
(See Resource Section)

School Without Walls Senior High School
21st & G Sts, NW, Washington, DC 20037

Emily Crandall, Prin, 202-724-4889
Type: public choice
9–12th grade
College prep; internships, apprenticeships, independent
    study in conjunction with GWU; concentrated humanities
    and integrative learning.

Magnet School Assistance Program
400 Maryland Ave SW #2056, Washington, DC 20202
Sylvia Wright, Branch Chief
Type: Montessori

West Virginia

Gesundheit Institute (1971)
HC 64 Box 167, Hillsboro, WV 24946
Dr. Patch Adams, Dir, 304-653-4338
Type: independent
Teacher qualifications: interested in creating the school
Building a free hospital on 310 acres with alternative school
    for children of staff and patients, sick children and local
    area children; staff live on-site.

Alternatives in Education
Rt 3 Box 305, Chloe, WV 25235
304-655-7232
Type: home-based

Laurelbrook Montessori
400 Swarthmore Ave #1, Charleston, WV 25302
Lori Ann Flanigan

Christian Home Educators of West Virginia
Box 8770, S Charleston, WV 25303
304-776-4664

Mountaineer Montessori (1978)
308 20th St SE, Charleston, WV 25304
Mary E. McKown, Dir, 304-342-7870
Tuition: $2,200-3,350/yr
98 students, ages 3–12
Affiliations: NCME, AMI, AMS
Governance by director, administrator, and parent board
Extensive field trips; multi-aged classes; no letter grades;
    urban location; interns accepted.

Montessori, Etc
869 Sherwood Rd, Charleston, WV 25314
Mary Esther McKown

West Virginia Home Educators Association, Inc
PO Box 3707, Charleston, WV 25337-3707
304-733-4735, 800-736-9843

Charleston Montessori School
PO Box 4443, Charleston, WV 25364
Eleanor Kawsek

Berkeley Springs Community Preschool
302 Warren St, Berkeley Springs, WV 25411
Type: Montessori

The Learning Tools Company
PO Box 657, Berkeley Springs, WV 25411
Ellen Gould
Type: Montessori

Tri-State Montessori School
773 Norway Ave, Huntington, WV 25705-3830
Judith Smith

Children's House
203 S Kanawha St, Beckley, WV 25801-5616
Type: Montessori

Mount de Chantal Montessori School
410 Washington Ave, Wheeling, WV 26003
Margaret Erickson

Salomi's Montessori School
35 G C & P Rd, Wheeling, WV 26003
Salomi Jayasekera

De Sales Hts Academy
37 Willowbrook Dr, Parkersburg, WV 26104-1002
Type: Montessori

Mid-Ohio Valley Montessori School
PO Box 4106, Parkersburg, WV 26104-4106

Montessori Early Learning Center (1979)
1002 S Davis Ave, Elkins, WV 26241-3528
Virginia Longtain Zuboy, 304-636-2075
Tuition: $1,278/2,655/yr
1 teacher, 4 assistants, 65 students, ages 3–6
Governance by teacher/owner
Interns accepted.

Highland School (1981)
Rt 83 Box 56, Highland, WV 26346
Dr. Charlotte Landvoigt, Dir, 304-869-3250
Type: independent, boarding, non-profit; tuition: day 60, bdg
    560/mo
3 teachers, 14 students, ages 5–18
Governance by democratic school meeting
Teacher qualifications: B.A. minimum; willingness to be equal
    member of democratic community
Located on 480 acres: woods, pond, streams, fields, wildlife;
    international visitors and exchanges; stresses individual
    interests, responsibility; apprenticeships in oil and gas, vet-
    erinary science, office skills; PSAT administered; no letter
    grades; non-compulsory class attendance; multi-aged
    classes; interns accepted.

Alternative Learning Center
417 Holland Ave, Morgantown, WV 26505

Saint Luke's Montessori School
RR 6 Box 145-CC, Morgantown, WV 26505-9806

Wisconsin

Amy Montessori School
305 N Calhoun Rd, Brookfield, WI 53005-3403

Prairie Hill Waldorf School (1987)
N 14 W 29143 Silvernail Rd, Pewaukee, WI 53072
Sally Sommer, Adm Coord, 414-691-8996
Non-profit; tuition: $1,950-3,200/yr, scholarships
18 teachers, 142 students, ages 3.5-12, K-8th grade
Governance by faculty and board of trustees
Teacher qualifications: Waldorf training
Weekly French, German; clay modeling; written evaluations;
　　suburban location; interns accepted.

Montessori Children's House
1701 Vogt Dr, West Bend, WI 53095

Guadalupe Montessori School
PO Box 368, Burlington, WI 53105-0368

Switch
(See Resource Section)

Kenosha Montessori School
5900 Seventh Ave, Kenosha, WI 53140

Montessori Children's House of Kenosha
4601 8th Ave, Kenosha, WI 53140-3301
Marcia Ray

Rosehart Montessori School
1711 74th St, Kenosha, WI 53143-5379

Montessori School of Waukesha (1964)
2600 Summit Ave, Waukesha, WI 53188
Jane Walrath, Adm, 414-547-2545
Non-profit; tuition: $2,127-2,860/yr
7 teachers, 5 assistants, 126 students, ages 3-9
Governance by administrator
Childcare; suburban location.

Milwaukee
PO Box 2181, Wilwaukee, WI 53201-2181
Howard Fuller, 414-475-8393
Type: charter
Affiliation: WI DPI

Lincoln Center Middle School
820 E Knapp St, Milwaukee, WI 53202
Hector Perez-LaBoy, 414-272-6060
Type: magnet
6-8th grade
Creative arts.

Waldorf School of Milwaukee (1977)
718 E Pleasant St, Milwaukee, WI 53202
Lucas G. Hendrickson, Teacher, 414-272-7727
Non-profit; tuition: $3,000-4,000/yr, scholarships
12 teachers, 96 students, ages 3.5-11, K-5th grade
Affiliation: AWSNA
Governance by teachers and board
Teacher qualifications: openness to Anthroposophy, willing-
　　ness to learn
Teachers show LOVE to the students daily; struggles shared
　　openly; multi-cultural; no letter grades; interns accepted.

Kagel Elementary
1210 W Mineral St, Milwaukee, WI 53204
Rose Guajardo, 414-647-1552
Type: magnet
K-5th grade
Bilingual gifted and talented.

Brown St Academy
2029 N 20th St, Milwaukee, WI 53205
Mack Hughes, 414-933-4011

Type: magnet
Student ages 3+,-5th grade
Talent development.

Elm Elementary
900 W Walnut St, Milwaukee, WI 53205
Darrel Jacobs, 414-562-1000
Type: magnet
Student ages 4+,-5th grade
Creative arts.

Lloyd St Elementary
1228 W Lloyd St, Milwaukee, WI 53205
Helen Harris, 414-562-5893
Type: magnet
Student ages 4+,-5th grade
Multi-unit; individually guided.

Multilingual Elementary Academy
2035 N 25th St, Milwaukee, WI 53205
D. Guzman-Estevez, 414-933-7500
Type: magnet
Student ages 4+,-5th grade

NOVA: Northwest Opportunities Vocational Academy
(1993)
3718 W Lancaster Ave, Milwaukee, WI 53205
Felita Daniels, Dir, 414-438-8320, FAX: -8325
Type: public/independent at-risk
8 teachers, 70 students, mainly at-risk, ages 12-17, 7-12th
　　grade
Affiliation: NCSG
Governance by teachers, principal, democratic school
　　meeting
Teacher qualifications: BA, desire to work with at-risk
School-to-work; competency-based; college prep, credit;
　　internships, extensive business community involvement;
　　multi-aged classes; urban location; interns accepted.

Roosevelt Middle School
800 W Walnut St, Milwaukee, WI 53205
Michael Hickey, 414-263-2555
Type: magnet
6-8th grade
Creative arts.

Shalom High School (1973)
1749 N 16th St, Milwaukee, WI 53205
Gwendolyn Spencer, Dir, 414-933-5019, FAX: -5433
Type: independent at-risk, non-profit
80 students, mainly at-risk, ages 14-19, 9-12th grade
Affiliation: NCSC
Governance by teachers, principal, democratic school
　　meeting, board
Teacher qualifications: BA
Competency-based; at-risk students catch up to age group;
　　multi-aged classes; urban location; interns accepted.

Urban Day School (1967)
1441 N 24th St, Milwaukee, WI 53205
Bob Rauh, Prin, 414-937-8400, FAX: -8406
Type: independent, non-profit; scholarships, state choice
28 teachers, 620 students, ages 3-14, K-8th grade
Governance by a board of staff, parents, and community
　　volunteers
Teacher qualifications: degree, certification
Many staff are parents; interns accepted.

Urban Waldorf Elementary
2023 N 25th St, Milwaukee, WI 53205
Dorothy St Charles, 414-933-4400
Type: magnet
Student ages 4+,-5th grade
Educating the Heart, Hands and Mind.

Multicultural Community HS
1645 N 25th St, Milwaukee, WI 53205-1435
Carl Hedman
Type: independent

Franklin Elementary
2308 W Nash St, Milwaukee, WI 53206
James Henry, 414-873-0771
Type: magnet
K-5th grade
Multi-age; multi-unit.

Clement Ave Elementary
3666 S Clement Ave, Milwaukee, WI 53207
Janetta Trotman, 414-482-2720
Type: magnet
K-5th grade
Individualized; ungraded.

Montessori Institute of Milwaukee (1989)
3195 S Superior St #L 428, Milwaukee, WI 53207
Allyn S. Travis, Adm, 414-481-5050
Non-profit; tuition: $4,500/yr
Student adult ages
Affiliation: AMI; accreditation: MACTE
Governance by administrator
Elementary teacher training; one year full-time course; along
   Lake Michigan.

Tippecanoe Elementary
357 E Howard Ave, Milwaukee, WI 53207
Patricia Holmes, 414-769-3220
Type: magnet
K-5th grade
Humanities.

Highland Community School
2004 W Highland Blvd, Milwaukee, WI 53208
Tim Souers, Prin, 414-342-1412
Type: Montessori; tuition: ability to pay
6 teachers, 75 students, ages 2.5–10, pre K–3rd grade
Governance by parent cooperative
Teacher qualifications: Montessori background, community
   involvement
Focus on empowerment and liberation through loving, supportive, politically active staff, parents, students; no letter
   grades; multi-aged classes; extensive field trips; interns
   accepted.

Milwaukee Montessori School
4610 W State St, Milwaukee, WI 53208-3198

Northwest Opportunities Vocational Academy (NOVA)
3718 West Lancaster Ave, Milwaukee, WI 53209
414-428-8320
Type:public at-risk
9-10th grade
seeks to create an academic climate for at-risk youth to
   become college bound; opportunity to earn college
   credits; internships.

Thurston Woods Campus Elementary
5966 N 35th St, Milwaukee, WI 53209
Joyce Taylor, 414-536-8664
Type: magnet
Student ages 4+,-3rd grade
Ungraded.

38th St Elementary
2623 N 38th St, Milwaukee, WI 53210
Donna Zoble, 414-449-9624
Type: magnet
Student ages 4+,-5th grade
Open education.

Sherman Elementary
5110 W Locust St, Milwaukee, WI 53210
Dolores K. Jackson, 414-449-0918

Type: magnet
K-6th grade
Multi-cultural arts.

Family Montessori School
5806 W Burleigh St, Milwaukee, WI 53210-1516

Dr Martin Luther King, Jr Elementary
3275 N 3rd St, Milwaukee, WI 53212
Josephine Mosely, 414-562-4174
Type: magnet
K-5th grade
African-American immersion.

Meir Elementary
1555 N Martin Luther King, Milwaukee, WI 53212
Albin Kacsmarek, 414-271-6840
Type: magnet
3-5th grade
Gifted and talented.

Rethinking Schools
(See Resource Section)

Fratney Street
3255 N Fratney St, Milwaukee, WI 53212-2297
Carol Schmuhl, 608-264-4840 x182
Type: public choice

Granville Elementary
9520 W Allyn St, Milwaukee, WI 53215
Debrorah Bent, 414-355-1230
Type: magnet
K-5th grade
Multi-aged, multi-unit; IGE.

Greenfield Elementary
1711 S 35th St, Milwaukee, WI 53215
Debra Jupka A/P, 414-647-2767
Type: magnet
Student ages 3+,-5th grade
Montessori.

65th St Elementary
6600 W Melvina St, Milwaukee, WI 53216
Kay Mantilla, 414-464-5005
Type: magnet
K-5th grade
Comprehensive; multi-cultural.

New World Montessori School
217 W Dunwood Rd, Milwaukee, WI 53217-3108

Turning Point School
5460 N 64 St, Milwaukee, WI 53218
Ellen Smith
Type: independent

Lowell Elementary
4360 S 20th St, Milwaukee, WI 53221
Claudette St. Clair, 414-282-6560
Type: magnet
K-5th grade
High achievement.

Victory Elementary
2222 W Henry Ave, Milwaukee, WI 53221
Estell Sprewer, 414-282-9050
Type: magnet
K-5th grade
Multi-aged; multi unit; IGE; ungraded.

Thoreau Elementary School
7878 N 60th St, Milwaukee, WI 53223
Judith Rick, 414-354-3650
Type: magnet
K-6th grade
Multi-age; multi-unit; IGE

Emerson Elementary
9025 W Lawrence Ave, Milwaukee, WI 53225
Roberta Wilkerson, 414-464-9550
Type: magnet
K-5th grade
Ungraded.

Morse Middle School
4601 N 84th St, Milwaukee, WI 53225
Rogers Onick, 414-466-9920
Type: magnet
6-8th grade
Gifted and talented.

River Trail Elementary
12021 W Florist Ave, Milwaukee, WI 53225
Barbara Birks, 414-353-0370
Type: magnet
K-5th grade
Multi-unit.

Grand Ave Middle School
2430 W Wisconsin Ave, Milwaukee, WI 53233
Thomas McGinnity, 414-933-9900
Type: magnet
6-8th grade
Global education; multiple intelligences.

MacDowell Elementary
1706 W Highland Blvd, Milwaukee, WI 53233
John Schmuhl, 414-933-0088
Type: magnet
Student ages 3+,-5th grade
Montessori.

Milwaukee High School of the Arts
2300 W Highland Ave, Milwaukee, WI 53233
Jo Alice Bender, 414-933-1500
Type: magnet
9-12th grade

Scott Middle School
1017 N 12th St, Milwaukee, WI 53233
James Townes, 414-344-6200
Type: magnet
6-8th grade
Individualized.

Red Apple Elementary
914 St Patrick St, Racine, WI 53402
Sheryl Esch, 414-637-5635
Type: magnet
K-5th grade

Bull Fine Arts Elementary
815 DeKoven Ave, Racine, WI 53403
Frank Germinaro, 414-632-8931
Type: magnet
1-5th grade

Lighthouse Gifted & Talented Elementary
1722 W 6th, Racine, WI 53403
Steve Miley, 414-632-5147
Type: magnet
K-5th grade

Racine Montessori School (1963)
520 21st St / DeKoven Foundation, Racine, WI 53403
Rita C. Lewis, Adm, 414-637-7892
Non-profit; tuition: $1,544-2,780/yr
9 teachers, 2 assistants, 130 students, ages 3-12
Accreditation: AMS
Governance by board
Historic buildings in park-like setting on Lake Michigan; child-
    care; urban location; interns accepted.

Walden III (1972)
1012 Center St, Racine, WI 53403
Charles Kent, Prin, 414-633-1321

Type: public choice
30 teachers, 405 students, ages 11-18, 6-12th grade
Affiliation: CES since 1986
Governance by democratic school meeting
Oldest comprehensive Portfolio Evaluation Program in the
    US; no exceptional education labeling; multi-aged classes;
    urban location; transportation; interns accepted.

Racine
2220 Northwestern Ave, Racine, WI 53404
Major Armistead, Jr, 414-631-7171
Type: at-risk charter
Affiliation: WI DPI

Wisconsin Christian Home Educators
2307 Carmel Ave, Racine, WI 53405
414-637-5127
Affiliation: WI DPI

Burdge Elementary
321 Olympian Blvd, Beloit, WI 53511
Barbara Hickman, 608-364-6055
Type: magnet
K-6th grade
Expressive arts.

Morgan Elementary
Lee Lane, Beloit, WI 53511
Anthony Beardsley, 608-364-6090
Type: magnet
K-6th grade
Expressive arts.

Families in Schools at Home (FISH)
4639 Conestoga Trail, Cottage Grove, WI 53527

De Forest
520 E Holum St, De Forest, WI 53532
James Stillman, 608-846-6500
Type: charter
1-8th grade
Affiliation: WI DPI
1-5th at Leeds Elementary.

LIFE: Learning is ForEver
c/o Deforest Middle School
500 S Cleveland St, DeForest, WI 53532
Barb Fossum, At-risk Facilitator, 608-846-6560
Type: public at-risk
6-8th grade
Parent participation; develops communication between
    school, home, and student.

Lake Mills
318 College St, Lake Mills, WI 53551
Donald Childs, 414-648-2215
Type: charter
6-8th grade
Affiliation: WI DPI

Little Friends Montessori
6273 University Ave, Middleton, WI 53562

Middleton-Cross Plains
7106 South St, Middleton, WI 53562
Gen Thieleke, 608-828-1600
Type: charter
K-2, HS
Affiliation: WI DPI
K-2: reading-based w/business participation.

Children's Community School (1976)
211 Parkway, Mt Horeb, WI 53572
Pence Revington, 608-437-4121
Type: Montessori, non-profit; tuition: $80-420/mo
2 teachers, 10 assistants, 85 students, ages infant-6
Affiliations: WECA, 4-C's; accreditations: AMS, WI
Governance by board
Creative use of natural resources in Practical Life, geography;
    childcare; rural location; transportation; interns accepted.

Verona
700 N Main St, Verona, WI 53593
Dr Bob Gilpatrick, 608-845-6451
Type: charter
Affiliation: WI DPI
Will be either a new elementary school or a "school without walls" high school.

Wisconsin Parents Association
PO Box 2502, Madison, WI 53701
Type: state home-based

Middle School 2000
545 W Dayton St, Madison, WI 53703
Cheryl Whilhoyte, 608-266-6270
Type: charter
Affiliation: WI DPI
Proposed on south side.

Countryside Montessori
721 Northport Dr, Madison, WI 53704
Deborah Nicholson

HOME (1983)
c/o 5745 Bittersweet Pl, Madison, WI 53705
Alison McKee, 608-238-3302
2 teachers, 2 students
Governance by parents
Inclusive.

Madison Central Montessori
4337 W Beltline Hwy, Madison, WI 53711

Wingra School (1972)
3200 Monroe St, Madison, WI 53711
Ann Jarvella Wilson, Dir, 608-238-2525
Type: independent, non-profit; tuition: $4,500, scholarships
18 teachers, 146 students, ages 4-14, K-8th grade
Affiliations: NCACS, Network of Progressive Schools
Governance by principal, board
Teacher qualifications: teacher training programs of several area colleges
Thematic; integrated; problem-solving; communication skills; independent thinking; encourages interest in local and world communities; no letter grades; multi-aged classes; extensive field trips; interns accepted.

Quest Learning Center, Inc (1991)
PO Box 9174, Madison, WI 53715
Donna R. Mahr, Dir, 608-255-1080
Type: independent, non-profit; tuition: $25/day, scholarships
6 teachers, 12 students, ages 6-16, K-12th grade
Governance by parent cooperative, board, democratic school meeting
Mini-classes; activities; tutoring; equipment; individual learning plans; extensive field trips; no letter grades; multi-aged classes; interns accepted.

Woodland Montessori School
1124 Colby St, Madison, WI 53715-2008

Montessori Children's House
5530 Medical Cir, Madison, WI 53719-1202

Beaver Dam (1994)
705 McKinley St, Beaver Dam, WI 53916
Dr Richard Fitzpatrick, 414-885-7300
Type: at-risk charter
70 students, MS, HS
Affiliation: WI DPI

JTPA The Bike Farm (1993)
2780 230th St, Cushing, WI 54006
Steve Clark, Adm, 715-648-5519, FAX: same
Type: home-based, non-profit
2 teachers, 3-12 students, mainly at-risk, ages 13-18, 7-12th grade
Governance by democratic school meeting

Work on Ice Age Trail and other community service; organic sustainable living; student-led; no letter grades; non-compulsory class attendance; multi-aged classes; transportation; interns accepted.

Hudson Children's House
605 North End Rd N, Hudson, WI 54016-9570
Rebecca Janke and Noreen Teachout
Type: Montessori

Pass/ Mini Pass Program
c/o CESA #8
223 W Park St, Gillett, WI 54124-0320
Frank Kazmierczak, WI PASS Coord, 414-855-2114
Type: public at-risk

Nicolet Elementary School (1981)
109 E 8th St, Kau Kauna, WI 54130
John P. Moore, Prin, 414-766-6124
Non-profit
18 teachers, 210 students, ages 5-9, K-3rd grade
Governance by teachers, principal
Kagan cooperative learning strategies; Marie Clay reading recovery; no letter grade; interns accepted.

Children's House of Manitowoc
4020 Memorial Dr; PO Box 506, Manitowoc, WI 54220
Pam Eggebrecht
Type: Montessori

Children's House (1985)
4020 Memorial Dr, Two Rivers, WI 54241-3221
Janice Schaden, 414-793-2629
Type: Montessori, non-profit; tuition: $1,600/2,900/yr
2 teachers, 30 students, ages 3-6
Affiliation: AMS
Governance by board
Multi-aged classes; rural location; interns accepted.

Aldo Leopold Alternative Program at Allouez School (1976)
116 W Allouez, Green Bay, WI 54301
Dr Margaret A. Hutchison, Prin, 414-448-2140
Type: public choice
23 teachers, 400 students, ages 5-14, K-8th grade
Governance by principal, district BE, parents, teachers.
Teacher qualifications: WI Certification, MA
Experiential; whole language; cooperative learning; integrated curriculum; a peer teaching; environmental issues; no letter grades; non-compulsory class attendance; multi-aged classes; extensive field trips; urban location.

Montessori Children's Village, Inc (1990)
214 Sherman St, Wausau, WI 54401
Patricia Filak, Adm, 715-842-9540
Tuition: $220/315/325/mo
2 teachers, 3 assistants, 57 students, ages infant-9
Affiliations: AMS, NAEYC, WECA
Governance by administrator
100-year old school building; childcare; urban location; interns accepted.

Montessori School of Wausau Inc. (1970)
1921 Wagner Street, Wausau, WI 54401
Ursula Velm, 715-842-7917
Non-profit; tuition: $135/320/mo.
3 teachers, 3 assistants, 80 students, ages 3-6
Affiliations: IMS, CMNE
Governance by board, administrator

Providing Alternative Credit Education
c/o Mosinee High School
1000 High St, Mosinee, WI 54455
Steve Smolek, Assistant Prin, 715-693-2550
Type: public at-risk

Stevens Point
1900 Polk St, Stevens Point, WI 54481
Dr Richard Eisenhauer, 715-345-5444

Type: at-risk charter
110 students, senior high
Affiliation: WI DPI
School within a school; student/teacher-designed schedule and curriculum.

International Institute
(See Resource Section)

Montessori Children's Center
445 Chestnut St, Wisconsin Rapids, WI 54494-4803

Montessori North
PO Box 24, Rhinelander, WI 54501

Montessori of Rhinelander (1977)
121 N Stevens / PO Box 24, Rhinelander, WI 54501
Diane Reupert, Adm, 369-4830
Tuition: $10-17.50/day
1 teacher, 2 assistants, 23 students, ages 3-6
Accreditation: NAEYC
Governance by administrator, parent board
Emphasis on local and global peacekeeping; childcare.

Lakeland High School
8669 Old Highway 70 West, Minocqua, WI 54548
John Eckardt, Youth At Risk Coord, 715-356-5252
Type: public at-risk

An Alternative Program
c/o Phillips High School, Phillips, WI 54555
Scott A. Johnson, Prin, 715-339-2141
Type: public at-risk

An Alternative Program
c/o Prentice School District
PO Box 110, Prentice, WI 54556
David Christoffersen, Guidance Dir, 715-428-2811
Type: public at-risk

La Crosse Montessori Preschool (1966)
1818 Redfield St, La Crosse, WI 54601
Peggy Parry or Georgia Maas, Co-Dir, 782-3320
Non-profit; tuition: $85-140/wk
2 teachers, 1 assistant, 49 students, ages 3-6
Accreditation: AMS
Governance by democratic school meeting
Childcare; urban location.

Pleasant Ridge Waldorf School (1979)
321 E Decker St, Viroqua, WI 54665
Kate Walter, Development, 608-634-2746
Non-profit; tuition: $1,250-2,400/yr, scholarships
15 teachers, 97 students, ages 4.5-11, K-5th grade
Affiliations: AWSNA, WI ANS
Governance by faculty
Teacher qualifications: at discretion of faculty
No letter grades; rural location.

Children's House Montessori School
510 S Farwell St, Eau Claire, WI 54701-3723

Ashland High School
1900 Beafer Ave., Ashland, WI 54806
715-682-7089
Type: public at-risk

Homebound
c/o Bayfield High School
PO Box 5001, Bayfield, WI 54814
Robert H. Lind, Prin, 715-779-5666
Type: public at-risk

Unschooling Families
1908 N. Clark St, Appleton, WI 54911
414-735-9832
Type: home-based

Montessori Adventure Schools, Inc
900 N Mason St, Appleton, WI 54914-3669

An Alternative Program
c/o Clintonville Senior High School
255 N Main St, Clintonville, WI 54929
Lynn Schevers, Assistant Prin, 715-823-2174
Type: public at-risk

Weyauwega-Freemont
PO Box 580, Weyauwega, WI 54983
Robert Hecht, 414-867-2148
Type: at-risk charter
Senior high
Affiliation: WI DPI
Business participation in design of curriculum.

Wyoming

High School III
2201 Morrie Ave, Cheyenne, WY 82001
Durla M. Cockley, Counselor, 307-771-2500, FAX: -2383
Type: public choice
17 teachers, 200 students, mainly at-risk, ages 14-21, 9-12th grade
Governance by principal
Teacher qualifications: WY certification
Outcome-based; technology-based vocational courses; community-oriented; work programs, explorations; multi-aged classes; extensive field trips; outreach programs with college and adult learning center; interns accepted.

Montessori School of Cheyenne
3619 Evans Ave, Cheyenne, WY 82001-1427

The Village School
5307 Hynds Blvd, Cheyenne, WY 82009-4053
Type: Montessori

Riverton Alternative High
2002 W Sunset Dr, Riverton, WY 82501
Mike Kouris, Dir

Wyoming Unschoolers (1993)
23 Dance Hall Rd, Lander, WY 82520
Cynthia W. Howdyshell, 307-332-6941
Secular; support; open to all; connections to isolated homeschoolers.

Roosevelt High School (1977)
140 E K St, Casper, WY 82601
Dr Carl Madzey, 307-577-4630, FAX: 307-577-4633
Type: public at-risk
15 teachers, 170 students, ages 14-21, 9-12th grade
Governance by teachers, principal, parent cooperative
Teacher qualifications: Behavioral MS
Whole-school activities; projects; multi-aged classes; extensive field trips; rural location; transportation; interns accepted.

Montessori School of Casper
224–226 S David; PO Box 684, Casper, WY 82602

Montessori Family Development Center
PO Box 684, Casper, WY 82602-0684

Homeschoolers of Wyoming
Box 926, Evansville, WY 82636
307-237-4383

Rock Springs Alternative High School (1978)
1600 College Dr; PO Box 1089, Rock Springs, WY 82901
Don White, Director, 307-382-4851
Type: public at-risk
7 teachers, 70 students, mainly at-risk, ages 16–21, 9–12th grade
Governance by teachers and principal
Teacher qualifications: state certification
Self-paced and directed; contracts; no letter grades; multi-aged classes; extensive field trips; rural location; interns accepted.

Rock Springs Alternative High
Western Wyoming College Campus
Rock Springs, WY 82901
Robert L. Plant, Prin

Western Wyoming High School (1988)
Box 568, Jackson, WY 83001
Terry Roice, Prin/Tch, 307-733-9116, FAX: -6443
Type: public choice
4 teachers, 23 students, 9–12th grade
Affiliation: Teton SD #1
Governance by advisory board; faculty and student reps
Teacher qualifications: WY certification
Outcome-based; performance assessment; portfolios; senior project; community service; expeditional, experiential learning; flexible schedule; multi-aged classes; interns accepted.

Canadian Alternatives

Alternative High School
5003–20 St SW, Calgary, AB, Canada
Jim Hoeppner, Prin, 403-287-9500, FAX: -9500
Type: public at-risk
11 teachers, 120 students, 10–12th grade
Weekly democratic meeting
Flexible; first name basis with staff; "beyond the walls" community use; multi-aged classes; extensive field trips; urban location; interns accepted.

Medicine Hat Montessori Society
410 6th St NE, Medicine Hat, AB, Canada T1A 5P1
Pres/Dir

Calgary Waldorf School
1915 36th Ave SW, Calgary, AB, Canada T2T 2G6
Faculty Chair

Calgary Alternative High School (1974)
5003 20th St SW, Calgary, AB, Canada T2T 5A5
Jim Hoeppner, Prin, 403-287-9500, FAX: -9485
Type: public choice; tuition: $140/mo
11 teachers, 120 students, ages 15–19, 10–12th grade
Governance by democratic school meeting
Informal community atmosphere; extensive field trips; multi-aged classes; interns accepted.

Bishop Carroll High School (1971)
4624 Richard Rd SW, Calgary, AB, Canada T3E 6L1
Gerald Fijal, Vice Prin, 403-249-6601, FAX: 403-240-1141
Type: public choice
52 teachers, 57 assistants, 1,180 students, ages 15–19
Affiliation: CES
Governance by principal
Teacher qualifications: Alberta certification
Completely individualized, self-directed study; holistic teacher-advisory program; flexible class times; urban location.

Bilingual Montessori Learning Centre
9003 168th St, Edmonton, AB, Canada T5R 2V7

Homeschoolers Association of Alberta
8754 Conners Rd, Edmonton, AB, Canada T6C 436
403-988-4652

Alberta Home Education Association c/o Aine Stasiewich
Box 3451, Leduc, AB, Canada T9E 6M2

The Pembina Institute
(See Resource Section)

Plenty Valley Montessori School
315 Aqueduct Rd, Diamond Creek, Victoria, BC, Canada
J. P. Puckey

Vancouver Public Schools
6330 Sophia St, Vancouver, BC, Canada U5W 2W6
Debbie Adams
Type: Montessori

Kelowna Waldorf School
Box 93, 429 Collett Rd, Okanaga Mission, BC, Canada V0H 1S0
Faculty Chair

Home Learning Resource Centre
Box 61, Quathiaski, BC, Canada V0P 1N0

Gabriola Homeschoolers
PO Box 223, Gabriola Island, BC, Canada V0R 1X0

Nelson Waldorf School (1983)
Box 165, 3468 Ymir Rd, Nelson, BC, Canada V1L 5P5
Deborah Kranenburg, Adm, 604-352-6919
Non-profit; tuition: $2,960/yr, scholarships
13 teachers, 135 students, ages 4–15, K–8th grade
Governance by college of teachers and faculty
Teacher qualifications: Waldorf training or experience, college teaching certificate
35 mountainside acres; hiking, cross-country ski; French; rural location; transportation.

Canadian Home Educators Association of BC
4684 Darin Ct, Kelowna, BC, Canada V1W 2B3
604-764-7462

Schoool District 27 Montessori Program
1894 9th Ave, Prince George, BC, Canada V2M 1L7
Don Reimer

High Glen Elementary School
290 Voyageur Dr, Prince George, BC, Canada V2M 4P2
Bonnie Addison
Type: Montessori

Montessori Elementary School Society
RR2 Site 23 Comp 32, Prince George, BC, Canada V2N2H9
Cynthia Christensen

East Canyon Springs Montessori School
2910 Walton Ave, Coquitlam, BC, Canada V3B 2W3
Halina Pisarski

Western Montessori
16-800 Egmont Ave, Coquitlam, BC, Canada V3J 4J8
Carol Scarratt

Strawberry Hill Annex
12028 75th Ave, Surrey, BC, Canada V3W 2S5
Type: Montessori

Boundary Bay Montessori House
PO Box 237, Delta, BC, Canada V4K 3N7
Montessori in Delta Society

Wondertree Educational Society
PO Box 38083, Vancouver, BC, Canada V52 4L9
604-739-5943, FAX: -6903
Type: independent

Wondertree Education Society
1940 Napier St, Vancouver, BC, Canada V5L 2N5
Karen Martin
Type: independent

Community Association of Montessori Parents
1461 E 19th Ave, Vancouver, BC, Canada V5N 2H9
Fran Tanner

Typee Elementary Montessori Alternative
3525 Dumfries St, Vancouver, BC, Canada V5N 3S5

Little Learners Preschool
2175 W 14th Ave, Vancouver, BC, Canada V6K 2V8
Rita deGraaf
Type: Montessori

Greater Vancouver Home Learners Support Group
Box 39009 Pt Grey RPO, Vancouver, BC, Canada V6R 4P1
Diana Sandberg, 604-228-1939, 298-6710

University Colleges
Head Office: 548 Beatty St, Vancouver, BC, Canada V6V2L3
604-685-7095
Accreditations: MACTE, IMI
International consortium of institutions and programs;
   awards Montessori teaching degrees; correspondence
   courses.

Vancouver Waldorf School
2725 St Christopher's Rd, N Vancouver, BC, Canada V7K 2B6
Colin Price

Windsor House
714 Westmorland Crescent, North Vancouver, BC, Canada V7P
   2G7
Helen Hughs, 604-985-7315
3 teachers, 1 assistant, 80 students, ages 5-18
Governance by democratic school meeting
Teacher qualifications: BC Ministry certification
Strong parent involvement; bicameral system for rule-
   making; community-oriented; public choice school is ages
   5-12, 56 students; independent high school with 25 students; no letter grades; non-compulsory class attendance;
   multi-aged classes; extensive field trips; urban location;
   interns accepted.

Education Advisory
2267 Kings Ave, W Vancouver, BC, Canada V7V 2C1
Type: home-based

Montessori Centre of Victoria
1530 Lionel St, Victoria, BC, Canada V8R 2X8
Karen Colussi

Sundance Elementary
1625 Bank St, Victoria, BC, Canada V8R 4V5
Type: public choice

IAPM
301-667 Head St, Victoria, BC, Canada V9A 5S9
Angela Martin, Pres
Type: Montessori

Maria Montessori Academy
637 Head St, Victoria, BC, Canada V9A 5S9
Milo Coldren

Cowichan Valley Christian Homelearners Support Group
1050 Marchmont Rd, Duncan, BC, Canada V9L 2M7

Cowichan Valley Trade School
81 Trunk Rd, Duncan, BC, Canada V9L 2N7
Joanne Pastor, Coord, 604-748-6255, FAX: -4997
Type: independent
4 teachers, 45 students, ages 20+
Affiliations: PCTA, Chamber of Commerce
Teacher qualifications: degree from recognized institute and
   6 mo experience
Job entry/re-entry; project-based training; no letter grades;
   multi-aged classes; urban location.

The Cowichan Valley Open
c/o SD #65, 2557 Beverly St, Duncan, BC, Canada V9L 2X3
Type: public choice

Cowichan Valley Alternate
1843 Tzhouhalem Rd, RR #5, Duncan, BC, Canada V9L 4T6
G. Harvey, Prin
Type: public at-risk
15-18 students, ages 13-19
Voc, emphasis on Cowichan Valley logging industry; monthly
   allowance based on academic/work performance.

Consulting in Free Range Learning and Deschooling
   (1987)
RR 7, Duncan, BC, Canada V9L 4W4
Juanita Haddad, 601-746-5129
Critical consciousness; reclaim parental responsibility, trust;
   heal from forced separation; rural location.

Sunrise Waldorf School (1979)
4344 Peters Rd, RR #7, Duncan, BC, Canada V9L 4W4
Lynda Curry, Adm, 604-743-7253
Non-profit; tuition: $250-300/mo, scholarships
132 students, ages 3.5-13, pre K-8th grade
Governance by teacher/parent board
Teacher qualifications: BC certification, Waldorf training
Language; orchestra; PE; Bothmar; rural location.

Charles Hoey VC School
756 Castle Place, Duncan, BC, Canada V9L 4Y3
Students mainly developmentally disabled, ages 5-19
Self-directed.

Kootenay Home Educators (1989)
PO Box 814, Nelson, BC, Canada VIL 6A5
Sarah Sherk, 604-352-9496, FAX: 604-352-3400
Student all ages
Affiliation: Canadian HEA
Unstructured curriculum; art; skating; foreign languages.

Personal Power Press International, Inc
(See Resource Section)

Maxwell International Baha'i School
Bag 1000, 2371 E Shawnigan Lake Rd, Shawnigan Lake, BC,
   Canada V0R 2W0
Type: independent
Whole-person approach.

Manitoba Education and Training
Office: 507-1181 Portage Ave, MB, Canada
Brian Hanson, Asst Dir, 204-948-2154, FAX: same
Type: public choice
Group of 9 secondary, vocational/technical, cooperative, and
   adult education schools.

Manitoba Association for Schooling at Home
89 Edkar Cres, Winnipeg, MB, Canada R2G 3H8

Manitoba Association for Schooling at Home (1982)
98 Baltimore Ave, Manitoba, MB, Canada R3L 1H1
Keith Michaelson, Pres
Non-violence; positive socialization.

New Brunswick Association of Christian Homeschoolers
RR 1 Site 11 Box 1, Hillsborough, NB, Canada E0A 1X0
506-734-2863

Schole (1985)
Box 10 RR #1, Margaree Valley, NS, Canada
Donald Knight, 902-248-0601
Type: Independent, home-based, boarding; cost: C$12,000/yr,
　　scholarships
2-3 teachers, 4-6 students, ages 6-16, 1-12th grade
Governance by board
Wilderness setting; extensive travel, eg, to Latin America,
　　1994-95 to Europe; no letter grade; interns accepted.

Nova Scotia Homeschool Support Group
RR 1, Pleasantville, NS, Canada B0R 1G0
Laura Uhlman

Primavera Montessori School
5303 Tobin St, Halifax, NS, Canada B3H 1S3

Indian Way School
Box 732, Kahnawake Quebec, ON, Canada J0L 1B0
Dianne Delaronde, 514-632-3258
Type: independent

Alexander Montessori School
188 Billings Ave, Ottawa, ON, Canada K1H 5K9

Quest, The Home Educators' Journal
(See Resource Section)

Ottawa Waldorf School
10 Coral Ave, Nepean, ON, Canada K2E 5Z6
Paul Power

Canadian Montessori Academy
2 Peter St, Nepean, ON, Canada K2G 1K2
Sherie De Mel

Catholic Homeschoolers Association
(See Resource Section)

Kanata March Montessori School
355 Michael Cowpland Dr, Kanata, ON, Canada K2M 2C5
Erin Gailor, Prin

Rideau Valley Home Educators Association
Box 313 North Gorler, Ottawa, ON, Canada K0A 2T0
Ellen Hackett, 613-228-8145

Pinewood Alternative School (1986)
RR 3, Millbrook, ON, Canada L0A 1G0
Melisande Neal, Prin, 705-932-3129
Type: home-based, non-profit
Student ages 6-16
Affiliations: Canadian Alliance of Homeschoolers, FTP
Rural location.

Halton Waldorf School
83 Campbellville Rd E, Campbellville, ON, Canada L0P 1B0
Helmut Krause

Orilla Homeschoolers Support Group
45 Albert St N, Orilla, ON, Canada L3V 5K3
M. Black, 705-326-5260

Pickering College (1842)
16945 Bayview Ave, Newmarket, ON, Canada L3Y 4X2
J.F. Lockyer, Dir of Devp, 416-895-1700, FAX: -9076
Type: Quaker
22 teachers, 200 students, ages 9-19, 4-13th grade

Governance by board
U prep; suburban location; interns accepted

Rudolf Steiner Centre
9100 Bathurst St #4, Thornhill, ON, Canada L4J 8C7
Diana Hughes
Type: Waldorf

Toronto Waldorf School (1968)
9100 Bathurst St #1, Thornhill, ON, Canada L4J 8C7
Brenda Kotras, Registrar, 905-881-1611, FAX: 881-6710
Non-profit; tuition: $6,815/yr
35 teachers, 370 students, ages 3-18, pre K-12th grade
Governance by democratic school meeting
Teacher qualifications: Waldorf training
Two languages; suburban location.

Sheridan College Montessori
1430 Trafalgar Rd, Oakville, ON, Canada L6H 2L1
Vi Matheson

Dearcroft Montessori School
1167 Lakeshore Rd E, Oakville, ON, Canada L6J 1L3
Gordon Phippen

MUDPUDL
c/o 25 Magill St, Hamilton, ON, Canada L8R 2Y4
Lisa Weintraub, 416-577-9491
Type: home-based, non-profit; cost: max $18/wk
1 teacher, max 15 students, ages 5-12, K-6th grade
Parent cooperative
Traditional curricula and student-directed environment;
　　based on John Holt's "unschooling"; non-compulsory
　　attendance; non-sectarian; urban location.

Beaches Alternative School at Kimberley PS
50 Swanick Ave, Toronto, ON, Canada M4E 1Z5
416-393-1451
Type: public choice
Pre K-6th grade
Field trips; individualized.

SOLE c/o Greenwood Secondary School
24 Mountjoy Ave, Toronto, ON, Canada M4J 1J6
416-393-0756
Type: public at-risk
Max 100 students, ages 16+, 9-OAC
Independent study.

Subway Academy One
c/o Eastern High School of Commerce
16 Phin Ave, Toronto, ON, Canada M4J 3T2
416-393-9466
Type: public at-risk
Max 70 students, ages 16+, 9-OAC
Independent study.

Quest Alternative Senior School at Withrow PS
25 Bain Ave, Toronto, ON, Canada M4K 1E5
416-393-9430
Type: public choice
7-8th grade
Individualized math, science; experiential; French exchange;
　　extensive computer ed; 3 one-week field trips.

Our Schools Our Selves
(See Resource Section)

First Nations School of Toronto at Dundas PS
935 Dundas St E, Toronto, ON, Canada M4M 1R4
416-393-0555
Type: public choice
Pre K-8th grade
Governance by executive committee, parents, community
　　support representatives
Instruction in Ojibwe and English; curriculum centered
　　around four seasons; stress on spiritual and cultural her-
　　itage of Native Way of life; day care.

The Student School
c/o Eastdale C.I.
701 Gerrard St E, Toronto, ON, Canada M4M 1Y4
416-393-9639
Type: public at-risk
Max 120 students, ages 16+, 11-OAC
Small classes; active student involvement in all decision-making.

Spectrum Alternative Senior School at Eglinton PS
223 Eglinton Ave E, Toronto, ON, Canada M4P 1L1
416-393-9311
Type: public choice
7-8th grade
Small classes; individualized goal-setting and evaluation; field trips; community-based projects; intensive research in areas of interest.

The Schoolhouse (1971)
243 St Clair Ave W, Toronto, ON, Canada M4V 1R3
Laura Schein, Prin, 416-920-0972
Type: independent, non-profit; tuition: $6,300/yr
3 teachers, 4 assistants, 50 students, ages 4-12, pre K-6th grade
Governance by teachers and principal
Teacher qualifications: we train asst staff w/out certification
No letter grades; multi-aged classes; interns accepted.

CONTACT
410 Sherbourne St, Toronto, ON, Canada M4X 1K2
416-393-1455,-1457
Type: public at-risk
145 students, age 18 (avg), 9-12th grade
Community liaison; student-run nutrition program.

Inglenook School
19 Sackville St, Toronto, ON, Canada M5A 3E1
416-393-0560
Type: public choice
Max 120 students, 10-OAC
Advanced level courses only; emphasis on community; parent involvement; outreach program 1 day/wk required.

SEED (1970)
22 College St Suite 500, Toronto, ON, Canada M5G 1K3
416-393-0564
Type: public choice
Max 135 students, 10-OAC
Individualized; seminars; extensive resources and visiting staff from community.

Alternative Primary School at North Preparatory PS
1100 Spadina Ave, Toronto, ON, Canada M5N 2M6
416-393-9199
Type: public choice
Pre K-6th grade
Governance by parent cooperative, board, teachers, principal
Field trips; group projects; multi-age activities; day care.

Alan Howard Waldorf School (1987)
228 St George St, Toronto, ON, Canada M5R 2N9
Barbara Ackerman, Adm, 416-975-1349
Non-profit; tuition: variable, scholarships
15 teachers, 130 students, ages 3-12, nursery-8th grade
Affiliation: AWSNA
Governance by faculty and board
Teacher qualifications: Waldorf certification
Interns accepted.

Green Teacher
(See Resource Section)

Subway Academy Two
304 Brunswick Ave, Toronto, ON, Canada M5S 2M7
416-393-1445
Type: public at-risk
Max 75 students, 9-OAC

Credit earned on-site, at other Toronto schools, or through accredited community resources, eg, Conservatory of Music.

West End Alternative
70 D'Arcy St, Toronto, ON, Canada M5T 1K1
416-393-0660
Type: public at-risk
Max 120 students, 9-12th grade
Individualized; work-study.

Horizon Alternative Senior School at Kensington PS
401 College St, Toronto, ON, Canada M5T 1S9
416-393-1298
Type: public choice
7-8th grade
Flexible grouping; individualized goal-setting and evaluation; field trips; integrated and term projects; extensive CAI; non-competitive PE.

Oasis Alternative
707 Dundas St W, Rm 3, Toronto, ON, Canada M5T 2W6
416-393-9830
Type: public at-risk
Max 75 students, 9-12th grade
Independent and work-study; Alexandra Park Outreach for adults.

Downtown Alternative Alpha School at Brant St School
20 Brant St, Toronto, ON, Canada M5V 2M1
416-393-1880,-1882
Type: public choice
Pre K-8th grade
Multi-age grouping; daily school mtg; problem solving; day care; families volunteer at least half-day/week, serve on committee; whole language; team-learning; hands-on math, science; peacemaking.

Reading Circles
c/o The Second Floor Community Library, 61 Humewood Dr, Toronto, ON, Canada M6C 2W3
Edmund P. Fowler, Coordinator, 416-651-9772
Type: independent; tuition: $50 for 5 sessions, scholarships
1 teacher, 10 students, adult ages
Small group discussion; no letter grades; non-compulsory class attendance; multi-aged classes.

Hawthorne II Bilingual School
50 Essex St, Toronto, ON, Canada M6G 1T4
416-393-0727
Type: public choice
Pre K-6th grade
Instruction in English and French; student-centered; experiential; field trips; extensive use of community resources; non-competitive PE; day care.

Delta Senior Alternative School at Montrose PS
301 Montrose Ave, Toronto, ON, Canada M6G 3G9
416-393-9730
Type: public choice
7-8th grade
Contracts; voluntary service; community; enriched lunch-time; extracurriculars.

Indoor Park (1985)
c/o 242 Havelock St, Toronto, ON, Canada M6H 3B9
Jutta Mason, 416-533-0153
Inclusive meeting place structured around food, free play, swapping, gardening, gossip.

City School
315 Osler St, Toronto, ON, Canada M6N 2Z4
416-393-1470
Type: public choice
Max 113 students, 10-OAC
Consortiums with other alternative schools; interdisciplinary courses.

High Park Alternative School at Annette St PS
265 Annette St, Toronto, ON, Canada M6P 1R3
416-393-9050
Type: public choice
Pre K-6th grade
Governance by parent cooperative
Self-paced; activity-centered; multi-aged grouping; non-
competitive evaluations.

Mountview Alternative School at Keele St PS
99 Mountview Ave, Toronto, ON, Canada M6P 2L5
416-393-9037
Type: public choice
Pre K-6th grade
Groupings based on needs, skills, interests; team teaching;
themes; school paper; newsletter; field trips; day care.

Foundation for Montessori Education
3 Riverview Gardens, Toronto, ON, Canada M6S 4E4

Canadian Association of Montessori Teachers
#818-6 Humberline Dr, Etobicoke, ON, Canada M9W 6X8
Tracy Gilmour

The Rural Learning Association
PO Box 1588, Guelph, ON, Canada N1H 6R7

Montessori School of Cambridge
Box 56, Cambridge, ON, Canada N1R 5S9
Marilyn Herrriot

London Waldorf School
1697 Trafalgar Sq, London, ON, Canada N5W 1X2
Merwin Lewis

Gibbons Park Montessori School
29 Victoria St, London, ON, Canada N6A 2B1
Maia Burghardt

Lakeview Montessori School
13803 Riverside Dr E, St Clair Beach, ON, Canada N8N 1B5

Canadian Alliance of Home Schoolers
(See Resource Section)

Oneida Learning Center
RR 2, Southwold, ON, Canada N0L 2G0
Bruce Elijah, 519-652-6367, FAX: -9603
Type: independent
4 teachers, 38 students, pre K-14th grade
Total Oneida immersion; oral tradition; agriculture; field expe-
riences; rural location.

Immanuel Christian School
PO Box 1991, Charlottetown, PEI, Canada C1A 7N7
Type: independent

Institute for Bioregional Studies (1982)
449 University Ave, Suite 126, Charlottetown, PEI, Canada C1A
8K3
Phil Ferraro, Dir, 902-892-9578
Type: higher education, boarding
1-6 teachers, 11 students, ages 17+
Affiliation: York University
Governance by faculty, student reps, board
Teacher qualifications: MA, licensed
Integrated resource management training; summer camp;
apprenticeships; community resources include organic
farms, eco land trust, Fundy Folk Society; interns accepted.

Grace Christian School
50 Kirkdale Rd, West Royalty, PEI, Canada C1E 1N6
Type: independent

Les Ecoles Montessori
1357 Van Horne, Montreal. PQ, Canada H2V 1K7
Ann Lendman

Montreal Homeschoolers' Support Group
5241 Jacques Grenier, Montreal, PQ, Canada H3W 2G8
514-481-8435

L'Ecole Rudolf Steiner de Montreal
8205 Rue Mackle, Cote St-Luc, PQ, Canada H4W 1B1
Sasha Manacas
Type: Waldorf

Montreal Home Schoolers (1989)
730 Pine Beach Blvd, Dorval, PQ, Canada H9P 2L5
Sheryl Farrell, 514-636-8534

Quebec Homeschool Association
(See Resource Section)

Survival School
Kahnawake, PQ, Canada J0L 1B0
Type: independent

Système Montessori Chez Denyse (1989)
548 Village, Morin Heights, PQ, Canada J0R 1H0
Denyse Richard, Dir, 514-226-8369
Tuition: variable
1 teacher, 2 assistants, 25 students, ages 3-6
Affiliation: AMI
Governance by administrator
Situated in the Laurentian Mountains near ski resort areas;
150 year-old building; nature study; geography; bilingual
program; childcare; interns accepted.

Au Grand Bois (1980)
RR 1, Ladysmith, PQ, Canada J0X 2A0
A & L Prost, Co-Dirs, 819-647-3522
Type: independent, boarding, non-profit; scholarships
20 teachers, 50 students, ages 8-16
Governance by staff, co-directors, much input from campers.
Summer program; organic gardens; 565-acre semi-
wilderness; non-competitive; campers choose avtivities;
promotes understanding and respect for self, others,
natural environment.

Allegro Montessori School
2606 Broadway Ave, Saskatoon, SK, Canada 57J 026
Ursula Hodgson, Adm Dir

Community Folk Schools of Saskatchewan
Box 22114, Regina, SK, Canada S4S 7G7
Type: independent

Saskatoon Montessori School (1979)
432 10th St E, Saskatoon, SK, Canada S7N 0C9
Patricia Janetzki, 306-244-1027
Non-profit; tuition: $1,850/2,930
1 teacher, 2 assistants, 34 students, ages 3-6
Affiliations: NAMTA, CAMT
Governance by administrator and board of trustees
Suburban location.

Montessori School of Regina
2935 Regina Ave, Regina, SK, Canada SHS 0G7
Maggie Volke

Selected International Alternatives

The movement of educational alternatives is truly world-wide. Although the major focus of this book is educational alternatives in the United States and Canada, we want to provide the tools to access the innovations taking place around the globe. We are aware of many thousands of these, in many countries, and I recently attended alternative education conferences in England, Holland, Vienna, and Russia which included representatives from over 40 different countries. However, we do not have space to list all of the international schools of which we are aware. For these purposes we will provide information about how to find out about them, with several examples which have been sent to us by readers of *AEROGRAMME,* and with at least one contact in each country where we have information, and contacts for major networking organizations.

Escuela Del Siglo Nuevo (1987)
Olleros 3855, Buenos Aires, Argentina 1427
Gabriella Roncoroni de Christeller, 553-4872,-9689, FAX:
5418145264
Also parent and teacher program.

CONNECT, The Newsletter of Youth Participation in Education
(See Resource Section)

Schulproject Wienerwald (1988)
Nimmersdorf 27, 3041 Asperhofen, NO, Austria
Michael Pichler, 0277218444
Type: home-based
2 teachers, 19 students, ages 6-10
Governance by parent cooperative
Teacher qualifications: university study, Montessori training
Student-centered, directed, and paced; rural location.

Colegio Bilingue "Jorge Emilio Gutierez"
Apdo Aereo 101634, Bogota, DE, Columbia SA
Alejandro Acero, 011571-2150051
Type: independent, boarding
60+ students, partly international, indigenous, K-12th grade
Summerhill philosophy; outdoor classes on mountainside; exchange program.

La Casa de los Ninos Montessori
Apartado 1108-1250, Escazu, Costa Rica
Alexandra Franco de Olher

Global Personal Teachers' Transformation (1993)
Myslfkova 7, Prague 1, Czech Republic 100 00
Dr Miluse Kubfekova, 24913899, FAX: 295561
Type: higher education, non-profit
Affiliation: Pedagogika Fakulta Uk Praha
Governance by board
Improving pre/postgraduate teacher training based on research of professional attitudes and personal needs.

Lib Ed
(See Resource Section)

Education Otherwise
36 Kinross Rd, Leamington Spa, England CV32 7EF
0926-886828
Type: home-based
For everyone who practices or supports the right of students to learn without schooling.

Summerhill School (1921)
Leiston, Suffolk, England IP16 4HY
Zoe Redhead, 0728-830540
Type: independent, boarding; tuition: $£5,000/yr
12 teachers, 70 students, mainly international, ages 6-17

Governance by democratic school meeting
Teacher qualifications: dictated by position
Founded by A.S. Neill as a pioneering free school and democratic community; 12 acres; no letter grades; non-compulsory class attendance; multi-aged classes; rural location; interns accepted.

Brockwood Park Krishnamurti Educational Centre (1969)
Bramdean, Hampshire, England SO24 0LQ
Scott Forbes, 962-771-744, FAX: 962-771-875
Type: independent, boarding, non-profit
30 teachers, 60 students, ages 14-19
Affiliation: Krishnamurti Schools
Governance by all faculty with school meeting
Holistic; in 1769 Georgian mansion and park; no letter grades; multi-aged classes; extensive field trips; rural location.

Small School (1982)
Fore St, Hartland, Bideford, Devon, England EX39 5EA
Caroline Walker, Co-Head Tch, 0237441672, FAX: 0237441203
Type: independent, non-profit
6 teachers, 10 assistants, 36 students, ages 11-16
Affiliation: Human Scale Education
Governance by consensus in parent-teacher-pupil meeting
Teacher qualifications: willingness to work for little pay
Equal emphasis on creative, spiritual, practical, academic; multi-aged classes; extensive field trips; rural location; interns accepted.

Sands School (1987)
48 East St, Ashburton, Devon, England TQ13 TAX
Sean Bellemy, 0364 653666
Type: independent, non-profit; tuition: $£3,000/yr, scholarships
6 teachers, 30 assistants, 10-18 students
Governance including staff selection by democratic school meeting
Teacher qualifications: staff ranges from no degree to PhD
Minimum rules; no system of punishments; cooking, cleaning, gardening by students and staff; non-compulsory class attendance; multi-aged classes; no letter grades; urban location; transportation; interns accepted.

Park School
Park Road, Dartington, Totnes, Devon, England TQ9 6EQ
Chris Nichols, Coord Tch, 0803-864588, FAX: -866676
Type: independent, non-profit; tuition: £1,738/yr, scholarships
5 teachers, 60 students, ages 3-11
Governance by democratic school meeting, board
Teacher qualifications: degree, certification
Students-parents-teachers partnership for a broad, creative education; no letter grades; multi-aged classes; extensive field trips; rural location.

Theleme (1984)
3 Rue Des Chalets, Vernet, France 66820
Michel Ferre, Head, 68056585
Type: independent, non-profit
4 teachers, 25 students, ages 12-18
Governance by teachers and principal, democratic school
    meeting, parent cooperative
Teacher qualifications: no official qualifications
"Learning space" approach; student-centered; multi-cultural
    approach through international travel; deeply environmen-
    tally-oriented; no letter grades; multi-aged classes; non-
    compulsory class attendance; rural location.

Agence Information Enfance
(See Resource Section)

European Forum for Freedom in Education (EFFE)
(See Resource Section)

Handbook of Alternative Schools in Europe
(See Resource Section)

World List of Rudolf Steiner (Waldorf) Schools,
    Herausgeben vom Bund der Freien Waldorfschulen
(See Resource Section)

Montessori School of Hong Kong (1977)
99 Caine Rd, 1st Flr, Hong Kong
Dr George E. Caruso, Dir, 852-559-0066, FAX: 852-547-7807
Tuition: $4,000/6,000/yr
175 students, mainly international, ages 3-6
Affiliations: MSHK, AMS, NAMTA; accreditations: AMI, AMS,
    NAEYC, HKED, MSA of HK
Governance by board of trustees
Bilingual program: English/Mandarin, English/Cantonese;
    parent education program; cultural studies; childcare;
    urban location; transportation; interns accepted.

Rogers Person Centered School Foundation
Szeher Ut 29, Budapest, Hungary
Dr. Anna Gador
Type: higher education

Budapest: Waldorf School (1989)
Kozseghaz St 8-10, Budapest, Hungary 1028
Tamas Vekerdy, 2120 Dunakeszi, Baratsag Str 21, Ph: 176-
    5609, FAX: 201-2908
Non-profit; tuition: none
18 teachers, 187 students, ages 7-13, 1-6th grade
Governance by board
Bio-gardening; eurythmy; hand crafts; religious studies;
    school under construction; no letter grades;
    transportation.

Godolloi Waldoff Iskola (1990)
Godolloi Waldorf Pedagogiai Alap., Erzsebet Krt 27, Godollo,
    Hungary 2100
Attilla Giecse, 06-28/320-495
Type: Waldorf; tuition: $2,500
4 teachers, 35 students, 3rd grade
Governance by college of teachers
Teacher qualifications: teacher's diploma
Urban location.

Montessori College at Mount St Mary's
Dundrum Rd, Milltown, Dublin, Ireland 14
Susan Goldman, Adm, 01-269-2499
Tuition: £1,675/1,780/yr
Affiliations: AMI, UNESCO
Governance by AMI
3-year AMI teacher training course; credit transfers accepted
    from AMI centers in US, Mexico, Canada, Italy, Sweden,
    Japan.

Democratic School of Hadera
Brandeis Grove, Hadera, Israel
Yakov Hecht
Type: public choice, teacher education

300 students, K-12th grade
Governance by democratic school meeting
Computers, including Lego room; exchange program; drama;
    networking; in eucalyptus grove; no letter grades; non-
    compulsory class attendance; extensive field trips; multi-
    aged classes.

Centre for Educational Technology
Man in His Environment Department (1975)
16 Klausner St, POB 39513, Ramat Aviv, Israel 61394
Ayala Yiftah, 03-6460160, FAX: 03-6422619
Type: resource, teacher education
Affiliations: Ministry of Ed, Trans, Labour; Inst for Occupational
    Safety & Health
Contracts; programs on safety, life stages/cycles, individual in
    community; books and articles.

Adam Institute
(See Resource Section)

AMI Centro Internazionale Montessori
Via Abruzzi 2, Perugia, Italy 06100
Type: Montessori teacher education

AMI Montessori Institute of Tokyo
332-19 Unomori, Sagamihara-shi 228, Japan
Type: Montessori teacher education

Tokyo Shure (1986)
1-9-19 Kishimachi Kita-Ku, Tokyo, Japan 9-933-137
Keiko Okuchi, Dir
100 students, ages 5-18
Affiliation: NCACS
Two Tokyo locations.

Global School
(See Resource Section)

La Casa del Niño
Collegio 300, Pedregal San Angel, Mexico City, Mexico 01900
Type: Montessori

Centro de Estudios de Educacion
Canal de Miramontes Esquina y Estrolla Binaria, Prados de
    Coyoacan, Mexico 04810DF
Type: Montessori teacher education

Instituto Montessori del Norte
Carbonel 4108 Ave, Chihuahua, CHI, Mexico
Zulema Ruiz or Josefina Espino
Type: Montessori teacher education

Colegio Waldorf de Cuernavaca (1988)
Jesus H Preciado 103 Col. San Anton, Cuernavaca, MOR.,
    Mexico 62020
Rosa Barocio, Faculty Chair or Martha Nanez, 18-85-76, FAX:
    11-30-06
Non-profit; scholarships
16 teachers, 140 students, ages 3-12, K-6th grade
Affiliation: AWSNA
Governance by faculty, college of teachers, board
No letter grades; interns accepted.

Montessori Sierra Madre School (1965)
Juarez 250 Sur, San Pedro Garza Garcia, NL, Mexico 66200
Adriana Vega, Dir, 83-338-0924, FAX: 83-338-5879
Non-profit; tuition: $2,990-5,500/yr
29 teachers, 10 assistants, 267 students, ages infant-15
Accreditation: AMS
Library; music; athletics; computer science; cafeteria; A/V
    room; urban location.

Tamariki School (1967)
PO Box 19506, 83 Rutherford St, Christchurch, New Zealand
Pat Edwards, 00613-38490141
Type: independent, non-profit; tuition: $1,240
4 teachers, 55 students, ages 5-14, P1-F2nd grade
Governance by democratic school meeting

Teacher qualifications: NZ certification, emotionally literate
Emphasis on basic emotional health; family and student-centered; everyone, students & staff, learns; no letter grades; non-compulsory class attendance; multi-aged classes; urban location; interns accepted.

Ripple Educational Community (1989)
493 Manchester St, Christchurch, New Zealand 8001
Marsha Morgan; Pauline Matsis, 011-643-365-7770, FAX: 011-643-379-2544
Type: home-based Montessori; cost: NZ$3,000/yr
2 teachers, 22 students, ages 5-11
Governance by teachers and Prin
In Victorian house; working garden; parents teach, learn with students; no letter grades; field trips; urban location.

Eureka Free University (1989)
Novokosinskaya 27-151, Moscow, Russia 111672
Alexander Adamsky, 7095-350-3157, FAX: 7095-350-3157
Type: higher education, resource
Russia's first private university; on-site alternative teacher training throughout former S.U.; seminars in England, US, and other countries; internships; see AERO for more info.

English Montessori Educational Group
Avda Alfonso XIIII 40, Madrid, Spain 28002
Maria Olaechea

AMI Montessori Primary Course at Uppsala University
Dept of Teacher Training, Box 2136-S750 02, Uppsala, Sweden
Type: Montessori teacher education

Sacred Heart Montessori (1980)
Upper De Gannes Street, Arima, Trinidad, West Indies
Sister Jerome Boland, S.J.C., 809-667-4279
1 teacher, 5 assistants, 100 students, ages 3-6
Affiliation: London Montessori
Governance by administrator

Leicester Montessori School (1990)
137 Loughborough Rd, Leicester, UK
Dr Dayah, 0533-610022, FAX: same
Tuition: variable
8 teachers, 15 assistants, 115 students, ages infant-12
Affiliations: LMC, MENSA; accreditation: CHI (support society for children of high intelligence)
Governance by administrator, board
Childcare; urban location; transportation.

Cherry Trees School (1982)
Flempton Rd, Risby, Bury St Edmunds, Suffolk, UK IP28 6QJ
Wendy E. S. Compson, 0284-760531
Type: Montessori; tuition: $£70-1,270/term
10 teachers, 4 assistants, 216 students, ages infant-15
Affiliation: ISIS; accreditations: MATS, ISAI
Governance by principal
French house in Normandy for ages 7+; childcare; rural location; interns accepted.

Stork Family School
Ul Stakhurskogo 62 Kv 40, Vinnitsa, Ukraine 70432265577
Type: independent; tuition: $5/mo
70 students, ages K-17
Family cooperative; emphasis on English language, crafts, fine arts, music; teacher education with Eureka Free University.

Scarborough Montessori Center (1985)
Glen Rd, Scarborough, Tobago, West Indies
Susan Sandiford, Prin, 639-5195
Tuition: $550/610
6 teachers, 1 assistant, 250 students, ages 3-12
Affiliation: London M Center
Governance by administrator

Resources

A+ Discount Distributors and Educational Warehouse
Spring Valley, NY
800-443-7900
For K-12.

"A Voice For Children"
7 Casa Del Oro Ct, Santa Fe, NM 87505-3718
Summerhill philosophy newsletter

ABeka Catalog and Correspondence School
Box 18000, Pensacola, FL 32523
800-874-BEKA
Curriculum; free catalog.

Activities for Learning
21161 York Rd, Dept BK, Hutchingson, MN 55350
612-587-9146

Adam Institute
Jerusalem Forest, POB 3353, Jerusalem, Israel 91033
Uki Maroshek-Klarman, Ed Dir, 2-419184
Promoting democracy in education; opening International Center for Education for Democracy in a Multi-cultural Society; '93 conference attended by 400 from 40 countries; books and publications.

Agence Information Enfance
29 Rue Davy, Paris, France F 75011
Roger Auffrand
National ed alternatives clearinghouse; newsletter POSSIBLE; directory.

ALLPIE: The Alliance for Parental Involvement in Education (1989)
PO Box 59, East Chatham, NY 12060
Katharine Houk, Exec Dir; Seth Rockmuller, Pres, 518-392-6900
Non-profit
Affiliations: NCACS, NHA, ERIC, Parent Ed Network
Newsletter; book; resources catalog; mail-order lending library; annual conference; workshops.

Alpha Omega
800-622-3070
Curriculum; free catalog.

Alpha Plus
PO Box 185, Chewsville, MD 21721
301-733-1456
Math counseling, advice, products; free brochure.

Alternative Education Resource Organization (AERO)
417 Roslyn Rd, Roslyn Hts, NY 11577
Jerry Mintz, Dir, 516-621-2195, FAX: 516-625-3257
Non-profit
Helped create Handbook of Alternative Education; sponsored by School of Living; helps people who want to home-school, find or start alternative schools, restructure existing schools or programs; publishes networking newsletter, AERO-GRAMME, $15/yr; many videos; speaking and consulting services; interns accepted.

Alternative Schools Network
1807 W Sunnyside, Suite 1D, Chicago, IL 60640
Jack Wuest, 312-728-4030, FAX: 312-728-3335
Clearinghouse; support; assistance.

American Home Academy, Latter Day Saints Home Educators' Association (1989)
2770 S 1000 W St, Perry, UT 84302
Joyce Kinmont, Founder, 801-723-5355
Materials including books, math manipulatives, Brite music, health products; LDS: quarterly newsletter; annual conference.

American Montessori Consulting (1988)
PO Box 5062, 11961 Wallingsford Rd, Rossmoor, CA 90721
Frances Henderson
Publishes books which reflect the teachings of Montessori, used also by homeschoolers.

American School
850 E 58th, Chicago, IL 60637
Type: home-based

American Science and Surplus
601 Linden Pl, Evanston, IL 60202
708-475-8440

Anatomical Chart Company
8221 Kimball Ave, Skokie, IL 60076
800-621-7500
Science books and kits.

Anthroposophic Press
RR 4 Box 94 A1, Hudson, NY 12534
518-851-2054
Books by Rudolf Steiner and others.

Aquarian Research Foundation (1970)
5620 Morton St, Philadelphia, PA 19144-1330
Art Rosenbloom, Dir, 215-849-3237
Non-profit
Promotes Earth's positive future through science, intuition, freedom; new social movements; computer networking; students may donate toward expenses and/or share poverty communally; newsletter, Aquarian Alternatives.

Aristoplay, Ltd
PO Box 7529, Ann Arbor, MI 48107
Educational games.

Association for Experiential Education
2885 Aurora Ave #28, Boulder, CO 80303-2252
Maria Riley, 303-440-8844
Sponsors regional, national conferences; publishes Journal of Experiential Education, Jobs Cearinghouse, other books, periodicals.

Association Montessori Internationale
170 W Scholfield Rd, Rochester, NY 14617
Virginia McHugh, 716-544-6709

Association of Waldorf Schools
3750 Bannister Rd, Sacramento, CA 95628
David Alsop

Atrium Society
PO Box 816, Middlebury, VT 05753
802-388-0922, FAX: 802-388-1027
Non-profit
Education for Peace program focuses on creative, non-violent conflict resolution; publications; seminars; training; community events; open forums.

Audio Memory Publishing
1433 E 9th St, Long Beach, CA 90813
Learning tapes.

Backyard Scientist
Box 16966, Irvine, CA 92713
Jane Hoffman

Bellweather School and Family resource Center (1995)
120 S. Borwnell Rd, Williston, VT 05495
Ron Miller, 802-865-9752
Tuition: $4500, scholarships
3 teachers, 25 students, ages 3–10
Ungraded; democratic meeting; ecological focus; holistic curriculum; services for homeschoolers

Blue Mountain Book Peddler
15301 Grey Fox Rd, Upper Marlboro, MD 20772
Free catalog.

Bluestocking Press
PO Box 1014, Dept 5, Placerville, CA 95667-1014
American History learning materials.

Bob Jones University Press
Greenville, SC 29614
800-845-5731
Christian; for K-12; free catalog.

Brain-Compatible Information
Box 427, New Rochelle, NY 10802
Leslie Hart, 914-632-9029

Brigham Young U- Dept of Independent Study
206 Harman Continuing Ed Building, Provo, UT 84602

Brook Farm Books
Box 246, Bridgewater, ME 04735
Donn Reed
Type: home-based

Builder Books
PO Box 5291, Lynwood, WA 98046
Free catalog.

Bureau of Federal School Improvement, Dept of Education
Grimes State Office Bldg, Des Moins, IA 50319
Ray Morley

Canadian Alliance of Home Schoolers (1979)
272 Hwy 5 RR 1, St George, ON, Canada NOE 1NO
Wendy Priesnitz, Coord, 519-448-4001, FAX: same
"Natural Life" magazine; also info on alt schools in Canada.

Carden Education Foundation
Box 659, Brookfield, CT 06804

Career Publishing Inc
905 Allanson Rd, Mundelein, IL 60060
Book/cassette phonics program.

Cassidy and Nells
PO Box 24133, Huber Hts, OH 45424
800-453-6114
Type: home-based
Publishes Home Education, Answers for Ohio Parents; materials; free catalog.

Catholic Home School Newsletter
688 11th Ave NW, New Brighton, MN 55112

Catholic Homeschoolers Association
PO Box 24145; 300 Eagleson Rd, Kanata, ON, Canada K2L 3M3

Center for Public Montessori Programs
Box 8354, Minnenapolis, MN 55408-0354
612-823-6348

Centre for Educational Technology: Man in His Environment Department (1975)
16 Klausner St, POB 39513, Ramat Aviv, Israel 61394
Ayala Yiftah, 03-6460160, FAX: 03-6422619
Affiliations: Ministry of Ed, Trans, Labour; Inst for Occupational Safety & Health
Teacher education; contracts; programs on safety, life stages/cycles, individual in community; books and articles.

Changing Schools Newsletter
c/o Colorado Options in Education
98 N Wadsworth Blvd #127 Box 191, Lakewood, CO 80226
Mary Ellen Sweeney, 303-331-9352

Charlotte Mason Research & Supply
PO Box 172, Stanton, NJ 08885
Newsletter.

Children's Art Foundation, Stone Soup Magazine (1973)
PO Box 83, Santa Cruz, CA 95063
Gerry Mandel, William Rubel, Editors, 408-426-5557
School; museum and national magazine of students' work.

Children's House/Children's World Magazines
PO Box 111, Caldwell, NJ 07006
Montessori teaching materials

Chinaberry Book Service
2830 Via Orange Way, Suite B, Spring Valley, CA 92078-1521

Christian Liberty Academy Satellite Schools (1968)
502 W Euclid Ave, Arlington Hgts, IL 60004
708-259-8736
Type: home-based, non-profit
Student ages 4-60, K-12th grade
Governance by church board
Curriculum from 30 publishers; self-publications; flexible;
    comprehensive; suburban location.

Clonlara School Home Based Education Program (1967)
1289 Jewett, Ann Arbor, MI 48104
Pat Montgomery, 313-769-4515, FAX: -9629
Non-profit; cost: $450/yr per family
Student ages 5+, K-12th grade
International guidance, assistance with completion of forms,
    and upkeep of cumulative records; transfer reports;
    diplomas.

Coalition of Essential Schools
Brown U Ed Dept Box 1938, Providence, RI 02912
Theodore Sizer

Cobblestone Publishing
7 School St, Peterborough, NH 03458
800-821-0115
Cobblestone (US history), Calliope (world history), Faces (cul-
    tures) magazines.

Community Service, Inc
PO Box 243, Yellow Springs, OH 45387
Jane Morgan, 513-767-2161; 767-1461
Non-profit
Mail order book service; annual conference; newsletter;
    correspondence.

Compu-Educare BBS
RR #2 Box 324, Summerville, SC 29483
Brian Comstock, 803-873-1050
Computer bulletin board for Charleston area; games; down-
    load educational programs; part of nationwide group.

**CONNECT, The Newsletter of Youth Participation in
    Education** (1979)
12 Brooke St, Northcote, Victoria, Australia 3070
Roger Holdsworth, 03 489-9052
$10/yr (6 issues)

Core Knowledge Foundation
2012-B Morton Dr, Charlottesville, VA 22901
800-238-3233
What Your ** Grader Should Know series and related
    materials.

Creative Teaching Materials
PO Box 7766, Fresno, CA 93747
800-767-4282
Catalog.

Critical Thinking Press
PO Box 448, Pacific Grove, CA 93950
800-458-4849
Books; software; secular; for K-12.

Design-A-Study
408 Victoria Ave, Wilmington, DE 19804
Books, including The Natural Speller; for K-8.

Designs for Learning
449 Desnoyer, St Paul, MN 55104
Wayne B Jennings, 612-645-0200

**Directory of Global Education Resources in North
    America**
PO Box 83916, Fairbanks, AK 99708
Lisa Brosseau, 907-479-9093
Descriptions of organizations which promote economic
    justice, environmental protection, racial and gender equity,
    human rights, media literacy, indiginous people, peace
    education, area studies; resources, curriculum, audio-
    visual.

Dover Publications, Inc
31 E 2nd St, Mineola, NY 11501
Coloring books; dioramas; classics; free catalog.

Duke UniversityTalent Identification Program
1121 W Main St, Suite 100, Durham, NC 27701
Educational Opportunity Guide, Directory of Programs for
    the Gifted.

Eagle Voice Center
Box 44, Glenelg, MD 21737
Henry Niese, 301-531-6166

Early School Materials
Rt 2, Celina, TN 38551
Jake Rockwood
Type: Montessori

Early Work
PO Box 5635, Petaluma, CA 94955-5635
Montessori resources for classrooms and parents.

Educational Futures Project (1976)
Box 2977, Sacramento, CA 95812
Don Glines, 916-393-8701
Consulting group; workshops, articles, books on educational
    alternatives, human potential, year-round continuous
    learning.

Educational Reform Group (1993)
76 Glenview, Wilton, CT 06897
Linda Moore, 203-834-0144, FAX: 203-761-1479
Publicizes, promotes and distributes video and audio tapes
    of select educational reformers.

Educator's Publishing Service (EPS)
75 Moulton St, Cambridge, MA 02138-1104
800-225-5750
Secular materials.

Enthusiasm for Learning Foundation
Sander Feinberg, Exec Dir, 800-ELF-5270
Non-profit regional centers in CA, KS, OR; R&D in progressive
    ed through learning communities, coop ed, consensus,
    entrepreneurial projects; teen college for ages 13-19.

ESP Publishers, Inc
7163 123rd Circle N, Largo, FL 34643

Eureka Free University (1989)
Novokosinskaya 27-151, Moscow, Russia 111672
Alexander Adamsky, 7095-350-3157, FAX: 7095-350-3157
Russia's first private university; on-site alternative teacher
    training throughout former S.U.; seminars in England, US,
    and other countries; internships; see AERO for more info.

European Forum for Freedom in Education (EFFE) (1989)
Annener Berg 15, Witten, Germany D 58454
Eginhard Fuchs, Speaker, 49-2303-699-442, FAX: 49-3202-669-443
Over 500 members from 30 countries; semi-annual conferences; teacher education; publications and surveys in English and German.

Family Christian Academy
487 Myatt Dr, Madison, TN 37115
Robin Scarlata, 800-788-0840; 615-860-3000
Umbrella school; newsletter; teacher training; testing; seminars; bookstore; unit studies; Bible-based books; Saxon math; Learning Language Through Literature; publications.

Family Learning Center
Rt 2 Box 264, Hawthorne, FL 32640
904-574-5869
Learning Language Arts Through Literature series; Valerie Bendt's unit study books; free catalog.

Farm Country General Store
Rt 1 Box 63, Metamora, IL 61548
800-551-FARM
Curriculum; kits; free catalog.

Fearon Teacher Aids
Box 280, Carthage, IL 62321
Secular; catalog.

Fernbank Science Center
156 Heaton Park Dr, Atlanta, GA 30307
Mary Hiers, 404-378-4311
K-12th grade
Exhibition hall, forest, botanical gardens, greenhouse, planetarium, observatory, meteorological lab, electron microscopy lab, human development classroom, library.

Florida Associationof Alternative School Educators
1201 NE 191st St, G117, N Miami Beach, FL 33197

"Florida at Home"
4644 Adanson St, Orlando, FL 32804-2024
407-740-8877
Magazine by Circle Christian School for homeschoolers

Folk Education Association of America
107 Vernon St, Northampton, MA 01060
Christopher Spicer
Based on Scandinavian folk HSs; newsletters; journal; annual conference; networking; study tours; exchange programs.

Forestry Education Assistance Program
Oregon Department of Forestry (1992)
801 Gales Creek Rd, Forest Grove, OR 97116
Ric Balfour, Public Use Coord, 503-357-2199, FAX: -4548
Students mainly at-risk
Acess to 2-acre arboretum, 350,000-acre state forest; staff available, self-sufficiency encouraged.

Foxfire Teacher Outreach (1975)
PO Box 541, Mountain City, GA 30562-0541
Hilton Smith, 706-746-5318, FAX: 706-746-5829
Collaborative process; community-based; respect for elders and what they have to teach us; summer courses; networking; workshops; also Urban Foxfire Network.

Friendly Foreign Language Learning
29481 Manzanita Dr, Campo, CA 91906
Newsletter/catalog; tapes; software; flashcards.

Friends Council on Education
1507 Cherry St, Philadelphia, PA 19102
Kay Edstone, Dir, 215-241-7245
Coordinates N. American Quaker schools; consultants; workshops; referrals; newsletter; film library.

Gentle Wind School
Box 184, Surry, ME 04684
Type: home-based

Geode Educational Options
PO Box 106, West Chester, PA 19381
Materials for teaching and parenting.

Global Alliance for Transforming Education (1990)
Box 21, Grafton, VT 05146
Phil Gang, Dir, 802-843-2382, FAX: 802-843-2300
Network of holistic educators, social change agents; promotes vision of education that fosters personal empowerment, peace, social justice and sustainable living; Gateways newsletter.

Global School (1985)
525-3 Imazu-Machhi, Takasago-Cho, Takasago, Hyogo, Japan 676
Kazuhiro Kojima, 0794-42-1473
Natural curiosity is starting point; references and info; conferences; scholarships; non-compulsory class attendance.

Global Voice Education Project for C Band Satellite (1993)
1017 Van Ness, San Francisco, CA 94110
Julie Ward, 415-647-6374
Creative learning broadcasts; emphasis on SE, home, alternative, and rural schools.

Green Teacher
95 Robert St, Toronto, ON, Canada M5S 2K5
Tim Grant, 416-960-1244

Greenleaf Press
1570 Old LaGuardo Rd, Lebanon, TN 37087
615-449-1617
History units, books; free catalog.

Growing Without Schooling
2269 Massachusetts Ave, Cambridge, MA 02140
Magazine and group founded by John Holt.

Handbook of Alternative Schools in Europe
Padagogische Hochschile Murwiker Strasse77, Flensburg, Germany D-2390
Ehrenhard Skiera
A directory of alternative schools in Europe, by country, in German

Hands-On History
201 Constance Dr, New Lenox, IL 60457
Kits; books; study materials.

Hands-On Science
12642 E Calle Tatita, Tucson, AZ 85749
602-749-1263

Hearthsong
PO Box B, Sebastopol, CA 95473-0601
Materials include Waldorf items, toys, gifts.

Heinemann Educational Books
361 Hanover St, Portsmouth, NH 03801-3959
603-431-7894

Hewitt Research Foundation (1964)
PO Box 9, 2103 B St, Washougal, WA 98671
Donna Fisher, Dir of Student Services, 800-348-1750, 206-835-8708, FAX: 206-835-8697Charles Jakiela, 802-247-8312
"Holistic Education Review" and What Are Schools For? by Ron Miller.

Holt Associates
2269 Mass Ave, Cambridge, MA 02140
Pat Farenga, 617-864-3100
Books and materials for unschoolers and homeschoolers in general; beginners packets; "Growing Without Schooling" networking newsletter.

Home Education Press
PO Box 1083, Tonasket, WA 98855
4 teachers, 1200 students, ages 5-18, K-12th grade
Non-profit homeschooling services and products include
testing for grades 3-8, phone counseling, evaluations,
special needs dept.

Holistic Education Press
39 Pearl St, Brandon, VT 05733-1007
509-486-1351
Type: home-based resource
"Home Education Magazine", Alternatives in Education, and
other publications.

Home Educator's Almanac
18515 Murphy Springs Ct, Morgan Hill, CA 95037

Home School Advantage
Box 8190, Phoenix, AZ 86066-8190
Donna Hamill

Home School Legal Defense Association
PO Box 159, Paeonian Spgs, VA 22129
703-338-5600

Home School Supply House
PO Box 7, Fountain Green, UT 84632
800-772-3129
Secular; mainstream texts.

Home Study Directory/National Home Study Council
1601 18th St NW, Washington, DC 20009

Home Study Institute
6940 Carroll Ave, Takoma Park, MD 20912
202-723-0800

Homeschool Associates of New England
116 Third Ave, Auburn, ME 04210
Steve Moitozo, 800-882-2828
Yearly homeschool conference; consultation service; radio
show; books and resource materials.

Homeschooling in Oregon, the Handbook
PO Box 80214, Portland, OR 97280
Ann Lahrson, 503-244-9677
$14.95

Homeschooling Today
Box 1425, Melrose, FL 32666
Dale Simpson

Homeward
17020 Hamilton Dr, Lakeville, MN 55044
Joan Torkildson
South Metro Families for Home Education; newsletter.

Imagination Times
1811 Tartan Court, Charlotte, NC 28212
Stories; fingerplays; recordings; games; crafts.

In Other Words
2000 Floral Drive, Boulder, CO 80304
Spanish and French language Montessori curriculum
materials.

Innovative Program Center
526 Mt Pleasant Rd, Thomson, GA 30824
Lynne Entrekin, Coordinator, 404-595-9742
Pre K-12th grade
State support.

InPrint for Children
2270 Mt Carmel Ave, Glenside, PA 19038-4610
Supplemental Montessori classroom materials.

Institute for Alternative Futures
108 N Alfred St, Alexandria, VA 22314
Chris Bui, 703-684-5880

Institute for Democracy in Eastern Europe
48 East 21st 3rd Floor, NY, NY 10010
Irena Lasota, 212-677-5801

Institute for Democracy in Education
119 McCracken Hall, Ohio U, Athens, OH 45701-2979
George Wood

Institute for Independent Education (1984)
1313 N Capitol St NE, Suite 200, Washington, DC 20002
Joan Ratteray, 202-745-0500
Technical assistance and policy development; works with
community-based schools serving African-American, Hispanic, Latin-American, Native American, and Asian American communities, numbering over 350; located primarily in
inner cities.

Institute for Mutual Instruction (1993)
4875 San Joaquin Dr, San Diego, CA 92109-2318
E.M. "Mac" Swengel, Founder/Pres, 619-272-1935, FAX: 619-
272-1935
Non-profit; comprehensive; focus on individual tutoring; students teach what they learn.

Institute for Responsive Education
605 Commonwealth Ave, Boston, MA 02215
Owen Heleen

Institute of General Semantics (1938)
163 Engle St, Englewood, NJ 07631
Marjorie Zelner, Exec Sec, 201-568-0551, FAX: 569-1793
Theory of evaluation based on scientific method and leading
to critical evaluation; seminars on theory and its
application.

Interaction Book Company
7208 Cornelia Dr, Edina, MN 55435
612-831-9500

International Alliance for Invitational Education
c/o School of Ed, UNC Greensboro, Greensboro, NC 27412
919-334-5100
Promotes humanistic, individualized, respectful approach.

**International Association for the Study of Cooperation
in Education**
Box 1582, Santa Cruz, CA 95061
408-426-7926
Publishes Cooperative Learning Magazine.

International Institute
N6128 Sawyer Lake Rd, White Lake, WI 54491
715-484-5002, FAX: same
Type: home-based

International Montessori Society
912 Thayer Ave, Silver Spring, MD 20910
Lee Havis, 301-589-1127
Tuition: $2,100
1 teacher, 30 students
Governance by board
Independent study, correspondence to prepare for Montes-
sori teaching; primary and elementary levels; Trust Tutoring
Program.

Italic Handwriting Series at Portland State University
PO Box 1394, Portland, OR 97202
Tena Spears, 503-725-4846, FAX: 503-725-4840
Student K-adult ages
Small press; comprehensive, self-directed program; italic is
logical, based on printing, easy to write and teach.

Joyful Child
Box 5506, Scottsdale, AZ 85261
Peggy Jenkins

Kagan's Cooperative Learning
27134 Paseo Espada, Suite 302, San Juan Capistrano, CA 92675
800-933-2667

Kew Resources
79-12 154th St, Kew Gardens, NY 11367
Anthony Cardo, 718-969-3454

Kids Art
PO Box 274, Mt Shasta, CA 96067
916-926-5076
Arts and crafts books and projects; magazine $10/yr.

Kids Discover Magazine
PO Box 54205, Boulder, CO 80322-4205
Use for unit study.

Kids Lib News
Box 28, Naalehu, HI 96772
Type: home-based

KONOS
PO Box 1534, Richardson, TX 75083
214-669-8337
Christian unit studies/time line; free catalog.

La Leche League International
PO Box 1209, Franklin Park, IL 60131
Early child-raising, breastfeeding ed.

Landmark
PO Box 849, Fillmore, CA 93016
Lori Harris, 805-524-2388, FAX: 805-524-7334
Type: home-based
Governance by board
Materials for K-12; focus on ability to research, record, reason, relate the history of any subject; facilitates Master Teachers.

Learning All Ways
7 Canyon Oaks Dr, McLoud, OK 74851
Carol Tofani, 405-386-5979
Type: home-based

Learning Things, Inc
68A Broadway; PO Box 436, Arlington, MA 02174
Microscope viewers; slide sets; catalog $3.

Lib Ed
Phoenix House, 170 Wells Rd, Bristol, England BS4 2AG
Richard Musgrove, 0272-778453
Magazine (3/yr) & books for the liberation of learning, including No Master High or Low, Libertarian Education and Schooling; conferences.

Liedloff Continuum Network
PO Box 1634, Sausalito, CA 94966
415-332-1570
For people wanting to incorporate The Continuum Concept into their lives; newsletter; members list; consultations with Jean Liedloff in Sausalito or by phone.

Lifetime Books and Gifts
3900 Chalet Suzanne Dr, Lake Wales, FL 33853
Homeschoolers Complete Reference Guide; curriculum items.

Linda Tagliaferro
248-44 Thebes Ave, Little Neck, NY 11362
718-423-0928
Author, lecturer, long-time home educator.

LORD/Elizabethtown Montessori School
100 Gray St, Elizabethtown, KY 42701-2608
Montessori materials and classroom furniture.

Magnet Schools of America
2111 Holly Hall Suite 4203, Houston, TX 77054
Don Waldrip, 800-462-5526
11,000 members in over 300 schools; directory (2,452 entries), $65; annual conference.

Mankato Wilson Campus School Remembered: Video (1968)
PO Box 2977, Sacramento, CA 95812
Don Glines, 916-393-8701
Featured completely individualized curriculum, student-selected facilitators, optional attendance, and no textbooks or homework.

Materials Company of Boston
PO Box 378, Salem, NH 03079
Ben Feldman and Bonnie LaMothe, 603-641-1339
US-made Montessori materials.

Math Products Plus
PO Box 64, San Carlos, CA 94070
415-593-2839

Merlyn's Pen (1985)
PO Box 1058, East Greenwich, RI 02818-0964
Valerie English, Assoc Ed, 800-247-2027, FAX: 401-885-5222
Student ages 11-18
National magazine; authors/artists submit original fiction, essays, poetry, book reviews, artwork; circulation 100,000; Parent's Choice Award recipient.

Michael Olaf Company
PO Box 1162, Arcata, CA 95521
Susan or Jim Stephenson, 707-826-1557
Montessori supplies; publication.

Minnesota Association of Alternative Programs (MAAP) Area Education Center
1102 Willow St, Brainerd, MN 56401
Lorin Ellertson, 218-829-2915
Over 100 member programs; information; assistance; workshops; meetings; tours; conferences; newsletter.

Montessori Foundation
4157 Mountain Rd, Pasadena, MD 21122
Tim Seldin
"Tomorrow's Child" magazine; seminars; consultation; resource center.

Montessori Institute of America
5901 NW Waukomis, Kansas City, MO 64151

Montessori Requisites–USA
314 West Main St, Norristown, PA 19401
800-365-0671
Montessori materials from Sri Lanka.

Montessori Services
228 S A St, Santa Rosa, CA 95401
Supplemental educational and practical life skills materials for the home and Montessori classroom.

Moore Academy
Box 1, Camas, WA 98607
Dr Raymond S. Moore, Chair/CEO, 206-835-5500, FAX: -5392
Type: home-based, non-profit; cost: $125-400/mo
Student ages 6-20, K-12th grade
Affiliation: Dr. Moore affiliated with 6 universities
Governance by teachers and Principal
Balances study, work and service; students have never been rejected for college; no early formal school; interns accepted.

Mothering Magazine
PO Box 1690, Santa Fe, NM 87504
800-827-1061

Multicultural Education c/o Caddo Gap Press
3145 Gaeary Blvd #275, San Fransisco, CA 94118
415-750-9978
Quarterly journal addresses stereotypes, racism, democracy
and diversity; reviews and extensive resource listings.

NAM Enterprises
PO Box 67, Keene, TX 76059
800-262-1069
Supplies.

National Association of Charter Schools
2722 E. Michigan Ave, Suite 201, Lansing, MI 48912
Greg Morris, 517-772-9115
Type: resource, non-profit
Provides technical and moral support to charter schools and
charter school founders; helps state legislators and citizens' groups interested in enacting meaningful charter
school laws; organizes a national conference.

**National Association of Private Nontraditional Schools
and Colleges**
182 Thompson Rd, Grand Junction, CO 81503
Earl Heusser, 303-243-5441

National Center for Fair and Open Testing (FairTest)
342 Broadway, Cambridge, MA 02139
617-864-1410

National Center for Montessori Education
PO Box 1543, Roswell, GA 30077
404-434-1128

National Center for Restructuring Education (NCREST)
Box 110, New York, NY 10027
212-678-3432
Major network and clearinghouse for new progressive,
learner-centered approaches within public ed.

National Coalition of Advocates For Stududents
100 Boylston St, Suite 737, Boston, MA 02116

National Coalition of Educational Activists (NCEA)
PO Box 679, Rhinebeck, NY 12572-0679
Debi Duke, 914-658-8115
Supports change within the public school system.

National Coaltion of Alternative Community Schools
(1976)
Box 15036, Santa Fe, NM 87506
Ed Nagel, Office Mgr, 505-474-4312
Governance by board and annual membership meeting
A national organization of educational alternatives; annual
and regional conferences; National Directory of Alternative
Schools; quarterly newsletter; information on alternative
schools; school accreditation program through NALSAS.

National Dropout Prevention Center
Clemson U, Clemson, SC 29634-5111
National Dropout Prevention Newsletter, 803-656-2599
A partnership between concerned business and education
leaders and schools and communities throughout the
United States; technical assistance for drop-out preven-
tion; database; consultant services, publications.

National Home Education Research Institute
5000 Deer Park Dr SE, Salem, OR 97301-9392
Brian D Ray, PhD, Pres, 503-375-7018
Non-profit clearinghouse; identifies effective educational
approaches; lectures; quarterly journal, Home School
Researcher; court testimony.

National Homeschool Service
PO Box 167, Rodeo, NM 88056
505-557-2250

National Institute for Christian Home Education
Rt 3 Box 543, Rustburg, VA 24588

National Society For Internships
3509 Haworth Dr S 207, Raleigh, NC 27609
Sally Migliore, 919-787-3263

NE Foundation For Children
71 Montague City Rd, Greenfield, MA 01301
Chip Wood

Network of Educators on the Americas
1118 22nd St NW, Washington, DC 20037
Deborah Menkart, Dir, 202-429-0137, FAX: 202-429-9766
Works with schools, communities to develop, promote peda-
gogies, resources, cross-cultural understanding for social,
economic justice in the Americas; books; workshops.

Network of Progressive Educators (1989)
PO Box 60308, Passadena, CA 91116
Neal Wrightson, 818-797-6890
Type: resource, non-profit

New Horizons For Learning (1980)
PO Box 15329, Seattle, WA. 98115
Dee Dickinson, CEO; Teri Howatt, Coordinator, 206-547-7936
Tuition: $50/yr membership
Network of people, programs, products dedicated to innova-
tive learning; synthesizes and communicates successful
research; supports lifespan learning communities; has net-
working electronic "building" in Bitnet; newsletter: "New
Horizons for Learning."

New Moon Publishing (1992)
PO Box 3587, Duluth, MN 55803
Nancy Gruver, Publisher, 218-728-5507, FAX:-1812
Girls ages 8-15 and adults produce bi-monthly, international
"New Moon, the Magazine for Girls and Their Dreams";
interns accepted.

Nienhuis Montessori USA
320 Pioneer Way, Mountain View, CA 94041-1576
800-942-8697
Montessori materials from Holland.

North American Montessori Teachers' Association
11424 Bellflower Rd NE, Cleveland, OH 44106
216-421-1905
Videos and publications for staff development, administrators, and parent education.

Northwest Earth Institute (1993)
921 W Morrison, Suite 532, Portland, OR 97205
Jennifer West, Development Dir, 503-227-2807, FAX: -2917
Non-profit; study groups in deep ecology, voluntary simplic-
ity in the home or workplace; special focus on youth;
"EarthMatters" newsletter; Lawyers for Env Responsibility.

Ohio Alternative Education Organization
1512 Woodward Ave, Springfield, OH 45506
Ruth Chapman

Open Court Publishing
PO Box 599, Peru, IL 611354-0599
815-223-2520
Specify math and reading catalog.

Oregon Association of Alternatives in Education
1005 NW Galveston Ave #A, Bend, OR 97701
Montessori resource

Our Schools Our Selves
1698 Gerrard St, Toronto, ON, Canada M4L 2B2
George Martel, 416-463-2637, 563-3657

Parent-Child Press
PO Box 675, Hollidarpburg, PA 16648
Montessori art appreciation curriculum; books and posters
for parent education

Personal Power Press International, Inc
Box V-49, Bowen Island, BC, Canada VON 1GO
Terry Carruthers, 604-947-2739, FAX: 604-947-0706
Books by Dr Maurice Gibbons on self-directed learning, integration; how-to guidebooks for students and teachers; compatible with Education 2000 Guidelines.

Pinewood School
112 Road D, Pine, CO 80470
Olivia Loria, Dir, 303-670-8180
Type: home-based, non-profit; cost: $425 or 125
4 teachers, 200 students, ages 4-21, K-12th grade
Affiliations: NCACS, NHA, CHEA, NALSAS
Governance by annual general meeting
Teacher qualifications: teaching certificate, experience
Individualized; diploma; on-line; resource center; international; no letter grades.

Pinyon Court School
7215 West 8th Pl, Lakewood, CO 80215
Mary Rothfeld, 303-238-3254
Type: home-based; cost: $30/family/yr
16 students, K-12th grade
Flexible curriculum and evaluation for homeschoolers.

Practical Homeschooling
Box 1250, Fenton, MO 63026
Mary Pride, 314-225-9790, 800-346-6322, FAX: 314-225-0743
Type: home-based resource
"Practical Homeschooling", Big Book of Home Learning, other publications.

Prairie
2545 Koshkonong Rd, Stoughton, WI 53589
Larry Kaseman
A bulletin on parental rights and responsibilities in education.

Priority Montessori Materials
10141 Rookwood Dr, San Diego, CA 92131
619-271-7312
Supplemental materials for the Montessori classroom.

Progressive Results
160 Old State Rd, Ballwin, MO 63021-5915
Walter A. De Anna, Pres, 314-394-7015, 800-966-1737, FAX: 314-394-2501
Skills Bank home tutoring software for grades 4-12; lessons; word problems; quizzes; tests.

Public School Montessorian
127 W. Lake St, Suite 1, Minneaplois, MN 55408
Dennis Schapiro

Quality Education Resources
PO Box 847, Cupertino, CA 95015-0847
408-252-2254
Free catalog.

Quebec Homeschool Association (1983)
1002 Rose Marie Rd, Val David, PQ, Canada J0T 2N0
Elizabeth Edwards, Editor, 819-322-6495
Quarterly newsletter; advice/support phone line; small library of books, magazines, catalogs.

"Quest, The Home Educators' Journal"
1144 Byran Ave, Ottawa, ON, Canada K2B 6T4
Andre Dubuc, Editor, 800-668-5878, FAX: 613-729-0117
$35/yr (US), 26/yr (Can) quarterly.

Rainbow Re-Source Center
PO Box 491, Kewanee, IL 61443
New and used curricula.

Resource Center for Redesigning Education
Po Box 818, Shelburne, VT 05482
Ron Miller, 802-865-9752
Hard-to-find books, videos, info on holistic ed, innovations; catalog; see books by Miller in bibliography.

Rethinking Schools
1001 E Keefe Ave, Milwaukee, WI 53212
414-964-9646
Independent journal published by Milwaukee area educators.

Riverside Schoolhouse
HCR 34 Box 181A, Bemidji, MN 56601
USBORNE books.

RSM Creative Services Inc
2600 Navarre Ave, Oregon, OH 43616
Supplemental materials for the Montessori classroom.

Saxon Publishers, Inc
1320 W Lindsey St #100, Norman, OK 73069-4310
405-329-7071
Math program for grades 4+.

Scholastic Book Clubs, Inc
PO Box 3745, Jefferson City, MO 65102
Teacher aids.

School of Living
Rd 1 Box 185 A, Cochranville, PA 19330
Ginny Green, 215-593-6988
Non-profit, $20/yr
60-year-old group founded by Ralph Borsodi; pioneer in environmental protection, consumer protection, land trust, home education, intentional communities, educational alternatives; "Green Revolution" newsletter.

Schools for the 21st Century
Old Capitol Bldg FG-11, Olympia, WA 98504-3211
John Anderson, 206-586-4512
Public alternatives.

Scientific Wizardry Educational Products
9925 Fairview Ave, Boise, ID 83704
208-377-8575

Shekinah Curriculum Cellar
967 Junipero Dr, Costa Mesa, CA 92626
Catalog $1

Sing and Learn Curriculum Supplies
2626 Club Meadow, Garland, TX 75043
Sarah Cooper, 214-840-8342
Type: home-based

"SKOLE " (1985)
72 Philip St, Albany, NY 12202-1789
Mary Leue, 518-465-0241
On ed alts, primarily by the grass-roots practitioners; $15/yr, two issues.

Society for Utopian Studies (1975)
U of MO, 8001 Natural Bridge Rd, St Louis, MO 63121
Lyman Sargent, Exec Dir

Southeast Educational Materials
1149 Rocky Lane, Monterey, TN 38574
615-839-3822
Type: Montessori

"Spirit of January"
Box 234162, Great Neck, NY 11023
Asiba Tupahache, 516-877-1630
Newsletter for homeschoolers.

States Educational Alternatives League (SEAL)
2550 University Ave W, Suite 347 N, St Paul, MN 55114-1052
612-645-0200, FAX: 612-645-0240
Comprised of state alt ed orgs.

Steward Ship
PO Box 164, Garden Valley, CA 95633
Choreganizers; send large SASE for brochure.

Study Circles Resource Center (1990)
PO Box 203, Pomfret, CT 06258
Phyllis Emigh, 203-928-2616, FAX: 206-928-3713
Non-profit adult ed
Networking services; topical discussion programs.

Summit Christian Academy
PO Box 802041, Dallas, TX 75380
Jan Bailey, Dir, 800-362-9180
Type: home-based; cost: $395/yr
1,000 students, K-12th grade
Alpha Omega curriculum; electives; educational games;
   achievement tests; diplomas; record keeping.

Switch
Box 403, Fontana, WI 53125
Alan Fiebig, 414-275-5497
Homeschool support group and magazine.

The 15th Street School Foundation (1983)
4 Jane St, New York, NY 10014
Betta Ehrenfeld, Pres, 212-243-1387
Clearinghouse for those interested in Summerhill model.

The American Montessori Society
150 Fifth Ave, New York, NY 10011
212-924-3209

The Book Cellar
87 Union Square, Milford, NH 06055
800-338-4257
Used curriculum.

"The Cheerful Cherub"
Box 262302-H, San Diego, CA 92196
Catholic catalog; magazine.

"The Drinking Gourd, Harambee"
PO Box 2557, Redmond, WA 98073
Donna Nichols-White, 836-0336
Multi-cultural homeschooling publication, support group;
   75% African American; Harambee means "Let's pull
   together."

The Eagle's Nest
1539 Oakwood Dr, Escalon, CA 95320
Supplies; free catalog.

**The Educational Association of Christian
   Homeschoolers** (TEACH)
PO Box 91, Bloomfield, CT 06002
203-677-4538, 800-205-7844

The Elijah Company
PO Box 12483, Knoxville, TN 37912-0483
615-475-7500
Educational programs; catalog.

"The Grapevine"
1702 Hwy 83 N, Seeley Lake, MT 59868
406-754-2481
Montana Homeschool News

"The Helping Hand"
5006 Barcelona Dr, Garland, TX 75043-5101
214-681-5161
Unit study curriculum for grades 3-6 based on children's
   classic literature; magazine.

The Home School
3131 Smokey Point Dr, Arlington, WA 98223
Huge inventory of materials.

The Home School Manual (1976)
c/o 1906 Niles-Buchanan Rd, Niles, MI 49120
Ted Wade, Gazelle Publications
Christian perspective with respect for all opinions; 55 chapters, 26 appendices; forms; by Theodore E. Wade and 38
   others; $21.95 pp.

The Home School Shopper
PO Box 11041, Spring Hill, FL 34610
813-856-5160
Used curriculum.

The Odysseus Group
295 8th St #3W, New York, NY 10009
John Taylor Gatto, 212-529-9327
1991 NY State Teacher of the Year; author of The Guerrilla
   Curriculum and Dumbing Us Down; goal that every
   student develops own learning style, interests and needs.

The Pembina Institute
PO Box 7558, Drayton Valley, AB, Canada TOE OMO
403-542-6272, FAX: 542-6464
The Canadian Environmental Education Catalogue

The Sycamore Tree
2179 Meyer Pl, Costa Mesa, CA 92627
Curriculum; umbrella school.

"The Teaching Home"
Box 20219, Portland, OR 97220-0219
503-253-9633
Christian perspective.

The Threefold Review
PO Box 6, Philmont, NY 12565
518-392-5728
Promotes R. Steiner's idea that education and other cultural
   pursuits should be kept separate from government
   control; special report on "Real Choice in Education."

Timberdoodle
E 1610 Spencer Lake Rd, Shelton, WA 98584
Supplies and games.

To Kids-For Kids-By Kids Newsletter
11119 Pucket Pl, Midlothian, VA 23112
Sherri Raynor
$4/yr; kids ages 6-18.

**TRANET: Transnational Network for Alternative/
   Appropriate Technologies**
PO Box 567, Rangeley, ME 04970
William Ellis, 207-864-2252
Assists grassroots workers and community developers
   through information distribution, meetings, conferences,
   and newsletter.

Tropical Homeschooler Newsletter (1992)
220 Waipalani Rd, Haiku, HI 96708
Ken and Adrienne Pinsky, Eds/Owners, 808-572-9289, FAX:
   808-572-0168
Local & national topics; bookstore/catalog.

Two Ragamuffins in Perpetual Search-mode (TRIPS)
c/o 10775 SW 133 Tr, Miami, FL 33176
Alan Muskat and efie womon
Affiliations: SoL, FIC, WWC, KOG
Directory production; consensus facilitation; herbal consulta-
   tions; mushroom and bargain hunting; cheezy clip-art.

"Under the Apple Tree" Magazine, Apple Tree Press
PO Box 8, Woodinville, WA 98072
Crafts; projects; hands-on studies; $18/yr.

Virginia Alternative Education Association
Box 310, Monroe, VA 24574
Ken Payne, 804-929-6931

Washington Alternative Learning Association (WALA)
   (1975)
PO Box 795, Port Townsend, WA 98368
Jane B. Ansley, Exec Dir, 206-385-9252
Funds scholarships and projects; liaison with State Office of
   Public Instruction; "Options in Education" newsletter;
   meetings; workshops; conferences.

Whole Language Umbrella
4848 N Fruit, Fresno, CA 93705
Debbie Manning

Wilcox & Follett
1000 W Washington Blvd, Chicago, IL 60607
Used curriculum; send request on school stationery.

World Future Society
7910 Woodmont Ave, Suite 450, Bethesda, MD 20814
Robert Schley, 301-656-8274, FAX: 951-0394

World List of Rudolf Steiner (Waldorf) Schools, Herausgeben vom Bund der Freien Waldorfschulen
Heidhofstrasse 32, Stutgart 1, Germany D-7000
0711-21042-0, FAX: 0711-21042-19

Zephyr Press (1979)
PO Box 66006, Tucson, AZ 85728
Amy Myers, 602-322-5090, FAX: 602-323-9402
Publisher; distributor; for K-12 teachers; student-centered curricula; multiple intelligence; multi-culturalism; language arts.

Charter Schools

Academy of Charter Schools, CO
Aishu Shule/W.E.B. DuBois Prep Public School, MI
Battle Rock Charter School, CO
Bay Mills Academy, MI
Bear Valley Charter School, CA
Beaver Dam, WI
Benjamin Franklin Classical Charter School, MA
Bennett Valley Charter School, CA
Bluffview Montessori, MN
Boston Renaissance Charter School, MA
Boston University Charter School, MA
Bowling Green Elementary School, CA
Canyon Charter School, CA
Cape Cod Lighthouse Charter School, MA
Carlin C. Coppin Elementary School, CA
Casa Maria Academy, MI
Cato School of Reason, CA
Cedar-Riverside Community School, MN
Charter Community School and Extended Day Program, CA
Charter Oak School, CA
Charter School for the Gifted and Talented, CO
Charter School Number 25, CA
Choice 2000 On-Line School, CA
Cities in Schools Learning Center, CA
City Academy, MN
City on a Hill Charter School, MA
Clayton Charter School, CO
Clear View Elementary Charter School, CA
Community Day Charter School, MA
Community Involved Charter School, CO
Community of Learners, CO
Constellation Community Charter Middle School, CA
Core Knowledge Charter School, CO
Creekside Oaks Charter Elementary School, CA
Dakota/Open Charter School, MN
Darnell E-Campus, CA
De Forest, WI
Denver Youth Academy, CO
Deterding Elementary School, CA
Discovery School, CA
Eagle County Charter Academy, CO
EDUTRAIN, CA
Emily Community Learning Center, MN
Excelsior Academy, CA
Fenton Avenue School, CA
Fenway II Charter School, MA
Florin Elementary, CA

Folsom Middle School, CA
Francis W. Parker Charter School, MA
Garfield Charter School, CA
Guajome Park Academy, CA
Home Tech, CA
Horizon Instructional Systems, CA
Horizons High School, MI
International Studies Academy, CA
Jefferson Academy, CO
Jingletown Charter Middle School, CA
Lake Mills, WI
Lincoln High School, CA
Linscott Charter School, CA
Louisiana Schnell Elementary School, CA
Lowell Charter School, MA
Lowell Middlesex Academy Charter School, MA
Marquez Charter School, CA
Metro Deaf, MN
Michigan Early Childhood Center, MI
Middle School 2000, WI
Middleton-Cross Plains, WI
Milwaukee, WI
Minneapolis Community Learning Center, MN
Minnesota New Country School, MN
Moreno Valley Community Learning Center, CA
Mountain Home School, CA
Mueller Elementary School, CA
Natomas Charter School, CA
Neighborhood House Charter School, MA
Nevada City Charter School, CA
Nevada City Home Study Charter School, CA
New Branches School, MI
New Heights Schools, Inc, MN
New Visions School, MN
Northlane Math and Science Academy, MI
O'Farrell Community School, CA
Options for Youth, CA
Palisades Charter High School, CA
Palisades Elementary Charter, CA
Parents Allied with Children and Teachers, MN
Peabody Charter School, CA
Pioneer Primary, Middle, CA
Prairie Island Dakota Community, MN
Pueblo School for the Arts and Sciences, CO
Racine, WI
Ready Springs Union Elementary Alternative Education School, CA

Renaissance School, CO
Rite of Passage School, CA
SAFE School, CO
Saginaw Chippewa Academy, MI
San Carlos Charter Learning Center, CA
San Francisco Charter Early Childhood School, CA
Santa Barbara Charter School, CA
Santiago Middle School, CA
Sci-Tech Academy, CO
Sheridan Elementary School, CA
Skills for Tomorrow, MN
Sonoma County Charter School, CA
Sonoma Valley Charter School, CA
South Shore Charter School, MA
Stevens Point, WI
Temecula Learning Center, CA
The Accelerated School Charter, CA
The Charter School of San Diego, CA
The Connect School, CO
The Discovery School, CO
The Eel River School, CA
The EXCEL School, CO
The Macomb Academy, MI
The Open Charter School, CA
The Waldorf Charter School, CA
Thurgood Marshall Charter Middle School, CO
Toivola Meadowlands, MN
Twin Ridges Alternative Charter School, CA
Vacaville Independent Charter School, CA
Vaughn Next Century Learning Center, CA
Verona, WI
Walden Academy Charter School, CA
Washington Charter School, CA
Wayne State University School, MI
West Michigan Academy of Environmental Science, MI
West Park Academy Charter School, CA
Western Massachusetts Hilltown Charter School, MA
Westwood Elementary School, CA
Weyauwega-Freemont, WI
Wheatland High School, CA
Windover High School, MI
Worcester Charter School at Assumption College, MA
YouthBuild Boston Charter School, MA
Yucca Mesa Charter School, CA

Colleges That Have Accepted Alternative School Graduates

The following colleges and universities were listed in the questionnaires returned to us as having accepted students graduating from their alternative schools or homeschool programs. Of course, this is not a complete list, but it indicates the spectrum of colleges which welcomes graduates from educational alternatives.

Aims CC
Alabama State U
Allan Hancock College
Am. River College
American Institute of Business
American River
Antelope Valley CC
Antioch
Arapaho CC
Arizona
Army Academy
Art Center
Art Inst. of Chicago
Austin Peay U
Baker Business College
Baker College
Bakersfield CC
Ball State
Barstow CC
Boston College
Boston U
Brandeis
Brown
Butte CC
BYU
Cabot College
California Arts
California State Hayward
California State U
Carson Newman College
Central Michigan U
Central Washington U
Central Wyoming CC
Chabot
Chaffey College
Clarkson
Cleveland Inst. of Music
Colgate
College of Sequoias
College of the Desert
College of the Redwoods
Collin County CC
Colorado Aerotech
Colorado State U
Colorado U
Columbia
Contra Costa JC
Cooper Union
Cornell
Cosumnes River College
CSU
Cuesta JC
CUNY
Curry
CW Post

Cypress CC
Davenport CC
Del Mar Tech
Delta CC
Delta College
Denison
Des Moines Area CC
Diablo Valley College
Dickinson
Dowling
Duke
E. Tennessee State U
E. Texas
Earlham
Easter State U
Harbor JC
El Camino JC
Evergreen
Ferris State U
Fort Lewis College
Fresno State
Front Rance CC
FSU
Ft. Lewis College
Fullerton CC
George Fox U
Georgetown U
Grand Valley Central Michigan U
Grandview College
Grossmant CC
Guilford
Hampshire
Hanover College
Harvard
Hawkey CC
Hayward State U
Healds Business College
Hofstra
Humboldt State U
Indiana Tech
Indiana U
Irvine Valley
ITT Tech Inst.
JFK U
Julliard
Kalamazoo Valley CC
Kendall School of Design
Kentucky State U
Kings County
Kirkwood CC
Lake Michigan College
Lakewood CC
Lansing CC
Laramie CC
Lawrence

LeMoyne-Owen College
Lincoln U
Loma Linda U
Long Beach State U
Los Angeles City College
Los Medanos College
Macomb CC
McAlister
McGill
Merced College
Metro State College
Michigan State U
Michigan Tech
Mid-Michigan CC
Middle Tennessee State U
Mira Costa CC
Mott CC
Mount San Jacinto CC
Mt. Royal
Mt. Sac
Mt. San Antonio College
N. Texas State
Napa Valley College
Nassau CC
NE Technical College
New College
Northeastern
Northeastern JC
nursing schools
NYU
Oakland CC
Oakland U
Oberlin
Oneida Area Vocational
Oregon
Palomar
Peralta Colleges
Pikes Peak CC
Pima CC
Pomona
Portland School of Art
Pratt
Princeton
PSU
Pueblo CC
Purdue
Radcliffe
Red Rocks CC
Reed
Richland
RISD
RIT
Roane State CC
S. Maine Tech. College
Sacramento City College

Sacramento State
Saddleback JC
San Diego City College
San Diego State
San Francisco College of Art
San Francisco State U
San Jose State U
UC Santa Barbara
UC Santa Cruz
Santa Monica City College
Sarah Lawrence
Seattle Pacific U
Shelby State CC
Sierra JC
Sierra Valley
Skadron Business College
Smith
SMU
Sonoma State
Southwestern
Southwestern Michigan College
St. Clair CC
St. Joseph's
Stanford
SUNY
Swarthmore
Syracuse
Tennessee State U
Tennessee Tech U

Texas A & I
Texas State Tech College
Tulane
U at New York
U Nacional Autonoma
U of Alabama
U of Arizona
U of Calgary
U of California
U of Colorado
U of Hawaii
U of Illinois
U of Lowell
U of Maine
U of Michigan
U of Missouri
U of N. Colorado
U of N. Iowa
U of New Hampshire
U of Northern Colorado
U of Penn
U of S. Maine
U of San Diego
U of Santa Clara
U of Tennessee
U of Victoria
U of Virginia
U of Washington
UC Berkeley

UC Irvine
UCLA
U of Louisville
U of N. Colorado
UNH
Union College
UNLV
UNR
USC
Victor Valley College
Virginia Tech
Warren Wilson
Washington State U
Washington U
Wayne State U
Western
Western Michigan College
Western Michigan U
Western Washington U
Western Wyoming CC
Whitman College
William & Mary
Wisconsin CCs
Wooster
Worcester Polytech.
Yale
Yuba City CC

Higher Education Alternatives

American Open University, NY
Antioch New England Graduate School, NH
Antioch University, OH
Aprovecho Research Center, OR
Bank Street College, NY
Barry University, FL
Burlington College, VT
California Institute of Integral Studies, CA
Center for the Study of Educational Alternatives, NY
College of the Atlantic, ME
Columbia Pacific University, CA
Echo Springs Transition Studies Center, ID
Eugene Lang College, NY
Eureka Free University, Russia
Friends World Program of Long Island University, NY
GAIA Permaculture Community, GA
Geocommons College, NH
Global Personal Teachers' Transformation, Czech Republic
Goddard College, VT
Hampshire College, MA
Hawthorne University, UT
Houston Montessori Center, TX
Institute for Bioregional Studies, PEI, Canada
International Montessori Society, MD
Johnson Center at University of Redlands, CA
Lesley College, MA
Marlboro College, VT
Montessori College at Mount St Mary's, Ireland
Montessori Education Center of the Rockies, CO

Montessori Institute of Los Angeles, Inc, CA
Montessori of Las Colinas School & Training Center, TX
Naropa Institute, CO
Naropa Institute-Early Education BA, CO
National Audubon Society Expedition Institute, ME
National-Louis University's Northern Virginia/Washington, DC Center, VA
NCACS Teacher Education Program, PA
New College, FL
New College of California, CA
New England Montessori Teacher Education Center, NH
New York Open Center, NY
Pendle Hill, PA
PLENTY, CA
Portland Community College, OR
Prescott College, AZ
Rogers Person Centered School Foundation, Hungary
Rowe Camp & Conference Center, MA
Rural Education Program, HOME Coop, ME
Saybrook Institute Graduate School, CA
School for International Training, VT
School of Education, Alternative Teacher Education, IN
School of Human Service, VT
Shimer College, IL
Umpqua Community College, OR
Union Institute, OH
Waldorf Institute of Sunbridge College, NY
Warren Wilson College, NC
World University, AZ

Alternative Boarding Schools

Andis Alternative Education Center and Drift Creek Farm for Youth
2204 SR 217, Kitts Hill, OH 45645
Earl Hutchinson, Dir, 614-532-8882, -9068
81 acres; voc; natural resources, agri. prod, work & family; lab work in forestry, soil conservation, hydroponic horticulture, food prep, nutrition; CAI.

Armand Hammer United World College (1982)
Box 248, Montezuma, NM 87731
Dan Tyson, Adms Dir, 505-454-4248, FAX: -4274
Type: independent, non-profit; tuition: $16,500/yr, scholarships
24 teachers, 200 students, ages 16-19
Governance by teachers; principal
Teacher qualifications: Masters in teaching field, international experience
IB curriculum, 6th form; equivalent to grades 12-13; students enter into UK 3-yr undergraduate programs or as sophomores in the US; extensive field trips; community service; rural location; transportation; interns accepted.

Arthur Morgan School (1962)
1901 Hannah Branch Rd, Burnsville, NC 28714
Johno Zakelj & Joy Montagano, Co-clerks, 704-675-4262
Type: Quaker, non-profit; tuition: $5,150-10,500, scholarships
12 teachers, 24 students, ages 12-15, 7-9th grade
Affiliations: NCACS, NAMTA, FEAA
Governance by staff, staff and student all-school meeting
Geared to meet specific needs of JHS students; challenging outdoor experiences; community service; daily work projects; caring community environment; based on Montessori's Erkinder model; no letter grades; multi-aged classes; extensive field trips; rural location; interns accepted.

Au Grand Bois (1980)
RR 1, Ladysmith, PQ, Canada JOX 2AO
A & L Prost, Co-Dirs, 819-647-3522
Type: independent, non-profit; scholarships
20 teachers, 50 students, ages 8-16
Governance by staff, co-directors, much input from campers.
Summer program; organic gardens; 565-acre semi-wilderness; non-competitive; campers choose avtivities; promotes understanding and respect for self, others, natural environment.

Boston University Charter School
775 Commonwealth Ave, Boston, MA 02115
Rear Admiral W. Norman Johnson, USN (Ret.), 617-353-4126
Type: at-risk charter
150-180 students, 7-12th grade
Affiliation: MA Executive Office of Ed
Uses military realignment for teachers and other resources.

Boynton School (1964)
RR 1, Box 31B, Orford, NH 03777
Arthur Boynton Jr, Director, 603-353-4874
Type: independent; tuition: $5,000
2 teachers; 7-12+
Governance by cooperative
Individualized help with languages, music, athletics; multi-aged classes; no letter grades; rural location; interns accepted.

Boys Totem Town
398 Totem Rd, St Paul, MN 55119
Dave Ardoff, 612-292-6295
Career exploration; work experience; year-round.

Brockwood Park Krishnamurti Educational Centre (1969)
Bramdean, Hampshire, England SO24 OLQ
Scott Forbes, 962-771-744, FAX: 962-771-875
Type: independent, non-profit
30 teachers, 60 students, ages 14-19
Affiliation: Krishnamurti Schools
Governance by all faculty with school meeting
Holistic; in 1769 Georgian mansion and park; no letter grades; multi-aged classes; extensive field trips; rural location.

Buxton School (1928)
PO Box 646, Williamstown, MA 01267
C. William Bennett, 413-458-3919, FAX: -9427
Type: independent, non-profit; tuition: $19,500/yr, scholarships
16 teachers, 80 students, ages 14-18, 9-12th grade
Governance by teachers and principal
Teacher qualifications: Bachelor's
Work program; the arts; students maintain school; entire school travels to major city for research projects and to perform touring play; no letter grades; extensive field trips; multi-aged classes; rural location.

Colegio Bilingue "Jorge Emilio Gutierez"
Apdo Aereo 101634, Bogota, DE, Columbia SA
Alejandro Acero, 011571-2150051
Type: independent
60+ students, partly international, indigenous, K-12th grade
Summerhill philosophy; outdoor classes on mountainside; exchange program.

Eagle Rock School (1993)
Box 1770, Estes Park, CO 80517
Robert Burkhardt, Head, 303-588-0600, FAX: 586-4805
Type: independent, non-profit; tuition: free
20 teachers, 96 students, partly at-risk, ages 15-18, HS
Affiliation: Honda
Governance by teachers, principal, democratic school meeting, board
650 acres; 1 mile from Rocky Mountain National Park; integrated; stresses service learning, outdoor ed, environmental stewardship, cross-cultural understanding; no letter grades; multi-aged classes; extensive field trips; interns accepted.

George School (1893)
Box 4000, Newtown, PA 18940
Karen S. Hallowell, Adms Dir, 215-579-6500, FAX: -6549
Type: Quaker, non-profit; tuition: res:$17,900/yr day:$11,650/yr, scholarships
70 teachers, 525 students, ages 13-18, 9-12th grade
Affiliation: Religious Society of Friends
Governance by consensus
Teacher qualifications: college degree
65 hours community service; work camps in developing countries; IB; suburban location.

Headwaters Academy (1990)
418 W Garfield St, Box 7258, Bozeman, MT 59715
Jill King, Off Mgr, 406-585-9997
Type: independent, non-profit; tuition: $4,950/yr, scholarships
10 teachers, 40 students, ages 11-18, ungraded
Affiliation: PNAIS
Governance by board
Teacher qualifications: credential or advanced degree
Cooperative; integrated; community study; travel to Baja, Spain, Guatemala; multi-aged classes; rural location.

High Mowing School (1942)
PO Box 850, Abbot Hill Rd, Wilton, NH 03086
Virginia R. Buhr, Adms Dir, 603-654-2391
Type: Waldorf, non-profit; tuition: $9,950-10,500 day,
$16,250-18,000 boarding/yr, scholarships
20 teachers, 85 students, ages 13-19, 9-12th grade
Affiliations: NEASC, NAIS, ISANNE, AWSNA, SATB
Governance by faculty
Teacher qualifications: BA, Waldorf interest/training, love
teenagers
College prep; extensive arts; social responsibility; interna-
tional community; multi-aged classes; rural location;
interns accepted.

Highland School (1981)
Rt 83 Box 56, Highland, WV 26346
Dr. Charlotte Landvoigt, Dir, 304-869-3250
Type: independent, non-profit; tuition: day 60, bdg 560/mo
3 teachers, 14 students, ages 5-18
Governance by democratic school meeting
Teacher qualifications: B.A. minimum; willingness to be equal
member of democratic community
Located on 480 acres: woods, pond, streams, fields, wildlife;
international visitors and exchanges; stresses individual
interests, responsibility; apprenticeships in oil and gas, veterinary science, office skills; PSAT administered; no letter
grades; non-compulsory class attendance; multi-aged
classes; interns accepted.

Horizons School
1900 Dekalb Ave, Atlanta, GA 30307
Dr Lorraine Wilson, Co-Adm, 404-378-2219, FAX: 404-373-
3650
Type: independent, non-profit; tuition: $3,800-8,000/yr,
scholarships: work, need
14 teachers, 145 students, ages 4-18, pre K-12th grade
Affiliation: NCACS
Governance by democratic school meeting; some decisions
by administration
Campus designed and built by students and staff; alt eval
methods in some classes; college prep; whole-person
approach; multi-aged classes; extensive field trips; urban
location; interns accepted.

Illinois Mathematics and Science Academy (1986)
1500 W Sullivan Rd, Aurora, IL 60506-1039
708-801-6000
Type: magnet
Student ages 13-18, 10-12th grade
State-funded; mentorships; near Fermi Accelerator Lab.

John Woolman School (1963)
13075 Woolman Ln, Nevada City, CA 95959
916-273-3183, FAX: 916-273-9028
Type: Quaker; tuition: $14,900/yr, scholarships
35 students, ages 14-17, 9-12th grade
Affiliation: NAIS
Governance by teachers, principal, board
Teacher qualifications: credentials, experience
Emphasizes truthfulness, simplicity, non-violence, respect,
listening to the Spirit Within; nurtures inquiry, creativity,
physical work, service; multi-aged classes; rural location.

Johnson Center at University of Redlands (1969)
PO Box 3080 1200 E Colton Ave, Redlands, CA 92373-0999
Yasuyuki Awada, Dir, 909-335-4071, FAX: 909-793-2029
Non-profit; tuition: $15,760/yr, scholarships
140 students
Accreditation: WASC
Governance by community consensus
Teacher qualifications: PhD, ABD
Students negotiate learning contracts with faculty; no letter
grades; student designed curriculum and majors; subur-
ban location.

Marlboro College (1946)
PO Box A, Marlboro, VT 05344
Wayne R. Wood, Adms Dir, 802-257-4333, FAX: -4154
Non-profit; tuition: $17,175/yr, scholarships
36 teachers, 270 students, ages 17-40
Governance by faculty and student reps
Self-designed; tutorials; small classes.

National Audubon Society Expedition Institute (1981)
PO Box 365, Belfast, ME 04915
Karen Woodsum, Office Mgr, 207-338-5859
Type: independent higher education; tuition: $9,300/yr,
scholarships
4 teachers, 20 students, HS, college, graduate school
Affiliation: Leslie College
Governance by consensus
Explores 1 region of US & Canada each sem; environmental
ed degrees; values-based, holistic approach; non-
authoritarian; self-paced, directed and evaluated; camping,
hiking, canoeing.

Nebraska Center for Children & Youth: Whitehall School
5701 Walker, Lincoln, NE 68504
402-471-3305
Type: public at-risk
K-12th grade
Work experience; cooperative programs; behavior modification, contracts; vocational, group, individual counseling.

North Country School (1938)
Box 187, Lake Placid, NY 12946
Christine Lefevre, Adms Dir, 518-523-9329, FAX: -4858
Type: independent, non-profit; tuition: $22,000/yr,
scholarships
30 teachers, 55 students, ages 9-14, 4-8th grade
Affiliation: Camp Treetops
Governance by board
Teacher qualifications: BA/BS and interest/experience
School-as-village model; outdoor ed; art; work program;
greenhouse; organic gardens; farm animals; maple-
sugaring; no letter grades; transportation; interns
accepted.

Oak Grove School
220 W Lomita Ave, Ojai, CA 93023
Mary Louise Sorem, HS Dir, 805-646-8236, FAX: -6509
Type: independent, non-profit
Pre K-12th grade
Affiliations: Krishnamurti Schools, NAIS; Accreditations: CAIS,
WASC
ES: no letter grades, nature study, arts; HS: college prep,
interscholarstic sports, camping, travel; rural location.

Olney Friends School (1837)
61830 Sandy Ridge Rd, Barnesville, OH 43713
Bonnie Irwin, Asst Head, 614-425-3655
Type: Quaker, non-profit; tuition: $13,230/yr, scholarships
12 teachers, 49 students, ages 13-19, 9-12th grade
Affiliations: ISACS, NAIS, FCOE
Teacher qualifications: BS with a major in subject to be taught
Whole-person approach; college prep; multi-aged classes;
rural location; interns accepted.

Owosso Alternative Education (1990)
120 Michigan Ave, Owosso, MI 48429
Shirley McNier, Coord, ?-723-5598
Type: public choice
7 teachers, 65 students, mainly at-risk, ages 16-18
Affiliation: MAEO
Governance by principal, faculty, student reps, board
Teacher qualifications: secondary certification
Electives; Glasser's control theory; reality therapy for behavior
control; hands-on projects; volunteer work; suburban loca-
tion; interns accepted.

Padanaram Village School (1972)
RR 1, Box 478, Williams In, IN 47470
Steven Fuson, Schoolmaster, 812-262-7252
Type: independent, non-profit; no tuition
9 teachers, 60 students, ages 5-18, K-12th grade
Governance by teachers and principal, parent cooperative
Community shares goods communally; 3 R's and strong cur-
ricula are blended with arts, hands-on learning, community
life; no letter grades; multi-aged classes; extensive field
trips.

Petrolia High School (1983)
Box 197, Petrolia, CA 95558
Seth Zuckerman, Director, 707-629-3509
Type: independent, non-profit
10 teachers, 24 students, ages 14-18, 9-12th grade
Governance by teachers and principal, democratic school
meeting, board
Year starts with 2 week backpacking; 6 week intercultural trip
with home stay, often in Mexico; involvement in local environmental restoration efforts; individually designed project
month; extensive field trips; rural location.

Phoenix International School for Peace
Box 336, Birch Tree, MO 65438
John Staniloiu, Dir, 314-292-3880
Type: independent
Student ages 8-16
320 acres; animals, rivers, caves; hands-on experiences.

Rock Point School
Institute Rd, Burlington, VT 05401
Russell Ellis
Type: independent
Students mainly at-risk, HS
Low ratio; counseling; tutoring; self-image/motivation; sub-
stance abuse counseling; 24 hr/day supportive environ-
ment; positive peer culture.

Sandhill Crane School (1989)
PO Box 160, Fall River, CA 96028
916-336-6582
Type: independent; tuition: $5,000/yr
2 teachers, 3 students, ages 9-15
Affiliations: Kempo International, Ch'uan Tao Assn
Governance by benevolent director
Teacher qualifications: outstanding athlete, min 7 yrs training
in Chinese martial arts
Does not advocate material gain, ego enhancement; vehicle
is mind-body training of Chinese martial arts; no letter
grades; multi-aged classes; extensive field trips; rural location; interns accepted.

Schole (1985)
Box 10 RR #1, Margaree Valley, NS, Canada
Donald Knight, 902-248-0601
Type: Independent, home-based; cost: C$12,000/yr,
scholarships
2-3 teachers, 4-6 students, ages 6-16, 1-12th grade
Governance by board
Wilderness setting; extensive travel, eg, to Latin America,
1994-95 to Europe; no letter grade; interns accepted.

Shining Mountain Waldorf School (1982)
987 Locust Ave, Boulder, CO 80304
Nancy Jane, Enrl Coord, 303-444-7697, FAX: 444-7701
Non-profit; tuition: $3,500-5,850/yr, scholarships
25 teachers, 326 students, ages 4-18, K-12th grade
Affiliation: AWSNA
Governance by teachers, principal, and board
Teacher qualifications: Waldorf training, certification
8 acres; extensive field trips; summer school; rural location;
interns accepted.

Stonesoup School (1979)
Star Rt 1, Box 127, Crescent City, FL 32112
Deborah Rogers, 904-698-2516
Type: independent, non-profit; tuition: $700/mo,
scholarships
3 teachers, 10 students, ages 8-18, -12th grade
Affiliation: NCACS
Governance by democratic school meeting
Free school approach to learning and living; freedom tem-
pered with responsibility and independence, cooperation;
encourages self-reliance, character development; self
paced tutorials; on 50 acres with lake; no letter grades;
non-compulsory class attendance; multi-aged classes;
extensive field trips; rural location; interns accepted.

Summerhill School (1921)
Leiston, Suffolk, England IP16 4HY
Zoe Redhead, 0728-830540
Type: independent; tuition: $£5,000/yr
12 teachers, 70 students, mainly international, ages 6-17
Governance by democratic school meeting
Teacher qualifications: dictated by position
Founded by A.S. Neill as a pioneering free school and democ-
ratic community; 12 acres; no letter grades; non-
compulsory class attendance; multi-aged classes; rural
location; interns accepted.

The Community School (1973)
Box 555-79 Washington St, Camden, ME 04843
Emanual Pariser, Dora Lievow, Co-Directors, 207-763-3000
Type: independent, non-profit; tuition: $17,000/yr,
scholarships
6 teachers, 8 students, mainly at-risk, ages 16-21, HS
Affiliations: NCACS, Nat Dropout Prev Net
Governance by democratic school meeting; faculty determines inalterable rules
"Real" work in community, maintenance, and meeting room
and board costs; applied home ec; conflict resolution and
anger mgmt; competency-based; new book: Changing
Lives: Voices From a School that Works; no letter grades;
multi-aged classes; extensive field trips; rural location;
interns accepted.

The Meeting School (1957)
Thomas Rd, Rindge, NH 03461-9781
Ed Miller, Admissions Director, 603-899-3366
Type: independent, non-profit; tuition: $15,000, scholarships
12 teachers, 27 students, ages 13-19, 9-12th grade
Affiliations: NCACS, ISEANNE
Governance by faculty consensus for some decisions; whole
community or board for some
Student/faculty co-op households; 4-hr work study: farm,
childcare, office; 4-week intersession project/travel;
apprenticeships, peace studies; student-run radio station;
no letter grades; multi-aged classes; extensive field trips;
rural location; interns accepted.

Timber Lake Job Corps CCC (1964)
59868 E Hwy 224, Estacada, OR 97023
Juanita Morin, Mgr, 503-834-2291
Type: public at-risk
7 teachers, 234 students, ages 16-21
Intensive; voc and life skills; GED/diploma.

Upattinas School (1971)
429 Greenridge Rd, Glenmoore, PA 19343
Sandra Hurst, Dir, 215-458-5138
Type: independent, home-based, non-profit
11 teachers, 80 students, ages 5-19, K-12th grade
Governance by democratic school meeting
Teacher qualifications: individually decided by school

Enrollment, materials, support for homeschooling; international student placement; I-20 authorization; exchanges, part time programs; HS diploma for in-school and ind study; no letter grades; non-compulsory class attendance; multi-aged classes; extensive field trips; rural location; interns accepted.

Veade Valley School (1948)
3511 Veade Valley School Rd, Sedona, AZ 86351
Roy E. Grimm, Head, 602-284-2272, FAX: 284-0432
Type: independent, non-profit; tuition: $17,325/yr, scholarships
24 teachers, 125 students, ages 13-18, 9-12th grade
Affiliations: NAIS, AEE
Governance by board
Teacher qualifications: prefer BA/MA

Emphasis on anthropology, intercultural understanding, environmental stewardship; classical college prep; experiential pedagogy; multi-aged classes; extensive field trips; rural location; interns accepted.

Wil Lou Gray Opportunity School (1921)
PO Drawer 280128, Columbia, SC 29228
Dr Mary Catherine Norwood, Superintendent, 803-822-5480, FAX: -8146
Type: public at-risk; scholarships
23 teachers, 170 students, ages 15+, 9-12th grade
Governance by board
Case management teams; outdoor education; vocational training; college residential setting; individualized; suburban location; interns accepted.

Bibliography

This is a partial listing of mostly new books and periodicals that would be useful in studying educational alternatives.

Armstrong, Thomas. *Awakening Your Child's Natural Genius*. Los Angeles: Jeremy P. Tarcher, 1991.

Avrich, Paul. *The Modern School Movement*. NJ: Princeton University Press, 1980. History of the movement pioneered by Spanish Anarchist Francisco Ferrer, with a special emphasis on the Stelton Community.

Barickman, Joan Estes. *Schoolwise, Teaching Academic Patterns of Mind*. New Hampshire: Heinemann/Boynton/Cook Publishers, 1992.

Bear, John. *College Degrees by Mail*. Berkeley, CA: Ten Speed Press, 1991.

Bear, John and Mariah Bear. *Bear's Guide to Earning College Degrees Nontraditionally, 12th Edition*. Benicia, CA: C&B Publishing, 1995.

Chapman, Judith D., Isak D. Froumin and David N. Aspin. *Creating and Managing the Democratic School*. Washington DC: The Falmer Press, 1995.

Chattin-McNichols, John. *The Montessori Controversy*. Delmar Publishers, 1992.

Colfax, David and Micki. *Hard Times in Paradise*. New York: Warner Books, 1992. *Homeschooling for Excellence*. New York: Warner Books, 1988. Stories by a homeschool family whose children went to Harvard.

Dewey, John. *Experience and Education*. London: Collier-Macmillan, 1938. Dewey's philosophy is the basis for progressive education.

Fellowship for Intentional Communities. *Directory of Intentional Communities: A Guide to Cooperative Living*. Rutledge, MO: Communities Publications Cooperative, 1991.

Fliegel, Seymour. *Miracle in East Harlem: The Fight for Choice in Public Education*. New York: Times Books, 1992.

Gatto, John Taylor. *Dumbing Us Down*. Philadelphia, PA: New Society Publishers, 1992. A veteran, award-winning teacher gets fed up with the system.

Gribble, David. *Considering Children: A Parents' Guide to Progressive Education*. London, England: Dorling Kindserly Limited.

Glasser, William. *The Quality School: Managing Students Without Coercion*. New York: Harper & Row, 1990.

Goldman, Jenifer. *My Life as a Traveling Homeschooler*. Roslyn, NY: Solomon Press, 1991. An 11-year-old girl writes about her experiences.

Greenberg, Daniel. *Announcing a New School: A Personal Account of the Beginnings of the Sudbury Valley School*. Framingham, MA: Sudbury Valley Press, 1973. *The Sudbury Valley School Experience*. Framingham, MA: The Sudbury Valley School Press, 1987.

Hainstock, Elizabeth G. *Teaching Montessori in the Home: The Preschool Years. Teaching Montessori in the Home: The School Years*. New York: Random House, 1968, 1971.

Hart, Leslie A. *Human Brain and Human Learning*. Oak Creek, AZ: Books for Educators, 1983. The implications of brain research for education.

Hegener, Mark and Helen. *Home Education Magazine*. Tonasket, WA: Home Education Press. *Alternatives in Education*. Tonasket, WA: Home Education Press, 1993.

Holt, John. *How Children Learn*, 1967. *How Children Fail*, 1964. NY: Pitman. *Teach Your Own*. New York: Delta/Lawrence, 1981. Evolution from school criticism and change to homeschooling.

Lamb, Albert. *Friends of Summerhill Trust Journal*. Leiston, Suffolk, England: Summerhill School, 1992. *Summerhill School, A New View of Childhood*. New York: St. Martin's Press, 1993. New and more recent editing of A. S. Neill's writings.

Llewellen, Grace. *Teenage Liberation Handbook: How to Quit School and Get a Life and Education*. Eugene, OR: Lowry House, 1991.

Loomis, Mildred Jensen, and Ralph Borsodi. *Reshaping Modern Culture; The Story of the School of Living and Its Founder*. Cochranville, PA: The School of Living, 1922.

Leue, Mary. *SKOLE, The Journal of Alternative Education*. Albany, NY: Down to Earth Books, summer 1991.

Luvmour, Sambhava and Josette. *Natural Learning Rhythms: How and When Children Learn.* Berkeley: Celestial Arts, 1993.

McCullough, Virginia. *Testing and Your Child,* New York, NY: Penguin Books, 1992.

Miller, Ron. *What Are Schools For: Holistic Education in American Culture.* Brandon, VT: Holistic Education Press, 1990. *The Renewal of Meaning in Education: Responses to the Cultural and Ecological Crisis of Our Times.* Brandon, VT: Holistic Education Press, 1993.

Mintz, Jerry. *AERO-GRAMME: The Newsletter of the Alternative Education Resource Organization.* Roslyn, NY. Networks spectrum of educational alternatives world-wide.

Moffett, James. *The Universal Schoolhouse: Spiritual Awakening Through Education.* San Francisco: Jossey Bass, 1994.

Montessori, Maria. *The Secret of Childhood.* Ballantine Books, 1973.

Nagel, Ed. *National Coalition News.* Santa Fe, NM: NCACS Publications.

Nathan, Joe. *Public Schools by Choice.* St. Paul, MN: The Institute for Learning and Teaching, 1989.

Neill, A. S. *Summerhill, A Radical Approach to Child Rearing.* New York: Hart, 1960.

O'Leary, Jenifer. *Write Your Own Curriculum.* Stevens Point, Wisconsin: Whole Life Publishing, 1993.

Rupp, Rebecca. *Good Stuff: Learning Tools for All Ages, second revised edition.* Tonasket, WA: Home Education Press, 1994. An educational resource guide with thousands of listings and reviews.

Sheffer, Susannah. *Growing Without Schooling.* Cambridge, MA: Holt Associates. Letters and reports from homeschoolers around the country.

Shotton, John. *No Master High or Low.* Bristol, England: Libertarian Education, 1993. History of libertarian education in England.

Sizer, Theodore R. *Horace's Compromise: The Dilemma of the American High School.* Boston: Houghton Mifflin, 1984.

Smith, Gregory. *Education and the Environment: Learning to Live With Limits.* Albany: SUNY Press, 1992.

Spring, Joel. *A Primer of Libertarian Education.* New York: Free Life Editions, 1977.

Trickett, Edison J. *Living an Idea: Empowerment and the Evolution of an Alternative High School.* Bookline Books, 1991.

Wade, Theodore E. *The Home School Manual.* Bridgman, MI: Gazelle Publications, 1993.

Wagner, Patricia. *Building Support Networks for Schools.* Santa Barbara, CA: ABC-Clio, 1992.

Weinstein, Miriam. *Making a Difference College Guide, Education for a Better World.* San Anselmo, CA: Sage Press, 1993. Selected descriptions of forward-looking colleges.

Wheelock, Anne. *Crossing the Tracks.* New York: The New Press, 1992.

Wood, George. *Schools That Work: America's Most Innovative Public Education Programs.* New York: Dutton, 1992.

About The Editors

JERRY MINTZ has been a leading voice in the alternative school movement for over thirty years. He has a B.A. from Goddard College, and a M.A. from Antioch. He was a public school teacher and a principal in alternative schools. He was the executive director of the National Coalition of Alternative Community Schools from 1985 to 1989. In 1989 he founded the Alternative Education Resource Organization, and he is editor of its publication, *AERO-GRAMME.* He has lectured and consulted with schools and organizations in the United States and around the world, and has published many articles and studies on educational alternatives.

RAYMOND SOLOMON is a partner in The Solomon Press, and works as editor, graphic designer, and science publisher. He was picture editor of the best-selling *Macmillan Illustrated Almanac for Kids.* He has published about fifty articles in various periodicals. He is a graduate of Forest Hills High School in New York and has a B.A. in government from Windham College. He is currently working on *The Science Almanac for Kids* and *The Modern Vegetarian Almanac.* He often writes as Reuven Solomon in the weekly paper *The Jewish Press.*

SIDNEY SOLOMON, the former Design Director of the Macmillan Publishing Company, is now a partner in The Solomon Press, book publishers. Sidney is a graduate of City College of New York. He was a jazz drummer and teacher in New York before going into publishing as an editor and art director. He is the co-author of the *Macmillan Illustrated Almanac for Kids.* He became a serious painter as an adult and has had eight solo shows.